PAGE 34

ON THE ROAD

YOUR COMPLETE DESTINATION GUIDE
In-depth reviews, detailed listings
and insider tips

Temples of Bagan > p149

Northern Myanmar p233

Mandalay & Around p199

Western Myanmar p268

Eastern Myanmar p166

Bagan & Central Myanmar p111

Around Yangon p73

Yangon p36

Southeastern Myanmar p91

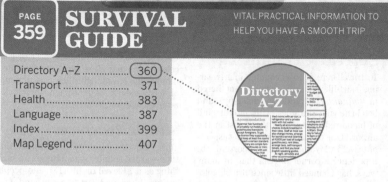

Directory A–Z

THIS EDITION WRITTEN AND RESEARCHED BY

**John Allen,
Allen John Smith, Jamie Smith**

welcome to
Myanmar
(Burma)

Surreal & Traditional

To travel here is to encounter men wearing skirt-like *longyi*, women smothered in *thanakha* (traditional make-up) and betel-chewing grannies with mouths full of blood-red juice – and that's just at the airport! One of the most fascinating aspects of travel in Myanmar is the opportunity to experience a corner of Asia that, in many ways, has changed little since British colonial times. Myanmar, for instance, has yet to be completely overwhelmed by Western clothing. It's also a country of many incredible and sometimes surreal sites. Contemplate the 4000 sacred stupas scattered across the plains of Bagan. Stare in disbelief at the Golden Rock teetering impossibly on the edge of a chasm. Ride a horse cart past colonial-era mansions. Meet multitalented monks who have taught their cats to jump, or feisty elderly Chin women, their faces tattooed with intricate designs.

Simple Pleasures

Turn back the clock with a trip to this time-warped country where there's no such thing as a 7-Eleven or an ATM, and people still use horse and cart to get around. Liberate yourself from your mobile multiphone (it won't work here) and the internet (you can get online, but connections are *sloooow*) and discover a culture where holy men are more revered than rock stars. Drift down the Ayeyarwady in an old river steamer,

'This is Burma', wrote Rudyard Kipling. 'It is quite unlike any place you know about.' How right he was: more than a century later Myanmar remains a world apart.

(left) Umin Thounzeh (p229); Sagaing Hill
(below) Fresh produce at a Nyaung U market

stake out a slice of beach on the blissful Bay of Bengal, or trek through pine forests to minority villages scattered across the Shan Hills. Dig into the myriad dishes of the local cuisine, from a hearty bowl of *mohinga* noodles for breakfast to the fermented tea-leaf mixture that's a popular finish to a Burmese meal. Swap cocktails and canapés for snacks and tea sweetened with condensed milk at teahouses where you can shoot the breeze with locals.

The Ethical Dimension

You no doubt know that Myanmar is a troubled land. In 2011, following the previous year's election, a quasi-civilian government was sworn in and Aung San Suu Kyi, at the time of research, had been released from house arrest. The tourism boycott that persuaded many to steer clear of the country for over a decade has been lifted. It's still up to you to decide whether it's time to visit (see p21). Keep in mind that the long-suffering people are everything the regime is not. Gentle, humorous, engaging, considerate, inquisitive and passionate, they want to play a part in the world, and to know what you make of their world. Yes, this is Burma – come with your mind open and you'll leave with your heart full.

Myanmar (Burma)

Top Experiences

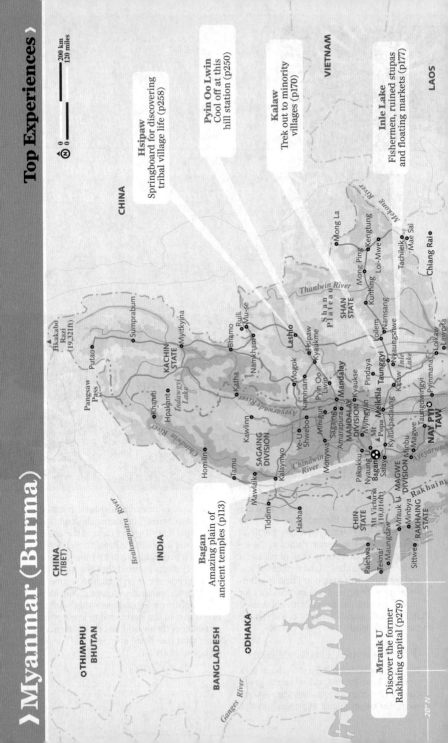

0 | 200 km
0 | 120 miles

Hsipaw
Springboard for discovering tribal village life (p258)

Pyin Oo Lwin
Cool off at this hill station (p250)

Kalaw
Trek out to minority villages (p170)

Inle Lake
Fishermen, ruined stupas and floating markets (p177)

Bagan
Amazing plain of ancient temples (p113)

Mrauk U
Discover the former Rakhaing capital (p279)

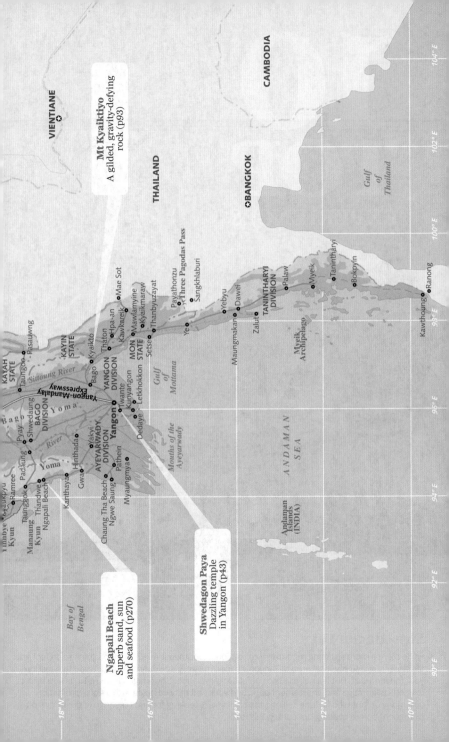

Mt Kyaiktiyo
A gilded, gravity-defying rock (p93)

Ngapali Beach
Superb sand, sun and seafood (p270)

Shwedagon Paya
Dazzling temple in Yangon (p43)

VIENTIANE

THAILAND

BANGKOK

CAMBODIA

Gulf of Thailand

Bay of Bengal

ANDAMAN SEA

Andaman Islands (INDIA)

Gulf of Mottama

Mouths of the Ayeyarwady

KAYAH STATE

KAYIN STATE

MON STATE

YANGON DIVISION

BAGO DIVISION

AYEYARWADY DIVISION

TANINTHARYI DIVISION

Yangon-Mandalay Expressway

Sittoung River

Bago Yoma

Yoma

Bago River

Three Pagodas Pass

104° E
102° E
100° E
98° E
96° E
94° E
92° E
90° E

18° N
16° N
14° N
12° N
10° N

Tilinbye Maaukpyu Kyun
Kamee
Taungok
Manaung Kyun
Thandwe
Ngapali Beach
Karthayana
Gwa
Chaung Tha Beach
Ngwe Saung
Myaungmya
Pathein
Hinthada
Padaung
Pyay
Shwedaung
Taungoo
Pasauwng
Kyaukto
Bago
Kunyangon
Twante
Letkhokkon
Dedaye
Yangon
Thaton
Kyaikto
Hpa-an
Kawkareik
Mae Sot
Mawlamyine
Kyaikmaraw
Thanbyuzayat
Setse
Payathonzu
Sangkhlaburi
Ye
Yebyu
Dawei
Maungmakan
Zalut
Myeik
Archipelago
Palaw
Myeik
Tanintharyi
Bokpyin
Kawthoung
Ranong
Yakyi

10 TOP
EXPERIENCES

Shwedagon Paya

1 Is there a more stunning monument to religion in Southeast Asia? We don't think so. In fact, the sheer size and mystical aura of Yangon's gilded masterpiece may even cause you to question your inner atheist. But it's not all about quiet contemplation: Shwedagon Paya (p43) is equal parts religious pilgrimage and amusement park, and your visit may coincide with a noisy ordination ceremony or fantastic fortune-telling session. If you're looking for one reason to linger in Yangon (Rangoon) before heading upcountry, this is it.

Inle Lake

2 Virtually every visitor to Myanmar (Burma) makes it here at some point, but Inle Lake (p177) is so awe-inspiring and large that everybody comes away with a different experience. If you're counting days, you'll most likely be hitting the hotspots: water-bound temples, shore-bound markets and floating gardens. If you have more time, consider day hikes or exploring the more remote corners of the lake. Either way, the cool weather and friendly folk and that placid pool of ink-like water are bound to find a permanent place in your memory.

ANDERS BLOMQVIST/LONELY PLANET IMAGES ©

Bagan

3 More than 3000 Buddhist temples are scattered across the plains of Bagan (Pagan; p149), site of the first Burmese kingdom. Dating back to between the 11th and 13th centuries, the vast majority of the temples have been renovated, as Bagan remains an active religious site and place of pilgrimage. Yes, there are tour buses and crowds at the most popular sunset-viewing spots, but they can be avoided. Pedal off on a bike and have your own adventure amid the not-so-ruined temples, or float over the temple tops in a hot-air balloon. Buddhist monks, Ananda Pahto Festival

Pyin Oo Lwin

4 Pyin Oo Lwin (Maymyo; p250) is a one-off curiosity that makes for an easy escape from sweaty lowland Mandalay. As the former British-era summer capital, it retains a wide scattering of colonial buildings big and small and a remarkable botanical garden that's one of Southeast Asia's most manicured. Today, local tourists and a new generation of elite fleeing the heat are treated to some of provincial Myanmar's best cuisine and most imaginative hotels. And to give it all a photogenic twist, the local taxi service is by colourful horse and cart. National Kandawgyi Gardens, Pyin Oo Lwin

BERNARD NAPTHINE/LONELY PLANET IMAGES ©

Mrauk U

5 While exploring the many temples, monasteries and ruined city walls of the former Rakhaing capital of Mrauk U (Myohaung; p279), you realise what an amazing place this sleepy town was at its zenith in the 16th century. Giant structures such as the Dukkanthein Paya and Kothaung Paya appear even more impressive amid the beguiling rural landscape of gently rounded hills and vegetable fields, through which the locals weave their way, aluminium water pots balanced on their heads. Stay an extra day and travel by boat to the Chin villages (p286) scattered along the Lemro River. Pagoda in the hills, Mrauk U

DENNIS WALTON/LONELY PLANET IMAGES ©

Thingyan

6 Myanmar in April is so hot that you'll enjoy getting soaked at Thingyan (Water Festival; p343), which marks the start of the country's new-year celebration. The festival involves lots of drinking, dancing, singing and theatre, with the emphasis on satire – even making (careful!) fun of the government. Cultural taboos are temporarily lifted, so women can 'kidnap' young men, blacken the men's faces with soot or oil, bind their hands and dunk their heads in buckets of water until they surrender and perform a hilarious monkey dance.

Ngapali Beach

7 Take with a pinch of salt the story about this beautiful beach reminding a homesick Italian of Naples. From its gently swaying palms, luxury resorts and appealing guesthouses to its pristine sands, tempting blue waters and delicious seafood caught fresh each day by local fishermen, Ngapali (p270) is the antithesis of the Italian city. Enjoy it for what it is: the perfect getaway and a chance to wind down – sunbathing, snorkelling and sipping fresh coconut juice as an ox-drawn cart trundles slowly across the fine, soft sand.

FRANK CARTER/LONELY PLANET IMAGES ©

Hsipaw

8 Attractive Hsipaw (p258) is ideally placed for quick, easy hikes into fascinating Shan and Palaung villages. The town's handful of guides offer just enough English-speaking help to make the experience comfortable, while the whole region feels far less 'discovered' than that around Kalaw. Hsipaw itself is a historic little town. It was once home to Shan princes and has its own (very) 'Little Bagan' of historic stupas. Fill out a few interesting days here with visits to a curious assortment of local, house-sized factories. Palaung home

Kalaw

9 Boasting an almost Himalayan atmosphere, Kalaw (p172) is Myanmar's ideal base for upcountry exploration. Hiking with Danu, Pa-O and Taung Yo villagers through the forests, fields, roads and trails that link the town and Inle Lake, you may even forget which country you're in. Trekking in the area is also one of the few travel experiences in Myanmar in which the authorities don't seem to mind if you stray off the beaten track. Children in Kalaw

Mt Kyaiktiyo (Golden Rock)

10 The good things in life never come easy. This is particularly so with the sweat-inducing, never-ending uphill slog to what is essentially a gilded stone. Sound questionable? Perhaps, but if you ask us, you can't say you've been to Myanmar if you haven't ascended Mt Kyaiktiyo (p93), home of the golden rock, the country's most important religious pilgrimage site after the Shwedagon Paya. The journey may be difficult, but at the top you'll be rewarded by a scene replete with scenic vistas and a uniquely Myanmar-style spiritualism.

need to know

When to Go

Mandalay
GO Nov-Feb

Pyin Oo Lwin
GO Nov-Feb

Bagan
GO Nov-Feb

Mrauk U
GO Oct-Mar

Yangon
GO Nov-Jan

Warm to hot summers, mild winters
Tropical climate, wet dry seasons

Your Daily Budget

Budget less than
$50
» Guesthouse: $10–20
» Local restaurant or street-stall meal: $1–3
» Travel on buses: $1–5

Midrange
$50– 100
» Double room in a midrange hotel: $20–60
» Two-course meal in midrange restaurant: $3–15
» Hiring a guide: $10 per day
» Puppet: $10–50

Top end over
$100
» Double room in top-end hotel: $60–500
» Two course meal restaurant plus bottle of wine: $20–30
» Driver and guide: $100 per day
» Fine lacquerware bowl: $200

High Season
(Dec–Feb)
» Rains least (if at all in places) and is not so hot.

Shoulder (Oct–Nov, Mar–Apr)
» March to May Yangon often reaches 104°F (40°C). Areas around Bagan and Mandalay are hotter.
» Cooler in the hill towns of Shan State.
» All forms of transport booked solid during Thingyan in April.

Low Season
(May–Sep)
» The southwest monsoon starts mid-May and peaks from July to September.
» The dry zone between Mandalay and Pyay gets the least rain. Rain can make roads impassable anywhere (especially in the delta region).

Money

» Cash only. Credit cards generally not accepted. Bring only pristine US bills for exchange.

Visas

» Needed by everyone. Maximum stay 28 days, non-extendable.

Mobile Phones

» No international roaming. Prepaid SIM cards available for locally bought phones.

Transport

» Buses and trains – both are pretty slow, especially trains. Flights to major tourist spots can get booked up quickly in high season.

Websites

» **Lonely Planet** (www.lonelyplanet.com) Good for pre-planning.

» **Irrawaddy** (www.irrawaddy.org) Thailand-based news and features site.

» **Myanmar Image Gallery** (www.myanmar-image.com) Pictures and text on myriad Myanmar-related subjects.

» **Online Burma/Myanmar Library** (www.burmalibrary.org) Database of books and past articles on Myanmar.

» **Demoractic Voice of Burma** (www.dvb.no) Norway-based media organisation.

Exchange Rates

The US dollar is the only foreign currency that's readily exchanged and/or accepted as payment for goods and services. The official exchange rate (US$1 equals around K6.5) is less than a tenth of the black-market rate, so do *not* change money at airport exchange booths or at banks. The best places to change money in Yangon are Bogyoke Aung San Market (p67) and your hotel.

Recent black-market rates in Yangon:

Australia	A$1	K750
Europe	€1	K1050
Japan	¥100	K9
UK	UK£1	K1200
US	US$1	K785

Important Numbers

Country code	☑95
International access code	☑00
Ambulance (Yangon)	☑192
Fire (Yangon)	☑191
Police (Yangon)	☑199

Arriving in Myanmar

Yangon International Airport If you haven't pre-arranged a transfer with you hotel or travel agent, a taxi from the airport to the city centre will be $8. Bring single bills with you (see below) so that you don't have to change money in the airport. Also see p71.

Cash-Only Economy

Myanmar ATMS don't accept international cards. With few exceptions, credit cards and travellers cheques aren't accepted either. Budget carefully and get the *right kind* of bills before your plane lands in Yangon. Otherwise, you'll end up in financial trouble.

US dollar bills must be 2006 or later bills that have colour and are in absolutely perfect condition: no folds, stamps, stains, writing marks or tears. On the black market, $100 bills get a better rate of exchange than lower values ones – but bring some of those, too.

We know of only one Yangon hotel (Parkroyal; p53) that is willing to provide cash against a credit card, but it does so at 12% commission. For more on money matters, see p364.

if you like...

Buddhas & Temples

Myanmar is one of the most devout Buddhist countries in the world. Yangon's Shwedagon Paya, Mandalay's Mahamuni Paya and Bagan's plain of temples shouldn't be missed, but there are also many other lesser-known Buddhist religious sites that will impress you with their beauty and spirituality.

Pyay (Prome) A 10-storeys tall, seated buddha watches over Pyay's hilltop Shwesandaw Paya, providing sweeping views of the town (p143)

Win Sein Taw Ya Gawp at the 560ft-long buddha reclining on the lush hillsides of Yadana Taung, accessible from Mawlamyine (p102)

Mrauk U (Myohaung) Fall under the spell of the old Rakhaing capital, dotted with ruined and restored temples and monasteries (p279)

Sagaing Leafy paths shade the routes to 500 hilltop and riverside stupas and a community of some 6000 monks and nuns (p228)

Mt Kyaiktiyo (Golden Rock) Join the pilgrims as they fix gold leaf squares on this incredible balancing boulder (p93)

Food & Drink

Not as spicy as other Southeast Asian food, Myanmar's cuisine reflects its multicultural mix of people. With the offerings ranging from Shan-style rice-noodle curries and soups to tamarind-flake sweets in Bagan and fresh grilled seafood in Rakhaing State, you're sure to find something new and delicious.

Street eats There are street vendors serving great, cheap snacks and meals everywhere in Myanmar, but the best selection is in Yangon (p61)

Tea time Breakfast or an afternoon snack at a Myanmar teahouse is a unique experience that provides more than a caffeinated kick (p334)

Cooking classes Learn how to cook like a native at classes in Bagan (p114)

Alcoholic beverages Raise a glass of toddy (p333) made from the sap of the palm, or wine produced from Shan Hills grapes (p191)

Superfresh Seafood At Ngapali Beach's restaurants (p285) dine on fish and shellfish caught the same day in the Bay of Bengal

Ethnic Variations Hunt out Jing Hpaw Thu (p237) in Myitkyina for authentic Kachin food, or Shan specialties at Shan Restaurant (p190) in Taunggyi

Handicrafts & Shopping

Going on a shopping spree of Myanmar's fine range of handicrafts is one of the best ways of ensuring your tourist dollars benefit the people rather than the military. It's also a wonderful eye-opener to browse one of the many local markets selling fresh produce and everyday items, photogenically laid out by stallholders.

Markets Drop by Yangon's Bogyoke Aung San Market (p67) for handicrafts from around the country, and the central markets in Pyay (p143) or Sittwe (p275) for colourful, lively shopping scenes

Lacquerware Watch artisans craft, paint and engrave lovely bowls, cups and other ornaments at workshops in Myinkaba (p123), New Bagan (p125) and Kengtung (p196)

Parasols Keep the sun off with the graceful, painted paper umbrellas that are a specialty of Pathein (p79)

Puppets If you enjoyed the classic marionette shows in Mandalay, why not adopt a puppet character of your own (p218)

» Buddhist monk with a jumping cat at Nga Hpe Kyaung (p185)

Activities & Adventures

Many activities take place under the hot Myanmar sun, from long-distance treks in Shan State to diving adventures around the islands of the deep south, best reached from Phuket. Adventures include floating over Bagan's temples in a hot-air balloon or admiring the gorgeous scenery from the deck of a river boat.

Overnight treks Head to Kalaw (p170), Pindaya (p176) or the less 'discovered' Hsipaw (p259) for short, easily arranged hill-tribe village treks

Balloon rides Marvel at Bagan's temples, bathed in the beautiful light of dawn, from the basket of a hot air balloon (p113), or save up for a balloon safari over Inle Lake (p187)

Boat journeys Ride sections of the Ayeyarwady (Irrawaddy) (p239); explore the Chindwin from Monywa (p132) or sail from Yangon to Pathein (p70)

Bicycling Pedal your way around Bagan (p115), or arrange a more challenging cross-country bike ride (p374)

Big Game Fishing Board the Barracuda in Ngapali Beach (p271) to go fishing for marlin, king mackerel or bluefin and yellowfin tuna

Surreal & Quirky Sights

Men wearing skirts (called *longyi*) and with faces slathered in *thanakha* (traditional make-up) – just one of Myanmar's litany of unusual and memorable sights that you'll encounter. Locals balance their Buddhist beliefs with a respect for supernatural *nats* (spirits) – keep an eye out for *nat* effigies at village temples and shrines as well as larger complexes, such as Mt Popa (p126).

Nay Pyi Taw In a country of intermittent power supply and pot-holed roads, the 24-hour-street lights and empty, pristine highways of Nay Pyi Taw are a surreal sight (p139)

Jumping cats Applaud the kitties that have been trained to leap through hoops by the monks at Inle Lake's Nga Hpe Kyaung (p185)

Giant spectacles Sometimes even Buddha needs spectacles; the faithful believe the buddha wearing a massive pair at Shwedaung can cure eyesight afflictions (p147)

Holy snakes Whether draped around their favourite buddha statue or being tenderly washed at 11am, Paleik's star residents are its pythons (p231)

Ethnic & Tribal Diversity

Apart from Buddhist temples, Yangon has religious sites that are important to Hindus, Muslims, Jews and various Chinese communities. But you need to leave Myanmar's biggest city to encounter some of the country's estimated 135 different ethnic groups; try to schedule your trip to coincide with one of the major ethnic or religious festivals, too (p16).

Kengtung Mingle with Shan and tribal people from the surrounding hills at the central market and twice-weekly water-buffalo market (p193)

Hsipaw Trek out of this low-key country town to encounter Shan and Palaung tribal villagers (p259)

Mawlamyine Soak up the laid-back atmosphere of this tropical town that's the heart of Mon culture (p96)

Myitkyina Proud of its Kachin culture and host to two huge, colourful tribal festivals, including a new one that reunites Lisu villagers from both sides of the Chinese border (p236)

month by month

Nearly every active *paya* (Buddhist temple) or *kyaung* (Buddhist monastery) community hosts occasional celebrations of their own, often called *paya pwe* or 'pagoda festivals'. Many occur on full-moon days and nights from January to March, following the main rice harvest, but the build-up can last for a while. All such festivals follow the 12-month lunar calendar (p368) and so their celebration can shift between two months from year to year.

January

Peak season and, if Chinese New Year falls within the month, even busier with local tourists and those from the region. Plan well ahead to secure transport tickets and hotels of choice. Note New Year's Day is not a public holiday in Myanmar.

Independence Day

Celebrating the end of colonial rule in Burma, this major public holiday on 4 January is marked by nationwide fairs, including a week-long one at Kandawgyi Lake (p48) in Yangon.

Manao Festival

Costumed dancing, copious drinking of rice beer and 29 cows or buffalo sacrificed to propitiate *nats* (traditional spirits) are part of this Kachin State Day event, held in Myitkyina on 10 January (p236)

Ananda Pahto Festival

Stretching over a couple of weeks in January (but sometimes in December, depending on the Myanmar lunar calendar) this is one of the biggest religious festivals in Bagan (p158).

February

Still a busy travel season, with the weather beginning to get warmer. If Chinese New Year happens to fall in this month, watch out for a boost in travel activity.

Shwedagon Festival

The lunar month of Tabaung (which can also fall in March) signals the start of the Shwedagon Festival (p51), the largest *paya pwe* in Myanmar.

April

While joining in the water frolics of Thingyan can be fun, note that it's steaming hot in Myanmar during this month. Also, with many locals off work and on the move during the New Year celebrations, securing transport, booking hotels and even finding a restaurant open for a meal can be tricky – plan well ahead!

Buddha's Birthday

The full-moon day of Kason (falling in April or May) is celebrated as Buddha's birthday, the day of his enlightenment and the day he entered *nibbana* (nirvana). Watering ceremonies are conducted at banyan trees within temple and monastery grounds.

Water Festival (Thingyan)

Lasting from three days to a week, depending on whether the holiday falls over a weekend, this celebration welcomes in Myanmar's New Year. See p11 and p343 for more details.

★ Dawei Thingyan
The male residents of the tropical seaside town of Dawei (Tavoy; p110) don huge, 13ft bamboo-frame effigies and dance down the streets to the beat of the *kalakodaun*, an Indian drum.

June

Pack your raincoat and a sturdy umbrella, as this month Myanmar is doused by monsoon rains. Roads can be flooded and flights to coastal destinations are sharply reduced.

★ Start of the Buddhist Rains Retreat
The full moon of Waso is the beginning of the three-month Buddhist Rains Retreat (aka 'Buddhist Lent'), when young men enter monasteries and no marriages take place. Prior to the full-moon day, a robe-offering ceremony to monks is performed.

August

The monsoon is still in full swing so be prepared for damp days and transport hitches.

★ Taungbyone Nat Pwe
Myanmar's most famous animist celebration is held at Taungbyone, 13 miles north of Mandalay (see p210) and attracts thousands of revellers, many of them homosexual or transgender.

September

The rainy season starts to wind down. Watch out for boat races in places such as Inle Lake.

★ Thadingyut
Marking the end of Buddhist Lent, this festival of lights celebrates the descent of Buddha from heaven. People place candles in their windows and it's a popular time for weddings and monk pilgrimages.

October

Rain still a possibility but that means everything is very green – making this a great time to visit Bagan, for example.

★ Tazaungdaing
The full-moon night of Tazaungmon (which can also fall in November), known as Tazaungdaing, is a second 'festival of lights', particularly famous for the fire-balloon competitions in Taunggyi (see p189).

November

The start of the main tourist season sees cooler weather and still-lush landscapes.

★ National Day
Held on the waning of Tazaungmon (usually in late November), this public holiday celebrates student protests back in 1920, seen as a crucial step on the road to independence.

December

Peak travel season with many visitors heading to the country over the Christmas–New Year break. Christmas itself is celebrated by many Christian Kayin, Kachin and Chin people.

★ Kayin New Year
On the first waxing moon of Pyatho (which can also happen in January), the Kayin New Year is considered a national holiday, with Kayin communities (clustered in Insein near Yangon and Hpa-An) wearing traditional dress.

Whether you've got a week or a month, these itineraries provide a starting point for the trip of a lifetime. Want more inspiration? Head online to lonelyplanet.com/thorntree to chat with other travellers.

itineraries

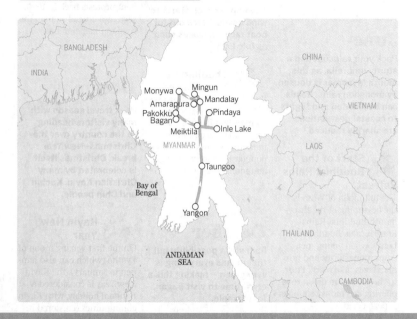

Two Weeks
Myanmar's Highlights

Starting in **Yangon**, visit the **Shwedagon Paya** at night, when its golden *zedi* (stupa) glows under floodlights. The next day, follow our walking tour of the city centre and shop for handicrafts at **Bogyoke Aung San Market**. Take a bus or flight to **Mandalay**, then climb **Mandalay Hill** and see the famed **Mahamuni Paya** and **Moustache Brothers**. The next day take a morning boat trip to **Mingun**, home to a giant earthquake-cracked stupa, following up with a sunset boat ride past U Bein's Bridge at **Amarapura**. Catch a bus to **Monywa**, climb halfway up inside the world's tallest standing buddha or take day trips to quiet riverside villages like **A Myint**. Continue by road to **Pakokku**, then board the afternoon boat to **Bagan**; set aside two or three days to explore the thousands of ancient temples. Fly or settle in for the long bus ride to beautiful **Inle Lake**, where motor-powered dugout canoes take you to floating markets under the flight path of egrets. Make a day trip to the **Shwe Oo Min Cave** near Pindaya to see 8000 buddha images. If you're not flying directly back to Yangon, consider breaking your road journey at either the relaxing lakeside town of **Meiktila** or the pilgrimage town of **Taungoo**.

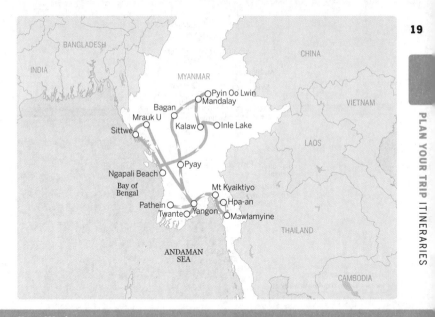

Four Weeks
A Month in the Country

This itinerary, which doesn't require any special travel permits, takes maximum advantage of the 28-day tourist visa. Week one sees you heading south, by bus or train, from **Yangon**. First stop: the amazing, golden boulder stupa balanced atop Mt Kyaiktiyo. Next up, **Mawlamyine**, a beguiling, melancholic town that was once a stomping ground of both Kipling and Orwell. Linger long enough to make a few day trips, such as to the coconut-crazy island Bilu Kyun, the giant reclining buddha Win Sein Taw Ya, or Thanbyuzayat War Cemetery, last resting place of the prisoners who died building the infamous Burma–Siam Railway.

Time your departure from Mawlamyine to coincide with the Monday or Friday boat service to Kayin State's underrated capital, **Hpa-an**. Give yourself enough time here to climb nearby Mt Zwegabin, before taking the overnight bus back to Yangon.

Week two starts with a journey north along the Yangon–Bagan Highway, pausing at historic **Pyay**, famed for its pilgrimage site, Shwesandaw Paya, and the ancient city ruins of Thayekhittaya. Continuing north, switch buses in Magwe, to reach the amazing temple-strewn plains of **Bagan**. A boat ride away is **Mandalay**, bigger and less exciting than many visitors imagine, but a great base for visiting several ancient-city sites.

If the heat is getting you down, drive two hours and breathe fresh cool air in the colonial-era getaway of **Pyin Oo Lwin**. Chill out even more around the shores of magical **Inle Lake**, perhaps getting there via an overnight trek from **Kalaw**.

Fly from Heho direct to Thandwe for some R&R on beautiful **Ngapali Beach**. Tan topped up, head north by plane or boat to Rakhaing State's regional capital of **Sittwe**. Linger a day to catch its atmospheric market and breezy seaside promenade, then take a river trip to **Mrauk U**. Once a powerful, cosmopolitan city, it's now one of Myanmar's most atmospheric backwaters, an idyllic location dotted with hundreds of ancient stupas and monasteries. Reserve a day for another river trip to visit nearby Chin villages.

Fly back to Yangon where you can do some last minute sightseeing and shopping, perhaps making a day trip to the Delta town of **Twante** for pottery, or taking an overnight break in **Pathein** to pick up some paper parasols.

No Fees Please!
Down the Ayeyarwady

24-28 Days
Down the Ayeyarwady

18 Days
No Fees Please!

Fly to **Myitkyina**, capital of Kachin State and home to two of Myanmar's most colourful festivals. A pair of one-day river-boat rides descend through the Ayeyarwady River's first defile to attractive old **Bhamo** with an overnight stop along the way in the delightful car-less village of **Sinbo**. Choose a fast boat or slow ferry to historic **Shwegu** through the grander, shorter second defile, and then continue on to **Katha**, a former colonial outpost where George Orwell based his *Burmese Days*. From Katha express boats can zoom south all the way to Mandalay in one day. Alternatively, continue down river by slow ferry, spending a couple of nights aboard, and possibly jumping ship at **Kyaukmyaung** with its fascinating riverside pottery factories. An hour's drive west is the former Burmese capital **Shwebo**, from which you can head by road to Mandalay or to appealing **Monywa** and colourful **Pakokku**. From Pakokku you can board a ferry to Myanmar's multi-temple masterpiece, **Bagan**. If you head direct from Katha to **Mandalay**, visit the nearby ancient city sites, including Mingun and Inwa, before jumping on an Ayeyarwady boat to Bagan, or even a plumping for a bargain four-day river odyssey all the way to **Pyay**.

Limit the amount of money that goes to the government by following this itinerary; it ventures off the beaten track and covers mainly private businesses. In **Yangon** visit the 2000-year-old **Sule Paya** while on a downtown walking tour. Hop on a ferry to explore nearby rural villages **Thanlyin** and **Kyauktan**, returning to Yangon to catch an overnight bus to **Mandalay**. Skip the $10 government fee by visiting alternative sights, such as Yankin Paya, and by making a day trip to **Amarapura**. Bus or taxi into the Shan Hills at **Hsipaw** and take a privately guided rural trek to Palaung villages. After two nights, taxi downhill to **Pyin Oo Lwin** for a night in the old British hill station. Bus hop from Mandalay back to Yangon via the lakeside town of **Meiktila** and the 16th-century capital of **Taungoo**, which offers a delightful guesthouse overlooking a beguiling rural scene. From Yangon, take either a boat or a bus to low-key **Pathein** to pick up a sun parasol from private workshops, then finish with a couple of days sunning yourself with the locals at either **Chaung Tha Beach** or **Ngwe Saung Beach**.

Responsible Travel

Key Points

» Travel independently rather than in a big tour group.

» Where possible, avoid using businesses owned by the government or those closely linked with it.

» Spread your money around, ie buy souvenirs across the country, not just in Yangon.

» Don't compromise locals by your actions or topics of conversation.

» Do talk to locals – they relish outside contact.

» Contribute to local charitable causes.

Advance Reading

Culture Shock! Myanmar, Saw Myat Yin
To Myanmar with Love, ed Morgan Edwardson
Burma/Myanmar: What Everyone Needs to Know, David I Steinberg
The River of Lost Footsteps, Thant Myint-U
Freedom From Fear, Aung San Suu Kyi
Perfect Hostage, Justin Wintle
Nowhere to Be Home, eds Maggie Lemere and Zoë West

Geographically beautiful and populated by gentle people, Myanmar is also notorious for its human rights abuses. The United Nations, Amnesty International and Human Rights Watch are among the many respected bodies who have called the country's military rulers to account for their imprisonment and mistreatment of political dissidents, use of forced labour, and violent crackdowns on peaceful demonstrations, as witnessed in September 2007.

Many countries, including the US, Canada, Australia and those of the European Union, have and continue to apply economic sanctions. In 1995 the NLD also called for a tourism boycott (see p318), which led to criticism of previous editions of this guidebook. In 2010 this controversial travel boycott was officially dropped by the NLD, who now welcome independent tourists who are mindful of the political and social landscape; however, those on large group package tours are discouraged.

Lonely Planet believes the answer to the question of whether to visit Myanmar is something that everyone has to decide for themselves; the box on p22 sums up the major pros and cons. If you do go, this guide has been researched and designed to maximise how much of your travel budget goes directly to local people and minimise how much goes to the regime.

The chapters on p290, p293 and p315 are all good starting points for getting to grips with the past and current situation in Myanmar.

TO GO OR NOT TO GO?

The Pros

» When researching this book, we found that the vast majority of locals – including democracy supporters – welcomed visitors.

» Tourism creates badly needed jobs in a country with a per capita income of $435.

» A savvy independent traveller should be able to ensure that the majority of his or her travel dollars go to the private sector and not to the government (p24).

» Through 'direct aid' efforts (p25), visitors can help improve living conditions for a local community.

» Tourism facilitates contact between Myanmar's locals and the outside world: locals see that they're not forgotten and visitors take away images and stories to share with friends and relatives at home, which helps people stay informed about what is going on inside this traditionally closed nation.

The Cons

» It's impossible to visit without some money going to the government.

» International tourists can be seen as a symbolic stamp of approval for the government, whose human rights abuses and corruption are well documented and continuing; there are over 2000 political prisoners, for example.

Avoid Package Tours

'We want people to come to Burma, not to help the junta, but to help the people by understanding the situation: political, economic, moral – everything. To have a very big cruise ship with hundreds of tourists coming in – that's a lot of money for the regime, and so we don't like such big business.'

U Win Tin, NLD leader and former political prisoner

This guidebook is geared for independent travellers, rather than those on group tours. You not only get more out of a trip travelling independently and meeting locals, but also you have more control over where your money goes.

Many locals who support tourism favour individual travellers over package tourists; this is the approach encouraged by Aung San Suu Kyi and the National League for Democracy (NLD).

Generally, the more luxurious the tour the greater the chance that a large percentage of its cost is going to businesses with strong links to the government. And in many cases, travellers pay for tours before they arrive in Myanmar, which means less of their money

finds its way into the pockets of ordinary citizens. Tours also tend to provide less interaction with locals while you're in the country.

For tips and advice on arranging your own tour, including securing permits and deciding where to stay and what modes of transport to use, see p27. If you prefer working with tour agents in your own country or in Mynamar, ask them the following questions:

» Who are your owners and do they have any links to the government?

» What are your policies with regard to using the services of government or government-linked businesses?

» Do you have any charitable programs in place to assist local communities and/or individuals?

» Can I contribute directly to a clinic, school or orphanage as part of a trip (always do this in person)?

» Can I hire different guides at each destination rather than travel with one guide for the whole trip?

Choose Goods & Services Carefully

Responsible visitors to Myanmar try to minimise the amount of money they spend on government owned, or government-friendly business and services. However, disentangling the complex web of financial connections in Myanmar's economy is like unpicking the Gordian knot. The government has recently been divesting itself of certain nationalised businesses – the supply of petrol being a key example – but it still controls large chunks of the economy.

While some cronies are easily identifiable (see p26), other 'private' companies are run by government members or supporters on the sly, or by their family members. Such links can be difficult to trace, partly because there is no equivalent of surnames in Myanmar, so each member of the family has his or her own name.

When researching this guide, we made every effort to identify government-owned or government-friendly businesses. Where there is a good alternative to such businesses, that service is reviewed instead of the crony-owned one. Where there is no alternative business or service (ie trains, or the only hotel in a location), a note of the government affiliation is made in the review.

It should not be assumed, however, that all other reviewed businesses in this guide have no involvement with the government. Ownership is frequently murky, and as in any country, taxes (both the official kind and the bribes that are a necessary part of getting things done) are a fact of life in Myanmar, with no business being able to avoid financial dealings with those in power. Also, when it comes to buying souvenirs and products, keep in mind who may be supplying them; see p319 for details about precious stones and jewellery.

Bottom line: the only way ensure that none of your money will benefit the government is to not visit Myanmar.

Spread Your Money

Critics of independent travel argue that travellers' spending usually bottlenecks at select places, even if those spots are privately run. Familiarity can be reassuring – such as your trishaw-driver buddy, or the plate of noodles that didn't make you sick – but the more places at which you spend money, the greater the number of locals likely benefit. A few things to consider:

» Don't buy all of your needs (bed, taxi, guide, meals) from one source.

» Be conscious that behind-the-scenes commissions are being paid on most things you pay for when in the company of a driver or guide. If all travellers follow the same lead, the benefits go to only a select few.

» Plan en-route stops, or take in at least one off-the-beaten-track destination, where locals are less used to seeing foreigners.

» Mix up the locations from which you catch taxis and trishaws – and try to take ones from drivers who aren't lingering outside tourist areas.

» Try to eat at different family restaurants, and if you're staying at a hotel, eat out often. In Ngapali Beach, for example, local restaurants are just across the road from the beach and hotels.

» Buy handicrafts directly from the artisans as you travel around the country, or if you're spending most of your time in the same location, don't get all your souvenirs from one private shop.

MY LIFE AS A TREKKING GUIDE

Some of the benefits, and dilemmas, of tourism in Myanmar are illustrated in this interview we conducted with a trekking guide in Shan State, who wished to remain anonymous:

'I've been leading treks since 1990. I was a civil servant for 15 years but in 1988 I took part in the democracy movement and was put in jail for three months. They couldn't find me guilty of anything and when I was released, I didn't want to work for the military government. So I started doing this after helping some visiting foreigners.

'It's a good job: I have a lot of chance to speak English and improve [my language skills]. I'm even reading books in English now. But after I help my son through university I'd like to become a monk.

'I think tourists should come to Myanmar. If tourists come, then our people can earn money. But [the downside is that] all hotels have to pay money to the government – this means that the military generals have more money to buy weapons and guns.'

Interact, But Don't Endanger

One way you can positively help people is to talk and talk and talk, and make new friends. Many locals cherish outside contact because they have so little. This means the two-way exchange that comes from it is reassurance for them that Myanmar isn't forgotten. If you're spending all your time with one guide, or on your own, you're not really seeing Myanmar right. The temples and mountains and markets are lovely, but ultimately a trip to Myanmar is mostly about its people.

This said, bear in mind that Myanmar is a country that imprisons its people for disagreeing with the government's line. Ensure you don't behave in a way that will get locals into trouble. John Yettaw's impromptu visit to Aung San Suu Kyi (see p356) provides a salient lesson on the dangers of compromising locals.

Some things to keep in mind:

» Don't raise political questions and issues in inappropriate situations; let a local direct the conversation. For example, don't come out with something like: 'Did you march with the monks in 2007?' or anything about Aung San Suu Kyi or the NLD where there are others who may be listening in.

» Show equal caution regarding what you ask or say on the phone or via email. Internet shop operators may get into trouble if you log onto banned sites, for example.

» Exercise care when handing over to a local anything that could carry political overtones (such as a copy of the *Economist* or Myanmar-related books).

» Be wary of places that treat minority groups as 'attractions'. The 'long-necked' Padaung women in Shan State (p192) have led to a zoo-like tourist event.

» Think very carefully before accusing anyone of cheating you or of theft. Innocent people can suffer greatly by implication. For example, a bus driver can end up in very hot water if you report your camera stolen during a bus ride – indeed, several bus companies no longer carry foreigners for fear of such problems.

» Don't try to make contact with political prisoners who are on conditional release.

WHERE THE MONEY GOES

This table estimates how much on average the government may get from different types of traveller. We have based our calculations on our own on-the-ground experiences and conversations with locals. The figures include government taxes such as a visa, fees and a 10% tax on all purchases.

In some places, there are ways around the imposed fees, such as in Mandalay (p208). Also see p20 for an itinerary that bypasses all sites and destinations that require government fees.

TRAVEL BUDGET	THE GOVERNMENT RECEIVES	TYPE OF TRIP
$0	$0	People who stay at home and read about Myanmar
$420	$72	A two-week trip skipping all government fees (eg Bagan, Inle Lake) and services, and sticking with family guesthouses and public buses
$420	$97	Another shoestring trip, but one that includes government fees at Shwedagon Paya, Bagan and Inle Lake
$1000	$150	A two-week trip that includes three flights, a boat ride to Bagan and accommodation at midrange hotels
$1500	$200	A two-week trip with a private car for a week and accommodation at midrange hotels
$2000+	$250+	A one-week trip staying at higher-priced hotels, taking several guided day trips, eating at hotels and taking four domestic flights
$5000	$500	A deluxe cabin on a seven-night luxury cruise

THE PERILS OF MASS TOURISM

Despite the country's serious problems, there's a tendency among visitors, expats and some locals to talk about Myanmar as an 'unspoiled' tourist destination, one where the atmosphere, values and friendliness of 'old Asia' prevail – as fairytale-ish as such an assumption is. One of the reasons for this view is Myanmar's relatively tiny number of tourist visitors, in the region of 300,000 per year. Contrast that with the 14 million who descend on neighbouring Thailand annually for their holidays and you get an idea of how under-developed tourism is in the country.

While we met many people who would like tourism to continue to grow, we also spoke with others, such as Thant Myint-U, author of *The River of Lost Footsteps*, who told us of their concerns. 'For years I've tried to advocate tourism, as a way to create jobs for ordinary people and help open up the country,' says Thant. 'But now that tourism is beginning to take off and seems set to grow significantly over the coming years, I think we need to also have a serious public discussion about both the potential dangers as well as the benefits of mass tourism, learning lessons from the experience of nearby countries, and looking at concrete options for how tourism might best be managed.'

The NLD, who are now cautiously encouraging independent tourists to visit Myanmar, recognise the perils of mass tourism and have urged the government and businesses to avoid further damaging the environment in the process of developing tourism infrastructure.

Charity & Direct-Aid Volunteerism

Tourism isn't going to fix all of Myanmar's problems, of course, but there are some small things you can do to help during your visit. Ask guesthouse owners, agents, teachers and monks about where you can donate money for medical or school supplies. Or stop at a village school and ask what materials they lack. Often less than $100 can get a book, notepad and pen for everyone needing them.

One remote Chin village we visited in Rakhaing State sees occasional tourists, and donations to the village leader had resulted in something they quickly pointed out: a corrugated metal roof on a stilt house. 'Tourists paid for the roof of our school', the leader told us.

Outside of small donations, some NGOs prefer tourists to stick with their trips and leave bigger projects for them. Joel Charny at Refugees International, who supports tourism in the private sector, told us, 'I am not a fan of tourists trying to turn into development workers. Let tourists be tourists.'

During research for past editions of this guide, however, we met several retired travellers who acted as 'direct-aid volunteers'. They felt there wasn't time to wait for aid to reach locals, so they come twice yearly to fund projects on their own. One, who has built and overseen many new school projects, told us: 'When I finish one, I only have to drive 10 minutes to the next village to find another in need.' In *Tony Wheeler's Bad Lands* the founder of Lonely Planet writes about how he and his wife financed the construction of a 300m wooden bridge connecting the floating village of Maing Thauk to land at Inle Lake.

Another charity-minded traveller told us: 'Never give money. Go in a shop and buy a kilo of rice for someone. Ask what they need and get it, not money.'

For further information on volunteering, see p370.

Giving Gifts & Donations

Travellers handing out sweets, pens or money to kids on hiking trails or outside attractions have had a negative impact (as you'll certainly see when begging kids follow you around a pagoda). It's not the best way to contribute to those in need, and many locals will advise you not to give to children anyway. If you want to hand out useful items keep this in mind:

» Try to give directly to schools, clinics and village leaders, not kids. A rewarding way to spend a day is going to a village school, asking a teacher what

WHO ARE THE CRONIES?

In a rare interview published in the magazine *Future* in April 2011, Tay Za, founder of the Htoo group of companies, said that when he started in business in 1984 he had just US$12 to his name. Today, the 46-year-old is considered Myanmar's richest private individual. He made his billions through a string of government-favoured businesses that includes exporting timber, gems and jade (he's the president of the Myanmar Gems and Jewelry Entrepreneurs' Association).

This pantomime baddy of Myanmar's economy is also the owner of Air Bagan and two luxury hotel chains: Aureum Palace (in Ngwe Saung, Ngapali, Bagan, Nay Pyi Taw and Pyin U Lwin) and Myanmar Treasure Resort (in Yangon, Pathein, Ngwe Saung, Mawlamyine, Bagan and Inle Lake), as well as the Popa Mountain Resort and Malikha Lodge in Putao. Myanmar experts we spoke to while researching this guide believe that the airline Asian Wings is also under his control.

Tay Za is on the sanctions lists of the EU, the US, Canada, Australia and Switzerland. Sanctions are also imposed on his wife, Thidar Zaw, and his son, Pye Phyo Tay. Alongside him on the cronies blacklist is Zaw Zaw, managing director of the Max Myanmar (www.max-myanmar.com) group of companies. Among Zaw Zaw's properties are Hotel Max in Chaung Tha Beach and the Royal Kumudra in Nay Pyi Taw, as well as a string of petrol stations (Tay Za also owns petrol stations).

In his defence, Tay Za says his enterprises create jobs and encourage young citizens who have gone abroad to 'come back home and work' in Myanmar. And some of his luxury hotels are remarkable achievements, notably the reconstructed British-era Governors' Palace at Pyin Oo Lwin.

supplies are lacking, buying them and handing them out to each of the students.

» Foreign-made gifts (eg pens) are generally cherished items, and more likely to find a place in a bookcase than actually get used. If you want to give useful items, buy locally. This puts money into the local economy, and locals are more likely to use the gift!

» Give only to those with whom you have made some sort of personal bond, not to random supplicants who happen to ask. Otherwise you'll encourage a culture of begging.

» If you do decide to help a begging family, ask what they need. Often you can accompany them to the market and pick up food (a bag of rice, some vegetables, some fish).

» Some items from outside the country are greatly appreciated, though. It's a good idea to carry books and magazines. It's best, however, to be discreet about giving them to people you meet (for instance, leaving one behind in a guesthouse), particularly if there are any potential political overtones.

Back at Home

Your trip to Myanmar doesn't have to end once you're back home.

» Alert Lonely Planet and fellow travellers via the Thorn Tree discussion board (www.lonelyplanet.com/thorntree) if you've found a new or changed government-operated service or have advice on how to minimise money going to the government or any other tips about how to travel in Myanmar.

» Consider posting photos and perceptions of your trip on a blog – but make sure your words don't have repercussions for locals you may have met while travelling.

» Write to your local Myanmar embassy and elected politicians to express your views about the human-rights situation.

» Contact the various prodemocracy activist groups in your country.

» Email the people in Myanmar you became friendly with – let them know they are not forgotten.

Planning Your Trip

Don't Forget

» Your visa
» All-purpose electrical-plug adapter
» Torch (flashlight)
» Warm jacket for chilly overnight bus rides
» Colour passport photos for permits
» Flip flops or sandals
» Bug spray
» Prescription medicines
» Brand-new US dollars
  Vaccinations (see p383)
» Short-wave radio for BBC & VOA broadcasts

Travel Literature

The Trouser People Andrew Marshall
Finding George Orwell in Burma Emma Larkin
The Native Tourist Ma Thanegi
Golden Earth Norman Lewis
Burma Chronicles Guy Delisle
Bad Lands Tony Wheeler

Travel Advisories

Australia (www.smarttraveller.gov.au)
Canada (www.voyage.gc.ca)
New Zealand (www.safetravel.govt.nz)
UK (www.fco.gov.uk/travel)
USA (travel.state.gov/travel)

When to Go

November to February Peak travel season
October and March Shoulder season is also worth considering

Getting Your Visa

Everyone requires a visa to visit Myanmar – for full details, see p369. If you're applying for a tourist visa at home you should start the process no later than three weeks before your trip, a month before to be safe. For most people, getting a visa will be a relatively straightforward process. It's certainly far easier and less costly than the process Myanmar people have to go through to get a passport – see http://tinyurl.com/44b25e2 – let alone a visa for foreign travel!

It's possible to get a tourist visa at the **Myanmar Embassy in Bangkok** (☑662-233-2237; 132 Sathorn Nua Rd) within 24 hours if you apply in person; the cost for this service is 1010 baht.

Arranging Permits

There are large areas of Myanmar that are firmly off limits, or accessible only with permission. Securing such permission

» takes time – a minimum of at least two weeks, but more commonly around a month

» requires the help of an experienced travel agency – for a list of reputable Yangon-based agencies, see p69

» involves paying fees to the government – usually via the government-owned travel agency, MTT, even if you're dealing with another agency

» usually means dancing to the MTT's tune when it comes to how you visit the area in question and who you go with.

DON'T VISIT MYANMAR IF...

If you don't like to compromise on such things as food and hotel quality, and/or have a low tolerance for last-minute changes of plan or being denied conveniences such as guaranteed round-the-clock power, use of ATMs and credit cards, your mobile phone and the internet, then perhaps Myanmar isn't for you.

Don't come here if your holiday priorities revolve around nightlife and partying. Myanmar's evening entertainment options, including bars, are very limited, if they exist at all – Yangon (Rangoon), the largest city, included.

And in Myanmar, like many developing countries, there are questions around travel safety and health.

Sometimes areas that were possible to visit with or without a permit, suddenly become off-limits; that's how it is in Myanmar.

Exiting Myanmar by a land border (only three possible; see p375) will require permits and 'guide' fees and plenty of advanced notice.

Areas of Restricted Travel

Plan accordingly if your travel itineraries involve the following places:

» **Border Crossings** (p375) Permission is needed to exit Myanmar by all open land border crossings; entering the country this way is also subject to travel restrictions.

» **Kayah State** (p198) Only accessible on a government-sanctioned package tour, which aren't allowed to stray too far from the state capital, Loikaw.

» **Mt Victoria** (p287) Bypass the government guide by going with a private one, but you'll still need a permit. Mt Victoria is in Chin State.

» **Putao** (p266) Putao is in Kachin State.

» **Tanintharyi (Tenasserim) Region** (p110) No permission needed to go to Dawei (Tavoy), Myeik (Mergui) and Kawthoung, but access in and out is by flight only and you must stay within the city limits.

Picking Hotels

This guidebook lists hundreds of hotels and guesthouses that are believed to be privately run with no links to the government. Bear in mind that a tax of at least 10% goes to the government no matter where you stay. Visitors who want to ensure that the least amount of their money goes to the government can stick with budget family-run guesthouses and minihotels. Those who want their stay to benefit the most people may prefer midrange and top-end hotels, which can employ staff of 100 or more and often fund community projects. See p22 for more details about how we decided which hotels to review for this guide.

If you want to stay at a particular hotel or guesthouse, advance bookings are advised for the busiest holiday season in December and January. Otherwise, you usually shouldn't have a problem finding places to stay once you're in Myanmar. Note that some high-end hotels import their furnishings, supplies and even food; ask before booking. Staying at hotels that use local products can keep more of your money in the country.

Family-Run Guesthouses

Often with just five or so rooms and a lounge, which are shared with three or four generations of a family living in-house, these budget-level guesthouses can be a highlight of your trip, offering connections with local life and cheap deals (often $10 to $15 for a double). Most rooms come with a fan or some sort of air-conditioning unit, though electricity frequently cuts out after midnight. Some are better than others, however, and like budget hotels, you'll find some with squashed mosquitoes left on the walls.

Budget Hotels

In many towns your only options will be a couple of four-floor, modern, 'Chinese-style' hotels. In some there are dark cell-like rooms with a shared bathroom on the ground floor (usually for locals only), and

TRAIN, BOAT, ROAD OR TRAIN

The following places are only accessible by flights: Dawei, Kawthoung, Kentung (if approaching from within Myanmar), Myeik and Putao. Sittwe is accessible by airplane and by boat from Taunggok. Keep the following in mind when choosing your mode of transport:

MODE OF TRANSPORT	PROS	CONS
Air	Fast; reasonably reliable schedules	Relatively expensive; more money goes to government or crony-owned business
Boat	Chance to interact with locals; pleasant sightseeing	Slow; big ferries are government-owned and infrequent; only covers certain destinations
Bus	Frequent; reliable services; generally privately owned	Some services go overnight and have inconvenient departure/arrival times; can be uncomfortable
Car	Total flexibility; see more of the country	Can be expensive and is slower than flying; can only drive to some locations if you have a government-approved guide and driver.
Train	Chance to interact with locals; see the countryside	Uncomfortable; very slow and often delayed; government-owned

two types of nicer rooms on upper floors. Some have lifts. Some keep their generators on 24 hours; others just for a few hours at night and in the morning. Most cost $20 to $40 for a double.

Have a look before taking the higher-priced 'deluxe' rooms; they often cost an extra $10 for a refrigerator and writing desk you may not use. Others deluxe rooms offer more space, nicer flooring and maybe satellite TV.

Government Hotels

Very few hotels are still run by the government's Ministry of Hotels & Tourism (MHT), and they're generally dated, empty and poorly cared for. These hotels are usually easy to identify: they are often named for the town they're located in (eg Sittwe Hotel in Sittwe) and fly a Myanmar flag out front – and the staff are often quite up front about it if you ask!

There's little reason for staying in a directly run government hotel. They are haphazardly run and are frequently vacant because of it; often they are leased out to private individuals who may or may not be friendly with the government. Throughout this book we point out government hotels so that you can avoid them if you choose.

Joint-Venture Hotels

A number of foreign hotel groups operate hotels – technically via a lease with the government. These are all top-end, electricity-all-day hotels and are often the nicest options.

Though these hotels work on the whole as private hotels, it's unclear how much beyond the 10% tax, and their 'licence' fee, goes to the government. Because of this murkiness, some travellers opt to skip joint-venture hotels. On the other hand, some are known to fund community projects, such as the building of medical clinics, and are said to pay a slightly higher-than-average salary to their staff.

Other Private Hotels

It's hard to be sure where your money goes at these hotels, namely upper-midrange and top-end hotels owned and run by various local entrepreneurs. Some are former government hotels now leased to local owners. Some owners are simply part of Myanmar's tiny middle class and aren't linked with the government. Conversely, other owners are members of the generals' families or cronies of the government – for example, the owners of the Aureum Palace and Myanmar Treasure chains (p26).

HOW TO SKIP OVERNIGHT BUSES

There's not one obvious way to travel by bus between Myanmar's four big destinations: Yangon, Inle Lake, Mandalay and Bagan. Most travellers start in Yangon and bus to Mandalay one night, then pick between Inle Lake or Bagan next; this requires at least a couple of overnight buses. Also note, there's a dearth of direct buses from Mandalay to the Inle Lake area that are willing to take foreigners, and there's only one direct bus daily going to Kalaw/Taunggyi from Nyaung U, departing at 4am.

If you like being able to see scenery out the window, or sleeping in beds, you can travel to these places without taking an overnight bus. But it takes pre-planning and a bit more time – around a week of travel time and a total cost of K44,900 if you take the following buses and/or pick-up trucks:

ROUTE	DURATION (HR)	COST (K)
Yangon-Taungoo	9	3500-4300
Taungoo-Meiktila	6½	4000
Meiktila-Taunggyi (for Inle Lake)	6	2500-4000
Taunggyi-Kalaw	3	2500
Kalaw-Mandalay	9	8000-10,000
Mandalay-Nyaung U (for Bagan)	7-8	6500
Bagan-Magwe	8	5500
Magwe-Pyay	7	4000
Pyay-Yangon	7	4100

Putting Together Your Own Package

If you're used to having a car at the airport waiting for you, and guides showing you where to go, that can be done *and* arranged privately. Just because many roads are rough doesn't mean you have to sacrifice all comforts. Either contact a Yangon-based agent (p69) before a trip, or give yourself a couple of days to do so once you arrive. The agent can help set up private guides, transport and hotels. Ask to pay as you go to ensure that your money is spread out and to use different guides at each destination rather than one guide for the whole trip (see p21). Talk with more than one agent, telling them what you want, to gauge offers.

We know that some agents are keen to ensure you have adequate travel insurance covering medical emergencies for your trip. Their concerns are well-founded, as quality medical care in Myanmar isn't readily available. Therefore an insurance policy that covers medi-vac is wise.

Budgeting

Having decided on all the above, you'll be in a position to budget more accurately for your trip. If you need extra help, see p12.

In the vast majority of cases, you'll be paying for everything in cash – either US$ or the local currency, kyat – once you get to Myanmar (see p364). With a few very rare exceptions, credit cards are not accepted for local payment. Sometimes, if you're dealing with a travel agent, you can pay in advance for some of your expenses, on top of which a processing fee of around 5% is charged.

Also remember to bring brand new greenbacks. Myanmar ATMs don't accept international cards, and with one exception, it will also not be possible for you to get a cash advance on a credit card. Thus, you need to bring all the cash you think you'll need with you – and not just any cash. Brand-new US dollars – 2006 or later bills that have colour and are in absolutely perfect condition: no folds, stamps, stains, writing or tears – only will be accepted for payment or exchanged for kyat; see p13 for more details.

regions at a glance

Yangon

Temples ✓✓✓
Shopping ✓✓
Food ✓✓

Temples
Home to Shwedagon Paya, the most important religious pilgrimage site in the country, not to mention many, many other visitworthy paya and buddhas, Yangon is practically overrun with monuments to Buddhism. However, if all the Buddhist architecture is starting to look the same, the city's Hindu shrines, mosques, colonial-era churches and lone synagogue provide a worthwhile contrast for the templeweary.

p36

Shopping
Decades of international isolation have prevented Yangon from competing with neighbouring Bangkok as a shopping hotspot, but the city is home to a decent selection of shops stocked with quality handicrafts, quirky cultural items and one-of-a-kind art you're unlikely to encounter elsewhere. In particular, Yangon is home to some great antique stores stocking some genuine treasures. And if you prefer browsing, Yangon's open-air fresh markets are some of the more vibrant and interesting in the region.

Food
Home to some of the country's best Burmese food (a new cuisine for most visitors), Yangon is also has a plethora of restaurants serving tasty takes on more familiar cuisines, from subcontinental to Italian. And as soon as you're able to distinguish your *mohinga* from your *mondhi,* the city also offers a vibrant street-food scene that ranges from Indian to Shan.

Around Yangon

Temples ✓✓
Beaches ✓
Boats ✓✓

Temples
For temples, the former capital of Bago (Pegu) would probably outdo just about any city in Myanmar, but the water-bound Yele Paya at Kyauktan and the Shwemokhtaw Paya in Pathein make the entire region an area worth investigating for temple freaks.

Beaches
Chaung Tha Beach and Ngwe Saung Beach probably won't fit everybody's notion of a picture-postcard deserted beach, but they're clean, sunny and the easiest beaches to reach in Myanmar.

Boats
If you're still bearing the scars from your last crowded, hot, bumpy and never-ending Burmese bus ride, consider the region's water-bound transport. The easiest option is the five-minute river-crossing ferry to Dalah, while more intrepid travellers can take the two-hour boat to Twante or the overnight ferry to Pathein.

p73

Southeastern Myanmar

Caves ✓✓✓
Temples ✓✓✓
Culture ✓✓

Caves
For those who love the dark side, this is your region, particularly the countryside surrounding Hpa-an. There are countless caves, some with ancient Buddhist art, others largely untouched, all ripe for exploration.

Temples
There are enough temples in and around Mawlamyine alone to keep you busy for a lifetime, but the indisputable highlight of the region is Mt Kyaiktiyo (Golden Rock) – a must-do religious pilgrimage for every man, woman, child and tourist in Myanmar.

Culture
You will probably never have heard of the Mon people before, so let one of the excellent Mawlamyine-based guides introduce you to the culture via the area's tidy sugar-palm-lined towns, seaside temples and island-bound villages.

p91

Bagan & Central Myanmar

Temples ✓✓✓
Shopping ✓✓
Elephants ✓✓

Temples
You'll find thousands of them in Bagan, but also worth seeking out are the Nat shrine at Mt Popa and the pilgrimage temples of Shwesandaw Paya in Taungoo, Shwesandaw Paya in Pyay, and Shwemyetman Paya in Shwedaung.

Shopping
Bagan is also famous for its exquisitely decorated lacquerware; watch artisans create it in workshops in Myinkaba and New Bagan. Across the Ayeyarwady River, Pakoku is famous for its patterned blankets.

Elephants
The new capital, Nay Pyi Taw, has a couple of white elephants beside its giant Uppatasanti Paya, as well as a herd of regular elephants at its zoo. You can also watch elephants working at jungle logging camps on trips to teak plantations outside Taungoo.

p111

Eastern Myanmar

Outdoors ✓✓✓
Culture ✓✓✓
Food ✓✓

Outdoors
Tramping between tea plantations in Pindaya; buzzing around in a boat on Inle Lake; scaling mountains outside Kalaw; visiting a Loi longhouse outside Kengtung... These are just a few of the outdoor options possible in eastern Myanmar.

Culture
The country's far east boasts exceptional cultural diversity – even by Myanmar standards. Visit and learn about Pa-O culture around Inle Lake or learn about Shan culture and language and their similarities with those of neighbouring Thailand in Kengtung.

Food
From *shàn k'auq-swèh,* Shan-style noodle soup, to *ngà t'ămìn jìn,* a turmeric-tinged rice dish, a stay in eastern Myanmar is your chance to try authentic Shan food at the source.

p166

Mandalay & Around

Temples ✓✓
Culture ✓✓
Shopping ✓

Temples

As Burma's last royal capital, Mandalay has retained many fine monastic buildings. Arguably more interesting are the older stupas and temples on the sites of several older former capitals, including what would have been the world's biggest stupa (Mingun) had it been finished.

Culture

Mandalay is considered Myanmar's cultural capital, so it's a convenient place to see intimate traditional dance performances and marionette shows, while the dissident Moustache Brothers' vaudevillian rants are an eternal talking point.

Shopping

Numerous antique shops don't necessarily stock real antiques, but even if you're only window-shopping there's an impressive range of craft work, notably stuffed embroidery, silk, stone carving and the manufacture of gold leaf. The stone carving and the hammering of gold leaf are fascinating to watch.

p199

Northern Myanmar

Outdoors ✓✓
Culture ✓✓
Boats ✓✓

Outdoors

Lace up your boots and hike to unspoilt hill-tribe villages that are easily accessible on short yet easy-to-arrange hikes from Hsipaw and Kyaukme. Given permits and serious money, intrepid travellers can trek deep into Myanmar's Himalayan foothills from Putao.

Culture

Immerse yourself in this region's cultural panoply. Observe the contrasts between the predominantly Chinese Lashio, Palaung and Shan villages around Hsipaw and Kachin, and Lisu populations in Myitkyina, home to two of Myanmar's biggest 'minority' festivals.

Boats

Bump elbows with locals in no-frills public boats chugging down the mighty Ayeyarwady River. You'll barely see another foreigner here. But if you want something even remoter, you could join a relatively exclusive tour that takes you rafting or boating on the dramatic Malikha River near Putao.

p233

Western Myanmar

Temples ✓✓✓
Beaches ✓✓✓
Boat Trips ✓✓

Temples

Explore the ruined and functioning temples and palace remains scattered across the lush hillsides of the old Rakhaing capital of Mrauk U. Sittwe's giant Lokananda Paya and the teak buildings of the Shwezedi Kyaung monastic complex are also worth searching out.

Beaches

Idyllic stretches of palm-fringed sand hardly come more perfectly formed than that at Ngapali Beach. You can also watch the sunset over the Bay of Bengal from the beach and viewpoint a short walk or cycle south of Sittwe.

Boat Trips

The only way to reach Mrauk U or the remote Chin village further up the Lemro River is by a leisurely boat ride. For the really adventurous there's also the day-long coastal hop from Sittwe to Taunggok via the island port of Kyaukpyu.

p268

Look out for these icons:

 TOP Our author's
CHOICE recommendation

 A green or
sustainable option

FREE No payment
required

See the Index for a full list of destinations covered in this book.

On the Road

Yangon

Includes »

Best Places to Eat

» Aung Thukha (p60)

» Nilar Biryani & Cold Drink (p58)

» Feel Myanmar Food (p58)

» SK Hot Pot (p60)

» 999 Shan Noodle Shop (p58)

Best Places to Stay

» Strand Hotel (p52)

» Mother Land Inn 2 (p52)

» Panorama Hotel (p53)

» Governor's Residence (p53)

» Three Seasons Hotel (p53)

Why Go?

Many travellers tend to give Yangon (ရန်ကုန်) short shrift, sacrificing the city for extra time in Myanmar's high-profile upcountry destinations. This is a pity, as the city is – in its own quirky way – one of the more distinctive in Southeast Asia. In addition to possessing what is quite possibly the most awe-inspiring religious monument in the region, international isolation over the last five decades has left Yangon with an enduring colonial charm that has all but disappeared elsewhere. And although a sense of melancholy is a frequent backdrop to this setting, your memories are more likely to be of Yangon's vibrant and colourful streets, its hectic open-air markets, some of the friendliest urbanites anywhere and what is most likely your first experience with an entirely unfamiliar cuisine.

When to Go

Weather in Yangon follows the familiar pattern of hot in the summer (March to May) and relatively comfortable in the winter (November to January), with average highs of 84°F to 97°F (29°C to 36°C) and average lows of 64°F to 77°F (18°C to 25°C). Winter is the best time to visit, as the days are tolerable and the evenings often cool. As elsewhere in Myanmar, you can expect daily showers during the rainy season, from approximately June to November, although these are often short and shouldn't generally inconvenience your visit.

Yangon Street Names

The English terms 'street' and 'road' are often used interchangeably in Yangon for the single Burmese word *làn*. Hence, some local maps may read Shwegondine Rd, while others will say Shwe Gone Daing Rd or Shwe Gone Daing St; in Burmese, it's simply Shwe Gone Daing Làn. This chapter uses the most common English version that travellers encounter.

And as the previous examples demonstrate, different maps may also present the actual names of streets differently; eg Shwegondine Rd is Shwegondaing Rd on some local maps.

DANGERS & ANNOYANCES

Yangon is an incredibly safe city: you are far less likely to be robbed here than almost any other big city in Southeast Asia. Having said that, rich foreigners and badly lit side streets at night don't mix, and you should show some caution at such times. A far bigger danger is getting hit by a belligerent motorist, stumbling on the uneven paving slabs in central Yangon or even disappearing completely into a sewage-filled pot hole. Keep your eyes peeled for such obstacles and carry a torch at night.

Worth Noticing in Yangon

» Driving me crazy – Yangon is most likely where you'll first encounter Myanmar's unique driving situation: right-hand-drive cars being driven on the right side of the road.

» Smooching – Myanmar people get somebody's attention by making a kissing sound.

» No late nights here – just about the entire city closes down by 9pm.

» Motorcycle free – if you believe the rumours, a high-ranking military leader's car was hit by a motorcycle several years ago, leading him to issue a total ban on the two-wheeled vehicle on the streets of Yangon.

» Betelgeuse – red stains and even redder teeth will tip you off that this is betel nut country.

» Weird sex – on the streets of Yangon you'll see stalls selling bizarre sexual aids. In addition to flavoured condoms, we saw dodgy pills, penis enlargers and scary looking rings with hair and beads.

» Powerless – the lack of a consistent power source means noisy smoke-pumping generators are ubiquitous on the streets of Yangon.

Fast Facts

» Population: c4,348,000

» Telephone code: 01

» Elevation: 46ft

Planning Your Trip

» Be sure to arrange your Myanmar visa ahead of time – at the time of research, visa on arrival had temporarily been suspended.

» Bring cash – ideally US$ – and make sure it's in perfect condition.

Resources

» The **Irrawaddy** (www.irrawaddy.org) has put together an 'Alternative Tourist Trail' of lesser-known historical and political sights in Yangon at www.irrawaddy.org/article.php?art_id=6862.

Yangon Highlights

1 Offer a slack-jawed prayer of wonder at the **Shwedagon Paya** (p43), the pyramid of gold that is the Burma of old

2 Pick up some Burmese-style slippers or a new *longyi* at **Bogyoke Aung San Market** (p67)

3 Massage the person-sized toes of the jewel-bedecked enlightened one at the **Chaukhtatgyi Paya** (p47)

4 Have your palm read on the watercolour streets and search for a glittering paya and Chinese dragons on our **downtown Yangon walking tour** (p54)

5 Caffeinate, eavesdrop on the gossip and grab a snack at one of Yangon's **teahouses** (p63)

6 See Yangon's 'burbs from a very crowded train on the **Yangon Circle Line** (p50)

7 Witness the treasures of Myanmar's past at the poorly maintained but worthwhile **National Museum** (p41).

WHITE MARBLE & WHITE ELEPHANTS

There are numerous Buddhist monuments in the suburbs surrounding Yangon, but Kyauk Daw Kyi (Map p38; Bargaryar St; admission free; ☉6am-6pm), an immense seated Buddha, is undoubtedly the most impressive. Carved from a single piece of marble found outside Mandalay in 1999, the partially finished statue was painstakingly transported to Yangon by boat and train (on a specially built track) a year later, events that are depicted in the complex's modern murals. After the detailing was finished, the Buddha was positioned at its current home at the top of a hill and encased in glass.

Couple a visit here with the nearby Hsin Hpyu Daw (Map p38; admission free; ☉8am-5pm), an unmarked park across the street where two white elephants are held. The elephants – actually light pink in colour – were found upcountry and brought to Yangon in 2002, their discovery regarded, by the military at least, as a good omen for the country.

In late 2007 Yangon was the centre of huge nationwide fuel protests, which were led by Buddhist monks. The protests quickly escalated into antigovernment demonstrations, which resulted in the deaths of many protestors and worldwide condemnation.

In May 2008 the worst natural disaster in Myanmar's recent history hit the south of the country (see p305 for more). Yangon was declared a disaster area by Myanmar's government. Many of the city's pagodas, temples, shops and hotels had minor to serious damage from falling trees, lampposts and fences. However, when reconstruction work began, it was found that most of the city had escaped major structural damage. By mid-June 2008 electricity and telecommunications were back to normal, and shops and restaurants had reopened with brand-new corrugated-tin roofs.

History

Myanmar's biggest city, Yangon is comparatively young. It became the capital only in 1885 when the British completed their conquest of northern Myanmar, and Mandalay's brief period as the centre of the last Burmese kingdom ended.

Despite its short history as the seat of national government, Yangon has been in existence for a long time – although mostly as a small town – in comparison to places such as Bago (Pegu), Pyay (Prome) or Thaton. In 1755 King Alaungpaya conquered central Myanmar and built a new city on the site of Yangon, which at that time was known as Dagon. Yangon means 'end of strife': the king rather vainly hoped that with the conquest of central Myanmar, his struggles would be over. In 1756, with the destruction of Thanlyin (Syriam) across the river, Yangon also became an important seaport.

In 1841 the city was virtually destroyed by fire; the rebuilt town again suffered extensive damage during the Second Anglo-Burmese War in 1852. The British, the new masters, rebuilt the capital to its present plan and corrupted the city's name to Rangoon.

In 1988 around 15% of Yangon's city-centre population – all squatters – were forced to move to seven *myo thit* (new towns) northeast of the city centre. Many of the old colonial buildings once occupied by the squatters have now been refurbished for use as offices, businesses and apartments.

The city changed dramatically following the 1989 banishment of socialism. Starting in the early 1990s, the government began sprucing up the city's appearance by cleaning the streets and painting many public buildings. Since 1992, when the procapitalist General Than Shwe took power, new cars and trucks have taken to city roads, mobile phones are commonly seen in the city centre and satellite dishes dot the horizon.

In November 2005, quite unexpectedly, the government announced that the newly constructed city of Nay Pyi Taw in central Myanmar was to be the nation's capital. Despite the government upping sticks for the new capital, Yangon remains the commercial and diplomatic capital and by far the largest city.

☉ Sights

CITY CENTRE

Botataung Paya　　　　　BUDDHIST TEMPLE

ဗိုလ်တထောင်ဘုရား

(Map p42; Strand Rd; admission $2, camera $1) One of Yangon's 'big three' payas, and said to contain hair relics of the Buddha, the Botataung Paya was named after the 1000 military leaders who escorted relics of the Buddha from India to Myanmar over 2000 years ago (*Bo*

YANGON IN...

Two Days

Start the morning with a traditional Myanmar breakfast of **mohinga** (soup of thin rice noodles and fish broth). Before the heat becomes oppressive, take a walk around the city centre following our suggested **walking tour**. Allow yourself plenty of time to play in the markets, dawdle in the temples and fawn over the rickety architecture. Rest your feet before the day's highlight: the **Shwedagon Paya** at sunset. End your day with dinner at a nearby restaurant such as **SK Hot Pot**.

Dedicate your second day to exploring the sights outside the city centre. After a **teahouse breakfast**, take the **ferry** to Dalah, on the other side of the Yangon River, to provide a taste of delta life. Back on dry ground, the **Botataung Paya** near the jetty is the next logical stop. For lunch, take a taxi to **Aung Thukha** and try authentic Burmese food. Spend the remainder of the afternoon cruising around temples north of the city centre, including the **Chaukhtatgyi Paya** and nearby **Ngahtatgyi Paya**. Then, if time allows, take a stroll around **Kandawgyi Lake**, and maybe stop in for a drink at one of the lakeside restaurants or hotels.

Four Days

The sensible should try to give themselves more time to devote to the city, and if you're one of the lucky blighters able to do this, Yangon has some treats in store! Spend the first two days following the Yangon in Two Days suggestions and then, after another teahouse breakfast on day three, head to the **National Museum** to swoon over treasures that would make Aladdin jealous. Wander around the embassy district until you arrive at your lunch destination, **Feel Myanmar Food**. In the evening, hit up Chinatown and the incense-clouded temple **Kheng Hock Keong**, and finish with a streetside **grilled feast** on 19th St. By day four you'll probably feel the need to stretch your wings a little, so choose from one of three easy day trips out of the city. The first involves floating temples and off-beat adventure around **Thanlyin** and **Kyauktan**. The second involves more water with a slow ferry ride and temple tour of **Twante**. The third is for those for whom one Buddha is never enough: temple-packed **Bago** is where you're off to today.

means leader, usually in a military sense, and *tataung* means 1000). For one six-month period this paya is said to have harboured all eight strands of the Buddha's hair before they were distributed elsewhere. It's not as breathtaking as the Shwedagon, or as striking for being so out of place like Sule Paya, but Botataung's spacious riverfront location and lack of crowds give it a more down-to-earth spiritual feeling than the other two.

Its proximity to fresh air and the Yangon wharves were less fortuitous when a bomb from an Allied air raid in November 1943 scored a direct hit on the unfortunate paya. After the war the Botataung was rebuilt in a very similar style to its predecessor, but with one important and unusual difference: unlike most *zedi* (stupa), which are solid, the Botataung is hollow, and you can walk through it. There's a sort of goldleaf-coated maze inside the stupa, with glass showcases containing many of the ancient relics and artefacts, including small silver-

and-gold Buddha images, which were sealed inside the earlier stupa. Reconstruction also revealed a small gold cylinder holding two small body relics and a strand of hair, said to belong to the Buddha, which is reputedly still in the stupa. Above this interesting interior, the golden stupa spire rises to 131ft.

To the western side of the stupa is a hall containing a large **gilded bronze Buddha**, cast during the reign of King Mindon Min. At the time of the British annexation, it was kept in King Thibaw Min's glass palace, but after King Thibaw was exiled to India, the British shipped the image to London. In 1951 the image was returned to Myanmar and placed in the Botataung Paya. Also on the grounds is a *nat* pavilion containing images of Thurathadi (the Hindu deity Saraswati, goddess of learning and music) and Thagyamin (Indra, king of the *nat*) flanking the thoroughly Myanmar *nat* Bobogyi.

There's also a large **pond** full of hundreds of terrapin turtles. Most are fairly small but every now and again a truly monstrous one sticks its head out of the water.

A short walk from Botataung Paya at Botataung jetty, you can watch ferries and oared water taxis cross the Yangon River.

Sule Paya
BUDDHIST STUPA

ဆူးလေဘုရား

(Map p46; cnr Sule Paya & Mahabandoola Rds; admission $2) It's not every city whose primary traffic circle is occupied by a 2000-year-old golden temple. Surrounded by government buildings and commercial shops, the tall *zedi* at Sule Paya is another example of the strange incongruity of the Yangon cityscape. Yet, it's this mix of modern Asian business life melding with ancient Burmese tradition that is the highlight of the Sule Paya. Early evening, just after the sun has gone down and workers have rushed home for the night, is the most atmospheric time to both visit the temple and make a turn of the streets surrounding it. Many take the time to pause by the Sule Paya to pray and meditate on the day's events.

The central stupa's name, Kyaik Athok, translates in the Mon language as 'the stupa where a Sacred Hair Relic is enshrined'. As with many other ancient Myanmar shrines, it has been rebuilt and repaired many times over the centuries, so no one really knows exactly when it was built.

The golden *zedi* is unusual in that its octagonal shape continues right up to the bell and inverted bowl. It stands 151ft high and is surrounded by small shops (including an internet café and a guitar shop) and all the familiar nonreligious activities that seem to be a part of every *zedi* in Myanmar. Besides its significance as a landmark and meeting place, maybe its most mundane function is

as a milestone from which all addresses to the north are measured.

National Museum
MUSEUM

အမျိုးသားပြတိုက်

(Map p46; ☏371 540; Pyay Rd; admission $5; ⏱10am-4pm) Try to ignore the fact that the priceless collection at the National Museum is appallingly labelled and lit, and just focus on the treasures that lie within this cavernous building.

Highlights of the collection include the 26ft-high Sihasana (Lion Throne), which belonged to King Thibaw Min, the last king of Myanmar. It's actually more of an entrance doorway than a throne but let's not quibble, because it's a damn sight more impressive than your front door! Further signs that the kings of old didn't understand the meaning of the word 'subtlety' are the jewel-encrusted beds, silver and gold rugs, flashy palanquins (one of which is palatial in its size and splendour), kitchen chairs made of ivory, some breathtaking ceremonial dresses and a large collection of betel-nut holders and spittoons, which alone could make the British Crown Jewels look like cheap tack picked up at an 'everything for a dollar' shop.

The upper floors are less impressive and take you on an amble through natural history, prehistory and a very poorly lit art gallery.

Mahabandoola Garden
PARK

မဟာဗန္ဓုလပန်းခြံ

(Map p42; admission K500) Just southeast of the Sule Paya, this square urban park offers pleasant strolling in the city centre's heart, especially in the early morning when the air hasn't yet filled with traffic fumes. Occupying the centre of the northern half of the park is the

---

THE GRAVE OF THE LAST MUGHAL

In 1858, 27 years before they banished Burma's last king Thibaw to Ratnagiri, India, the British executed a similar regime change in Delhi. Following the failed Sepoy Mutiny, Bahadur Shah Zafar II, India's last Mughal emperor, was exiled to Rangoon with his wife Zeenat Mahal and remaining members of his family. The ex-emperor, who had a reputation as a talented Urdu poet, died four years later in November 1862.

William Dalrymple, who chronicles Bahadur Shah Zafar's life in *The Last Mughal*, writes of how his shrouded corpse was hastily buried in an anonymous grave in his prison enclosure, so that, as the British Commissioner in charge insisted, 'No vestige should remain to distinguish where the last of the Great Mughals rests.'

A mausoleum – the **Dargah of Bahadur Shah Zafar** (Map p46; Ziwaca St; admission free) – was later built on the location of the prison, but the grave itself remained a mystery until 1991 when workmen discovered it 3½ feet underground during excavations for a new structure at the site. Covered in silks and strewn with sweet-smelling petals, it is now a place of pilgrimage for Indians, Muslims and others interested in the history of the Raj.

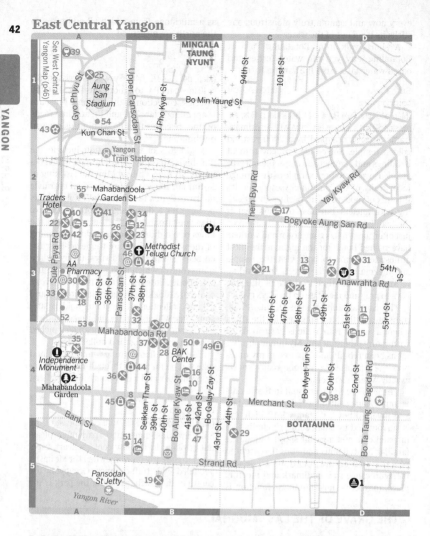

Independence Monument, an obelisk surrounded by two concentric circles of *chinthe*.

For a year or two following the 1988–90 prodemocracy uprisings, the park was occupied by soldiers; many of the more violent events of the time took place nearby.

Other Temples & Shrines

For a change of scenery check out the dragons and incense of the **Kheng Hock Keong** (Map p46; Strand Rd; admission free; ⊙24hr), the largest Chinese temple in Yangon. Supported by a Hokkien association, the 100-year-old temple is most lively from around 6am

to 9am when it's thronged with worshippers offering candles, flowers and incense to the Buddhist and Taoist altars within.

The impressive **Moseah Yeshua Synagogue** (Map p46; 85 26th St), near Mahabandoola Rd, was founded in 1894 by Sephardic Jews from India and Baghdad. Watched over by trustee Moses Samuels, one of Yangon's now tiny community of Jews, its lovingly maintained interior contains a *bimah* (platform holding the reading table for the *torah*) in the centre of the main sanctuary and a women's balcony upstairs. The wooden ceil-

Map p42

Christians get in on the act in Yangon as well with **St Mary's Cathedral** (Map p42; cnr Bo Aung Kyaw St & Bogyoke Aung San Rd), built in a bizarre red brick (and with an equally bizarre red, green and white interior), which will excite colonial buffs.

OUTSIDE CITY CENTRE

Shwedagon Paya   BUDDHIST STUPA

ရွှေတိဂုံဘုရား:

(Map p48; admission $5; ⊙5am-10pm) Heart stopping at any time, the Shwedagon Paya glitters bright gold in the heat of the day. Then, as the sun casts its last rays, it turns a crimson gold and orange, magic floats in the heat and the mighty diamond at the spire's peak casts a beam of light that reflects sheet white, bloody red and jealous green to the far corners of the temple platform. It can be quiet and contemplative or colourful and raucous, and for the people of Myanmar it is the most sacred of all Buddhist sites, one that all Myanmar Buddhists hope to visit at least once in their lifetime.

Visible from almost anywhere in the city, Shwedagon is located to the north of central Yangon, between People's Park and Kandawgyi.

The admission fee, which goes to the government (see p21), includes a lift ride to the raised platform of the stupa. Of course, like most local visitors, you may walk up one of the long graceful entrances, by far the more exciting method of entry. The north gate is especially photogenic at night.

The following details the history and attributes of the main structure. Freelance guides (they'll locate you before you can find them) at the stupa can fill in the details about the surrounding elements.

History

The great golden dome rises 322ft above its base. According to legend this stupa – of the solid *zedi* (conelike) type – is 2500 years old, but archaeologists suggest that the original stupa was built by the Mon people some time between the 6th and 10th centuries. In common with many other ancient *zedi* in earthquake-prone Myanmar, it has been rebuilt many times, and its current form dates back only to 1769.

During the Bagan period of Myanmar's history (10th to 14th centuries), the story of the stupa emerged from the mists of legend to become hard fact. Near the top of the eastern stairway you can see an inscription recording the history of the stupa to 1485.

ing features the original blue-and-white Star of David motif.

Several colourful Hindu temples can be found in the centre of the city, including **Sri Kali** (Map p46; Anawrahta Rd; ⊙5-11am & 3-9pm), between 26th and 27th Sts, and the **Sri Devi** (Map p42; cnr Anawrahta Rd & 51st St; ⊙6.30-11.30am & 4.30-8.30pm), both of which are Technicolor temples following the classic South Indian style of towers. These are the centres for the city's annual Murugu Festival, famous for colourful street processions featuring acts of ritual self-mutilation.

In the 15th century, the tradition of gilding the stupa began. Queen Shinsawbu, who was responsible for many improvements to the stupa, provided her own weight (88lb) in gold, which was beaten into gold leaf and used to cover the structure. Her son-in-law, Dhammazedi, went several better, offering four times his own weight and that of his wife in gold. He also provided the 1485 historical inscription on the eastern stairway.

The *zedi* suffered from a series of earthquakes during this time, which caused great damage. In 1612 Portuguese renegade adventurer Filipe de Brito e Nicote raided the stupa from his base in Thanlyin and carried away Dhammazedi's great bell, with the intention of melting it for cannons. As the British were to do later with another bell, he accidentally dropped it into the river. During the 17th century, the monument suffered earthquake damage on eight occasions. Worse was to follow in 1768, when a quake brought down the whole top of the *zedi*. King Hsinbyushin had it rebuilt to virtually its present height, and its current configuration dates from that renovation.

British troops occupied the compound for two years immediately after the First Anglo-Burmese War in 1824. In 1852, during the Second Anglo-Burmese War, the British again took the paya, the soldiers pillaged it once more and it remained under military control for 77 years, until 1929. In 1871 a new *hti* (the umbrella-like decorative top of a stupa), provided by King Mindon Min from Mandalay, caused considerable head-scratching for the British, who were not at all keen for such an association to be made with the still-independent part of Myanmar.

During the 20th century, the Shwedagon Paya was the scene for much political activity during the Myanmar independence movement – Aung San Suu Kyi spoke to massive crowds here in 1988 and the temple was also at the centre of the monks' protests in 2007. The huge earthquake of 1930, which totally destroyed the Shwemawdaw in Bago, caused only minor damage to Shwedagon. Less luck was had the following year when the paya suffered from a serious fire. After another minor earthquake in 1970, the *zedi* was clad in bamboo scaffolding, which extended beyond King Mindon's 100-year-old *hti*, and was refurbished.

Design

There are four covered walkways up Singuttara Hill to the platform on which Shwedagon stands. The southern entrance, from Shwedagon Pagoda Rd, is the one that can most properly be called the main entrance. Here, and at the northern entrance, there are lifts available, should you not feel fit enough for the stroll up the stairs. The western entrance features a series of escalators in place of stairs, and is the only entrance without vendors. The eastern stairway has the most traditional ambience, passing adjacent *kyaung* (monasteries) and vendors selling monastic requisites, such as alms bowls and robes.

Two 30ft-high *chinthe* (legendary half-lion, half-dragon guardian figures) loom over the southern entrance. You must remove your shoes and socks as soon as you mount the first step. Like the other entrances, the southern steps are lined with a series of shops, where devotees buy flowers – both

Once upon a time in the land of Suvannabhumi, a great king was presented with a gift of eight strands of hair. The bearers of these gifts, two merchant brothers who had journeyed from faraway lands after looking for an enlightened one, told King Okkalapa that he should guard these strands well for they were no ordinary hairs.

The king set to his task with zeal and on the summit of a 10,000-year-old sacred hill he enshrined the hairs in a temple of gold, which was enclosed in a temple of silver, then one of tin, then copper, then lead, then marble and, finally, one of plain iron-brick.

real and beautifully made paper ones – for offerings. Buddha images, ceremonial paper umbrellas, books, golden thrones, incense sticks and antiques are also on sale. However hot it may be outside, you'll find the walkway cool, shady and calm. It's this quiet, subdued atmosphere on the entrance steps that makes the impact so great as you arrive at the platform.

Also linked to the Shwedagon complex's southern gate is the Maha Wizaya Paya (Map p48; U Htaung Bo St; admission K200; ☉24hr). It's a rather plain but well-proportioned *zedi* built in 1980 to commemorate the unification of Theravada Buddhism in Myanmar. The king of Nepal contributed sacred relics for the *zedi's* relic chamber and Myanmar military strongman Ne Win had it topped with an 11-level *hti* – two more levels than the *hti* at Shwedagon.

You emerge from semi-gloom into a dazzling explosion of technicoloured glitter, for Shwedagon is not just one huge, glowing *zedi* (stupa). Around the mighty stupa cluster an incredible assortment of smaller *zedi*, statues, temples, shrines, images and *tazaung* (small pavilions). Somehow, the bright gold of the main stupa makes everything else seem brighter and larger than life.

Stupas – indeed, all Buddhist structures – should be walked around clockwise, so turn left at the top of the steps and, like the crowds of locals, start strolling. During the heat of the day, you'll probably have to confine yourself to the mat pathway laid around

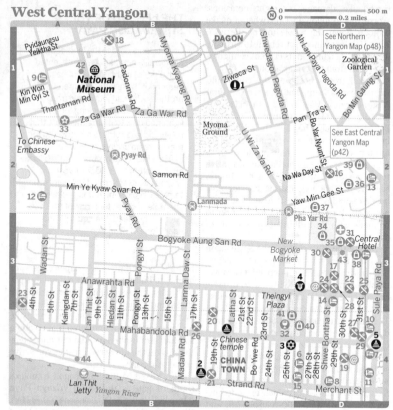

See Northern Yangon Map (p48)

DAGON

Zoological Garden

National Museum

See East Central Yangon Map (p42)

Myoma Ground

To Chinese Embassy

New Bogyoke Market

Central Hotel

Bogyoke Aung San Rd

Anawrahta Rd

Mahabandoola Rd

Theingyi Plaza

Chinese temple

CHINA TOWN

Lan Thit Jetty   *Yangon River*

Strand Rd   Merchant St

---

the platform – unless your bare feet can take the heat of the uncovered marble paving.

The Stupa & Its Treasures

The hill on which the stupa stands is 190ft above sea level and the platform covers over 12 acres. Prior to the British takeover of southern Myanmar there had been defensive earthworks around the paya, but these were considerably extended by the British. The emplacements for their cannons can still be seen outside the outer wall.

The main stupa, which is completely solid, rises from its platform in a fairly standard pattern. First there is the plinth, which stands 21ft above the clutter of the main platform and immediately sets Shwedagon above the lesser structures. Smaller stupas sit on this raised platform level – four large ones mark the four cardinal directions, four medium-sized ones mark the four corners of the basically square platform and 60 small ones run around the perimeter.

Various planetary posts around the base conform to the days of the week, and locals pray at the station that represents the day they were born. If you know what day you were born, locals can point you to the appropriate post. The one for Mars (Tuesday) corresponds to Aung San Suu Kyi's birthday – this is where she prays whenever she visits the shrine; look up and you'll note a closed-circuit TV camera trained on the spot.

From this base, the *zedi* rises first in three terraces, then in 'octagonal' terraces and then in five circular bands – together these elements add another 98ft to the stupa's height.

The shoulder of the bell is decorated with 16 'flowers'. The bell is topped by the 'inverted bowl', another traditional element of stupa architecture, and above this stand the mouldings and then the 'lotus petals'. These consist of a band of down-turned petals, followed by a band of up-turned petals.

The banana bud is the final element of the *zedi* before the *hti* tops it. Like the lotus petals below, the banana bud is actually covered with no fewer than 13,153 plates of gold, measuring 1 sq ft each – unlike the lower elements, which are merely covered with gold leaf. The seven-tiered *hti* is made of iron and again plated with gold. Even without the various hanging bells, it weighs well over a ton.

The *hti* tiers get smaller from bottom to top, and from the uppermost tier projects the shaft, which is hung with gold bells, silver bells and various items of jewellery. The topmost vane, with its flag, turns with the wind. It is gold- and silver-plated and studded with 1100 diamonds totalling 278 carats – not to mention 1383 other stones. Finally, at the very top of the vane rests the diamond orb – a hollow golden sphere studded with 4351 diamonds, weighing 1800 carats in total. The very top of the orb is tipped with a single 76-carat diamond.

Chaukhtatgyi Paya & Ngahtatgyi Paya
BUDDHIST TEMPLES

ချောက်ထပ်ကြီးဘုရား နှင့် ငါးထပ်ကြီးဘုရား

Fifty years ago there was a giant standing Buddha poking his head above the temples and monasteries here, but one day he got tired and collapsed into a heap on the floor, whereupon he was replaced with the

See West Central Yangon Map (p46)

monster-sized lazy **reclining buddha** you see today. One of Myanmar's more beautiful reclining buddhas, the placid face of the Chaukhtatgyi Buddha (Map p48; Shwegondine Rd; admission free; ☺24hr) is topped by a crown encrusted with diamonds and other precious stones. Housed in a large metal-roofed shed, only a short distance northeast of the Shwedagon Paya, this huge figure is surprisingly little known and hardly publicised at all. Close to the Buddha's feet is the small shrine to Ma Thay, a holy man who has the power to stop rain and grant sailors a safe journey.

Attached to the temple complex is the **Shweminwon Sasana Yeiktha Meditation Centre**, where large numbers of locals gather to meditate. It's not hard to find someone to show you around the adjoining monasteries.

Virtually across the street from Chaukhtatgyi Paya is a gorgeous seated Bud-dha image at the Ngahtatgyi Paya (Map p48; Shwegondine Rd; admission $2; ☺24hr). Sitting in calm gold and white repose with a healthy splash of precious stones to boot, it's one of the most impressive **sitting buddhas** in southern Myanmar. In fact, it's worth going to see for its carved wooden backdrop alone.

Kandawgyi Lake LAKE

ကန်တော်ကြီး

(Map p48; admission K2000) Occupying prime Yangon real estate, this natural lake close to the city centre is a good place for a stroll. Don't expect untamed nature or meditative quiet here, as the footpath surrounding the circumference of Kandawgyi also runs alongside a busy road. Also known by its literal translation, Royal Lake (Dawgyi Kan), the lake is most attractive at sunset, when the glittering Shwedagon is reflected in its calm waters. You'll find the best sunset view from the lake's eastern edge.

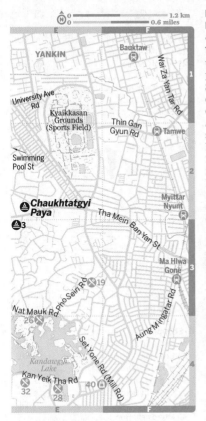

ကမ္ဘာအေးဘုရား နှင့် မဟာပါသာနလှိုင်ဂူ

When the designers were asked to come up with a suitable blueprint for the 'world peace' *zedi*, which was built for the 1954–56 Sixth Buddhist Synod, they obviously decided that Mickey Mouse and friends were the epitome of world peace, because the Kaba Aye Paya (Map p38; Kaba Aye Pagoda Rd; admission free; ☺24hr) has a Disneyesque feel and look to it. The 112ft-high paya also measures 112ft around its base. It stands about 5 miles north of the city centre, a little beyond the Inya Lake Hotel. The interior of the monument is hollow and contains some nice Buddhist sculptures, including a *lei-myet-hna* (four-sided Buddha sculpture).

Just north, Mahapasana (Map p38; Kaba Aye Pagoda Rd; admission free; ☺24hr), the 'great cave', is a totally artificial. It was here that the Sixth Buddhist Synod was held in 1954–56 to coincide with the 2500th anniversary of the Buddha's enlightenment. This enormous cave (measuring 456ft by 371ft; it can accommodate up to 10,000 people) took only 14 months to build. It helped that there were 63,000 labourers. The cave is still used to hold grand religious ceremonies.

Several of the city's embassies, clinics and smaller hotels are in the lake's vicinity, the majority north of the lake. Just east of the Kandawgyi Palace Hotel, on the southern side of the lake, floats a **Shin Upagot shrine**. Upagot is a Bodhisattva (Buddhist saint) who is said to protect human beings in moments of mortal danger.

The eastern side of the lake is dominated by a very expensive government-financed project including a small park and a playground for children, as well as the fanciful or monstrous (depending on your taste) **Karaweik**, a reinforced concrete reproduction of a royal barge. Apart from being something of a local attraction in its own right, the Karaweik (Sanskrit for Garuda, the legendary bird-mount of the Hindu god Vishnu) is also the name of a government-owned restaurant nearby.

Inya Lake   LAKE

အင်းလျားကန်

Inya Lake (Map p48) is roughly five times larger than Kandawgyi, but to see actual water you must explore on foot and brave the powerful sun. There aren't many opportunities for shade, only scattered umbrellas, which are popular with young couples sneaking a little alone time.

Before reclusive dictator Ne Win died in December 2002, he lived on University Ave Rd at one end of the lake while Aung San Suu Kyi, who was released from house arrest at number 54 in November 2010, was at the other end. For years these two important figures in contemporary Myanmar history resided like powerful *nat* locked in a battle of wills.

Myanmar Gems Museum &
Gems Market   MUSEUM

မြန်မာ့ကျောက်မျက်ရတနာပြတိုက် နှင့် ကျောက်မျက်အရောင်းပြခန်း

(Map p38; ☎665 365; 66 Kaba Aye Pagoda Rd; admission $5; ☺9am-5pm Tue-Sun) Just north of Parami Rd, this government-owned museum is meant to impress – starting with the world's largest sapphire, which comes

Northern Yangon

Top Sights
- Chaukhtatgyi Paya ... E2
- Shwedagon Paya ... C4

Sights
- 1 Bogyoke Aung San Museum ... D3
- 2 Maha Wizaya Paya ... D4
- 3 Ngahtatgyi Paya ... E3
- 4 People's Park ... C4
- 5 Yangon Zoological Gardens ... D4

Activities, Courses & Tours
- 6 Happy World ... A4
- 7 Happy World ... C4
- 8 Mahasi Meditation Centre ... D2
- 9 Panditarama Meditation Centre ... C2
- 10 Seri Beauty & Health ... C3

Sleeping
- 11 Alamanda Inn ... D2
- 12 Classique Inn ... C2
- 13 Comfort Inn ... C3
- 14 Guest Care Hotel ... C3
- 15 Savoy Hotel ... C3
- 16 Sedona Hotel ... D1
- 17 Summit Parkview ... C4
- 18 Winner Inn ... C2

Eating
- Alamanda Inn ... (see 11)
- 19 Ashoka Indian Restaurant ... E3
- Aung Thuka ... (see 31)
- 20 Black Canyon Coffee ... C4
- 21 Café Dibar ... C3
- Coffee Circles ... (see 14)
- 22 Green Elephant ... B1
- 23 Hla Myanma Htamin Zain ... C3
- 24 House of Memories ... B3
- 25 Le Planteur ... D3
- 26 Royal Garden ... E4
- 27 Sabai @ DMZ ... C3
- 28 Seit Taing Kya ... E4
- Sharky's ... (see 14)
- 29 Sharky's ... C3
- Singapore's Kitchen ... (see 17)
- 30 SK Hot Pot ... D3
- 31 Thai Kitchen ... C3
- 32 Yin Fong Seafood Restaurant ... E4

Drinking
- Captain's Bar ... (see 15)
- 33 Ginki Kids ... D2
- 34 Inya 1 ... C2
- 35 Mr Guitar Café ... D2

Entertainment
- JJ City ... (see 40)
- Pioneer ... (see 20)
- YGN Bar ... (see 20)

Shopping
- 36 Augustine's Souvenir Shop ... A1
- 37 Beikthano Gallery ... D1
- 38 Blazon Centre ... C3
- 39 Dagon Centre ... B3
- Elephant House ... (see 22)
- 40 Mingala Zei ... E4
- 41 Monument Books ... C3
- 42 Nandawun ... B4

Information
- 43 Alliance Francaise ... B2
- Myanmar Himalaya Trekking ... (see 17)

from Mogok (to the northeast of Mandalay). The sapphire measures 6.7in in height, and is nearly 26lb in weight – this somehow translates to 63,000 carats. The museum also boasts the world's largest jade boulder, rough ruby and star sapphire. Other not-so-impressive claims include the only mineral with 'imperial' in its name.

Bogyoke Aung San Museum MUSEUM
ဗိုလ်ချုပ်အောင်ဆန်းပြတိုက်
(Map p48; Bogyoke Aung San Museum St; admission free) Now open only once a year on 19 July, Martyrs' Day, the former home of General Aung San and his wife Daw Kin Kyi contains remnants of another era. Inside the 1920s house you will find several old family photos, which of course include daughter Aung San Suu Kyi as a little girl.

Activities

Massage

After a long day slogging around the city, what could be better than a massage? A professional centre with no dodgy side is **Seri Beauty and Health** (Map p48; ☎534 205; 118 Dhama Zedi Rd; massage per hr K5000; ⏲9am-6pm).

Train Ride

More in the category of sightseeing rather than transportation, the **Yangon Circle Line** (tickets $1) is a slow-moving, not particularly comfortable three-hour trip around Yangon and the neighbouring countryside. However, it's a great way to experience commuter life in the big city. You can always hop off at any station and take a taxi back to the city centre. Trains leave at 8.30am, 10.30am, 11.30am, 1pm and 2.30pm from platform 6/7 at the **Yangon Train Station** (Map p42; Bogyoke Aung San Rd). Be aware that the trains don't always do the full circuit; after reaching a station two hours from Yangon, our train simply headed back the way we came! Only US$ or FECs (Foreign Exchange Certificates; see p365) are accepted for the fare (you'll also need your passport), and the train is least crowded at weekends.

➤ Courses

Meditation

Several monasteries in Yangon welcome foreigners to meditation courses. The most famous centre in Yangon is the **Mahasi Meditation Centre** (Map p48; ☑541 971; http:// web.ukonline.co.uk/buddhism/mahasi.htm; 16 Thathana Yeiktha Rd, Bahan Township), founded in 1947 by the late Mahasi Sayadaw, perhaps Myanmar's greatest meditation teacher. The Mahasi Sayadaw technique strives for intensive, moment-to-moment awareness of every physical movement, every mental and physical sensation and, ultimately, every thought. The centre only accepts foreigners who can stay for six to 12 weeks.

Two of the Mahasi centre's chief meditation teachers, Sayadaw U Pandita and Sayadaw U Janaka, have established their own highly regarded centres in Yangon: **Panditarama Meditation Centre** (Map p48; ☑535 448; www.panditarama.net; 80-A Than Lwin Rd, Bahan Township) and **Chanmyay Yeiktha Medita-**

tion Centre (Map p38; ☑661 479; www.chanmyay. org; 55-A Kaba Aye Pagoda Rd). Both have second branches with private quarters, especially geared for foreigners, who must commit to a stay of one week. **Panditarama's forest meditation centre** (☑949 450) is 2 miles northeast off the highway to Bago. Chanmyay's **branch** (☑620 321), set among gardens in Hmawbi, is a 50-minute drive north of Yangon; one-month stays are preferred.

✪ Festivals & Events

Crowds of pilgrims descend on the Shwedagon for a *paya pwe* (pagoda festival), one of the more important Myanmar holidays. This takes place over the March full moon day, the last full moon before the Myanmar New Year. In the Western calendar it normally falls in late February/early March.

Other major festivals in Yangon:

Independence Day (4 January) Includes a seven-day fair at Kandawgyi; see p16.

Water Festival/Thingyan (April) The Myanmar New Year is celebrated in wet pandemonium; see p16 for more details.

Buddha's birthday (April/May) Celebrate Buddha's enlightenment; see p16.

Martyrs' Day (19 July) Commemorates the assassination of Bogyoke Aung San and his comrades. It's also the only day his former home is open to the public – see p50.

Murugu Festival (March or April depending on lunar calendar) Held at Yangon's Hindu temples (see p43), it involves colourful processions.

⌂ Sleeping

The price of accommodation in Yangon is largely the same as it was a few years ago, and

---

YANGON FOR CHILDREN

There aren't a whole lot of attractions in Yangon meant to appeal directly to the little ones, but there's no lack of locals willing to provide attention.

The most convenient option is **Happy World** Kandaw Mingala Garden (Map p48; ☑243 434; Shwedagon Pagoda Rd; admission K1200; ☺9am-9pm); Thirimingala Zei (Map p48;☑212 678; 3rd fl, Thirimingala Zei, Lower Kyee Myin Dyaing Rd; admission K1200; ☺9am-9pm). The Thirimingala Zei branch has indoor tunnels and ball pits, and the Kandaw Mingala Garden branch, located near the south entrance to Shwedagon Paya, resembles an outdoor amusement park.

A less palatable option is the **Yangon Zoological Gardens** (Map p48; Kan Yeik Tha Rd; admission K2000; ☺8am-6pm), although many of the animals were relocated to Nay Pyi Taw Zoo in 2008. The expansive grounds, which date back to 1901, also include an aquarium and amusement park.

Hotels with swimming pools, including the Governor's Residence, the Parkroyal, the Savoy and the Sedona, charge $10 per nonguest for single-day use of their swimming facilities.

HOW THINGS CHANGE...

Today, the Strand is easily the most expensive hotel in Yangon. Things were quite different back in 1979, when Tony Wheeler reviewed the hotel for the first edition of this guidebook:

'Staying at the Strand is full of amusing little touches – beside the reception desk there is a glass faced cabinet labelled "lost & found". Most of the articles were clearly lost half a century ago, not many ladies carry delicate little folding fans around these days. The single lift is ancient but smoothly operating. In the restaurant the maitre de is grimly efficient in a crumpled grey suit in which he looks very ill at ease. The waiters call everybody sir, male or female. Both the bar and restaurant close at 9pm but a small cache of Mandalay Beer from the Peoples' Brewery is kept behind the reception desk should you wish to continue drinking. By 11pm you are likely to be feeling pretty lonely in the lounge area, though, just the occasional Strand rat scampering across the floor to keep you company. On the last night of one Burma visit, to my utter amazement hot water came from the shower when I turned on the tap.'

that means guesthouses and hotels are still relatively cheap. There's virtually nil in the way of fresh new faces, particularly in the budget and midrange categories, and much of the city's budget accommodation is as dank and dreary as ever.

The prices quoted here are high-season walk-in rates, but almost all midrange and top-end hotels offer discounts of up to 50%. Many of the midrange and top-end hotels also provide perks such as airport pick-up, internet access and full-service business centres, and all provide some form of breakfast. Only one hotel accepted credit cards at research time and some high-end places also add a 10% service charge and a 10% government tax.

It's worth noting that all large hotels will have taken part in some financial agreement with the ruling junta to establish their business. Some, like the large **Traders Hotel** (Map p42) in central Yangon, are joint ventures between foreign companies and the military. Others, such as the **Kandawgyi Palace Hotel** (Map p48) or the **Central Hotel** (Map p46), are owned outright by the government or by those with close military connections. As far as we are aware, those listed here have a fairly minimal government ownership share – if any. See p21 for more information.

CITY CENTRE

Strand Hotel　　　　　BOUTIQUE HOTEL **$$$**
(Map p42; ☎243 377; www.ghmhotels.com; 92 Strand Rd; ste $550-1100; ✸@☎) The Strand is a relic of the same colonial-era legacy as the Oriental in Bangkok, the Raffles in Singapore and the Eastern & Oriental in George-

town, but boasts what is arguably a more 'colourful' history than its peers.

Opened in 1901 by the famed Sarkies brothers, the hotel in its early years hosted the likes of Rudyard Kipling, George Orwell and Somerset Maugham. During WWII, the Strand was used to house Japanese troops, and Burmese nationals were allegedly not allowed to stay in the hotel until 1945. And from 1962 to 1989, in what was quite possibly its darkest period (see boxed text) the hotel was owned and managed by the Burmese government.

The latest incarnation of the Strand dates to 1995. It's very much a luxury affair, with heaps of charm and history – even the bathroom fixtures are vintage – and a high level of service. But it's worth mentioning that the Strand doesn't have the same modern comforts as other hotels of this class (the TVs are non-flatscreen and small, internet is available only in the lobby or business centre, and don't even bother looking for an iPod jack). Note also that, at the time of research, only cash in US$ dollars was accepted, so book online or make sure you have a lot of cash.

Even if you can't afford the rent, the Strand is well worth a visit for a drink in the bar, high tea ($18; ☺2.30-5pm) in the lobby lounge or a splurge lunch at the café.

TOP
CHOICE **Mother Land Inn 2**　　　BUDGET HOTEL **$**
(Map p42; ☎291 343; www.myanmarmother landinn.com; 433 Lower Pazundaung Rd; dm $8, r $10-25; ✸@) Take a pinch of backpacker bohemia, a dollop of professional service, a massive portion of cleanliness, mix well with a generous helping of travel advice

and services, leave to marinate with enviously attired and proportioned rooms and, voila, it's the Mother Land Inn 2. There are of course downsides, namely it's often fully booked and is located in a slightly dodgy 'hood a long walk or a short taxi ride from the centre. But the free airport transfer, fast internet access (per hour $1) and a solid breakfast more than make up for them.

Governor's Residence
BOUTIQUE HOTEL **$$$**

(Map p46; ☎229 860; www.governorsresidence.com; 35 Taw Win St; r $154-242, ste $279-319; ❋@🛜☀) If you'd like to live like a sovereign, this UK-owned teak mansion of period elegance and modern luxury in the leafy embassy district is for you. In the '20s the Governor's Residence was a guesthouse for important nationals of the Kayah ethnic group, but now, after a masterful restoration, it's a tourist's ideal of colonial luxury. A waiter with a crystal cocktail is always on hand and the pool merges gently into the lawns and sparkles in reflected beauty. The glorious rooms have ever-so-lightly perfumed air, teak floors, cloudy soft beds and stone baths with rose-petal water.

Panorama Hotel
HOTEL **$$**

(Map p42; ☎253 077; panoramaygn@myanmar. com.mm; 294-300 Pansodan St; r $30-40, ste $45-50; ❋@🛜) Within walking distance of the train station and Bogyoke Market, and boasting distant views over the Shwedagon Paya, the aptly named 10-storey Panorama offers some of the best value in this price range. All rooms are equally vast and similarly well appointed, so unless you really require a bathtub, save yourself some money by going for one of the cheaper standard rooms.

May Shan Hotel
HOTEL **$$**

(Map p46; ☎252 986; www.mayshan.com; 115 Sule Paya Rd; s/d/tr $20/25/40; ❋@🛜) It's not exactly a steal, and the single rooms are pretty tight and lack windows, but the combination of convenient location, gracious service and ample amenities (TV, air-conditioning, wi-fi) make the May Shan the best option in the area immediately surrounding Sule Paya. If you can afford it, the triple rooms (ask for room 601) are spacious and have arguably the best views of any hotel in the city.

Three Seasons Hotel
GUESTHOUSE **$**

(Map p42; ☎293 304; phyuaung@mptmail.net.mm; 83-85 52nd St; s/d $12/18; ❋) The nine rooms in this homey guesthouse are large, spotless and well endowed with everything that would make your granny smile. The outdoor terrace, with tree shade, is a nice place to sit and watch the world cruise by. And to top it off, it's very friendly and helpful and is located on a block that is especially quiet at night, so you should be able to sleep undisturbed.

Okinawa Guest House
HOTEL **$**

(Map p46; ☎374 318; 64 32nd St; dm/s/d $5/14/18;❋) A brief walk from Sule Paya is the red pitched roof of this charming bougainvillea-fronted guesthouse. The interior is a bizarre hotchpotch of decorations and building styles that blend wood, bamboo and red brick. The handful of rooms are small and dark but very clean, although noise – both from the street and the staff – can be an issue here. It also has a cosy dorm upstairs for penny-pinchers and a number of communal areas with old wooden chairs and tables.

Parkroyal
BUSINESS HOTEL **$$$**

(Map p46; ☎250 388; enquiry@parkroyalhotels. com.mm; 33 Ah Lan Paya Pagoda Rd; r $90; ❋@🛜☀) This smart, newish, centrally located business hotel is the Yangon branch of a Singaporean chain. If you're haven't booked a room through an agent, you'll only have access to their very capable deluxe rooms, which feature all the amenities you'd expect from a hotel of this price. The Parkroyal is also the only hotel we're aware of in Yangon that accepts a credit card (in this case, Visa only) – at a hefty 12% commission.

Thammada Hotel
HOTEL **$$**

(Map p42; ☎243 3639; www.thamadahotel.com; Ah Lan Paya Pagoda Rd; r/ste $44/88;❋) Located in the same complex as the Thamada Cinema, this longstanding joint venture with Singapore boasts old-school rooms with lots of worn wood and heavy, handsome furnishings. Take a look at a few, as some rooms are markedly smaller than others. The ground-floor **365 Café** is convenient for eats, drinks and wi-fi.

Yoma Hotel
HOTEL **$**

(Map p42; ☎299 243; www.yomahotelone.com; 146 Bogyoke Aung San Rd; r $10-18;❋) Although it's a bit of a hike from the city centre, this is one of the tidier and better-run midrange places in town. The rooms are a bit frumpy and clearly date from another era, but are well equipped and clean. There are five floors and no lift, so if you're on the top floor you can eat that extra cake without guilt. A tip: avoid the rooms on Floor G unless you desire the combination of comically low ceilings and furry friends.

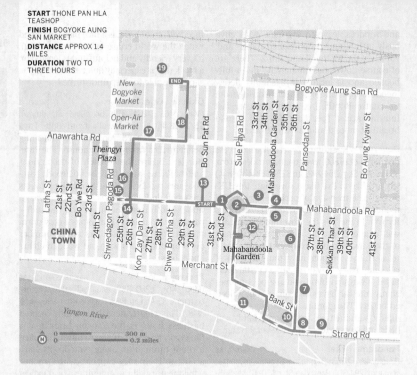

START THONE PAN HLA
TEASHOP
FINISH BOGYOKE AUNG
SAN MARKET
DISTANCE APPROX 1.4
MILES
DURATION TWO TO
THREE HOURS

Downtown Yangon
Walking Tour

❯ Yangon is a great city to explore on foot,
and this tour takes in the best of colonial
Yangon, flirts with Indian flamboyance, gets
serene in Buddhist temples, lightens your
wallet in the markets and throws in some
crystal-ball-gazing for good measure. Supplement your walk with *Historical Walks in
Yangon: A Myanmar Heritage Trust Guide
Map* – map available from **Silkworm Books**
(www.silkwormbooks.com).

We recommend starting this tour in the
cool hours of the morning, so kick it off with
a caffeine boost and Burmese-style breakfast at a teahouse such as ❶ **Thone Pan
Hla**, a typical Burmese teahouse. From here
it's only a short walk to the 2200-year-old
❷ **Sule Paya**, the geographic and commercial heart of the city, and where the British-
designed grid street pattern was centred.
Make a circle or two around the monument
to get just the right angle for your photograph, but don't feel obligated to go inside,
as the largely unremarkable interior is
probably not worth the $2 entry fee. After

a complete rotation or two and an inside
visit, cross the busy traffic circle to the east
and you'll find the twice-rebuilt ❸ **City
Hall**, a yellow colonial building with oriental
overtones. On the next corner further east
on Mahabandoola Rd is the ❹ **(former)
Immigration Office**, once one of the largest
department stores in Asia, now seemingly
abandoned. Across the street is the
❺ **Immanuel Baptist Church**, originally
built in 1830, though the present structure
dates from 1885.

Continuing east on Mahabandoola Rd
you'll pass a couple of alleyways crammed
with food stalls, many selling the type of
deep-fried snacks and sweets that the
Burmese seem to love so much. Consider
refuelling and take the next major right
onto Pansodan St, where on the east side
of the street you'll find several stalls selling
second-hand and photocopied books. The
Burmese are big readers and this strip is
colloquially referred to as Yangon's open-air
library.

About halfway down this block you'll see the **6** **High Court Building** on your right – in name at least, the highest legal authority in the land. Continuing along this wide and generally empty section of Pansodan St. It's hard not to feel minuscule, particularly when walking by the huge **7** **Inland Water Transport** offices and the even grander **8** **Myanma Port Authority** building. Continue south to Strand Rd, the last east-west thoroughfare before the Yangon River.

Two blocks to your left is the **9** **Strand Hotel**, whose restored façade evokes another era. You may not be able to afford a room, but the air-conditioned lobby, café and bar make a good rest stop along the way.

When you're ready to brave the heat and uneven sidewalks again, walk west along Strand Rd for a block past Pansodan St, where you'll see on your right the **10** **Customs House**, built in 1915, and on your left the **11** **Law Court**, an impressive-looking colonnaded building. Police will prevent you approaching this last building, so turn north, just past the Customs House, and then left onto boisterous Bank St and up onto Sule Paya Rd, where you can discover how the remainder of your walking tour will pan out by consulting one of the many fortune-tellers who hang out under the trees.

Bordering this street is a 55yd obelisk, a monument to the country's independence, standing in the middle of the heat-stained **12** **Mahabandoola Garden**. A glance through the fence is enough to give you an idea of what goes on here – no need to pay the K500 entry fee.

This brings you back to the Sule Paya, from where you can continue west down Mahabandoola Rd through the chaotic Indian and Chinese quarters of the city. Roughly speaking, the Indian quarter extends as far west as the Shwedagon Pagoda Rd, while the Chinese quarter begins at about 21st St and extends several blocks further west. A good drink stop and an appropriate taste of Yangon's Little India is the open-air lassi stall **13** **Shwe Bali**, near the corner of Bo Sun Pat Rd.

Continue west along Mahabandoola before detouring south onto 26th St in order to pay a visit to **14** **Moseah Yeshua Synagogue**. Retrace your steps to Mahabandoola and carry on westwards a little further until you reach the bursting **15** **Theingyi Zei** market. If you arrive early enough (ideally before 9am), you can catch the action along the adjacent **16** **open-air market** on 26th St.

Exit onto Anawrahta Rd and head east until you crash into the **17** **Sri Kali temple**. Continue east along Anawrahta St, turning left down 29th St, where **18** **Danu Phyu Daw Saw Yee Myanma Restaurant**, one of central Yangon's most lauded Burmese restaurants, is your lunch stop.

From here it's only a short hike north to the sprawling mess of **19** **Bogyoke Aung San Market**, where you can begin a new sort of tour, a slightly more difficult one that combines walking *and* shopping.

Beautyland Hotel II
HOTEL $

(Map p42; ☑240 054; www.goldenlandpages.com/beauty; 188-192 33rd St; r $8-24;❄) A convenient location near central Yangon's attractions, restaurants and internet shops, and exceedingly tidy rooms with friendly and confident service make this one of the better budget choices in central Yangon. The cheapest rooms don't have windows while the more expensive front-side rooms boast heaps of natural light, so depending on your budget, look at a few.

Panda Hotel
HOTEL $$

(Map p46; ☑212 850; www.myanmarpandahotel.com; 205 Wadan St; r $33-45; ❄@) One of the more appealing hotels in this price range is this 13-storey high-rise west of the city centre. It has bright and enticing rooms with excellent bathrooms. It's in a peaceful residential area, but is close enough to downtown to be worthwhile. Popular with tour groups.

May Fair Inn
GUESTHOUSE $

(Map p42;☑253 454; maytinmg@gmail.com; 57 38th St; s/d $12/15;❄) This family-run inn has freshly painted rooms that are a little spartan but ever reliable. It's more equipped to deal with the traveller looking for tranquillity rather than a party, and it has a loyal clientele of returnees for a good reason. The complimentary breakfast is served in the small communal area. Only US$ dollars accepted.

Ocean Pearl Inn
HOTEL $

(Map p42; ☑297 007; www.oceanpearlinn.com; 215 Bo Ta Taung Pagoda Rd; s/d/tr $13/18/23;❄) A paint job and rooms washed and polished by a team of cleaning addicts make the Ocean Pearl one of the tidiest choices in the budget range (admittedly not much of an accomplishment in Yangon). Another perk is free airport pickup – mention it when booking or look for the Ocean Pearl sign when you arrive in Yangon.

Queen's Park Hotel
HOTEL $$

(Map p42; ☑296 447; www.qpyangon.com; 132 Anawrahta Rd; r/ste $15-33/32-36; ❄@) Unusually for a hotel in this category, the rooms are more appealing than the dowdy reception area – though only by a little. The staff are sweet, and slow days mean easy discounts.

White House Hotel
HOTEL $

(Map p46; ☑240 780; whitehouse.mm@gmail.com; 69/71 Kon Zay Dan St; s/d $8-15/14-20;❄) The positives in this long-running backpacker joint are the generous breakfasts, rooftop hammocks, cold beer, expansive views and useful travel desk. The negatives are a thigh-burning number of stairs, small and sometimes windowless rooms and basic bathrooms (both shared and private). Kon Zay Dan St is located between 26th St and 27th St.

Tokyo Guest House
HOTEL $

(Map p42; ☑386 828; tokyoguesthouse.yangon@gmail.com; 200 Bo Aung Kyaw St; s/d $9/14;❄) Highlights at this friendly budget hotel are the sunny terrace with views and the room cleanliness. Lowlights are the fact that said rooms are windowless and very cramped.

Some more centrally located budget and midrange options:

New Aye Yar Hotel
HOTEL $$

(Map p42; ☑256 938; www.newayeyarhotel.com; 170-176 Bo Aung Kyaw St; s $25, d $30, ste $30-35; ❄@) This good-value high-rise has avoided the tropical rot that has struck down so many of its cousins.

Eastern Hotel
HOTEL $$

(Map p42; ☑293 815; www.myanmareasternhotel.com; 194-196 Bo Myat Tun Rd; s/d $15/20; ❄@) The 40 rooms here are utterly unremarkable, but are clean and boast amenities such as satellite TV, hot water and fridge.

Cherry Guest House
HOTEL $

(Map p42; ☑340 623; 278/300 Mahabandoola Garden St; s $8-12, d$14;❄) One of the few new places we encountered on this research trip, the Cherry looks its age and its 13 rooms have wall-mounted flatscreen TVs. It's located on the 4th floor of this (relatively) quiet street – look for the street-level sign that says 'Guest House'.

Golden Smile Inn
HOTEL $

(Map p46; ☑373 589; myathiri@gmail.com.mm; 644 Merchant St; r $14, with shared bathroom $12; ❄) Located up a slightly scary stairway, the Golden Smile is rather dark and dank, and is not much of a bargain, but its popularity and the communal balcony make it a good choice for those who emphasise socialising over comfort.

Garden Guest House
HOTEL $

(Map p46; ☑253 779; 441-445 Mahabandoola Rd; r fan $5, air-con $6-12) The location steps away from Sule Paya is great (if rather noisy), but we suspect that the boxlike rooms, which don't have windows and need a paint job, will have you spending most of your time in the communal areas.

Sunflower Hotel
HOTEL $

(Map p46; ✆240 014; www.myanmarsunflower-hotel.com; 259-263 Anawrahta Rd; r $6-22;✻) Located in the heart of the busy Indian quarter. The cheapest rooms are little more than fan-cooled closets with shared bathroom, while the corner suites are quite spacious and airy with great city views.

Daddy's Home
HOTEL $

(Map p46; ✆252 169; daddyhomehotel@gmail. com; 107 Kon Zay Dan St; r $12, with shared bathroom $6) A drab tower-block hotel with the largest bathrooms in the budget category. The cleaners need to purchase a broom, but otherwise it's friendly and adequate. Kon Zay Dan St is located between 26th St and 27th St.

OUTSIDE CITY CENTRE
The suburbs are generally quieter than central Yangon. They're also convenient for walking to Shwedagon Paya and Kandawgyi Lake, but are not great for budget accommodation.

Classique Inn
BOUTIQUE HOTEL $$

(Map p48; ✆525 557; www.classique-inn.com; 53B Golden Valley Rd; r $40-60; ✻@☎) Located in a villa in Yangon's posh Golden Valley neighbourhood, this leafy, family-run place offers eight cosy, attractive rooms. The rates aren't exactly a steal, particularly for the rather tight ground-floor single rooms, and you'll need taxis to get around town, but warm service (including travel arrangements), good breakfast and a homey atmosphere make up for this.

Savoy Hotel
BOUTIQUE HOTEL $$$

(Map p48; ✆526 289; www.savoy-myanmar.com; 129 Dhama Zedi Rd; s $90, d $95, ste $125-135; ✻@☎✻) Everything inside the Savoy is done so well it's easy to forgive the fact that it's situated on a busy street corner. Hallways, rooms and even the lavish bathrooms are stocked with photographs, antiques, handicrafts and sculptures, and it takes little imagination to feel as if you are some Raj-like king. Basically what you get at this Myanmar-German joint venture is Strand Hotel standards without the price tag.

Alamanda Inn
BOUTIQUE HOTEL $$$

(Map p48; ✆534 513; alamanda.inn@gmail.com; 60B Shwe Taung Gyar Rd/Golden Valley Rd; r $60-65; ✻@) Yet another colonial-villa-turned-B&B in the quiet, leafy embassy district. The French-run Alamanda hotel combines five

spacious and attractively decorated rooms, the most expensive of which is the suite in the old servants' quarters with its own private garden. The French-style breakfast gets good reports and there's an excellent attached French restaurant and bar (see p62).

Winner Inn
BUDGET HOTEL $$

(Map p48; ✆535 205; www.winnerinnmyanmar. com; 42 Than Lwin Rd; r $20-30, ste $35; ✻@) If it weren't for its somewhat remote location, the Winner would be one of our faves. This low-slung building is in a quiet, leafy suburb and has spotless rooms with desks, and pictures on the walls. The communal areas have plenty of well-positioned chairs waiting for you to collapse into with a book.

Sedona Hotel
BUSINESS HOTEL $$$

(Map p48; ✆666 900; www.sedonasmyanmar. com; 1 Kaba Aye Pagoda Rd; r $100-160, ste $350-900; ✻@☎✻) You know exactly what you'll be getting at the Singapore-owned Sedona: peace, quiet and very professional service. What you won't be getting is any indication you're in Myanmar, but as you sink into one of the comfortable beds, you probably won't be that bothered.

Summit Parkview
BUSINESS HOTEL $$$

(Map p48; ✆211 888; www.summityangon.com; 350 Ahlone Rd; r $65-70, ste $95-100; ✻@ ☎✻) How many hotels do you know of with breathtaking views over one of the wonders of the universe? If a bargain-rated, orderly and civilised room overlooking the jewel-encrusted Shwedagon Paya isn't for you, feel free to take the same type of room overlooking the pool (open to nonguests for $5 per day).

Guest Care Hotel
HOTEL $$

(Map p48; ✆511 118; www.guestcarehotel.com; 107 Dhama Zedi Rd; r $20-22, ste $32; ✻@☎) There are several classes of room here (with little noticeable difference between them), and it's worth taking a look at a few before committing, as some are in much better nick than others. For character you'll find a few bits of beautifully carved wooden furniture tossed about the place.

Comfort Inn
BUDGET HOTEL $$

(Map p48; ✆525 781; www.comfyland.biz; 4 Shweli Rd; s/d $15/25;✻) A family-run guesthouse on a side street close to the Bangladeshi embassy and within walking distance of the Shwedagon Paya. The wood-panelled rooms are decent enough, but do little to set the imagination alight. The tens of caged birds, on the other hand, may inspire a variety of thoughts and emotions.

✕ Eating

Eating at a Burmese restaurant, with its seemingly never-ending courses and side dishes, is an experience in itself. And as Yangon is the gateway to Myanmar for most visitors, it's here that many travellers' first experience Burmese cuisine. As such, be sure to arm yourself with a bit of culinary knowledge (p328) before hitting the restaurants, street stalls and teahouses of Yangon.

But it's not all about Burmese eats; Yangon is the culinary capital of the country, and its culinary diversity is an unexpected highlight of a visit to the city. You're likely to encounter more than your fair share of Chinese (Burmese Chinese, actually) while upcountry, so unless you're a huge fan of the genre, it's probably worth investigating the other options.

Myanmar people love their Shan food, and the cuisine is not difficult to find in Yangon. Along Anawrahta Rd, west of Sule Paya Rd towards the Sri Kali temple, are a number of shops serving Indian food, much of it southern Indian in origin and Muslim-influenced. Much of the city's Western-style food is disappointing, but it's probably the most authentic you'll encounter in Myanmar, so it's worth taking advantage of.

Eat early – by 10pm all but a couple of places and a few large hotel restaurants will be closed. Travellers keen to avoid government-owned places (see p21) should bypass the Karaweik Palace Restaurant, which is a remarkable-looking structure on Kandawgyi.

HAVE YOUR SAY

Found a fantastic restaurant that you're longing to share with the world? Disagree with our recommendations? Or just want to talk about your most recent trip?

Whatever your reason, head to lonelyplanet.com, where you can post a review, ask or answer a question on the Thorntree forum, comment on a blog, or share your photos and tips on Groups. Or you can simply spend time chatting with like-minded travellers. So go on, have your say.

CITY CENTRE

Nilar Biryani & Cold Drink   MUSLIM INDIAN $
(Map p46; 216 Anawrahta Rd; meals from K800; ☺all day) Giant cauldrons full of spices, broths and rice bubble away at the front of this bright and brash Indian joint. It's never less than packed, and with good reason: the biryanis are probably among the best your lips will meet. The chicken has been cooked so slowly and for so long that the meat just drips off, the rice is out of this world and the banana lassi is divine. Nothing on the menu costs more than K1800, and most is a fraction of that. It's far and away the best of several similar nearby places.

Danuphyu Daw Saw Yee Myanma
Restaurant   BURMESE $
(Map p46; 175/177 29th St; meals from K2000; ☺lunch & dinner) Ask locals where to eat Burmese food in central Yangon and they'll most likely point you in the direction of this longstanding shophouse restaurant. There's a brief English-language menu, but your best bet is to have a look at the selection of curries behind the counter. All dishes are served in the Burmese style with sides of soup du jour (the sour vegetable soup is particularly good) and *ngapi ye*, a pungent dip served with par-boiled vegies and fresh herbs.

999 Shan Noodle Shop   SHAN $
(Map p42; 130/B 34th St; noodle dishes from K500; ☺breakfast & lunch) A handful of tables are crammed into this tiny, brightly coloured eatery behind City Hall, a short walk from Sule Paya. The menu includes noodles such as *Shàn k'auq swèh* (thin rice noodles in a slightly spicy chicken broth) and *myi shay* (Mandalay-style noodle soup) and tasty non-noodle dishes such as Shan tofu (actually made from chickpea flour) and the delicious Shan yellow rice with tomato.

Feel Myanmar Food   BURMESE $$
(Map p46; 124 Pyidaungsu Yeiktha St; meals from K3000; ☺lunch & dinner) This sophisticated jungle-shack restaurant is reminiscent of a north Myanmar house. It's a superb place to get your fingers dirty experimenting with the huge range of tasty Burmese dishes, which are laid out in little trays that you can just point to. It's very popular at lunchtime with local businesspeople and foreign embassy staff.

New Delhi Restaurant   INDIAN $
(Map p46; Anawrahta Rd; mains from K500; ☺all day) This grubby place serves tasty Muslim-

MA THANEGI: WRITER ON ALL THINGS MYANMAR

Myanmar cuisine does not use coconut, green chillies or sugar like in Thailand. It is neither as delicate as the steamed dishes of China nor as fiercely hot as Sichuan cuisine. It does not use as many aromatic spices as India.

Best Dishes

The salads we call *athoke* or *let thoke*, meaning a 'mixture' or 'mixed with hand'. You must also try the pickled tea leaves, eaten in a salad with roasted or deep-fried nuts and beans, sesame, etc. The prepared tea-leaf pulp tastes like pesto, and can have lime or chillies added to it for different tastes.

Best Noodle Dish

I love all, but my favourite is the Delta region noodle *mohinga*, thin rice noodles eaten with a thick fish broth cooked with lots of lemongrass and slices of the inner banana stem for crunch. My favourite upcountry noodle is *mondhi*, the thick, soft rice noodles eaten with a curry of chicken strips, onion oil, roasted chickpea powder, sliced fried fish cakes and sliced raw onions.

Best Yangon Restaurants

For Burmese food, clean but not fancy, I like Feel Myanmar (p58). For teahouses, Lucky Seven (p63) because it has a huge selection of snacks, one-dish meals and noodles.

Best Eating Tip

If you don't like the oil in the curries, simply leave it in the bowl and don't spoon it onto your plate, just take the meat or fish. This is what we do; not all Myanmar people go for oily food.

---

influenced South Indian dishes such as an insanely rich mutton curry, as well as meat-free options including *puris* (puffy breads), *idli* (rice ball in broth), various *dosai* and banana-leaf *thalis*.

365 Café INTERNATIONAL, JAPANESE **$$**
(Map p42; Ah Lan Paya Pagoda Rd; mains K3300-7800; ☺24hr; ❋ 🛜) This stylish café, located on the ground floor of the Thamada Hotel, serves coffee drinks (K2200 to K3150) and a largely Japanese-influenced menu, with a few Western and Chinese dishes thrown in for good measure. Wi-fi is available at 15 hours for K5000.

Shwe Mei Tha Su MUSLIM BURMESE **$**
(Map p46; 173 29th St; meals from K2000; ☺lunch & dinner) Located next door to the more famous Danuphyu Daw Saw Yee, and lacking a roman-script sign, this is the Muslim version of the traditional Myanmar curry house, where the sour soup is replaced with a hearty dhal, the meat-based curries are rich and spicy, and sides include pappadum and a smoky *balachaung*.

Be Le CHINESE **$$**
(Junior Duck; Map p42; Pansodan St Jetty; dishes from K1200; ☺lunch & dinner) Virtually the only place in town taking advantage of a riverfront location, this former ferry terminal is one the best places in town to soak up a view and some breezes. The Chinese food isn't amazing, but it's decent, and most go for the roast duck.

Ingyin New South India Food Centre SOUTHERN INDIAN **$**
(Map p46; Anawrahta Rd; mains from K600; ☺all day) The cheery staff here do the crispiest and tastiest *dosai* in central Yangon. It's a good place for a *thali* as well, and it has tea and Indian sweets if you require dessert.

Aung Mingalar Shan Noodle Restaurant SHAN **$**
(Map p46; Bo Yar Nyunt St; mains from K1000; ☺breakfast & lunch) Aung Mingalar is an excellent place to indulge simultaneously in people-watching and noodle sipping. It's a simple and fun restaurant with trendy city-café overtones.

Zawgyi House
BURMESE, INTERNATIONAL **$$**

(Map p46; 372 Bogyoke Aung San Rd; mains K2300-7800; ☺all day;❋) This coffee shop is a bold display of what could be if the city was ever allowed out of its doldrums. It's very much a hang-out for expats and passing business-people, all of whom appreciate the expensive shakes, juices, ice creams and sandwiches.

Hong Lau Lau
NORTHERN CHINESE **$$**

(Map p46; 416-418 Strand Rd; mains from K1800; ☺lunch & dinner; ❋) Allegedly where the Chinese embassy staff eat when feeling homesick, this unassuming joint serves northern Chinese staples, from hand-pulled noodles to freshly rolled dumplings, under the supervision of a Chinese chef.

Japan Japan
JAPANESE **$$**

(Map p42; 239 Pansodan St; mains K2500-3000; ☺lunch & dinner; ❋) A kitschily decorated but strangely cool Japanese restaurant (the sign says 'Japan Style'), with Japanese staff who like to make a fuss over you. The food is cheap, filling and mouthwatering with some superb sushi.

Nam Kham Family Shan Restaurant
SHAN **$**

(Map p42; 134 37th St; meals from K700; ☺all day) This tiny restaurant, located conveniently near the centre of town, serves the usual Shan noodle dishes plus a variety of point-and-choose curries, soups, stir-fries and other dishes served over rice.

Monsoon
SOUTHEAST ASIAN **$$$**

(Map p42; ☏295 224; www.monsoonmyanmar.com; 85-87 Thein Byu Rd; mains from K2200; ☺lunch & dinner; ❋) Located in an airy colonial town house, Monsoon is a good option for those intimidated by Yangon's more authentic options. The menu also spans the rest of mainland Southeast Asia, with sections from Thailand, Vietnam, Cambodia and Laos. Upstairs is **Loft**, a good handicraft shop.

Bharat Restaurant
SOUTHERN INDIAN **$**

(Map p42; ☏281 519; 356 Mahabandoola Rd; mains from K1000; ☺all day) Specialising in southern Indian dishes, Bharat's tidy interior and marble-topped tables make a nice change from the long cafeteria-style tables at the Indian places on Anawrahta Rd.

Ichiban-Kan
JAPANESE **$$**

(Map p42; 17-18 Aung San Stadium; noodle dishes $5-7; ☺lunch & dinner; ❋) An intimate and tasteful restaurant, which seems to have been lifted straight from the Tokyo backstreets of yester-

year. The food is as well presented and created as the décor, and the small menu focuses on soup and noodle dishes.

Ciao Pizzeria Italiana
ITALIAN **$$**

(Map p42; 262 Pansodan St; pizzas K4000-7500; ☺lunch & dinner; ❋) Small and simple Italian restaurant without any unnecessary fuss, and with passable imitations of Rome's finest, including spaghetti with seafood and a decent selection of pizzas. The Myanmar chef has been trained by an Italian.

Lotaya
SHAN **$**

(Map p46; Bogyoke Aung San Market; mains K1000-3800; ☺lunch Tue-Sun) A shack-like place located at the back of Bogyoke Market serving Shan noodles and Thai- and Chinese-style dishes, in addition to iced coffees and fruit drinks. They're not the best Shan noodles in town, but it's a good place to refuel while shopping.

Maw Shwe Li Restaurant
SHAN **$**

(Map p46; 654 Strand Rd; mains from K1000; ☺lunch & dinner) The most recent incarnation of this popular restaurant is something of a Shan-themed sports bar. Several screens broadcast football while Shan-style snacks (spicy salads, deep-fried tofu) and draught beer entertain the mouth.

OUTSIDE CITY CENTRE

⬛TOP CHOICE Aung Thukha
BURMESE **$**

(Map p48; Dhama Zedi Rd; meals from K2000; ☺all day) This longstanding institution just might be our favourite place in town for Myanmar food. There's heaps of choice, with everything from rich, meaty curries to light, freshly made salads, and the flavours are more subtle here than elsewhere, emphasising herbs rather than oil and spice. And despite the fact that it's almost constantly busy, Aung Thuka manages to maintain gentle, friendly service and a palpable old-school atmosphere, making the experience akin to eating at someone's home.

Minn Lane Rakhaing Monte & Fresh Seafood
RAKHAING BURMESE **$$**

(Map p38; cnr Parami Rd & Pyay Rd; mains from K2000; ☺lunch & dinner) If you want spicy, skip Thai and head directly to this boisterous Rakhaing-themed grilled seafood hall, popular with local families on a night out. The eponymous *monte* (actually *moún-di*) is a noodle soup featuring rice noodles and an intensely peppery broth. If you prefer the latter on the side, order Rakhaing salad, a spicy noodle salad. And of course there's all

It doesn't take long to see that much of life in Yangon takes place on the streets. Likewise, for the average Burmese, eating at a proper restaurant is an infrequent extravagance and most eating is done at home or on the street.

Yangon's street-food options can be both overwhelming and challenging (pork offal on a skewer, anyone?), so as a guide in this jungle of meals, the below are some of our favourite street eats and the best places to eat them.

» **Samusa thoke** During the day a line of **vendors** (Map p42; Mahabandoola Garden St; K500) near Mahabandoola Park sell this 'salad' of sliced samosas served with a thin lentil gravy.

» **Fruit juice** Several vendors at Bogyoke Aung San Market sell refreshing **fresh-squeezed juice** (Map p46; Bogyoke Aung San Rd; from K1000; ⏰10am-5pm) – don't miss the creamy avocado, sweetened with condensed milk.

» **Bein moun & moun pyar thalet** These delicious 'Burmese pancakes' (K200), served sweet (*bein moun*) or savoury (*moun pyar thalet*), can be found at most Yangon corners at all times of the day and night.

» **Dosai** At night along Anawratha St, several street-side vendors sell this thin southern Indian crepe (from K500), known in Burmese as *to-shay*.

» **Mohinga** This soup of thin rice noodles and fish broth is available just about everywhere, but our favourite bowl is at **Myaung Mya Daw Cho** (Map p42; 158 51st St; from K500; ⏰4.30-9am). There's no English sign here; simply look for the green sign near some trees.

» **Grilled food** Every night, the strip of 19th St between Mahabandoola and Anawrahta Rds hosts dozens of stalls and open-air restaurants serving delicious **grilled snacks** (Map p46; meals from K5000; ⏰5-11pm) and draught beer.

» **Lassi Shwe Balee** (no roman-script sign; Map p46; Bo Sun Pat Rd; per glass from 600K; ⏰10am-9pm) serves deliciously curdy glasses of this Indian yogurt drink.

» **Buthi kyaw** Every evening a lone **vendor** (Map p42; cnr Anawratha & Thein Byu Rds; K500; ⏰4-9pm) sells this tasty snack of battered and deep-fried chunks of gourd served with a spicy/sour dipping sauce.

» **Burmese sweets** Every afternoon in front of FMI Centre a handful of street-side vendors sell delicious **Burmese sweets** (Map p46; Bogyoke Aung San Rd; from K50) ranging from *shwe-t'aumi'n* ('golden' sticky rice) to *mou'n-se'in-ba'un* (a type of steamed cake topped with shredded coconut).

---

manner of grilled crab, oyster, shrimp, squid and shellfish, all for low prices.

K Hot Pot HOT POT $$$
(Golden Happy Hot Pot; Map p48; Ko Min Ko Chin Rd; meals from K10,000; ⏰dinner) This vast hall is Yangon's most famous and most popular hot-pot joint. Join hundreds of other diners in choosing the raw ingredients then cooking them in vats of a spicy Sichuan-style broth. Not exactly cheap, but good, tasty fun. Dinner only.

Le Planteur FRENCH $$$
(Map p48; ☎541 997; www.leplanteur.net; 22 Kaba Aye Pagoda Rd; mains $19-32, set lunch/dinner $25/79; ⏰lunch & dinner; ❄) Widely considered the best restaurant in Yangon and with meal prices to match its exalted reputation. If you can fit it into your budget, Le Planteur's set dinner runs the gamut from foie gras to prime rib. If you can't, then try the Business Lunch set, which runs at a third of the cost, or if you find yourself in Nyaungshwe, try Swiss chef Boris Granges' other venture, Viewpoint (p182).

Ashoka Indian Restaurant NORTHERN INDIAN $$
(Map p48; 28B Pho Sein Rd; mains from K2000; ⏰lunch & dinner; ❄) The creamy curries of north India are the main event here. The portions are small, so it's a good idea to consider one of the expansive set meals ($7 to $9), which also include vegetarian options. The colonial villa the restaurant is housed in is as gorgeous as the food.

L'Opera Restaurant ITALIAN $$$
(Map p38; ☑665 516; www.operayangon.com; 62D U Tun Nyein St; mains from $10; ☺lunch & dinner; ❋) One of the better and more elegant restaurants in Yangon, L'Opera boasts well-trained and smartly dressed waiters, but more important is the Italian owner and chef's meticulous preparation. The outdoor garden seating is a bonus in good weather. The restaurant is located off Kaba Aye Pagoda Rd, at the northern end of Inya Lake.

Alamanda Inn FRENCH $$
(Map p48; ☑534 513; 60B Shwe Taung Gyar Rd/ Golden Valley Rd, Bahan; meals K7000-10,000; ☺lunch & dinner) In a quiet residential neighbourhood, this breezy open-air restaurant and bar under a covered patio is a relaxing place to put the cares of Yangon behind you. The house speciality is tagines, but it also does good steaks and sandwiches as well as killer cocktails, all reasonably priced.

House of Memories BURMESE, INTERNATIONAL $$
(Map p48; ☑525 195; 290 U Wi Za Ra Rd; ☺lunch & dinner) Housed in a mock Tudor colonial villa stuffed with antiques and old photos (and including an office where General Aung San once worked), this an interesting place to dine on dishes such as a hearty beef curry and an authentically smoky-tasting grilled eggplant salad. Although it also boasts a 'piano bar', the live music is sporadic – call ahead to see when the next performance will be. Located off U Wi Za Ra Rd.

Green Elephant BURMESE $$$
(Map p48; www.greenelephant-restaurants.com; 519A Thirimingalar St; mains K1500-18,000; set lunch K8000; ☺lunch & dinner) Popular with tour groups, the Green Elephant is a safe but tasty enough introduction to Myanmar cuisine. The open-air wooden dining room boasts a romantic atmosphere and the restaurant also includes an upmarket crafts shop.

Hla Myanma Htamin Zain BURMESE $
(Map p48; 17 1st St; mains from K1500; ☺lunch & dinner) This longstanding place is a traditional Myanmar-style restaurant, where a blasting TV fills in for interior design. This place, which doesn't have a roman-script sign, is sometimes called Shwe Ba because a famous actor of that name once had his house nearby.

Inlay Amathaya SHAN $
(Map p38; cnr Kaba Aye Padoga Rd & Kanbe Rd; mains from K500; ☺lunch & dinner) There's neither a roman-script sign or an English menu. However, the menu does feature tiny pictures to guide you through the basics of Shan cuisine. Most head straight for the noodle dishes, but this is a great place to try Shan rice dishes such as *weq-thà jeh* (rice steamed with blood – much better than it sounds) or *ngà t'avmìn hneiq,* turmeric rice with fish.

Sabai @ DMZ THAI $$
(Map p48; 232 Dhama Zedi Rd; mains from K2500; ❋) This semi-formal Thai-owned place boasts a Thai chef and an extensive and appetising menu. The range of salads is particularly impressive for someone craving a light lunch in the heat of the day.

Singapore's Kitchen SINGAPOREAN $$
(Map p48; 333 Ahlone Rd; mains from K2500; ☺all day; ❋) Located next door to Summit Parkview hotel, the menu here has pages devoted to cheap and tasty Singapore hawker food (think Hainanese chicken rice, *rojak*, *mee goreng*) as well as Chinese-influenced seafood dishes.

Thai Kitchen THAI $$
(Map p48; 126 Dhama Zedi Rd; mains from K2000; ☺all day; ❋) This place boasts a thick, illustrated menu, with a variety of dishes given the stamp of approval by Thai tourists.

Yin Fong Seafood Restaurant CHINESE $$$
(Map p48; Kan Yeik Tha Rd; dishes from K4500; ☺lunch & dinner; ❋) The setting, beside a busy main road, isn't ideal, but the seafood sure is. This pricey restaurant has carved a well-founded reputation as one of the top Chinese restaurants in Yangon.

Black Canyon Coffee INTERNATIONAL, THAI $$
(Map p48; Ahlone Rd; dishes from K2000; ☺lunch & dinner; ❋🖰) Located next door to the Summit Parkview hotel, this is a swish little Thai restaurant, which also delves into fusion foods, eg spicy pasta. The noodles are decent, as are the Wellington boot-shaped coffeecups.

Coffee Circles INTERNATIONAL $$
(Map p48; 107 Dhama Zedi Rd; mains from K3000; ☺all day; ❋🖰) Located in front of the Guest Care Hotel, this chic restaurant-café is the place to go if you want to forget you're in Yangon. In addition to real coffee, it offers a menu that ranges from Thai to burgers, and has fast wi-fi to boot.

Café Dibar INTERNATIONAL, ITALIAN $$
(Map p48; Inya Rd; mains from K4000; ☺lunch & dinner; ❋) Like your corner Italian place back home: not outstanding, but always reliable.

Specialising in pizza and pasta, but with a few other dishes (sandwiches, salads, burgers) thrown in.

Royal Garden CHINESE **$$**
(Map p48; ☑546 923; Nat Mauk Rd, Bahan; mains K7000; ⊙6.30am-10.15pm) Kicking off with dim sum for breakfast and rolling through to roasted duck for dinner this big lakeside restaurant offers up a tasty and keenly priced selection of Chinese goodies.

Quick Eats

Yangon is home to a handful of domestic fast-food chains and several Western-style bakery-cafés. Most are open for lunch and dinner and have basic snacks and dishes that start at about K500.

For Burmese-style teahouses, see p63, and for street food, see p61.

Café Aroma CAFÉ **$**
(Map p42; Sule Paya Rd; ❀) The Starbucks of Yangon, this café has several outlets

YANGON'S CAFÉ CULTURE

Yangon's numerous teahouses are not just places to have cups of milk tea and coffee or tiny pots of Chinese tea. They're also places to grab a snack. They're places to catch up with a friend. They're almost certainly a better place for breakfast than your guesthouse (see p334), and they're also where gossip is passed around, deals made and, if you believe the rumours, government spies are rampant.

But back to the tea. Depending on the size of your sweet tooth and your caffeine tolerance, to order tea in Yangon you'll need a short language lesson:

» *lăp'eq·ye* – black tea served sweet with a dollop of condensed milk

» *cho bawq* – less sweet version of *lăp'eq·ye*

» *kyauk padaung* – very sweet; the phrase comes from a famous sugar-palm-growing region near Bagan

» *cho kya'* – strongest tea, also served with condensed milk.

Once you've mastered the lingo, it's time pull up a tiny plastic stool and drink. The following is our shortlist of teahouses in Yangon. All are open from approximately 6am to 4pm. A cup of tea should set you back about K250, and snacks and light meals start at about K400:

Lucky Seven (Map p42; 49th St) Located west of the centre of town, this is our all-around favourite Yangon teahouse – tidy, lively and with excellent food. The *mohinga* here is outstanding, as are most other Burmese-style noodle dishes.

Shwe We Htun (Map p42; 81 37th St) A buzzing old-school teahouse that serves better-quality food than most. There's no roman-script sign, but you'll know it by the crowds.

Thone Pan Hla (Map p46; 454 Mahabandoola Rd) This centrally located teahouse doesn't have a roman-script sign, but it does have an English-language menu of teahouse staples, from *shàn k'auk swèh* to fried rice.

Shwe Khaung Laung (Map p46; cnr Bogyoke Aung San Rd & 31st St) In addition to good tea, this Chinese-style teahouse serves decent steamed buns and noodles and baked cakes and pastries. There's no English sign, but it's located right on the corner.

Man Myo Taw Café (Map p42; cnr Mahabandoola Rd & 39th St) Also representing the Chinese end of the Yangon teahouse spectrum, this tidy place offers good steamed buns and coffee.

Golden Tea (Map p46; Bo Sun Pat Rd) This centrally located Muslim-run teahouse is busy at breakfast, but we prefer to come later in the day when they serve tasty *s'uanwi'n-mauk'in* (semolina cakes).

Seit Taing Kya (Map p48; 53 Za Ga War St) A lauded hall-like place, this is very popular – probably because the tea here actually tastes of tea, unlike the sugar and condensed milk of most teahouses.

Yatha Teashop (Map p42; 353 Mahabandoola Rd) A classic Muslim-style teahouse, providing fresh samosas and *palata*.

around the city. The Sule Paya Rd branch is the most central and offers fine, freshly brewed coffee and fruit smoothies (from about K800).

Parisian Cake & Café
CAFÉ $
Sule Paya Rd (Map p42; Sule Paya Rd; ✷); Mahabandoola St (Map p46; 778 Mahabandoola St; ✷) It certainly ain't as chic as a café in its namesake city, but it's cool and relaxing and has an arm-length list of teas and coffees (from K800), as well as cold juices and shakes, a variety of cakes and light pasta lunches.

Mr Brown Café
CAFÉ $
(Map p42; Mahabandoola Garden St; ✷) Another place to get a break from the heat, sip a cold drink and chow down on a cake.

Tokyo Fried Chicken
FAST FOOD $
(Map p46; Shwe Bontha St; mains K1500; ✷) TFC is Yangon's own KFC.

Self-Catering

City Mart
SUPERMARKET
Shwe Bontha St (Map p46; Shwe Bontha St; ◷9am-9pm); Anawrahta Rd (Map p42; cnr Anawrahta Rd & 47th St; ◷9am-9pm) Can't live without peanut butter? These relatively well-stocked supermarkets near the city centre have a pretty good selection of imported goods (including tampons) and a pharmacy.

Ruby Mart
SUPERMARKET
(Map p42; cnr Bogyoke Aung San Rd & Pansodan St; ◷9am-9pm) Centrally located, modern grocery store with all the staples and then some.

Sharky's
DELI
Dhama Zedi Rd (Map p48; 117 Dhama Zedi Rd; ◷9am-10pm); Inya Rd (Map p48; 131 Inya Rd; ◷9am-10pm) The two nearly adjacent locations of this modern deli have good selections of fresh and preserved Western-style foods and meals.

🍷 Drinking & Entertainment

We hope you had your fun in Bangkok, because things are quiet here... Most places close by 10pm and the main form of local nightlife is hanging out in beer gardens, teahouses or 'cold drink' shops.

Bars

Yes, there is alcohol in Yangon, and just about every neighbourhood has a grubby beer-garden-type restaurant, but places that fit the Western concept of a bar are few and far between.

Strand Bar
HOTEL BAR
(Map p42; Strand Hotel, 92 Strand Rd; ◷to 11pm; ✷🛜) Primarily an expat scene, this classic bar inside the Strand Hotel has any foreign liquors you may be craving behind its polished wooden bar. Friday afternoon and early evening is a two-for-one happy hour (there's a standard happy hour all other days from 5pm to 7pm).

Mr Guitar Café
LIVE MUSIC
(Map p48; 22 Sayasan St; ◷6pm-midnight; ✷) Founded by famous Myanmar vocalist Nay Myo Say, this café-bar features live folk music from about 7pm to midnight nightly. Well-known local musicians drop by frequently to sit in with the regular house group. There's food, and the clientele is a mix of locals and expats.

50th Street Bar & Grill
BAR
(Map p42; 9-13 50th St; ◷11am-2.30pm & 5pm-late Mon-Fri, 10.30am-late Sat & Sun; ✷🛜) The teak and heavy leather furniture here inspire thoughts of an elite men's club. It's popular with locals and expats on Wednesday nights, when it has $6 pizzas to soften the drinking.

Inya 1
RESTAURANT
(Map p48; 1 Inya Rd; ◷lunch & dinner; ✷) Though technically a restaurant, Inya 1's inviting garden and modern Balinese design theme make it one of the best choices in Yangon for a sophisticated sundowner.

British Club Bar
BAR
(Map p42; off Gyo Byu St; ◷1st Fri evening of month until midnight) Think ambassadors sit around at night discussing world peace? Think again! Once a month the ever-so-prim British Club throws open its doors and discussion moves from world peace to beer consumption. Expats (of all nationalities) rate this as the social event of the month. Bring your passport.

Zero Zone Rock Restaurant
BAR
(Map p46; 4th fl, 2 Theingyi Zei market) This rooftop bar is more fun than the unintentionally self-deprecating name suggests. Live karaoke-like music starts at 7pm, the draught beer is cheap and the cool breezes free.

Sky Bistro
BAR
(Map p42; 20th fl, Sakura Tower, cnr Sule Paya Rd & Bogyoke Aung San Rd; ◷9am-10pm; ✷) Certainly not the sexiest place in Yangon for a night out, but the views from the 20th floor are pretty impressive and there's a generous happy hour from 4pm to 10pm. Bar snacks and other dishes are also available.

Captain's Bar
HOTEL BAR

(Map p48; Savoy Hotel, 129 Dhama Zedi Rd; ⊘to midnight; ❋🛜) This bar at the Savoy is popular with locals and expats, especially on Wednesday and Friday nights, when there's live music.

Ginki Kids
BAR

(Map p48; Kan Baw Sa Rd; ⊘to midnight) A cosy bar popular among expats and upper-class locals.

Clubs

Lagging behind Yangon's already thin bar scene is its club scene. There are a few dance clubs, but they're so full of local quirks that they're more appropriate for anthropological investigation than a night on the town.

JJ City
CLUB

(Map p48; Mingala Zei, Set Yone Rd (Mill Rd); ⊘8pm-2am) Just your typical, bog-standard wet market by day, multi-storey entertainment complex by night... Enter lifts stained with betel spit to emerge at one of several floors of fun: **JJ** is ostensibly a disco, but most appear to come for the bizarre 10pm fashion show, in which the 'JJ Queen' is chosen on a nightly basis. Your entrance fee of K3000 gets you a beer. On the fifth floor of the same complex is **Channel V**, a slightly more downmarket disco with lots of teenage boys and not enough air-conditioning. This place charges a K4500 entry fee. Foreign patrons are rare, and so may be given VIP treatment.

Pioneer
CLUB

(Map p48; Ahlone Rd; admission K6000; ⊘7pm-3am) This disco sees a relative mix of people, from upper-class locals to profit-seeking 'dancing girls'. Like other clubs in Yangon, it's similar to your first school dance: a handful of girls actually hit the floor while the guys fidget nervously.

YGN Bar
CLUB

(Map p48; Ahlone Rd; no cover; ⊘7pm-3am) This place can't decide whether it's a bar or a club. There's no entrance fee, so you can do as the locals do and sip a beer while staring at the handful of girls who dare to dance. On Saturday nights the place has a distinctly pink vibe.

Cinemas

There's no better city for Myanmar cinephiles than Yangon. By a conservative estimate there are over 50 cinemas. Half a dozen of these cinemas (Map p42) are found along Bogyoke Aung San Rd, east of the Sule Paya. Tickets start at about K600 per seat. Critically acclaimed films are in short supply; rather there is a succession of syrupy Myanmar dramas, Bollywood musicals and kung-fu smashups, plus a few Hollywood blockbusters.

Nay Pyi Daw Cinema
CINEMA

(Map p42; Sule Paya Rd) This cinema across from Traders Hotel and next to Café Aroma has showings throughout the day. It's one of the busiest cinemas in the city.

Thamada Cinema
CINEMA

(Map p42; 5 Ah Lan Paya Pagoda Rd) Easily the best cinema for foreigners, Thamada is comfortable and shows fairly recent international (including Hollywood) films.

American Center
CULTURAL CENTRE

(Map p46; 14 Taw Win St) This US-sponsored centre shows free American movies at 1pm from Tuesday to Saturday.

🔒 Shopping

While it isn't quite the shoppers' Mecca that Bangkok is, Yangon does offer a more manageable alternative, as there are fewer and smaller outlets, and prices tend to be cheaper all around.

Arts & Handicrafts

There is quite a bit of interesting art, furniture and antiques to be bought in Yangon. Unfortunately much of it is too large to fit in most people's luggage.

Augustine's Souvenir Shop
ANTIQUES

(Map p48; www.augustinesouvenir.com; 20 Thirimingalar St; ⊘11am-7.30pm Mon-Fri, 2-7.30pm Sat & Sun) Walk through a garden of abandoned vintage cars into this handsome house, which doubles as one of Yangon's most captivating shopping destinations. A virtual museum of Myanmar antiques, there's a particular emphasis on wooden items, including carved figures, chests and wall hangings. It's a short walk from the Green Elephant Restaurant.

Pansodan Gallery
GALLERY

(Map p42; 1st fl, 286 Pansodan St; ⊘10am-6pm) This loft-like gallery has a variety of Myanmar contemporary and antique art, the latter including some truly unique antique prints, advertisements and photos. Owner-artist Aung Soe Min is knowledgeable about Myanmar art, and can point you in the right direction of that special souvenir you didn't even know you needed.

FREE XB Shop
HANDICRAFTS

(Map p46; 106 20-B Yaw Min Gee St; ⊘9am-6pm) The showroom of this international NGO, dedicated to fighting poverty and AIDS, has fabric-based products, including adorable soft toys, cushions, rugs and other crafts.

Nandawun
SOUVENIRS

(Map p48; cnr Baho Rd & Ahlone Rd; ☺9am-6pm) This house-bound shop spans two storeys and just about every Myanmar souvenir, from lacquer vessels to replicas of antique scale weights. The upstairs bookshop has a good selection of titles on obscure Myanmar topics.

Gallery Sixty Five
GALLERY

(Map p46; http://gallerysixtyfive.webstarts.com; 65 Yaw Min Gee St; ☺9am-8pm) Housed in a beautiful colonial-era mansion, the ground floor of this private gallery is dedicated to revolving exhibits of contemporary local art.

Loft
SOUVENIRS

(Map p42; 2nd fl, Monsoon, 85-87 Thein Byu Rd; ☺10am-10pm) Above Monsoon restaurant is this craft shop selling high-quality products for prices that don't send waves of shock through your body.

J's Irrawaddy Dream
SOUVENIRS

(Map p42; 1st fl, Strand Hotel, 92 Strand Rd; ☺10am-8pm) This shop features high-quality Myanmar textiles, clothes, lacquer and other handicrafts. It's an especially good place to find stylish women's dresses.

Elephant House
HANDICRAFTS

(Map p48; Green Elephant, 519A Thirimingalar Rd; ☺10am-9pm) Attached to Green Elephant restaurant, this shop sells a decent selection of Burmese housewares, primarily high-quality and attractive lacquerware.

Beikthano Gallery
GALLERY

(Map p48; 133/3 Kaba Aye Pagoda Rd; ☺10am-8pm) Suburban gallery featuring the work of contemporary Myanmar artists.

Bookshops

It's worth checking out the many bookstalls (Map p42) around Bogyoke Aung San Market or along 37th St, which is also regarded as something of a university library for the people. Several stalls have small selections of novels and nonfiction books in English, French and German.

English-language newspapers such as the *Bangkok Post* and the *International Herald Tribune* are sold by vendors in front of **Zawgyi House** (Map p46; 372 Bogyoke Aung San Rd), and a small selection of magazines is also available at **Black Canyon Coffee** (Map p48; Ahlone Rd). In addition to the following shops, **Nandawun** (Map p48; cnr Baho Rd &

Ahlone Rd; ☺9am-6pm) also has a good selection of English-language books on Myanmar.

Bagan Book House
BOOKSHOP

(Map p42; ☑377 227; 100 37th St; ☺9am-5.30pm) This Yangon institution has the most complete selection of English-language books on Myanmar and Southeast Asia, and owner U Htay Aung really knows his stock: we asked for a book on the Shan language and were handed an original text from 1887! The front gate pulled across the entrance doesn't necessarily mean the place is closed unless the door inside the gate is closed too.

Monument Books
BOOKSHOP

(Map p48; 150 Dhama Zedi Rd; ☺9am-8pm) The newest branch of this Southeast Asian chain is Yangon's most modern and well-stocked bookshop. In addition to a good selection of books on topics local and international, there's an attached café-restaurant.

Inwa Bookshop
BOOKSHOP

(Map p42; 301 Pansodan St; ☺9am-6pm) This bookshop sells a small selection of English-language books as well as back issues of foreign magazines such as *Newsweek* and the *Economist*.

Malls

There are a number of modern Western-style shopping malls selling everything from hipster jeans to flat-screen TVs. The largest and most convenient:

Blazon Centre
MALL

(Map p48; 72 U Wi Za Ra Rd)

Dagon Centre
MALL

(Map p48; 262-264 Pyay Rd)

FMI Centre
MALL

(Map p46; 380 Bogyoke Aung San Rd) Just east of Bogyoke Aung San Market.

La Pyat Wun Plaza
MALL

(Map p46; 37 Ah Lan Paya Pagoda Rd) Not far north of the train station.

Markets

Shopping at the *zei* (markets, often spelt *zay*) in central Yangon can be fun, educational and a chance to interact with the locals. Fans of fresh markets should make a point of visiting the hectic **morning market** (Map p46; ☺6-10am) along 26th St, adjacent to Theingyi Zei. Another photogenic **morning market** (Map p42; ☺5-9am) unfolds along the southernmost end of 42nd St, and a tiny but lively **night market** (Map p42; cnr Anawrahta Rd

& 38th St; ◷5-9pm) is held every evening near the Methodist Telugu Church.

Bogyoke Aung San Market   MARKET

(Map p46; Bogyoke Aung San Rd; ◷10am-5pm Tue-Sun) Half a day could easily be spent wandering around this 70-year-old sprawling market (sometimes called by its old British name, Scott Market). Besides the fact that it has over 2000 shops and the largest selection of Myanmar handicrafts you'll find under several roofs, the market is a fantastic opportunity to smile, laugh and haggle alongside local shoppers. You'll find a whole variety of interesting souvenirs, from lacquerware and Shan shoulder bags to T-shirts and puppets. Pick up some nice slippers here, convenient for all the on-and-off demanded by paya protocol. Gems and jewellery are also on hand. Shops worth seeking out include **Yo Ya May** (1st fl), specialising in hill tribe textiles, particularly those from Chin State, and **Heritage Gallery** (1st fl), which has a good selection of reproduction and authentic antiques with an emphasis on lacquerware.

Theingyi Zei   MARKET

(Map p46; Shwedagon Pagoda Rd) The biggest market in central Yangon, this is especially good for locals, who find Bogyoke Aung San Market a little too pricey. Most of the merchandise is ordinary housewares and textiles, but the market is renowned for its large selection of traditional herbs and medicines, which can be found on the ground floor of the easternmost building. Traditional herbal shampoo, made by boiling the bark of the Tayaw shrub with big black *kin pun* (acacia pods), is sold in small plastic bags; this is the secret of Myanmar women's smooth, glossy hair.

Mingala Zei   MARKET

(Map p48; cnr Ban Yar Da La St & Set Yone Rd) A little southeast of Kandawgyi, this market proffers textiles, clothes, electrical appliances, plasticware, preserved and tinned foodstuffs, modern medicines, and even cosmetics from China, Thailand and Singapore. Amazingly, at night a section of this market transforms into a nightclub, JJ City (p65).

Tailors

Yangon isn't a place you'd usually think of for tailor-made clothes, but prices are among the lowest in Southeast Asia.

Tip-Top Tailors   TAILOR

(Map p42; cnr Mahabandoola Rd & 43rd St) A friendly tailor shop, which is open 'everyday, except some of the days when we are shut'. Some of the days when it is most likely to be shut are Fridays and Sundays.

Globe Tailoring   TAILOR

(Map p46; 367 Bogyoke Aung San Rd) Well regarded by local expats for women's and men's tailoring.

ⓘ Information

Cultural Centres & Libraries

At Shwedagon Paya (p71), you can visit the Library & Archives of Buddhism, located in the western arch. There is no public library system in the country.

Alliance Française (Map p48; ☑536 900; http://afrangoun.org; 340 Pyay Rd; ◷9.30am-12.30pm & 2-5.30pm Mon-Fri, 9.30am-12.30pm & 2-6pm Sat) French culture, reading material and various French-language evening courses.

American Center (Map p46; ☑223 140; 14 Taw Win St; ◷9am-4pm Mon-Sat, 9am-noon Thu) Behind the Ministry of Foreign Affairs. It also has a collection of books and magazines, including a good Burma section. American films are shown here Tuesday to Saturday at 1pm.

British Council Library (Map p42; ☑254 658; www.britishcouncil.org/burma; 78 Strand Rd; ◷8.30am-6pm Mon-Fri, 9am-6pm Sat, 9am-1pm Sun) A very modern and plush facility connected to the British embassy. It has a small library of English-language magazines, books and videos and one of the most complete collections of English-language history books on Myanmar.

Emergency

Your home embassy (see p362) may be able to assist with advice during emergencies or serious problems. It's a good idea to register with your embassy upon arrival or, if possible, register online before you arrive, so that embassy staff will know where to reach you in case of an emergency at home.

There isn't always an English-speaking operator on the following numbers; you may have to enlist the aid of a Burmese speaker.

Ambulance (☑192)
Fire department (☑191)
Police (☑199)
Red Cross (☑383 680)

Internet Access

Most top-end hotels and many midrange ones offer wi-fi access, as do a steadily growing number of small hotels and cyber cafés (see boxed text, p68). Rates are by the hour – usually pro rata if under an hour – and most of the central cyber cafés (as well as many hotels) know how to outwit the censors, meaning that you can normally log onto pretty much any website. Server

WI-FI

Yangon is definitely not as online as other Asian cities, but wi-fi is available at a handful of hotels, restaurants and bars. In the hotel lobbies it's generally free (or you're at least expected to buy a drink or snack); otherwise it costs about $1 per hour. Although the hotel lobby connections are usually for guests, we had no problem 'borrowing' them for a short time, particularly if just using a smart phone.

A non-authoritative list of wi-fi hotspots in Yangon:

» **365 Café** (p59; 15 hrK5000)

» **50th St Bar & Grill** (p64) Free.

» **BAK Center** (Map p42) Free with purchase of instant coffee.

» **Black Canyon** (p62) Free.

» **Coffee Circles** (p62) Free.

» **Click Me Quick** (p68) Per hour K4000.

» **Kandawgyi Palace Hotel** (Map p48) Free.

» **May Shan Hotel** (p53) Per hour $1.

» **Panorama Hotel** (p53) Free.

» **Savoy Hotel** (p57) Free.

» **Sedona Hotel** (p57) Free.

» **Strand Hotel & Bar** (p52) Free.

» **Summit Parkview** (p57) Free.

» **Traders Hotel** (Map p42) Free with drink purchase.

speeds have improved over the last couple of years, but still tend to be frustratingly slow in comparison to almost any other country.

Internet shops can be found in just about every corner of central Yangon these days, but if you're in a hurry, make a beeline for one of the following:

Castle Internet & Café (2nd fl, 142-146 Sule Paya Rd; per hr K400; ⊙7am-11pm)

Click Me Quick (97 38th St; per hr K400; ⊙8am-11pm) This quiet and relatively fast internet café also provides wi-fi (per hour K4000).

Hero Cyber Café (33rd St; per hr K300; ⊙9am-10pm)

Internet & Games (Bo Sun Pat Rd; per hr K400; ⊙9am-10pm) Centrally located and relatively fast, although it suffers from loud teenage boys playing online games.

Net 2 Go (cnr Anawrahta Rd & 37th St; per hr K400; ⊙9am-10pm)

Virus III Cybercafe (283-302 Anawrahta Rd; per hr K400; ⊙9am-11pm) Centrally located and, unlike most places, not filled with screaming teenagers playing online games. There are a couple of similar places in the area.

Laundry

Almost all of Yangon's budget and midrange guesthouses and hotels offer inexpensive laundry services including ironing for about K100 per item. Rates at the top-end hotels are not cheap. Another option is **Ava Laundry** (Map p42; 305 Mahabandoola Rd, btwn 41st & 42nd Sts; ⊙8am-8pm). Though it's no quicker than the guesthouses and is relatively expensive, the proprietor is a lovely chap to talk to.

Medical Services

There are several private and public hospitals in Yangon, but the fees, service and quality may vary. There are also some useful pharmacies in town.

AA Pharmacy (Map p42; 142-146 Sule Paya Rd; ⊙9am-10pm) Just north of Sule Paya.

International SOS Clinic (☑667 879; www.internationalsos.com; Inya Lake Hotel, 37 Kaba Aye Pagoda Rd; ⊙8.30am-5.30pm Mon-Fri, 8.30am-12.30pm Sat) This is your best bet in Yangon for emergencies. The clinic also claims to be able to work with just about any international health insurance. Located at Inya Lake Hotel (Map p48).

Pun Hlaing International Clinic (Map p46; ☑243 010; 4th fl, FMI Centre, Bogyoke Aung San Rd; ⊙9am-7pm Mon-Sat & 10am-7pm Sun) Located in the FMI Centre, this is your best bet for centrally located healthcare.

Money

If you're not aware of the various money-related issues involved in visiting Myanmar, you may be in for a big surprise. Be sure to pay close attention to our boxed text (below) and be sure to also read p364.

In Yangon, you can pay for your taxi from the airport to the city in US dollars and there's no reason to buy kyat in the terminal. Most hotels and guesthouses sell kyat for rates slightly lower than the usual street rate. Bogyoke Aung San Market is the best place to change money; odds are you'll be approached if you wander down the centre aisle. Before you go, ask around to establish the going rate. You should not pay any commission or tip for such services.

At the time of research, there appeared to be a near total freeze on credit cards, and not even the Strand was accepting them. The only place we found accepting and/or giving cash advance on credit cards was the Parkroyal hotel, and this was only for Visa cards, with cash advances susceptible to a 8% service charge and a maximum of $200 per day. Also forget about travellers cheques – they're useless in Myanmar (see p364).

Post

DHL (Map p46; [phone]664 434; Parkroyal hotel, 33 Ah Lan Paya Pagoda Rd; ⊙8am-6pm Mon-Fri)

Main post office (Map p42; Strand Rd; ⊙7.30am-6pm Mon-Fri) A short stroll east of the Strand Hotel. Stamps are for sale on the ground floor but go to the 1st floor to send mail.

Tourist Information

Myanmar Travels & Tours (MTT; Map p42; [phone]374 281; 118 Mahabandoola Garden St; ⊙8.30am-5pm) Once you wake them up from their nap, the people at this government-run information centre are actually quite friendly and helpful, although their resources are very limited. This is the place to go to apply for per-

MONEY MATTERS

» Do not change money at the airport or at banks – the official exchange rate is a fraction of the black market rate. Your best bet for changing money in Yangon is Bogyoke Aung San Market or your hotel.

» US dollar bills must be the latest version (multi-coloured bills from 2006 or later) and in *absolutely perfect* condition: no folds, stamps, stains, writing or tears.

» Myanmar ATMs don't accept international cards – take all the cash (ideally in US$) you'll need.

» Parkroyal hotel is the only hotel in Yangon that accepts credit cards.

mits to the Delta region (Dalah, Twante) or – if you're determined to do things yourself and have the requisite four to six weeks – to request permission for a government-sanctioned trip to destinations such as Kayah State (p198), Tanintharyi (Tenasserim) Region (p110) or Chin State (p287).

Travel Agencies

Most visitors to Myanmar use private domestic travel agencies to book a tour, hire a car or book a domestic flight (air-ticket prices are usually cheaper through a private travel agency). However, of the more than 100 enterprises in Yangon calling themselves travel agencies, only a handful can be considered full-service, experienced tour agencies, and they're essential in arranging government-sanctioned visits to more remote places in Myanmar.

Among the more reliable agencies:

Asian Trails (Map p46; [phone]211 212; www.asiantrails.info; 73 Pyay Rd) This outfit can arrange specific-interest tours of Myanmar, including cycling and mountaineering, and can facilitate visits to far northern Myanmar and other remote areas.

Ayarwaddy Legend Travels & Tours (Map p42; [phone]252 007; www.ayarwaddylegend.com; 107 37th St; ⊙9am-5pm Mon-Fri, 9am-noon Sat & Sun) Professional agency that can provide advice on visiting off-the-beaten track areas.

Columbus Travels & Tours (Map p42; [phone]255 123; www.travelmyanmar.com; 3rd fl, Sakura Tower, cnr Bogyoke Aung San Rd & Sule Paya Rd)

Diethelm Travel ([phone]662 898; www.diethelm travel.com/myanmar; Inya Lake Hotel, 37 Kaba Aye Pagoda Rd) At Inya Lake Hotel (Map p48).

Exotissimo Travel (Map p42; [phone]255 266; http://myanmar.exotissimo.com/travel/tours; 3rd fl, Sakura Tower, cnr Bogyoke Aung San Rd & Sule Paya Rd)

Good News Travels (Map p46; [phone]375 050, 09-511 6256; www.myanmargoodnewstravel.com; 4th fl, FMI Centre, 380 Bogyoke Aung San Rd; ⊙9am-5pm Mon-Sat) The owner, William Myatwunna, is extremely personable and knowledgeable, and can help arrange visits to remote parts of Myanmar. Highly recommended.

Myanmar Himalaya Trekking (Map p48; [phone]227 978; www.myanmar-explore.com; Room 205, Summit Parkview hotel, 350 Ahlone Rd; ⊙9.30am-5pm Mon-Fri, 9am-noon Sat)

Websites

Lonely Planet (http://www.lonelyplanet.com/myanmar-burma/yangon-rangoon)

ⓘ Getting There & Away

Air

See p371 for information on international air travel, and p372 for details on domestic air travel to and from Yangon.

Boat

There are several jetties along the Yangon River, but those interested in travelling by boat only need to be familiar with two – all other departure points are for cargo or are for routes that don't allow foreign passengers.

The **Pansodan St Jetty** (Map p42), located at the foot of Pansodan St, near the Strand Hotel, is the jumping-off base for daytime river-crossing boats to Dalah (round trip K2000, five minutes), which leave roughly every 20 minutes from the early morning to the evening. Keep in mind that, as Dalah is technically part of the Delta Region, you'll need to apply for permission from Myanmar Travels & Tours (p69) to board this boat. Pansodan St Jetty is also where you board ferries to Twante ($1, two hours), which depart at 6.30am on Tuesday and 7am on Wednesday and Saturday.

Farther west along Strand Rd, **Lan Thit jetty** (Map p46) is where **IWT** (Inland Water Transport; Map p46; ☎381 912, 380 764; Lan Thit jetty) run Chinese triple-decker ferries to Pathein every day at 5pm (deck class/private cabin $7/42, 17 hours). Foreigners must buy tickets from the deputy division manager's office next to Building 63 on Lan Thit jetty.

There are several privately owned companies that operate luxury cruises from Yangon to Bagan and Mandalay (see p376).

Bus

There are two major bus terminals that service Yangon: **Aung Mingalar Bus Terminal** (Map p38) and **Hlaing Thar Yar Bus Terminal** (off Map p38).

Most signs at the bus terminals are in Burmese; however, English-speaking touts anxious to steer you in the right direction are in abundance. To avoid the hassle and attention make sure your taxi driver (both of the major terminals are around 45 minutes from the city centre) knows where you want to go and, even better, the name of the specific bus company. Showing the driver your ticket will do; if you don't have a ticket, ask a Burmese speaker to write the information on a slip of paper.

Both bus stations are located far outside town, but most companies have offices alongside Aung San Stadium; expect to pay a couple thousand kyat more than for tickets bought at the station. Many hotels can book tickets for you.

Bus companies with offices at the Aung San Stadium:

Maw (Map p42; ☎393 384) Departures for Bagan, Chaung Tha, Inle, Kalaw, Kyaiktiyo, Mandalay, Ngwe Saung, Pyay and Taunggyi.

PTT Express (Map p42; ☎252 212) Departures for Mawlamyine.

Shwe (Map p42; ☎249 672) Departures for Bagan, Chaung Tha, Inle, Kalaw, Kyaiktiyo, Mandalay, Mawlamyine, Ngwe Saung and Taunggyi.

Shwe Zin (Map p42; ☎704 253). Departures for Bagan, Chaung Tha, Inle, Kalaw, Mandalay, Ngwe Saung and Taunggyi.

Teht Lann Express (Map p42; ☎255 557) Departures for Lashio, Mandalay and Pyin Oo Lwin.

BUSES FROM AUNG MINGALAR

DESTINATION	FARE (K)	DURATION (HR)	DEPARTURE	TYPE
Bagan	18,000	13	4pm	air-con
Bago	1500	2	every 30min 6am-6pm	air-con
Hpa-an	8600	8-10	6.30-8pm	air-con
Kalaw	11,000	12	4pm	air-con
Kyaiktiyo/Kinpun (for Golden Rock)	7000	5	7-10.30am	air-con
Mandalay	11,000	12-15	7am & 5-7pm	air-con
Mawlamyine	8600-10,000	8-10	6-8am	air-con
Pyay	4000	6	every hr 7.30am-8pm	air-con
Taunggyi (for Inle Lake)	11,000-18,000	15-17	5-7pm	air-con
Thandwe (for Ngapali Beach)	12,000	18	3-4pm	air-con

DESTINATION	FARE ($) ORDINARY/ UPPER/SLEEPER	DURATION (HR)	DEPARTURE
Bago	2/4/-	3	5am, 5.30am, 6am
Kyaikto	3-4/8-10/-	4-5	2am, 6.30am, 7.15am
Mandalay	11-15/30-35/33-40	15½	5am, 5.30am, 6am, 12.15pm
Mawlamyine	5-7/14/-	9-11	2am, 6.30am, 7.15am
Pyay	5/13/-	7-8	1pm
Taungoo	5/13/-	6	5am, 5.30am, 6am, 8am, 11am
Thazi	9/24/-	12	5am, 5.30am, 6am

AUNG MINGALAR BUS TERMINAL (Highway Bus station; Map p38) Located about 3 miles northeast of the airport as the crow flies, Aung Mingalar is the only official bus terminal for all 150 bus lines leaving for the northern part of Myanmar, as well as for Kyaiktiyo (Golden Rock), Mawlamyine and destinations to the south. A taxi here costs $7.

Keep in mind that journey times can differ immensely from the estimates we've given, and depend on road conditions and the health of your bus.

HLAING THAR YAR BUS TERMINAL This is the bus terminal for travel to the Delta region (often called Ayeyarwady Division) and to destinations west of Yangon. By taxi (K7000) the terminal is 45 minutes to an hour west of the city centre on the other side of the Yangon River on Hwy 5 (Yangon-Pathein Rd). More than 20 bus lines operate out of here.

From here you can catch buses to Chaung Tha Beach (K8000, six to eight hours, departure 6am, air-con bus), Ngwe Saung Beach (K8000, five to seven hours, departure 6am, air-con bus) and Pathein (K6000, four hours, departures 5.30am to 2pm, non-air-con buses).

Car

Many people choose to forgo both public transport and package tours by hiring a guide and car. For some this combines the best of both worlds: relative comfort and safety, and flexibility and personalised itineraries. Rates run approximately $60 per day within Yangon and $100 per day upcountry. Yangon-based **Zayar** (☏09-519 8486; zayar_gs@gmail.com) speaks English well, knows every road in the country and is a good driver. Otherwise, a driver can be arranged through a travel agent or hotel front desk.

See p378 for information on car rental.

Train

Yangon's train station (Map p42; ☏202 178; ⏰6am-4pm) is located a short walk north of Sule Paya, although advance tickets must be purchased at the adjacent **Myanmar Railways Booking Office** (Map p42; Bogyoke Aung San Rd; ⏰7am-3pm).

See p381 for more information on rail travel within Myanmar.

ℹ Getting Around

To/From the Airport

Taxi drivers will approach you before you exit the airport terminal. The standard fare for a ride from the airport to anywhere in the city is $7. It's best to have a few single bills so that you don't have to change money in the airport. From the city centre to the airport it can cost slightly less ($5).

Bus

With taxis in Yangon being such a fantastic deal, you'd really have to be pinching pennies to rely on buses. They're impossibly crowded, the conductors rarely have change, the routes are confusing and there's virtually no English, spoken or written.

If you're determined, there's a useful **poster** (Map p42) near Sule Paya that describes the various bus routes. The typical fare within central Yangon is K100 (use small bills – again, bus conductors don't tend to have change). Prices often double at night, but they're still cheap and still crowded.

Some useful bus routes from the Sule Paya stop:

Shwedagon Paya Bus 43 (၄၃).

Yangon Airport Bus 51 (၅၁), 53 (၅၃), 132 (၁၃၂), 136 (၁၃၆), 231 (၂၃၁) all go to 10th Mile bus stop, from where it's possible to transfer to a pick-up truck to the airport.

Aung Mingalar Bus Station Bus 43 (၄၃).

Taxi

Yangon taxis are one of the best deals in Asia. Although the meter and air-conditioning are never turned on and you might see the street through the holes in the floor, most drivers speak at least

RAISING BUS FARES

Prior to the summer of 2007 most local bus fares used to be K5, but overnight, due to government fuel price hikes, prices rose by 2000% to K100. The majority of Yangon workers, who earn just K9000 a month, suddenly found themselves forking out K6000 for transport to and from work. It was anger over these price increases that eventually led to the huge September protests. Depending on fuel prices, the cost of bus tickets may also fluctuate in the future.

some English (although it's advisable to have someone write out your destination in Burmese) and are almost universally honest and courteous. All licensed taxis have a visible taxi sign on the roof. The less expensive licensed taxis are the usually older, midsized Japanese cars, many missing their door handles and other 'extras'.

Most drivers charge about K1000 for a short hop, K1500 to K2000 to go from one part of town to another, and K2500 or K3000 to go across town. From downtown to either bus ter-

minal, drivers ask for K7000 and the trip takes from 45 minutes to an hour. You can also hire a taxi for about K4000 an hour or about $25 for a half-day. For the entire day, you should expect to pay approximately $40 to $60, depending on the quality of the vehicle and your negotiating skills. Be sure to work out all details before you agree to a price and itinerary.

For all types of taxi the asking fares usually leap by 30% or so after sunset and on weekends, when rationed petrol isn't available. Late-night taxis – after 11pm or so – often cost double the day rate, mainly because the supply of taxis is considerably lower than in the day, so the drivers are able to charge more.

Train

Yangon Circle Line loops out north from Yangon to Insein, Mingaladon and North Okkalapa townships and then back into the city. For more info, see p50.

Trishaw

Every Asian country seems to have its own interpretation of the bicycle trishaw. In Myanmar, trishaw passengers ride with the driver, but back-to-back (one facing forward, one backward). These contraptions are called *saiq-ka* (as in side-car) and to ride one across the city centre costs about K500.

Around Yangon

Best Temples

» Shwethalyaung Buddha (p86)

» Shwemawdaw Paya (p87)

» Yele Paya (p75)

» Shwemokhtaw Paya (p76)

Best Places to Stay

» Emerald Sea Resort (p83)

» Bay of Bengal Resort (p83)

» Shwe Ya Min Guesthouse & Restaurant (p80)

» Shwe Hin Tha Hotel (p83)

» Bago Star Hotel (p89)

Why Go?

Like the spokes of a wheel jutting out from Yangon, you can find fun and adventure if you head a short distance in just about any direction.

Immediately south of Yangon are the vast, squelchy swamps and river channels of the Delta region. Travel here might be tough, but the rewards include starry nights on chugging river ferries and pagodas that float on water.

West, across more rivers and past paddy field after gorgeous green paddy field, is sticky Pathein, home of golden monuments to love and a Buddha who sailed on a raft from far away Sri Lanka. Beyond that charming city are carefree Chaung Tha Beach and the refined sands of Ngwe Saung.

And heading east out of Yangon it's only a short hop to Bago (Pegu), the former capital born of a chivalrous bird. Today Bago might look a little down at heel, but it has treasures to make any monarch jealous.

When to Go

Not surprisingly, the weather in this region follows many of the same trends as Yangon: hot in the summer (March to May) and relatively comfortable in the winter (November to January), with an average high of 89°F (32°C). Rainy season rice planting (from approximately June to October) makes the Delta region the greenest part of Myanmar.

DELTA REGION

A vast, wobbly mat of greenery floating on a thousand rivers, lakes and tributaries, like a squishy waterbed, the Delta region south of Yangon is one of the most fertile and dazzlingly green regions of Myanmar. All this water irrigates millions of hectares of farmland, making the delta essentially one of the rice bowls of the country. In addition, the estuarine environments along the coast provide much of Myanmar's saltwater and freshwater fish harvest.

Thanlyin & Kyauktan

သံလျင် နှင့် ကျောက်တန်း

📞 056 / POP C5000

One of the easiest escapes from the glamour and noise of Yangon is to the small, rural towns of Thanlyin and Kyauktan, just across the river from Yangon. The official goals of the trip are a couple of interesting religious sites, but the true purpose is just getting into the groove of rural Myanmar.

During the late 16th and early 17th centuries, Thanlyin was the base for the notori-

---

ⓘ TRAVEL RESTRICTIONS

At the time of research, a permit was still required to visit those parts of the Delta region that were particularly damaged in 2008 by Cyclone Nargis, namely Dalah and Twante.

---

ous Portuguese adventurer Filipe de Brito e Nicote. Officially a trade representative for the Rakhaing (Arakan), he actually ran his own little kingdom from Thanlyin, siding with the Mon (when it suited him) in their struggle against the Bamar. In 1599 his private army sacked Bago, but in 1613 the Bamar besieged Thanlyin and de Brito received the punishment reserved for those who defiled Buddhist shrines: death by impalement. It took him two days to die, due, it is said, to his failure to take the recommended posture for the stake to penetrate vital organs.

Thanlyin continued as a major port and trading centre until it was destroyed by Bamar King Alaungpaya in 1756, after which Yangon took over this role. Today Thanlyin

Around Yangon Highlights

① Pretend you're a local on holiday at family-friendly **Chaung Tha Beach** (p80)

② See a less-visited side of Myanmar in **Pathein** (p76)

③ Stroll the virtually people-free sands of **Ngwe Saung Beach** (p83)

④ Cycle around ancient pagodas in **Bago** (p86)

⑤ Boarding a crowded local ferry for the day trip to **Twante** (p76)

is a low-key industrial town as well as the home of a large Hindu community.

◉ Sights

Thanlyin is a relaxing place, with shaded streets and a busy market to stroll through, but there is little of the ancient city to be seen.

A short bus ride out of town will take you to the **Kyaik-khauk Paya** (admission $1), a scaled-down Shwedagon with stupendous views from its hilltop location. It's said to contain two Buddha hairs delivered to the site by the great sage himself. Most likely the first stupa on this hillock was erected by the Mon 600 to 800 years ago. A Kyauktan-bound bus can drop you off here, or if you were dropped off at Thanlyin's market, a motorcycle taxi will take you for K1000.

Thanlyin was also the first place in Myanmar to receive Christian missionaries and the first place to have its own church. You can visit the remains of the Portuguese-built **church**, which was constructed in 1750.

Yele Paya (admission $2) at Kyauktan, 7.5 miles southeast of Thanlyin, is a sparkling floating temple adrift on a chocolate river. You can re-enact *Jaws* by feeding the massive catfish splashing about at the temple complex's edge. To reach the islet, catch one of the **launch ferries** (K5000 return) reserved for foreigners from the riverbank. Also in the town is a small pagoda perched on the top of a hill beside the river and a hectic, flyblown and rather fishy market, which reaches its climax in the morning.

In the third week of January Thanlyin's Hindu community celebrates (or endures depending on your opinion) **Thaipusam**, the ritual of penitence in which devotees repent bad deeds by impaling themselves with hooks and nails and walking over hot coals.

◫ Sleeping & Eating

There is no licence for foreigner accommodation in either town. For eats, **Pwint** (☑21400; set meals K2000-6000; ☺lunch & dinner), a self-proclaimed 'high-class' Myanmar restaurant, about a mile from Thanlyin's market, is allegedly the best in town (there's no roman-script signage).

If you've hired a driver, ask to refresh at **Shwe Pu Zun** (☑553 062; 14A Minnandar Rd, Dawbon Township; ice cream & drinks from K650;✤), a huge modern complex located between Yangon and Thanlyin specialis-

ing in sweets; the *faluda* ('fa-lu-da' on the menu; a mixture of custard, ice cream and jelly) here is famous.

Near the ferry landing in Kyauktan are several **food vendors**.

ⓘ Getting There & Away

The most convenient way to visit both Thanlyin and Kyauktan on the other side of the river is to hire a taxi in Yangon (K25,000 for a half-day). By taxi, it takes about 30 minutes to get to Thanlyin.

However, if you're passionate about Myanmar's uncomfortable local transport or are counting kyat, buses to Thanlyin (K200, one hour, 16 miles) leave frequently throughout the day from Sule Pagoda; look for lines 173 (၁၇၃), 189 (၁၈၉) and 217 (၂၁၇).

In Thanlyin, motorcycle taxis can take you to Kyaik-khauk Paya (K1000) and Yele Paya (K3000).

Twante

တွံတေး

☑045 / POP C5000

The small town of Twante was noted for its pottery, cotton-weaving and an old Mon paya complex. Much of the town was destroyed by Cyclone Nargis in May 2008, but in the years since, life has largely returned to normal.

The journey to Twante, by rickety ferry, is the best reason for coming. You'll glide past fishers in little wooden boats hauling in nets, larger cargo boats steaming towards Yangon and, on land, small villages where kids spill out from thatched huts to play.

◉ Sights

Shwesandaw Paya   BUDDHIST STUPA

ရွှေဆံတော်ဘုရား

(camera fee K200) Standing 250ft tall, the Shwesandaw Paya is a Mon-built *zedi* (stupa), just a

ⓘ GETTING AROUND THE DELTA

» Due to slow and infrequent public transport in the Delta, this is one region where you might consider hiring a driver (p71).

» If you've bought a deck ticket for the ferry to Pathein (p79), consider buying a mat and/or a blanket.

few years younger than Yangon's Shwedagon Paya, making it over 1000 years old. One corner of the compound commemorates King Bayinnaung's (also spelt Bayint Nyaung) defeat of a local rebellion.

Near the southern entrance is a 100-year-old sitting bronze buddha in Mandalay style. Instead of focusing on the floor, the buddha's eyes stare straight ahead. Along the western side of the *zedi* stand some old bronze buddhas.

Other Sights

Pottery is a major cottage industry in Twante, which supplies much of the Delta region with well-designed, utilitarian containers of varying shapes and sizes. The pots were made in huge thatched-roof sheds in the **Oh-Bo Pottery Sheds** (အိုးဘိုလှုပ်ဝင်း) in the Oh-Bo district south of the canal, about 15 minutes' walk from the dock.

❶ Getting There & Around

The easiest way to hit up Twante from Yangon is via a short cross-river ferry and a ride on a public jeep or pick-up truck. Pedestrian ferries from Pansodan St jetty (near the foot of Pansodan St and opposite the Strand Hotel) take passengers across the Yangon River to Dalah (round trip K2000, five minutes) – remember that you'll need your letter of permission from MTT in Yangon (see boxed text, p74); the process involves writing a letter stating that you don't plan to stay overnight and that you will 'not engage in any way of any of matters of political natures'. There's another brief form, to be copied in triplicate, and will need your passport. The entire process took us only about five minutes and doesn't cost anything. You'll need to hand over a copy of the permit when buying tickets for the river crossing ferry at Pansodan St Jetty

Arriving at the jetty in Dalah, a variety of vehicles will compete to take you to Twante; a seat on a pick-up costs K2000 (45 minutes), a motorcycle taxi will take you there and back for K10,000 and a taxi for about K17,000.

By far the most enjoyable way of getting to Twante is to take the slow ferry from Yangon. For details on this trip, go to p70.

The return ferry to Yangon leaves late in the evening, and since an overnight stay is not allowed, your best bet is to return to Dalah by pick-up or motorcycle.

Technically, from the ferry dock to Shwesandaw Paya a horse cart shouldn't cost more than K500, but in reality you'll pay K1500 return with waiting time.

Pathein

ပုသိမ်

☑ 042 / POP C200,000

Pathein, Myanmar's fourth city and the most important delta port outside Yangon, lies in the heart of a major rice-growing area that produces the finest in Myanmar, including *pawsanmwe t'ămìn* (fragrant rice). The growth of the delta trade, particularly rice exports, has contributed to a general air of prosperity in the city, which has a busy, buzzy atmosphere. Most travellers only stop off on their way to the beaches, but the workshops that produce colourful, hand-painted parasols, along with the shady, tree-lined village lanes to the northeast of the market, are worth a little more than this token glance.

Adding to the allure is the fact that Pathein can be reached by boat. The overnight trip, where large boats are laid up on the mud flats like dinosaurs taking their last gasp of air, is a rare window on the pattern and pace of the everyday lives of locals in the Delta region.

History

The town was the scene of major clashes during the struggle for supremacy between the Mon and the Bamar. Later it became an important trade relay point for goods moving between India and Southeast Asia. The city's name may derive from the Burmese word for Muslim – *Pathi* – due to the heavy presence of Arab and Indian Muslim traders here centuries ago. The colonial Brits – or more likely their imported Indian civil servants – corrupted the name to Bassein.

Today, Pathein's population includes large contingents of Kayin (Karen) and Rakhaing. Once part of a Mon kingdom, Pathein is now home to only a few Mon. During the 1970s and '80s, the Kayin villages surrounding Pathein generated insurgent activity that has since generally calmed.

◉ Sights & Activities

The following sights don't charge an admission fee.

Shwemokhtaw Paya   BUDDHIST STUPA

ရွှေမုဌောဘုရား

Looming with grace over central Pathein is the golden bell of the Shwemokhtaw Paya. This large complex is unusually well layered in legend. One states that it was originally built by India's Buddhist King Ashoka in 305 BC. Standing just 7.5ft tall, this original

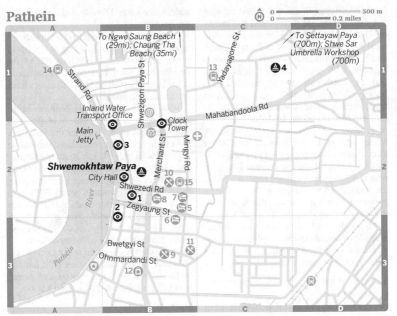

stupa supposedly enshrined Buddha relics and a 6in gold bar.

Another legend says a Muslim princess named Onmadandi requested each of her three Buddhist lovers build a stupa in her honour. One of the lovers erected Shwemokhtaw, the others the less distinguished Tazaung and Thayaunggyaung Paya.

Whichever story you choose to believe, Bagan's King Alaungsithu is thought to have erected a 46ft stupa called Htupayon over this site in AD 1115. Then, in 1263, King Samodagossa took power, raised the stupa to 132ft and changed the name to Shwemokhtaw Paya, which means Stupa of the Half-Foot Gold Bar.

The *hti* (umbrella-like pinnacle) consists of a topmost layer made from 14lb of solid gold, a middle tier of pure silver and a bottom tier of bronze; all three tiers are gilded and reportedly embedded with a total of 829 diamond fragments, 843 rubies and 1588 semiprecious stones.

The southern shrine of the compound houses the **Thiho-shin Phondaw-pyi** sitting buddha image, which, the story goes, floated to the delta coast on a raft sent from Sri Lanka during ancient times. According to the legend, an unknown Sinhalese sculptor fashioned four different buddha images using pieces from the original Bodhi tree mixed with cement composite. He then placed the images on four wooden rafts and set the rafts adrift on the ocean. One landed in Dawei (Tavoy), another at Kyaikkami (Amherst), another at Kyaiktiyo (this one is now at Kyaikpawlaw); and the fourth landed near Phondawpyi, a fishing village about 60 miles south of Pathein, from where it was transferred to Pathein.

A **marble standing buddha** positioned in a niche in the fence running along the western side of the stupa marks a spot where Mon warriors once prayed before going off to battle. In the northwestern corner of the compound is a **shrine** dedicated to Shin Upagot, the Bodhisattva who floats on the ocean and appears to those in trouble. Turtles swim in the water surrounding the small pavilion.

Also in this northwest corner is an unusual golden **Ganesh shrine**, dedicated to the elephant-headed god worshipped by Hindus as the god of wisdom and wealth.

Settayaw Paya
BUDDHIST TEMPLE

စက်တော်ရာဘုရား

Of the several lesser-known shrines in Pathein, perhaps the most charming is Settayaw Paya, dedicated to a mythical Buddha footprint left by the Enlightened One during his legendary perambulations through Southeast Asia.

The paya compound in the northeast of town wraps over a couple of green hillocks that are dotted with well-constructed *tazaung* (shrine buildings) – altogether a nice setting and a change from the flat paya compounds near the river. The footprint symbol itself is an oblong, 3ft-long impression.

Other Religious Monuments

The Twenty-Eight Paya is a rectangular shrine containing 28 sitting and 28 standing buddha images. None of them are particularly distinguished except that the latter appear in the open-robe style rather than the closed-robe pose that is typical of Mandalay standing images.

At one end of the hall stands a group of crude sculptures depicting a scene from the Buddha's life in which he teaches a disciple the relativity of physical beauty by comparing a monkey, the disciple's wife and a *deva* (celestial being). You may have to ask the caretaker to unlock the building.

More interesting from an artistic perspective is Tagaung Mingala Zeditaw (Tagaung Paya), south of town, which is centred on a graceful stupa that sweeps inward from a wide, whitewashed base to a gleaming silver superstructure.

Look for the small squirrel sculpture extending from the western side of the upper stupa, representing a previous life of the Buddha as a squirrel. One of the pavilions at the base of the stupa contains a very large sitting buddha image.

West of Tagaung Mingala Zeditaw, a little way towards the river, stands Mahabodhi Mingala Zedi, patterned after the Mahabodhi stupa in Bodhgaya, India. Leikyunynaung Paya, about a mile directly south of Mahabodhi, was renovated by the State Law & Order Restoration Council (Slorc), now the State Peace and Development Council (SPDC), in the early 1990s to create a facsimile of Ananda Paya in Bagan. Few people outside the government worship here now, reportedly because forced labour was used in the renovation.

These paya are located south of town off Merchant St, but can be somewhat hard to find. Your best bet is to hire a trishaw driver, who will probably charge around K2000.

Markets

At the night market (Strand Rd) that is set up each evening in front of Customs House, teenagers cruise, flirt and hang out while vendors purvey food, clothing and tools and just about every other requisite for daily life at low prices. Just south of Shwemokhtaw Paya is the central market (⊘Mon-Sat), and just south of that is a new market (⊘Mon-Sat), with all manner of goods.

✦✦ Festivals & Events

Vesakha
RELIGIOUS

The people of Pathein celebrate the Buddha's birth, enlightenment and passing away with a huge *paya pwe* (pagoda festival) during the full moon of Kason (April/May). The festival is held at the Shwemokhtaw Paya.

🛏 Sleeping

The sleeping options in this city are a sorry lot, no doubt because most people race right on through to the beaches. The hotels' electricity supplies are at the mercy of the city-wide rationing schedule, which means power is usually available from early evening to early morning.

Those wishing to avoid government-owned properties (see p21) should steer clear of the Pathein Hotel, a two-storey building on spacious grounds near the bus station.

Taan Taan Ta Guest House
HOTEL $

(☏22290; 7 Merchant St; r $6-10; ✳) This, the best and most popular budget guesthouse with locals and foreigners alike, has tidy and colourful rooms and friendly staff, but the secret's out and it fills up quickly. If you're not on a shoestring, check out the double rooms on the top floor, which feature air-conditioning, TV and fridge.

La Pyae Wun Hotel
HOTEL $$

(☏24669; 30 Mingyi Rd; s/d $20/33; ✳) The town's most prestigious address offers white-tiled rooms that are as polished as the staff. The huge bathrooms, rather bizarrely, only have cold showers. Breakfast isn't included and loving couples will be delighted to hear that it's twin rooms only – so we'll have none of that hanky-panky, please!

Paradise Hotel
HOTEL $

(☏25055; 14 Zegyaung St; s/d $14/15; ✳) Tucked down a side street away from road noise, this place features unremarkable rooms in a large modern building. This wouldn't be too bad for Pathein, except for the fact that, on our visit, there were lots of people seemingly just hanging about, giving the place a slightly dodgy feel. Perhaps they're associated with the attached karaoke lounge.

Sein Pyae Hlyan Inn
HOTEL $

(☏21654; 32 Shwezedi Rd; s/d with shared bathroom $5/8, r with bathroom $14-15; ✳) Certainly the cheapest hotel in town, and it shows, particularly in the cheapest rooms. Consider the slightly nicer double rooms with air-con, TV and fridge, but ask to see a few, as standards vary. The owner claims that the hotel uses its generator 24/7, so you may even get to use the amenities you're paying for.

✖ Eating

Zone Pan
BURMESE $

(Bwetgyi St; meals from K1500; ☺all day) This typical Myanmar curry house features a good range of tasty curries, soups and salads. To cut the grease of a Myanmar meal, try their mouth-puckeringly tart *shauk-thi dhouq* (lemon salad). There's no English sign here; instead look for the light blue shopfront.

New City Tea Centre
TEAHOUSE $

(Mingyi Rd; snacks from K200; ☺breakfast & lunch) Next to La Pyae Wun Hotel and perfect for replacing the breakfasts that your hotel doesn't provide. This shady teahouse provides plates of nan and chickpeas and other snacks and a morning caffeine kick.

Myo Restaurant
BURMESE $

(5 Aung Yadana St; mains from K1000; ☺lunch & dinner) A bustling, retro bar and restaurant that extends a loving welcome to all-comers. The meals, which focus on all your favourite Bamar staples, are done with more style than most places and, to keep you entertained while you wait for your supper, there is a TV playing all the premiership matches, and draught beer to boot.

Shwe Zin Yaw Restaurant
BURMESE $

(24/25 Shwezedi Rd; meals from K1500; ☺lunch & dinner) Oh you lucky, lucky taste buds, finally you're going to get something different, including goat curry and sardine salad! A handy place for lunch before hopping on a bus out of here.

🛍 Shopping

Most of the 'umbrellas' made in Pathein are actually parasols; that is, they aren't waterproof, but are used to counter the hot Delta sun. There are a few workshops scattered throughout the northern part of the city, particularly in the vicinity of Twenty-Eight Paya, off Mahabandoola Rd, and at the southern end of Merchant St.

The parasols come in a variety of bright and bold primary colours. One type that can be used in the rain is the saffron-coloured monks' umbrella, which is waterproofed by applying various coats of tree resin; a single umbrella may take five days to complete, including the drying process. Parasols and umbrellas can be ordered in any size directly from the workshops, and are cheap.

Workshops welcome visitors who want to observe this craft, which is a lot more interesting than it might sound.

Shwe Sar Umbrella Workshop
PARASOLS

(☏25127; 653 Tawya Kyaung Rd; ☺8am-5pm) This family-run affair with high-quality work is just around the corner from the Settayaw Paya.

ℹ Information

Despite the city being one of Myanmar's largest, there are no banks here offering foreign exchange. Internet is available at **Lynn Internet Café** (Shwezigon Paya St; per hr K400; ☺9am-11pm).

ℹ Getting There & Around

Boat

For boats from Yangon, see p70.

To Yangon, boats leave daily at 5.30pm, arriving in Yangon the next day at noon. Tickets cost $7 for deck class and $42 for cabin class (although we've yet to encounter the cabin), and are available in the morning at the **Inland Water Transport Office** (Mahabandoola Rd; ☉10am-noon), located in a wooden colonial-era building near the jetty, or from 3pm onward at the jetty itself.

Bus

For buses from Yangon, see p71.

Inconveniently, the bus stations for various destinations are spread throughout central Pathein. This is confusing, but probably easier than having to schlep all the way to the town's bus station, located well outside the city centre.

If you're bound for Yangon (K6000, four hours), head to the informal **bus company offices** (Shwezedi Rd) located directly east of Shwe Zin Yaw Restaurant. There are departures at 3.30am, 5.30am, 6.30am and 1.30pm; arrive early and a shuttle truck will transport you to the station and your bus. The 6.30am departure is the only air-con one.

Insanely uncomfortable minibuses ply the route from Pathein to Chaung Tha Beach (K2500, 2½ hours, 36 miles) at 7am, 11am, 1pm and 3pm, departing from an informal **bus station** (Yadayagone St) a couple of blocks northeast of the clock tower.

To Ngwe Saung Beach (K4000, two hours, 29 miles), buses leave from yet another **bus station** (Strand Rd) at 9am, 11am and 3pm.

Taxi

Share taxis for up to four people can be arranged from your hotel in Pathein for Chaung Tha (K50,000), Ngwe Saung (K40,000) and Yangon (K100,000).

Chaung Tha Beach

ချောင်းသာကမ်းခြေ

♩042 / POP C2000

Chaung Tha Beach, 25 miles west of Pathein, is a place of holiday excess for the Myanmar middle class. There's paddling in the water, floating about on rubber rings, plodding up and down on ponies, wasting money on tacky souvenirs, boisterous beach football games and happy family picnics. As with other beaches of this type in Southeast Asia, it's not the most awe-inspiring piece of coastline you'll ever encounter, but if you need to squeeze some sand and sun into your visit to Myanmar, it is the most convenient option.

◉ Sights & Activities

The village market is most active from 6am to 9am. East of the main village area is a mangrove wetland and a canal beach with a wooden jetty. It isn't hard to persuade a fisherperson to take you up the river and around the mangroves for a few thousand kyat.

Boating Trips

A modest coral reef lies a short way offshore with decent **snorkelling** possible both here and around the headland at the beach's northern end. During the rainy season the water clarity is terrible.

The best snorkelling, though, is about a two-hour boat ride away. Boats, which should be arranged through your hotel, cost K50,000 per hour for six people. If you haven't got your own gear some of the hotels might conjure up a tatty snorkel and mask for your use – ask at Myanmar Travel Beach or the Shwe Hin Tha Hotel.

The appropriately named Whitesand Island, which is visible a short way offshore, can be explored in a day trip from Chaung Tha Beach. Boats (K3000 one way, 15 minutes) leave from the jetty at the south end of the village every hour or so from 8am (last one back leaves at 5pm). There's good **swimming** and **snorkelling** around the island, but very little shade. Bring plenty of water and, finally, don't attempt to swim over – it's a very long way and around the halfway point the *Jaws* theme tune gets lodged in your head!

Other Activities

You can rent canoes for about K10,000 a day, or bicycles for about K2000 a day, at hotels and guesthouses.

🛏 Sleeping

Of all the beach destinations in Myanmar, Chaung Tha offers the most affordable accommodation. Yet at research time, the beach was experiencing something of a mini boom and there will undoubtedly be even more top-end places by the time you read this. Those keen to avoid places with close links to the military should avoid the Hotel Max (see p21).

All but a few hotels close down from 15 May to 15 September; those that remain open discount room rates. Most places, including even the most expensive resorts, have electricity only from 1pm to 3pm and 6pm to midnight or morning.

If none of the budget places recommended here are available, there are several similarly priced off-beach guesthouses south of the bus station, along the way to the pier.

All hotels are located along Main Rd.

MR GEORGE: LOCAL GUIDE

I'm from Pathein, but I've lived at Chaung Tha Beach for 15 years. I've worked in tourism since 1996, and in 2000, I got a wife from here.

Best Beach

Most Europeans like Ngwe Saung Beach (p83) because it's a long beach and it's quiet, with fewer people. But there is no village there, only huge resorts. If you like nature, Chaung Tha Beach is better, but the beach is small and doesn't have white sand or clear water.

Best Time to Visit

November to April is the best time because the region has a lot of seafood and good weather. After April the monsoon comes and the water isn't so clear because the rainwater and river water mix. At Ngwe Saung Beach many hotels are closed during the rainy season, but the hotels at Chaung Tha Beach are open all year.

Secret Spot

About 9 miles from Chaung Tha Beach is a place called Chauk Maung Na Ma (p82). It's very similar to Ngwe Saung: it's quiet, and you can snorkel, fish and meet local people. It's also a good place for a picnic.

Shwe Ya Min Guesthouse & Restaurant
HOTEL **$**

(☑42127; s/d $5/10; ❄) Although located on the opposite side of the road from the beach, the bright rooms here are scrubbed clean, neatly tiled and come with desk, soft bed (bring your own mosquito net) and a bathroom with highly original washbasins. The attached restaurant serves a justifiably well-regarded pancake breakfast, and gracious, friendly service rounds out the package.

Belle Resort
RESORT **$$$**

(☑42112; www.belleresort.com; r $55-180; ❄❄) The rooms are understated sophistication with stone walls, sprawling beds, massive windows with equally massive ocean views and satellite TV. Enter the bathrooms, made of stylish black stone, and things get even better. And best of all, they claim to provide more electricity than other places, giving you the chance to take advantage of the electronic amenities offered at this price tag.

Grand Hotel
HOTEL **$$**

(☑42329; r $30-35; ❄) The cute whitewashed bungalows here aren't the newest or flashiest accommodation along the beach, but represent good value. Along with an atmosphere of yesteryear, the spacious rooms have tall windows, TV, fridge and a huge bathroom with big old-school tubs.

Golden Beach Hotel
RESORT **$$**

(☑42128; r $25-40; ❄❄) This vast resort (56 rooms) doesn't have the park-like manicured grounds that others do, but the hotel-room-style duplex bungalows have recently been renovated. There is a well-used pool table and a little-used pool. The stretch of sand out the front is especially popular with middle-class Myanmar tourists.

Shwe Hin Tha Hotel
HOTEL **$$**

(☑42118; r $7-12, bungalows $20-25; ❄@) Located near the bus drop-off point and boasting budget prices, this is Chaung Tha's most popular backpacker choice. The rooms and bungalows are unremarkable, but it's located at the quiet northern end of the beach and has intermittent internet and a tourist information centre (p82), where equipment can be rented and tours organised.

Diamond Hotel
HOTEL **$$$**

(☑13109; d/tr $50/65; ❄) The bungalow-based rooms here are large enough, but leave you rather close to your neighbour. Rooms come with amenities such as TV and fridge but, other than the rainbow-coloured balustrade on the balconies, not a whole lot of character.

Dream Light Guest House
HOTEL **$**

(☑42201; bungalows $8-35; ❄) All in all the large and airy bungalows here have seen better times, but they are just a sandy step from the tranquil northern part of the

BUSES FROM CHAUNG THA BEACH

DESTINATION	FARE (K)	DURATION (HR)	DEPARTURE	TYPE
Yangon	7000	6-7	6am	bus
	10,000		10.30am	air-con bus
Pathein	3800	2½	7am, 9am, 11am, 1pm	minibus

beach. Communicating in English can be a problem here, as the 'Check out time 11.00 noon' sign at the reception suggests.

Hotel Ayeyarwady
HOTEL $

(☑42332; s/d/tr $12/15/20; ❋) Located across the road from the beach just south of the market intersection, this is a 1960s-style 'motel' complex in bright aquamarine with simple but tidy rooms.

Dream Light
HOTEL $

(☑42201; s/d $5/10; ❋) If you don't need a room right on the beach, this pastel-hued castle-like complex near the market intersection is an adequate, although slightly musty budget choice.

Shwe Chaung Tha Hotel
GUESTHOUSE $

(☑42249; s/d $5/8) The rooms in this large wooden house across from the beach are rather run down, but are clean and certainly cheap.

✕ Eating

Unlike at nearby Ngwe Saung, there aren't many independent restaurants here, so plan on eating most of your meals at your resort.

A standout during our visit was **Shwe Ya Min Restaurant** (mains K1500-2000; ☺all day), where the service is charming (we were ceremoniously presented our bottle of Myanmar Beer for approval) and more than a bit of care goes into the food. The menu at this attractive guesthouse-based restaurant is largely seafood-based and includes all the Myanmar and Chinese-Burmese staples. And even if you're not staying here, you'd be well advised to consider the restaurant's famous breakfast, which features thick, sweet Myanmar-style pancakes.

ℹ Information

In addition to being the only hotel with internet, Shwe Hin Tha Hotel is also home to Chaung Tha's unofficial information centre, **Myanmar Travel Beach** (☑09 520 0617; www.myanmartravel beach.weebly.com). The go-to man for all things

local is Mr George, who can arrange snorkelling trips, day trips to Ngwe Saung or Chauk Maung Na Ma, a nearby white-sand beach, as well as transport etc.

ℹ Getting There & Around

The rough 25-mile road between Chaung Tha and Pathein can be traversed in two hours by private car; buses and minibuses usually take about 2½ hours. The route passes through jungle hills – well, OK, ex-jungle – it's a depressing example of the effects of deforestation. Over half the villages passed along the way are Kayin.

Bus

For buses from Yangon, see p71.

It's theoretically possible to travel north via the town of Gwa all the way to Ngapali without first having to go through Yangon and Pyay. It's an exciting, beautiful but very demanding two-day journey on very local minibuses.

Motorbike & Boat

Motorbike taxis can be hired to take you to Pathein (K10,000) or directly to Ngwe Saung Beach. In fact, the trip to the latter is a real highlight of a beach holiday. The route, which takes about two hours, is through wild and glorious country and involves three river crossings on small wooden country boats that have just enough room for the motorbike and a couple of passengers. You will pass serene beaches, several untouched villages and heavy forests and whiz over tracks and trails between shocking-green rice paddies. It costs at least K15,000 per person. Ask your hotel a few hours in advance to organise it.

If it's calm you can also hire a boat (seats six; K65,000, two hours) to and from Ngwe Saung. This is handy if you're in a group but be prepared to wade ashore with your bags and ask to be dropped as close to your hotel as possible. Bring plenty of water and sunblock. Again organise this through your hotel or Myanmar Travel Beach a few hours in advance.

Taxi

Share taxis for up to four people to Pathein (K50,000) and Yangon (K150,000) can be arranged with your hotel's assistance.

Ngwe Saung Beach

ငွေဆောင်ကမ်းခြေ

🗘 042 / POP C2000

Forgive us for thinking that Ngwe Saung Beach may have begun to show symptoms of bipolar disorder. These days the northern end of the beach has the air of a weekend getaway destination for nouveau riche Yangonites, and is home to an uninterrupted chain of walled, upscale resorts. At the southern end a palpable abandoned aura – not unlike that of Kep in Cambodia – pervades, and this is where you'll find foreign backpackers and budget bungalows. The factor linking these two disparate places is an attractive 13-mile string of sand and palms that, although it won't rate as one of the region's best beaches, has finer sand and clearer and deeper water than nearby Chaung Tha Beach.

👁 Sights & Activities

Above all else Ngwe Saung is an indulgent, lie-back-and-do-absolutely-nothing sort of beach and most visitors are happy to comply. However, if sitting around doing nothing more strenuous than wiggling your toes in the sand sounds boring then there are a few calorie-burning activities you can take part in.

A boat trip out to **Bird Island**, just visible way out on the horizon, for a day of snorkelling and, dare we say it, bird-watching, is the most popular water-based excursion. Boats can be arranged through many hotels for between $65 and $85, depending on the size of your group and the boat it will require.

If you don't have the stomach or budget for a boat trip, at low tide you can simply walk over to **Lovers' Island**, a handsome strip of sand located at the southern end of the beach. The water surrounding this island is also a good place to **snorkel** among dancing clouds of tropical fish. Masks and snorkels can be hired from some hotels (Shwe Hin Tha Hotel and Treasure Resort are the most reliable) for K2500 per day.

Several of the resorts can arrange day trips to an **elephant camp** (p85) halfway between Ngwe Saung and Pathein.

🛏 Sleeping

In the last few years Ngwe Saung has gentrified significantly and an uninterrupted chain of resorts now backs the northern end of the beach. Many of these are aimed at the upper price range and some, like the Aureum Palace Resort, Myanmar Treasure Resort and Myanmar Treasure II, are owned by those with close government links (see p21).

Making it even more difficult for budget travellers is that many of the cheap places have folded in recent years and the few that remain are at the far southern end of the beach. Getting between these hotels and the village is a pain, but enough trishaws drift on past to allow some means of escape.

Electricity is a rare commodity at Ngwe Saung, even if you are paying hundreds of dollars a night, and is generally available only from 1pm to 3pm and 6pm to midnight.

Shwe Hin Tha Hotel   HOTEL $$
(🗘40340; bungalows $15-35; ❄) Set at the blissful southern end of the beach, this place is almost within paddling distance of Lovers' Island. It has a magnetic pull for backpackers who agonise over whether to opt for cheap-and-simple bamboo huts or one of the more solid and luxurious bungalows. Either way they can be sure that it will be clean and well maintained and that hot water will appear on request. There's a book exchange, various travel services and plenty of like-minded clientele to waste away the days with. It's the sister hotel of the one in Chaung Tha but comes with much higher recommendations.

Emerald Sea Resort   RESORT $$$
(🗘40247, in Yangon 01-520 0890; www.emerald seahotel.com; r $45, bungalows $55-75; ❄❄) Located south of the village, this cosy resort may not be as flashy as the newer places along the beach, but it makes up for it with heaps of atmosphere and excellent service. The rooms themselves are beautifully created with minimal decor making the virgin-white, and very comfortable, interiors all the more classy. There's a decent restaurant (advance notice is often required) and a beautiful stretch of beach out front, but it's the staff that really make this place as good as it is.

Bay of Bengal Resort   RESORT $$$
(🗘40304; www.bayofbengalresort.com; r $85-95, ste $115-135; ❄@❄) Quite possibly the poshest beach resort in Myanmar, this immense new compound at the far northern end of Ngwe Saung feels something like a timeshare condo community in Florida. The ground-floor Bengal Suites have a spacious sitting area and huge balcony, and bathrooms with a stone tub and an open-air shower. Reasons to leave your room include tennis courts, a huge pool and a spa. It's also one of the only places in the area to offer internet, at a whopping $4 per hour.

Silver Coast Beach Hotel RESORT **$$**
(☑40324, in Yangon 01-254 708; htoo.maw@mpt
mail.net.mm; r $38; ❀) About as far down the
beach from the village as you can get, this
secluded resort is a bargain hunter's fantasy,
featuring delightful beachside bungalows
with finesse and character. There's plenty of
space, lots of light and hardly a soul around
to disturb the peace of your own slab of
palm-bedecked perfection.

Sunny Paradise Resort HOTEL **$$$**
(☑40227; www.sunnyparadiseresort.com; r $15-
160, bungalows $130-180, ste $170-180; ❀@❀)
Yet another imposing compound north of
the village, Sunny Paradise has attractive
wooden bungalows offering the accommodation and amenities you'd expect at this
price range. A pleasant surprise, for those
on a budget at least, is the associated Sunny
Villa, located just across the street, where
similar rooms, also decked out with TV,
fridge and air-conditioning, are available for
a fraction of the price.

Yamonnar Oo Resort HOTEL **$$**
(☑40338, in Yangon 01-530 722; kbzinfo@bzbank.
com.mm; r $37-45, bungalows $38-70) Down at
the southern end of the beach this mod-
ern hotel offers good value for money. The
rooms and bungalows were being exten-
sively renovated and refurbished at research
time, making them an even better deal. The
landscaped gardens are another highlight.

Silver View Resort HOTEL **$$**
(☑40317, in Yangon 01-502 681; silverviewresort@
gmail.com; r $30-50) Also located south of the
village and popular with vacationing locals, this attractive compound offers green,
condo-like, duplex bungalows, most offering sea views. Packages with transportation
from Yangon are available.

✗ Eating

You should try your hardest to break out of
your hotel restaurant at least once in order
to eat in the village, where there is a good
range of cheap restaurants. There is little to
distinguish one from another – most places share a facsimile menu that focuses on
seafood-based dishes prepared in the Chinese style. They're open for breakfast, lunch
and dinner.

**Ngwe Hline Si
Restaurant** CHINESE, BURMESE **$$**
(mains K3500) Maybe the pick of the bunch
in the village, the Ngwe Hline Si has all

the usual seafood and mixes it up with
pastas and a variety of tasty starters.

**Golden Myanmar
Restaurant** CHINESE, BURMESE **$**
(mains from K1000) When asked for a good
place to eat, most locals will point you in
the direction of this seafood shack, located
in the middle of the village.

Kaung Kaung Lay CHINESE, BURMESE **$**
(mains from K1500) This restaurant has the
same facsimile menu as the others, but
does Burmese dishes, including a good
chicken curry, quite well. Located in the
centre of the village.

Happy Restaurant TEAHOUSE **$**
(dishes from K400) If you didn't fork out for
a hotel breakfast, or simply want some-
thing local, head to this buzzing teahouse
where you can get Myanmar-style break-
fast faves such as *mohinga* (noodle soup)
or deep-fried sticks of dough.

❶ Information

Located towards the northern end of the vil-
lage, **Sandalwood** (☑09 856 8130), a cafe-
information centre, is the place to go for local
information. Tom Tom may have a few ragged
copies of a good local map printed by the
Myanmar Hotelier Association, can arrange
a day trip or snorkelling excursion, and rents
motorcycles. If he's not here, Tom Tom can also
be found at his second office at the Shwe Hin
Tha Hotel.

❶ Getting There & Around

To get to Ngwe Saung from Yangon, see p71.

A bus leaves for Yangon every morning at
6.30am (K8000, six hours) from the cross-
roads between the village and the beach
resorts.

Minibuses from Pathein (K3000, two hours)
stop first at the intersection between the be-
ginning of the village and the Treasure Beach
Resort. If you're staying further south, the
bus should be able to drop you at your resort;
conversely, you should be able to catch the bus
leaving Ngwe Saung (7am, 8am, 9am, 11am and
3pm) by waiting by the side of the road.

Taxis can be arranged for Pathein (K40,000)
and Yangon (K110,000).

For information on motorbike taxis and boats
between Ngwe Saung and Chaung Tha Beach
see p82.

There are a few trishaws available to
carry you between the resorts and the village
(K1000), and motorbikes can be hired via

BIRD-SPOTTING

Myanmar isn't known for its environmental awareness and the nation's few national parks and protected areas are largely inaccessible to foreigners. **Moeyungyi Wetlands** (မိုးယွန်းကြီးရေနက်ကွင်း), about an hour northeast of Bago and close to the village of Pyin-bongyi, is the one real exception to this rule.

The wetlands originally started life as an artificial water storage reservoir in the 19th century, but over time the reservoir naturally morphed into a 15-sq-mile lake and marsh. Sitting on a migration route of birds fleeing the icy Siberian winter and attracting thousands of local waders, the wetlands will bring a big grin to any birder's face. The last census revealed some 125 different species including great flocks of egrets, cormorants, white stalks and large numbers of the beautiful swamp hen (purple gallinule) as well as sarus cranes with their brilliant red heads.

Your best chance of seeing exotic birds is from December to February and during this time a small 'resort' offers excellent boat tours (up to six people) on the lake for $15 per person for about two hours. As well as the boat driver, you will be accompanied by a guide – normally the very knowledgeable and informative Mr Aung Ko Oo. The boat will take you whizzing over the lake to the marshy reed beds in the centre where the birds congregate in vast numbers.

Should you want to stay, the resort offers **accommodation** (☎70113; per person $55) in floating houseboats from November to March. The price includes three meals and a boat ride and it's essential that you book in advance. The rooms, though novel, are somewhat overpriced and even serious birders may prefer to make a half-day tour from Bago.

The resort is privately owned by Myanmar businesspeople, though the wetlands themselves belong to the government (see p21).

Sandalwood or from some hotels for about K12,000 per day.

Around Ngwe Saung

ELEPHANT CAMP
Around half an hour's drive from Ngwe Saung is an **elephant camp** (admission $5, elephant rides $5; ☺8am-noon). Though the dozen elephants here are working elephants, the camp itself is purely for tourists and no logging actually takes place. It's possible to go for a half-hour elephant ride through the forest – the romance of which wears off in about 30 seconds. If you thought horses attracted a lot of large biting insects, just wait until you get on the back of an elephant!

The camp used to be government run but is now a joint venture tied to the Treasure Resort in Ngwe Saung, which in turn is owned by Tay Za (p21).

The camp is located approximately halfway between Ngwe Saung and Pathein. To get there, hop on any outbound bus, or Tom Tom at Sandalwood can arrange a motorcycle taxi for about $10.

NORTH OF YANGON

Taukkyan

ထောက်ကြံ့
☎01 / POP C5000

On the road to Bago, beyond Yangon's airport at Mingaladon, you reach Taukkyan, where you will find the huge **Taukkyan War Cemetery**, maintained by the Commonwealth War Graves Commission.

It contains the graves of 6374 Allied soldiers who died in the Burma and Assam campaigns of WWII. There is also a memorial bearing the names of the almost 27,000 soldiers who died with no known grave. Slowly, as you walk around reading the names of those who died and the epitaphs commemorating them, the heat of the sun seems to fade and the noise of the road recedes, leaving you alone in the silence of your own thoughts in this immensely sad place.

You can get to Taukkyan on bus 9 (၉) from Yangon or aboard any Bago-bound bus from the Aung Mingalar Bus Terminal (p71).

Bago (Pegu)
ပဲခူး

📞 052 / POP C200,000

Bago, a former capital, is a Disney-flavoured theme park of gaudy religious sites. It would be fair to say that this small and scrappy town probably contains a greater density of blissed-out buddhas and treasure-filled temples than any other similar-sized town in southern Myanmar. All this makes Bago a superb and simple day trip from Yangon, or the ideal first stop when you leave the city behind.

History

Bago was reputedly founded in AD 573 by two Mon princes from Thaton, who saw a female *hamsa* (mythological bird) standing on the back of a male *hamsa* on an island in a huge lake. Taking this to be an auspicious omen, they founded a royal capital called Hantha-wady (from the Pali-Sanskrit 'Hamsavati', meaning the 'kingdom of the *hamsa*') at the edge of the lake. During the later Mon dynastic periods (1287–1539), Hanthawady became the centre of the Mon kingdom of Ramanadesa, which consisted of all southern Myanmar.

The Bamar took over in 1539 when King Tabinshwehti annexed Bago to his Taungoo kingdom. The city was frequently mentioned by early European visitors – who knew it as Pegu – as an important seaport. In 1740 the Mon, after a period of submission to Taungoo, re-established Bago as their capital, but in 1757 King Alaungpaya sacked and utterly destroyed the city. King Bodawpaya, who ruled from 1782 to 1819, rebuilt it to some extent, but when the river changed its course the city was cut off from the sea and lost its importance as a seaport. It never again reached its previous grandeur.

◉ Sights & Activities

Many of Bago's monuments are actually centuries old, but don't look it, due to extensive restorations. This is an excellent place to explore by bicycle, as most attractions are near each other. Bikes are available for rent at Bago Star Hotel.

Shwethalyaung Buddha   MONUMENT
ရွှေသာလျောင်းဘုရား

Once upon a time a nasty king, who went by the name of Mgadeikpa, ruled the lands around what is today Bago. His reign was marked by corruption and violence, but one day his son was out hunting in the forests when he came upon the village of Suvannabhumi, where his eye fell upon a Mon girl who caused his heart to flutter. Even though she was a Buddhist and he, like everyone in his father's kingdom, worshipped pagan idols, the two became lovers and married after he promised her that she could continue to practise Buddhism.

Back at the court the king was furious when he discovered this and ordered the execution of both the girl and his son. Yet when the new bride prayed in front of the pagan idol it cracked and broke. The king was seized with fear and, realising the error of his ways, he ordered the building of a statue of the Buddha and the conversion of the population to Buddhism.

The gorgeous reclining buddha that you see here today is said to be the result of this doomed love. Measuring 180ft long and 53ft high, the Shwethalyaung is certainly the

Bago

kind of overwhelming object you would expect to be constructed by an absolute monarch with a guilt complex – the little finger alone extends 10ft.

Since its original construction the statue underwent several restorations before the destruction of Bago in 1757. The town was so completely ravaged that the huge buddha was totally lost and overgrown by jungle. It was not rediscovered until 1880 and restoration began in 1881. The 1930s saw another flurry of renovation activity, as a mosaic was added to the great pillow on which the buddha's head rests.

Near the huge head of the image stands a **statue of Lokanat** (Lokanatha or Avalokitesvara), a Mahayana Buddhist deity borrowed by Burmese Buddhism.

A Japanese war cemetery, **Kyinigan Kyaung**, can be seen on the grounds of a monastery just north of Shwethalyaung.

Shwemawdaw Paya
BUDDHIST STUPA
ရွှေမောဓောဘုရား:
A pyramid of washed-out gold in the midday haze and glittering perfection in the evening

gloss, the 376ft-high Shwemawdaw Paya stands tall and proud over the town. According to murky legend the original stupa was a small, ramshackle object, built by two brothers, Kullasala and Mahasala, to enshrine two hairs given to them by Gautama Buddha. In AD 982 a sacred tooth was added to the collection; in 1385 another tooth was added and the stupa was rebuilt to a towering 277ft. In 1492 strong winds blew over the *hti* and a new one was raised.

The stupa has collapsed and been rebuilt many times over the last 600 years; each time it has grown a little taller and the treasures mounted in it have grown a little thicker. The last time it was destroyed was in 1930 when a huge earthquake completely levelled it and for the next 20 years only the huge earth mound of the base remained.

Today the gaudy golden top of the stupa reaches 46ft higher than the Shwedagon in Yangon. At the northeastern corner of the stupa, a huge section of the *hti* toppled by the 1917 earthquake has been mounted into the structure of the stupa.

The Shwemawdaw Paya is a particularly good destination during Bago's annual pagoda festival, in March/April.

Hintha Gon
BUDDHIST STUPA
ဟင်္သာကုန်း:
Located behind the Shwemawdaw, this shrine was once the one point in this whole vast area that rose above sea level and so was the natural place for the *hamsa* to land.

A statue of the bird, looking rather like the figures on opium weights, tops the hill. The stupa was built by U Khanti, the hermit monk who was the architect of Mandalay Hill. Walk to it by taking the steps down the other side of the Shwemawdaw from the main entrance. This paya is also a big spot for *nat* (spirit beings) worship and festivals and with a bit of luck you'll catch the swirling, veiled forms of masculine-looking *nat* dancers accompanied by the clanging and crashing of a traditional orchestra.

Kyaik Pun Paya
MONUMENT
ကျိုက်ပွန်ဘုရား:
The Gautama Buddha and his three predecessors can all be found hanging out together about a mile south of Bago just off the Yangon road.

Built in 1476 by King Dhammazedi, the Kyaik Pun Paya consists of four 100ft-high sitting buddhas placed back to back around a huge, square pillar. According to legend,

ℹ️ ENTRANCE FEES & OPENING HOURS

Though foreigners can visit the town for free, officially they must buy an entrance ticket ($10) valid for all the town's sights. During our visit, this could be purchased only at the Shwemawdaw Paya, but should also be available at the Shwethalyaung Buddha. Nearly all of the sights charge an additional K300 for camera and K500 for videocameras. All the sights are open from just before sunrise until well after dark.

four Mon sisters were connected with the construction of the buddhas; it was said that if any of them should marry, one of the buddhas would collapse. One of the four buddhas disintegrated in the 1930 earthquake, leaving only a brick outline (since restored) and a very old bride.

Maha Kalyani Sima (Maha Kalyani Thein) BUDDHIST TEMPLE
မဟာကလျာဏီသိမ်တော်ကြီး

This 'Sacred Hall of Ordination' was originally constructed in 1476 by Dhammazedi, the famous alchemist king and son of Queen Shinsawpu. Like almost everything in Bago it has suffered a tumbledown history and has been destroyed and rebuilt many a time.

Next to the hall are 10 large tablets with inscriptions in Pali and Mon describing the history of Buddhism in Myanmar.

If you can't get enough of buddha statues then across the road from the Maha Kalyani Sima is the Four Figures Paya, with four buddha figures standing back to back. An adjacent open hallway has a small reclining buddha image, thronged by followers, and some macabre paintings of wrongdoers being tortured in the afterlife.

Relaxing in the sun next to these two monuments is the Naung Daw Gyi Mya Tha Lyaung, a reclining buddha sprawled out over 250ft, which is almost as long as its name. It was built in 2002 with donations from the people and, though locals adore it, you probably won't find it all that interesting.

Mahazedi Paya BUDDHIST STUPA
မဟာစေတီဘုရား

The design of the Mahazedi Paya (Great Stupa), with its whitewashed stairways leading almost to the stupa's summit, is unusual for southern Myanmar and certainly one of the more attractive religious buildings in Bago.

Originally constructed in 1560 by King Bayinnaung, it was destroyed during the 1757 sacking of Bago. An attempt to rebuild it in 1860 was unsuccessful and the great earthquake of 1930 comprehensively levelled it, after which it remained a ruin. This current reconstruction was only completed in 1982.

The Mahazedi originally contained a Buddha tooth, at one time thought to be the most sacred of all Buddha relics, the tooth of Kandy, Sri Lanka. After Bago was conquered in 1539, the tooth was moved to Taungoo and then to Sagaing near Mandalay. Together with a begging bowl supposed to have been used by the Buddha, it remains in the Kaunghmudaw Paya (p229), near Sagaing, to this day.

Shwegugale Paya BUDDHIST STUPA
ရွှေဂူကလေးဘုရား

A little beyond the Mahazedi, this *zedi* has a dark *gu* (tunnel) around the circumference of the cylindrical superstructure. The monument dates to 1494 and the reign of King Byinnya Yan. Inside are 64 seated buddha figures. In the evening many locals venture out here.

From the zedi, cross a rickety wooden footbridge and you'll arrive at a **nat shrine** with life-sized statues of Ko Thein and Ko Thant, the *nat* of the temple compound.

Kanbawzathadi Palace PALACE
ကမ္ဘောဇသာဒီနန်းတော်

The original site of Hanthawady, which surrounded Kanbawzathadi Palace, a former Mon palace, was excavated just south of the huge Shwemawdaw Paya. Walled in the Mon style, the square city measured a mile along each side and had 20 gates.

THE HAMSA

In deference to legend, the symbol for Bago is a female *hamsa* (*hintha* or *hantha* in Burmese; a mythological bird) standing on the back of a male *hamsa*. At a deeper level, the symbol honours the compassion of the male *hamsa* in providing a place for the female to stand in the middle of a lake with only one island. Hence, the men of Bago are said to be more chivalrous than men from other Burmese areas. In popular Burmese culture, however, men joke that they dare not marry a woman from Bago for fear of being henpecked!

Other Attractions

Kha Khat Wain Kyaung
MONASTERY

The is one of the three largest monasteries in the country and watching the long line of monks and novices file out in the early morning for their daily round of alms is quite a sight.

Busloads of tourists visit the monks at lunchtime (10.30am). You're free to wander around the eating hall, and most of the monks think it's hilarious that tourists come and watch them eat, but the atmosphere is a bit like a zoo. Prior to the protests of 2007 there were supposedly 1500 monks in residence here but afterward that figure fell to just 400.

Snake Monastery
MONASTERY

A short distance from the Kanbawzathadi Palace and Museum is the Snake Monastery, where you'll find a former head of a monastery in Hsipaw reincarnated in the form of an enormous 118-year-old Burmese python. Apparently the snake told its owner up north the exact address he needed to go to in Bago in order to complete the construction of a stupa begun in a previous life. Streams of pilgrims come to pay fearful homage to the snake.

Even if the snake isn't actually a monk, it is amazing simply because of its sheer size. Burmese pythons are regarded as one of the world's largest snakes but this one, which chows down 11lb of chickens every 10 days, has to be at least 17ft long and a foot wide, making it probably one of the largest in the world. Don't worry though, it's harmless. There's a **zedi** nearby on a small hilltop that's great for watching sunsets.

The temple and *zedi* are somewhat hard to find, so unless you can speak Burmese, it's probably a good idea to hire a guide.

★ Festivals & Events

Shwemawdaw Paya Festival
RELIGIOUS

On the full moon of the Burmese lunar month of Tagu (March/April) this festival attracts huge crowds of worshippers and merrymakers.

🛏 Sleeping

The quality of accommodation reflects the fact that many travellers visit Bago only for the day. Most of the options are on the busy and – make no mistake about this – noisy main road, so rooms towards the back of these hotels are the choice pickings. Electricity is generally available only from the evening to early morning.

DON'T MISS

BAGO ON TWO WHEELS

With impressive temples, emerald rice fields and a buzzing city all within cycling distance of your hotel, you could easily spend a day or two exploring Bago on two wheels.

Travellers keen to avoid government-owned hotels should bypass the Shwewatun Hotel, out towards the Shwemawdaw Paya.

Bago Star Hotel
RESORT **$$**

(☏30066; http://bagostarhotel.googlepages.com; 11-13 Kyaikpon Pagoda Rd; s/d $24/30; ❄❄) The Star, one of the better choices in Bago, is located just off the highway and only a short walk to the ever-watching eyes of the Kyaik Pun Paya. The business card describes the accommodation as 'Country style, Bangalow type Hotel' and the A-frame wooden rooms and pool do give the place a summer-camp feel. The showers are hot, the swimming pool is murky and the restaurant is echoing and formal. Bikes can be rented for K1000 a day. Generators keep the air-conditioning humming.

Emperor Hotel
HOTEL **$**

(☏21349; Main Rd; s/d $6-14; ❄) This place is the best of the downtown budget lot. Rooms have recently been repainted, in a very sexy pink, of course, and the more expensive have a bit of light and space. The hotel's size allows some respite from the city noise, and rooftop offers great views of the surrounding religious monuments.

Gandamar Hotel
HOTEL **$$**

(☏201629; Shwemawdaw Paya Rd; s/d $20/25; ❄) That rarest of things in Myanmar, a new hotel! The 35 rooms here are located outside of the city centre, a short walk from Shwemawdaw Paya. Also working in its favour is a generator that provides electricity 24/7. The bad news? The generator also provides juice for an adjacent karaoke lounge.

San Francisco Motel
HOTEL **$**

(☏22265; 14 Main Rd; r $4-10; ❄) The rooms are rough and ready but fear not, for this is an excellent budget hang-out in the true sense of the word. The guys who run it organise excellent motorbike tours of Bago's sights and are so knowledgeable that by all rights they should actually be a tourist office.

TRAINS FROM BAGO

DESTINATION	FARE ORDINARY/ UPPER ($)	DURATION (HR)	DEPARTURE
Yangon	2/5	3	6am-8pm
Mawlamyine	5/12	7-9	8.18am, 9.07am
Mandalay	10/27	14	6.11am, 6.51am, 7.21am, 7.50am, 1.50pm

Mya Nanda Hotel   HOTEL $
(☎19799; 10 Main Rd; r $6-15; ✸) An acceptable, if grubby, budget choice, and the staff here can arrange motorbike taxis and guides so that you can check out the sights.

✖ Eating

Hanthawaddy   CHINESE, BURMESE $$
(192 Hintha St; mains K2000-8000; ⊙lunch & dinner) The food here isn't amazing, but it's the only restaurant in Bago with a bit of atmosphere. Located across from the football pitch and a short walk from Gandamar Hotel, the open-air upper level is breezy and offers great views of Shwewawdaw Paya. And perhaps the food situation will change when, as we were told, they get a Thai chef.

Three Five Restaurant INTERNATIONAL, BURMESE $
(10 Main Rd; mains K1200-4000; ⊙all day; ✸) A friendly, but shabby, place a few doors west of the Emperor Hotel. The menu is a combination of Bamar, Chinese, Indian and European; the food is cheap and good, and the menu includes 'goat fighting balls' (goat testicles), prepared in a number of ways.

Hadaya Café   TEAHOUSE $
(⊙breakfast & lunch) Opposite the Emperor Hotel, this popular teahouse has a nice selection of pastries and good-quality tea and coffee.

ℹ Information

STG Computer Center (Yangon-Mandalay Rd; per hr K500; ⊙5am-5pm) Offers basic internet service east of the river. Other similar cafes can be found northwest of the clock tower along Yangon-Mandalay Rd.

ℹ Getting There & Away

Bus

For buses from Yangon, see p70.

Bago's **bus station** (Yangon-Mandalay Rd) is about halfway between the town centre and the Bago Star Hotel, located across from the Hindu temple. Many buses passing through Bago can also be waved down from outside your hotel, though unless you have booked a ticket in advance there is less likelihood of a seat.

Buses to Yangon (K1500, two hours) depart approximately every 45 minutes from 6.45am to 5.15pm.

Going south, buses to Kinpun, the starting point for Mt Kyaiktiyo (Golden Rock), leave every hour or so during the day (K5000, three hours). During the rainy season (May to October), buses go only as far as Kyaikto, 10 miles from Kinpun. Departures for Mawlamyine are at 7.45am, 8am and 9am (K8000, seven hours).

Heading north, for Mandalay there are departures at 5.30pm and 8pm (K11,500). It's also possible to hop on one of the buses coming from Yangon – try to book ahead and ask your hotel to help. For Taungoo and Inle Lake, you might be able to grab a seat on one of the buses originating in Yangon between 1.30pm and 4pm (K14,000 to K16,000, 12 hours).

Taxi

A more expensive but more convenient alternative is to hire a taxi for a day trip from Yangon. With bargaining this should cost about $60, but it does give you the additional advantage of having transport between sites once you get to Bago and saves traipsing all the way out to the bus station in Yangon. One-way taxis back from Bago straight to your hotel in Yangon cost about K40,000.

A guide and driver to Mt Kyaiktiyo (Golden Rock, p93) can be hired for around $55 return.

For any of the above, you can inquire at the town's **taxi stand** (Yangon-Mandalay Rd) or through any of the central Bago hotels.

Train

For trains from Yangon see p71.

ℹ Getting Around

Trishaw is the main form of local transport in Bago. A one-way trip in the central area should cost no more than K500. If you're going further afield – say from Shwethalyaung Buddha, at one end of town, to Shwemawdaw Paya, at the other – you might as well hire a trishaw or motorcycle for the day, either of which should cost about K6000.

Southeastern Myanmar

Best Places to Eat

» San Ma Tau Myanmar
Restaurant (p107)

» Beer Garden 2 (p100)

» Mi Cho Restaurant (p100)

Best Places to Stay

» Cinderella Hotel (p99)

» Golden Sunrise Hotel
(p95)

» Hotel Zwegabin (p106)

» Soe Brothers Guesthouse
(p106)

» Mountain Top Hotel (p95)

» Breeze Guest House (p99)

Why Go?

Although virtually unknown to the outside world, the plea-sures of southeastern Myanmar are diverse and wonderful, and exist on a variety of levels.

The caves around sleepy Hpa-an will escort visitors to unparalleled depths and darkness, while the ascent to the sacred golden boulder at Mt Kyaiktiyo might have you be-lieving that you've gone to heaven. And somewhere in the middle, the romantic ferry ride from Hpa-an to Mawlamy-ine (Moulmein) features some of the best of what Middle Earth has to offer.

Yet another inspiring intersection of land and water is Tanintharyi (Tessarim) Division, Myanmar's Deep South and home to some of the most gorgeous coastline in Southeast Asia. Unfortunately, access to this area is strictly limited to a trio of towns or by pre-arranged government-sanctioned luxury package tours, which essentially makes it out of bounds for all but the most determined.

When to Go

The weather in the southeast is largely similar to that of the rest of Myanmar. Temperatures can reach as high as 86°F (30°C) during the summer (from March to May), and the days are relatively cool during the winter (from November to January), with an annual high temperature of around 90°F (32°C). The region sees more rain than elsewhere in the country during the wet season (from approximately June to October), and annual rainfall in Mawlamyine can reach 190in.

Southeastern Myanmar Highlights

1 Reach for enlightenment at the golden, gravity-defying **Mt Kyaiktiyo** (Golden Rock; p93)

2 Discover seemingly hidden lakes, hanging Buddhist art and a sparkling spring in the **caves** (p108) around Hpa-an

3 Taking what could very well be one of the last trips along the Thanlwin River (Salween River) on the double-decker **Mawlamyine to Hpa-an ferry** (p107)

4 Compose prose to rival Kipling's 'By the old Moulmein Pagoda, lookin' lazy at the sea' in go-slow **Mawlamyine** (p96)

5 Exploring the **remote ruins, sacred temples** and unknown **beaches** around Mawlamyine (p101)

6 Scale Hpa-an's **Hpan Pu Mountain** (p108) for one of the best views in Myanmar.

7 Give back to the community with a volunteer teaching stint at Kinpun's **Seik Phu Taung Youth Development Centre** (p94)

> ## ⓘ TRAVEL RESTRICTIONS
>
> Foreigners are restricted from travelling by land south of Thanbyuzayat in Mon State. Southeastern Myanmar has two land crossings officially open to foreigners, but visits must be within the city limits, and you're generally expected to exit the way you came in.
>
> Confusing things even more, if you've come to Myanmar via Yangon, it is possible to fly, without advance permission, to the southern cities of Dawei (Tavoy), Myeik (Mergui) and Kawthoung but, once there, you're not allowed to leave the city limits and you must also return by air.
>
> Visiting the untouched beaches and islands of southern Myanmar's Tanintharyi (Tenasserim) Region is a whole other bag of worms. For details on the hoops you have to jump through to reach this region, see p110.

MON STATE

Magnificent Mon State (မွန်ပြည်နယ်) is so full of wonders that it's a wonder that the whole world isn't wondering about holidaying here! There are two dominant colours: the gold of a zillion breathtaking temples and the green of a million, zillion flouncy palm trees. Travelling in this region is generally easy (at least, for Myanmar) and distances short; yet, strangely, few visitors seem to make it down here.

History

Once native to a broad region stretching from southern Myanmar to Cambodia, the Mon have been absorbed – sometimes willingly, sometimes unwillingly – by the more powerful Bamar and Thai cultures in Myanmar and Thailand respectively over the last thousand years.

Though no one knows for sure, the Mon may be descended from a group of Indian immigrants from Kalinga, an ancient kingdom overlapping the boundaries of the modern Indian states of Orissa and Andhra Pradesh. They are responsible for much of the early maintenance and transmission of Theravada Buddhism in mainland Southeast Asia.

Since 1949 the eastern hills of the state (as well as mountains further south in Tanintharyi Region) have been a refuge for the New Mon State Party (NMSP) and its tactical arm, the Mon National Liberation Front (MNLF), whose objective has been self-rule for Mon State.

In 1995, after years of bickering and fighting, the NMSP signed a ceasefire with the Myanmar government. Still, reports continue of fighting, instances of forced labour and harassment of Mon villagers. Partly because of this, there remains much emigration to Thailand.

Mt Kyaiktiyo (Golden Rock)
ကျိုက်ထီးရိုးတောင်
♪ 057

Floating in atmospheric clouds high above the coastal plains and, it seems, almost within touching distance of the heavens is the prayer- and wish-drenched, balancing boulder stupa of Kyaiktiyo.

This sublime and magical monument is a major pilgrimage site for Burmese Buddhists. Its image adorns many a local's car windscreen or family hearth and every good Buddhist dreams of the day they finally set eyes on this holiest of shrines.

The atmosphere surrounding Kyaiktiyo during the height of the pilgrimage season (from November to March) is charged with magic and devotion, especially when the glinting boulder is bathed in the purple, sometimes misty, light of dawn and dusk. Pilgrims chant, light candles and meditate all through the night. Men (only) are permitted to walk along a short causeway and over a bridge spanning a chasm to the boulder to affix gold leaf squares on the rock's surface.

For a mere tourist, Mt Kyaiktiyo is a sight and an experience to rival the wonders of the Shwedagon Paya or the breathtaking beauty of Bagan. Like any proper pilgrimage, a visit here involves a certain amount of hardship and nobody should approach this holy mountain lightly.

The constructed plaza around Kyaiktiyo is the typical Myanmar mix of religious iconography and commercial development: monks and laypeople meditate in front of golden buddha statues while, several yards away, rosary beads and toy wooden rifles are for sale (these are especially popular with monks!).

There are several other stupas and shrines scattered on the ridge at the top of Mt Kyaiktiyo, though none is as impressive as Kyaiktiyo itself. Even so, the interconnecting trails sometimes lead to unexpected views of the valleys below.

LEGEND OF THE BALANCING BOULDER

Legend states that the boulder at Mt Kyaiktiyo maintains its precarious balance due to a precisely placed Buddha hair in the stupa. Apparently King Tissa received the Buddha hair in the 11th century from a hermit who had secreted the hair in his own topknot. The hermit instructed the king to search for a boulder that had a shape resembling the hermit's head, and then enshrine the hair in a stupa on top. The king, who inherited supernatural powers as a result of his birth to a *zawgyi* (an accomplished alchemist) father and *naga* (dragon serpent) princess, found the rock at the bottom of the sea. Upon its miraculous arrival on the mountain top, the boat used to transport the rock then turned to stone. This stone can be seen approximately 270yd from the main boulder – it's known as the Kyaukthanban (Stone Boat Stupa).

Further behind the pagoda plaza area, down a stairway, there is a village of restaurants, souvenir shops and guesthouses for Myanmar citizens.

Orientation

Too many towns with similar-sounding names make orientation confusing. The town of Kyaikto is the least important. This is the town along the highway between Bago and places further south. There is no reason to get out here or to stay here: most buses turn off the highway and end their journeys in Kinpun at the base of the mountain, about 6 miles from the Hwy 85.

Climbing the Mountain

From Kinpun, the base camp for the mountain, there are two ways to get to the rock. The first is to hike all the way there. This is approximately 7 miles and takes between four and six hours. The trail begins past the bazaar of souvenir shops in Kinpun and there are numerous 'rest camps' along the way where weary pilgrims can snack and rehydrate. Not many people, even the true devotees, choose to hike all the way up and back. The way down takes from three to four hours and should not be attempted in the dark even with a torch; it's too easy to stumble.

The second way to the rock, which most people do both ways, is to ride one of the large trucks (*lain-ka;* per person K1500) up the winding road to the Yatetaung bus terminal, the end point for all passenger vehicles. The truck beds are lined with wooden slats for benches and seat 35 or so people. Five passengers are allowed in the much more comfortable front seats (per person K2000) but these are usually reserved in advance by groups or families. As an individual traveller it's difficult to secure a front seat, while a group of five has a better chance. Regardless, you could be in for a wait of an hour or more, as trucks don't leave until they are completely packed to the brim.

The ride to the bus terminal takes 45 minutes and usually includes a stop around halfway up to allow trucks coming from the opposite direction to pass. The first truck in the morning leaves at 6am and the last truck down departs at 6pm, though you should try to be at the Yatetaung bus terminal earlier to avoid the risk of being stranded for the night.

From the terminal (nothing more than a dirt lot surrounded by snack and souvenir shops), it takes 45 minutes to an hour to hike up the remaining steep, paved switchback path to the rock. Those with accessibility concerns, or royal fantasies, might want to be carried the rest of the way in a sedan chair – a canvas litter held aloft by four perspiring Burmese men. (A one-way ticket costs $5 to $7.) Walking or reclining, you pass through an array of vendors along the way to the stupa area at the top.

There is a $6 government entrance fee and $2 camera fee, payable at the checkpoint near the top, just after the Mountain Top Hotel. The ticket is valid for 30 days, so you may visit again without paying the government another $6. Men wearing shorts or women wearing trousers, miniskirts or skimpy tops risk being denied entry.

Hiking & Other Activities

If you have the time to extend your stay in the vicinity there are several other rewarding hikes that take in eye-popping views and quiet religious meditation. You can start your journey from Kinpun, the Yatetaung bus terminal, or even the shrine itself.

From Kinpun the most obvious short hike is to **Maha Myaing Pagoda**, a miniature Kyaiktiyo, an hour's climb from Kinpun. Any of the Kinpun hotels can point you in the right direction.

From Yatetaung bus station it's a 45-minute climb to the top of **Mt Ya-The**, a 30-minute walk down to **Mo-Baw Waterfall** and a 1½-hour walk to the **Sa-ma-taung paya and kyaung** (monastery).

From Kyaiktiyo itself a trail continues along the crests of the surrounding peaks for another couple of hours to the **Kyauk-si-yo Pagoda** and **Kyaiktiyo Galay Zedi**.

If you'd like to spend more time in the area or want to give something back to the community, the Seik Phu Taung Youth Development Centre (✆60353), located between Kyaikto and Kinpun, is an established, temple-based orphanage that accepts volunteer English teachers. Basic food and lodging is provided and a minimum stay of two weeks is the norm.

🛏 Sleeping

Although Kyaiktiyo can be visited as a day trip from Bago and, in theory, Yangon, this isn't recommended; the advantage of staying near the shrine is that you can catch sunset and sunrise – the most magical times. Foreigners aren't permitted to stay in one of the many *zayat* (rest shelters) for pilgrims at the top, nor are they permitted to camp in wooded areas on the mountain.

In the town of Kyaikto along the main road from Bago there are several guesthouses, none of them very appealing, and there really is no reason to stay here rather than in Kinpun.

ON THE MOUNTAIN

If you want to catch the best light and most enchanting atmosphere at the shrine (and yes, you do) then you simply have no choice but to stay at one of the three overpriced hotels near the top.

Mountain Top Hotel HOTEL $$$

(✆in Yangon 01-502 479; grtt@goldenrock.com.mm; r $50-78; ❄) Yes, the rooms in the Mountain Top Inn are overpriced but they're clean and well maintained, with good service. They're also situated right on the summit of the mountain only a couple of moments' stroll to the shrine complex – an unbeatable position. The more expensive 'deluxe' rooms have air-con, a TV, a mini bar and great views.

Kyaiktiyo Hotel HOTEL $$

(✆in Yangon 01-663 341; s/d $40/50) This former government-owned hotel is where most package tourists stay. It's unremarkable, but has the benefit of being located a short walk from the Golden Rock. We've come across reports of things missing from rooms here, so take care to look after your valuables if you choose to stay.

Golden Rock Hotel HOTEL $$$

(✆70174; grtt@goldenrock.com.mm; r $46-72; ❄) The Golden Rock Hotel, just a few minutes up from the Yatetaung bus terminal, but at least 45 minutes from the shrine, is in a lovely spot and has larger and marginally more endearing rooms than the Mountain Top Hotel. The only problem is that its positioning – halfway between everywhere but not really anywhere – makes it a little inconvenient.

KINPUN

⎡TOP⎤
⎣CHOICE⎦ **Golden Sunrise Hotel** HOTEL $$

(✆in Yangon 01-701 027; gsunrise@myanmar.com.mm; s $20, d $30-35; ❄) A few minutes' walk outside the centre of Kinpun village in the direction of the highway, the Golden Sunrise is one of the best value hotels in southeastern Myanmar. There are eight bamboo-heavy bungalows with a touch of class. The spacious rooms are undisturbed by noise and immaculately clean and, for once, the bathrooms are a sheer delight to spend time in! The private verandahs overlooking the secluded gardens are the perfect place to relax at the end of the day with a drink.

Sea Sar Guest House HOTEL $

(✆60367; r $5-15; ❄) In the heart of the town, but set in spacious gardens a little way back from the pilgrimage noise, the more expensive rooms at the Sea Sar are memorable for all the right reasons. They're clean, with hot showers, silky soft beds and wooden floors – you can't really go far wrong. The cheaper rooms, though, are more disappointing and look as dark and messy as a crime scene. The staff are dialled into travellers' needs and can provide local maps with marked walks, taxi services and bus tickets. The restaurant can do a variety of basic Burmese dishes for K1500 to K2000.

Pann Myo Thu Inn GUESTHOUSE $

(✆60285; r $5-20; ❄) This green-themed inn (the building is green and it's full of green plants and lots of green, flowering orchids) is another great choice. The cheap rooms are better value than those at the Sea Sar, but the pricier ones are not quite as neat. It has a friendly home-away-from-home feel – probably because it is in fact the owner's home.

✕ Eating

Because Kinpun is the starting point for Mt Kyaiktiyo, there are numerous Chinese and Bamar restaurants running up and down the town's main street, capitalising on the mountain's popularity.

In addition to the food stalls at Kinpun and all along the footpaths, there is a veritable food court of restaurants at the summit, past the shrines and plaza area and down the steps.

Mya Yeik Nyo   BURMESE $
(meals from K2000) This is the pick of the bunch, and the one that all taxi drivers will recommend. It's very close to where the trucks depart for the mountain.

❶ Information

Kinpun is where you'll find most of the accommodation for foreigners – besides a few hotels near the top of the mountain itself. It's also the starting point for trips up the mountain to Kyaiktiyo. There is no internet access.

❶ Getting There & Away

For individual travellers, Bago makes a better starting point for road trips to Kyaiktiyo than Yangon, as Bago hotel staff are adept at arranging inexpensive alternatives. A guide and driver to Kyaiktiyo can be hired through any of the central Bago hotels (p89) for $55.

Bus & Pick-Up Truck

For buses from Yangon, see p70.

Win Express run air-con buses from Kyaikto to Bago (three hours) and Yangon (five hours) at 8.30am, 10am, 12.30pm, 2pm. Despite where you're getting off, you'll have to pay the full fare to Yangon (K7000). Tickets can be purchased in Kinpun across from Sea Sar Guest House. The ticket price includes truck fare to Kyaikto, where you'll board the bus.

Similar air-con buses also run to Mawlamyine (K7000, 4½ hours) at 5am, 6am, 7.30am, 8.30am and 10.30am.

Small pick-up trucks leave from Kinpun to Hpa-An (K5000, five hours) from 6am to 1pm, or there is a more comfortable bus (K7000) that has a useful departure time of 1.30pm.

Pick-ups cruise the road between Kyaikto and Kinpun every half an hour or so (K500).

Train

For times and prices of trains from Yangon, see p71. Trains run to Yangon (ordinary $3 to $4, upper $6 to $9; five hours; departure 10am, 1.20pm, 3.40pm) and Mawlamyine (ordinary $3, upper $6 to $7; four hours; 6.20am, 10.40am, 12.30pm).

Trucks run between Kyaikto's train station and Kinpun every half an hour or so (K500).

Mawlamyine (Moulmein)
မော်လမြိုင်
♪057 / POP C300,000

With a ridge of stupa-capped hills on one side, the sea on the other and a centre filled with mosques and crumbling colonial-era buildings, Mawlamyine is a unique combination of beauty and melancholy. If you've ever wondered what life was like during the Raj, Mawlamyine is about as close as it comes to a living time capsule.

But it's not all about history; the area around Mawlamyine has enough attractions – from beaches to caves – to keep a visitor happy for several days.

Mawlamyine (some maps may show it as Mawlamyaing) served as the capital of British Burma from 1827 to 1852, during which time it developed as a major teak port. A great deal of coastal shipping still goes on, although Pathein and Yangon have superseded it as Myanmar's most important ports. The city is composed roughly of 75% Mon, or some mixture of Mon, plus Kayin, Bamar, Indian, Chinese and other ethnic groups.

◉ Sights & Activities

Mon Cultural Museum   MUSEUM
မွန်ယဉ်ကျေးမှုပြတိုက်
(cnr Baho Rd & Dawei Jetty Rd; admission $2; ⏰9.30am-4.30pm Sun-Fri) This government-run, two-storey museum is dedicated to the Mon history of the region. It's on the corner of Baho Rd (formerly Dalhousie St). The museum's modest collection includes stelae with Mon inscriptions, 100-year-old wooden sculptures depicting old age and sickness (used as *dhamma*-teaching devices in monasteries), ceramics, silver betel boxes, royal funerary urns, Mon musical instruments and wooden buddha altars.

This is all well and good, but unfortunately the collection is so poorly lit that many of the exhibits are actually impossible to see without a torch!

Buddhist Monuments

Unknown Mawlamyine has inspired two of history's finest writers of the English language – George Orwell and Rudyard Kipling. Orwell lived here for some years (the famous essay 'Shooting an Elephant' is about an experience he had as a police officer in Maw-

LOCAL KNOWLEDGE

MR ANTONY: LOCAL GUIDE

I'm a Karen Christian who has lived in Mawlamyine for 12 years, but I only speak a little bit of Mon. I work at Breeze Rest House and as a local guide.

Best Village

On Bilu Kyun (Ogre Island; p101) there are many villages. Tourists can see the traditional Mon way of life, including villages that make good-quality walking sticks and rubber bands from local rubber. Sometimes, during a festival, tourists can see traditional kickboxing.

Best Temple

Seindon Mibaya Kyaung (p96) has some artistic wooden crafts and antiques. There's a very old throne and some carvings from ivory donated by King Mindon's wife.

Best Beach

Setse Beach (p104) is the only beach around Mawlamyine. It's a quiet place and not far from Kyaikkami and the Yele Paya.

Best Day Trip

Nwa-La-Bo Pagoda (p102) is a rock pagoda on the top of a hill, like the famous Golden Rock. It's only a half-hour drive from Mawlamyine but not many tourists go there.

Secret Spot

From a viewpoint between U Zina Paya and Kyaikthanlan Paya (p96), on the high peak looking over the town, you can see what many tourists say is the most beautiful sunset in Southeast Asia.

lamyine), and generations of his family were born and bred here. Kipling's visit was shorter, just three days, but resulted in a few lines of prose that turned Burma into an oriental fantasy: 'By the old Moulmein Pagoda, lookin' lazy at the sea...' The spirit of the poem 'Mandalay', from which these words arise, lives on in Mawlamyine in the form of the golden poems of Buddhist stupas sprawled across the jungle ridge behind the town.

At the northern end of this ridge is **Maha-muni (Bahaman) Paya**, the largest temple complex and easily the most beautiful in Mawlamyine. It's built in the typical Mon style with covered brick walkways linking various shrines. The highlight is the Bahaman Paya itself, a jewel-box chamber shimmering with mirrors, rubies and diamonds and containing a century-old replica of its namesake in Mandalay (p208).

Farther south along the ridge is **Kyaik-thanlan Paya**, the city's tallest and most visible stupa. Impressive though the paya is, it didn't do much for Kipling, who was later to comment of it: 'I should better remember what the pagoda was like had I not fallen deeply and irrevocably in love with a Burmese girl at the foot of the first flight of

steps. Only the fact of the steamer starting next noon prevented me from staying at Moulmein forever.' He was certainly not the last to think like that...

Just below the paya, you can admire the view over the city; it's a favoured spot for watching the sunset. The best way to approach the paya from town is via the long covered walkway that extends from Kyaikthan St.

Below Kyaikthanlan is the 100-year-old **Seindon Mibaya Kyaung**, a monastery where King Mindon Min's queen, Seindon, sought refuge after Myanmar's last monarch, King Thibaw Min, took power. On the next rise south stands the isolated silver-and-gold-plated **Aung Theikdi Zedi**.

U Khanti Paya was built to commemorate the hermit architect of Mandalay Hill fame; supposedly U Khanti spent some time on this hill as well. It's a rustic, airy sort of place centred around a large buddha image.

U Zina Paya, on the southern spur of the ridge, was named after a former monk who dreamt of finding gems at this very spot, then dug them up and used the proceeds to build a temple on the same site. One of the shrine buildings contains a very curvy, sensual-looking reclining buddha; there are

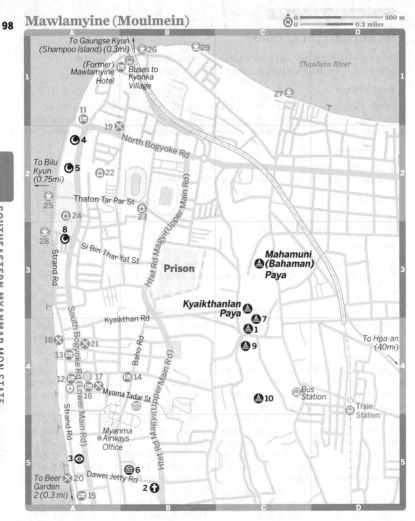

also statues depicting Gautama Buddha's meeting with a sick man, an old man, a dead man and an ascetic – encounters that encouraged him to seek a meaning behind human suffering.

Other Religious Monuments

In the centre of town towards the waterfront, on South Bogyoke Rd, are three mosques built during the colonial era when many Indians arrived to work for the British. Since the Indian exodus of the 1970s, Muslim congregations have declined substantially, but the survival of these grand old buildings makes a walk here a fleeting exercise in nostalgia.

The **Kaladan Mosque** was designed by Sunni Muslims in an elaborate 'wedding-cake' style. Further south, on the same side of the street, is the smaller **Moghul Shiah Mosque**, a Shi'ite place of worship that was under construction at the time of research. A couple of blocks further, south of the central market, the Sunni **Surtee Sunni Jamae Masjid** fills a similar space but presents a more multi-coloured facade.

Just up from Dawei jetty, on the eastern side of Strand Rd, the small but colourful

Mawlamyine (Moulmein)

Htyan Haw Chinese Temple serves the local Chinese community. Of historic interest is the sturdy brick **First Baptist Church** (cnr Htet Lan Magyi Rd & Dawei Jetty Rd), also known as the Judson Church; this was Myanmar's first Baptist church.

Gaungse Kyun (Shampoo Island) ISLAND
ခေါင်းဆေးကျွန်း

This picturesque little isle just off Mawlamyine's northern end is so named because,

during the Ava period, the yearly royal hairwashing ceremony customarily used water taken from a spring on the island.

You can hire a boat out here from the **pier** at the north end of town, not far from the former Mawlamyine Hotel, for K2000 return. Peace rather than sights are the reason for venturing out here, but you can visit **Sandawshin Paya**, a whitewash-and-silver *zedi* (stupa) said to contain hair relics, and a nearby Buddhist meditation centre. Many nuns, with a menagerie of pet dogs, live on the island.

🛌 Sleeping

Most of Mawlamyine's accommodation is a K1000 motorcycle taxi ride from the train station, bus station or boat pier.

TOP CHOICE **Cinderella Hotel** HOTEL $$
(📞24411; www.cinderellahotel.com; 21 Baho Rd; s/d/tr $18/30/40; 🌀@🌐) Where else could you afford to stay in the nicest place in town? This shockingly purple structure has numerous and capable staff who look after huge rooms with heaps of amenities: 24-hour electricity, TV, air-con, wi-fi and a huge fridge stuffed with junk food.

Breeze Guest House BUDGET HOTEL $
(Lay Hnyin Tha; 📞21450; breeze.guesthouse@gmail.com; 6 Strand Rd; s $6-12, d $16; 🌀) The rooms aren't much but the Breeze, an attractive, blue, colonial-style villa on Strand Rd, produces its charms in other ways. The staff are an endless source of information, pleasant conversation and superb guiding skills. Try to snag one of the more expensive rooms, which are quite spacious and have large, modern bathrooms with air-con.

Attran Hotel HOTEL $$
(📞25764; Strand Rd; r $25-60; 🌀) Overlooking the sultry river waters, the Attran is suitably reminiscent of a beach resort. Tour groups enjoy the series of orderly bungalows spread across the green pastures. It's exceptionally friendly and helpful, but there is no getting away from the fact that it's a little overpriced. The hotel restaurant, on a deck by the river and lit up at night, is a nice place to eat.

Sandalwood Hotel HOTEL $$
(📞27253; 278 Myoma Tadar St; r $15-35; 🌀) A modern and clean multi-storey hotel, conveniently located near the town's attractions, restaurants and internet cafés. Communicating in English can be problematic

if the friendly English-speaking owner isn't around.

Ngwe Moe Hotel   HOTEL $$
(☎24703; cnr Kyaikthoke Paya & Strand Rd; s/d $27/36; ☀) The three-storey Ngwe Moe on Strand Rd is frequented by groups. The rooms are fresh and comfortable but lack character.

Aurora Guest House   HOTEL $
(☎22785; 277 South Bogyoke Rd (Lower Main Rd); r $5-18; ☀) The more expensive rooms in this rather dark and dreary budget hotel have a private bathroom and air-con; others only have a fan and a shared bathroom. Breakfast is not included.

✗ Eating

For a city of this size, the eating options are scarce. The Attran Hotel and Ngwe Moe Hotel have restaurants that serve lunch and dinner. An atmospheric **teahouse** (South Bogyoke Rd (Lower Main Rd); snacks from K400; ☺6am-6pm) near the Aurora Guest House serves good tea and snacks.

TOP CHOICE Beer Garden 2   BEER GARDEN $
(58 Strand Rd; meals from K3000; ☺dinner) Ignore the misleading English-language menu they'll dust off for foreigners and instead head straight for the barbecued snacks: these guys are truly talented grillers. Simply point to select your vegies and proteins from the refrigerators and staff will slather them with a delicious, spicy sauce and grill them for you. Couple your skewers with a glass of what must be the coldest draught beer in Myanmar, and you've got Mawlamyine's best meal.

Mi Cho Restaurant   MUSLIM, BURMESE $
(North Bogyoke Rd; meals from K1500; ☺lunch & dinner) This busy hole in the wall, a short walk from Attran Hotel, serves excellent Muslim-style Myanmar cuisine, in particular a rich biryani and a delicious dhal soup. Worth the walk.

Mya Than Lwin
Restaurant   CHINESE, BURMESE $$
(Dawei jetty, Strand Rd; mains from K2000; ☺all day) This restaurant, in what appears to be a former warehouse, is now a popular hangout. You can dine on the wooden planked floor outside and feel like you're on a boat at sea or in the smokier, and more bar-like, indoors. There's an extensive menu of soups,

chicken and seafood, including an abundance of shrimp- and prawn-based dishes.

Help Grandfather and Mother
Restaurant   CHINESE, BURMESE $
(Strand Rd; mains from K500; ☺all day) Does what it says on the label: the money raised here goes to a charity helping the town's elderly. If that weren't reason enough to eat here, it's also a delightful waterfront restaurant in its own right and absolutely the place to watch the sunset with a cup of tea. The sign is written in Burmese only; look for silhouettes of old people walking with canes.

Chan Thar Restaurant   CHINESE, BURMESE $$
(4 Myoma Tadar St; mains from K2000; ☺all day) You could easily mistake this restaurant for a cinema and walk right on past. The sweet and sour stir-fry is unusually good and the chef can even whip up a mean fruit salad. There's beer and conversations on tap and a TV tuned to the UK premiership football.

Peking Restaurant   CHINESE, BURMESE $$
(235 South Bogyoke Rd (Lower Main Rd); mains from K3000; ☺lunch & dinner) Despite the name, this isn't the place to go for northern Chinese specialties. Rather, they do an acceptable, if somewhat overpriced and greasy take on Chinese-Burmese standards.

🔒 Shopping

Mawlamyine has a number of busy markets including the **Zeigyi** (central market), the **Big Market** and the even bigger **Myine Yadanar Market**. Though locals distinguish between all of them, you probably won't as they virtually meld into one another and you'll be too engrossed in the melange of smells, sights and tastes to care anyway.

ℹ Information

A police station is located over the road from the government jetties. The post office is a couple of blocks further inland.

Grace Internet Cafe (South Bogyoke Rd (Lower Main Rd); per hr K500; ☺9am-10pm) Not entirely reliable internet connections are available at this shop in the centre of town. There are a couple of similar places in the area.

ℹ Getting There & Away
Air

Myanma Airways fly to Yangon ($30) and Myeik (Mergui; $65) every Sunday at 7am, although

DESTINATION	FARE (K)	DURATION (HR)	DEPARTURE	TYPE
Yangon	5100	8	8am, 9am, 7pm, 7.30pm	air-con buses
Bago	5100	6	8am, 9am, 7pm, 7.30pm	air-con buses
Kyaikto	5100	4	8am, 9am, 7pm, 7.30pm	air-con buses
Hpa-an	1050	2	6am-4pm	non-air-con-buses

flights are anything but consistent. Tickets can be purchased at the **Myanma Airways office** (☏21500, 09-871 8220; ◷9am-3pm), located in a colonial-era building (no English-language sign) behind the park on Baho Rd.

Boat

Double-decker ferries leave from the **Kyaik Hpa Nai Jetty** in Mawlamyine at 12.30pm on Mondays and Fridays for the trip up the Thanlwin River to Hpa-an ($2, at least five hours).

For boats from Hpa-an, see p107.

Bus

For information about reaching Mawlamyine by bus from Yangon, see p70. It's worth noting that if you are coming from Yangon on an evening or night bus you will have the pleasure of getting to the edge of the bridge linking Mawlamyine with the north only to find that you have to wait until dawn before being allowed to cross! If you happen to be reading this bit while you're on the night bus, well, don't get disheartened – it's only another five hours until daybreak...

Train

For trains from Yangon, see p71.

Foreigners travelling south by train are allowed only as far as Ye, due to insurgency in the area. Trains from Mawlamyine:

YANGON Ordinary $5 to $7, upper $14 to $16; nine hours; departures 6am, 8.15am, 11.25am.

BAGO Ordinary $5 to $8, upper $7 to $10; six hours; 6am, 8.15am, 11.25am.

KYAIKTO Ordinary $3 to $5, upper $6 to $7; four to five hours; 6am, 8.15am, 11.25am

ⓘ Getting Around

MOTORCYCLE TAXI AND TRISHAW The main form of public transport around the city, most found on South Bogyoke Rd (Lower Main Rd) in front of **Zeigyi** (short trips, K500; longer journeys, K800). Motorcycle taxi from train/bus station to town costs K1000.

CHEVY TRUCK Old WWII-era American style and used as a minibus. for the town and its

environs. From the train/bus station into town (K150).

Around Mawlamyine

If you're finding Mawlamyine a bit too sleepy, you'll be delighted to find that the town functions a great base for a variety of day trips.

Many people save themselves time and hassle by hiring a car (K45,000 per day) and guide ($12) for two or three days in order to explore fully. The best place to organise this is through the Breeze Rest House, where Mr Antony and Mr Khaing are both highly informed and entertaining guides.

BILU KYUN
ဘီလူးကျွန်း

Bilu Kyun (Ogre Island) isn't quite as scary as it sounds. Rather than a hideaway for nasty monsters, it's a fascinating self-contained Mon island directly east of Mawlamyine. It comprises 64 villages linked by rutted dirt tracks that promise adventure.

Some of the villages on this large island are involved in the production of coconut fibremats and even coconut-inspired and created cutlery and teapots. You can spend an interesting day exploring by taking the daily ferry ($1) at 9.45am and 10.45am from the **pier** at the northern end of Strand Rd. Once on the island, all local transport is by horse and cart, though the more distant villages can be linked by one of the few rattling buses.

To get back to Mawlamyine you must be at Nut-Maw village by 3pm in order to catch the final ferry back to town. Foreigners are not allowed to stay overnight on the island (that's when the ogres come out to get you) and, in order to keep things running smoothly, it's a good idea to go with Mr Antony or Mr Khaing at Breeze Rest House. They charge $12 for the tour, which typically runs from 9am to 5pm.

SOUTHEASTERN MYANMAR AROUND MAWLAMYINE

NORTH OF MAWLAMYINE

◉ Sights & Activities

Nwa-la-bo Pagoda
BUDDHIST TEMPLE

နွားလဘိုတောင်ဘုရား

In the jungle-cloaked hills to the north of Mawlamyine the Tolkienesque side of the country comes to life in an extraordinary fashion at the Nwa-la-bo Pagoda. A local pilgrimage site, Nwa-la-bo is still relatively unknown outside Mon State and, currently, very few foreigners make it out here. This is surprising because the pagoda is a smaller but, geologically at least, far more astonishing version of Kyaiktiyo. Unlike at that shrine, where just one huge boulder perches on the cliff ledge, Nwa-la-bo consists of three sausage-shaped **gold boulders** piled precariously atop one another and surmounted by a stupa. The result is lifted straight from the fairytale world of Middle Earth or could it possibly be that Middle Earth is actually lifted straight from the fairytale world of the Burma of old?

ℹ Getting There & Away

Getting to Nwa-la-bo is fairly easy (except during the rainy season when it can't be reached) and makes a perfect half-day trip from town. Try to go on a weekend when pilgrims will add more flair to the scene and transport is a little more regular.

Bus & Pick Up Truck

From Mawlamyine you'll have to wait at the roundabout before the bridge for a northbound bus or pick-up to Kyonka village (K600), located around 12 miles north of town. From here clamber into the back of one of the pick-up trucks that crawl slowly up to the summit of the mountain (K1600 return) in 45 minutes. Allow plenty of time as the trucks don't leave until beyond full, and don't leave your descent too late in the day as transport becomes scarcer after 3pm. Alternatively, motorcycle taxis will do the trip for K7000.

SOUTH OF MAWLAMYINE

◉ Sights & Activities

Pa-Auk-Taw-Ya Monastery
BUDDHIST MONASTERY

ဖားအောက်တောရဘုန်းကြီးကျောင်း

(☑22853; www.paauk.org) Only 9 miles south of Mawlamyine, the monastery teaches *satipatthana vipassana* (insight-awareness meditation) and, at 500 acres, is one of the largest meditation centres in Myanmar. Foreigners can visit for the night or several days; sleeping and eating is gratis.

Win Sein Taw Ya
BUDDHA

If you thought you'd seen some big old buddhas, just wait till you get a load of this one. Draped across a couple of green hillsides at Yadana Taung, and surrounded by a forest of other pagodas and shrines, is this recently constructed, 560ft-long reclining buddha. It's easily one of the largest such images in the world.

Many other stupas and standing buddhas dot the area, including 500 statues lining the road to the Win Sein Taw Ya. Aside from inflated buddhas, the area affords some gentle walks with wonderful panoramas.

Every year around the first couple of days of February a crazy coloured **festival** takes place here to celebrate the birthday of the monk who constructed the buddha. As well as a host of itinerant traders, monks and nuns, magic men and the odd hermit or two, the festival often hosts a major kickboxing tournament, which leads to the slightly surreal sight of hundreds of cheering monks baying for blood in the ring!

Kyauktalon Taung
BUDDHIST MONUMENT

ကျောက်တစ်လုံးတောင်

Kyauktalon Taung is a strangely shaped, sheer-sided crag rising out of the surrounding agricultural land and crowned with stupas. It's a sticky 20-minute climb to the summit. On the opposite side of the road is a similar but smaller outcropping surmounted by a Hindu temple.

Kandawgyi
LAKE

ကန်တော်ကြီး

This lake formed by **Azin Dam** (a water storage and flood-control facility that's also used to irrigate local rubber plantations) also boasts a tidy recreation area and is a favourite picnic spot with locals – don't miss the *buthi kyaw,* tasty deep-fried gourd, sold here. At the northern end of the lake stands the gilded stupa of **Kandawgyi Paya**.

Thanbyuzayat
HISTORICAL SITE

သံဖြူဇရပ်

Thanbyuzayat (Tin Shelter), 40 miles south of Mawlamyine, was the western terminus of the infamous Burma–Siam Railway, dubbed the 'Death Railway' by the thousands of Allied prisoners of war (POWs) and Asian coolies who were forced by the Japanese military to build it.

About a mile south of the town centre's clock tower, a locomotive and piece of track commemorating the railway are on display.

There also used to be a WWII museum, but the government let it turn to ruin as, according to one local, 'They do not even want us to remember this history.'

Half a mile west of the clock tower towards Kyaikkami, on the southern side of the road, lies the **Thanbyuzayat War Cemetery**. This lonely site contains 3771 graves of Allied POWs who died building the railway. Most of those buried were British but there are also markers for American, Dutch and Australian soldiers. As you walk around this simple memorial, maintained by the Commonwealth War Graves Commission, reading the heart-rending words inscribed on the gravestones it's impossible not to be moved to the brink of tears.

Some are simple and state only that 'One day we will understand', which of course we never did. Others are personal messages of love and remembrance, such as: 'I waited, but you did not come. Life was cruel to us. Dorothy' – GE Wright, died age 28.

Daw Pu (⊗breakfast & lunch), a Burmese restaurant located across from the pick-up-truck stand, west of the clock tower, is a good place to eat.

ℹ Getting There & Away
Bus & Pick-Up Truck

Hop on a bus or pick-up from the eastern side of *zeigyi* (Mawlamyine's main market) heading in the direction of Mudon (K1000, 45 minutes) and ask to be dropped at the junctions for any of the above places (with the exception of Thanbyuzayat). Note you will have to pay the full fare to Mudon.

For Thanbyuzayat there are six departures (K1000, two hours) from the east side of *zeigyi*, all before noon. As there is no legal lodging in Thanbyuzayat, start early so you can catch the last bus back to Mawlamyine at 3pm.

KYAIKKAMI
ကျိုက်ခမီ

Located 5.5 miles northwest of Thanbyuzayat, Kyaikkami was a small coastal resort and missionary centre known as Amherst during the British era. Adoniram Judson (1788–1850), an American missionary and linguist who has practically attained sainthood among Myanmar Baptists, was sailing to India with his wife when their ship was blown off course, forcing them to land at Kyaikkami. Judson stayed on and established his first mission here; the original site is now a **Catholic school** on a small lane off the main road.

The town is an atmospheric seaside destination, although you'll probably not do any swimming at the rocky and rather muddy beach. Instead, the main focus is **Yele Paya**, a metal-roofed Buddhist shrine complex perched over the sea and reached via a long two-level causeway; the lower level is submerged during high tide. Along with 11 Buddha hair relics, the shrine chamber beneath Yele Paya reportedly contains a buddha image that supposedly floated here on a raft from Sri Lanka in ancient times (see Thihoshin Phondaw-pyi on p76 for more details on this legend). A display of 21 Mandalay-style buddha statues sits over the spot where the Sinhalese image is supposedly buried.

THE DEATH RAILWAY

The strategic objective of the 'Burma–Siam Railway' was to secure an alternative supply route for the Japanese conquest of Myanmar and other Asian countries to the west.

Construction on the railway began on 16 September 1942 at existing terminals in Thanbyuzayat and Nong Pladuk, Thailand. At the time, Japanese engineers estimated that it would take five years to link Thailand and Burma by rail, but the Japanese army forced the POWs to complete the 260-mile, 3.3ft-gauge railway in 13 months. Much of the railway was built in difficult terrain that required high bridges and deep mountain cuttings. The rails were finally joined 23 miles south of the town of Payathonzu (Three Pagodas Pass); a Japanese brothel train inaugurated the line. The railway was in use for 21 months before the Allies bombed it in 1945.

An estimated 16,000 POWs died as a result of brutal treatment by their captors, a story chronicled by Pierre Boulle's book *Bridge on the River Kwai* and popularised by a movie based on the book. Only one POW is known to have escaped, a Briton who took refuge among pro-British Kayin guerrillas.

Although the statistics of the number of POWs who died during the Japanese occupation are horrifying, the figures for the labourers, many from Myanmar, Thailand, Malaysia and Indonesia, are even worse. It is thought that 80,000 Asians, 6540 British, 2830 Dutch, 2710 Australians and 356 Americans died in the area.

Pilgrims standing at the water's edge place clay pots of flowers and milk into the sea in order to 'feed' the spirits.

The only accommodation in town is **Kaday Kywe Guest Villa** (☎75019; Bogyoke Rd; r 50,000, without bathroom K6000; ✹). A short walk from Yele Paya, this hotel has tidy but overpriced air-con rooms with attached bathrooms, while the shared bathrooms are little more than fan-cooled closets. There's a basic restaurant directly across the street.

During the early half of the day there are pick-up trucks to Kyaikkami from Thanbyuzayat for K500 per person. From Mawlamyine, a Kyaikkami-bound bus (K1050, 2½ hours) leaves from the Thanbyuzayat stop near the market.

SETSE BEACH
စက်စဲ

Not a picture postcard beach by any stretch of the imagination, but as the grime of travel washes away you probably won't care. This low-key Gulf of Mottama (Martaban) beach is a very wide, brown-sand strip. The beach is lined with waving casuarina trees and has been a popular spot for outings since colonial times. Though a few locals stop by for a swim, almost no foreigners visit this area and facilities are minimal. At low tide you can walk along the beach to the small temple on the rocks at the northern end.

You can stay at the privately owned **Shwe Moe Guesthouse** (☎09-870 3283; r $20), which has spacious but run-down beach bungalows. A few modest restaurants offer fresh seafood, including the **Pyay Son Oo Restaurant**, which is very close to the hotel.

Pick-ups run between Setse and Thanbyuzayat on a fairly frequent basis (K500). The last one leaves for Thanbyuzayat at 4pm.

EAST OF MAWLAMYINE
KYAIKMARAW
ကျိုက်မရော

This small, charming town of wooden houses lined with flowering plants, 15 miles southeast of Mawlamyine, is the site of an important temple. Yet more impressive than the temple is the drive to get there, which passes through bright green rice fields studded with sugar palms and picturesque villages.

Kyaikmaraw Paya BUDDHIST TEMPLE
ကျိုက်မရောဘုရား

The pride of the town is this temple of serene, white-faced buddhas built by Queen Shin Saw Pu in 1455. Among the temple's many outstanding features are multicoloured glass windows set in the outside walls, an inner colonnade decorated in mirrored tiles, and beautiful ceramic tile floors. Painted reliefs appear on the exterior of several auxiliary buildings.

Covered brick walkways lead up to and around the main square sanctuary in typical 15th-century Mon style. The huge main buddha image sits in a 'European pose', with the legs hanging down as if sitting on a chair, rather than in the much more common cross-legged manner. A number of smaller cross-legged buddhas surround the main image, and behind it are two reclining buddhas. Another impressive feature is the carved and painted wooden ceiling.

ⓘ Getting There & Away

BUS Buses nip between the eastern side of *zeigyi* (Mawlamyine's main market) and Kyaikmaraw every hour during the daylight hours for K800.

KHA-YON CAVES
ခရုံ

Spirited away in the back of the little-known, dark and dank Kha-Yon Caves, a short way along the road to Hpa-an, are rows of ghostly buddha statues and wall paintings that come lurching out of the dark as the light from a torch catches them. Close by is another, smaller, cave system. This one is more of an open cavern and contains further statues, as well as a small cave-dwelling stupa. Bring a torch or buy candles from the stall near the entrance.

The statues and shrines in these caves make for a popular stop for local tourists and pilgrims alike. There is something unnerving about stumbling upon a meditating monk sitting in utter darkness at the foot of a cobweb-stained shrine.

To get here from Mawlamyine, head to the bus station and take any bus towards Hpa-an (K1050, 10 departures between 6am and 4pm) and ask to be dropped at the junction for the caves.

KAYIN STATE

The limestone escarpments and luminous paddy fields, coupled with a fascinating ethnic mix, would make Kayin State (ကရင်ပြည်နယ်) a Myanmar highlight but sadly, like so much of the nation's border regions, much of the area is very much off limits to foreign visitors.

Mae Sot is – at least when things are calm – a legal border crossing to Myanmar. Yet as with all of Myanmar's land crossings, the situation is volatile and, on our visit, the border was firmly shut due to fighting between the Myanmar Armed Forces and splinter groups of the Democratic Karen Buddhist Army (DKBA). Even when the border eventually does reopen, it's possible to cross only from Thailand to Myanmar, and like other land crossing points, visits are restricted to a limited number of days within a limited area, you have to leave your passport at the border and you're expected return the same way you came in.

If things change by the time you read this, immigration procedures are taken care of at the **Thai immigration booth** (☎Thailand 0 5556 3000; ⊙6.30am-6.30pm) at the Friendship Bridge. It takes a few minutes to finish all the paperwork to leave Thailand officially, and then you're free to walk across the arched 420m Friendship Bridge.

At the other end of the bridge is the **Myanmar immigration booth**, where you'll fill out permits for a one-day stay, pay a fee of US$10 or 500B and leave your passport as a deposit. Then you're free to wander around Myawadi, as long as you're back at the bridge by 5.30pm Myanmar time (which is half an hour behind Thai time) to pick up your passport and check out with immigration. On your return to Thailand, the Thai immigration office at the bridge will give you a new 15-day visa.

Myawadi is a fairly typical Burmese town, with a number of monasteries, schools, shops and so on. The most important temple is **Shwe Muay Wan**, a traditional bell-shaped *paya* gilded with many kilos of gold and topped by more than 1600 precious and semiprecious gems. Another noted Buddhist temple is **Myikyaungon**, named for its crocodile-shaped sanctuary. A hollow pagoda at Myikyaungon contains four marble Mandalay-style buddhas around a central pillar, while niches in the surrounding wall are filled with buddhas in other styles, including several bronze Sukhothai-style buddhas. Myawadi's thousand-year-old earthen city walls, probably erected by the area's original Mon inhabitants, can be seen along the southern side of town.

For further information, head to shop.lonelyplanet.com to purchase a downloadable PDF of the Northern Thailand chapter from Lonely Planet's *Thailand* guide.

Ever since Myanmar attained independence from the British in 1948, the Karen have been embroiled in a fight for autonomy. The struggle continues today, and is said to be the word's longest-running internal conflict. The main insurgent body, the Karen National Union (KNU), controls parts of the northern and eastern parts of the state, although recent Yangon military victories have left the KNU and its military component, the Karen National Liberation Army (KNLA), severely weakened. In 2010 the KNU aligned with five other insurgent armies and, as recently as 2011, parts of the state, particularly those near the Thai border, still remain a battleground.

Some parts of Kayin State are possible to visit, though, including Hpa-an, the regional capital, an easy and highly recommended trip from Mawlamyine or Yangon. Kayin State itself, homeland to around a million Karen, has probably received more foreign visitors, who have crossed over – unofficially – from Thailand, than from other parts of Myanmar. Many international volunteers have ventured into the frontier area to assist with refugee concerns.

Hpa-an

ဘားအံ

☎058 / POP C50,000

Though Hpa-an has only a limited number of official tourist attractions, the atmosphere is energetic and the colours on the streets rich and vibrant. The real draw is in the surrounding countryside, which contains art galleries housed in caves, sacred mountains and cloud-scraping islands. In addition to this, the boat trip between Hpa-an and Mawlamyine is a gentle cruise through rural bliss.

◉ Sights & Activities

The town of Hpa-an itself is of limited interest. The town's vibrant **Morning Market** is fun to explore and **Shweyinhmyaw Pagoda**, down by the waterfront, is a good place from which to watch the world sail on by. Some might also describe the central **Clock Tower**

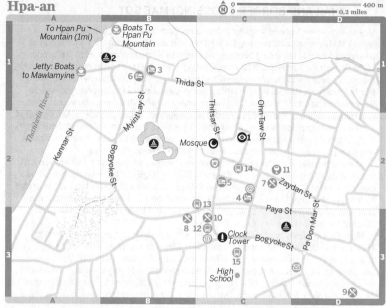

as a 'sight' at night when it's lit up like a gaudy lollipop – it's certainly memorable.

If you're bound for Mawlamyine and you've got the time, consider taking one of two weekly ferries from Hpa-an. It's worth the trip if only because this dirt-cheap riverboat passes through stunning scenery of limestone mountains and sugarcane fields. It's not usually crowded and there are a few sun chairs, perfect front-row seats for the river show. Bring your own food and drinks. For details on the trip, see p107.

🛏 Sleeping

Options are fairly limited in Hpa-an and, unless you have your own transport, you're relegated to the cheaper places in town that inspire little to write home about.

TOP CHOICE Soe Brothers Guesthouse HOTEL $
(☎21372; 2/146 Thitsar St; s/d $10/14, without bathroom $5/10) This is an excellent backpackers' choice and though the basic rooms here don't have much space in which to stretch, they are clean and cool and the communal bathrooms are kept ship-shape. The two 'luxury' rooms have a bit more space and no queues for the toilet. There are lots of welcoming communal areas to relax or chat. Phoekhwarr, one of the eponymous Soe

Brothers, in addition to being a great guide, has put together maps of the town and environs and is very tuned in to travellers' needs.

Hotel Zwegabin HOTEL $$
(☎22556; Hpa-an-Mawlamyine Rd; r $30-50; ✳) Located about 4 miles outside Hpa-an along the road to Mawlamyine, this hotel boasts a park-like atmosphere in a stunning location at the foot of limestone karsts and facing Mt Zwegabin. The best rooms are the very spacious duplex bungalows with balconies taking in the view, while the cheapies are in a two-storey condo-like bloc. All in all, not bad value but not a very convenient place to stay if you don't have your own wheels.

Parami Motel HOTEL $$
(☎21647; cnr Ohn Taw St & Paya St; s/d $26/28; ✳) Large and comfortable rooms that come with satellite TV and hot-water bathrooms make this an ideal midrange rest stop. The friendly staff don't speak much English and aren't as foreigner savvy as the Soe Brothers. Nevertheless, in comparison to that hotel the Parami is the last word in luxury.

Grand Hill Hotel HOTEL $$
(☎22286; Sin Phyu Shin St; s/d $25/35; ✳) This hotel takes the form of a suburban compound with cosy pink and white bunga-

Hpa-an

lows chock full of amenities (air-con, TV, fridge, hot water). They're comfortable and new, with more rooms being added at research time, but the hotel's location, about 2 miles east of the clock tower, isn't exactly convenient.

Tiger Hotel   HOTEL $$
(🖉21392; cnr Myint Lay St & Thida St; r $25; ✸) Located near the jetty to Mawlamyine, this is a modern four-storey hotel with clean but rather musty rooms that aren't particularly good value.

Golden Sky Guest House   BUDGET HOTEL $
(🖉21510; 2 Thida St; s/d $15/20; ✸) Also located mere steps from the jetty, the rooms here are large and clean, but the multicolour mishmash of tiles, furniture and furnishings is not particularly attractive. Staff can hardly be described as friendly.

✗ Eating & Drinking

As with hotels, the selection of restaurants is limited.

TOP CHOICE San Ma Tau Myanmar Restaurant   BURMESE $
(1/290 Bogyoke St; meals from K2000; ⊘lunch & dinner) This local institution is one of our favourite restaurants anywhere in the country. The friendly and popular place serves an almost overwhelming variety of excellent curries, soups and stir-fries, all served with fresh vegies and herbs and several types of spicy *balachaung* (chilli-based dips). The restaurant also doubles as an internet cafe.

White   TEAHOUSE $
(cnr Thitsar St & Bogyoke St; snacks from K200; ⊘breakfast & lunch) This teahouse, located near the clock tower, serves decent tea and freshly baked naan – great for breakfast.

New Day   CAFE $
(3/624 Bogyoke St; drinks from K600; ⊘breakfast & lunch) This modern cafe features real coffee, tasty fruit shakes and a variety of baked goods.

Khit-Thit Restaurant   CHINESE, BURMESE $
(New Age Restaurant; Zaydan St; mains from K800; ⊘lunch & dinner) A typical mixed Burmese and Chinese menu in a quiet backstreet restaurant.

Lucky 1   CHINESE, BURMESE $
(Zaydan St; mains from K800; ⊘lunch & dinner) This grubby place is the closest thing Hpa-an has to a bar and, in addition to draught beer, also serves decent Chinese-style dishes.

ⓘ Information

The **post office** is on a side road off Bogyoke St on the way to the bus station.

Frustratingly slow internet connections are available at **San Ma Tau Myanmar Restaurant** (World Gate; 1/290 Bogyoke St), at the **bus ticket stalls** (clock tower) and **Scare Crow Internet** (Ohn Taw St); all are open from 9am to 9pm and charge K500 per hour.

ⓘ Getting There & Away

Boat
Twice a week, double-decker ferries travel the scenic route between Hpa-an and Mawlamyine. The **jetty** is located near Shweyinhmyaw Pagoda. Because new bridges and roads have made commuting by bus much faster and more convenient, only a handful of people take the ferry nowadays and we reckon this particular route is on its last legs.

Boats leave Hpa-an at a very user-unfriendly 5.30am on Mondays and Fridays ($2, four hours). The predawn departure means that you will actually miss the best of the scenery so, though the journey from Mawlamyine is longer, it's better to use Mawlamyine as your starting point for this boat trip.

WORTH A TRIP

HPAN PU MOUNTAIN

Across the Thanlwin River from Hpa-an, Hpan Pu Mountain is a craggy, pagoda-topped peak that can be scaled in one sweaty morning. Getting there involves hopping on one of the river crossing boats from the informal **jetty** (K500, every 30 minutes from 7am to 5pm) near Shweyinhmyaw Pagoda. Upon reaching the other side, you'll walk through a quiet village then begin the steep but relatively short ascent to the top. The views of the river, the surrounding rice fields and limestone cliffs (including Mt Zwegabin) are astounding.

For information on boats from Mawlamyine, see p101.

Bus & Pick-Up Truck

For information on getting to Hpa-an by bus from Yangon, see p70.

Hpa-an's bus station is inconveniently located about 4 miles north of the clock tower, but tickets can be bought and buses boarded at a few centrally located **ticket stalls** (clock tower). Staff at Soe Brothers can also arrange tickets.

There are three daily buses to Yangon (K4000 to K8000, seven to eight hours) at 7am, 8am and 7pm, with stops in Kyaikto (four hours) and Bego (six hours); even if you're getting off in these towns you're expected to pay the full fare to Yangon.

To Mawlamyine (K1100, two hours), buses leave the bus station every hour from 6am to 4pm. Every second bus makes a brief stop to pick up passengers at a **stand** on Bogyoke St, not far from the clock tower.

Pick-up trucks to Eindu (K700), which pass Kaw Ka Thawng Cave and terminate part of the way to Saddar Cave, depart from a **stop** on Zaydan St. There's also a single daily **pick-up** to Mt Zwegabin (K1000, Monday to Friday) at 8am, departing from the high school.

Around Hpa-an

The real highlights of the Hpa-an area are all scattered about the divine rural countryside out of town. While most of these sights are accessible by public transport you will need to devote several days to them and be prepared to give your leg muscles a workout. Therefore, almost everyone takes a motorbike (or motorised trishaw) tour organised by the Soe Brothers Guesthouse, which cir-

cumnavigates Mt Zwegabin, stopping at all the sights mentioned below. A full day tour costs K30,000.

Some of the closer attractions can also be explored by bicycle. Bikes can be rented at Soe Brothers (K1500 per day), who have also put together a good map of the surrounding area and its attractions.

Mt Zwegabin   LANDMARK
ဇွကပင်ေတာင်

Hpa-an is hemmed in by a wrinkled chain of limestone mountains. The tallest of these is Mt Zwegabin, about 7 miles south of town, which as well as being a respectable 2372ft is also a home of spirits and saintly souls.

It's a demanding two-hour hike to the summit – up more steps than you'd care to count – but once at the top the rewards are staggering views, a small monastery and a stupa containing, yes, you guessed it, another hair from the Buddha. If you arrive at the top before noon you can take advantage of a complimentary lunch (rice, orange and tea) and the 11am **monkey feeding** – different primates, different menus.

Kaw Ka Thawng Cave   CAVES
ေကာကေသာင်ဂူ

More popular among locals than travellers, this compound actually consists of three caves, only two of which are generally open to the public. The first cave you'll come to, Kaw Ka Thawng, has been quite gentrified and has a tile floor and numerous buddha statues. Continuing along a path, you'll pass the stairway to another somewhat concealed cave that's not normally open (allegedly a monk found a used condom here and decided to lock it). Near the end of the path, you'll reach an inviting spring-fed **swimming hole**, popular with local kids, and another water-filled cave that also serves as a swimming hole.

Splitting from the path, a long bridge leads to Lakkana Village, a picturesque Kayin village, the backdrop to which includes Mt Zwegabin and has been featured in numerous Myanmar films and videos. The countryside here is drop-dead gorgeous and you could easily spend a day walking and swimming.

Kaw Ka Thawng Cave is about 7 miles from Hpa-an along the road to Eindu. To get there hop on a pick-up truck to Eindu (K700) and ask to be dropped off at Kaw Ka Thawng Cave. Both Kawgun and Yathaypyan caves are about 7 miles from Hpa-an, and the only public transport will leave you a good 45-minute walk from the caves, so you'll most likely have to hire a tuk-tuk (K5000) or motorcycle taxi (K3500) from Hpa-an.

Kawgun Cave CAVE

ကော့ဂွန်းဂူ

(admission K3000, camera K500) Ferreted away in these remote southern hills is a secret gallery of Buddhist art and sculpture. The 7th-century artwork of the Kawgun Cave consists of thousands of tiny clay buddhas and carvings plastered all over the walls and roof of this open cavern.

Down at ground level newer buddha statues stand and recline in various lazy positions. This gallery was constructed by King Manuaha after he was defeated in battle and had to take sanctuary in these caves. Impressive as it is today you can only imagine what it was like a few years back, before a cement factory, in its quest for limestone, started dynamiting the nearby peaks – the vibrations caused great chunks of the art to crash to the floor and shatter.

Yathaypyan Cave CAVE

ရသေ့ပြန်ဂူ

Just over a mile away from Kawgun Cave and built by the same exiled king, is the Yathaypyan Cave, which is a proper cave rather than a cavern and contains several pagodas as well as a few more clay wall carvings. If you're there during the dry season (approximately November to April) and have a torch you can traverse the cave, which takes about 10 minutes, after which you'll emerge at a viewpoint.

Kyauk Kalap MONASTERY

ကျောက်ကလပ်

Standing proud in the middle of a small, artificial lake is Kyauk Kalap, a tall finger of sheer rock mounted by one of the most unlikely pagodas in Myanmar. The rock offers great views of the surrounding countryside and nearby Mt Zwegabin, and is allegedly the best place to see the sunset over this mountain.

The compound is a working monastery and is closed every day from 12pm to 1pm to allow the monks to meditate. The 30 or so monks here are vegetarian and free vegetarian food is served from the temple from 9am to 5pm.

The monastery is also where the highly respected monk **U Winaya**, whose solid support of democracy leader Aung San Suu Kyi is well known in Myanmar, first resided. U Winaya passed away several years ago and his body was entombed in a glass case at **Thamanyat Kyaung**, another monastery about 25 miles southeast of Hpa-an. On one night in April 2007, the monk's body was stolen (allegedly by soldiers) and has yet to be recovered.

To get to Kyauk Kalap, you can hire a motorcycle taxi from Hpa-an (K2500) or take a motorised trishaw from Hpa-an market area to Kawd Kyaik village (along the road to Mawlamyine) for K500. From there it's an easy 10-minute walk.

The descent down the east side of the mountain takes around 1½ hours, and from the bottom it's another 2 miles to the main road from where you can catch a pick-up truck back to town. The whole trek takes roughly six hours or about half a day.

To get to the mountain, there's a pick-up (K1000, Monday to Friday) at 8am on Ohn Taw St in Hpa-an, in front of the high school. You'll be dropped off at the Zwegabin junction, where it's a 15-minute walk through a village to the base of the mountain on the west side past hundreds (1150 to be precise – don't believe us? Get counting!) of identical buddha statues lined up row after row. Alternatively, a motorcycle taxi from Hpa-an to the base of the mountain costs K2500. It's possible to overnight on the floor of the monastery compound on the summit (give a healthy donation), which means you can also appreciate the fantastic sunsets. Hiring your own transport – someone to drop you off on one side and pick you up on the other – makes everything run smoother.

Saddar Cave CAVE

ဆဒ္ဒန်ဂူ

This huge cave is simply breathtaking. As you enter the football stadium-sized cavern you'll be greeted by (what else?) dozens of buddha statues, a couple of pagodas and some newer clay wall carvings, but the real treat lies beyond these relics. In absolute darkness (bring a torch; otherwise for a donation of K3000, they'll turn on the lights for you) you can scramble for 15 minutes through black chambers as high as a cathedral, truck-sized stalactites and, in places, walls of crystal.

To add to the general atmosphere, thousands, possibly hundreds of thousands, of **bats** cling to the cave roof. In places the squealing from them is deafening and the ground underfoot becomes slippery with bat excrement!

Emerging at the cave's far side, the wonders only increase and the burst of sunlight reveals an idyllic secret **lake** full of ducks and flowering lilies hidden in a bowl of craggy peaks. There is another cave on the far side of the lake that is actually half flooded, but local

Kawthoung (also known as Victoria Point), at the far southern end of Tanintharyi (Tenasserim) Region, is a legal crossing point for foreign tourists. Yet, as with all of Myanmar's land crossings (or, in this case, water crossings), visits are restricted to a limited number of days within a limited area, you have to leave your passport at the border, and you're generally expected to return the same way you came in. We've received a couple reports of travellers having entered Myanmar via Yangon and, with advance permission from MTT, exited via Kawthoung, but the official line is that you can cross the border here and proceed onward only if you've already arranged a visit via Mergui Princess or Andaman Club. For details on doing this, see below.

From Thailand, several travel agencies in Ranong offer 'visa trips' for about 400B, but the trip is easy enough to do unassisted. Boats to Kawthoung leave the Saphan Pla pier, located about 6 miles from Ranong, regularly from 8am till 4pm (round-trip 200B, 40 minutes). After getting your passport stamped by Thai immigration, board one of the boats near the immigration office and you'll be taken to the Myanmar immigration office, where you must surrender your passport and pay a fee of $10 or 500B for a permit that allows you to stay in Kawthoung for up to 14 days. If you decide to stay, sights include the town's busy **waterfront** (Strand Rd) and a hilltop temple, **Pyi Taw Aye Paya**. Your best bet for accommodation is the centrally located but overpriced **Honey Bear Hotel** (☎592 1352; Strand Rd; s/d $36/48; ❇).

It's worth noting that, if you're crossing at Ranong to get a fresh Thai tourist visa, they're now limited to only 15 days.

fishers occasionally paddle through the cave for 10 minutes to yet another lake. You may be able to persuade one to take you along.

Saddar Cave can be traversed only during the dry season (about November to April) and is 17 miles from Hpa-an along the road to Eindu. To get there, take a pick-up to Eindu (K700). From the village take a motorbike taxi (K3000) for the remaining 2 miles to the cave.

TANINTHARYI (TENASSERIM) REGION

The deep south of Myanmar, known as Tanintharyi Region (တနင်္သာရီတိုင်း), appears to be a beach bum's dream. The coastline consists of a seemingly untouched archipelago of bridal-white beaches, and is said to be home to over 4000 islands, though British surveyors recognised only 804. Most are uninhabited, though a few are home to the Moken, or 'sea gypsies', a nomadic seafaring people (p312).

Unfortunately, for all intents and purposes, visiting these beaches and islands remains largely a dream.

It's possible for independent foreign travellers to cross by boat from Thailand to Kawthoung (see boxed text), or to take a domestic flight (on Tay Za's Air Bagan or government-owned Myanma Airways) to the southern towns of Dawei (Tavoy), Myeik

(Mergui) and Kawthoung, but once you hit the ground you're restricted to the city limits, defeating the purpose of visiting this beachy region. Based on our talks with Myanmar Travels & Tours and several knowledgeable tour operators, the only generally approved way to explore the beaches and islands of this region is through pre-arranged package tours with companies that have strong government ties. Alternatives include booking a seat with **Mergui Princess** (www.merguiprincess.com), an outfit that runs six-day cruises from Kawthoung to Mergui, or a stay at **Andaman Club** (www.andamanclub.com), a luxury resort on Thahtay Kyun Island. With advance notice of at least four weeks, these entities will file the required paperwork for you, which, we're told, can get you permission to cross the border at Kawthoung and receive a 28-day visa that allows you to exit the country via Yangon.

If you're determined to see the region, but don't want to contribute money to those closely linked to the military, the only real alternative is to join a live-aboard diving tour departing from southern Thailand. Recommended outfits with experience in the Mergui Archipelago include **Colona Liveaboards** (www.diving-thailand-phuket.com), **Moby Dick Adventures** (www.moby-dick-adventures.com) and **Sea Fun Divers** (www.seafundivers.com), all operating out of Phuket.

Bagan & Central Myanmar

Best Places to Eat

» Aroma 2 (p118)

» Be Kind to Animals the Moon (p122)

» Grandma Café (p144)

» Golden Rain Tea Center (p142)

» Maw Khan Nong (p141)

Best Places to Stay

» Hotel @ Tharabar Gate (p122)

» Thazin Garden Hotel (p124)

» Mya Yatanar Inn (p129)

» Myanmar Beauty Guest House II, III & IV (p138)

Why Go?

This heartland of Bamar culture has been the location of three former Burmese capitals – Bagan, Pyay and Taungoo – as well as the current one, Nay Pyi Taw. Of this quartet, it's Bagan with its wondrous vista of pagodas and stupas, many dating back to the 12th century, that's the star attraction. The tallest and most majestic of Bagan's temples – built of brick, decorated inside with beautiful frescos and topped with gilded *hti* pinnacles – mix Hindu and Buddhist images with locally brewed *nat* (spirits) in nooks.

Most visitors fly directly to Bagan, but central Myanmar also provides scenic rewards for adventurous travellers. It may be known as the 'dry zone', but the region is far from a desert. Beside highways and rickety train tracks amble ox carts through rice fields and rolling plains, all rimmed by the Shan Mountains to the east and the snaking Ayeyarwady (Irrawaddy) River to the west, creating scenes that hark back centuries.

When to Go

This area comprises the bulk of the 'dry zone' of Myanmar, and it remains hot and dusty for much of the year. Most visitors come in winter (November to February), when daytime temperatures are a relatively chilly 86°F (30°C) during the day and about 50°F (10°C) at night. From March to May, the hottest season, daytime temperatures boil at up to 109°F (43°C). Rains peak in June and October, but run throughout the months between. There are several temple festivals in Bagan (p158) and elsewhere that you may want to try and build your itinerary around or avoid, depending on your interests.

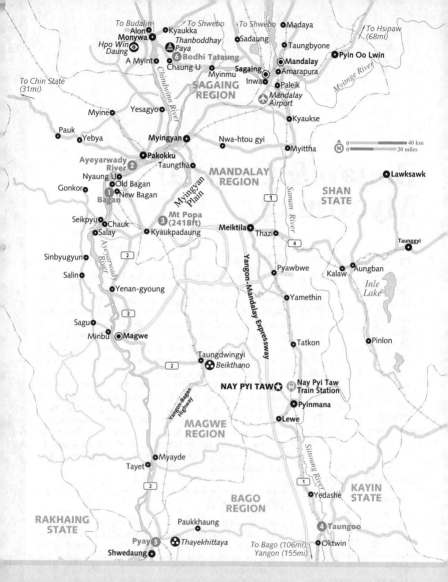

Bagan & Central Myanmar Highlights

1 Watch from a **hot-air balloon** (p113) as the sun rises or sets over the temple-studded plain of Bagan

2 Hit the **Ayeyarwady River** on a Bagan–Mandalay boat (p120), or on a half-day trip to nearby temples (p165)

3 Pay respects to Myanmar's 37 *nat* at their spiritual home, the monkey-arama volcanic mountaintop temple at **Mt Popa** (p126)

4 Hang with elephants at a working camp east of **Taungoo** (p137)

5 Explore the colourful riverside market in the morning and the hilltop Shwesandaw Paya in the afternoon at **Pyay** (p143)

6 Ponder what the Buddha would have felt to see his likeness fashioned as a 30-storey concrete statue at **Bodhi Tataung** (p133)

History

Moving armies led by various people – the Pyu, the Mon, the Burmese – have swish-swashed across this central plain, the 'heart of Myanmar', over the centuries. The area around Pyay served as the Pyu capital from the 5th to 9th centuries AD; some consider the Pyu to be founders of Myanmar's 'first empire', though little is known of this vanished group.

Bagan's burst of energy ran two-and-a-half centuries, beginning in 1047 and ending as the pounding footfall of Kublai Khan's raiders approached in 1287. See p149 for more on Bagan's history. The latest empire to lodge in the area is the military junta, which founded the new capital of Nay Pyi Taw in 2005.

ⓘ Getting There & Away

Nyaung U is the principal gateway for Bagan, with a train station, a jetty and an airport. Most visitors by boat come downriver from Mandalay or Pakokku. Most long-haul bus routes (eg Yangon–Mandalay) miss Bagan, instead stopping at Meiktila. But there are a few direct bus links between Bagan and Yangon, Mandalay and Inle Lake. Trains to the Bagan area are slow and impractical. The more interesting road route from Yangon to Bagan is via Pyay and Magwe.

BAGAN

♪ 061

One of Myanmar's top attractions, the area known as Bagan (ပုဂံ) or, bureaucratically, as the 'Bagan Archaeological Zone', occupies an impressive 26-sq-mile area 118 miles south of Mandalay and 429 miles north of Yangon. The Ayeyarwady River drifts past its northern and western sides.

The area's most active town and chief transport hub is Nyaung U, in the northeast corner. About 2.5 miles west, Old Bagan is the former site of the village that moved to 2 miles south to New Bagan in 1990. Between the two is Myinkaba, a village boasting a long-running lacquerware tradition.

Connecting the towns are paved roads making a 12-mile oval. In between and around these towns, of course, is the bulk of the Bagan action: the plain, featuring most of the temples, all connected with a vast network of bumpy dirt roads and trails. At times, you'll be about a mile from the nearest paved road.

This section includes sleeping, eating and transport options; see p149 for the history and descriptions of the temples themselves.

ⓘ GOVERNMENT FEES

All foreign visitors to the Bagan Archaeological Zone are required to pay a $10 entrance fee, which goes to the government. If you arrive by boat or air, the fee will be collected at the river jetty or airport. You'll be given a credit-card-sized plastic ticket embossed with a number, for which you'll be asked when you check in at nearly all accommodation. The fee covers a one-week visit, but it's unlikely you'll be asked to pay again if you stay longer. Entrance fees to the Archaeological Museum and Palace Site also go into government coffers; see p21.

⚡ Activities

Boat Trips

Sunset chasing in Bagan isn't restricted to the tops of temples. An interesting alternative is a dusk boat trip ($10-15) on the Ayeyarwady. The hour-long tours offered by the boat folk at the Old Bagan jetty tend to cater to package tourists, but drop by to arrange your own ride.

You can also arrange an interesting boat and taxi side-trip to the mountaintop Tan Kyi Paya (see p155), one of four stupas that marked the original edges of the city. Another possible boat trip is to three temples north of Nyaung U (p165).

Ballooning

The best way to truly appreciate Bagan's size and sprawl is from the basket of a hot-air balloon belonging to Balloons over Bagan (Map p121; ♪ 60058; www.balloonsoverbagan.com; office in Bagan Thiripyitsaya Sanctuary Resort; per person stand-by rate $290). These magical 45-minute rides over one of the world's most highly acclaimed ballooning spots only run from October to March. Sometimes sunrise flights are booked up to a month or more in advance, but *if* there's space, any hotel or guesthouse should be able to arrange a ticket.

The slickly run Burmese company, owned by an Australian-Burmese couple and employing British pilots and some 80 locals, has five balloons that usually fit eight to 10 passengers and a pilot. The experience begins with a pick up from your hotel in one of their fleet of lovingly restored, pre-WWII Chevrolet CMP buses partly made of teak. You can have coffee and snacks while watching the UK-made balloons fill with hot air, and sparkling wine and snacks after you land and watch them get packed up again.

Although sunset flights are offered (depending on weather conditions), the sunrise ones are preferable as the cooler dawn air allows pilots to fly the balloons at lower altitude for a closer view of the temples. See p187 for details of the company's balloon safaris in Shan State and Bagan.

🎓 Courses

Flavour of Myanmar Cooking Class COOKING
(☑09-863 5066, in Yangon 01-375 050; www.myanmarcookingclass.com; US$50) This Good News Travels cooking course is a half-day food-focused experience that can be tailored to the level of cooking you're comfortable with and is interesting even for those not wanting to learn to prepare Myanmar food. Kicking off

around 8am, participants visit New Bagan's market to go shopping for ingredients. Several dishes are then prepared at a fully equipped outdoor kitchen at the cooking school in New Bagan, with some of the food afterwards being packed up into tiffin boxes and taken to a local monastery to present to the monks. The morning ends with lunch back at the cooking school.

Bagan Thiripyitsaya Sanctuary Resort COOKING
(☑60048,60049; www.thiripyitsaya-resort.com) This resort offers a variety of courses, including a three-hour cooking course covering four or five traditional dishes for a maximum of four participants ($60 each). Other classes include a photography tour ($230; six hours) with a local professional shooter, Burmese-language lessons ($100; six hours), medita-

---

LOCAL KNOWLEDGE

LEE HOOPER: HOT-AIR BALLOON PILOT

Best temple

Dhammayangyi Pahto (p159). It's the most mysterious. You can spend hours there learning about its history, and still learn new things.

Best non-temple thing to do

A sunset cruise on the river (p113) can be a great way to end the day.

Best shopping

Tun Handicrafts/Moe Moe's (p126). Run by a lovely lady who produces good-quality laquerware. The range on display is just the tip of the iceberg – ask to see the special room, with the really nice bits. All the prices are negotiable, and Moe Moe does lots of charity work and generally has a good heart.

Best restaurant

The Black Bamboo (p118).

Best nightlife

Shwe Ya Su (p119). It's the only nightlife in Bagan! A great place to unwind with a cold beer.

Best place to hang out with locals

Sarabha III/Gyi Gyi's (p122). All the locals love eating there, which is always a good sign. The beef curry is amazing.

Secret spot

Bagan is the country's only producer of *pon yay gyi*, a black bean curd used in a lot of Myanmar cooking. It's basically the Burmese version of Marmite or Vegemite. The factory in Nyaung U, called Lucky Owl, is an amazing place to see the fascinating process, which is one of the most environmentally friendly I have ever seen. Peanut husks are used as fuel for cooking and the left-over beans are used as pig feed, so there are literally no waste products.

Lee Hooper, Chief Pilot for Balloons over Bagan, has been flying hot-air balloons over Bagan since 2003

» **Old Bagan** (p121) Closest to the big-time temples. Most of Bagan's high-end hotels cluster in and around the riverside and the old palace walls. It's a central location (particularly good for quick visits to Bagan), with plenty of day-time eating options, but less nightlife than Nyaung U. Doubles from $35.

» **New Bagan** (p124) Not the most charming village. However, New Bagan has by far the best midrange choices, with excellent-value rooms from $25. There's also a couple of pleasant riverside restaurants.

» **Nyaung U** (p116) The budget heart of Bagan, with the liveliest restaurant scene and the bulk of the transport connections, Nyaung U is a real town, with guesthouses from $8. On the downside it's a 2-mile bike ride to the bulk of the temples.

tion training with a monk ($45; one hour) and lacquerware painting ($90; five hours).

ℹ️ Information

For travel information, try Nyaung U's Ever Sky Information Service (p119) or the government-run MTT office in New Bagan (p126).

Nyaung U and New Bagan have post offices. You can get online in Nyaung U, New Bagan and at select hotels.

Bagan used to have two area codes. A few listings may still use the old ☑02 area code, which we indicate, but nearly all local numbers now use the ☑061 area code.

The Map of Bagan (www.dpsmap.com/bagan; K1000) is sold at most hotels and at the airport. It shows many of the area's paths, but isn't always 100% accurate.

ℹ️ Getting There & Around

To orient themselves, many visitors opt for a 'greatest hits' tour of the temples on horse cart or by car, then follow it up by checking more remote or lesser-known temples by bike. See also the Getting There & Away and Getting Around sections of Nyaung U (p119), Old Bagan (p123) and New Bagan (p126) for details on getting to Yangon, Inle Lake, Mandalay and other destinations.

To/From the Airport

Taxis between Nyaung U Airport and hotels in Nyaung U, Old Bagan and New Bagan cost K5000, K6000 and K7000 respectively. Horse carts and taxis are cheaper from the Old Bagan or Nyaung U jetties, if you arrive by boat.

Bicycle

Bikes are widely available and can be an ideal way of getting around, despite the direct exposure to sun and some dirt roads that slow you up. Essentially all accommodation places rent bicycles: in Nyaung U it costs about K1500 or K2000 per day; in Old Bagan and New Bagan it's more like K3000 or K4000 per day.

Traffic is pretty light on all roads. Early-morning or late-afternoon rides along the sealed Bagan–Nyaung U Rd are particularly pleasant. It's worth planning ahead a little, as the bulk of the temples in the Central Plain (p159) have little shade and nowhere to get lunch. The most convenient eating options are in Old Bagan (p122).

Horse Cart

A popular but uncomfortable and slow way of seeing the ruins is from the shaded, padded bed of a horse cart. Drivers speak some English (at least), know where to find the 'keyholders' to locked sites and can point out temples with few or no tourists around. (Some might stop by a shop in the hope of securing a commission; it's OK to say 'no thanks'.) A cart works best for two passengers, but it's possible to go with three or (in a pinch) four.

In Nyaung U a day with a horse cart and driver costs about K10,000; a half-day is K5000 or K6000. It's about K5000 more if taken from Old Bagan or New Bagan.

Pick-Up Trucks

A pick-up (K200; hourly 7am to 3pm) runs from outside the Nyaung U market, ending near the junction in New Bagan and passing Wetkyi-in, Old Bagan and Myinkaba on the way. This could be used to jump from one place to the next, then walk around the temples, particularly on the North Plain (p156) or around Old Bagan (p154).

Taxi

Hiring a shared taxi for the day in Nyaung U costs about $25. Old Bagan hotels will charge anything up to $95 to hire an unshared taxi. Hired taxis are also convenient ways of making day trips to Mt Popa and Salay.

Trishaw

There's little trishaw activity outside Nyaung U, where you can get one at the jetty or bus station; the pedal into town is around K2000.

BAGAN & CENTRAL MYANMAR

Nyaung U

ညောင်ဦး

ⓙ061

A bustling river town with more happening than you'll find elsewhere in Bagan, Nyaung U is where most independent travellers hang their hat (or backpack). Roaming the back roads towards the jetty or stopping at scrappy teashops will attract friendly wide-eyed looks. There are a handful of temples to see, including the Shwezigon Paya (p164), and a lively market. Visitors staying in New or Old Bagan tend to make it here, if not for the restaurant scene (the closest the Bagan area gets to nightlife) then for the transport links.

Guesthouses and roadside restaurants now push a couple of miles west, along the road to Old Bagan, reaching the small village of Wetkyi-in (Giant Pig). The town was named for a mythical pig that, per local legend, inhabited the lake there and killed a lot of people before being killed by a future king of Bagan.

◉ Sights & Activities

FREE **Thanakha Gallery**   MUSEUM, SHOP
(ⓙ60179; cnr Yarkinnthar Hotel Rd & Main Rd; ◷9am-9pm) Claiming that it's the 'Only One Thanakha Gallery In the World', this sizeable complex has a small gallery devoted to the myriad medicinal and cosmetic uses of the thanakha tree (*Limonia acidissima*) – from its roots to its bark. It has a small plantation of the trees, around which bounce a posse of cute bunny rabbits, to which you can feed bunches of greens. Really, the place is a glorified shop for the thanakha cosmetics of **Shwe Pyi Nann** (www.shwepyinann.com), as well as a good range of other Bagan and Myanmar souvenirs. A restaurant, internet cafe and beauty salon round out the complex.

Bagan Nyaung U Golf Club   GOLF
(ⓙ60035; www.bagangolfresort.net/golfclub.html; green fee incl clubs & caddy $42; ◷6am-6pm) Just south of town, this government-owned facility run now by the Amazing Bagan Resort has about half a dozen pagodas scattered around its 18-hole, par-72 course.

🛏 Sleeping

Nyaung U's main road has several cheap, interchangeable guesthouses (not listed below), which offer rooms for about $10. For that price you can expect a boxy room with a lazy ceiling fan, concrete or tiled floors and attached bathroom with (supposedly) hot water, and sometimes even an old air-conditioning unit. Guesthouses off Yarkinnthar Hotel Rd (aka Restaurant Row) are away from traffic noise.

Nyaung U

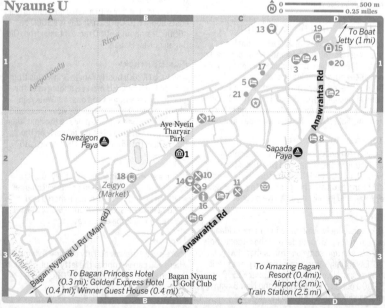

All of the following include breakfast in their rates, which may drop a dollar or three off-season.

TOP CHOICE **New Park Hotel** HOTEL **$**
(☎60322, 60484, in Yangon 01-290073; www.newparkmyanmar.com; 4 Thiripyitsaya; s $10-20, d $14-30; ✳@) Perhaps the best of the bunch on the leafy backstreets off Restaurant Row, the 24-room New Park has three classes. The older rooms, with bungalow-style front decks, are comfortable, wood-floor set-ups, with spic-and-span bathrooms (a big upgrade from the main-road choices). The newer wing gets you more space, a fridge and a TV.

Amazing Bagan Resort RESORT **$$$**
(☎60035, in Yangon 01-297 766; www.bagangolfresort.net; s/d $55/58, ste s/d $74/83; ✳@🛜🗚) Formerly the Bagan Golf Resort, this pleasantly designed 59-room property – the nicest in Nyaung U – is now run by a Yangon-based businessman. The bungalow suites in brick buildings mimicking old Bagan architecture are best. Has nice touches, such as sun hats in the rooms, free internet and bikes. Located next to the golf club.

Golden Express Hotel HOTEL **$$**
(☎02-60034, 02-60381; www.goldenexpresstours.com; Bagan-Nyaung U Rd; s $21-35, d $25-44; ✳@🗚) With cartoon colours and some pagodas next door, this complex features four bright motel-style units. The best value of the four classes are the superior single/double rooms ($29/34), with wood floors, a bit more space and tubs. There's a nice pool, and a big buffet breakfast is served on the grounds.

Bagan Princess Hotel HOTEL **$$**
(☎60661, in Yangon 01-222 797; www.baganprincesshotel.com; Bagan-Nyaung U Rd; r $35-40; ✳@🛜🗚) Built around a small pool, this curiously designed new complex in Wetkyi-in offers good rooms, all with separate Jacuzzi bathrooms as well as showers in the main bathrooms. Pay the extra $5 for upper-level rooms, which have more light and direct pool access.

Thante Hotel HOTEL **$$**
(☎60315, in Yangon 01-664 424; nyaunguthante@gmail.com; Anawrahta Rd; s/d $30/40; ✳🗚) Just off the main road, this 37-room hotel offers roomy bungalows on shady grounds and has a decent swimming pool ($3 for nonguests). The rooms are starting to show a few nicks, but they're spacious and come with satellite TV, twin beds, refrigerator, bathtub, wooden floor and deckchairs on the small porch. The hotel's staff members are very welcoming, plus it has a good bakery and restaurant on site.

May Kha Lar Guest House GUESTHOUSE **$**
(☎60304, 60907; Main Rd; s $8-14, d $12-18; ✳) The best kept of the main-road budget choices, with lots of handy traveller info and a shrine room! On the ground floor the cheap, gaudily tiled rooms are compact, with air-conditioning, ceiling fan and attached bathroom. Nicer upstairs options have wooden floors and TV.

New Heaven
GUESTHOUSE $

(⏰60921; off Yarkinnthar Hotel Rd; s $10-12, d $15-18; ❄) A quick stroll from Restaurant Row, this place offers clean, compact rooms with small decks overlooking the peaceful lawn. The bigger, pricier rooms include a TV.

Eden Motel
GUESTHOUSE $

(⏰60815, 60812; Anawrahta Rd; s/d from $8/15; ❄) Split in two by the busy road to the airport, Eden isn't exactly a garden party. The rooms in the newer Eden Motel II have bigger, tiled rooms and an over-touted bathtub, but we prefer the ones in the original – particularly the ones with all-bamboo walls and hardwood floors. The friendly management told us they 'have an idea' to upgrade all the rooms.

Inn Wa Guest House
GUESTHOUSE $

(⏰60902, 60849; Main Rd; s $8-10, d $13-15; ❄) If you just need a cheap bed, this three-floor, 16-room choice near the market works, offering minigolf-green carpets in boxy rooms and simple attached bathrooms with hot water. Rooms 206 and 306 have more window light (and less street noise). Breakfast is served on the open roof deck. Advance booking gets you a free transfer from your point of arrival.

Winner Guest House
GUESTHOUSE $

(⏰61069; Main Rd, Wetkyi-in; s $5-7, d $7-10; ❄) If money's tight, opt for this little family-run guesthouse on the road to Old Bagan. The cheapest rooms share the common bathroom. Simple concrete-floor rooms with an air-conditioning unit and tiled bathroom attached are just as good as the cheapies in town. Other pluses are that it's nearer the temples, and there are appealing roadside restaurants around.

Golden Myanmar Guest House
GUESTHOUSE $

(⏰60901, 09-204 2064; www.goldenmyanmar guesthouse.com; Main Rd; s $7-8, d $11-15; ❄) More bare-bone than its neighbour Inn Wa, with the cheaper rooms sharing a common bathroom. Go with room 108: it's got more light and has direct access to the roof deck, where breakfast is served.

Golden Village Inn
GUESTHOUSE $

(⏰60921; off Yarkinnthar Hotel Rd; s $8-10, d $12-16; ❄) Behind New Heaven (and with the same owners), the Village is another shady spot near the restaurant strip, with comfortable bungalow-style rooms. Higher-priced rooms have TV, desk and tub.

✖ Eating & Drinking

Nyaung U's Yarkinnthar Hotel Rd (aka Restaurant Row) is a strip of atmospheric open-air eateries geared towards foreign visitors. It's touristy, but easily the hub(bub) of Bagan action. Many of the restaurants are copycats, with similar 'everything goes' menus (Chinese, Burmese, Thai, Indian, pizza and 'Western' options).

TOP CHOICE Aroma 2
INDIAN $$

(Yarkinnthar Hotel Rd; dishes K2000-7000; ⏰11am-9pm or 10pm) 'No good – no pay' is the mantra of this justifiably confident operation serving delish vegie and meat curries on banana leaves (or plates) with an endless stream of hot chapattis and five dollops of condiments (including tamarind and mint sauces). If you order one day in advance, it can also whip up various biryani rice dishes.

TOP CHOICE Black Bamboo
EUROPEAN $$

(⏰09-650 1444; off Yarkinnthar Hotel Rd; dishes K3500-6000; ⏰9am-9.30pm) Run by a French woman and her Burmese husband, this garden-set café and restaurant is something of an oasis: a lovely place to relax over a decent steak and chips, a well-made espresso or delicious homemade ice cream. Service is friendly but leisurely.

Red Pepper Diner
THAI, EUROPEAN $$

(⏰09-4926 0229; cnr Anawrahta Rd & Thirpyitsaya 3 St; meal K4000-12,000; ⏰11am-3pm, 6-10pm) Serving a broad range of Thai dishes, freshly made with an authentic spicy kick, this yellow house takes a stab at sophistication with silky pillows on concrete benches in a courtyard facing the main road.

San Kabar Restaurant & Pub
ITALIAN $$

(Main Rd; pizza K4000-6000, salads K1500-2700; ⏰7am-10pm) Famous as the birthplace of Bagan pizza, the San Kabar's streetside candlelit courtyard is all about its thin-crusted pies and well-prepared salads.

Pyi Wa
BAMAR, INTERNATIONAL $$

(Yarkinnthar Hotel Rd; noodles & dishes K1500-3000; ⏰7am-9pm or 10pm) Slightly less stylish than some, but Pyi Wa is the operation on Restaurant Row with a Bagan-era *zedi* (stupa) as a neighbour – staff light up its base at night. The best dishes are Chinese, but do start off with the 'potato cracken' (fried potato wedges that go particularly well with a bottle of Myanmar Beer).

The following table provides a quick comparison of the various ways of getting to Nyaung U from Yangon and Mandalay

TO/FROM YANGON	DURATION	COST	FREQUENCY
Air	70min	$82-85	6-8 flights daily
Boat	6 days	$18-36	weekly
Bus	11hr	K15,000	daily
Car	10hr	$80	n/a
Train	16hr	$30-50	daily

TO/FROM MANDALAY	DURATION	COST	FREQUENCY
Air	30min	$38-40	6 daily
Boat (slow)	2 days	$10	2 weekly
Boat (fast)	11hr	$36	2-4 times weekly
Boat (luxury cruise)	2 days	$280	weekly
Bus	7-8hr	K6500	2 daily
Car	7hr	$80	n/a
Train	8hr	$5-10	daily

Shwe Ya Su BEER STATION **$$**
(Yarkinnthar Hotel Rd; dishes K1500-3000; ⊙7am-10.30pm) Since this place started selling draught Myanmar Beer (look for the illuminated sign outside), it's become quite the local hangout. It's a pleasant spot to revive with twinkling fairy lights hanging from the trees and tasty barbecued-pork snacks.

Beach Bagan Restaurant & Bar PAN-ASIAN **$$**
(12 Youne Tan Yat; dishes K4000-8000; ⊙8am-9pm) Signs lead past backstreets from the Nyaung U market to this slick, breezy spot with plenty of parking space for tour buses that may or may not come. The restaurant overlooking the river has wicker chairs and offers Thai, Chinese and Myanmar dishes. Try the roof-top bar for a sunset cocktail (K3000); all drinks are 10% off from 4pm to 6pm.

🛍 Shopping

There's also a good selection of souvenirs at the Thanakha Gallery and at shops along Restaurant Row.

Mani-Sithu Market MARKET
(⊙6am-5pm Mon-Sat) Near the roundabout at the east end of the main road, this market offers a colourful display of fruit, vegetables, flowers, fish and textiles and is best visited early in the day to see it at its liveliest. You'll find many traveller-oriented goods (wood-carvings, T-shirts, antique pieces) at its northern end.

ℹ Information

Ever Sky Information Service (✆60895; 5 Thiripyitsaya; ⊙7.30am-9.30pm) On the restaurant strip, this friendly place has travel and transport information and a used bookshop. Staff can get share taxis (to Mt Popa, Kalaw, Salay, around Bagan) for the cheapest rates you'll find.

Internet (Thanakar Complex, Yarkinnthar Hotel Rd; K600 per hr; ⊙9am-9pm)

Post office (Anawrahta Rd; ⊙9.30am-7pm)

Telephone Stands around town follow the same set prices: it's $5 per minute to call Europe or Australia and $6 to call North America.

ℹ Getting There & Away

See Mt Popa and Salay Getting There & Away sections for transport details to those nearby attractions.

Air

The Nyaung U Airport is about 2 miles southeast of the market. Airlines connect Bagan daily with Mandalay ($38 to $40; 30 minutes), Heho ($60 to $62; 40 minutes) and Yangon ($82 to $85; 70 minutes).

Travel agencies sell tickets a bit cheaper than airline offices. Try **Seven Diamond** (✆60883; Main Rd) or **Sun Far** (✆60901) in front of the Golden Myanmar Guest House.

Boat

Boats to Mandalay go from either Nyaung U or Old Bagan, depending on water levels. The Nyaung U jetty is about half a mile northeast of the Nyaung U market.

The government-run IWT ferry (aka 'slow boat') heads to Mandalay on Monday and Thursday at 5am ($10, two days) and overnights near Pakokku. Meanwhile the south-bound government ferry leaves weekly to Magwe ($5, two days) and Pyay ($9, three days). If open (unlikely!) the IWT office, about 300yd inland from the jetty, sells tickets; alternatively book a ticket through your hotel or one of the agencies listed above, who can also secure tickets for the faster **Malikha 2** ($32; 11 hours) boat to Mandalay.

From the Nyaung U jetty, small local boats leave for Pakokku (K4000, 2½ hours) a few times daily (at research time: 6am, 9am and noon), the last returning to Nyaung U at 2pm. To charter a private boat to Pakokku costs about K10,000 one way.

Bus

The main bus station serving Bagan is on the main road in Nyaung U.

During peak season, it's wise to book bus tickets for Mandalay, Taunggyi (for Inle Lake) and Yangon a couple of days in advance. You can call ☎60743 for information on the Magwe, Mandalay and Taunggyi buses, but it's better to drop by the office at the bus station.

Note, some Mandalay-bound buses go via Myingyan, others via Kyaukpadaung and Meiktila; if you want to get off at these intermediate stops, you still pay the full fare to Mandalay. The Yangon-bound service goes via Meiktila and Nay Pyi Taw. Services:

Magwe (K6500; four to five hours; 7am; minibus)
Mandalay (K6500; seven to eight hours; 4am, 7am, 8.30am, 9am, 7pm; local, no air-con)
Meiktila (K6500; three to four hours; 7am, 9am, 7pm; local, no air-con)
Myingyan (K6500; three hours; 4am, 8.30am, 8am; local, no air-con)
Kalaw (K10,500; nine to 10 hours; 4am; Taunggyi bus)
Taunggyi (K10,500; nine to 10 hours; 4am; local)
Yangon (K15,000; 11 hours; 5pm; air-con)

Pick-Up Trucks

The lone daily pick-up service to Mt Popa (K3000 each way, one hour) leaves at 8.30am from in front of the south entrance to the market, and returns at 1pm. From the bus station half-hourly pick-ups go to Chauk (two hours), where you can connect via pick-up to Salay (one hour).

Pick-ups between Nyaung U, Old Bagan and New Bagan run along the main street, starting from the roundabout outside the Nyaung U market.

Taxi

As Bagan has limited bus connections to other major destinations, many travellers hire share taxis – often quite old cars, some with open backs, most without air-con and seating up to three people – to destinations around the country. Ask at Ever Sky (p119) or at your hotel. Some sample taxi fares: Inle Lake ($170, 12 hours), Kalaw ($150, 10 hours), Magwe ($70, five hours), Mt Popa ($35, 1½ hours), Salay ($35, two hours), Mt Popa and Salay ($55).

Train

The Bagan train station is about 2.5 miles southeast of Nyaung U. The shop **Blue Sea** (☎60949; Main Rd) sells tickets and charges a $2 commission. The train to Mandalay takes eight hours and departs at 7am (ordinary/upper class $5/10), while the train to Yangon takes 16 hours and departs at 4.30pm (ordinary/upper class/sleeper $30/40/50).

MALIKHA 2 BOAT TO MANDALAY DEE MACPHERSON AND BONNIE MCMILLAN

'It was a pretty nice boat – part of the outside deck is open and part is covered. There's also an upstairs and downstairs inside part that is air-conditioned. The boat left at 6am (promptly!) and the trip upriver took about 11½ hours. There is free coffee/tea and toast/jam available for a few hours after departure, which was nice. Halfway through the morning, they come around and take your order for lunch – fried noodle or fried rice for 3000K. It was actually quite good food! There is also beer/pop/water available for sale.'

'Our boat was maybe half full, so it was quite comfortable. There was outside seating available for pretty much everyone who wanted it, either in a chair or on the benches around the back. When you buy your ticket, you are assigned a seat inside the air-conditioned part. We were told by someone to go outside immediately and lay claim to a chair to ensure we got one – good advice because there aren't enough for everyone, especially if the boat is full. The boat has a capacity of 129, and if you choose to sit inside, you certainly can see outside – the windows are fairly large.'

Old Bagan

ပုဂံမြို့ဟောင်း

♪061

The core of the Bagan Archaeological Zone contains several of the main temple sites, city walls, a museum, a reconstructed palace, restaurants, a few shops and a cluster of mid-range to top-end hotels. It's right on a bend of the Ayeyarwady River – sometime during your stay, wander down to the waterfront and watch the coming and going of the river trade.

In 1990 the government forcibly relocated a village that had grown up in the 1970s in the middle of the walled area of 'Old Bagan'. We're told one of the reasons for this was the increased incidence of treasure hunting and gold prospecting around the ruins in the wake of the 1988 street protests, when the authorities' attentions were diverted elsewhere.

Some claim the villagers had a week's notice of the move; others say it was longer and they put off the inevitable to the last minute. Either way, there was certainly resistance to the uprooting of homes and belongings for a new home in a peanut field, now developed as the village of New Bagan.

◉ Sights

See p149 for information on temples in Old Bagan.

Archaeological Museum MUSEUM
(Bagan-Nyaung U Rd; admission $5; ⊙9am-4.30pm) Housed in an out-of-place, 19th-century-style temple, this government-run museum (see p21) features many fine pieces from Bagan (reclining Buddhas, original images, inscribed stones and mural re-creations) and an unexpected room of modern-art renderings of the temples.

Bagan Golden Palace PALACE
(Bagan-Nyaung U Rd; admission $5; ⊙9am-4.30pm) Following similar government-mandated palace reconstruction jobs in Bago, Mandalay and Shwebo, this towering concrete-and-steel-reinforced edifice was opened to much fanfare in 2008. Built opposite the excavated site of the actual palace just in from the Tharabar Gate, it's unlikely to bear much resemblance to the original. Either way, it's a sign of the encroaching Disneyfication of Bagan.

🛏 Sleeping

Old Bagan's hotels provide views of the river, proximity to the temples and nice pool areas, but don't necessarily offer much more com-

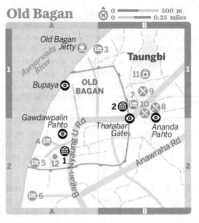

Old Bagan

fort than you get at New Bagan's best – and less expensive – accommodation. Also, they can fill up months in advance of peak season.

All places listed have restaurants, bars and pools, plus satellite TV and extras like a minibar in the room. Prices listed here are walk-in rates during peak season, and don't include the 10% service charge and 10% government tax. Yangon agents often arrange discounted rates.

TOP CHOICE **Hotel @ Tharabar Gate** HOTEL $$$
(✆60037, 60042, in Yangon 01-211 888; www.thar abargate.com; r $160-200, ste $300; ❋@🖳🏊) If you can live without river views, this 86-room hotel is a fine option (particularly when you beat those rack rates by booking on the internet or via agents, some of whom can offer good deals). Lush gardens of tropical plants and bougainvillea line walkways to the roomy wood-floor bungalows with decks. The two-room suites at the far end go traditional, with gold-coloured ogres and *naga* spirits on the walls.

Aye Yar River View Hotel HOTEL $$$
(✆60352, 60313, in Yangon 01-537 961; www.bagan ayeyarhotel.com; r $75-95; ❋@🖳🏊) Following a major make-over, this former government hotel (we're told it's owned by a 'private business person' in Yangon) is very appealing. The most expensive rooms are set in spacious bungalows with river views, while those closer to the pool are pretty nice, too.

Bagan Thiripyitsaya Sanctuary Resort RESORT $$$
(✆60048, 60049; www.thiripyitsaya-resort.com; r $130-175, ste $300; ❋@🏊) It's hard not to wish for more midday shade in this nice Japanese joint-venture hotel on the river, about 500m south of the Old Bagan walls. There's a pool and rooms are away (mostly) from direct river views in ageing four-room bungalow-style duplexes with covered decks. The restaurant is good with panoramic river views and there's a wide range of activities offered (see p114).

Bagan Thande Hotel HOTEL $$
(✆60025, 60031; www.hotelbaganthande.com; s $28-66, d $33-75, ste $200; ❋@🏊) Opened for King Edward VIII in 1922, this riverside hotel carries a bit of dated formality. The simple, but fine, midpriced 'superior' bungalows have decks looking over the pool and nearby Gadawpawlin Pahto. Best for views, though, are the riverfront deluxe rooms at the river's edge. Breakfast is served under tree shade with river views too.

Bagan Hotel HOTEL $$$
(✆60032; www.kmahotels.com; r from $60; ❋@🖳🏊) More modern and stylish than Thande, this 107-room hotel has bungalows with teak floors in a nice setting. The owner is friendly with the government (see p21).

🍴 Eating

Old Bagan's restaurants (between the Ananda Pahto and Tharabar Gate) are a logical central point for lunch. The nearby hotel restaurants add a little style (and kyat) to your meal.

TOP CHOICE **Be Kind to Animals the Moon** VEGETARIAN, BAMAR $$
(off Bagan-Nyaung U Rd; dishes K1500-3000; ⊙7am-10pm; 🖋) The original among the couple of vegetarian restaurants clustered near Tharabar Gate, this place offers a friendly welcome and delicious food including pumpkin and ginger soup, aubergine curry and a lime and ginger tea that the owners claim is good for stomach upsets.

Sarahba III/Gyi Gyi's VEGETARIAN, BAMAR $
(off Bagan-Nyaung U Rd; dishes from K300; ⊙6am-6pm) Join the crowds under a shady tree near the Tharabar Gate squatting on low chairs at green-painted tables and tucking into some of Bagan's best tucker, all freshly prepared and supremely tasty. There's no sign – the name is what local's jokingly call the place.

Scoopy's ICE CREAM $
(off Bagan-Nyaung U Rd; dishes from K300; ⊙11am-6pm) Run by the French-Burmese owners of the Black Bamboo in Nyaung U, this relaxed café and ice-cream parlour is something of a godsend. Toasted sandwiches, homemade muffins and treats such as Western chocolate bars are available – all great for picnic snacks while touring the temples.

Sarabha II CHINESE, INTERNATIONAL $$
(dishes K1200-8000; ⊙11am-9pm) Of the two Sarabhas back to back by the Tharabar Gate, we like the one behind best, away from the road. It's a great midday resting point for shade and its range of food (Chinese, Thai, Burmese, pizza). The food's good, and cheaper than hotel restaurants, but best are the cold towels handed out to wipe the dust off your face.

Golden Myanmar BAMAR $$
(Bagan-Nyaung U Rd; buffet K3000; ⊙10am-10pm) Keep-it-real seekers (and lots of horse-cart drivers) prefer this excellent roadside eatery with shaded seats on a brick floor. The 'buffet' (your pick of chicken, pork, fish or mutton curry) comes with the usual tableful of condiments. There's another location near Ananda Pahto.

Apart from the floating over Bagan by balloon, there are a couple more ways to see the temples in grand style. Indulge your inner princess by hiring the Cinderella-style **Victoria Horsecart** (☑60782, 09 650 1444; half/full day $35/55), a 120-year-old wooden horse-drawn carriage made in England that seats up to four passengers. It's owned by the same Burmese-French couple who run the Black Bamboo and Scoopys.

A Yangon-based Burmese-Italian couple are the driving force behind **Elephant Coach** (☑in Yangon 01-661 731, 09 503 7366; www.asiaelephantcoach.com), which has one of its three lovingly restored Chevrolet buses based in Bagan; the other two are in Yangon. An Orient Express compared to the typical clapped-out coach trundling Myanmar's roads, these beauties, decorated with teak and ironwood, seat six in high colonial comfort. Hiring one for six/12 hours of sightseeing, including driver and hostess serving fresh hand towels and soft drinks, costs US$250/380.

Shopping

Shwe War Thein Handicrafts Shop
HANDICRAFTS

(☑67032; shi@mptmail.net.mm; ☺6am-10pm peak season) Just east of Tharabar Gate (and well signed off the Bagan–Nyaung U Rd) is this popular treasure trove of Myanmar trinkets. The collection includes antique and new puppets (starting from $5), woodcarvings, chess sets, lacquerware and bronze pieces. Ask to see the antique section at the rear. Lacquerware selections are wider in Myinkaba and New Bagan.

Getting There & Away

Depending on water levels, boats from Mandalay arrive in Old Bagan near the Aye Yar Hotel. See p120 for more on boats leaving Nyaung U, the major gateway for buses, trains and planes out of Bagan.

Myinkaba

မြင်းကပါ

☑061

Like lacquerware? Bagan's most famous shopping zone is this otherwise sleepy village, about half a mile south of Old Bagan, which has been home to family-run lacquerware workshops for generations. At least a dozen workshops and storefronts are located around the smattering of choice *pahto* (temples) and stupas (p161) from the early Bagan period. And King Manuha, respectfully called the 'Captive King', built the poetic Manuha Paya while held here in the 11th century.

Shopping

Before pulling out your wallet, it's wise to stop at a handful of places to compare varying styles (and prices). Workshops (like the ones that follow) will show you the many stages of lacquerware-making and how lacquer is applied in layers, dried and engraved. There's refreshingly little pressure to buy at any of the workshops. But quality varies; often the best stuff is kept in air-conditioned rooms at the back. Most workshops and stores keep long hours (roughly 7am to 9pm during peak season).

Generally, you can bargain about 10% off the quoted prices – and no more. We priced higher-quality 14-layer (or higher) vases for $35, full tea sets with tray for $110, tea cups or rice bowls for $15 to $25 and jewellery boxes from $12. Seven-layer pieces are cheaper.

A few places to check out:

Art Gallery of Bagan
LACQUERWARE

English-speaking Maung Aung Myin has two rooms and a busy workshop on the road 200yd north of Mahamuni. Apart from the full range of lacquerware – including some beautiful and pricey cabinets and casks – it also has antique and new puppets ($20 to $150).

Family Lacquerware Work Shop
LACQUERWARE

Smaller workshop off the east side of the road, with a few more modern styles with less layers of lacquer and untraditional colours such as blue and yellow.

Golden Cuckoo
LACQUERWARE

Just behind the Manuha Paya, this family-run workshop spans four generations and focuses on 'traditional' designs, which are applied to some unusual objects, including a motorbike helmet ($250) and a guitar ($500).

ℹ Getting There & Away

Pick-ups running between New Bagan, Old Bagan and Nyaung U stop here.

New Bagan (Bagan Myothit)

ပုဂံမြို့သစ်

🎵061

Not as bustling as Nyaung U, even though it's closer to the juicy temples, New Bagan sprung into existence in 1990 when the government relocated the village from the Old Bagan area. The people have done the best to make the most of their new home, with a network of shady, dusty roads away from the river. It's laid-back and definitely the site of Bagan's best midrange accommodation and riverside restaurants.

🛏 Sleeping

All prices here include breakfast and all places claim to have hot water.

TOP CHOICE Kumudara Hotel　　HOTEL $$

(✆65142, in Yangon 01-295 472; www.kumudara -bagan.com; superior s/d $18/22, junior ste s/d $26/30, ste $40; ❖ ☀ @ ☀) No hotel boasts better balcony views of the mighty sprawl of red-brick temples than Kumudara. Opt for the chic junior suites and suites in a green

geometrical building that fits well with the arid, desert-like setting. Inside, rooms have a playful mix of wood panelling, modern art and retro-style safe boxes. Kumudara has a pool and a restaurant, plus half an hour of free internet access in the business centre.

Thazin Garden Hotel　　HOTEL $$

(✆65035, in Yangon 01-537 898; www.thazingarden hotel.net; s $45-55, d $55-65; ☀ ☀) Set down a dusty path near a clutch of small temples, this oasis of palms and flowers and shaded walkways is an irresistible choice. The deluxe 'bungalows' are built in a paya-style red-brick complex with a sea of dark luxurious teak inside and a balcony overlooking a 13th-century pagoda within the grounds – dinner is served on the lawn in front. The 'superior' rooms are just as inviting with hanging paper umbrellas, a chess board and deck area. It has a pool (nonguests can swim for $5), a spa and a billiards table.

Thiri Marlar Hotel　　HOTEL $$

(✆65050, 65229; thirimarlar@mptmail.net.mm; s/d $23/25; ☀) The teak walkways leading to the 15 lovely rooms are wrapped around a small pagoda-style dining room, though most guests eat breakfast (or prearranged dinners) on the roof deck with temple views. Spotless rooms are rather compact but inviting, with

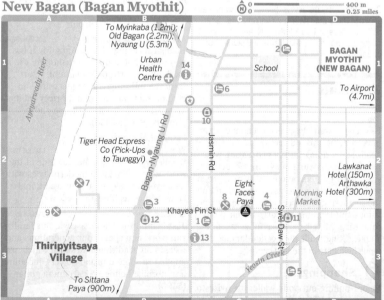

New Bagan (Bagan Myothit)

shiny wood floors, small rugs and views of bougainvillea draping over the wall outside.

Arthawka Hotel
HOTEL $

(☎65321, in Yangon 01-502 479; www.visitmyanmar.net/hotels; 160 Cherry Rd; s $25-30, d $30-35) Big glazed clay pots and wicker chairs dot the spacious lobby of this friendly 60-room hotel. It offers spacious rooms sporting wood floors and white tiled bathrooms. In the centre of the complex is a saltwater pool, shaded by palms.

Lawkanat Hotel
HOTEL $$

(☎65046; s/d $25/30; ❄) This 20-room complex, just off the main road, has black-tiled decks leading to simple green-carpeted rooms with giant front windows, which look out over the peaceful gardens. It works.

NK Betel Nut Hotel
HOTEL $$

(☎65054, 09-204 2052; Khayea Pin St; s/d $20/25; ❄) A bit overpriced for what you get, this funny group of cabins – a few at the front with log facades – offers OK rooms with red carpet, a little TV and an old tiled bathroom. You can find the same for less in Nyuang U, but it's clean and the management are welcoming.

Bagan Central Hotel
HOTEL $

(☎65057, 65265; Main Rd; s/d from $15/20; ❄) These good-value bamboo-style rooms with pebbled facades are compact and clean and set around a tree-shaded courtyard where breakfast is served. For rooms with tubs add $5 to the rates.

Kyi Kyi Mya Guest House
HOTEL $

(☎65092; Main Rd; s/d $15/20; ❄) This simple, shady complex has straightforward rooms with scruffy carpets laid atop concrete floors, old air-con unit, tiny TV, and attached bathroom. There is a portrait of General Than Shwe in the reception, which is also decorated with Bambi and Thumper print curtains.

✖ Eating

New Bagan's Main Rd is lined with several Chinese and Burmese restaurants. Many foreigners grab a meal on the riverside, just west – there are several and you can either be lost amid the tour groups or have the place to yourself.

Green Elephant
BAMAR, ASIAN $$

(mains K7000-9000; ⊙11am-4pm & 6-10pm) The good-value and tasty Myanmar set meal (K8000) comes with a couple of curries, vegetable tempura, soup, dessert and coffee. There are small and large portions of other dishes (including local curries). But it's the setting that's the deal, with shaded tables on a lawn overlooking the Ayeyarwady River.

Silver House
BAMAR, ASIAN $$

(Main Rd; mains K5000; ⊙7am-10pm) A welcoming family-run restaurant that offers large, tasty portions of dishes such as traditional Myanmar chicken curry and tomato salad.

The King Si Thu
BAMAR, ASIAN $$

(☎65117; mains K4500; ⊙8am-10pm) Another riverside setting, another Myanmar restaurant mainly serving Chinese and Thai dishes such as sweet-and-sour pork, or fish with ginger. Order one hour ahead for Burmese food. There's a half-hour puppet show at 7.30pm.

🔒 Shopping

New Bagan has several good options for lacquerware – at all you can watch artisans at work.

TOP CHOICE Black Elephant Studio
LACQUERWARE

(www.lacquerinstitute.org; 1-25 Swel Daw St; ⊙8am-5pm) Set up by British-Ukrainian

New Bagan (Bagan Myothit)

artist Veronica Gritsenko in 1999, this small studio produces lacquerware in the traditional style, but with exquisite unique and unusual designs.

Tun Handicrafts/Moe Moe's LACQUERWARE
(Main Rd; ⊗8am-9pm) A large showroom with mix of traditional and modern lacquerware (exposed-bamboo tea cups for $4 and rice bowls from $7).

Bagan House LACQUERWARE
(9 Jasmin Rd; www.baganhouse.com; ⊗8am-7pm) Worth seeking out on the backstreets, this stylish showroom has a mix of cheap and higher-priced lacquerware, as well as the usual artisans at work. Unlike other places, it does accept credit cards if you spend over $100, with the usual 5% surcharge.

ℹ Information

Exotissimo (☑60383; ⊗9am-6pm Mon-Fri, 9am-noon Sat) High-end agent, which can arrange Mt Popa tours ($65 including guide and car) or rent sturdy mountain bikes ($10 per day).

Internet Available at several places along the main street.

Myanmar Travels & Tours (MTT; ☑65040; ⊗8.30am-4.30pm) The government-run tourist office can help organise excursions to visit Chin State (see p287).

ℹ Getting There & Around

See Nyaung U for most transport connections.

Tiger Head Express Co (Bagan-Chauk Rd) sends daily pick-up trucks to Kalaw and Taunggyi (K12,000, front seat K15,000), departing at 5am.

There are airline offices on Main Rd. **U Zaw Weik** (☑65017; zawweik@myanmar.com.mm; Main Rd) helps with air tickets or can get you a taxi to Mt Popa (K42,000), Mt Popa and Salay (K42,000), around Bagan (K30,000) or to Kalaw or Mandalay ($115).

Bicycle rental starts at K5000 per day; you can get a mountain bike at Exotissimo. See p115 for more on getting around the Bagan site.

AROUND BAGAN

Mt Popa

ပုပ္ပါးတောင်
☑02

Like a Burmese Mt Olympus, Mt Popa is the spiritual HQ to Myanmar's infamous '37 nat' and thus a premier venue for nat worship; for more on these pre-Buddhist spirits, see p338.

Mt Popa proper is the 4980ft extinct volcano covered in lush forests protected within the Popa Mountain Park and home to the exclusive Popa Mountain Resort; on the mountain's lower flank is Popa Taung Kalat, a towerlike 2418ft volcanic plug crowned with a gilded Buddhist temple accessed by 777 steps. The volcano last erupted some 250,000 years ago (some locals suggest 40 million years ago). One local told us: 'Popa is like the sun or moon; no one can guess how old it is.'

From the temple there are mammoth views back towards the Myingyan Plain and beyond. It's gorgeous, but only a few visitors come on a half-day trip from Bagan, and of those who do, many shrug their shoulders because they don't have a guide to enliven the experience with stories and explanations – going on a day trip to Mt Popa without some sort of guide is like watching a foreign-language film without subtitles.

One revered guide to Mt Popa is U Taung Hwin (per day $20), a gentle old soul with good English and plenty of experience leading travellers around the culturally rich area. Ask for him by name at the Shwe Taung Tarn Restaurant, on Nyaung U's main road.

Myanmar superstition says you shouldn't wear red or black on the mountain, nor should you curse, say bad things about other people or bring along any meat (especially pork). Any of these actions could offend the resident nat, who might then retaliate with a spate of ill fortune. And no-one likes a mad nat.

◎ Sights

Mother Spirit of Popa Nat Shrine NAT SHRINE
Before climbing Popa Taung Kalat, drop by the tiger-guarded shrine in the village at the foot of the mountain (just across from the steps guarded by elephant statues – there are loads of critters around here). Inside you'll find a display extending left and right from an inner hallway door of mannequin-like figures representing some of the 37 official nat, plus some Hindu deities and a few necromancers (the figures with goatees at the right end of the shrine).

In the shrine there are also other nat not counted among the official '37', including three principal figures: the **Flower-Eating Ogress** (aka Mae Wunna, or 'Queen Mother of Popa') and her two sons (to her left and right) **Min Gyi** and **Min Lay** (see p127).

A few other interesting nat here caught our attention. The plump Pyu goddess **Shin Nemi** (Little Lady) is a guardian for chil-

NAT MORAL: FULFIL YOUR DUTIES!

Sometimes it's hard being a *nat*. The namesake figure of the Mother Spirit of Popa & Nat Shrine is Mae Wunna. She was famous for her love of Byat-ta, one of King Anawrahta's servants – a flower-gathering Indian with superhuman powers – who neglected his duties and was executed for it.

Their two sons, Min Gyi and Min Lay, supposedly born atop Mt Popa, followed their father's tradition. They became servants of the king (often going to China), grew neglectful of their duties, and then *they* were executed. King Anawrahta, however, ordered a shrine built at the place of their execution (at Taungbyone, north of Mandalay), now the site of a huge festival (see p127). Many worshippers come to offer a blessing to these three. Mae Wunna and her sons are the central figures facing the entry to the shrine.

dren, and gets toy offerings during school exam time. She's the cute little thing clutching a green umbrella and a stuffed animal, midway down on the left of the shrine.

There have been a few Kyawswas in Myanmar spirit history, but the most popular is the Popa-born **Lord Kyawswa** (aka Drunk Nat), who spent his few years cockfighting and drinking. He boasts: 'If you don't like me, avoid me. I admit I'm a drunkard.' He's the guardian of gamblers and drunks and sits on a horse decked in rum and whiskey bottles, to the right.

Locals pray to **Shwe Na Be** (Lady with Golden Sides) when a snake comes into their house. She's the woman holding a *naga* (serpent) near the corner to the left.

Mt Popa Temple   BUDDHIST TEMPLE
From the *nat* shrine start up the steps under a covered walkway and past the usual rows of trinket and souvenir shops and shrines to a revered local medicine man, Pomin Gawng. At a steady pace it shouldn't take you more than 20 minutes to reach the top of this impressive rocky crag crowned with a picturesque complex of monasteries, stupas and shrines. Along the way, you'll pass platoons of cheeky monkeys and a small army of locals selling drinks and endeavouring (not always successfully) to keep the steps clean of monkey poo – for this they'll request a tip.

Views from the top are fantastic. You may be fortunate enough to spot one of the slow-walking hermit monks called *yeti,* who wear tall, peaked hats and visit occasionally.

Popa Mountain Park   HIKING
A variety of **hiking trails** thread through the Popa Mountain Park, leading to the rim of the volcano crater and to viewpoints and waterfalls. Along the way, you'll be able to observe the difference in the vegetation. The heights capture the moisture of passing clouds, causing rain to drop on the plateau and produce a profusion of trees, flowering plants and herbs, all nourished by the rich volcanic soil. In fact, the word *popa* is derived from the Sanskrit word for flower.

Trekking here is best done with local guides. Ask at the turn-off, a mile or so back from Popa village (towards Bagan), or enquire at the Popa Mountain Resort, half-way up the peak. From the resort, the hike to the crater takes around four hours.

If you come by taxi, ask the driver to point out bits of **petrified forest**, which are strewn along either side of the road west of Popa village.

✨ Festivals & Events

Mt Popa hosts two huge **nat pwe** (spirit festivals) yearly, one beginning on the full moon of Nayon (May/June) and another on the full moon of Nadaw (November/December). Before King Anawrahta's time, thousands of animals were sacrificed to the *nat* during these festivals, but this practice has been prohibited since the Bagan era. Spirit possession and overall drunken ecstasy are still part of the celebration, however.

There are several other minor festivals, including ones held on the full moons of Wagaung (July/August) and Tagu (March/April), which celebrate the departure and return of the famous Taungbyone *nat* (Min Gyi and Min Lay). Once a year, the Taungbyone *nat* are believed to travel a spirit circuit that includes Mt Popa, Taungbyone (about 14 miles north of Mandalay) and China.

🛏 Sleeping

Most visitors find a couple of hours with Mt Popa's monkeys enough. However, there are a couple of guesthouses in Popa village (rooms about $15). There's also the lovely, lonely

FRUIT OF THE PALMS

On the way to or from Mt Popa have your driver pause at one of the several toddy and jaggery (palm sugar) operations that are set up along the road. The operators will give you a basic demo of how the alcoholic drink and sweets are made from the sap of the toddy palm. After, you can taste and buy the products.

Popa Mountain Resort (☏69169, in Yangon 01-503 831; rsvpopa@myanmar.com.mm; r superior $70, r deluxe garden/mountain view $150/200; ✳@≋≋), owned by Htoo Trading Company, a business affiliated with the government (see p21).Nonguests can take a dip in the pool ($5) or have a meal (Myanmar set menu for $12) at the good restaurant while overlooking the pagodas atop Popa Taung Kalat.

ⓘ Getting There & Away

Most travellers visit Mt Popa in half a day by share taxi or by organised tour from their hotel. In Nyaung U, guesthouses could get you a slot in a share taxi (without guide); a whole taxi is $35 and, at a squeeze, can fit four plus the driver.

At research time a pick-up truck left Nyaung U's bus station at 8.30am for Mt Popa (K3000, two hours); it left Popa for Nyaung U at 1pm. Less conveniently, you could take an hourly pick-up from Nyaung U to Kyaukpadaung (90 minutes) and then another to Mt Popa (45 minutes). This would take a full day.

Salay

ဝင်္လ
☏063

This Bagan-era village, 22 miles south of Bagan, is rooted in the 12th and 13th centuries, when Bagan's influence spread. It remains an active religious centre, with something like 50 monasteries for the 7000 or so residents! Day-trippers make it here to visit a few of the 19th-century wooden monasteries and some select Bagan-era shrines, and peek at a handful of untouched British colonial buildings.

It can be paired with Mt Popa on a full-day trip, though the two are in different directions from Bagan. Eating choices tend to be better in nearby **Chauk** (famous for its production of the sweet tamarind flakes that are served at the end of all meals in Bagan),

but you can get noodles in the Salay market. There are no hotels.

◉ Sights

Youqson Kyaung   BUDDHIST MONASTERY
ရပ်စုံကျောင်း

(☏09-4721 5427; admission $5, camera fee $2; ⊙9am-4.30pm) Designed as a copy of the Crown Prince House in Mandalay, and built from 1882 to 1892, the huge wooden monastery is the best place to start a visit in Salay.

Along two of its exterior sides are detailed original carvings displaying 19th-century court life and scenes from the Jataka (stories of the Buddha's past lives) and Ramayana (one of India's best-known legends); sadly another side's pieces were looted in the 1980s. Inside, the 17th- to 19th-century pieces are behind glass cases, while the Bagan-era woodcarvings (including a massive throne backdrop) stand in open view.

The monastery was renovated twice in the 1990s and the government's Department of Archaeology runs the site (see p21); on-site staff can point you to other nearby sites in and outside town.

Bagan-Era Monuments   BUDDHIST TEMPLES
Little of the history of Salay's 103 ruins is known outside a small circle of Myanmar archaeologists working with limited funds. It is said that most of the monuments in Salay weren't royally sponsored, but were built by the lower nobility or commoners – thus there's nothing on the grand scale of Bagan's biggest structures.

In the pagoda-filled area about 110yd east of Youqson Kyaung, you can see Paya Thonzu (Temples 18, 19 and 20), which is a small trio of brick shrines with *sikhara* (Indian-style corncob-like temple finials) and some faded murals inside. The westernmost shrine (to the left if you come from the museum) has the most visible murals and also a narrow set of stairs leading to a small terrace. If it's locked, ask at Youqson Kyaung.

A more interesting feature is the modern makeover of the Bagan-era Shinpinsarkyo Paya (Temple 88), about 4 miles southwest of town via a dodgy road (and a couple of dodgy bridges). Inside the glass- and tile-filled pagoda, you'll find an original 13th-century wood Lokanat (Mahayana Bodhisattva guardian spirit).

The nearby northern entrance passageway features interesting 19th-century 3-D murals (some are torture to see). Original woodcarvings abound, some of which are painted afresh in original design.

Another mile or so south of Shinpinsarkyo (most taxis won't drive it, but it's an easy 15-minute walk) is Temple 99, an unassuming 13th-century shrine that features 578 painted Jataka scenes inside. The last 16 paintings to the left as you enter represent the '16 Dreams of King Kosala'.

Other Sights

An interesting aspect of Salay is the faded colonial-era buildings dotted around town, a few of which still feature the Royal Crown high up on their facades (look around the market area, about 220yd west of the museum). This area is especially worth visiting, as few buildings in Myanmar still sport the lion-guarded crown.

In the complex about 500yd west of the Paya Thonzu, the Mann Paya is a modern pagoda housing a 20ft gold Buddha made of straw lacquer. As the story goes, the Buddha image was originally located near Monywa and was washed downstream during an 1888 monsoon – all the way to Salay. Ask for a peek inside from the latched door at the back.

North 500yd of the Paya Thonzu, the monastery and meditation centre of Sasanayaunggyi Kyaung (a stop-off point for day-trippers) features a lovely 19th-century glass armoire with painted Jataka panels and 400-year-old scripture in Pali inside. The monks are chatty and friendly, and will ask for a donation for their on-site school.

ℹ Getting There & Away

Salay is 22 miles south of Bagan on a road that's often flood damaged. You pass through the larger town of Chauk on the way. From Chauk, another road goes east to Kyaukpadaung, with a turn-off for Magwe.

A hired taxi for a four- or five-hour trip to Salay from Nyaung U runs from $45. It's technically possible to come by pick-up truck from Nyaung U in three hours (not including a change in Chauk), but it's not advisable, as some sites in Salay aren't close to the drop-off point.

Pakokku

ပခုက္ကူ

☑062

A transit point for wayward travellers on the west side of the Ayeyarwady River, Pakokku was a quiet backwater until 2007, when it found itself front-and-centre in international headlines. Monks from the Myo Ma Ahle

monastery here kick-started the nationwide protests against rising petrol prices that became the ill-fated 'Saffron Revolution'.

Since then Pakokku – famed for its tobacco and *thanakha* – has reverted to type as an interesting and friendly place, even if you just have a couple of hours before catching a bus to Monywa or a boat to Nyaung U. Should you choose to linger, there's a riverside homestay that's basic, but which many guests rank as a highlight of their trip. One of the town's biggest *pwe* festivals, **Thihoshin**, is held during Nayon (May/June).

A new bridge – the longest in Myanmar – across the Ayeyarwady is under construction and, when completed in the next couple of years, will speed up connections between Pakokku and Bagan, which is only 16 miles south.

◉ Sights

If time is limited, you'll get the most out of Pakokku by seeing its market, checking out some of its temples and monasteries – including one monastery with a giant clocktower – or just wandering its picturesquely decrepit, slightly tropical side streets, which feature old homes backing onto the Ayeyarwady River.

About 17 miles northeast, on the way to Monywa, are the remains of Pakhangyi, a 19th-century wooden monastery. About 3 miles east of Pakhangyi (via the road behind the big modern pagoda) is the destroyed frame of Pakhanngeh Kyaung, which was once the country's largest wooden monastery. Many of its 332 teak pillars still stand, and the area – near the fork of the Ayeyarwady and Kaladan Rivers – makes for interesting exploration. A taxi here from Pakokku is K25,000 to K30,000.

⊨ Sleeping

TOP CHOICE Mya Yatanar Inn   HOMESTAY $
(☎21457; 75 Lanmataw St; r per person K6000, with shared bathroom K5000) Charming, English-speaking grandma Mya Mya, her daughter and four granddaughters will welcome you to their 100-year-old home on the river, a couple of blocks east of the market. Rooms are super-basic and grubby, but bearable once you fall under the hospitable spell of these women. Electricity is mostly off during the day (as with all of Pakokku), and most rooms share the cold-water bathroom and squat toilet. They can rustle up a delicious meal for under K1000, help you get a taxi

deal to see the sights, or show you to local pagodas or where tattooing is done.

Tha Pye No Guest House   GUESTHOUSE **$$**
(☎21166, 23166; 68 Myoma Rd; r K12,000-20,000; ✹) If you need things like 24-hour electricity, satellite TV, minibar fridge or even a night dress, then the newly built superior rooms here are a reasonable choice. Instant pot noodles, coffee or green tea constitute breakfast. Skip the cheaper cell-like rooms, which share a bathroom with a cold shower.

① Getting There & Away

Minibuses shuttle to and from Monywa (K1300, three hours) leaving at 6am, 9am, 11am and 2pm from the corner of Tinda and Aung Taw Mu Sts. From the main bus station on Myoma Rd there are three services daily to Mandalay (K3000, seven hours).

Ferries to Nyaung U (K3400, two hours) leave at 5am, 10am and 1.30pm.

Monywa
ဝ
☎071 / POP 180,000

Pronounced in two syllables (mon-ywa), Monywa is an engaging if slightly scrappy trade town that makes a sensible stopping point if you're looping between Mandalay

and Bagan via Pakokku. A series of interesting attractions in the surrounding countryside (p132) can happily fill a couple of days, and for the adventurous few who boat-hop the Chindwin, Monywa is the logical start/end point. The town itself is big, hot and flat, with relatively little to see beyond the markets and the pleasant Chindwin riverside setting, though two large, central pagoda complexes, **Shwezigon Paya** and **Su Taung Pye Zedi** are well worth a wander.

🛏 Sleeping

Breakfast is included in all three hotels reviewed. If these three are full, you'll be stuck with the central but miserable **Golden Arrow Hotel** (☎21548; Bogyoke Rd; s/d from $10/16) or the inconveniently located Great Hotel down by the bus station.

Win Unity   RESORT HOTEL **$$**
(☎22438, 22013; tintinmoe@mptmaill.net.mm; Bogyoke Rd; s $35-50, d $45-65, tr $60-80; ✹@☒) Easily Monywa's swankiest option, the Win is a series of tile-roofed modern bungalow rooms set on the lakeside, less than half a mile north of the central area. They're all irreproachably neat and comfortable, but think low-rise condo rather than colonial gem. Lake-view rooms (s/d/tr $50/65/80) command a premium. Beware that the nine

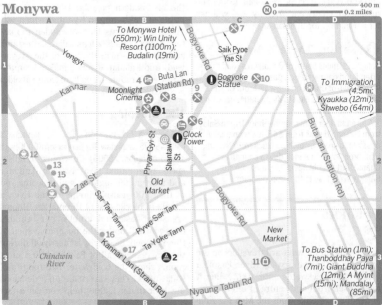

far plainer 'standard' rooms (s/d $25/30) are hidden away above staff workstations and are aimed more for drivers rather than for guests. The inviting pool has a swim-up bar and Jacuzzi area, but mosquito repellent is advised.

Monywa Hotel   HOTEL **$$**
(☑21581, 21549; Bogyoke Rd; s $20-25, d $25-30; ✱) Set well back from the busy street amid birdsong and creeper-draped trees, this well-maintained series of multiroom cabins is popular with small tour groups. Interiors feel a little dated and the colour schemes are hideous, but even the cheaper rooms are fair-sized with effective air-conditioning, desk, fridge, piping-hot showers, satellite TV and comfy beds. Superior rooms score a bathtub and a chair on your terrace.

Shwe Taung Tarn   BUDGET HOTEL **$**
(☑21478; 70 Station Rd; r per person $8-12; ✱) For years Shwe Taung Tarn has been Monywa's most popular budget choice. The facade looks unkempt – and it's worth skipping the front building's $8 rooms, which are worse – but behind is an unexpectedly pleasant little garden area and a pair of newer two-storey buildings. Rooms there remain good value for the price, but while they were once relatively stylish, many now suffer seriously scuffed floors and gob-stained walls.

131

🍴 Eating & Drinking

Shwe Taung Tarn has a restaurant section beside its budget hotel that cooks fine Chinese food and has an unexpectedly chic rooftop section.

Pleasant Island   CHINESE **$$**
(Myakanthar Lake, Bogyoke Rd; mains K3000-8000, rice/beer K500/3500; ⊘7am-10pm; 🅟) Monywa's finest restaurant occupies a tiny lake island across upper Bogyoke Rd from the Win Unity Hotel. It's a photogenic spot at sunset, linked to the shore by a roly-poly wooden bridge. Fine if pricey Chinese food is served at open pavilions: bring mosquito repellent. If you want (partial) lake views at far lower prices, walk 200m further south and cross the side-road, where there's a simpler Sino-Burmese eatery.

Yad Khel Taung   BEER STATION **$**
(Bogyoke St; mains K1500-4000; ⊘8am-10pm) This friendly if typical draft beer station serves Shan and Chinese food, but is most remarkable for the tiny amuse-bouche plates of *namakyien,* a delicious local sesame-based humus that arrive free with most meals.

Aung Pan   BURMESE **$**
(Phyar Gyi St; meals K2000; ⊘9am-9pm) The typically generous multi-dish spread arriving with your choice of curry includes a superlative *khayandi thuk* (mashed roast eggplant). The setting is unremarkable, but helpful Bagyi in the attached computer-repair shop speaks English. Similar meals are served at **Su** and **Zwe Mahn**, both on Station Rd.

Shine's Shine   CHINESE **$**
(Saik Pyoe Yae St; mains K2000-4500, rice/draft beer K100/600; ⊘10am-10pm) Oddly recycled from a vehicle-repair yard, but shaded by fine trees full of coloured lights, this large, busy outdoor space serves fair-priced delicacies, including eel, duck and catfish. The crumbed Slavia fish in lemon sauce (K2800) was scrumptious if MSG-loaded.

Night Market   FOOD STALLS **$**
(Bogyoke St; ⊘5-10.30pm) Various cheap eats between the clock tower and Bogyoke (Aung San) statue.

Monywa

❶ Information

Netizen (Shantaw St; per hr K500; ☺8am-10pm) Comfortable downstairs room with fast connections. English spoken.

Nan Chung (Zae St; ☺7.30am-6pm) Kyat for dollar exchange at bearable rates from this olde-worlde Chinese grocery (yellow shutters at the corner of Kannar St).

❶ Getting There & Away

Air

The airport is 12km north, off the Budalin road. Some Tuesdays the government's Myanma Airways (see p21) stops in Monywa between Mandalay and Homalin, but as usual the decision to fly is only made the day before, so tickets can't be reserved until Monday afternoon.

Boat

There is no public service downriver to Pakokku, but daily boats link the towns and villages of the upper Chindwin River. Foreigners need permits, but permits for the journey to Kalewa are usually organised within a day or two (see boxed text). Express boats to Kalewa (foreigner/local K15,000/5000, around 13 hours) depart 4.30am daily, operated by one of three Strand Rd companies on a rotating cycle, **MGRG** (☎22987), **Ngwe Shwe Oo** (☎23051) or **Shwe Nadi** (☎23488). Buy tickets one day before, permit in hand. Stops should include the attractive old settlements of Kani, Mingin and Kan/Kyidaw. Departing Thursdays at 7am, the IWT (government; see p21) river ferry moves slower than political evolution. Allow up to four days from Monywa to Kalewa in the dry season. In the rainy season IWT boats become more frequent and travel further north.

Bus

Monywa's bus station is just over a mile southeast of the clock tower down Bogyoke St, hidden behind the Great Hotel.

MANDALAY Several companies, including Mahanwe and AGB, operate hourly buses 5am to 4pm (K1700, 3¼ to four hours).

PAKOKKU AGB buses (K1300, 4½ hours) leave at 6.30am, 8.30am, 12.30pm and 3pm. Other companies leave at 8am, 10.30am and 1.15pm. Take the first bus if you want to to be sure of a same-day ferry connection from Pakokku to Nyaung U (last departure 1.30pm).

SHWEBO Once or twice hourly from 5am to 1pm plus at 3pm (K1100, 3½ hours). The attractive rural route passes through **Kyaukka**, famed for its lacquerware cottage industry, but local help is needed if you want to see much there.

Train

MANDALAY Departs noon ($3, six hours). The trip, in an uncomfortable three-box-car train, takes twice as long as the bus and costs almost twice the price.

❶ Getting Around

Motorbikes/trishaws/three-wheelers to the centre from the bus station cost K1000/1000/1500. All, along with white, plain-clothes taxis, linger near the northern Shwezigon Paya entrance, while outside the Shwe Taung Tarn you might find **Saw Tha Hla**, a calm-driving, super-helpful guide/motorcycle taxi driver who speaks functional English.

Around Monywa

If you have only one full day, the most popular option is to visit Hpo Win Daung caves followed by Thanboddhay and Bodhi Tataung. The latter is west-facing, and so is best seen in afternoon sunlight.

SOUTH OF MONYWA

A Myint   ANCIENT VILLAGE

Little visited by foreigners apart from occasional Chindwin cruise groups, A Myint is a charmingly unspoilt riverside village dominated by a series of 336 higgledy piggledy **ancient stupas** in varying stages of collapse. All are compactly ranged around a

---

CHINDWIN PERMITS

To travel as far north as Kalewa, the permit procedure can prove comparatively painless. Apply Monday to Thursday before 4pm at the Monywa immigration office (four miles east of centre towards Shwebo) and the necessary letter should be ready within 24 hours. To continue further north (eg Mawleik, Homalin or Khamti), the permits are far more complicated to organise: generally they're limited to organised groups and you'll need to contact Yangon agencies for help. Allow at least three weeks' preparation. This is usually done in tandem with an expensive cruise program. The **Pandaw** (www.pandaw1947.com) made one such 10-day cruise in 2010 (s/d $4090/6300), and **GMT** (www.myanmartravelagent.com) can organise tailor-made small-boat cruises. A few Yangon travel agencies can get permits for those on semi-independent packages where you stay in local guesthouses and use local boats, but the cost is still prohibitive at around $2000 per person.

In 1056 the King of Bago became a vassal of Bagan's ascendant ruler, Anawrahta, who later sent his armies to bolster Bago against the Khmers. Among the tribute gifts that symbolised the relationship was one of four Buddha hair relics sent to Bagan and now enshrined within Bagan's Shwesandaw pagoda. Another 'gift' was the King of Bago's beautiful daughter Princess Manisanda (aka Khin U). To collect these priceless prizes, Anawrahta sent his most trusted commanders, the 'four paladins', led by his son and foremost general Kyanzittha. But as they returned Kyanzittha was overcome by temptation for the future queen, kicking off a classic love triangle. Once their affair was discovered, Kyanzittha was bound and sentenced to death by his furious father. However, the magic lance that was supposed to execute him instead broke the ropes that bound him and Kyanzittha made a fairy-tale escape, grabbing the lance and fleeing in a fishing boat. After a series of similarly implausible triumphs against Anawrahta's search parties, Kyanzittha settled in Kaungbyu, before finally returning to Bagan in 1077, only to rekindle the affair with Manisanda. Today, there is some controversy as to where Kaungbyu was, but Monywa guides are adamant that it was the delightful little village of A Myint (p132).

little **wooden monastery** and a few retain interior murals. Another minor attraction is the **British-era house** (62 Seidan St) of the former village chief. It's private and still owned by the charming original family, who might wind up their gramophone for you or show off their 1920s sepia photos.

A major attraction is the lovely 15-mile ride through agricultural villages from Monywa on a lane that's narrow but unusually well asphalted. Around half way look northeast for brief, distant views.

SOUTHEAST OF MONYWA

If you're driving between Mandalay and Monywa, the following sites can be conveniently visited as a short detour en route. However, if you're using public transport, you'd be wiser to visit on a return excursion from Monywa, costing around K5000/8000 by motorbike/three-wheeler and taking around three hours.

Thanboddhay Paya   BUDDHIST TEMPLE
သမ္မုဒ္ဓဘုရား

(Monye Sambuddhe) The central feature of this carnivalesque complex is a large mid-20th-century temple whose unique roof is layered with rows of gilt mini-stupas. Its flanks burst gaudily bright colours and are flanked by 30ft-high concrete obelisks set with uncountable minuscule Buddha shapes. The multiply arched **temple interior** (admission $3; ⊙6am-5pm) is plastered with so many Buddha images, large and small, that it feels like you're walking through a Buddha house of mirrors. However, while intriguing, you'll get the idea in two minutes and some visi-

tors make do with peeping in for free. Thanboddhay's kitschfest continues in the surrounding pastel-hued monks' quarters and with two huge white concrete elephants at the site's gateway. It's 1.5km off the Mandalay road, 10km from Monywa.

Bodhi Tataung   WORLD'S BIGGEST BUDDHA
ဗောဓိတစ်ထောင်

Another 8km east from Thanboddhay, the name of this vast hillside Buddha-rama translates as '1000 Buddhas'. But for most visitors, only two of them really count. Opened in 2008, the glimmering 424ft **standing Buddha** is claimed to be the world's tallest, and it utterly dominates the landscape for miles around. Inside the multi-storey torso, seemingly interminable stairways link painted galleries, many lower ones depicting gruesome hell scenes. You might hope that climbing to Buddha's head would take you, artistically at least, to Nirvana. However, so far at least, visitors' progress is blocked at the 16th floor, barely half way up. A spiritual message? The interior closes at 5pm.

Lower down the hillside lounges a slightly smaller but still enormous 312ft **reclining Buddha**. It's hardly refined and the dark interior contains poorly maintained tableaux: enter through the left buttock.

Note that both giant Buddhas face west, so for best photos come in the late afternoon.

If you're feeling inspired, the Bodhi Tataung site hosts many other minor fascinations, including a whole garden of identical sitting Buddhas under concrete parasols, and the gilded 430ft stupa **Aung Setkya**

SPIRULINA

An algae that grows in alkaline, subtropical lakes, Spirulina is named for its coiled spiral (or more accurately helix) shape, which you'll only notice when looking through a microscope. Harvested and dried, Spirulina was once a food-source for Aztec people. Today it's a popular dietary supplement said to help reduce cholesterol, lower blood pressure and counter hay fever. In Myanmar, Spirulina is best known as an ingredient of Mandalay Brewery's popular 'anti-aging' beer. You can visit a government Spirulina 'farm' at Twin Daung and buy a few Spirulina products at the government emporium (see p21), upstairs within a dowdy Monywa shopping centre.

Paya, which has lovely views from its upper rim (climbed via an inner passageway).

Carry your sandals to save your feet from gravel dents on connecting roads.

NORTH OF MONYWA

Wizened old neem trees and many an attractive stupa enliven the busy, well-paved road leading north from Monywa. After 19 miles, Budalin is a small junction settlement with a basic noodle-shop, from which it's still rather a slog to reach the area's minor attractions. But you'll certainly be getting far, far off the tourist radar.

Twin Daung   CRATER LAKE

Twin Daung is one of four volcanic crater lakes in Myanmar, from whose swirling green waters Spirulina is cultivated (see p134). You can visit the lakeside **Spirulina factory** (admission free, ☺8am-4.30pm Mon-Sat) to see the concrete cultivation tanks, peer through a microscope at the algae's incredible spiral form and see a range of packaged Spirulina-based products (manufactured elsewhere and not for sale here). The palm-fronted lakeside has a certain south-sea charm and views from the crater rim are very wide without being enormously spectacular.

Access is by a 13km unpaved lane that doubles back to the southwest, starting just a few yards after the toll gate as you arrive in Budalin from the south.

Payagyi   BUDDHIST MONASTERY

The large Payagyi stupa and its oversized chinthe face an abrupt twin-peaked hill, topped with a stupa and castle-like rocky outcrop and said to have an indelible footprint of Bagan-era King Kyanzittha at its base. Now boxed within concrete walls and tin roof, the empty front prayer hall retains its 170-year-old teak pillars. Its carved-stone floor tiles, telling Ramayana tales, have been moved for safe keeping to a museum shed: notice number 274 featuring Hanuman (the monkey god)

riding a sheep and smoking a cheroot. The lovable wooden monastery building seems oversized for five novices, one monk and the young abbot (who speaks a little English).

It's 30km from the central junction in Budalin (marked by a golden horseback Bandula statue, 500m north of the Twin Daung turning), where you veer left. Keep left again after 3km then continue 22km to Ta Kook Ta Nel. Turn right after the little row of teahouses then follow the track 5km to Payagyi. It's a long way to come for one monastery, but the rural scenes en route are very attractive, especially along the asphalted first 9km after Budalin through cottonfields, sunflowers and Palmyra palms to Nyaung Kai/Ywathar, which has a massive Shwezigon pagoda in a field at its southeast edge.

WEST OF MONYWA

Hpo Win Daung   BUDDHA CAVE-NICHE COMPLEX
ဖိုးဝင်းတောင်

(admission $2) Monywa's biggest draw for antiquity-hunters, this rural complex of 492 buddha chambers was carved into a limestone hillside between the 14th and 18th centuries. None of the 'caves' are more than a few yards deep, and many are just big enough for a single image but a few of the best (notably caves 478 and 480) have retained some colourful, well-executed murals. The area is fairly large and there's no map so some visitors prefer to engage an informal guide (around K4000) who is likely to be friendly but not especially informative. Without a guide, just head up and left from the starting point and don't worry – you don't need to climb nearly as high as the hilltop stupas that loom high on the ridge above. Around the complex, cheeky monkeys are all too keen to let you gain merit by donating to them food.

Some 700m beyond the restaurants and souvenir stands of Hpo Win 'village' lies **Shwe Ba Taung** (admission $2), a smaller, contrastingly different set of 46 cave chambers accessed from pathways cut around 25 feet vertically down into the limestone. The buddha images are larger and far newer than those of the main site but the intriguing overall effect is of a Buddhist Disneyland set in a miniature Petra. Squint at Hpo Win Daung as you return and you might see why locals think the hill looks like a reclining buddha.

ℹ️ Getting There & Away

The fastest access to the sites from Monywa is to cross the Chindwin River by boat then continue 23km west (the caves are 6km southwest of the main Pale road). From Strand Rd in Monywa, simple open-top ferry boats take locals across the Chindwin River for K200 each but foreigners must charter a whole boat, K2500 each way for up to five people plus K700 per motorbike. Boats run approximately 6am to 8pm.

Once across, waiting jeeps (carrying up to six at a pinch) want K15,000 return including waiting time. Motorbike drivers on the west bank won't take foreigners due to the jeep monopoly but you can bring a bike (and driver) across with you. Renting a chauffeured motorbike costs around K8000 return (plus boat charges).

Visiting by taxi/motor-trishaw from Monywa (K20,000/35,000 return) you'll need to cross the big Chindwin Bridge. That adds 9 extra miles but allows a stop at the brilliantly perched if brash Shwe Taung Oo pagoda for 360-degree river and plain views. The route also passes some apocalyptic copper-mining shack-villages backed by a vast industrial-scale open pit. By motorbike you could go out by boat, back by bridge (K10,000 plus boat charges) and enjoy sunset from Shwe Taung Oo.

Myingyan
☎️🅕:🅑
♫ 066

On the Ayeyarwady River 45 miles north of Nyaung U (towards Mandalay), sprawling Myingyan (sorta rhymes with 'engine') sees very few travellers, as the major bus routes avoid the bumpier roads that pass through town. Some cycling groups pedal through, and occasionally long-distance boats stop at the Ayeyarwady River docks.

Most famous for its big prison, scrappy Myingyan boasts only a couple of slim reasons to pause here. About 1 mile east of the bus station, across the railway line, is the Bodhi Dat Taw Taik (meaning 'depository of Buddha's relics'), where you can see relics (teeth, hair, bone and even skin) of saintly monks down the ages housed in what was once the walk-in safe of a British colonial bank; you'll be given

a torch to peer at the relics stored in jars in the gloomy interior.

Roughly 1 mile south of the town's central market, via the north–south Mandalay–Meiktila Rd, is the Soon Lu Kyaung, a small monastery where you can see the remains, draped in monastic robes, of the revered monk Soon Lu Sayadaw. He died in 1951, though his body is (relatively) well preserved.

🛏️ Sleeping & Eating

One Star Drive In Inn   GUESTHOUSE $
(☎️21389; Myo Pat St, 16th quarter; r per person K8000; ❄️) This odd group of bungalows on a dusty side street is about half a mile southeast of the bus station. Mattresses are thin, and in the less than appealing attached bathrooms the showers are cold.

New Sein Moe Bamaw
Restaurant   CHINESE $$
(7/96 8-St; ◎10am-9pm) A block west of the busy central market, this serviceable restaurant offers standard, just edible fried rice, noodles and vegies – most of the patrons seem more interested in downing K600 mugs of beer. Next door, on the corner, is the Mr Tea teahouse.

ℹ️ Getting There & Away

Frequent buses and pick-up trucks leave from the station just east of the Myingyan to Meiktila road, a couple of blocks south of the market. Services go to Meiktila (back/front seat K1500/3000, three hours, half hourly 4am to 2.30pm) and Mandalay (K2000, five hours, eight or nine daily). A pick-up goes to Nyaung U (back/front seat K1500/3000, 2½ hours, 11am).

The slow daily train between Mandalay and Bagan stops in Myingyan.

YANGON–MANDALAY HIGHWAY

There are two routes buses and cars ply between Yangon and Mandalay: the pot-holed old Hwy No 1, which some call the 'high road' (though it runs west of the Shan Hills); and the new Yangon–Mandalay Expressway, dubbed the 'big road'. Neither are particularly gorgeous drives but both provide access to a couple of places of interest en route to the north: the former capital of Taungoo and the modern-day 'royal capital' of Nay Pyi Taw, a visit to which plunges you into the deepest depths of the bizarre.

Taungoo

တောင်ငူ

📞 054, POP C120,000

A busy highway town, Taungoo (also spelled Toungoo) is a popular overnight stop for both tourists and truckers. Sporting several interesting temples, a lively central market and a pretty lake, it has more to keep your interest for a couple of hours than any other town on the Yangon–Mandalay Expressway. A great guesthouse on the town's outskirts makes it easy to stay an extra day, and can also be used as a base for visiting elephant camps in the hills to the west.

King Mingyinyo founded his capital here in 1510, and his dynasty ruled the country for the next 150 years. However, WWII bombing wrecked most of Mingyinyo's Katumadi Palace (only sections of the old walls and moat can still be seen). In celebration of the town's 500th anniversary in 2010 a couple of impressive new gates were built, as well as a massive statue of the king, unmissable on the old Yangon-Mandalay road, east of the palace walls.

The Karen hills to the east are famed for their vegetables and coffee. The area is also known for its bounteous areca (betel) palms. In Myanmar, when someone receives unexpected good fortune, they are likened to a betel-lover receiving a paid trip to Taungoo.

Kayin State is less than 22 miles east and Kayah State another 40 miles further east. Karen and Kayah insurgents have been known to operate within these areas. A dry-weather road continues east all the way to Loikaw, but any travel beyond the Sittoung (Sittang) River a couple of miles east of Taungoo requires special permission. Permission is typically arranged through a travel agent; see p69.

◉ Sights & Activities

Apart from visiting the sights listed below, it's fun to **hire a bike** and spend half a day pedalling around the town's sights and into the countryside. Bikes can be rented from Beauty Guest House for K2000 a day.

Shwesandaw Paya
BUDDHIST TEMPLE

ရွှေဆံတော်ဘုရား

Situated in the centre of town, around 500m west of the main road, this is Taungoo's grandest pilgrimage spot. The central stupa, a standard-issue bell shape, is gilded and dates back to 1597; local legend says an earlier stupa on the site was built centuries before and contains sacred-hair relics. Entering from the north, to your right is a display of Taungoo kings (and a rather busty

---

THE NEW ROAD TO MANDALAY

When Rudyard Kipling romanticised the road to Mandalay in his famous song, it's unlikely he had in mind the kind of highway – over half a century in the making – that now links Myanmar's capital of Naw Pyi Taw with the country's two major cities. Compared to the old bumpy and tarred 432-mile route between Yangon and Mandalay, this relatively smooth, concrete four-lane expressway, illuminated by solar-powered lights, is a revelation, slashing the drive time between the two from around 12 hours to eight. However, travel along it, and you'll rarely see another vehicle.

The Yangon–Mandalay Expressway's emptiness is down to combination of factors, including high tolls, which put off the majority of drivers. The road passes through unpopulated areas and has a dearth of facilities along its route, making it potentially treacherous should your vehicle breakdown. Heavy, road-punishing lorries and trucks are barred, but not long-distance buses, which usually traverse the road at night when its surface is cooler and thus less likely to overtax old engines and threadbare tyres.

At the 115-mile mark, just over halfway between Yangon and Nay Pyi Taw, there's a rest camp (services station) with several good 24-hour restaurants, including Feel Express, a branch of the Yangon dining favourite Feel Myanmar. A hotel is also under construction.

The expressway's origins date back to 1959 when the US provided $37 million in aid to General Ne Win's first military government, part of which was used for the expressway's initial survey by US Army engineers. It takes a long time to build a road when using forced and manual labour, the main impetus for finishing its construction being the junta's desire for faster access to Nay Pyi Taw. However, like many new things in Myanmar, the expressway is far from flawless. Apparently parts of it flood during the rainy season because of a lack of surface drains.

VISITING THE ELEPHANT CAMPS

Myanmar has the largest population of domesticated elephants in the world and is the only country where they are still used on a large scale in industry – in particular for logging carried out under the auspices of the state-owned Myanmar Timer Enterprise (MTE). In a mountainous area of Karen villages and teakwood plantations, 35 miles northwest of Taungoo, it's possible to visit logging camps and see up close working elephants and their *oozies* (the Myanmar word for mahouts) continuing a pattern of life unchanged for centuries.

With at least three days' notice (two weeks is better), trips of a day or longer can be arranged to this otherwise restricted area through **Dr Chan Aye** (drchanaye@gmail.com) of the Myanmar Beauty Guest House.

Day trips, starting at 6am and returning to Taungoo around 5pm, cost $90 per person for two people, with prices dropping the larger the group. Included in the rates are the necessary permits, return transport, a walk into the forest, an elephant ride, a lunch of rice and curry, and plenty of bottled water. Bamboo rafting and motorbiking in the jungle can be added for additional fees.

Overnight trips with a stay in either Shwe Daung or Ngwe Daug, both Karen villages, cost $220 per person; it's also possible to do this trip and continue onward to Pyay the next day for $300. The doctor provides free medical service to villagers in the area.

queen), and a round building housing a reclining Buddha surrounded by *devas* (celestial beings) and monastic disciples.

Nearby, on the western side of the stupa, there's a 12ft bronze, Mandalay-style sitting Buddha, given to the paya in 1912 by a retired civil servant who donated his body weight in bronze and silver for the casting of the image. He died three years after the casting at age 72; his ashes are interred behind the image.

On the east side, there's a shrine to Thurathati – a goddess borrowed by Buddhists from Hindus – atop a mythical *hintha* bird. Fine-arts students come to pray to her before exams.

Myasigon Paya   BUDDHIST TEMPLE
မြစဉ်းခုံဘုရား:
About 250m south of Shwesandaw, off Pagoda St, this lovely modern pagoda features a gold *zedi* and many glass mosaics. On the north side, an open building has a faded mural of Taungoo kings. A nearby squat white building is actually a **museum** (to have it opened, ask in the pagoda; it usually costs K1000). The museum has bronze images of Erawan (the three-headed elephant who serves as Indra's mount) and assorted Buddha images, but is more interesting for its random secular collection of British colonial-era memorabilia, including an ancient Kodak camera, 80-year-old plates and a cream soda bottle.

Kandawgyi Lake   LAKE/PARK
ကန်တော်ကြီး:
This pretty ornamental lake dates from the days when Taungoo (then known as Katumadi) was capital and Bayin Naung ruled. Strolling or cycling around its perimeter, lined with shady trees, is a pleasant way to pass an hour or so.

While nobody swims in the lake itself, on its eastern (town) side, you'll find a small **swimming pool** (for 2hr K500; ⏰7am-6pm) at the Evergreen Cafe, which also has friendly owners.

On the lake's western flank, sandwiched between the old palace walls and moat, is the **Kyet Minn Nyi Naung Amusement Park**, built by the firm responsible for the neighbouring Royal Katumadi Hotel. Apart from various places to eat and drink here, you can play snooker (K1000 per hour) and tennis (K3000 per hour) or hire the karaoke room (K5000 per hour). There's a free kids' playground, but we were told the pedal boats on the lake were 'not for foreigners'.

Kawmudaw Paya   BUDDHIST TEMPLE
ကောင်းမှုတော်ဘုရား:
One of Taungoo's oldest religious sites, this countryside temple is around 1 mile west of the lake through the new Sin Gate Arch. In the temple's southwest corner, look for a small pillar in a sandbox (with barefoot prints) – locals come here and walk around it to conquer personal problems.

🛏 Sleeping

TOP CHOICE Myanmar Beauty Guest House II, III & IV
GUESTHOUSE $$

(☎23270, 23527; Pauk Hla Gyi St; fourdoctors@mptmail.net.mm; r in III $10-15, s/d in IV $15/25;❄) This three-part, 20-room rural complex at the edge of town is reason enough to stop in Taungoo. The Beauty has a grab-bag of rustic, all-wood, bungalow-style rooms. Don't get confused by the numbers – the higher the number, the nicer the room. The spacious IV rooms face the fields and have air-con and a good hot shower; III is a step down, and II is usually used by drivers and guides. Staff are super, as is the wildly local breakfast, with samosas, sticky rice and exotic fruits – and lots of it. It's about 1.5 miles south of the turnoff from the old Yangon–Mandalay Highway into the centre of Taungoo and is a K1000 to K1500 trishaw ride from the centre. **Myanmar Beauty Guest House I** (☎23270; 7/134 Bo Hmu Pho Kun St; r $10-15), in town, isn't really worth considering.

Myanma Thiri Hotel
HOTEL $$

(☎23764; mthirihotel@myanmar.com.mm; Magalar Rd; s/d from $25/33; P❄❄) Set a block or so back from the main highway behind the sports field is this old government hotel now leased to a private company (see p21). The cheaper rooms, in the British colonial building, are big with overly soft mattresses. There are a few deluxe rooms in separate new chalets and a 20m-long swimming pool in the grounds.

Royal Kaytumadi Hotel
HOTEL $$$

(☎24761; www.kmahotels.com; Royal Kaytumadi St; r $50-65; ❄@❄) Hogging the west side of the lake is Taungoo's fanciest option, with very comfortable rooms and plenty of facilities and nice decorative details. The property is owned by a businessman affiliated with the government (see p21). The same businessman also bankrolled the new city gates and giant statue of Mingyinyo erected to celebrate the city's 500th anniversary.

Mother's House Hotel
HOTEL $$

(☎24240; mhh@banganmail.net.mm; 501-502 Yangon-Mandalay Highway; s/d $20/25; ❄) This 32-room bungalow hotel right on the highway and a little closer to town than the Beauty grants you 24-hour electricity, satellite TV and clean and comfy bungalow-style rooms with wood floors and fudge-and-banana colour schemes.

Hotel Amazing Kaytu
HOTEL $$

(☎23977; www.amazing-hotel.com; 8th St Ohtkyauttan; s/d from $30/35; ❄) 'Hotel Dependable If a Little Overpriced & Generic Kaytu' is more apt. It's a bit north of the main turn off from the old Yangon–Mandalay Highway into the centre of Taungoo; its 18 rooms are perfectly fine – with round-the-clock electricity, satellite TV and plain tiled bathrooms, plus a clock set to Spanish time in the lobby. The cheapest rooms are stuck at the back and a little dark.

Pun Swe Taw
HOTEL $$

(☎25595; ponswetaw@gmail.com; 8/15 Yangon-Mandalay Highway; s/d $35/40; ❄) Centrally located, this four-storey hotel offers reasonably clean and big rooms overlooking the moat on the east side of the old city. However, it also suffers from highway traffic noise.

🍴 Eating

Around Taungoo's tea shops, try asking for *yo yo* (normal coffee), which should get you a cup of 'Taungoo coffee' (actually it comes from the Karen mountains to the east).

At the night market, which convenes next to the central market, vendors specialise in chapattis and meat-stuffed *palata* (fried flatbread). On the old Yangon–Mandalay Highway, particularly to the south, are many Chinese and Myanmar restaurants; the restaurant at Mother's House Hotel is particularly inviting.

Yagon Food Villa
PAN-ASIAN $$

(185 Bo Hmu Pho Kun St; dishes K1500-2500; ⏱8.30am-9.30pm) Colourful fake-leather sofas and chairs add a bright note to this reliable option serving the usual mix of rice and noodle dishes, with burgers and fish and chips on the menu, too.

ℹ Information

Arena Net Cafe (Bo Hmu Pho Kun St; per hr K500; ⏱9am-4pm) Arena is next to Myanmar Beauty Guest House 1. Internet cafes are abundant, but don't expect speedy connections.
Dr Chan Aye (☎23270; Myanmar Beauty Guest House I) Runs a clinic and speaks good English.

ℹ Getting There & Away

The 62-mile unpaved logging road from Oktwin (9 miles south of Taungoo) to Pakkhaung provides a shortcut to Pyay. Foreigners are not allowed to travel along this road unless on a tour; Dr Chan Aye (see p137) can make this trip

DESTINATION	FARE ORDINARY/UPPER ($)	DURATION (HR)	DEPARTURE
Mandalay	7/17	9	11.18am, 12.15pm, 12.45pm
Nay Pyi Taw	2/6	3	2.15pm, 5.24pm
Thazi	4/11	5	11.18am, 12.15pm, 12.45pm
Yangon	5/13	7	8.40am, 11.40am, 1.10pm, 2.15pm

with you, including a one- or two-night stop in a village or jungle camp along the way (from $300 per person for two people, including accommodation, meals and transport).

Road travel east across the Sittoung River, towards Loikaw, is also restricted.

Bus

Most buses leaving Taungoo originated elsewhere. Generally stops are at private bus company offices scattered along the old Yangon–Mandalay Highway, just south of the turn-off to the 'centre'. It's easiest to have your local accommodation arrange a seat.

Yangon (K3500 to K4300; nine hours; departures 7am, 7pm) Buses with and without air-con.

Nay Pyi Taw (K1800; 3½ hours; departures 7am, 9am, noon, 2pm)

Meiktila (K4000; 6½ hours; departure 10.30am) Minibus, no air-con.

Mandalay (K6500; 10 hours; departure 6.30pm) Air-con bus.

Train

The Taungoo **train station** (☑23308) has a military presence, following some Karen 'attacks' on trains passing in the night.

Nay Pyi Taw
နေပြည်တော်

☑067 / POP C925,000

In 2005, following the tradition of Burma's ancient kings, the military relocated Myanmar's capital to a more strategically central location, about 240 miles north of Yangon. At untold expense (some reports have it at over $4 billion), Nay Pyi Taw was built on scrub ground amid rice paddies, villages and small towns such as Pyinmana on the old Yangon–Mandalay Highway. Most government ministries and their staff have been relocated here, but with a couple of exceptions the diplomatic community have dug in their heels in Yangon.

Absurdly grandiose in scale, Nay Pyi Taw (one translation is 'Royal City of the Sun')

is a sprawling, shoddily constructed city with eight-lane highways, 24-hour electricity, and zones for shopping, government housing and hotels, ministry buildings and generals' homes. Apart from the roadblocks that protect the roads leading to the generals' mansions, ministry buildings and the parliament, it's surprisingly open. Visits to some of its sights, including a giant gilded pagoda and a zoo and safari park, allow you to mingle freely with locals while putting a dollar or two into the private economy.

◉ Sights

You don't come to Nay Pyi Taw for the sights so much as for its surreal atmosphere. Besides, the city is very much a messy work in progress.

If approaching from the new Yangon–Mandalay Expressway, you'll first enter Nay Pyi Taw along the 'hotel zone' of Yarza Thingaha Rd. At the road's northern end near the Thabyaegone roundabout (one of the city's several gigantic, grassy road hubs) is the newly built convention centre, Maniyadanar Kyauk Sein Khanma. This is the location of the quarterly jade and precious stones fair, Emporium – about the only time Nay Pyi Taw fills up with visitors. Next door is the Gems Museum and northeast of the roundabout is the Water Fountain Garden.

Continue northeast from here to the Yarza Thingaha roundabout and hang a right to find the Uppatasanti Paya, Nay Pyi Taw's main sight. If you're approaching the city from the old Yangon–Mandalay Highway via the long-established town of Pyinmana, you'll hit the golden pagoda first.

Be careful where you point your camera in Nay Pyi Taw: photography of official buildings or military officials is prohibited. The giant **statues of three kings** (Alaungpaya, Anawrahta and Bayinnaung), seen in some publicised photos of Nay Pyi Taw, are in a military zone in the hills to the east, and are not accessible to the public.

Uppatasanti Paya
ဥပ္ပါတသန္တိစေတီ

BUDDHIST TEMPLE

An act of merit-making by General Than Shwe and his wife, this 321ft tall golden pagoda – 1ft smaller than Yangon's Shwedagon Paya – is impressive from afar (especially when illuminated at night), but close up betrays its hasty construction with poor finishes. Nevertheless, the vast interior is lined with some vivid carved-stone murals depicting the life and legend of Buddha and key scenes from Myanmar's Buddhist history. Foreigners are supposed to pay a $5 entry charge, but no one asked us for it when we showed up.

At the foot of the pagoda's east side is a covered, open-sided enclosure where two fabled **white elephants** – 38-year-old Buddawadi and 18-year-old Nandawadi – stand chained and munching bamboo. Along with two females, who are more dusky pink than white, there's also a regular two-year-old black elephant for comparison. Between 10am and 4pm the elephants are unchained and disappear from public view to roam the grazing ground to the rear.

Zoological Garden & Safari Park
တိရစ္ဆာန်ရုံ နှင့် ဆာဖာရီဥယျာဉ်

ZOO

(zoo admission $10, photo charge K2000; ⊘8.30am-8pm Tue-Sun) A good 45-minute drive northeast of the hotel zone (and closer to Pyinmana) are these animal-focused attractions, both run by the government. As zoos go, it's not a badly kept place – many of its inhabitants were shifted here from Yangon's decrepit colonial-era zoo. Spread across 612 acres are over 80 different species of animal, bird and reptile, including hippos, lions, deer, bison, crocodiles and several elephants. There's also an air-conditioned pool house for black-footed and Humboldt penguins, and a planetarium.

Next door, more wild beasts roam the **safari park** (admission $20; ⊘8.30am-4.30pm), which opened in 2011 and is toured on electric canopy-covered buggies – you'll be glad of these in the heat of the day. The 35-acre facility, home to zebras, rhinos, tigers and a pair of giraffes, is divided into sections showcasing the fauna of Africa, Asia and Australia.

Other Sights

Water Fountain Garden
PARK

(admission K200, camera charge K1000; ⊘8.30am-8.30pm) More or less at the heart of Nay Pyi Taw is this government-built grassy park, which boasts a viewing platform, water features (perhaps turned on) and cheaply constructed and already crumbling decorative structures bedecked with twinkling fairy lights at night.

Gem Museum
MUSEUM

(Yarza Thingaha Rd; entrance $5; ⊘9.30am-4.30pm Tue-Sun) The one-room exhibition hall at this government-run museum is a snooze. Have some fun walking around faster than the attendants who scuttle behind switching on and off the lights in cabinets displaying, among other things, pearls, rubies, silverware, jade and a big lump of coal. Downstairs, listless jewellers and gem merchants hawk their wares.

National Museum
MUSEUM

This new museum was under construction in the north of the city during our visit; we're told it's likely that original pieces currently in Yangon will be replaced by copies and the originals will be moved here.

🛏 Sleeping

Foreign visitors must stay in the hotel zone where new complexes are sprouting like daisies next to the villa-style resort Aureum Palace and Royal Kumudra, owned by businesses affiliated with the government (see p21). Forced to build quickly, construction and decorative standards are woeful and most places are overpriced. However, a couple of the smaller places are worth considering if you decide to overnight.

Tungapuri Hotel
HOTEL $$

(☎422 020; www.tungapurihotel.com; 9/10 Yarza Thingaha Rd; s/d from $25/35; ❋🛜) A Shan constructor built this small hotel, which has some appeal. The cheapest rooms are in the basement, where the singles don't even have windows; it's better to pay an extra $10 or more for the superior and deluxe rooms on the upper floors. Staff are very welcoming.

Oasis Hotel
HOTEL $$

(☎422 088; oasis.naypyitaw@gmail.com; 12 Yarza Thingaha Rd; r/ste $50/200; ❋@) The most stylish of Nay Pyi Taw's smaller hotels, the Oasis' suites are overpriced, but do come with Jacuzzi baths and small kitchenettes. Not open at the time of research, but in the works, is a fancy Chinese restaurant.

🍴 Eating & Drinking

There's a cluster of places to eat and drink atop what is known as Golden Hill, including the fancy but quiet Golden Hill Restaurant. At the foot of the hill, in the evenings, food and tea stalls set up shop. There's also a couple of places to eat in the **Junction mall**, where you'll also find a cinema (K1500).

TOP CHOICE **Maw Khan Nong** BAMAR **$**
(Golden Hill; meals K1500; ☺7am-10pm) Join government workers at this canteen and beer station with a spacious outdoor terrace. Order the good value 'Bagan bowl' meal, which includes a choice from the menu of one vegetable and two meat dishes plus rice.

TOP CHOICE **Santino** INTERNATIONAL **$$**
(Golden Hill; meals K2500-5000; ☺7am-10pm) The menu at this appealing Western-style café, bakery and restaurant has something for everyone, kicking off with full American-style breakfasts (K4000) and continuing with things such as burgers, club sandwiches and pizza.

Café Flight INTERNATIONAL **$$**
(☑422 122; info@skypalace.asia; 3 Yarza Thingaha Rd; mains K3500-9000; ☺8am-10pm) The safest way to board a Myanma Airways plane is to board this one, parked in front of the Sky Palace Hotel, and turned into a café-bar serving draught Tiger beer (K850), coffee, noodles, pasta and pizza.

ℹ Getting There & Away

Air

A new international airport is under construction 10 miles southeast of the city. The government's Myanma Airways runs a 'daily' flight here, but in reality it runs very irregularly.

Buses

Nay Pyi Taw has two bus stations. The closest to the hotel zone is at Mymoma Market, west of the Thabayaegone Roundabout. The Bawga Thiri bus station is on the Pyinmana side of town, around 1 mile east of Uppatasanti Paya; services from this station depart for Yangon at 6am, 5pm and 9pm (K5900, five hours) and Mandalay at 9pm (K4600, six hours).

Trains

Several miles northeast of the Uppatasanti Paya is the ridiculously massive new train station with an old steam locomotive as decoration out front. There are trains to Yangon and Mandalay:

Yangon (sleeper/ordinary/upper $21/19/7; nine to 10 hours; departures 6am, 9.10am)

Mandalay (sleeper/ordinary/upper $17/15/7; six to seven hours; departures 2.15pm, 9.15pm)

ℹ Getting Around

Nya Pyi Taw is no place for walking and there's nothing approaching a public bus service. The best way around is by private car, taxi or private motorbike taxis. From the bus and train stations to the hotel zone costs around K5000 by taxi. Four hours by motorbike taxi around the city from Pyinmana should cost you around K10,000.

Nay Pyi Taw Taxi & Car Rental Services (☑414 994, 09-4921 0613) Run by government-affiliated Max Myanmar group; see p21.

Meiktila
မိတ္ထီလာ
☑064

This attractive lakeside town, on the crossroads between Yangon, Mandalay, Bagan and Inle Lake, is a busy little trade centre with plenty of locals in uniform issued from the air-force bases outside town. It's not terribly exciting, but a bike ride around the lake can be fun – and you can peek at the old British officers' house where Aung San Suu Kyi and Michael Aris honeymooned.

Legend goes that King Anawrahta, founder of Bagan, had a pond here broadened into the current lake that looms west of town. When the king asked if the lake extended all the way to Mt Popa, the report came back: 'Lord, it doesn't go that far.' The name 'Meiktila' is an abbreviation of that bad-news report.

Between February and March 1945, the British killed 20,000 Japanese soldiers based here in the final WWII battle for control of Burma. Much of the city was flattened. Sadly that trend has continued: town-engulfing fires devastated the city in 1974 and 1991; another big one took out several buildings in 2003.

◉ Sights

Lake Meiktila is the town's premier attraction. There are no boating options, but you can cycle around some of it. Between the road and rail bridges, west of the city centre, you won't miss **Phaung Daw U Paya**, a temple housed in a giant floating barge shaped in the form of a golden Karaweik, a mythical bird.

Cross the road bridge to reach the wooden pier leading to the pretty **Antaka Yele Paya**, a small pagoda perched on an island in the lake. Back on the main road is an **Aung San statue**.

About 270yd southwest of the bridge is a building that was once a **British colonial diplomat house**. The building was used as an interrogation centre by the Japanese in WWII, and many years later Aung San Suu Kyi and Michael Aris honeymooned here. The house is to the east of the Lakeside Wunzin Hotel.

BAGAN & CENTRAL MYANMAR MEIKTILA

Meiktila

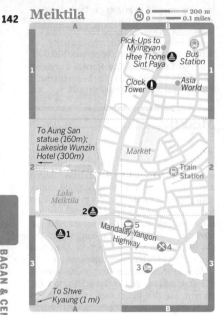

N 0 ——— 200 m
0 ——— 0.1 miles

A mile around the west end of the lake, **Shwe Kyaung** is a walled monastery on the inland side of the road with Japanese signs leading to a **WWII monument** that British and Japanese survivors put up in 1972. Monks will show you around. Just past the monument, a picturesque path leads between the lake and (usually) flooded rice fields.

Don't keep going to the south side of the lake, as the path leads into the no-go zone of a military compound.

🛏 Sleeping

Honey Hotel HOTEL **$$**
(☏25755, 23588; Panchan St; r $10-30;❄) Right on the lake in town, this converted mansion is Meiktila's best bet. If available, opt for room G2, which has views directly across the lake. Newly built, more expensive rooms at the front of complex substitute fresh paint, linens and TVs for the lack of lake view.

Lakeside Wunzin Hotel HOTEL **$$**
(☏23848, 23559; 49A Than Lwin Rd; economy/superior/deluxe s $8/24/30, d $12/30/36;❄) Showing its years, the pricier, huge rooms here overlook the lake from a quiet backstreet out of the centre. Staff are happy to join you for tennis on the scrappy court outside.

🍴 Eating & Drinking

Meiktila's not much for fancy eats.

Shwe Ohn Pin CHINESE **$$**
(Mandalay-Yangon Rd; dishes K2500-4500; ⏱7am-10pm) This clean tiled restaurant, located in the centre, hands you an English menu for its tasty Chinese and Myanmar dishes.

Golden Rain Tea Center TEAHOUSE **$**
(tea K200; ⏱5am-9.30pm) This popular place, just off the Mandalay–Yangon Rd, has all the usual milky, sweet drinks and filling chicken or pork steamed buns. Mix with locals at the low tables shielded by a rattan roof cover.

ℹ Getting There & Away

Buses

Express buses zooming between Yangon and Mandalay stop on the road east of the clock tower (and not at the local bus station). Along this road you'll find half a dozen ticket-sales shops, including **Asia World** (☏09-4301 1348) opposite the Thiri Minglar Mosque.

Buses from Meiktila go to the following destinations: Bagan (K6000, five hours, daily at 4pm), Lashio (K9000, eight hours, two daily), Magwe (K5500, eight hours, four daily), Mandalay (K2000, three to four hours, several daily), Nay Pyi Taw (K2000, three to four hours, several daily) and Yangon (K8500, 10 to 12 hours, three daily)

Pick-Up Trucks

From the bus station, pick-ups for Taunggyi (K2500 to K4000, six hours) leave regularly, stopping in Kalaw for the same price.

Pick-ups for Myingyan (K4000, 2½ hours) leave regularly from the main road in front of the Htee Thone Sint Paya, north of the clock tower.

Train

There's a small train station in town, catching slow trains heading east–west. A more useful station is in Thazi, about 16 miles east, at the crossroads of the Yangon, Mandalay and Taung-gyi lines.

YANGON–BAGAN HIGHWAY

This western route north of Yangon to Bagan is less heavily trafficked than the Yangon–Mandalay Expressway. Sometimes called the 'low road', or 'Pyay Hwy', this route is debatably more attractive than the old Yangon–Mandalay Highway. It follows the eastern bank of the Ayeyarwady River and rises over lovely hills and valleys north of Magwe. At Pyay, connections to Thandwe (and Ngapali) head west over the mountains.

Pyay (Prome)
ပြည်

♪ 053

With a breezy location on the Ayeyarwady River, Pyay is the most interesting stop on the Yangon–Bagan Highway. The city's glory days date back to the ancient Pyu capital of Thayekhittaya, the partially excavated remains of which lie 5 miles east of Pyay's other stellar attraction: the dazzling Shwesandaw Paya.

Myanmar folk alternate the town's pronunciation between 'pyay' and 'pyi'. The Brits, apparently, couldn't deal with the confusion and called it Prome.

The current town site became an important trading centre during the Bagan era. The Mon controlled it when King Alaungpaya conquered it in 1754. Pyay boomed, along with the British Irrawaddy Flotilla Company in the 1890s. Today, it remains an important transit point for goods between northern and southern Myanmar. Soak up its lively atmosphere along the riverfront and at the roundabout, at the centre of which is a gilded equestrian statue of Aung San.

◉ Sights

Shwesandaw Paya & Around BUDDHIST TEMPLE
ရွှေဆံတော်ဘုရား
Set on top of a hill in the town centre, the stunning Shwesandaw Paya (and the surrounding pagodas and monasteries) is not only Pyay's major point of interest, but also one of the country's biggest Buddhist pilgrimage sites. Just over 1yd taller than the main *zedi* at Yangon's Shwedagon, the Shwe-

sandaw stupa follows the classic Bamar design seen at Bagan's Shwezigon (p164).

Legend goes that it was built in 589 BC, and that the golden *zedi* houses four strands of the Buddha's hair (the Golden Hair Relics).

Atop the *zedi* are two *hti* (umbrella-like pinnacles), unusual for Myanmar. The lower, bigger one dates from Pyay's days as a Mon city. The higher, smaller one was added by King Alaungpaya as a symbol of peace between his realm and the Mon, after brutally capturing the city in 1754. In the southwest corner of the complex, the **Sacred Tooth Hall** is said to house an original tooth from the Buddha. It's in the golden bell (locked) behind the glass. The locks come off once a year for the November full-moon festivities.

The panoramic views from the pagoda are pretty great too. To the east, you'll see the **Sehtatgyi Paya** (Big Ten Storey), a giant (maybe not 10 storeys, though) seated Buddha, eye-to-eye with the Shwesandaw and watching over it. The smaller gold stupa on the highest hill southeast of Shwesandaw is the **Wunchataung Paya** (Apology Mountain Pagoda), where people can say 'sorry' for misdeeds. They get the best view of Shwesandaw and the mountains across the river while they're at it. You can reach it via Sehtatgyi Rd, east of the Shwesandaw.

Central Market MARKET
Follow Strand Rd north of a morning to catch all the action at the lively and colourful central market which spreads over several blocks. As you approach, you'll pass an ornate **Chinese Temple** dedicated to the goddess Guan Yin on the corner of Ya Yoke Tann St. A little further on are giant clay water pots and a row of thanakha wood sellers. Continue along the riverside north of the market to find the Shwepaliamaw Paya.

Payagyi Paya BUDDHIST TEMPLE
ဘုရား:ကြီး
Once marking one of Thayekhittaya's four corners, this towering pagoda is a half-mile east of the bus station. It probably dates from the 5th or 6th century AD. Three terraces encircle the slightly swollen, breastlike structure from its base; 'ladies' are not allowed on the upper one. The modern *hti* is lit up at night.

🛏 Sleeping

All of the following options include breakfast in the price.

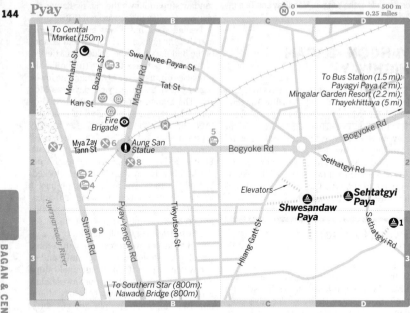

N 0 ————————— 500 m
0 ————————— 0.25 miles

To Central Market (150m)

Merchant St
Swe Nwee Payar St
Bazaar St 3
Madaw Rd
Tat St
Kan St
Fire Brigade
Mya Zay Tann St 7 6
Aung San Statue
8
2 4
Strand Rd
Pyay-Yangon Rd
Tikyutson St
9
Ayeyarwady River

To Bus Station (1.5 mi);
Payagyi Paya (2 mi);
Mingalar Garden Resort (2.2 mi);
Thayekhittaya (5 mi)

Bogyoke Rd
5
Bogyoke Rd
Sethatgyi Rd
Elevators
Shwesandaw Paya
Sehtatgyi Paya
Hliang Gatt St
Sethatgyi Rd
1

To Southern Star (800m);
Nawade Bridge (800m)

TOP CHOICE **Lucky Dragon** HOTEL **$$**

(☑24222; http://luckydragon.com; 772 Strand Rd; r $30-40; P❀❂✽) Leaving all other town centre hotels standing, this enclave of modern, bungalow-style, wood-floored rooms across from the river is reasonably priced and has pleasant, helpful staff. Another plus is the small pool, long enough for a few cooling laps after touring Pyay's sights.

Smile Motel HOTEL **$**

(☑22523, 25169; 10-11 Bogyoke Rd; r $18; ❀) The long corridor leading to the simply furnished rooms may have a shabby carpet and remind you of *The Shining*, but it's all pretty clean and the staff are nice, if a bit surprised at your existence.

Mingalar Garden Resort HOTEL **$$**

(☑28662; Flying Tiger Garden, Aung Chan Tha Quarter; s/d standard $30/36; superior $36/42; ❀@) Near Payagyi Paya and closer to Thayekhittaya than the Ayeyarwady River, this quiet garden complex of spacious bungalows is set in the grounds of a former cheroot manufacturer. It's worth springing a few extra dollars for the more modern superior rooms, all of which overlook an ornamental lake.

Myat Lodging House HOTEL **$**

(☑25695; 222 Bazaar St; r $6-12; ❀) This small back-street guesthouse has well-loved but simple rooms (green carpet, writing desks) a block from the Pyay 'action'. The cheapest rooms have fan and shared bathroom (which are kept clean); only the highest-priced rooms come with a private bathroom. Friendly English-speaking staff give out maps of Pyay and Thayekhittaya.

Pyay Strand Hotel HOTEL **$$**

(☑24874; Strand Rd; r standard/superior $25/35; ❀) Offers 32 simple rooms similar to Smile's, which are thus overpriced compared to Lucky Dragon. Higher-priced rooms get hot water and look out over the river.

✗ Eating & Drinking

The night market on Mya Zay Tann St, between the Aung San statue and the river, is atmospheric and well worth browsing for its cheap eats.

TOP CHOICE **Grandma Café** KOREAN, INTERNATIONAL **$$**

(Mya Zay Tann Rd; dishes K1500; ⏱8am-10pm) Owner Banyar Aung learned to make Korean food while working at various restaurants in Kuala Lumpur, then returned home and taught his wife. Together they run this

Pyay

Top Sights
Sehtatgyi Paya....D2
Shwesandaw Paya....C2

Sights
1 Wunchataung Paya....D3

Sleeping
2 Lucky Dragon....A2
3 Myat Lodging House....A1
4 Pyay Strand Hotel....A2
5 Smile Motel....B2

Eating
6 Grandma Café....A2
7 Hline Ayar Restaurant....A2
Night Market....(see 6)
8 Pyay Star Restaurant....B2

Transport
9 IWT Office....A3

cute place that turns out very tasty *dolsot bibimbap* and *kimchi ramen*, along with less adventurous dishes such as sandwiches, burgers and pasta.

Southern Star CHINESE $$
(☎25484; Strand Rd; dishes K4000-5000; ⊙10am-11pm) Enjoy river views from the terrace of this big restaurant serving good food, close by the Nawade Bridge. In the evenings there's karaoke, unless it's a weekend when they screen English Premier League soccer matches.

Pyay Star Restaurant CHINESE $$
(cnr Bogyoke Rd & Pyay-Yangon Rd; dishes from K1800-3000) The Star is a great spot: a two-floor beer hall with plenty of buzz and a balcony on which to eat tasty Chinese fare and down draught Myanmar beer or ABC stout.

Hline Ayar CHINESE, MYANMAR $$
(Strand Rd; dishes veg K1200, meat K2800-4000, fish K3000-6500; ⊙9am-9pm) Over on the river, this live-music spot shows its years (plus cheesy pop singers at 7pm), but it has tables looking over the Ayeyarwady.

Information

Cosmic (Kan St; per hr K400; ⊙7.30am-11pm) For internet, try here. It's in the same building as a cinema.

My Space Another internet provider; across the road from Cosmic.

Getting There & Away

Boat

Routes along the Ayeyarwady River start and stop in Pyay, heading either north or south. Few foreigners use either service.

The **IWT office** (☎24503; Strand Rd; ⊙9am-5pm Mon-Fri) is helpful on ever-changing times for slow-going government ferries. At research time, a ferry left at 5.30am on Wednesday for Mandalay (deck/cabin $9/18, about five days), and another cargo boat left Tuesday night for Yangon (deck/cabin $9/18; about three days).

Bus

Pyay is located at the junction of roads to Yangon, Bagan and Thandwe (for Ngapali Beach). The highway bus station is about two miles east of the centre (just off Bogyoke Rd).

Several companies run buses to Yangon (K4100, seven hours) throughout the day, including **Asia Express** (☎28145). There are no direct buses north to Bagan from Pyay, but you can catch a bus that left from Yangon for the full Yangon–Bagan fare (K15,000 to K18,000, 12 to 13 hours). Or take the 8.30am bus run by **Sun Moon** (☎09-4950 0521) to Magwe (K4100, six to seven hours), from where a 6am or 7am bus the next day leaves for Bagan.

Heading to Ngapali by bus is possible, but not terribly convenient. Thile Lone Kyaw run minibuses to Taunggok (K10,000, 11 hours) leaving at 5pm.

Train

A lone daily train leaves Pyay's central train station at 11.30pm for Yangon (sleeper/upper/1st/ordinary class $14/13/10/5, 8½ hours). From Shwethekar station, 3 miles east of the city towards Thayekhittaya, you can also board the Yangon to Bagan train as it takes a three-minute pause at 10pm (sleeper/upper/1st $28/26/23), before arriving in Bagan 8am; the Bagan to Yangon train arrives at 2.30am, before continuing on to Yangon.

Getting Around

Trishaws and blue taxi pick-up trucks are the main ways of getting around. A trishaw ride to/from the bus station is around K1000, and K1500 by blue taxi. A regular pick-up truck service runs along Bogyoke Rd to the bus station (K200).

Around Pyay

THAYEKHITTAYA

သရေခေတ္တရာ

It's no Bagan, but this ancient **site** (admission $5, incl museum $10; ⊙8am-5pm), about 5 miles east of Pyay centre, can make for a fun

BUSSING IT ACROSS THE BAGO YOMA

Victoria Tofiq and John Greenhalgh, British travellers we met in Ngapali in 2011, told us about their overland journey from Pyay via Taunggok, which took 18 hours and involved three changes of transport:

VT: When we went to Pyay bus station, the people pointed to a picture of a minibus. We found a tiny van seating just eight.

JG: They were worried about my height – it was very uncomfortable, impossible to sleep in.

VT: There were 10 checkpoints on the road between Pyay and Taunggok – our guest-house in Pyay prepared 10 photocopies of our passports and visas for the driver to hand out at each one. We arrived at the final checkpoint very early in the morning, so had to wait several hours until it opened at 4.30am.

JG: When it did open, we found we could have easily walked from there to Taunggok bus station! We decide to continue on to Ngapali when we found a big open-top pick-up truck leaving at 7am for Thandwe – that cost K2500.

VT: It was packed with people and piled with sacks of produce, but had lots of atmo-sphere. We saw the sunrise and drove past beautiful landscapes and waving children.

JG: At Thandwe we boarded a smaller pick-up that brought us to Ngapali for K2000 each.

VT: The road was bumpy all the way, so we didn't sleep and it was very tiring – it's really roughing it! But it was also the most interesting journey of our visit. And Ngapali is a beautiful place at which to recover.

few hours of laid-back exploration, often in isolation. Known to Pali-Sanskrit scholars as Sri Ksetra (Fabulous City), Thayekhittaya is an enormous Pyu city that ruled in the area from the 5th to 9th centuries AD. Local legend links its origin to the mythical King Dut-tabaung, who supposedly worked with ogres and other supernatural creatures to build the 'magical city' in 443 BC. The earliest Pali inscriptions found here date back to the 5th or 6th centuries.

Seeing the 5.5-sq-mile site means either walking the 7.5-mile loop around it or hopping on the back of an **ox-drawn cart** (K5000; 3hr) for a bumpy, dusty journey past the spaced-out temples, most just outside the oval city walls. It's a good idea to have a knowledgeable guide as well. Bicycles aren't permitted. Note that the site and museum fees go to the government (see p21).

☉ Sights

At the entrance to the site is the small, government-run **Sri Ksetra Museum** (admission $5; ☉ Tue-Sat 10am-4pm) with its posted map of the area and various artefacts from excavations, including Hindu deities, 6th-century Buddha images, Pyu beads and silver coins.

Behind the museum to the south, the road soon follows the remains of the old palace walls. Ox-cart drivers – at a speed that ebbs and flows according to the mood of the ox – make a counterclockwise loop of the following sites.

The first stop will be at a recent excavation: a large brick building that is thought to have been a **palace**. After 2.5 miles or so, the road passes **Rahanta Gate**, where fragments of the overgrown brick gate run alongside the dirt road. Immediately south is the **Rahanta cave temple**, thought to date to the Bagan period and last repaired in the 1920s, with eight Buddha images lined along the south wall.

About a mile south, the **Bawbawgyi Paya** (Big Grandfather Stupa) is Thayekhittaya's most impressive site: a 50yd cylindrical stupa with a golden *hti* on its top. It's among the oldest and least obviously renovated Pyu sights, dating back to the 4th century. It's the prototype of many Myanmar pagodas.

Two-hundred yards northeast is the smaller cube-shaped **Bebe Paya**, which has a cylindrical top and a few Buddha images inside; its thought to date to the 10th century. Just north is the squat **Leimyethna Paya**, which has a visible iron frame keeping it together. Inside four original Buddha reliefs (a bit cracked, some faces missing) are visible. On either side of the roads around here, look out for long ruts in the ground; they were once brick moats.

A couple of hundred yards to the north is a fork in the road: to the right (north) is a tin-roofed **cemetery**; to the left (west), on the way to 'Thaungpye Mound', is the better (but bumpier) way back to the museum.

Take the left and after half a mile you'll pass by a gap in the 3m-thick city walls, which has become a gate. Continue another mile, through a booming farming village of thatch huts, with piles of radishes and other produce. Towards the north end of the village is the 13th-century East Zegu Paya, a small four-sided temple with overgrown walls and (usually) locked doors. It's off the main road, but is worth visiting for the walk past the fields and farmers.

ⓘ Getting There & Away

The turn-off here is a couple of miles east of Payagyi Paya. A return taxi between Thayekhittaya and Pyay should cost about K10,000. No direct pick-up truck connects the Pyay town centre with the site. You can bike to the site, but not around it.

SHWEDAUNG

ေရႊေတာင္

This small town about 9 miles south of Pyay, via the road to Yangon, contains the famous Shwemyetman Paya (Paya of the Golden Spectacles), a reference to the large, white-faced sitting buddha inside the main shrine. The buddha wears a gargantuan set of eyeglasses with gold-plated rims. Coming south from Pyay, the turn-off for Shwemyetman is located on the right-hand side of the road; a green-and-white sign in English reads 'Shwe Myet Hman Buddha Image – 1 Furlong'.

Spectacles were first added to the image during the Konbaung era, when a no-bleman offered them to the temple in an attempt to stimulate local faith through curiosity. Word soon spread that the bespectacled buddha had the power to cure all ills, especially afflictions linked to the eyes. The first pair of spectacles was stolen at an early stage, and a second pair was made and enshrined inside the image to protect it from thieves.

An English officer stationed in Pyay during the colonial era had a third pair fitted over the buddha's eyes after his wife suffered from eye trouble and the abbot suggested such a donation. Naturally, as the story goes, she was cured. (This pair is now in a small shrine to the right of the image.)

On the southern side of Shwedaung, about 3 miles from Shwemyetman, is the attractive hilltop Shwenattaung Paya (Golden Spirit Mountain), which reportedly dates back to the Thayekhittaya era. Among the many images of buddha is a serene one carved from marble. A large *paya pwe* (pagoda festival) is held here each year on the full moon of Tabaung (February/ March).

To get to Shwedaung, hop on a pick-up truck headed towards Yangon. Pick-up trucks leave frequently from the Pyay bus station and pass by the Aung San statue before hitting the highway.

AKAUK TAUNG

အေကာက္ေတာင္

Carved into cliffs overlooking the Ayeyarwady, about 19 miles downstream from Pyay, are dozens of buddha images at Akauk

---

MEET THE FAMILY SIMON RICHMOND

'My name is Ku Tan Swe and this is my husband U Aye Cho, my brother U Ken Lu and my sister Luin Luin May; she's 82.' Sitting demurely behind a dusty table in the big, high-ceilinged entrance room, the old lady peered kindly at me through her circular glasses, not in the least bit fazed by having a perfect stranger drop by unexpectedly. A moment before I'd been outside taking a photograph of their home, a grand 1924 mansion a few blocks south of the Shwemyetman Paya in Shwedaung, when Ku Tan Swe – one of the several people who lived there – invited me inside.

Pointing at one of the many framed sepia photos hanging on the walls, Ku Tan Swe continued with the introductions. 'That's my grandfather U Aung Kyw – he built this house.' She then turned to the opposite wall to indicate the portrait of her grandmother Dohla. U Aung Kyw was a talented man: another of his fancy colonial-mansion creations, built in 1926, can be seen a block south of the Shwemyetman Paya.

Looking around, I noticed another fading, crumbling image, this one in colour and of an English-looking woman in army uniform. 'Is that another relation?' I asked. 'No, it's Elizabeth', replied U Ken Lu laughing. Taking a closer look, I saw it was, indeed, Princess Elizabeth, now the Queen.

Taung (Tax Mountain). The mountain is named for the crafty toll-takers from the mid-19th century, who spent the hours between taxing boats by carving reclining and meditating buddhas into the steep cliff.

To get there, you'll need to taxi across the Ayeyarwady to **Htonbo** (ထုံးဘိုရွာ), a village about 90 minutes by road from Pyay, then hire a boat (about K15,000) for the 45-minute look. To do so, you must bring a copy of your passport or visa to show the *strict* immigration officers in Htonbo.

For some visitors, it's too much travel for minimal payoff. A return taxi to Htonbo from Pyay (sometimes with Shwedaung thrown in) takes around two hours one-way and costs about $20.

Magwe

မကွေး:
☎063

About 155 miles north of Pyay and 93 miles south of Salay, Magwe's locale on the Ayeyarwady River is nice enough, as is the impressive 1.8-mile **Magwe Bridge**. Beyond this, however, it's a place of dilapidated buildings running along a confusing web of leafy streets and limited services, and not particularly good accommodation. Still, if you're travelling along the bumpy road connecting Bagan and Pyay, you'll probably want to break your journey here and the stretch your legs around the 'sights'.

Famously, the capital of Magwe Division sat out of the 1988 prodemocracy marches.

◉ Sights

Magwe's chief pagoda, the 1929 **Mya Tha Lun Paya**, a mile north of the bridge, features a gilded stupa and occupies a hilltop site with great river views.

Just across the river, about the same distance north of the bridge, is Minbu and the fun **Nga Ka Pwe Taung** (Dragon Lake), a burping pool of butane gas and mud that has (over the years) built a few acres of lunar-like terrain with bubbling pools atop four odd mounds. The sludge isn't hot; if your toes slip in, wash them off below at a small pagoda. The largest mound is named Thu Sei Ta and the second largest Nanda, for the mythical Dragon King's daughter and son, respectively. It's about a 30-minute taxi ride here from the centre.

🛏 Sleeping & Eating

Sein San Guesthouse GUESTHOUSE $
(☎23799; B-185 16th St, Ywathit Quarter; r $15, s/d with shared bathroom $8/12; ❄) Very simple, with stone floors, mint-green walls and thin mattresses on the beds. But the staff are friendly and speak English and the price is appropriate. It's on a quiet backstreet, midway between the bus station and the river.

Htein Htein Tar HOTEL $$
(☎23499; 234 17th St, Ywathit Quarter; s/d $25/40; ❄) Around the corner from the Sein San. Laughably overpriced, this motel-like place offers big but tatty rooms.

Rolex Guest House GUESTHOUSE $
(☎23536; cnr Mya Than Lun Rd & Ayeyarwady Bridge; s/d with air-con K10,000/18,000, with fan K8000/12,000; ❄) This bare-bones guesthouse, on the roundabout facing the bridge entry, has simple concrete-floored rooms with cold-water bathrooms attached. It's easy to find, but suffers from traffic noise.

Central Restaurant CHINESE $$
(Pyitawthar Rd; dishes K2000-4000; ◷7am-10pm) Handy for the bus station, this reasonably clean-looking Chinese restaurant serves the usual noodle and rice dishes, including hot and sour chicken. It's next to the Zin Yaw Guesthouse, which doesn't accept foreigners.

Monalizar 2 CHINESE, BAMAR $$
(dishes from K1500; ◷7am-10pm) On the river, just south of the bridge, this is a very popular drinking spot that also serves passable food. As the sun dips across the river, locals (mostly guys) hit the beer and whisky as a crew of 11 start up the 7pm music and dance show.

❶ Getting There & Around

Magwe's highway bus station is about 1.5 miles east of the central market. Yangon-bound buses also stop in Pyay, but you'll still need to pay the full fare to Yangon even if you get off there. Buses from Magwe go to the following destinations: Nyaung U (K6000, four hours, departure 6am or 7am), Pyay (K4000, seven hours, departure 9am), Yangon (K7500, 12 hours, departure 5.30pm), and Mandalay (K5500, 10 hours, departure 6.30pm).

IWT ferries between Pyay and Mandalay stop in Magwe. The **IWT office** (☎21503) is one block towards the river from the market's north side.

Motorised trishaws – with room for you and a few mates – tout their services at the bus station. A ride from the station to Nga Ka Pwe Taung and a stop at Monalizar 2 costs about K8000.

Temples of Bagan

Best Temple Murals

» Upali Thein (p158)

» Nandamannya Pahto (p164)

» Payathonzu (p164)

» Ananda Ok Kyaung (p158)

» Abeyadana Pahto (p162)

Best Sunset Spots

» Shwesandaw Paya (p159)

» Buledi (p158)

» Pyathada Paya (p160)

» Thabeik Hmauk (p160)

» Tan Kyi Paya (p155)

Why Go?

Marco Polo, who may or may not have visited on his travels, described Bagan as 'one of the finest sights in the world'. Despite centuries of neglect, looting, erosion, regular earthquakes (including a massive one in 1975), not to mention questionable restoration, this temple-studded plain remains a remarkably impressive and unforgettable vision.

In a 230-year building frenzy up until 1287 and the Mongol invasions, Bagan's kings commissioned over 4000 Buddhist temples. These brick and stucco religious structures are all that remain of their grand city, with the 11th to 13th century wooden buildings having long gone.

Many restoration projects have resulted in a compromised archaeological site that can barely be described as in ruins. Often the restorations bear little relation to the building styles and techniques used at the time of original construction. Still, Bagan remains a wonder. Working temples like Ananda Pahto, give a sense of what the place was like at its zenith, while others conceal colourful murals and hidden stairways that lead to exterior platforms and jaw-dropping views across the plain.

When to Go

Bang in the midst of the 'dry zone', Bagan is hot. Avoid sizzling March to May and visit in 'cooler' November to February, the peak travel season. The rainy season (June to October) sees fewer visitors but is still pretty steamy. If you're interested in local religious rites, music and dance, time your visit to coincide with the festival lasting several weeks at Ananda Pahto in January.

Plan your daily temple viewing around a dawn/dusk itinerary, building in a leisurely lunch/siesta/poolside lounging session from around 12.30pm to 4pm. Temperatures at dusk and dawn will be more pleasant and the light is better for photographs.

History

Per Pali inscriptions found here, Bagan kings apparently flirted with a couple of different city names during its heyday: Arimaddanapura (City of the Enemy Crusher) and the less dramatic Tambadipa (Copper Land). The name Bagan may in fact derive from Pyugan, a name first written down by the Annamese of present-day Vietnam in the mid-11th century as Pukam. The British in the 19th century called the site 'Pagan' while

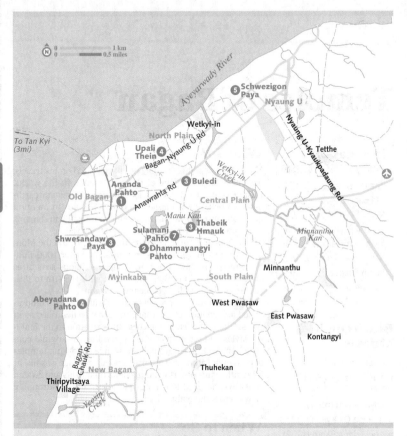

Temples of Bagan Highlights

1 Marvel at the perfectly proportioned **Ananda Pahto** (p156), which houses four giant buddha statues carved from teak

2 Speculate over what lies inside the bricked-up inner sanctum of mysterious **Dhammayangyi Pahto** (p159)

3 Take in all the colours of the sunset from **Shwesandaw Paya** (p159)

or **Buledi** (p158), or enjoy the spectacle, minus the crowds, at **Thabeik Hmauk** (p160)

4 Admire the intricate murals decorating **Upali Thein** (p158) and **Abeyadana Pahto** (p162)

5 Get acquainted with the 37 Nats at the beautiful zedi **Shwezigon Paya** (p164) in Nyaung U

6 Hire a private boat to cross the Ayeyarwady and make the trip to **Tan Kyi Paya** (p155), a gilded stupa providing sweeping views back towards Bagan

7 Inspect the fine internal ornamental work of **Sulamani Pahto** (p160), a temple known as the Crowning Jewel

c 950 Evidence from the remains of Pyu-style buildings are the earliest indication of a settlement on this bend in the Ayeyarwady (Irrawaddy).

1057 Temple building speeds up with the sacking of the Mon city of Thaton by Bagan's warrior king Anawrahta, a newly enthusiastic devotee of Buddhism.

c 1100-70 Temples become bigger and are better lit by broader windows, with more of an eye to vertical proportions than horizontal lines.

c 1170-1280 Bagan's late period of architecture sees more intricate pyramidical spires or adorning tile work added to the buildings, with an increased Indian influence.

1287 Bagan's decline is accelerated when the Mongols over-run the area, the Bamar having possibly abandoned the city already.

1975 An earthquake registering 6.5 on the Richter scale hits Bagan; many temples are damaged, but major reconstruction starts almost immediately with help of Unesco.

1990 Military forcibly relocate a village that had grown up in the 1970s in the middle of the walled area of 'Old Bagan' to 4km south of the main archaeological zone.

1996 Bagan placed on Unesco World Heritage Tentative List.

1998 Over US$1 million collected from local donations for the restoration of Bagan.

2008 An imaginary recreation of the 13th-century Bagan Palace is opened on a site opposite that of the original palace.

2011 Indian government pledges $22 million for the restoration of Ananda Pahto.

the military junta switched it back to Bagan in 1989.

GLORY DAYS

Bagan's two and a half centuries of temple building (from the 11th century to the 13th century) coincided with the region's transition from Hindu and Mahayana Buddhist beliefs to the Theravada Buddhist beliefs that have since characterised Myanmar. Legend has it that the main players were the monk Shin Arahan who came (sent by Manuha, the Mon king of Thaton; more on him in a bit) to convert Bamar King Anawrahta. To call his quest a success would be a landmark understatement. Inspired by his new faith, Anawrahta ordered Manuha to give him a number of sacred Buddhist texts and relics. When Manuha naturally refused, Anawrahta marched his army south and took everything worth carrying back to Bagan, including 32 sets of the Tripitaka (the classic Buddhist scriptures), the city's monks and scholars and, for good measure, King Manuha himself.

The self-assured Anawrahta then turned to architects to create something that befit Buddha. They built and built, and many of the greatest Bagan edifices date from their efforts, including Shwezigon Paya, considered a prototype for all later Myanmar stu-

pas; the Pitaka Taik (Scripture Library), built to house the Pitaka (scriptures); and the elegant and distinctive Shwesandaw Paya, built immediately after the conquest of Thaton. Thus began what the Myanmar people call the 'First Burmese Empire', which became a pilgrimage point for Buddhists throughout Southeast Asia.

King Anawrahta's successors, particularly Kyanzittha (r 1084–1113), Alaungsithu (r 1113–67) and Narapatisithu (r 1174–1211), continued scratching this phenomenal building itch, although the construction work must have been nonstop throughout the period of Bagan's glory.

DECLINE

Historians disagree on exactly what happened to cause Bagan's apparently rapid decline at the end of the 13th century. The popular Myanmar view is that hordes of Mongols sent by Kublai Khan swept through the city, ransacking and looting. A contrasting take holds that the threat of invasion from China threw the last powerful ruler of Bagan into a panic. Legend has it that, after a great number of temples were torn down to build fortifications, the city was abandoned so that the Mongols merely took over an already deserted city.

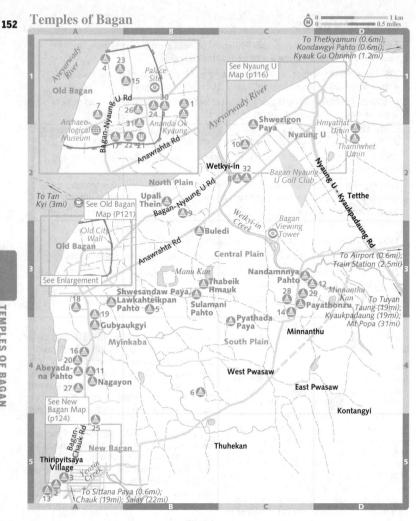

Bagan scholar Paul Strachan argues in *Pagan: Art and Architecture of Old Burma* that the city was never abandoned at all. Indeed evidence suggests Bagan continued as an important religious and cultural centre into the 14th century and beyond, after which its decay can be blamed on the three-way struggle between the Shan, Mon and Bamar. People began moving back in some numbers only after the British established a presence in the area in the late 19th century, but by that point the plain of temples had fallen victim to frequent earthquakes (there were at least 16 trembles that shook Bagan

between 1174 and the big one in 1975), general weathering and neglect.

CONTROVERSIAL RESTORATION

The enduring religious significance of Bagan is at the heart of the site's recent transformation from piles of picturesque ruins to a practically complete 13th-century city, minus the buildings, such as palaces, homes and monasteries, that would have been made of wood.

Dr Bob Hudson (see boxed text, p157) describes it as 'the most radical heritage management project in modern times', noting that, as of 2008, at least 1299 Buddhist temples, monasteries and stupas have been speculatively rebuilt from mounds of rubble since 1995, and a further 688 damaged buildings have received major repairs.

'There are now at least 3300 "sites" in Bagan and they are still digging up new ones', says Hudson, who points out that many international authorities have criticised the poor workmanship and historically inaccurate methods, styles and materials often being employed.

Putting this into perspective, Hudson notes that construction appears to have begun on new monuments every two weeks between 1200 and 1280. Down history these hastily built structures have been patched up, repaired and rebuilt. 'It's the ancestors of the same dodgy contractors who are doing the work today', he quips.

A LIVING RELIGIOUS SITE

Following the 1975 quake, Unesco spent 15 years and over US$1 million on restoration projects. But Bagan's current advanced state of restoration is mainly because of a hugely successful donations program initiated by the government in the mid-1990s and enthusiastically supported by many merit-making locals. The result, according to one Unesco official, is 'a Disney-style fantasy version of one of the world's great religious and historical sites'.

Defending the rebuilding programme, Culture Minister Win Sein was quoted in *The New Light of Myanmar* as saying 'it is our national duty to preserve, strengthen and restore all the cultural heritage monuments of Bagan to last and exist forever', pointing out that the temples are 'living religious monuments highly venerated and worshipped by Myanmar people'.

This conflict of interests aside, zoning restrictions continue to be broken in the Bagan archaeological area, the most notable recent examples being the construction of the Aureum Palace's Bagan Viewing Tower at the east end of the central plain and the new (2008) Bagan Golden Palace – both of which seem large and incongruous on the temple-strewn plain.

THE TEMPLES

This section covers the highlights of the thousands of temple sites you can visit in Bagan. For other details about Bagan, including

Many visitors set aside just two days in Bagan even though you can easily spend four or five days here and still leave much unexplored. Adapt the following itineraries to suit your plans or consider just renting a bike and heading off to view thousands of other random sights – the real pleasure of Bagan comes from a leisurely soaking up of its scale and time-slip atmosphere.

One Day

Stick to the **Old Bagan** area starting at the **Tharabar Gate** then heading south to Bagan's most popular temple, **Ananda Pahto** and west to **Thatbyinnyu Pahto**, near where you can climb up the old city wall.

Just west is where King Anawrahta stored all the non-Buddhist images at **Nathlaung Kyaung**. Back on the main road, backtrack towards Tharabar Gate and detour on the gravel road for a river view from **Bupaya**.

In the afternoon visit lacquerware shops in **Myinkaba**, climb up the hidden stairs in modern Manuha Paya and see the bas-relief figures in **Nan Paya**. Finish up at one of the choice sunset spots: **Pyathada Paya** is the adventurous option, east of Myinkaba on goat-herd trails, or play it safe with the easily accessible (hence crowded) **Shwesandaw Paya**, near Old Bagan.

Two Days

Having followed the one-day plan, now tick off other highlights starting with **Dhammayangyi Pahto**, Bagan's largest temple. Take the paths east to the gorgeous **Sulamani Pahto** and escape the crowds at its neighbouring 'mini-me' version, **Thabeik Hmauk**, which is also a good (and generally uncrowded) place to for sunset viewing.

Another lovely view can be had from the terrace of **Dhammayazika Paya** in the South Plain area east of Myinkaba. While out this way visit **Leimyethna Pahto** for its well-preserved frescoes and **Pyathonzu**, which also houses 13th-century murals.

Four Days

On day three many itineraries will have you heading out of the immediate Bagan area to **Salay**, another area sprinkled with old temples and monasteries, and/or **Mt Popa**, famous for its picturesque, *nat-* (spirit-) infested hilltop temple. Both places are interesting, but if you'd rather stay closer to Bagan, schedule visits to **Abeyadana Pahto** and **Nagayon** in Myinkaba and the frescoes in **Lawkahteikpan Pahto**. Adventurous half-day boat trips can be made down or across the Ayeyarwady (Irrawaddy) to more remote temples – the bonus being a chance to sail back into town at sunset.

additional sights, accommodation, eating and transport options, see p113. The temples are all shown on the map on p152.

Old Bagan

ပုဂံမြို့တော်

The most practical part of Bagan to tour by foot (with water and a hat), this roughly counterclockwise 1-mile circuit takes in temples within the old city walls.

Gawdawpalin Pahto   BUDDHIST TEMPLE
ဂေါ်တောပလ္လင်ပုထိုး

Standing 197ft tall, Gawdawpalin is one of the largest and most imposing Bagan

temples – though not necessarily the most inspiring, with its modernised altar and tile floors inside. Built during the reign of Narapatisithu and finished under that of Nantaungmya, it's considered the crowning achievement of the late Bagan period. Its name means 'Platform to which Homage is Paid'. The most recent homage was its heavy-duty reconstruction following terrific damage sustained in the 1975 earthquake (it stands near the quake's epicentre). The stairs to the top terrace are closed to visitors.

Mimalaung Kyaung   MONASTERY
မီးမလောင်ကျောင်း

A nice set of *chinthe* (half-lion/half-dragon deity) guards the stairway leading up this small, square monastery platform, constructed in 1174 by Narapatisithu. It's about 219yd south of Gawdawpalin, on the other side of the road. In front of the monastery is a brick-and-stucco Tripitaka library next to a large acacia tree. Atop the steps, a tiered roof (with a newer gold-capped *hti*, an umbrella-like decorated pinnacle) contains a large sitting buddha. Archaeologists discovered an intricately carved 2.5in votive tablet here that contained 78 sculpted figures.

Pahtothamya
BUDDHIST TEMPLE

ပုထိုးသားများ

On the dirt road 160yd east towards the dominating Thatbyinnyu, the Pahtothamya (or Thamya Pahto) was probably built during the reign of Kyanzittha, around the turn of the 12th century, although it is popularly held to be one of five temples built by the little-known king Taunghthugyi (aka Sawrahan; r 931–64). The interior of this single-storey building is dimly lit, typical of the early type of Pyu-influenced temples, with their small, perforated stone windows. In its prominent vertical superstructure and reconstructed lotus-bud *sikhara* (corncob-like temple finial), however, the monument is clearly beginning to move forward from the early period.

With a torch you can pick out super painting remnants along the interior passages, perhaps the earliest surviving murals in Bagan. Steps lead up to a roomy viewing platform.

Nathlaung Kyaung
HINDU TEMPLE

နတ်လှောင်ကျောင်း

Between Pahtothamya and Thatbyinnyu, this stubby building – the only Hindu temple remaining in Bagan – has a fascinating history. Named 'Shrine Confining Nat', it's where King Anawrahta stored non-Buddhist images, particularly ones for local *nat*, as he tried to enforce Buddhism. The king himself described the temple as 'where the *nat* are kept prisoner'. Severely damaged in the 1975 earthquake, only the temple's main hall and superstructure (with seven original Gupta-style reliefs) still stand.

A sign dates it to the early 11th century. Some say it was built in 931 by Taunghthugyi; if true, this was about a century before the southern school of Buddhism came to Bagan. The temple is dedicated to the Hindu god Vishnu.

The central square of brick supports the dome and crumbled *sikhara,* and once contained freestanding figures of Vishnu, as well as Vishnu reliefs on each of the four sides.

From the Old Bagan jetty you can hire a private boat to reach Tan Kyi village, where you can arrange a taxi ride (or hike) up to **Tan Kyi Paya**, the gold stupa atop the mountain, visible from much of Bagan. Views are terrific and unique, looking back over the river to Bagan's mighty sprawl. A ride for three or four people, including wait time, is about K15,000. You'll need three or four hours for the trip.

The statues were stolen by a German oil engineer in the 1890s, but the badly damaged brick-and-stucco reliefs can still be seen.

Thatbyinnyu Pahto
BUDDHIST TEMPLE

သဗ္ဗညုပုထိုး

Named for 'omniscience', Bagan's highest temple (about 160yd east of Nathlaung and 220yd south of Shwegugyi) is built of two white-coloured boxy storeys, each with three diminishing terraces rimmed with spires and leading to a gold-tipped *sikhara,* 207ft up. Its monumental size and verticality make it a classic example of Bagan's middle period – and neatly provide a chronological link between early-period Ananda and late-period Gawdawpalin, both nearby. Built in 1144 by Alaungsithu, its terraces are encircled by indentations for 539 Jataka. Plaques were never added, leading some scholars to surmise that the monument was never consecrated.

Visitors are barred from climbing Thatbyinnyu's inner passages. There are some original murals near the west entrance.

A couple of hundred yards south you can climb up on the southeastern corner of the **old city wall**. The small 'tally *zedi* (stupa)' just northeast of Thatbyinnyu Pahto was built using one brick for every 10,000 used in constructing the main temple.

Shwegugyi
BUDDHIST TEMPLE

ရွှေဂူကြီး

Built by Alaungsithu in 1131, this smaller but elegant *pahto,* 220yd north of Thatbyinnyu, is an example of Bagan's middle period of temple-building, a transition in architectural style from the dark and cloistered to the airy and light. Its name means 'Great Golden Cave' and its corncob *sikhara* is a scaled-down version of the one at Ananda.

Inside you'll find fine stucco carvings, a teak buddha and stone slabs that retell (in Pali) its history, including that it took just seven months to build. Missing from the scripts are details of its builder's demise – Alaungsithu's son brought his sick father here in 1163 to smother him to death.

Pitaka Taik
BUDDHIST LIBRARY

ပိဋကတ်တိုက်

Following the sacking of Thaton, King Anawrahta is said to have carted off some 30 elephant-loads of Buddhist scriptures in 1058 and built this library (just northeast of Shwegugyi) to house them. The square design follows the basic early Bagan *gu* (cave temple) plan, perfect for the preservation of light-sensitive palm-leaf scriptures. It's notable for the perforated stone windows, each carved from single stone slabs, and the plaster carvings on the roof, which imitate Myanmar woodcarvings.

Tharabar Gate
ARCHAEOLOGICAL SITE

သရပါတံခါး

Do stop on the east side of this former entrance of the original palace site. On either side of the arched gateway are two niches, home not to buddha images but to *nat* who guard the gate and who are treated with profound respect by locals. To the left is Lady Golden Face, and to the right her brother Lord Handsome.

Like most *nat*, Tharabar Gate's twosome had a tragic history. A king married Lady Golden Face to lure her brother Lord Handsome, whom he feared, out of hiding. When the king had Handsome burned at the stake, his sister jumped in too; only her face was saved from the fire.

Superstitious locals don't venture through the gate by motorbike, car or horse cart without first paying a one-time offering to the *nat* (usually a bunch of bananas and a couple of coconuts) to ensure protection against traffic accidents. Don't worry: bicycles are OK, blessing-free.

The gate is the best-preserved remains of the 9th-century wall, and the only gate still standing. Traces of old stucco can still be seen on the gateway.

A number of restaurants are past the former moat, about 220yd east.

Mahabodhi Paya
BUDDHIST TEMPLE

မဟာဗောဓိဘုရား

Unlike any other Bagan temple, this monument, located on the north side of the main road 380yd west of the gate, is modelled after the famous Mahabodhi temple in Bodhgaya, India, which commemorates the spot where the Buddha attained enlightenment. Built during the reign of Nantaungmya in 1215, the temple's unusual pyramidal spire is richly coated in niches enclosing seated buddha figures, rising from a square block. The stairway to the top is closed.

Inside is a modern makeover – with tile floor and carpet. The ruined buildings just north feature some original glazed painting fragments.

Bupaya
BUDDHIST TEMPLE

ဗူးဘုရား

On the bank of the Ayeyarwady (reached from the Nyaung U road, about 220yd northwest of the Mahabodhi Paya), this cylindrical Pyu-style stupa, named for *bu* (gourd), is said to date back to the 3rd century, further than any Bagan temple. Most likely it was erected around the same time as the city walls (around 850). What's seen now – a gold stupa above a row of crenulated terraces leading down to the water – is a reconstruction; the 1975 earthquake demolished the original.

Off the road to the southeast is the Pebinkyaung Paya, a 12th-century pagoda built in a unique Sinhalese style.

North Plain

The bulk of Bagan temples are scattered across the vast northern plain between Nyaung U, Old Bagan and New Bagan. This broad area runs between the Old Bagan walls and Nyaung U, and (mostly) between the two roads that connect the two. Sights are ordered (more or less) west to east.

Ananda Pahto
BUDDHIST TEMPLE

အာနန္ဒာ့ပုထိုး

With its shimmering gold, 170ft-high, corn-cob *hti* shimmering across the plains, Ananda is one of the finest, largest, best preserved and most revered of all Bagan souvenir stands, ur, we mean temples. Hawkers selling books, postcards and oil paintings surely know you'll be making it to this lovely terraced temple, but that shouldn't dissuade you from going.

It's roughly 490yd east of Thatbyinnyu, 550yd north of Shwesandaw and 1090yd northwest of Dhammayangyi Pahto. Most visitors access it from the northern side – where the highest concentration of hawkers are. For a quieter approach, enter from the east side.

A lack of primary sources means the 'histories' attached to Burma's early kingdoms are often a matter of opinion and creative interpretation. 'The best way to treat any legendary story is as a legend', says Sydney University's Dr Bob Hudson, an archaeological expert on Myanmar. He points out that some contemporary scholars have quite different interpretations of the story of Bagan.

'Michael Aung-Thwin, in his book *Mists of Rammana* (University of Hawaii Press), proposes that there was no conquest of Thaton, and that a Mon element in the population of Bagan got there because they had been pushed westward out of Thailand by the expansionist kings of Angkor. The appearance of Indian art styles at Bagan also did not need to come via Thaton. Following the conquest of Buddhist and Hindu principalities in eastern India by the image-shunning Muslims, the logical destination for an Indian artist who specialised in painting or carving human figures was the economically booming and devoutly Buddhist Bagan. The Indian art style became modified by local tastes and techniques, creating a distinctive Myanmar style.

'And the idea originally proposed by the 20th-century historian G H Luce, that the early, dark temples represent the brooding nature of the captive Mon, while the later high, airy temples show the outgoing nature of the Burmans, has an explanation that relies on architecture, not on imagined ethnic traits: the engineers of Bagan simply got better over time at using the arch, which they had adopted from India, and thus could build more spacious interiors.

'Doubt has also been cast on the tale of a Buddhist king of Bagan irreligiously tearing down temples to build fortifications against the advancing Mongols. This is more likely a 'cautionary tale' about the kinds of things that kings should never, never do. And while there was certainly a Mongol invasion of the northern borders of the kingdom in the late 13th century, there is no real evidence that they attacked the capital. There is indeed a painting of a Mongol archer on a pagoda wall at Bagan, but he is cheerfully shooting at a duck, while his senior officer lounges under a tree. The provincial lords in the north, who actually did fight off the Mongols, were so successful that, as the economy of Bagan deteriorated under the burden of temple construction, a new series of capitals slowly grew up around Mandalay and Ava. Bagan was not so much destroyed as relegated to the second division.

'Some of these interpretations remain contentious. You might find the discussions on some of the Burma/Mon history websites highly entertaining, especially if you thought academics are all full of reasoned arguments and civilised discourse!'

Thought to have been built between 1090 and 1105 by King Kyanzittha, this perfectly proportioned temple heralds the stylistic end of the early Bagan period and the beginning of the middle period. In 1990, on its 900th anniversary, the temple spires were gilded. The remainder of the temple exterior is whitewashed from time to time.

The central square measures 58yd along each side. Upper floors are closed to visitors. The entranceways make the structure a perfect Greek cross; each entrance is crowned with a stupa finial. The base and the terraces are decorated with 554 glazed tiles showing Jataka scenes, thought to be derived from Mon texts. Look back as you enter to see the huge carved teak doors that separate interior halls from cross passages on all four sides.

Facing outward from the centre of the cube are four 31ft standing buddha statues.

Only the Bagan-style images facing north and south are original; both display the *dhammachakka mudra* (a hand position symbolising the Buddha teaching his first sermon). The other two images are replacements for figures destroyed by fire in the 1600s. All four have bodies of solid teak, though guides may claim the southern image is made of a bronze alloy. Guides like to point out that if you stand by the donation box in front of the original southern buddha, his face looks sad, while from a distance he tends to look mirthful.

The western and eastern standing buddha images are done in the later Konbaung, or Mandalay, style. If looked at from the right angle, the two lions at the eastern side resemble an ogre. A small, nut-like sphere held between the thumb and middle finger of the east-facing image is said to resemble a herbal pill, and may represent the buddha offering *dhamma* (Buddhist teachings) as a cure for suffering. Both arms hang at the image's sides with hands outstretched, a *mudra* (hand position) unknown to traditional Buddhist sculpture outside this temple.

The west-facing buddha features the *abhaya mudra* (the hands outstretched, in the gesture of no fear). At its feet sit two life-sized lacquer statues, said to represent King Kyanzittha and Shin Arahan, the Mon monk who initiated Anawrahta into Theravada Buddhism. Inside the western portico are two symbols on pedestals of the Buddha's footprints.

Don't leave without taking a brief walk around the outside of the temple, where you can see many glazed tiles and lovely views of the spires and terraced roofs (often away from vendor hassle too).

Ananda Ok Kyaung
BUDDHIST CHAPEL

အာနန္ဒာအုတ်ကျောင်း

Just west of Ananda's northern entry, this small *vihara* (sanctuary or chapel) features some detailed 18th-century murals bursting with bright red and green, showing details of everyday life from the Bagan period. In the southeast corner, you can see Portuguese figures engaged in trade. Built in 1137, the temple's name means 'Ananda Brick Monastery'.

Upali Thein
ORDINATION HALL

ဥပါလိသိမ်

Just north of the Bagan-Nyaung U Rd, almost midway to Nyaung U, this squat mid-13th-century ordination hall houses some brightly painted frescoes depicting big scenes on the walls and ceilings from the late 17th or early 18th century. Sadly many pieces crumbled in the 1975 earthquake. The building, named for a well-known monk from the 13th century, is often locked to protect the art, but you can see in (a bit) from

the three gated doorways if the 'keyholder' isn't around. The roof battlements imitate Myanmar wooden architecture, and a small centre spire rises from the rooftop.

Htilominlo Pahto
BUDDHIST TEMPLE

ထီးလိုမင်းလိုပုထိုး

Across the road from Upali Thein, this 150ft-high temple (built in 1218) marks the spot where King Nantaungmya was chosen (by a leaning umbrella – that timeless decider), among five brothers, to be the crown prince. It's more impressive from the outside, with its terraced design, which is similar to Sulamani Pahto. Have a walk around the 140-sq-ft base to take in the fragments of the original fine plaster carvings, glazed sandstone decorations and nicely carved reliefs on the doorways. Inside are four buddhas on the lower and upper floors, though the stairways are closed. Traces of old murals are also still visible. Unfortunately it's Vendor Central.

Buledi
BUDDHIST TEMPLE

ဗူးလယ်သိ

Great for its views, this steep-stepped, pyramid-style stupa looks ho-hum from afar, but the narrow terrace has become something of an alternative sunset spot. It's about 660yd south of the Htilominlo, across Anawrahta Rd. It's also known as 'Temple 394' (not correctly labelled on some maps).

If persistent vendors are getting to you, try the miniature version, **Temple 405**, with several glazed tiles visible, just east of Buledi.

Gubyauknge
BUDDHIST TEMPLE

ဂူပြောက်ငယ်

Off Anawrahta Rd, almost a mile east of Htilominlo, this early-Bagan-period temple has some excellent stucco carvings on the outside walls (particularly on the north side) and some original paintings visible inside.

TEMPLE FESTIVALS

The following are Bagan's major temple festivals or *paya pwe*, listed in order of their celebration through the year. At them all expect religious chanting around the clock, religious paraphernalia stalls and music and drama performances.

» **Manuha Paya** Held on the full moon of Tabaung (February/March).

» **Gawdawpalin Pahto** Celebrated on the full moon of Thadingyut (September/October).

» **Shwezigon Paya** Celebrated on the full moon of Tazaungmon (October/November).

» **Ananda Pahto** This roughly two-week event culminating on the full moon of Pyatho (December/January) is Bagan's biggest festival, when hundreds of monks come to collect alms from thousands of merit-seeking locals.

Major temples that remain active places of worship such as Ananda Pahto and Shwezigon Paya are always open during the day. At many others to get inside you first have to find the 'keyholder' whose job it is to act as the caretaker of the site. Often they (or their kids) will find you first and open the gate for you. A bit of 'tea money' (say K500) is appreciated. We're told that the keyholders are assigned by the archaeology department.

The other constant of Bagan temples – even relatively remote ones – are souvenir hawkers, often selling (and sometimes creating) colourful sand paintings. Some of these replicate parts of the murals from inside the temples and are quite skilful with prices starting at as little as K500 for the smaller canvases, but rising sharply for more detailed and larger works; other images are pretty generic and found across all temple sites. Although some hawkers can be persistent, if you're not interested in buying, most will leave you alone.

We're told that official souvenir hawkers at the temples pay K45,000 a year for a licence, but it's likely that there are many more unofficial vendors given the potential for relatively easy money. 'Even if they only sell a few trinkets a week, it's an easy job,' said one frequent visitor to Bagan, 'as the alternative is a farm job which pays far less a day.' A guide also bemoaned that children in Bagan are starting to quit school in order to work as hawkers.

Wetkyi-In-Gubyaukgyi
BUDDHIST TEMPLE

ဝက်ကြီး;အင်း;ဂူပြောက်ကြီး;

Just west of Nyaung U and about 100yd east of Gubyauknge, this detailed off-the-main-circuit, 13th-century temple has an Indian-style spire, like the Mahabodhi Paya in Old Bagan. It's interesting for fine frescoes of scenes from the Jataka but, unfortunately, in 1899 a German collector surreptitiously removed many of the panels on which the frescoes were painted. Those that remain in the entry are in great shape. Steps inside lead to four buddha images and you can see Hindu figures engraved on the spire.

Central Plain

Extending from the edge of Old Bagan, this vast and lovely plain (roughly south of Anawrahta Rd between New Bagan and Nyaung U) is home to a few must-sees everyone gets to (Shwesandaw Paya and Dhammayangyi Pahto) and many pockets of temples that few ever see. It's great turf to follow your own whims, as you'll find goatherds and a bit of village life out here, but there is nothing in the way of restaurants or lunch options. Some temples are locked but a 'keyholder' should be in the area.

This list of well-worthy sites runs west to east (towards the clearly visible Bagan Tower construction site, near Nyaung U).

Shwesandaw Paya
BUDDHIST TEMPLE

ရွှေဆံတော်ဘုရား;

Bagan's most famous sunset-viewing spot, the Shwesandaw is a graceful white pyramid-style pagoda with steps leading past five terraces to the circular stupa top, with good 360-degree views. It's located roughly midway between Thatbyinnyu and Dhammayangyi. Its top terrace is roomy – just as well, considering the numbers of camera-toting travellers coming by taxi or bus before sunset. If you go during the day, you'll likely be alone.

Shwesandaw means 'golden holy hair': legend has it that the stupa enshrines a Buddha hair relic presented to King Anawrahta by the King of Ussa Bago (Pegu) in thanks for his assistance in repelling an invasion by the Khmers. The terraces once bore terracotta plaques showing scenes from the Jataka but traces of these, and of other sculptures, were covered by rather heavy-handed renovations. The now-gilded *zedi* (stupa) bell rises from two octagonal bases, which top the five square terraces. This was the first Bagan monument to feature stairways leading from the square terraces to the round base of the stupa.

The *hti,* which was toppled by the 1975 earthquake, can still be seen lying on the south side of the paya compound. A new one was fitted soon after the quake.

About 165yd north stands **Lawkahteikpan Pahto** – a small but interesting middle-period *gu* containing excellent frescoes and inscriptions in both Burmese and Mon.

Dhammayangyi Pahto
BUDDHIST TEMPLE

ဓမ္မရံကြီး;ပုထိ;

Visible from all parts of Bagan, this massive, walled, 12th-century temple (about 550yd east of Shwesandaw) is infamous for its

TEMPLES OF BAGAN CENTRAL PLAIN

mysterious, bricked-up inner passageways and cruel history.

It's said that King Narathu built the temple to atone for his sins: he smothered his father and brother to death and executed one of his wives, an Indian princess, for practising Hindu rituals. Narathu is also said to have mandated that the mortarless brickwork fit together so tightly that even a pin couldn't pass between any two bricks. Workers who failed in this task had their arms chopped off: just inside the west entrance, note the stones with arm-sized grooves where these amputations allegedly happened.

After Narathu died – by assassination in 1170 – the inner encircling ambulatory was filled with brick rubble, as 'payback'. (Others quietly argue the temple dates from the earlier reign of Alaungsithu, which would refute all this fun legend behind it.) It's also likely that this bricking up of the passages was a crude way of ensuring the massive structure didn't collapse.

The plan here is similar to Ananda, with projecting porticoes and receding terraces, though its *sikhara* is reduced to a stub nowadays. Walking around the outer ambulatory, under ceilings so high you can only hear the squeaks of bats circling in the dark, you can see some intact stucco reliefs and paintings, suggesting the work had been completed. The mystery goes on.

Three out of the four buddha sanctums were also filled with bricks. The remaining western shrine features two original side-by-side images of Gautama and Maitreya, the historical and future buddhas (it's the only Bagan site with two side-by-side buddhas).

The temple's bad karma may be the reason it remains one of the few temples not to have undergone major restoration. But that may change in the future, as China is said to be interested in donating funds for such a project. Perhaps then one of the great architectural mysteries of Bagan will be solved.

Sulamani Pahto
BUDDHIST TEMPLE

စူဠာမဏိပုထိုး

About half a mile east of Dhammayangyi, this broad two-storey temple is one of Bagan's most attractive, with lush grounds (and ample vendors) behind the surrounding walls. It's a prime example of later, more sophisticated temple styles, with better internal lighting.

This temple with five doorways is known as the Crowning Jewel and was constructed around 1181 by Narapatisithu. Combining the early period's horizontal planes with the

vertical lines of the middle period, the receding terraces create a pyramid effect. The brickwork throughout is considered some of the best in Bagan. The gilded *sikhara* is a reconstruction; the original was destroyed in the 1975 earthquake. The interior face of the wall was once lined with 100 monastic cells, a feature unique among Bagan's ancient monasteries.

There's much to see inside. Carved stucco on mouldings, pediments and pilasters represents some of Bagan's finest ornamental work and is in fairly good condition. Glazed plaques around the base and terraces are also still visible, as are many big and small murals.

Buddha images face the four directions from the ground floor; the image at the main eastern entrance sits in a recess built into the wall. The interior passage around the base is painted with quite big frescoes from the Konbaung period, and there are traces of earlier frescoes. The stairways to the top are closed.

Thabeik Hmauk
BUDDHIST TEMPLE

သပိတ်မှောက်

Facing Sulamani from 150yd east, and well worth visiting, this *sikhara*-topped temple looks like a miniature version of its more famous neighbour, but sees far fewer visitors (or vendors). Thabeik Hmauk means 'Boycott Temple', as it was made in response to the similarly designed Sulamani, which was ordered by the brutal king Narapatisithu. Much of its interior was damaged by the 1975 earthquake, but there are multiple stairways up to a wrap-around meditation chamber with little light (and a few bats). There are two outside terraces, reached by narrow stairs, with superb views.

Pyathada Paya
BUDDHIST TEMPLE

ပြဿဒါးဘုရား

About half a mile southeast of Sulamani, reached by dirt roads that sometimes get obscured in goat fields, this huge, impressive pagoda is a superb sunset-viewing spot, with a giant open terrace (Bagan's largest) atop the steps, and another small deck further up. The tour groups have discovered it so you're unlikely to have the place to yourself. Note how the top stupa isn't centred on the top platform.

Dating from the 13th century, during the latter period of temple building at Bagan, Pyathada's interior arches are still partly open to view. The architects used an inner relieving arch and a second upper arch to support the huge chambers, illustrating the point that temple styles changed in Bagan because the builders improved at arch construction (for more information, see p157).

Myinkaba Area
မြင်ကပါ

The sites north and south of Myinkaba village are all just off the main road and are easy to access. These are listed in order from north to south.

Mingalazedi Paya BUDDHIST TEMPLE
မင်္ဂလာစေတီ

Close to the riverbank, towards Myinkaba from the Thiripyitsaya Sakura Hotel, Mingalazedi Paya (Blessing Stupa) represents the final flowering of Bagan's architectural outburst, as displayed in its enormous bell-like dome and the beautiful glazed Jataka tiles around each terrace. Although many of the 1061 original tiles have been damaged or stolen, there are still 561 left. The smaller square building in the *zedi* grounds is one of the few Tripitaka libraries made of brick.

Gubyaukgyi BUDDHIST TEMPLE
ဂူပြောက်ကြီး

Situated just to the left of the road as you enter Myinkaba, Gubyaukgyi (Great Painted Cave Temple) sees a lot of visitors who are drawn by the well-preserved, richly coloured paintings inside. These are thought to date from the temple's original construction in 1113, when Kyanzittha's son Rajakumar built it following his father's death. In Indian style, the monument consists of a large vestibule attached to a smaller antechamber. The fine stuccowork on its exterior walls is in particularly good condition.

Perforated, Pyu-style windows mean you'll need a powerful torch to see the ceiling paintings clearly. If it's locked during off-season, ask in the village for the keyholder.

Next to the monument stands the gilded Myazedi (Emerald Stupa). A four-sided pillar in a cage between the two monuments bears an inscription consecrating Gubyaukgyi and written in four languages – Pyu, Mon, Old Burmese and Pali. Its linguistic and historical significance is great, since it establishes the Pyu as an important cultural influence in early Bagan and relates the chronology of the Bagan kings as well as acting as a 'Rosetta Stone' to allow scholars to decypher the Pyu.

Manuha Paya BUDDHIST TEMPLE
မနူဟာဘုရား

In Myinkaba village, about a third of a mile south of Gubyaukgyi, stands this active – and rather modern-looking, even though it dates back to 1059 – pagoda. It is named after Manuha, the Mon king from Thaton, who was held captive here by King Anawrahta.

In the front of the building are three seated buddhas; in the back is a huge reclining buddha. All seem too large for their enclosures – supposedly representing the stress and discomfort the king had to endure. However, these features are not unique in Bagan.

It is said that only the reclining buddha, in the act of entering *parinibbana* (final passing away), has a smile on its face, showing that for Manuha, only death was a release from his suffering. But if you climb to the top of this paya via the stairs in the back (ask for keys if it's locked), you can see the face of the sitting buddha through a window – from up here you'll realise that the gigantic face, so grim from below, has an equally gigantic smile.

Nan Paya BUDDHIST TEMPLE
နန်းဘုရား

Just south of Manuha Paya by dirt road, this shrine is said to have been used as Manuha's prison, although there is little evidence supporting the legend. In this story the shrine was originally Hindu, and captors thought using it as a prison would be easier than converting it to a Buddhist temple. It's worth visiting for its interior masonry work – sandstone block facings over a brick core, certainly some of Bagan's finest detailed sculpture. Perforated stone windows are typical of earlier Bagan architecture – in fact it was probably Bagan's first *gu*-style shrine.

In the central sanctuary the four stone pillars have finely carved sandstone bas-relief figures of three-faced Brahma. The creator deity is holding lotus flowers, thought to be offerings to a freestanding buddha image once situated in the shrine's centre, a theory that dispels the idea that this was ever a Hindu shrine. The sides of the pillars feature ogre-like *kala-ate* heads with open mouths streaming with flowers. Legend goes that Shiva employed these creatures of Hindu legend to protect temples, but they proved too ferocious so Shiva tricked them into eating their bodies, then fed them flowers to keep their minds off snacking on worshippers. In the centre of the four pillars is an altar on which once stood a standing

LOCAL KNOWLEDGE

U THEIN LWIN *DIRECTOR, DEPARTMENT OF ARCHAEOLOGY, BAGAN*

My recommendations for Bagan's most significant temples to see are as follows, in chronological order:

Ananda Pahto (p156)

Not only is it an outstanding example of Bagan temple architecture, Ananda is rich in decorative detail, including the four standing wooden images of Buddha, the life of Buddha depicted in niche carvings and the Jataka series tiles.

Nagayon (p162)

This is the last restoration project that Unesco was involved in and was built in the same period as Ananda. Look for the 28 images of Buddha under the main sculpture.

Abeyadana Pahto (p162)

This is my personal favourite – inside you can see 550 Jakata mural paintings and various Hindu deities paying homage to Buddha.

Gubyaukgyi (p161)

Famous for its frescoes, this is one of the last temples built in the 11th century – apart from life-of-Buddha illustrations, you can see scenes from four Buddhist synods held in ancient times.

Lawkahteikpan Pahto (p159)

Also very important for its frescoes, including eight great miracles of Buddha's life. You can read the Jakata scenes as a complete story. You start to see a distinct Myanmar style emerge here from the Mon influence.

---

buddha or (some locals believe) a Hindu god. Ask at Manuha if the temple is locked.

Abeyadana Pahto
BUDDHIST TEMPLE

အပါယ်ရတနာပုထို:

About 440yd south of Manuha Paya, this 11th-century temple with a Sinhalese-style stupa was supposedly built by Kyanzittha's Bengali wife Abeyadana, who waited for him here as he hid for his life from his predecessor King Sawlu. It's famed for its original frescoes, which were cleaned in 1987 by Unesco staff. With a torch, you can make out many figures that Abeyadana, believed to be a Mahayanist, would likely have asked for: Bodhisattvas such as Avalokitesvara, and Hindu deities Brahma, Vishnu, Shiva and Indra. The inner shrine contains a large, brick, seated buddha (partly restored); surrounding walls are lined with niches, most now empty. Inside the front wall are many Jataka scenes.

Ask at the caretaker's house to the south if the temple is locked.

Some visitors enjoy the sunset at the often-overlooked **Kyasin** across the road.

Nagayon
BUDDHIST TEMPLE

နဂါး:ရုံ

Slightly south of Abeyadana and across the road, this elegant and well-preserved temple was built by Kyanzittha. The main buddha image is twice life size and shelters under the hood of a huge *naga* (dragon serpent). This reflects the legend that in 1192 Kyanzittha built the temple on the spot where he was sheltered while fleeing from his angry brother and predecessor Sawlu – an activity he had to indulge in on more than one occasion.

Paintings also decorate the corridor walls. The central shrine has two smaller standing buddhas as well as the large one. The temple itself – with corncob *sikhara,* which some believe to be the Ananda prototype – can be climbed via tight stairs.

Somingyi Kyaung
BUDDHIST TEMPLE

စိုးမင်း:ကြီး:ကျောင်း:

Named after the woman who supposedly sponsored its construction, this typical late-Bagan brick monastery (about 220yd southwest of Nagayon) is thought to have been built in 1204. A *zedi* to the north and *gu* to the south are also ascribed to Somingyi. Many brick monasteries in Bagan were single-block structures; Somingyi is unique in that it has monastic cells clustered around a courtyard.

New Bagan Area
ပုဂံမြို့သစ်

Sights are a little scarcer heading south of New Bagan towards the outskirts of the Bagan area.

Seinnyet Nyima Paya & Seinnyet Ama Pahto   BUDDHIST TEMPLE
စိမ်းညက်ညီမ နှင့် စိမ်းညက်အစ်မ ပုထိုး

This stupa and shrine stand side by side (about 270yd north of New Bagan) and are traditionally ascribed to Queen Seinnyet in the 11th century, although the architecture clearly points to a period two centuries later. The *zedi* rests on three terraces and is topped by a beautiful stylised umbrella.

Lawkananda Paya   BUDDHIST TEMPLE
လောကနန္ဒာဘုရား

At the height of Bagan's power, boats from the Mon region, Rakhaing (Arakan) and even Sri Lanka would anchor by this riverside pagoda (about 270yd southeast of the New Bagan crossroads – a sign in Burmese points the way) with its distinctive elongated cylindrical dome. It was built in 1059 by Anawrahta. It is still used as a place of worship and is thought to house an important Buddha tooth replica. There are lots of benches for wide-open views of the Ayeyarwady, but it's sometimes hard to enjoy hassle-free.

Ashe (East) & Anauk (West) Petleik Paya   BUDDHIST TEMPLE
အရှေ့ နှင့် အနောက် ပက်လိပ်ဘုရား

Just inland to the northeast from Lawkananda Paya are the excavated remains of these twin 11th-century paya. Found in 1905, the lower parts of the pagodas are ho-hum from the outside but feature hundreds of terracotta Jataka lining the vaulted corridors (particularly impressive in Anauk Petleik Paya). A keyholder usually appears to unlock the door and turn on the fluorescent lights.

Sittana Paya   BUDDHIST TEMPLE
စစ်တနာဘုရား

About half a mile further south, this large, 13th-century bell-shaped stupa is New Bagan's most impressive structure. Built by Htilominlo, and showing some Hindu influences, it's set on four square terraces, each fronted by a standing buddha image in brick

and stucco. A rather rickety stairway leads up the stupa's southern side to the terraces, where you can circle the structure. At the southwestern corner is a closed-off chamber leading into an inner sanctum.

South Plain

This rural area, along Bagan's southern reaches, follows the main road between New Bagan and Nyaung U Airport, passing Pwasaw and Minnanthu villages on the way. Other than a few places, such as Payathonzu, most sights see few tourists. Many horse-cart drivers will take in the cluster of sights north of Minnanthu and go via dirt paths towards Central Plain sights, such as Sulamani Pahto. Views west from some temples here rival any other in Bagan in terms of scope of the site.

The following sites are listed in order from west to east.

Dhammayazika Paya   BUDDHIST TEMPLE
ဓမ္မရာဇိကဘုရား

About 2 miles east of the New Bagan crossroads, and standing north of the main road, this pentagonal *zedi* is similar to the Shwezigon but with a more unusual design. Set in the south-central end of Bagan, it also has lovely views from its highest terrace.

Sitting in lush garden grounds with a gilded bell, the Dhammayazika dates from 1196. An outer wall has five gateways. Up top, five small temples, each containing a buddha image, encircle the terraces; some of them bear interior murals added during the Konbaung era.

Watch out for ghosts here! Supposedly the stupa's construction began under a general who died before its completion. His likeness is said to appear in many photos of the site, including a fairly recent one of government officials.

It's possible, with perseverance, to cycle the thrilling dirt roads here from Dhammayangyi Pahto, a mile north.

Leimyethna Pahto   BUDDHIST TEMPLE
လေးမျက်နှာဘုရား

Built in 1222, this east-facing, whitewashed temple near Minnanthu village (almost 2 miles east of Dhammayazika on the north side of the road) stands on a raised platform and has interior walls decorated with well-preserved frescoes. It is topped by a gilded Indian-style spire like that on Ananda. The jar-like structures out the front were pillars of a building toppled by the 1975 earthquake.

Tayok Pye Paya BUDDHIST TEMPLE

တရုတ်ပြေးဘုရား:

A couple of hundred yards north of Leimyethna by dirt road, this spired temple gets attention for the views from its upper reaches (though its top level is now closed).

Payathonzu BUDDHIST TEMPLE

ဘုရားသုံးဆူ

Across the main road from Tayok, this complex of three interconnected shrines (the name means Three Stupas) is worth seeing for its 13th-century murals close up. It was abandoned shortly before its construction was complete. Each square cubicle is topped by a fat *sikhara;* a similar structure appears only at Salay (p128). The design is remarkably like Khmer Buddhist ruins in Thailand.

You enter the middle shrine. To the right (south) are scratched-up, whitewashed walls. The other two shrines (particularly the northernmost one) are home to lovely, vaguely Chinese- or Tibetan-looking mural paintings that contain Bodhisattva figures. Whether these indicate possible Mahayana or Tantric influence is a hotly debated issue among art historians. Some drawings are rather crudely touched up.

The three-shrine design hints at links with the Hindu Trimurti (triad) of Vishnu, Shiva and Brahma, a triumvirate also associated with Tantric Buddhism. You might also say it represents the Triple Gems of Buddhism (buddha, *dhamma* and *sangha*), except that such a design is uncommon in Asian Buddhist architecture, although it does appear in the Hindu shrines of India and Nepal.

Thambula Pahto BUDDHIST TEMPLE

သမ္ဗူလပုထိုး:

This square temple, surrounded by crumbling walls just north of Payathonzu, is decorated with faded Jataka frescoes and was built in 1255 by Thambula, the wife of King Uzana. It's often locked, but go to the (shaded at midday) doors and peek through the gate to see into wall and ceiling murals. A mural of a boat race can be seen from the southern entrance; good ceiling murals are seen from the north side.

Nandamannya Pahto BUDDHIST TEMPLE

နန္ဒာမညာ

Dating from the mid-13th century, this small, single-chambered temple has very fine frescoes and a ruined seated buddha image. It's about 220yd north of Thambula; a sign leads down a short dirt road. (It's the one to the right.)

Nandamannya earns its reputation from its mural of the 'Temptation of Mara', in which nubile young females (vainly) attempt to distract the Buddha from the meditation session that led to his enlightenment. The undressed nature of the females shocked French epigraphist Charles Duroiselle, who wrote in 1916 that they were 'so vulgarly erotic and revolting that they can neither be reproduced or described'. Times change: the topless women can be seen, without blushing, on the back left wall.

The murals' similarity with those at Payathonzu has led some art historians to suggest they were painted by the same hand.

Just behind the temple is the **Kyat Kan Kyaung**, a working underground monastery dating from the 11th century. Mats on the tunnel floors are used for meditation.

Nyaung U Area

ညောင်ဦး:

The main site in this area is the superb Shwezigon Paya.

Shwezigon Paya BUDDHIST TEMPLE

ရွှေစည်းခုံဘုရား:

At the west end of Nyaung U, this big, beautiful *zedi* is the town's main religious site, and is most famous for its link with the 37 *nat.*

Lit up impressively at dusk the gilded *zedi* sits on three rising terraces. Enamelled plaques in panels around the base of the *zedi* illustrate scenes from the Jataka. At the cardinal points, facing the terrace stairways, are four shrines, each of which houses a 13ft-high bronze standing buddha. Gupta-inspired and cast in 1102, these are Bagan's largest surviving bronze buddhas.

A 4in circular indentation in a stone slab, before the upwards-heading eastern steps, was filled with water to allow former Myanmar monarchs to look at the reflection of the *hti* without tipping their heads backwards (which might have caused them to lose their crowns).

The most important site here is the small yellow compound called **37 Nat** (in English) on the southeast side of the site. Inside are figures of all the 37 pre-Buddhist *nat* that were officially endorsed by Bamar monarchy in a compromising gesture towards a pub-

From Nyaung U's jetty you can negotiate a fun boat trip to see three temples just off the Ayeyarwady riverbank. Half a mile north, is 13th-century **Thetkyamuni**, with a few murals inside (hard to make out) and tight, dark steps leading up to a small terrace up top. On the hill nearby is the same-era **Kondawgyi Pahto**, with better preserved murals and views from the surrounding platform.

Another kilometre or so north is the 11th- and 12th-century **Kyauk Gu Ohnmin** cave temple, built in the side of a ravine. It's said during WWII Japanese soldiers hid out here. The inside tunnels lead about 55yd to blocked-off rubble. Some locals say the tunnel was intended to go, ahem, to Pindaya Cave near Inle Lake. You can climb on top of the temple from the new steps to the right.

These sights are accessible, with more difficulty, by road. A boat trip takes about two or three hours, and your driver will show you the temples. It costs about K15,000 for three or four people.

lic reluctant to give up all their beliefs for Buddhism. Ask around if the compound is locked. At one end stands an original stone figure of Thagyamin, king of the *nat* and a direct appropriation of the Hindu god Indra. This is the oldest known freestanding Thagyamin figure in Myanmar.

The site was started by Anawrahta but not completed until the reign of Kyanzittha. The latter is thought to have built his palace nearby.

A path on the north side leads down to the riverbank, where you can get some interesting views.

Kyanzittha Umin
BUDDHIST TEMPLE

ကျန်စစ်သားဥမင်

Although officially credited to Kyanzittha, this cave temple may actually date back to Anawrahta. Built into a cliff face 270yd southwest of Shwezigon, the long, dimly lit corridors are decorated with frescoes, some of which are thought to have been painted by Bagan's Tartar invaders during the period of the Mongol occupation after 1287. An attendant will usually greet you with a torch to lend and keys to unlock the doors. It's *very* quiet in there, and you can actually see the 700-year-old brush strokes.

Eastern Myanmar

Best Places to Eat

» Lin Htett Myanmar Traditional Food (p182)

» Viewpoint Restaurant (p182)

» Thu Maung Restaurant (p173)

Best Places to Stay

» Pindaya Inle Inn (p176)

» Golden Island Cottages (Thale U; p187)

» Pine Hill Resort (p172)

» Inle Princess Resort (p188)

» Teakwood Guest House (p180)

» Hotel Amazing Nyaung Shwe (p180)

» Aquarius Inn (p180)

Why Go?

The shaggy hills of Shan State are ground zero for some of the country's most fabled outdoor pursuits. Activities such as buzzing along Inle Lake in a motorised canoe and trekking among the Pa-O and Danu villages outside Kalaw are classic Myanmar (Burma) experiences, and should not be missed. Throw in even more opportunities for trekking, boating and caving in lesser-known areas such as Pindaya and Kakku, and we reckon even the most hopeless outdoor junkie will be sated.

Once you've caught your breath, eastern Myanmar is also the best region for a unique cultural experience. Because of the logistical difficulties of getting to Kengtung (Kyaingtong) and Kayah State, the border regions see far fewer visitors, but it's worth making the effort to reach these intriguing enclaves of ethnic Tai and hill-tribe culture.

When to Go

Eastern Myanmar is the place to head in winter (November to January); even though night-time temperatures dip perilously close to freezing, the daytime temperatures at the higher elevations are a comfortable 68°F to 79°F (20°C to 26°C). The hottest time of year is from March to May, when daytime temperatures climb close to 104°F (40°C), but the evenings and mornings remain cool. The rainy season is from June to October and it would be best to avoid this time, especially if you plan to do any trekking.

THAZI TO INLE LAKE

The rolling hills between Mandalay and Inle Lake have attracted travellers ever since Myanmar first opened up to international visitors in the early '90s. From the junction town of Thazi, a pitted highway cuts east across a series of mountainous ridges, divided by broad valleys covered in a multicoloured patchwork of fields, villages and hedges. After Yangon and Bagan, this is probably the most visited part of Myanmar – not least because of the enduring appeal of Inle Lake.

Thazi

သာစည်

☏064 / POP C10,000

Thazi crops up on travellers' itineraries for one reason only – the town marks the intersection of the Mandalay–Yangon rail line and the highway towards Inle Lake and the Thai border.

🛏 Sleeping & Eating

Moon-Light Rest House GUESTHOUSE **$**

(☏69056; Thazi-Taunggyi Hwy; r $3-10; ❋) On the main route to Taunggyi and located across the street from the road that leads to the train station, this simple guesthouse is run by the delightful Htun family. The basic rooms are clean, the atmosphere is wholesome, the welcome is genuine and the attached restaurant serves good food. Staff can help out with travel arrangements.

❶ Information

Internet (Thazi-Taunggyi Hwy; per hr K500; ☺9am-10pm) is available across the street from Moon-Light Rest House, in the post office compound.

❶ Getting There & Away

Most people arrive in Thazi by train – the station is about 300yd north of the main road. Buses drop off and pick up passengers along the highway near Moon-Light Rest House.

Bus

To reach Thazi from Mandalay, take a bus to Meiktila (K3000, three hours) from the highway bus station, then hop on a pick-up truck from Meiktila to Thazi (K500, one hour).

Heading east from Thazi, several buses leave between 7am and 11am daily bound for Kalaw (K2500, four hours), Shwenyaung (K3000, six hours) and Taunggyi (K4000, seven hours).

❶ TRAVEL RESTRICTIONS

Most places between Thazi and Taunggyi are open to foreigners, but the only way to reach Kengtung from inside Myanmar is by air. Even then, you are generally not allowed to exit the country at Tachileik, and must fly back the way you came (or to somewhere else within Myanmar).

Confusing things even more, tourists entering Myanmar from Thailand via Tachileik are only permitted to travel as far as Kengtung – it's not possible to cross to China nor will you be allowed to fly anywhere else in the country. For details on this border, go to p197.

Parts of Kayah State are open to foreign tourists, but only to those who have received advance permission and who have booked a government-sanctioned package tour. For details on arranging this go to p198.

Fares are typically doubled for foreigners. To get a seat on one of the more comfortable express buses between Mandalay and Taunggyi, you'll need to make an advance reservation – the staff at the Moon-Light can help.

Pick-Up Truck & Taxi

There are frequent pick-ups for Kalaw, Shwenyaung and Taunggyi, charging the same as buses but taking longer and not quite as comfortable.

A few long-distance taxis loiter around the station in Thazi charging $70 to Kalaw and $90 to Nyaungshwe (Yaunghwe) near Inle Lake. You'll need to bargain hard for a fair price.

Train

Thazi is an important stop on the rail route between Yangon and Mandalay, and also one end of the scenic mountain line to Shwenyaung. For information on getting here from Yangon see p71, and from Mandalay see p222.

A horse cart from the station to the bus stand will cost around K1000.

YANGON Ordinary $9 to $12, upper $24 to $28; 11 to 12 hours; departures 7.45am, 8.17am, 9am, 12.25am.

MANDALAY Ordinary $3, upper $8; three hours; departures 3.52am, 4.19am, 7.22am, 5.41am, 8.44am, 6.04pm.

SHWENYAUNG Fare $5; nine hours; departure 5am.

KALAW Fare $3; six hours; departure 5am.

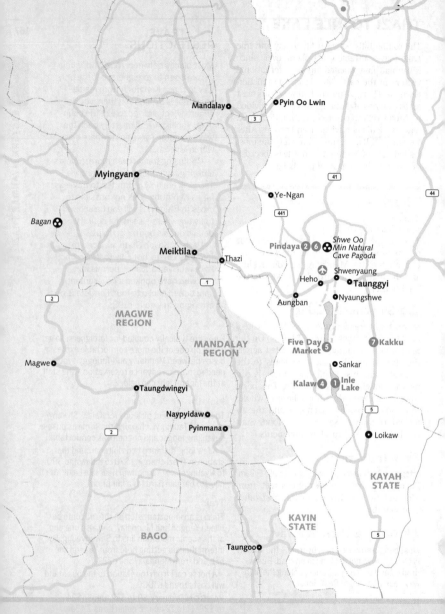

Eastern Myanmar Highlights

1 Drift around the backwaters, ruined stupas and tribal markets at **Inle Lake** (p177)

2 Gasp at the sight of more than 8700 golden buddhas in the atmospheric cave pagoda at **Pindaya** (p175)

3 Go pagoda hopping then trip out to traditional hill-tribe villages in **Kengtung** (p192)

Jinghong

Mong La

Wan Nyek & Wan Saen

CHINA

Pin Tau

④

③ Kengtung

Mong Yawng

SHAN STATE

Ho Kyim

Loi-mwe

LAOS

Tachileik

Mae Sai

Xieng Kok

Thanlwin River

Chiang Rai

Mae Hong Son

THAILAND

0 — 200 km
0 — 120 miles

④ Hike through mountains, fields and villages on the classic **trek from Kalaw to Inle Lake** (p172)

⑤ Pick up a unique souvenir (or at least some unique photos) at the Inle Lake area's **Five Day Market** (p183)

⑥ Get off the beaten track on an overnight trek through

the tea-tree-studded hills surrounding **Pindaya** (p175)

⑦ Witness 2478 seemingly abandoned stupas at **Kakku** (p192)

Kalaw

ကလော

☎ 081 / POP C10,000

Founded as a hill station by British civil servants fleeing the heat of the plains, Kalaw still feels like a high-altitude holiday resort: the air is cool, the atmosphere is calm, the streets are leafy and green, and the surrounding hills offer some of the best trekking in Myanmar.

In addition to foreign trekkers, Kalaw has a significant population of Nepali Gurkhas and Indian Hindus, Sikhs and Muslims, who came here to build the roads and railway line during the British period.

◉ Sights

Right in the centre of Kalaw is **Aung Chan Tha Zedi**, a glittery stupa (Buddhist ceremonial tower), covered in gold- and silver-coloured glass mosaics.

The town **market** (Merchant Rd; ⊘6am-5pm) is also worth a browse – several stalls sell dried fruit and local liqueurs. Every five days the market is swelled by traders from hill-tribe villages around Kalaw.

South of the market, the myriad stupas of **Hsu Taung Pye Paya** were restored from ruins using donations from visiting pil-

grims. For a good view over the market area, take the steps on the north side of Union Hwy to **Thein Taung Paya**, a modest Buddhist monastery with a small congregation of friendly monks.

There are more Buddhist monuments on the outskirts of Kalaw; see our suggested self-guided day hike in the Activities section for details.

🏃 Activities

Day Hike

Although trekking in the hills around Kalaw without a guide is not recommended, there are some interesting and easy-to-find sights just outside town that can be tackled in the form of a self-guided, half-day walk.

Starting at the market, head south on Min St, continuing to University St at the roundabout-like junction (the park will be on your left). Following the hilly, pine-lined road, and veering left at the junction after the Pine View Inn, it should take another ten to fifteen minutes to reach **Christ the King Church** (University Rd), which was run by the same Italian priest from 1931 to 2000. His successor, Father Paul, presides over an enthusiastic daily mass at 6.30am and a well-attended Sunday service at 8am and 4pm.

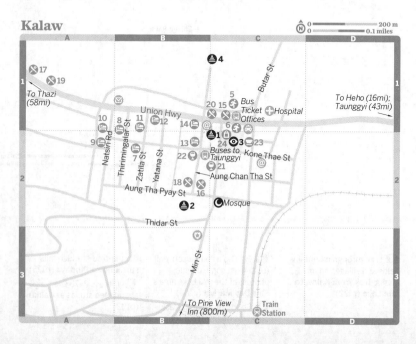

Return the way you came until you reach the intersection with Oo Min St (indicated by the sign for Pine Hill Resort). Turn left and continue about ten minutes or so until you see a group of pagodas on your left; this is **Shwe Oo Min Paya** (Oo Min Rd), a natural cave dripping with golden Buddha statues (and also just dripping – watch your footing on the slippery marble pathways).

After exploring the caves, continue along the road until you reach a T-junction. Turn right, as indicated by the wooden sign with gold letters; this and similar signs will lead you to **Hnee Pagoda**, home to 500-year-old, gold-lacquered bamboo Buddha.

After paying your respects, backtrack along Hnee Pagoda St and turn left at the intersection. Continue along this road until you reach the T-junction; turn right on Saitta Thukha St and after about ten minutes or so you'll merge with Thidar St just behind **Hsu Taung Pye Paya**.

Trekking

Almost everyone who comes to Kalaw goes trekking in the hills. The town is surrounded by Buddhist pagodas, hilltop viewpoints and the peaceful villages of the Palaung, Danu, Pa-O, Taung Yo and Danaw tribes, all set in a gorgeous landscape of forest-capped hills.

The level of development varies as you move from village to village. Some tribes wear traditional clothing and live without electricity or running water, while their immediate neighbours watch European football on satellite TV. The standard of living for tribal people across the region has been raised by development projects run by the UN and other international NGOs. Most villagers depend primarily on farming, but some subsidise their income by making handicrafts and providing meals and accommodation for visiting trekkers.

The most popular trek is undoubtedly the two- to four-day trek to **Inle Lake** (for details, see our boxed text on p172). A less common route is the multi-day trek to Pindaya, via Taung Ni. Popular destinations for one-day or overnight treks around Kalaw include the Myin Ma Hti Cave, the Pa-O villages south of Lamaing, and the Pa-O, Danu and Taung Yo villages near Myin Dike train station. Another popular route runs southwest from Kalaw to the Palaung villages of Ywathit and Tar Yaw and the **Viewpoint**, a rustic, Nepali-run restaurant with sweeping views over the hills. If you're interested in nature more than culture, Moteh, who can be found at the Viewpoint, offers a day or overnight 'jungle' trek through a protected forest. Trekkers sleep in the woods or stay overnight at a Taung Yo village; contact Ramu at Golden Lily Guest House (p173) for details on this trek.

On single-day treks, the only equipment you need is a pair of good walking shoes. Meals are usually included in the price of the trek, but you should buy and carry your own drinking water. Trekking goes on year-round, but expect muddy conditions during the rainy season (approximately June to October).

Trekking without a guide is not recommended – the trails are confusing, the

TREKKING FROM KALAW TO INLE LAKE

Instead of enduring another never-ending bus ride, consider walking the distance between Kalaw and Inle Lake. There are numerous alternative routes to take you to the lake shore and, depending on the route that you and your guide agree upon, the journey can take between two and four days.

Although scenic, it's important to understand that this trek is more of a cultural (or even agricultural) experience than a nature walk. The only real forest you'll encounter is just outside Kalaw and the bulk of the trek passes through relatively modern Pa-O and Danu settlements and extensive wheat, rice, tea, potato, sesame and chilli plantations. At some points you'll be walking on footpaths, while other parts of the trek are on roads (both paved and unpaved) or even along train tracks. You'll most likely spend one night with a Pa-O or Danu family and another at a Buddhist temple.

If you're doing the standard three-day option, expect to walk at least four hours a day. From Kalaw, the initial part of the trek passes through tall mountains fringed with tea plantations. The second day passes through hilly agricultural areas and the last day is a mix of the two. It's mostly level walking, the only truly steep part being the descent/ascent to/ from Thandaung at Inle Lake. There are numerous alternate long and short routes; some choose to go by car to Lamaing and walk to Inle Lake in two days, while other guides have found ways to extend the trip to four nights. Possible termination points at Inle Lake include Inthein, Tone Le, Thandaung or Kaung Daing. Discuss the options with your guide.

The winter months are the best time to do the trek, the only downside being that you'll almost certainly run into other trekkers – nights with as many as 50 people sleeping at the monastery have been reported. During the rainy season many of the roads are irritatingly muddy and slippery. Leeches and mosquitoes can also be a problem.

Guides can arrange to have your bags transported to a hotel in Nyaungshwe, so you carry only what you need for the walk – a towel and a torch (flashlight) are good extras to bring along.

If arranging your trek from Kalaw, expect to pay between $8 and $12 per person, per day, in groups of three or more; if going at it alone, the trek will be at least $60 for the three days. Keep in mind that cheaper day rates often don't include the cost of shipping your gear to your destination (at least K2000) and the boat fee at Inle Lake (about K13,000).

Guides with extensive experience on this particular route include Nyaungshwe-based Pyone Cho at Lotus Restaurant (p182) and the brothers Than Htay and Ko Htwe at Sunny Day Tour Services (p187), and in Kalaw, Naing Naing at **Ever Smile** (☑50683; Yuzana St), Harri and Rambo at Golden Lily Guest House, and **Sam's Trekking Guide** (☑50377; Union Hwy).

terrain challenging and few people in the hills speak English. The going rate for a guided walk ranges from $5 to $7 per day, in groups of three or more. Rates increase if you're hiking alone or if you're overnighting. For day treks, **JP Barua** (☑50549) gets good reviews, or you could try any of the Kalaw-based guides who also do the Kalaw to Inle Lake trek (p172).

🛏 Sleeping

Kalaw has a generous spread of hotels and guesthouses, many set up specifically for budget travellers. None of the hotels offer air-conditioning – in this climate they don't need to – and most places offer discounts in the low season (May to October).

TOP CHOICE ⧈ Pine Hill Resort   HOTEL **$$**
(☑50079; www.kalawpinehillresort.com; 151 Oo Min Rd; r $50-60) Set around an original colonial bungalow, this sophisticated modern hotel has rooms in wooden cottages sprawling through immaculate gardens. It's undoubtedly the most atmospheric place to stay in Kalaw, the only downside being that it's a good ten-minute walk from the city centre. To get here, follow Min St south, turning right at the second intersection, or hop on a motorcycle taxi (K500) near the market .

Dream Villa Hotel Kalaw   HOTEL **$$**
(☑50144; 5 Zatila St; dreamvilla@myanmar.com. mm; r $20-36) A cut above your average Myanmar hotel, the Dream Villa attracts tour groups and has tasteful, wood-panelled

rooms and lots of potted greenery. More expensive rooms have tubs and minibars and some have hill views.

Eastern Paradise Motel
HOTEL $
(⌨50315; 5 Thirimingalar St; r $7-15) Like much of the accommodation in Kalaw, this place calls itself a motel, but there's no need to be suspicious of the unintentionally self-deprecating moniker; large homey rooms and gracious service make this one of the best deals in town.

Honey Pine Hotel
HOTEL $
(⌨50728; 44 Zatila St; s/d/tr $10/20/30) Of the handful of new hotels going up in Kalaw, this was the only one finished at research time. The budget-priced rooms here include midrange amenities such as TV and fridge, although the single rooms lack windows and feel a bit tight.

Golden Lily Guest House
HOTEL $
(⌨50108; goldenlily@mandalay.net.mm; 5/88 Natsin Rd; r $3-10; @) A chalet mood pervades at this large, budget complex. The more expensive rooms share a wide balcony that looks over the town. They're also substantially nicer than the cheaper rooms, the shared bathrooms of which could really use some work. Trekking can be arranged here, although it's an annoying hard-sell. Slow internet access is available for K1000 for 30 minutes.

Pine View Inn
HOTEL $
(⌨50185; University Rd; s/d $10/15) If you'd rather stay in the leafy part of town, this quiet hotel offers plain but tidy rooms in a new bungalow block or an older wooden house. It's a ten-minute walk from the city centre. Follow Min St south or hop on a motorcycle taxi at the market (K500).

Golden Kalaw Inn
HOTEL $
(⌨50311; 5/92 Natsin Rd; s/d $5/8, with shared bathroom $3/6) The rooms here are about as basic as they come, but are clean. The balcony and front yard catch the afternoon sunshine.

New Shine Hotel
HOTEL $
(⌨50028; newshine@myanmar.com.mm; 21 Union Hwy; s/d $10/20) Targeting travellers on organised tours, the New Shine is cosier in than out.

Parami Motel
HOTEL $
(⌨50027; Kone Thae St; s/d $8/15, with shared bathroom $5/10) Set in two pale-blue blocks behind the Winner Hotel, the Parami has friendly owners and modest but inexpensive rooms.

Winner Hotel Kalaw
HOTEL $
(⌨50025; Union Hwy; s/d $15/18, with shared bathroom $6/12) A large, modern Chinese-style hotel on the main road, the Winner holds few surprises, but rooms are large, uncluttered and clean.

✖ Eating & Drinking
Kalaw has some decent places to chow down, many serving food with a distinctive Indian or Nepali flavour.

Thu Maung Restaurant
BURMESE $$
(Union Hwy; meals from K2500; ☺lunch & dinner) Probably the best Burmese restaurant in town, Thu Maung serves tasty chicken, pork and fish curries with all the usual Myanmar salads, pickles and trimmings. There's no English-language sign here, but it's the restaurant directly adjacent to the steps leading to Thein Taung Paya.

Pyae Pyae Shan Noodle
SHAN $
(Union Hwy; noodles from K500; ☺all day) This cosy, friendly shop sells delicious bowls of the eponymous noodle, as well as a short menu of rice-based dishes.

Sam's Family Restaurant
INTERNATIONAL, BURMESE $
(Aung Chan Tha St; mains from K1000; ☺all day) Run by the same family that operates Sam's Trekking Guide, this cosy little place serves Indian, Myanmar and Chinese standards and old-fashioned backpacker breakfasts.

Thirigayha Restaurant
INTERNATIONAL, BURMESE $$
(Seven Sisters; Union Hwy; meals from K5000; ☺lunch & dinner) If you want a romantic dinner, there's really only one choice in town. The menu ranges from Shan traditional meals to beef stroganoff, noodle soups and Indian curries and there's often a guitarist serenading diners.

Everest Nepali Food Centre
NEPALI $
(Aung Chan Thar St; set meals from K2000; ☺lunch & dinner) Relive memories of trekking in Nepal with a plate of *dhal baht* (rice served with lentils and other side dishes) at this convivial eatery run by a Nepali family who originally came to Myanmar from Pokhara.

FMD Indian Food
MUSLIM, INDIAN $
(Union Hwy; mains from K1500; ☺lunch & dinner) FMD specialises in rich, meaty Muslim-influenced Indian dishes. Stop in on Sunday when they do biryani.

3N South Indian Food
INDIAN $

(Union Hwy; meals from K1500; ☻lunch & dinner) Probably as authentic as that Italian restaurant you ate at in Nyaungshwe, but tasty and good for vegetarians.

There are several good teashops in Kalaw, many with a distinct Indian feel. All are open from breakfast to lunch, and a snack breakfast should set you back less than K1000.

Morning Star
TEAHOUSE $

(Kone Thae St) The sign's faded, but it's hard to miss this tidy, bright-blue teashop. Couple your sweet tea with equally sweet Indian sweets.

Ma Hnin Si Teahouse
TEAHOUSE $

(Butar St) This tiny teahouse on the east side of the market has no English sign but you can't miss it – just look for the crowds of locals enjoying plates of *pakoda* (vegetables fried in lentil-flour batter), Shan tofu and other tasty deep-fried snacks.

Tet Nay Win Teahouse
TEAHOUSE $

(Butar St) An Indian-style teahouse serving samosas, *nanbya, channa puri* (fried bread with chickpea curry) and other treats from the subcontinent.

Hi Snack & Drink
BAR

(Kone Thae St; ☻5-10pm) Hi is the size of a closet and boasts a palpable speakeasy feel. If you haven't had a rum here, you haven't been to Kalaw. Mr Myo is a welcoming host, and there's a ragged guitar that takes embarrassingly little prompting to get played.

Golden Wing
BEER STATION

(Min St; ☻5-10pm) South of the market, this typical Chinese beer station has Dagon and Skol beer on draught, as well as grilled snacks.

🔒 Shopping

A couple of art galleries around the market sell paintings of monks, tribal people and mountain scenery; some ordinary and others very good.

Rural Development Society Shop
HANDICRAFTS

(Min St; adr1992@gmail.com; ☻8.30am-6.30pm) On the west side of the market, this charitable enterprise sells fabrics, clothing and handmade paper produced by local tribes. Profits go towards development projects in local Shan and Pa-O villages.

ℹ Information

In addition to the two cafes below, internet is also available at Golden Lily Guest House (p173).

Cyber World Internet Café (Aung Chan Tha St; per hr K1000; ☻8am-11pm)

Sky Net (Kone Thae St; per hr K500; ☻noon-11pm)

ℹ Getting There & Away

Air

Kalaw has no airport of its own, but flights are served via Heho, about 16 miles away.

Air Mandalay (www.airmandalay.com) flies from Heho to Yangon at 9.30am, 9.40am and 4.30pm ($86, one to three hours), with the afternoon flight routing through Mandalay ($42, 25 minutes) and Nyaung U (for Bagan; $68, one hour). **Air Bagan** (www.airbagan.com), operated by Tay Za (see p21), also flies a similar route to Yangon at 8.45am, 9.45am and 4.40pm ($95, one to three hours), with the afternoon flight stopping in Mandalay ($53, 25 minutes) and Nyaung U (Bagan; $75, one hour). Air Bagan also operates a daily flight to Thandwe (Ngapali Beach; $122, one hour), **Asian Wings** (www.asianwingsairways.com) and Air Bagan also conduct flights between Heho and Kengtung ($85, one hour).

Taxis waiting at the airport charge K30,000 to Kalaw (1½ hours); a cheaper but less convenient option is to hike the near mile to the Union Hwy and wait for a pick-up truck or bus bound for Thazi (K2000, 1½ hours) or Meiktila (K1500, one hour), although you may face a long wait.

Bus & Taxi

For information on buses from Yangon see p70.

Several **bus ticket offices** across from the market book seats on the long-distance buses between Yangon and Mandalay and Taunggyi. These buses stop on the main road, in front of the market.

Small local buses bound for Taunggyi depart from a **stop** behind the Aung Chang Tha Zedi. Buses, minivans and pick-up trucks bound for Thazi will drop you in Shwenyaung (Inle Lake; two hours) for the same fare, or in Aungban (the junction for Pindaya; 20 minutes) for K1000.

Buses, minivans and pick-ups to Thazi (K2500, four hours) or Meiktila (K3000, five hours) stop periodically on the Union Hwy – fares for foreigners are routinely doubled along this route.

You can charter taxis from Kalaw to Pindaya (K35,000, two hours), Nyaungshwe (K35,000), Taunggyi (K40,000) and Thazi (K65,000).

Train

A single daily train departs from either end of the winding line that links Thazi and Shwenyaung. Stunning scenery makes up for the slow journey time and frequent delays. See p167 for

BUSES & PICK-UP TRUCKS FROM KALAW

DESTINATION	FARE (K)	DURATION (HR)	DEPARTURE	TYPE
Yangon	14,000	12-15	4pm-5.30pm	air-con buses
Mandalay	8000-10,000	9	8am, 8pm	air-con buses
Bagan	12,000-13,000	6-8	7am	air-con bus
Taunggyi	2000	3	6am, 6.30am, 7am	non-air-con bus, pick-up
Thazi	2500	4	6am-2pm	pick-up

information on departures from Thazi and p184 for departures from Shwenyaung (Inle Lake).

Heading to Shwenyaung, the train pulls into Kalaw around 10am ($3, three hours); to Thazi, departure is at 1pm ($5, six hours), but trains often leave hours behind the official departure times.

Getting Around

Most people choose to walk around town but motorcycle taxis at the northeast corner of the market can run you to Hnee Pagoda or the Shwe Oo Min caves and back for around K2000.

Pindaya

ပင်းဒယ

081 / C5000

The road to Pindaya cuts across one of the most densely farmed areas in Myanmar – at first glance, the patchwork of fields and hedges could almost be a landscape from central Europe or middle America. Along the way, you'll pass buffalo carts and groups of toiling farmers in black Danu tunics and checked Pa-O headscarves. The main reason to make this appealing journey is to visit the famous Shwe Oo Min Natural Cave pagoda, a massive limestone cavern filled with thousands of gilded buddha statues, but the hills around Pindaya are also home to a nascent trekking scene.

Sights & Activities

TOP CHOICE Shwe Oo Min Natural Cave Pagoda BUDDHIST CAVE PAGODA

ရွှေဥမင်သဘာဝလိုဏ်ဂူဘုရား

(admission $3, camera fee K300; 6am-6pm)

There are several 'Golden Cave' temples in Shan State, but Pindaya's Shwe Oo Min pagoda is by far the most impressive. Set high on a limestone ridge above Pone Taloke Lake, this winding complex of natural caves and tunnels is filled to bursting point with buddha images in an astonishing variety of shapes, sizes and materials, many gaudily daubed with gold paint.

At the latest count, the caves contained more than 8700 statues, some left centuries ago by Burmese pilgrims and others newly installed by Buddhist organisations from as far afield as Singapore, the Netherlands and the USA. The collection of alabaster, teak, marble, brick, lacquer and cement images is still growing – pilgrims arrive in a slow but steady stream, installing new images and meditating in tiny meditation chambers formed by natural cavities in the cave walls.

A series of covered stairways climb the ridge to the cave entrance. Most people arrive via the long stairway that starts near the gleaming white *zedi* (stupas) of **Nget Pyaw Taw Pagoda**, just south of the Conqueror Hotel. You can skip the last 130 steps to the cave mouth by taking the lift.

Two more covered stairways lead north from the lift pavilion. One descends gently back to Pindaya, while the other climbs to a second **cave pavilion** containing a monumental 40ft-high, gilded, Shan-style sitting buddha. The steps continue along the ridge to a third chamber with a large **reclining buddha** and more shrines and pagodas along the hilltop.

The easiest way to reach the caves is to walk along the tarmac road past the Golden Cave and Conqueror Hotels; it's about two miles and takes 20 minutes or so. Alternatively, an easy-to-follow track runs straight to the cave complex from the western shore of Pone Ta Loke Lake – just follow the road along the lake shore and turn right after the Pindaya Hotel; the path branches off to the left over a small bridge and, after a short walk, connects with the long sloping stairway that leads to the main cave. A horse cart from the market to the Nget Pyaw Taw pagoda entrance will cost K1000.

ALONG CAME A SPIDER

As you enter Pindaya, keep an eye out for the official town symbol – an archer and a giant spider. According to legend, seven princesses took refuge in Shwe Oo Min cave during a storm, and were imprisoned by an evil *nat* (spirit being) in the form of a giant spider. Luckily for them, Prince Kummabhaya of Nyaungshwe (Yaunghwe) was strolling nearby. Hearing their pleas for help, the heroic prince killed the spider with an arrow and freed the princesses from the cave. You can see some Disney-esque sculptures of the spider and prince by the entrance to the Shwe Oo Min cave complex.

Other Stupas

Downhill from the main cave on the dirt path to Pone Taloke lake, the gorgeous **Hsin Khaung Taung Kyaung** was constructed from carved teak panels in the late 19th century. The steps to the main cave start just beyond the *kyaung* (monastery) – the path is lined with ancient crumbling *zedi*.

At the north end of Pone Taloke Lake, the **Kan Tau Monastery** features some heavily restored stupas and a fine teak *kyaung* with a large collection of antique buddha images on ornate plinths.

Treks

A few local guides lead day and overnight treks in the area. Most head straight for **Yazagyi**, an attractive and modern Palaung village located in hilly tea-plantation country about five hours' walk from Pindaya. Treks start at about $10 a day per person, and experienced guides include U Myint Thaung at Old Home Tour Information Centre (p177) and Soe Soe at Golden Cave Hotel (p176).

✪ Festivals & Events

The main annual **paya pwe** (pagoda festival) at Shwe Oo Min takes place on the full moon of Tabaung (February/March). Expect all the usual singing, dancing and hand-operated fairground rides.

⌫ Sleeping

The only cheap option is in the town itself, a 20-minute walk from the caves.

TOP CHOICE **Pindaya Inle Inn** BOUTIQUE HOTEL $$$
(☑66029; www.pindayainleinn.com; Mahabandoola Rd; r/chalets $45/100) Located at the entrance to town, across the lake from Shwe Oo Min Pagoda, this is a surprisingly sophisticated place to stay – for a small town like Pindaya. Rooms are set in either bamboo or stone cottages in a lovingly tended garden centred on a longhouse-style restaurant and bar.

Conqueror Resort Hotel HOTEL $$$
(☑66106; www.conquererresorthotel.com; bungalows $55-80, ste $100;☀) There isn't a blade of grass out of place at this immaculately maintained resort hotel near the main entrance to the caves. Rooms are set in cottages around a central restaurant and a large, inviting pool. Choose from bamboo villas, wooden stilt houses or stone chalets – all are luxuriously appointed, with a TV, a minibar and a stylish bathroom.

Myit Phyar Zaw Gji Hotel HOTEL $
(☑66403; 106 Zaytan Quarter; s/d $10/15) Next to the market and close to the lake shore, this is the closest Pindaya has to budget accommodation. It's tidy and friendly and good value for money. Some rooms face the lake.

Golden Cave Hotel HOTEL $$
(☑66166; www.goldencavehotel.com; r $20-35) A warm welcome awaits at this unassuming midrange hotel a short walk from the start of the steps to the Shwe Oo Min cave. The smarter superior rooms in the annexe have balconies looking towards the caves, and are also equipped with a TV and a minibar.

✗ Eating

Most of Pindaya's dining scene is very workaday. If you don't require doilies with your dinner, check out one of the options below, otherwise you may want to stick with the restaurants at Conqueror Resort Hotel or Pindaya Inle Inn.

Green Tea Restaurant INTERNATIONAL, BURMESE $$
(mains K2000-7000; ☺lunch & dinner) Located between the market and Shwe Oo Min Pagoda, this open-air dining room looking over Pone Taloke Lake is definitely one of the posher places in town to dine. The menu spans several cuisines and the Myanmar food is better than you'd expect from a place like this. There are even a few local (Danustyle) dishes on the menu.

Dagon Beer Station   CHINESE, BURMESE $

(mains from K1500; ☺lunch & dinner) Mere steps from the town's market, this echoing beer hall is where local dudes come to have a drink after work. Visitors (including women) are welcome too, and you can accompany your draught Dagon with standard and not-so-standard Chinese-Burmese dishes, such as pig-lip salad!

Memento Restaurant INTERNATIONAL, BURMESE $$

(mains from K1500; ☺lunch & dinner) Also along the road that leads to Shwe Oo Min Pagoda, Memento is an example of a restaurant trying too hard to please day-tripping foreigners. The menu here includes dishes such as pork ball Vichy, and our 'traditional food' order was a very untraditional combination of fish and French fries fried with turmeric and ginger.

Kyan Lite Restaurant   CHINESE, BURMESE $

(mains from K1000; ☺all day) On the lake shore close to the market, Kyan Lite serves cold beers and a familiar menu of Myanmar Chinese dishes, as well as boxes of Shan tea.

ℹ Information

There was no functioning internet connection in Pindaya at the time of research.

Old Home Tour Information Centre (✆66188; ☺9am-5pm) Located at the market intersection. Here you'll find friendly local U Myint Thaung, who sells a small selection of books and antiques, and leads treks and day tours.

ℹ Getting There & Away

There is only limited public transport to Pindaya so unless you're willing to charter a taxi, you'll probably have to stay a night.

BUS Coming from Taunggyi, there are two daily buses at 1pm and 1.30pm (K2000, four hours). If starting from Nyaungshwe (Inle Lake), you can catch one of these buses up the road in Shwenyaung starting at 2pm (K2000, three hours).

Starting from Kalaw, your best bet is to take a bus or pick-up truck to Aungban – any of the Taunggyi-bound morning buses/trucks can drop you off here (K1000, 20 minutes). From Aungban, a single daily pick-up leaves at 8am (K1000, 1½ hours) from near Mikhine Restaurant, at the junction at the north end of town.

Leaving Pindaya, there are Taunggyi-bound buses at 5.30am and 5.45am (K2000), and a single daily pick-up departure to Aungban at 9am (K1000, 1½ hours), all of which depart from near the market intersection.

TAXI It is much more convenient, though much more expensive, to complete the journey from Aungban to Pindaya by taxi. Drivers loiter on the main street in Aungban, charging K25,000 for a drop-off in Pindaya and K30,000 for a return trip to the caves. Motorcycle taxis will take you to Pindaya from Aungban for about K6000.

INLE LAKE

Placid Inle Lake (အင်းလေးကန်) ranks among Myanmar's top five tourist attractions, which ensures that visitors come here in droves. The once-sleepy village of Nyaungshwe at the north end of the lake has grown into a bustling traveller centre, with dozens of guesthouses and hotels, a surfeit of restaurants serving pancakes and pasta, and a pleasantly relaxed traveller vibe. If Myanmar could be said to have a backpacker scene at all, it can be found here.

On paper Inle Lake is 13.5 miles long and 7 miles wide but up close it's hard to tell where the lake finishes and the marshes start. Looking down over the lake from the Taunggyi road, Inle sits like a puddle on an enormous carpet of greenery. Dotted around the lake are the **stilt-house villages** and **floating gardens** of the Intha tribe. You may also encounter Shan, Pa-O, Taung Yo, Danu, Kayah and Danaw tribal people at the markets that hopscotch around the lake on a five-day cycle.

Boats are the main means of transport around the lake – travellers tend to explore on motorised canoes (a little like Thai long-tail boats) but most Intha people get around using traditional flat-bottomed skiffs propelled by a single wooden paddle. The Intha technique of leg rowing – where one leg is wrapped around the paddle to drive the blade through the water in a snake-like motion – is unique.

The waters cool the surrounding air considerably. A pall of mist hangs over the lake before sunrise and during the morning, and evenings can be surprisingly cold. Bring a coat or buy a blanket in the market to keep off the wind chill on boat tours around the lake.

🎊 Festivals & Events

Inle comes alive during late September or early October for the **Phaung Daw Oo Paya Festival** at Phaung Daw Oo Paya. The four revered golden buddha images from the pagoda are ferried around the lake in a gilded barge shaped like a *hintha* (the golden swan of Burmese legend) visiting all the pagodas in the area. The festival lasts for 18 days and locals carry out energetic leg-rowing races on the channels between the villages.

The pagoda festival is closely followed by **Thadingyut**, which marks the end of Waso (Buddhist Lent).

ⓘ Information

There is a compulsory $5 government fee to enter the Inle Lake area, which you must pay on arrival at the **permit booth** (Map p178; ⊙6am-9pm) by the bridge at the entrance to Nyaungshwe. We cruised into town on an extremely packed bus from Taunggyi and circumvented paying the fee, and we were never asked to show proof of payment later, suggesting the authorities may not take it very seriously. Best to be on the safe side, though.

Nyaungshwe

ညောင်ရွှေ

☏ 081 / POP C10,000

The main traveller centre for the Inle Lake area, Nyaungshwe is a neat grid of streets next to the main canal, also known as Nan Chaung, leading down to the north end of the lake. Originally known by the Shan name Yaunghwe, the town was renamed Nyaungsh-

we (Golden Banyan) by the Bamar-dominated authorities after independence in 1948.

◎ Sights & Activities

Yadana Man Aung Paya   BUDDHIST TEMPLE
(Map p178; Phaung Daw Seiq Rd; ⊙6am-10pm) The oldest and most important Buddhist shrine in Nyaungshwe, this handsome gilded stupa is hidden away inside a square compound south of the Mingala Market. The stepped stupa is unique in Myanmar, and the surrounding pavilion contains a museum of treasures amassed by the monks over the centuries, including carvings, lacquerware and dance costumes.

Buddha Museum   MUSEUM
(Map p178; Museum Rd (Haw St); admission $2; ⊙9.30am-4pm Tue-Sun) Formerly the Museum of Shan Chiefs, this sprawling government-run museum has fallen victim to the government crackdown on symbols of Shan ethnic identity. Today the museum displays antique buddha images rather than any objects that might suggest a distinct Shan history and culture. It's worth coming here to see the stately brick-and-teak *haw* (palace) of the 33rd and last Shan *sao pha* (sky lord), Sao Shwe Thaike, who briefly served as the first president of Independent Burma, before the junta seized control.

Nyaungshwe

Mingala Market MARKET

(Map p178; Yone Gyi Rd) The busy *zei* (market) at the entrance to town is flooded with locals every morning, when traders from the lake bring in fresh fish and produce from the floating gardens. A few stalls sell local handicrafts but the focus is on day-to-day objects used by local people – food, begging bowls, machetes, fishing spears, you name it. The market doubles in size when it hosts the five-day rotating market (see boxed text, p183).

Other Religious Monuments

There are stupas and monasteries all over Nyaungshwe. Most of the monasteries are clustered around the Mong Li Canal, southeast of the market.

Hlaing Gu Kyaung (Map p178; off Yone Gyi Rd) has around 100 resident monks and an interesting collection of antique Buddha images. Nearby, **Shwe Gu Kyaung** (Map p178; Myawady Rd) has 130 novice monks and a huge central hall that echoes with the sound of synchronised chanting. A block further south, **Kan Gyi Kyaung** (Map p178; Myawady Rd) is the largest monastery in Nyaungshwe;

listening to 250 monks of all ages reciting the scriptures is quite an experience.

About a mile and a half north of town on the road to Shwenyaung, **Shwe Yaunghwe Kyaung** (off Map p178; Shwe Yan Pyay) is probably the most photographed monastery in Nyaungshwe; the unique oval windows in the ancient teak *thein* (ordination hall) create a perfect frame for portraits of the novices.

South of Nyaungshwe in the village of Nanthe, **Yan Aung Nan Aung Hsu Taung Pyi Pagoda** (Map p185) features a 26ft-high sitting buddha, surrounded by stucco *deva* (celestial beings) and *chinthe* (half-lion, half-dragon guardians). Although heavily restored, the statue is said to be more than 700 years old.

Boat Trips

Every hotel in town can arrange boat trips around the lake, and freelance boat drivers will approach you in the street. The going rate for a whole-day trip around the lake starts at K12,000.

Massage

Win Nyunt Traditional Massage (Map p178; off Myawady Rd; per hr K5000; ⊙8am-9pm) is the

Nyaungshwe

place to go to get the kinks out of your back if you've been sitting in a boat too long.

Trekking

There's opportunity for day and overnight hikes around Inle Lake, or you could do the trek to Kalaw. See p187 for some suggested destinations and recommended guides.

🛏 Sleeping

Nyaungshwe has dozens of hotels and guest-houses, ranging from basic backpacker hang-outs to comfortable midrange hotels. Most places offer low-season discounts from March to October, but rates are open to ne-gotiation most of the time because of the intense competition.

Almost all rooms have bathrooms with hot showers, but few places offer air-con because of the natural cooling effect of the breeze passing over the lake. As is the case in much of Myanmar, all room rates include breakfast.

For accommodation on Inle Lake itself see p187.

TOP CHOICE **Teakwood Guest House** GUESTHOUSE $
(Map p178; ☏209 250; teakwood.htl@gmail.com; Kyaung Taw Anouk Rd; r $10-25; @) Straddling the divide between budget and midrange, this attractive guesthouse is popular with older independent travellers. The best rooms are in the new block – big windows let in lots of light and the bathrooms are finished with small pebbles. The communal areas are great, but be ready for some assertive sales pitches from the owner for boat trips and excursions.

TOP CHOICE **Hotel Amazing Nyaung Shwe** BOUTIQUE HOTEL $$$
(Map p178; ☏209 079; www.amazing-hotel.com; Yone Gyi Rd; s/d $64/68, suite $86-130; ❄🖥📶) A league apart from the other hotels in Nyaung-shwe, this immaculate boutique hotel has gorgeous rooms decorated with murals and cultural artefacts. There's also an open-air breakfast pavilion on a bridge over the canal.

Aquarius Inn GUESTHOUSE $
(Map p178; ☏209 352; aquarius352@gmail.com; 2 Phaung Daw Pyan Rd; s/d $7/12) Charming own-ers make this small, family-run guesthouse a real home away from home. The cosy rooms contain an intriguing collection of local bric-a-brac and guests are treated to plates of fresh fruit and Chinese tea. There are tables and chairs in the plant-filled yard where you can sit and chat in the evenings.

Princess Garden Hotel HOTEL $$
(Off map p178; ☏209 214; princessgardenhotel@gmail.com; bungalows s/d $25/35; ❄) This hid-den gem was the newest place in town at research time and the only one with a swim-ming pool. The eight wooden bungalows are located in a shady garden and are looked af-ter by friendly, service-minded owners. Lo-cated near Mong Li Canal a brief walk south from the centre of town.

Nawng Kham – Little Inn GUESTHOUSE $
(Map p178; ☏209 195; Phaung Daw Pyan Rd; s/d $6/12) Opposite the Aquarius Inn, this small but perfectly formed guesthouse has just seven rooms. All have fans, bathrooms and hot showers and are set in a peaceful gar-den. Considering the number of rooms, it's a good idea to book ahead.

May Guest House GUESTHOUSE $
(Map p178; ☏209 417; 85 Myawady Rd; s/d/tr $7/12/16) Wagon wheels mounted in the front wall set the tone at this village-style guesthouse in the monastery quarter. The simple square rooms have fans and bath-rooms and the breakfast is said to be one of the best in town.

Hu Pin Hotel Nyaungshwe HOTEL $$
(Map p178; ☏209 291; www.hupinhotelmyanmar.com; r $36-50; ❄) The bland Chinese-style rooms here won't win any prizes for interior design, but everything is spotlessly clean, hot water is reliable and the hotel has its own boats for trips around the lake. The Hu Pin is Nyaungshwe's most imposing build-ing and is located along the canal that leads to Inle Lake.

Queen Inn GUESTHOUSE $
(Map p178; ☏209 544; queen.ine@gmail.com; r $7-20) Located on the opposite side of the Nan Chaung canal, this would be a bud-geter's dream if it weren't for the noise of boats. Rooms are simple, but the highlight is the homely feel, emphasised in the nightly family-style dinners for only K2000.

Inle Inn HOTEL $
(Map p178; ☏209 016; inleinns@gmail.com; Yone Gyi Rd; r $8-18) Potted plants and trellises create a pleasing cocoon of vegetation at this village inn on the eastern side of town. Rooms are arranged around a shady sitting area and restaurant.

Ming Ga Lar Inn HOTEL $
(Map p178; ☏209 198; mingalarinn@gmail.com; Phaung Daw Pyan Rd; r $7-18) A maze-like bud-

WORTH A TRIP

TOFU & HOT SPRINGS

Located on the northwestern shore of the lake, 5 miles from Nyaungshwe, **Kaung Da-ing** (ေ၁ှင်ထိုင်) is a quiet Intha village. It's known for its tofu, prepared using split yellow peas instead of soybeans, and its **hot springs** (Map p185; swimming pool K3000, private bathhouse K5000, mixed hot pool K5000; ☺6am-6pm), where hot water from the natural springs has been channelled into a swimming pool and a series of private bathhouses for men and women. The springs are also the start or end point of several trekking routes between Kalaw and Inle Lake – see p172 for details.

The attractions are admittedly low-key, and the real reason to come here is the bike ride through some beautiful Myanmar countryside. After renting a bicycle in Nyaungshwe, cross the bridge over the channel leading to the lake and follow the bone-shaking dirt track through the marshes until you reach the sealed road, then turn left. The trip to the springs will take around 40 minutes.

If you'd rather not expend so much energy, boat operators charge K3000 each way for the 30-minute trip across the lake, and motorcycle taxis at Mingala Market will ferry you to the springs and back for K5000, including a couple of hours waiting time while you bathe.

get place with a variety of room types. It's worth considering the larger, more expensive rooms, which have cleverly been fitted out with bamboo.

Gypsy Inn　　　GUESTHOUSE $
(Map p178; ☎209 084; 82 Kann Nar Rd; s/d $12/15, without bathroom $5/10) Handy for accessing the canal leading to the lake, this place has an old block containing budget rooms with shared bathrooms. There's also a much more appealing new block of rooms with private baths.

Joy Hotel　　　HOTEL $
(Map p178; ☎209 083; Jetty Rd; s/d $7/14, without bathroom $5/10) Set on the canal used by market traders delivering goods to Mingala Market, Joy has more of a local feel than the other budget guesthouses. The cheaper rooms with shared bathrooms are small and boxy but there are better rooms with private bathrooms and hot showers.

Four Sisters Inn　　　GUESTHOUSE $
(Map p178; ☎209 190; s/d $7/12) Away from the other guesthouses on the way to Yan Aung Nan Aung Hsu Taung Pyi Pagoda, this bright blue compound consists of small rooms around an old village house with a cosy restaurant. Communicating in English can be problematic.

Bright Hotel　　　HOTEL $
(Map p178; ☎209 137; 53 Phaung Daw Seiq Rd; r $7-25) The price is the drawcard rather than the atmosphere at this big white place near the boat jetty. The standard rooms are fairly

typical for this kind of hotel but the more inviting superior rooms have a tub, a TV and a minibar.

The following places straddle budget and midrange and take the very Nyaungshwe form of a main hotel structure and surrounding duplex bungalow-like buildings:

Nandawunn Hotel　　　HOTEL $$
(Map p178; ☎209 211; nandawunn@gmail.com; 80 Yone Gyi Rd; r $15-25; ✳@) In a residential part of town, east of the market, this tidy compound is probably the best of the lot for this style of hotel in Nyaungshwe.

Paradise Hotel & Restaurant　　　HOTEL $$
(Map p178; ☎209 321; www.inleparadise.com; 40 Museum Rd (Haw St); r $30-36, ste $65; ✳@) Paradise is probably overstating it, but this large chalet-style hotel near the museum is still a good choice. All rooms have a hot shower, a fridge, a TV and air-con.

Remember Inn Hotel　　　HOTEL $
(Map p178; ☎209 257; www.rememberinn.jimdo.com; Museum Rd (Haw St); r $8-15; ✳) Across from museum in a quiet and leafy part of town, the interior design won't draw you here, but the clean rooms, friendly service and cheap prices will.

Gold Star Hotel　　　HOTEL $
(Map p178; ☎209 200; goldstarhtl@mandalay.net. mm; cnr Kyauktein Rd & Phaung Daw Pyan Rd; r $8-25; ✳) A mish-mash of divergent rooms – some tiny and with a fan, some huge and with air-con – in different buildings, so look at a few.

✗ Eating

Unfortunately, Nyaugshwe's culinary scene doesn't quite live up to its atmosphere. Most restaurants tend to reach far beyond their culinary capabilities and there are relatively few places to find authentic local food. The good news – if you're a fan of quantity over quality, at least – is that serves tend to be rather large and there's an emphasis on Burmese- and Shan-style set meals, most starting at K3500.

For authentic local eats, check out the **food stalls** (Map p178; meals K1000; ⊙breakfast & lunch) in Mingala Market. Local specialities include Shan *kauq-sweh* (noodle soup), *maung jeut* (round, flat rice crisps) and *tofu thoke* (Shan tofu salad), prepared using yellow split-pea tofu, chilli, coriander and sesame oil.

Every evening from Comet Travel & Internet Cafe east to Mingala Market unfolds a basic **night market** (Map p178; Yone Gyi Rd; ⊙5-9pm) with dishes such as Shan noodles and tofu, grilled dishes, hot pot, roti and *murtabak* (stuffed pancake).

TOP CHOICE ★ Lin Htett Myanmar Traditional Food   BURMESE $$

(Map p178; Yone Gyi Rd; meals from K4000; ⊙lunch & dinner) Hands-down our favourite place to eat in Nyaungshwe, Lin Htett is as friendly as it is delicious. If you haven't yet encountered authentic Myanmar dining, here's the drill: choose a curry or two (refer to the pictures or, better yet, have a look behind the counter) and perhaps a salad (the pennywort salad, made from a fresh herb, is delicious). You'll find the accompaniments (rice, a sour soup, a vegetable soup, vegies, a fishy dip and three *balachaung*, chilli-based dips) will be supplied as a matter of course.

Viewpoint Restaurant   INTERNATIONAL, SHAN $$$

(Map p178; www.viewpoint.leplanteur.net; Taik Nan Bridge; mains from K2000, set meals K8000-14,000; ⊙lunch & dinner) Taking obscure local cuisines upscale is usually dangerous culinary territory, but the self-professed 'Shan nouvelle cuisine' at this, Nyaungshwe's most ambitious restaurant, is worth investigating. Although few of the menu items would ever have existed on a typical Shan family's dinner menu, the set meals and tasty Shan tapas are satisfying, regardless of their authenticity.

Lotus Restaurant   INTERNATIONAL, BURMESE $

(Map p178; Museum Rd (Haw St); mains from K1000; ⊙all day) With only five tables, this family-run place is as small as its menu is short. If even this is too much choice for you, go for the family-style dinner, which includes soup, salad, curry and a generous fruit plate for only K3500. Your host, Pyone Cho, is also an excellent trekking guide (see p187).

Golden Kite Restaurant   ITALIAN $$

(Map p178; cnr Myawady Rd & Yone Gyi Rd; pizzas from K5000, pasta from K3500; ⊙lunch & dinner) If you must seek Italian food in Nyaungshwe, you may as well do it here. This long-standing place claims to have got its recipes via an Italian lady from Bologna (you'll most likely get the spiel) – she's the source of the fresh basil. It makes its own pasta and serves decent pizzas.

Thu Kha Coffee   TEAHOUSE $

(Map p178; cnr Main Rd & Yone Gyi Rd; snacks from K200; ⊙5am-4pm) Ostensibly Nyaungshwe's only Muslim teashop, this tidy place serves good tea and, in the mornings, tasty *pakoda,* deep-fried vegetable dumplings. Come later in the afternoon for sweets such as roti, a type of sweet pancake.

Inle Pancake Kingdom   PANCAKES $

(Map p178; off Phaung Daw Seiq Rd; mains from K800; ⊙all day) Choose from a huge range of filled pancakes and toasted sandwiches at this cute little cabin on a narrow alley north of the sports field. Follow the signs from Phaung Daw Seiq Rd.

Hu Pin Restaurant   CHINESE, BURMESE $$

(Map p178; dishes from K1500) Close to the Hu Pin Hotel and run by the same team, this bright canteen has an illustrated menu of tasty Chinese soups and fried favourites such as sweet and sour pork. It gets very busy with tour groups at lunch time – come early or late for lunch or face a long wait.

Green Chili Restaurant   THAI, BURMESE $$

(Map p178; Hospital Rd; mains from K2000, set meals K5000; ⊙lunch & dinner) This new restaurant boasts one of the poshest dining rooms in town and, on the surface at least, the largely Thai-influenced menu here is also one of the more diverse and interesting. Unfortunately the flavours tend towards the timid tourist.

The majority of places in Nyaungshwe have a Burmese/Shan/Chinese/Thai/European menu – you'll recognise them from the billboards out the front, which tout everything from tofu to tagliatelle. If you're not put off by concepts such as Shan guacamole, the following places, generally open from 9am to 9pm, have been around for a while:

Unique Superb Food House INTERNATIONAL, BURMESE $
(Map p178; 3 Myawady Rd; mains from K2000) This simple restaurant in a village house has a menu that includes just about everything, but the Western-style food here gets good reports.

Smiling Moon Restaurant INTERNATIONAL, BURMESE $
(Map p178; Yone Gyi Rd; mains from K1500) A laid-back terrace restaurant serving Inle regional dishes, hill tribe food and the traveller holy trinity of Chinese, pasta and pancakes.

Miss Nyaungshwe Restaurant INTERNATIONAL, BURMESE $
(Map p178; Phaung Daw Seiq Rd; mains from K2000) Travellers gather at this cute bamboo-fronted restaurant for inexpensive Chinese and Bamar curries, plus pancakes, pasta and bottled beers.

Drinking & Entertainment

Despite the backpacker vibe, there's no bar scene in Nyaungshwe. The locals head to beer-based restaurants such as **Kaung Kaung** (Map p178; Main Rd; ☺lunch & dinner), which has Myanmar and ABC beers on tap, while tourists head to **Min Min's** (Map p178; Yone Gyi Rd; ☺all day), where the beer costs more but where the daring can order a caipirinha, Irish coffee or pina colada.

Aung Puppet Show PUPPET SHOW
(Map p178; Ahletaung Kyaung Rd; admission K3000; ☺show times 7pm & 8.30pm) Down the road opposite the Nandawunn Hotel, this place has two nightly shows of traditional Burmese puppetry.

Shopping

On any trip onto Inle Lake, you will be approached by dozens of vendors in canoes selling crafts objects and curios, so there isn't any great need to buy souvenirs in Nyaungshwe. It is, though, worth going out of your way to visit any of one of the five-day rotating market destinations (see the Marketing Strategy boxed text for details).

Information

Any guesthouse in town can arrange tours, boat trips, flights and bus tickets. Some hotels are willing to change US dollars into kyat for guests; otherwise money can be changed at Mingala Market.

See p183 for information on the permit fee.
Comet Travel & Internet Café (Map p178; ☑209 126; Yone Gyi Rd; ☺7am-11pm) Books flights and buses and has a few internet terminals.
Golden Island Cottages (Map p178; GIC; ☑209 551; Phaung Daw Seiq Rd; ☺8am-6pm) Come here to arrange guides to Kakku and Sankar.

MARKETING STRATEGY

A rustic market rotates among several cities and towns in the Inle Lake region. The most touted of these is the so-called floating market at Ywama, but this has become a victim of its own success, and the land-based options, where tribal people come down from the hills to trade livestock and produce, are much more interesting. The towns below Ywama host the market once every five days; hotels and guesthouses can advise you where the market will be heading next. Keep in mind that markets are not held on full moon days.

» **Heho, Thandaung** – Thandaung's market is small, but well off the beaten track.

» **Taunggyi, Floating Market (Ywama)** – The 'Floating Market' at Ywama has emerged to become the most touristy of the circuit – consider heading elsewhere.

» **Maing Thauk, Thaung Tho, Kyauk Taung** – Maing Thauk is close to Nyaungshwe and reachable by land or boat, but the Thaung Tho and Kyauk Taung markets, located at the far southern end of Inle Lake, are largely off the tourist circuit.

» **Shwenyaung, Kaung Daing, Kalaw, Inthein** – Inthein, although now fully on the tourist circuit, is still worth a visit for its size and setting. Kalaw's tidy market spills over to the streets on market day.

» **Nyaungshwe, Pindaya, Nampan** – On market day, Nyaungshwe's normally sleepy market swells to several times its normal size. Tiny Pindaya's central market also attracts vendors and buyers who come down from the surrounding hills.

K.K.O. Internet (Map p178; Yone Gyi Rd; per hr K1500; ⊙7am-10.30pm) International email accounts can be accessed via proxy servers at this small cafe.

Lin Internet (Map p178; Kann Nar Rd; per hr K1000; ⊙7am-10pm) Close to the boat jetty, above the Mini Mart, with decent connections.

❶ Getting There & Away

By far the easiest way to reach the Inle Lake region is to fly. Most long-distance road transport starts or finishes in Taunggyi – to reach Nyaungshwe, you'll have to change at the junction town of Shwenyaung on the highway between Taunggyi and Heho.

Air

The main airport for the Inle region is at Heho, 25.5 miles northwest of Nyaungshwe on the way to Kalaw – see p174 for flight details. There are no official airline offices in Nyaungshwe, but hotels and private travel agents can make bookings.

Taxis waiting at the airport charge K25,000 to Nyaungshwe (one hour); a cheaper but less convenient option is to hike the near mile to Hwy 4 and wait for a pick-up truck or bus bound for Taunggyi (K2000, 1½ hours); ask to be let off at Shwenyaung, from where you can change for Nyaungshwe. You may face a long wait.

Bus & Pick-up Trucks

Any bus travelling from Mandalay (see p221) or Yangon (see p70) to Taunggyi can drop you at Shwenyaung for the full Taunggyi fare.

To Yangon, overnight buses originating in Taunggyi reach Shwenyaung at 3pm (K14,000, 16 to 20 hours). Similarly, the Mandalay-bound bus arrives at Shwenyaung at 6pm (K10,000, 12 hours) and the bus to Nyaung U (Bagan) at around 5am (K10,000, eight hours). Hotels and travel agents in Nyaungshwe can book seats on these buses but be sure to be at the junction in Shwenyaung early so you don't miss your bus.

To reach Kalaw (K3000, four hours), Thazi (K5000, six hours) or Meiktila (K7000, seven hours), you must first take a pick-up or taxi to Shwenyaung. Once you reach the Hwy 4 junction, you can flag down local buses and pick-ups heading west.

From Nyaungshwe, pick-ups run to Shwenyaung (K500, 30 minutes) and Taunggyi (K1000, one hour) from 7am to 5pm. The **pick-up stand** (Map p178; off Yone Gyi Rd) is west of the market but pick-ups also stop near the bridge north of Mingala Market, although they're often full by then.

Taxi

The easiest way to find a taxi in Nyaungshwe is to ask at your hotel or, failing that, call **Ko Kyaw Kyaw Oo** (☑209 367); charter taxi fares include Shwenyaung (K10,000), Heho (K15,000),

Taunggyi (K25,000) and Kalaw (K40,000), and taxis have room for three or four passengers.

Motorcycle taxis at the **stand** (Map p178; Main Rd) near the market can transfer you to Shwenyaung for K3000.

Train

The train rumbling through the hills from Shwenyaung to Thazi is slow but the scenery en route is stunning. From Shwenyaung, the single daily departure leaves at 10am arriving in Kalaw after three hours ($3) and reaching Thazi at least another six hours later ($5).

For train times from Thazi see p167.

❶ Getting Around

Dirt tracks run through the marshes in all directions from Nyaungshwe – several shops on Yone Gyi Rd and Phaung Daw Pyan Rd rent out clunky Chinese bicycles for K1000 per day.

Motorcycle taxis at the **stand** (Map p178; Main Rd) near the market can take you to Kaung Daing hot springs for K5000 return.

The Lake

♩081

Almost every visitor to Nyaungshwe takes a boat trip on Inle Lake. But the lake is so large and the villages so spread out that Inle never feels too crowded. The exception is when the traditional five-day market rotation comes to Ywama or Inthein; every tour boat and souvenir vendor in the Inle region heads straight for the market and tourists jostle for space with tribal people trying to do their weekly shopping.

◎ Sights

Inthein　　　　　　　　　　　　VILLAGE
အင်းတိန်

West of Ywama, a narrow, foliage-cloaked canal winds through the reeds to the lakeside village of Inthein (Indein). As the channel leaves the reed beds, the jungle grows denser and denser on either side, before the village appears suddenly among the vegetation. The *Apocalypse Now* ambience evaporates somewhat when you see the waiting tourist boats and souvenir stalls, but no matter – the pagodas on the hilltop are still incredibly atmospheric despite the crowds.

The first group of ruined stupas is immediately behind the village. Known as **Nyaung Ohak**, the crumbling stupas are choked in greenery but you can still discern some ornate stucco carvings of animals, *deva* and *chinthe*.

From Nyaung Ohak, a covered stairway climbs the hill, flanked by stalls selling lacquerware, puppets and other souvenirs – quality is high but so are the prices. At the top is **Shwe Inn Thein Paya**, a complex of 1054 weather-beaten *zedi*, most constructed in the 17th and 18th centuries. Some of the *zedi* lean at crazy angles while others have been reconstructed (courtesy of donations from local Buddhists), which may ultimately be the fate of the whole complex. From the pagoda, there are great views across the lake and valley. For even better views, there are two more **ruined stupas** on conical hills just north of the village, reached via a dirt path behind Nyaung Ohak. You could easily spend a few hours exploring the various ruins here.

Part of the five-day inshore circuit, the **market** (see p183) at Inthein is one of the biggest and liveliest in the area.

Nga Hpe Kyaung
(Jumping Cat Monastery)   BUDDHIST TEMPLE
ငါးဖယ်ကျောင်း

(Map p185) On the eastern side of the lake, the Nga Hpe Kyaung is famous for its jumping cats, trained to leap through hoops by the monks during the slow hours between scripture recitals. The monks seem happy to put on a cat-jumping show for visiting tourists and the cats get treats for their efforts, so they seem fairly happy too. But don't expect a show when the monks are eating or meditating. A better reason to visit the pagoda is to see the collection of ancient buddha images. Constructed four years before Mandalay Palace, the huge wooden meditation hall has statues in the Shan, Tibetan, Bagan and Inwa (Ava) styles displayed on ornate wood and mosaic pedestals.

Ywama   VILLAGE
ရွာမ

(Map p185) Ywama was the first village to be developed for tourism and, as a result, it has the greatest number of souvenir shops and restaurants. It's still a very pretty village, with winding channels lined with tall teak houses, but the charm can be diminished by the crowds of tourist boats and paddling souvenir vendors.

The main attraction at Ywama is the famous **floating market** (see boxed text p183), though this has also been a victim of its own success. Held once every five days, the market is a traffic jam of tourist boats and

souvenir hawkers, with a few local farmers peddling vegetables in among the crowds.

Phaung Daw Oo Paya   BUDDHIST TEMPLE
ဖောင်တော်ဦးဘုရား

(Map p185; camera/video fee K200/300) A wide channel leads south from Ywama to the village of Tha Ley and Phaung Daw Oo Paya, the holiest religious site in southern Shan State. Enshrined within the huge tiered pagoda are five ancient buddha images that have been transformed into amorphous blobs by the sheer volume of gold leaf applied by devotees. During the annual Phaung Daw Oo festival (p194), the images are paraded around the lake in an ornate barge shaped like a *hintha*. Local families often bring their children here as part of the ordination rites for the *sangha* (Buddhist brotherhood) – a fascinating spectacle if you happen to be there at the right time.

LAKEFRONT VIEW

Cutting through the morning mist on Inle Lake is one of Myanmar's must-do experiences. Be sure to bring a coat or sweater (it can get cold out there), and in addition to the usual sights, be sure to hit the five-day market (p183).

Nampan
နမ့်ပန်
VILLAGE

South of Ywama, the peaceful village of Nampan is built on stilts over the water. It's off the main tourist circuit, but the Alodaw Pauk Pagoda (Map p185) is one of the oldest shrines on the lake. Built on stilts over the water, the whitewashed stupa enshrines a fabulous gem-encrusted, Shan-style buddha. Nampan has several small **cheroot factories** and there are some good restaurants on the edge of the village.

Floating Gardens
ကျွန်းမျော
GARDENS

(Map p185) North of Nampan are these famous gardens, where Intha farmers grow flowers, tomatoes, squash and other fruit and vegetables on long wooden trellises supported on floating mats of vegetation. In the morning and afternoon, farmers paddle up and down between the rows tending their crops. It's a bucolic scene made all the more photogenic by the watery setting.

In Phaw Khone
အင်းဖောပေါ့ခဲ
VILLAGE

(Map p185) This tidy village of teak stilt houses is famous for its **weaving workshops**. Buildings across the village vibrate with the clatter of shuttles and the click-clack of shifting loom frames. The workshops are a popular stop on the tourist circuit, and it's fascinating to see the skill of the weavers as they produce ornate, multicoloured fabrics on looms made from bamboo poles lashed together with rope.

Maing Thauk
မိုင်းသောက်
VILLAGE

(Map p185) On the eastern side of the lake, the village of Maing Thauk has a split personality – half the village is set on dry land, while the other half sits on stilts over the water, linked to the shore by a 450yd wooden bridge.

Inland from the village's main road, a few crumbling gravestones near the orphanage mark the location of the colonial-era **Fort Steadman.**

You can continue walking uphill to a peaceful forest monastery (Map p185) for good views over the lake. Maing Thauk is accessible by boat and by road – you can cycle to Maing Thauk in an hour or so along a dirt track leading southeast from Nyaungshwe.

Southern End of the Lake

At the southern end of the lake, the village of Thaung Tho (off Map p185) holds an important tribal market every five days. This market sees far fewer visitors than the one at Inthein. A long walkway leads uphill from town to a complex of whitewashed **Shan stupas**. There are more interesting stops in this part of the lake; the village of Kyauk Taung (off Map p185) is devoted to pottery-making and is also part of the market circuit, while nearby Kyaing Kan (off Map p185) specialises in weaving robes using lotus threads.

A long canal at the bottom of Inle Lake winds south through peaceful countryside to a second lake ringed by Shan, Intha and Pa-O villages. It takes around three hours from Shwenyuang to reach the largest village, Sankar (Samka; off Map p185), once the seat of a Shan hereditary prince. On the opposite side of the lake is **Tharkong Pagoda**, a collection of crumbling *zedi* and stucco sculptures that date back at least 500 years. The main attraction here is the almost total absence of other tourists – visits to this area have only been permitted since 2003 and foreigners must still be accompanied by a Pa-O guide. Guided boat trips to Sankar should be arranged through Golden Island Cottages (p183); guides cost $10 and there's a permit fee of $5.

Activities

Motorboat Trips

It is *de rigueur* to take at least one boat trip on the lake during a visit to Inle. Every morning, a flotilla of slender wooden canoes fitted with long-tailed outboard motors surges out into the lake, transporting visitors to various natural, cultural, religious, historical or commercial sites.

The lake itself is rich in wildlife, especially waterfowl. The area around the lake has been protected as the **Inle Wetland Bird Sanctuary**, an official bird sanctuary, since 1985 and you'll see herons, warblers, cormorants, wild ducks and egrets as you zip along the channels between the villages. But you won't hear them – or the comments of fellow passengers for that matter – over the thunder of the boat's motor. Bring ear plugs or sit right at the front, away from the thundering pistons.

Every hotel and guesthouse in Nyaungshwe can arrange motorboat trips or you can make your own arrangements directly with the boat drivers at one of the piers – although they'll most likely find you before you can find them. Prices for day-long boat trips start at K12,000, which typically includes visits to the famous sights in the northern part of the lake such as Phaung Daw Oo Paya in Tha Ley, the Nga Hpe Kyaung in Nga Phe village and the floating gardens. A trip to Inthein will raise the cost to about K15,000, while visits to destinations further south such as Thaung Tho or Kyauk Taung can run as high as K25,000. The fee covers the entire boat; drivers will carry five or more passengers in a single boatload and passengers get padded seats and life jackets.

Trekking

Inle Lake is the end point for several trekking routes from Kalaw. Trails run west from Kalaw through the villages of the Shan, Intha, Pa-O, Danu, Palaung and Danaw tribes, ending at villages on the western lake shore. These treks can be walked in either direction, though most people walk from Kalaw to Inle, as the final stages are mainly downhill.

The most popular start/end point for treks is Kaung Daing, but begging has become a problem on this route because of tour groups handing out sweets and money to children. More interesting places to start or end the walk to Kalaw include Inthein and Thandaung.

FLOATING OVER INLE LAKE

As beautiful as they are from the ground, the views across Inle Lake are even more stunning from the air. If you can gather up a minimum of four passengers, who are each prepared to stump up $5000, then the folks at Eastern Safaris (www.easternsafaris.com) can arrange a four-day, three-night hot-air balloon safari over the lake and surrounding hills. They're the same reliable and professional folks who run the balloon rides over Bagan (see p113). A six-day, five-night safari that also includes Bagan is also available and is usually scheduled for December, the best month for hot-air ballooning.

There are also some interesting day hikes and overnight treks north and south of Nyaungshwe, passing through rice paddies dotted with Shan stupa ruins. Trails into the hills east of town lead to Pa-O villages with panoramic views over the lake. Guides can talk you through the various treks and itineraries.

Day hikes cost around $10 a day, which includes a basic lunch of rice and curry (carry your own bottled or purified water). Overnight treks around Nyaungshwe are $25, while the two or three-day trek to Kalaw costs $30 per person in groups of three. Recommended guides in Nyaungshwe include Pyone Cho at **Lotus Restaurant** (Map p178; pyonechlotus@gmail.com; Museum Rd (Haw St), Nyaungshwe) and the brothers Than Htay and Ko Htwe at **Sunny Day Tour Services** (Map p178; htwe.sunny@yahoo.com; cnr Main Rd & Yone Gyi Rd, Nyaungshwe).

Swimming

The lake waters are very clear so a dip looks inviting, but the channels around the villages are shallow and full of weeds. The best place for a swim is out on the main body of the lake, though you need to be wary of speeding riverboats. One safe spot for a swim is the disused teak mansion known as **Inleh Bo The** (Map p185), near the mouth of the channel leading to Nyaungshwe.

🛏 Sleeping

Although many travellers choose to stay in Nyaungshwe, there are also a number of upmarket resorts built on stilts over the lake, where the sensation of sleeping over the water is very atmospheric. All of the resorts have their own boats and drivers but, as the resorts are quite isolated, most people eat where they stay.

Reservations are recommended in the high season, and discounts are often available for advance bookings. All rates include breakfast. All of the hotels arrange pick-ups and return boat trips to/from Nyaungshwe for K8000.

The majority of accommodation on Inle Lake is around Maing Thauk; prices grow progressively higher the further north you go. None of the following hotels appear to have government links, but Pristine Lotus and Myanmar Treasure Resort do.

TOP CHOICE **Golden Island Cottages** HOTEL $$$
Nampan (GIC; Map p185; ☎209 390, in Yangon 01-549 019; www.gicmyanmar.com; r $50-70; @) Thale U (GIC; Map p185; ☎209 389, in Yangon 01-549

019; www.gicmyanmar.com; r $50-70; @) Owned by a cooperative of Pa-O tribal people, the Golden Island Cottages resorts provide some of the best accommodation on the lake. The Nampan resort has a great location over open water while the Thale U resort is closer to shore. Both resorts offer attractive, raised cottages linked by wooden walkways, arranged around a central restaurant serving good Chinese, Pa-O and Shan dishes. The owners can arrange treks and boat trips to Kakku and Sankar – they have an office in Nyaungshwe on Phaung Daw Seiq Rd.

Inle Princess Resort   BOUTIQUE HOTEL **$$$**
(Map p185; ☑209 055; www.inleprincessresort. com; bungalows $160-250; ❄@) The Inle Princess is honeymoon material. The stylish wooden cottages would not look out of place in an Asian design magazine, with handmade furniture, luxurious fabrics, potted plants and ethnic artefacts on the walls. The more expensive bungalows have plant-filled sun decks facing the lake.

**Hu Pin Hotel Inle Khaung
Daing Village Resort**   HOTEL **$$$**
(Map p185; ☑209 291; www.hupinhotelmyanmar. com; Kaung Daing; r/cottage/ste $50-70/70-80/150) Owned by the same people as the Hu Pin Hotel in Nyaungshwe, this vast compound of 86 rooms and bungalows sits on dry land facing the lake. The wooden bungalows are comfortable and well cared for and feature great views over the lake.

Shwe Inn Tha   HOTEL **$$$**
(Map p185; ☑209445; www.myanmar-inleshweinntha -floatinghotel.com; Nam Pan; bungalow/ste $80/150; ❄@🏊) Open since 1996, this is the upscale version of the nearby Golden Island Cottages Nampan. Accommodation here takes the form of deluxe bungalows or suites elevated over water. Rooms are fully equipped and this is the only resort on Inle Lake with its own pool.

Inle Lake View   HOTEL **$$$**
(Map p185; ☑209 332; www.inlelakeview.com; Kaung Daing; r $120-130, ste $155-165, villa $220; @) Located on dry land at Kaung Daing, the rooms here are spread over several buildings a short walk from the shores of Inle Lake. There are only two free-standing villas, but all rooms are spacious and tastefully furnished.

Inle Resort   BOUTIQUE HOTEL **$$$**
(Map p185; ☑209 361; www.inleresort.com; Maing Thauk; cottages $75-120; ❄@) Opened in 2005, this handsome resort is centred on a palatial wooden restaurant and lobby. The stylish cottages feature huge picture windows and private sun decks facing the lake.

Sky Lake   HOTEL **$$$**
(Map p185; ☑209 128; www.inleskylake.com; Maing Thauk; bungalows $50-60) Sky Lake has the typical setup of a water-bound Inle Lake resort but with a slightly more aged feel than its direct neighbour, Paradise Inle Resort.

Paradise Inle Resort   HOTEL **$$$**
(Map p185; ☑209 586; Maing Thauk; bungalows $60-100; @) Next door to Sky Lake, this newer floating resort is similar to its neighbour, but feels comparatively overpriced.

✖ Eating

As well as the resorts, there are numerous floating restaurants in stilt houses on the lake that offer good Chinese and Shan food, cold beers and English-language menus. The greatest concentration of restaurants is in Ywama, but there are also some good choices around Nampan.

Inn Thar Lay   CHINESE, BURMESE **$$**
(Map p185; ☑209 451; Tha Ley; mains K5000-6000; ☺all day) This restaurant, with two branches near Phaung Daw Oo Paya, gets good reviews and has its own vegetable garden.

Around Inle Lake

TAUNGGYI
တောင်ကြီး
☑081 / POP C150,000

Although travellers make a beeline for Nyaungshwe, Taunggyi is the administrative capital for the whole of Shan State. Perched on top of a mountain, it's a busy trading post and the town markets are piled high with Chinese and Thai goods, freighted in daily via the border crossings at Mong La and Tachileik. Unless you've spent too much time in rural Shan State and are pining for the big city and/or consumer goods, there's really little of interest here for the average visitor.

◉ Sights

**Shan State Cultural Museum
& Library**   MUSEUM
ရှမ်းပြည်နယ်ယဉ်ကျေးမှုပြတိုက် နှင့်
စာကြည့်တိုက်
(Bogyoke Aung San Rd; admission $2; ☺9.30am-4pm Tue-Sun) With such a strong emphasis on tribal costumes, we reckon this place could

also be called the Shan Fashion Museum. Among the outfits you'll also find a handful of displays of weapons, musical instruments and jewellery.

MARKETS

The focal point of Taunggyi is the market area on the main road through town. The **Old Market** is dominated by foodstuffs and household goods while the **New Market** has clothes and black-market goods. Every five days the old market ground hosts a busy **tribal market** that attracts lots of traders from the hills.

RELIGIOUS MONUMENTS

The main downtown pagoda is the **Mya Le Dhamma Yon** (Bogyoke Aung San Rd) near the market and nearby is the huge **Gurdwara** (Sikh temple) used by Taunggyi's Sikh population. Taunggyi has a number of historic **churches** and there are several Burmese-style **mosques** on the alleyways southwest of the market.

Set among the pines above Circular Rd West, the **Yat Taw Mu Pagoda** contains a 33ft-high standing buddha, constructed using donations from Japanese Buddhists. Just north of Hotel Empire, **Min Kyaung** features gaudy statuary and a pagoda styled after the Mahabodhi temple at Bodhgaya in India.

On the outskirts south of town, the huge white **Sulamuni Paya** has a gilded corn-cob stupa that pays tribute to the Ananda Pahto in Bagan. You can continue uphill to the ridge-top paya of **Shwe Phone Pwint Paya** for dizzying views over Taunggyi and Inle Lake.

✩ Festivals & Events

As part of the full-moon celebrations during Tazaungmon (the eighth month of the Burmese lunar calendar), the city holds a huge **fire-balloon festival**, when hundreds of hot-air balloons in a kaleidoscope of colours and shapes are released into the sky to carry away sins. The three-day festival takes place in October or November and accommodation can be very hard to find in Taunggyi at this time.

🛏 Sleeping

Hotels in Taunggyi cater primarily to visiting traders, so there are few bargains to be had.

KBZ FC Hotel　　　　　　　　　　HOTEL **$$**
(☎22009; 157 Khwar Nyo St; s/d/ste $30/35/45; ❄) A recent renovation has changed the exterior and name of the former Paradise Hotel. The current emphasis appears to be on TVs:

Although they follow Buddhism and wear modern Burmese costume, the Intha people of Inle Lake are culturally quite distinct from their Shan neighbours. The ancestors of the Intha are thought to have migrated to Inle from Dawei in southern Myanmar. According to the most popular legend, two brothers from Dawei came to Yaunghwe (the original name for Nyaungshwe) in 1359 to serve the local Shan *sao pha* (sky lord). The chieftain was so pleased with the hard-working Dawei brothers that he invited 36 more families from Dawei; purportedly, all the Intha around Inle Lake are descended from these migrant families. A more likely theory is that the Intha fled southern Myanmar in the 18th century to escape wars between the Thais and Bamar.

the lobby boasts what is quite possibly the largest one we've ever seen, and each of the gigantic suites is fitted with two flat-screen TVs! Unfortunately the standard rooms have changed little and have the same aged furniture (and TVs) as its predecessor.

Hotel Empire　　　　　　　　　　HOTEL **$$**
(☎23737; 31 Bogyoke Aung San Rd; s/d $20/26) Another substantial Chinese business-style hotel, the Empire has modern rooms with TVs, and bathrooms with reliably hot showers. Staff here are more used to dealing with foreign visitors than at the other hotels in town.

Khemerat Hotel　　　　　　　　　HOTEL **$**
(☎22464; 4/B Bogyoke Aung San Rd; s/d $12/18) The closest Taunggyi has to budget accommodation, this faded block at the north end of town has large concrete rooms with rudimentary furnishings.

Eastern Hotel　　　　　　　　　　HOTEL **$$**
(☎22243; 27 Bogyoke Aung San Rd; r $15-36; ❄) Exceedingly tidy, with vast wood-floored suites and rather tight standard rooms.

Sun Minn Hotel　　　　　　　　　HOTEL **$$**
(☎22353; 137 Bogyoke Aung San Rd; r $15-35; ❄) Cosy feel and a variety of rooms; ask to see a few. The more expensive ones have wood floors and flat-screen TVs.

Taunggyi Hotel HOTEL $$
(☎21127; Shu Myaw Khin Rd; s/d $30/36) The hotel's park-like atmosphere is the highlight here, but it's such a hike from town that, unless you came with your own transportation, it's difficult to recommend.

✕ Eating

The street just south of the New Market has a number of inexpensive **food stalls** (meals from K1000; ⊙6.30am-5pm). At night this strip also functions as Taunggyi's **night market** (⊙6-10pm) serving *shan kauq-sweh* (Shan noodle soup) and other local staples.

Shan Restaurant SHAN $
(off Bogyoke Aung San Rd; mains from K500; ⊙breakfast & lunch) This open-air place serves yummy Shan treats such as *khao som (*sour rice with a garlic oil topping) and *kauq-sweh kai (*Shan-style chicken noodle soup). There's no English-language sign here;

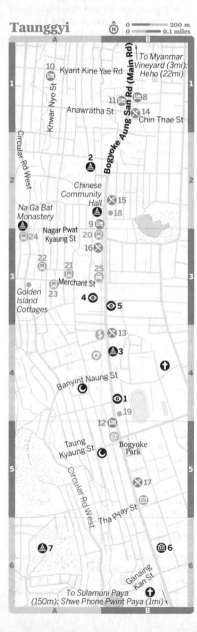

Taunggyi

look for the narrow alley with the rainbow-coloured umbrellas halfway down the block south of the Hotel Empire.

Lyan You
CHINESE, BURMESE $

(Bogyoke Aung San Rd; meals from K3000; ☺lunch & dinner) Lyan You has Skol and Dagon beer on tap and above-average Chinese food – we recommend the special assorted noodles and short ribs in soy sauce.

Shwe Min Thu Café
TEAHOUSE $

(Gold Mine; Bogyoke Aung San Rd; snacks from K400; ☺breakfast & lunch) Near the post office, this humble teahouse has posters of London on the walls and hot tea, coffee and cakes to warm your belly on cold mornings.

Saung Oo
SHAN $

(Chin Thae St; noodles from K500; ☺breakfast & lunch) North of the centre on a lane off the main drag, this popular noodle house serves hearty bowls of Shan-style noodle soup.

Sein Restaurant
BURMESE $

(Bogyoke Aung San Rd; meals from K2000; ☺lunch & dinner) Locals crowd into this busy restaurant at the north end of town for tasty Chinese food and Myanmar set-meals with all the trimmings. The fried snakehead fish goes down a treat.

ℹ Information

There is no tourist office, but hotels can advise on tours and transport. Also see www.lonelyplanet.com/myanmar-burma for further information on travelling in Myanmar.

Public Internet Access Centre (Bogyoke Aung San Rd; per hr K500; ☺8.30am-9pm) Fast access; near Bogyoke Park. There are several other internet cafes along Bogyoke Aung San Rd, most open from 10am to 10pm and charging K300 per hour.

Shan Pyi Thar (☑24549; 8 Bogyoke Aung San Rd; ☺9am-6pm) There's no English-language sign, but this ticket agency is located roughly across from Hotel Empire. It's the place to buy airline tickets as well as change money.

ℹ Getting There & Away

Air

The airport at Heho, about 22 miles west of Taunggyi, has regular flights to Yangon, Mandalay, Nyaung U (Bagan) and other cities – see p174. A taxi from Heho to Taunggyi costs K25,000; a cheaper but less convenient option is to hike the near mile to the Hwy and wait for a pick-up truck or bus to Taunggyi (K2000, 1½ hours).

Air Mandalay (☑21330; ☺8am-5pm Mon-Fri & 9am-1pm Sat & Sun) has an office on Bogyoke

THE BORDEAUX OF BURMA?

Myanmar probably isn't the first place that comes to mind when you think of fine wine, but all that may be set to change with the increasingly robust vintages coming out of two Shan state wineries. **Myanmar Vineyard** (☑in Yangon 664 386; www.myanmar-vineyard.com), located at Aythaya, 3 miles west of Taunggyi, was founded 1999 by German entrepreneur, Bert Morsbach. The vineyard sits at an elevation of 4290ft on well-watered, limestone-rich soils, providing good growing conditions for Shiraz, Cabernet Sauvignon, Sauvignon Blanc, Chenin Blanc and Moscato grapes. **Red Mountain Estate** (☑209 366; www.redmountain-estate.com) located in a valley just outside Nyaungshwe, grow similar varietals, as well as Pinot Noir.

Both vineyards are open daily for tours and tastings – see the websites for details. You can reach Myanmar Vineyard by taxi, or on any pick-up travelling between Taunggyi and Shwenyaung; Red Mountain is within cycling distance of Nyaungshwe.

Aung San Rd, as does **Air Bagan** (☑24737; ☺8am-5pm Mon-Fri & 9am-1pm Sat & Sun), which is owned by Tay Za (see p21).

Bus

Buses leave Taunggyi from several stands around town. The **offices** of companies running long-haul bus and van services to Yangon (K10,000; 2pm; 16 hours) and Mandalay (K6000; 5pm; 12 hours) are found along the west side of Bogyoke Aung San Rd, just south of Hotel Empire. The **office** for buses to Nyaung U (Bagan; K11,000; 4am; 10 hours) can be bought around the corner, on Nagar Pwat Kyaung St. Share taxis to Mandalay (K25,000 per person, 8 to 10 hours) can also be arranged here.

Buses to Kalaw (K2500; 1pm, 2pm & 3pm; 3 hours) and Pindaya (K2000; 1pm & 1.30pm; 4 hours) leave from the **Maw Cherry bus stand** (Circular Rd West), about a mile north of the town centre. Any of these buses can drop you in Shwenyaung or Heho. To get to the Maw Cherry bus stand, charter a taxi at the market in or front of Hotel Empire for around K1500.

For buses from Yangon, see p70.

Pick-Up Truck, Minivan & Taxi

PICK-UP TRUCKS leave regularly from a **stand** east of the New Market to Nyaungshwe (K700, one hour) between 6am and 4pm. Pick-ups to Thazi (K3000, seven hours) and Meiktila (K3000, eight hours) leave from a **stand** one block west of the New Market and from another **stand** on Circular Rd West, near the Na Ga Bat Monastery, during the day time.

MINIVANS to Heho (K2000, one hour) and Kalaw (K3000, five hours) leave from a **bus stop** just northwest of the New Market.

TAXIS loiter in front of the Hotel Empire or at a stand near the new market, offering charter rides to Nyaungshwe (K20,000) and Heho airport (K25,000).

KAKKU

ကက္ကူ

Arranged in neat rows sprawling over the hillside, the 2478 stupas at Kakku are one of the most remarkable sights in Shan State. According to local legend, the stupa garden was founded by the Buddhist missionaries of the Indian emperor Ashoka in the 3rd century BC. The stupas at Kakku were built in a bewildering variety of styles, marking the prevailing architectural styles when they were constructed. Some are simple and un-adorned while others are covered in a riot of stucco deities and mythical beasts. Among the tall Shan-style stupas are a number of small square 'monastery style' stupas that are unique to this region.

Like ancient sites across the country, Kakku is slowly being restored and modernised using donations from pilgrims – the stupa garden still has a palpable sense of antiq-uity but don't expect an Indiana Jones-style ruin in the jungle. The annual **Kakku Paya Pwe**, held on the full-moon day of the lunar month of Tabaung (March), attracts Pa-O pilgrims from across Shan State.

Kakku is surrounded by Pa-O villages and the site can be visited only with a Pa-O guide, arranged through Golden Island Cottages (☑ in Taunggyi 081-23136; 18 Circular Rd East, Taunggyi; ☺6am-5pm). There's a $3 entry fee for the site and a $5 fee for the guide and you must also arrange a taxi to the site – K30,000 from Taunggyi, including a few hours waiting at the stupas.

So far there isn't any accommodation at Kakku, but you can get a good meal at the Hlaing Konn Restaurant (☺lunch & dinner) overlooking the site.

KENGTUNG & BORDER AREAS

Beyond Taunggyi, the landscape rucks up into great folds, cloaked in dense forest and cut by rushing mountain rivers. This is the heartland of the Golden Triangle, where in-surgent armies battled for most of the last century to gain control of the opium trade between Myanmar, China, Laos and Thai-land. Ceasefires with the main rebel groups have allowed the region to finally move out of the shadow of civil war but drug traffick-ing and other illegal activities are common

---

THE PADAUNG

Originally from Kayah state on the Thai border south of Inle Lake, the Padaung tribe – Myanmar's famous 'giraffe women' – have become a victim of their own traditions. The ancient custom of fitting young girls with brass neck-rings has made the Padaung a ma-jor tourist attraction – and a major target for exploitation on both sides of the border.

Originally intended to make Padaung women less attractive to raiding parties from neighbouring tribes, the application of heavy brass neck-rings causes deformation of the collar bone and upper ribs, pushing the shoulders away from the head. Many Padaung women reach a stage where they are unable to carry the weight of their own heads with-out the rings as additional support.

These days, the rings are applied with a different purpose – to provide women from impoverished hill villages with the means to make a living posing for photographs. Many Padaung women are ferried across the border to Thailand to provide a photo opportunity for visiting tour groups. The UN has compared the treatment of Padaung women to the treatment of animals in a zoo.

Some souvenir shops on Inle Lake employ Padaung women to lure passing tourist boats. If you want to help the Padaung, purchase handloom fabrics and other Padaung crafts rather than take pictures of 'long-necked women'.

and travel to the border areas is still subject to government restrictions.

Kengtung (Kyaingtong)

ကျိုင်းတုံ

📋 084 / POP C20,000

The second-biggest city in Shan State, Kengtung (Kyaingtong), pronounced 'Cheng Dong', is the capital of the Golden Triangle region and one of the most attractive towns in Myanmar. In culture and appearance, it feels closer to the hill towns of northern Thailand and southern China, and the vast majority of the town's residents belong to one of several Tai ethnic groups: Shan, Tai Lü, Tai Khün and Tai Nuea.

For years, Kengtung was caught in the crossfire between rival drug lords, but peace has returned to the quiet, pagoda-lined streets. The rugged terrain of eastern Shan State contributes to the sense of isolation – Kengtung is an outpost of development in a sea of largely deforested mountains, where Wa, Eng, Shan, Akha and Lahu tribal people follow a way of life that has changed little in centuries. Needless to say, treks to hill-tribe villages are a major attraction.

◉ Sights & Activities

The **Central Market** draws people from all over the Kengtung district, including tribal people from the hills. The market has lots of stalls selling food and household items, including the coins, buttons, beads and threads used to decorate tribal costumes. Twice a week, there's a **water-buffalo market** on the road leading to Taunggyi. You probably won't be able to fit a buffalo into your backpack but it's interesting to watch the traders haggling for the best price on a used beast of burden.

The old British enclave in Kengtung was centred on the small **Naung Tung** lake, a popular spot for morning and evening strolls. There are several decaying colonial buildings above the lake shore, including the handsome **Colony House** (Mine Yen Rd). On the road leading towards Taunggyi, the **Roman Catholic Mission** and **Immaculate Heart Cathedral** have been providing an education for hill-tribe orphans since colonial times.

Monasteries & Temples

If there were many more Buddhist monasteries in Kengtung, people would have nowhere left to live. The town's many monasteries are called *wat* rather than *kyaung*, and local monks wear both orange and red robes, reflecting the close cultural links to Thailand.

The gilded stupa of **Wat Jong Kham** (Zom Kham) rises majestically above the centre of town. Legend dates the *wat* to a visit by Gautama Buddha but a more likely date for the stupa is the 13th-century migration from Chiang Mai. In the middle of the traffic roundabout below Wat Jong Kham, **Wat Mahamuni** (Maha Myat Muni) is a classic Thai-style *wat* with a richly painted interior. Just north of Airport Rd, **Wat In** contains a stunning collection of ancient gilded wooden buddha images in all shapes, sizes and positions. Chinese residents of Kengtung worship at the appealing **Chinese Buddhist temple** near the immigration office.

Pointing dramatically towards the mountains on a ridge overlooking Naung Tung lake, the 60ft-high standing buddha statue known as **Ya Taw Mu** is probably the most distinctive landmark in Kengtung. Next to the statue is a small **Cultural Museum** (⊙10am-4pm Tue-Sat; admission $2) with costumes, farming implements and other tribal objects, some inexplicably painted silver. Potentially interesting, but when we visited no-one knew where the key was.

You can see the dome-shaped stone **Mausoleums of the Tai Khün Princes** on the east end of Mine Yen Rd.

Day Trips Around Kengtung

The hills of eastern Shan State are dotted with the villages of the Eng, Lahu Akha, Palaung, Loi, Lishaw, Shan and Wa tribes, many of which can be visited on guided treks from Kengtung.

At research time, overnight trips were not allowed, and you will need to obtain advance permission from Kengtung's immigration office to visit any of the below.

The most popular destination is **Pin Tau**, only 9 miles north of town, where it's possible to visit the villages of several tribes in a single day.

Ho Kyim, approximately 10 miles south of Kengtung, is home to several Loi and Akha and Lahu villages. And **Wan Nyek** and **Wan Saen**, near the Chinese border at Mong La (မိုင်းလား), are two villages where the Loi people still live in traditional longhouses.

Loi-mwe (လွယ်ငွေ), 20 miles southeast of Kengtung, functioned as a second-tier hill station in the British era and you can still see a number of fading **colonial buildings** and a 100-year-old Catholic **church**.

EASTERN MYANMAR KENGTUNG & BORDER AREAS

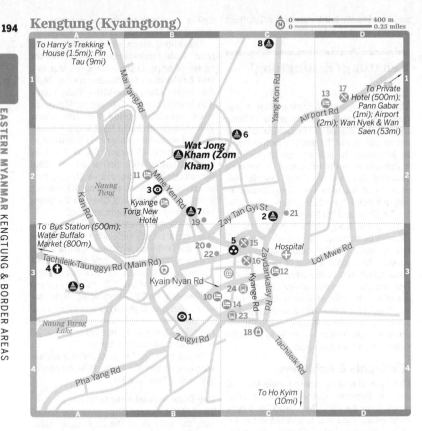

The main attraction, though, is the drive up here through a classically Asian landscape of dense forests and terraced rice fields.

Guide fees start at $15 per day, not including lunch. Keep in mind that you will also have to factor in the cost of getting to the trailheads by taxi – a further K36,000 to K65,000, depending on how far afield you go. Transportation can be arranged at Harry's Trekking House and Princess Hotel. Recommended guides include **Sai Leng** (☏09-490 31470; sairoctor.htunleng@gmail.com), **Freddie** (Yot Kham; ☏09-490 31934; yotkham@gmail.com) and **Paul** (Sai Lon; ☏09-490 30464, 22812).

If you don't have the time or funds for a trek, a good **self-guided walk** can be had along the former road to Mong La, now colloquially known as Yang Kon Rd. The area is home to several Shan families who earn a living by making **pottery** and *khao sen* (fermented rice noodles), the latter made

by a laborious process of boiling, pounding and squeezing. Your walk terminates at Wat Yang Kon, known among locals for the decorative robes covering the main buddha statue.

🎊 Festivals & Events

Kengtung's Chinese community celebrate the **Chinese New Year** in early February with the usual firecracker-charged festivities.

For Buddhists, the big calendar event is the **Water Festival** in April, when everyone gets a dousing, including visitors.

🛏 Sleeping

The accommodation scene in Kengtung will inspire few postcards home. As is the case elsewhere in Myanmar, breakfast is included in the fee and electricity is scarce; most hotels run generators from about 7pm to 10pm.

Kengtung (Kyaingtong)

The poshest option in town, the Kyainge Tong New Hotel by the lake, is government owned.

Princess Hotel   HOTEL $$
(☏21319; kengtung@mail4u.com.mm; s/d $30-50; ❄) The most popular midrange choice in town, the Princess Hotel has a great location near the market, and capable service. The rooms are large and come equipped with a television, air-conditioning, a fridge and a phone.

Sam Yweat Guest House   HOTEL $
(☏21235; cnr Kyaing Lan 1 Rd & Kyaing Lan 4 Rd; s/d $10/20) Bare but tidy rooms in a conveniently located residence. Some share a bathroom, but all rooms are the same price. Another 29 rooms should be finished by the time you read this. The same people run a far less inviting place on Airport Rd.

Private Hotel   HOTEL $$
(☏21438; www.privatehotelmyanmar.com; 5 Airport Rd; s/d $20/28) Away from the centre, on the road to the airport, this place offers plenty of creature comforts. The eccentric owner makes every effort to please and there's a cute lawn with benches where you can soak up the sun. Rooms have a TV, a minibar and 24-hour hot water.

Law Yee Chain Hotel   HOTEL $$
(☏21219; Kyain Nyan Rd; s/d $20/30; ❄) Above a Chinese bakery just south of the market, Law Yee Chain Hotel opened in late 2007 and everything still feels new. The smart rooms have air-con, TV and carpet, and immaculate bathrooms with hot showers.

Harry's Trekking House   HOTEL $
(☏21418; 132 Mai Yang Rd; r $7-20) Harry's is about 1½ miles north of the lake in Kanaburoy village. Most rooms are located in the two modern buildings and are outfitted with a TV and a bathroom, although there are also a few simple wooden rooms. Treks and transport can be arranged from here.

Saeng Tip Hotel   HOTEL $
(☏22445; Airport Rd; r $15; ❄) If you've ever stayed in a hotel in rural China, this starkly bare place will seem familiar. The good news is that they claim to provide electricity all day and night.

Noi Yee Hotel   HOTEL $
(☏21144; 5 Mine Yen St; s/d $5/10) A former royal residence, the Noi Yee has fallen on hard times. The faded colonial charm ends at reception – rooms are grungy and the shared bathrooms need some serious TLC.

✕ Eating

Many restaurants in Kengtung have a distinctively Thai flavour – no doubt thanks to the trickle of Thai tourists. The following restaurants are open for breakfast, lunch and dinner.

For local eats, your only options are the morning market or dinner with a generous local family.

THE SHAN

Eastern Myanmar is the heartland of the Buddhist Shan tribe, who have strong cultural links to the Tai peoples of northern Thailand. Many of the towns in eastern and northern Myanmar were once ruled by hereditary Shan chieftains known as *sao pha* (sky lords). With their strong sense of cultural identity and separatist leanings, the Shan have long been perceived as a threat by the central government.

Shan talk of succession from the Union of Burma was one of the triggers for the 1962 military coup. On the day of the takeover Sao Shwe Thaik, a Shan sao pha who had been Burma's first president, was arrested and his 17-year-old son shot dead – the only casualty of the coup. Sao Shwe Thaik died in prison within the year and an insurrection started that still simmers in parts of the state today.

In 2011, the ethnic Shan Dr Sai Mauk Kham, a politician from the military-backed Union Solidarity and Development Party (USDP), won a vote in parliament to become Myanmar's vice president. For more about the Shan see p312.

Lod Htin Lu Restaurant   CHINESE, BURMESE $
(Kyange Rd; mains from K1500) Downhill from the mausoleums of the Khün princes, this is another Chinese banquet restaurant with private tables for families screened off by partitions at the back. The menu features noodle soups, pork with cashews and other Chinese classics.

Golden Banyan Restaurant   CHINESE, BURMESE $
(mains from K2000) Yet another Chinese-style restaurant near the mausoleums of the Khün princes. Food is pretty standard for this kind of restaurant but the outdoor tables beneath a huge banyan tree create atmosphere.

Pann Gabar   THAI, BURMESE $
(Airport Rd; mains from K2000) If you fancy a break from Chinese food, this popular roadhouse by the bridge on the Airport Rd has indoor and outdoor seating and good Thai food – the chef doesn't scrimp on spices.

Seik Tie Kya Restaurant   CHINESE, BURMESE $
(Airport Rd; mains from K1500) This recommended Chinese restaurant has a cosy dining room at the back and tables under an awning in the yard. The spicy bean-curd hotpot is big enough for two.

🛍 Shopping

Kengtung's morning market has a couple of stalls selling hilltribe handicrafts.

U Mu Ling Ta   LACQUERWARE
(off Tachileik Rd) This fifth-generation, family-run shop specialises in lacquerware, from the ubiquitous multi-coloured Bagan style to the striking, black Kengtung style. Pieces are made on-site, so you can get a peek into the production process if you don't have the budget (they're not cheap). It's located at the top of an unmarked driveway on Tachileik Rd – locals should be able to point you in the right direction.

ℹ Information

Moneychangers in the market exchange kyat, US dollars, Thai baht and Chinese yuan.

gooGate (per hr K500; ⏰9am-9pm) Conveniently located internet access off Kyain Nyan Rd.

Immigration Office (cnr Zay Tan Gyi St & Yang Kon Rd; ⏰24hr) Down an alley north of the Paleng gate; issues permits for travel around Kengtung and to Tachileik.

Sunfar Travels (☏22626; 65 Loi Mwe Rd; ⏰9am-6pm) Sells tickets for all the private airlines.

ℹ Getting There & Away

The only way to reach Kengtung from inside Myanmar is by air, but road travel is permitted to Tachileik with a permit from Kengtung's immigration office.

ℹ TRAVEL RESTRICTIONS

From inside Myanmar, Kengtung is accessible only by air, and travellers entering Myanmar overland from Thailand cannot travel to the rest of the country.

Travel was previously possible between Kengtung and Mong La, on the Chinese border, but at research time this was off-limits.

Tachileik is a legal crossing point for foreign tourists. But, as with all of Myanmar's land crossings, there are several caveats and the following information is liable to change, so check the situation locally before you travel.

At the time of research, we'd received reports of a few travellers who had been permitted to cross into Thailand at Tachileik with advance permission from MTT in Yangon. Permits are issued in around two weeks and cost at least $50, but you may be required to book your flights and a taxi to the border through MTT. If you do obtain permission to cross into Thailand, the Thai authorities will issue you a 14-day Thai visa on arrival, or you can enter with a Thai visa obtained overseas.

If you're starting from Mae Sai, in Thailand, it's very straightforward to cross to Tachileik for the day and slightly more complicated to get a two-week visa and permission to visit Kengtung.

The Thai immigration office is open from 6.30am to 6.30pm. After taking care of the usual formalities, cross the bridge and head to the Myanmar immigration office. Here you pay 500B and your picture is taken for a temporary ID card that allows you to stay in town for the day; your passport will be kept at the office.

If you'd like to stay longer or visit Kengtung, you'll be directed to the adjacent Tourist Information office. There you'll need three photos, $10 and 50B to process a border pass valid for 15 days; your passport will be kept at the border. It's also obligatory to hire a guide for the duration of your stay. Guides cost 1000B per day (400B of this goes to MTT), and if you haven't already arranged for a Kengtung-based guide to meet you at border, you'll be assigned one by MTT and will also have to pay for your guide's food and accommodation during your stay. See p193 for some recommended Kengtung-based guides and p198 for details on getting to Kengtung.

For further information, head to shop.lonelyplanet.com to purchase a downloadable PDF of the Northern Thailand chapter from Lonely Planet's *Thailand* guide.

Air

Air Bagan (☑22790; www.airbagan.com), owned by Ta Za (p21), and **Asian Wings** (☑22300; www.asianwingsairlines.com) have offices in town and operate three flights a week between Kengtung and Heho ($85, one hour). If you're bound for Yangon ($130, three hours), you'll have to fly via Heho and Mandalay ($95, 1½ hours).

Taxis charge K5000 and trishaws K2000 for the 2-mile trip to/from the airport.

Bus & Pick-Up Truck

Foreigners can travel by road to Tachileik but the 280-mile road between Kengtung and Taunggyi is completely off-limits. Officials blame banditry and fighting between the government and Shan and Wa rebel groups, but the ban probably has more to do with the suspected smuggling of opium and methamphetamines through the Golden Triangle.

If you want to visit Tachileik by bus from Kengtung, you must first visit the immigration office in order to get written permission that will allow you to pass the route's numerous security checkpoints. The same procedure must be carried out at the Tachileik immigration office to return to Kengtung. In practice, it usually helps to get someone from your hotel to help with these arrangements.

Shwe Mya Taw Express (☑23145; Tachileik Rd) and **Thet Nay Wun** (☑23291; Kyain Nyan Rd) each run buses to Tachileik at 8am and noon (K10,000, five hours). Share taxis, which depart from 6am to noon from Kengtung's **bus station**, charge K10,000 to K15,000 per seat or about 2500 Thai baht, about US$75 for the entire car.

ⓘ Getting Around

Drivers of motorcycle taxis and trishaws wear coloured bibs. The going rate for a downtown trip is K1000. A trishaw from the airport to town costs K2000.

Taxis can be arranged at Harry's Trekking House and Princess Hotel; rates are cheapest at the former and start at K36,000 for a full day.

Tachileik

တာချီလိတ်

☑084 / POP C10,000

Facing the town of Mae Sai across the Thai-Myanmar border, this nondescript town is like border towns all over Asia – it's a border post and a magnet for black-market goods, and sports a handful of hotels catering to travellers en route to somewhere else. Thai baht is the accepted currency here.

🛏 Sleeping

If crossing the border into Thailand is an option, you'll find the accommodation there better in every respect. Hotels in Tachileik prefer payment in Thai baht, but some places will accept US dollars.

River Side Hotel   HOTEL **$$**
(☎51161; r 600B; ❄) Located on the river less than a block from the bridge that connects Myanmar and Thailand, this hotel has clean rooms with attached bathroom.

In Mae Sai, on the Thai side of the border, the Maesai Guest House on the river is recommended.

ℹ Getting There & Away

Air Bagan (www.airbagan.com), owned by Tay Za (see p21), and **Asian Wings** (www.asianwings airlines.com) fly from Tachileik to Kengtung ($42, 25 minutes) – but not in the opposite direction.

Buses depart from Tachileik's bus station, 2km and a 10B truck ride or a K1500/40B motorcycle taxi ride from the border, at 8am and noon (K10,000, five hours). Alternatively, you can charter a taxi for 2500B or, if you're willing to wait, get a front/back seat in a share taxi for K15,000/10,000.

KAYAH STATE

Like Tanintharyi (Tenasserim) Division in the south, Kayah State (ကယား:ပြည်နယ်) is yet another one of those uniquely Burmese destinations that's open to foreign tourists, but not really open.

Wedged between Shan State to the north and west, Kayin State to the west and south, and Thailand to the east, tiny Kayah State is home to a disproportionate number of **tribal groups**, including the Padaung, Yinbaw, Bre, Kayin (Karen) and Karenni (Red Karen).

It is indeed possible to visit Kayah State, but only with permission from the government and only on a prearranged, government-sanctioned package tour. The norm is a five-day trip that largely centres in and around Loikaw (the state capital) and terminates with a boat trip to Inle Lake. Sounds fun, but it's rather costly and the feedback we've heard from the handful of those who have done the trip wasn't all that inspiring. If you're determined, at least six weeks ahead of time, contact one of the Yangon-based travel agents in this book (see p69), who will initiate the necessary permits etc on your behalf.

Mandalay & Around

Best Religious Structures

» Bagaya Kyaung (p225)

» Mahamuni Paya (p208)

» Mingun Paya (p230)

» Pahtodawgyi (p225)

» Sagaing Hill monasteries (p228)

» Shwe In Bin (p209)

Best Views

» River scenes from View Point cafe (p216) or the rooftop of Ayarwaddy River View Hotel (p214)

» Chanthaya Paya and footbridge seen across the lake from the west (p211)

» U Bein's Bridge from the lake (p224)

Why Go?

For those who haven't been there – and that list included *The Road to Mandalay* author Rudyard Kipling – the mention of 'Mandalay' typically conjures up images of Asia at its most traditional and timeless. The initial reality can be a major anticlimax – a traffic-choked grid of interminable straight roads full of anonymous concrete buildings. But don't despair. Though it's a relatively 'young', dynamic city, Mandalay (မန္တလေး) is Myanmar's cultural capital. It's easy to escape the fumes and architectural banalities of the main streets in quarters full of craftworkers and tree-shaded monasteries. Temple-topped Mandalay Hill offers a welcomed exception to the city's pan-flat topography and several mini-theatres showcase traditional performing arts. Meanwhile, Mandalay is the ideal transport hub for northern Myanmar and offers a panoply of easy day-trip destinations, including three former royal capitals and the site of what would have been the world's biggest stupa, had it ever been finished.

When to Go

In the winter tourist season, days are still hot but evenings are mild and you might need a light jacket if you're riding a motorbike after sunset. By March you may find it hard to sleep without air-conditioning, while April and May really bake with temperatures sometimes reaching 104°F (40°C) by day and dust caking the trees (and the back of your throat). At such times, cool down by nipping up to nearby Pyin Oo Lwin (p250).

If you're not interested in participating in the water-throwing fun of Thingyan (see p16), it's generally best to avoid April, especially 12 to 21 April, when almost all public transport stops and shops are closed. Restaurants mostly close too, and those hotel eateries that still serve might double their prices.

In August, Mandalay regional transport can be overloaded for several weeks due to huge crowds heading to and from the vast *nat* festival at nearby Taungbyone, which culminates over the five days before the August (Wagaung) full moon.

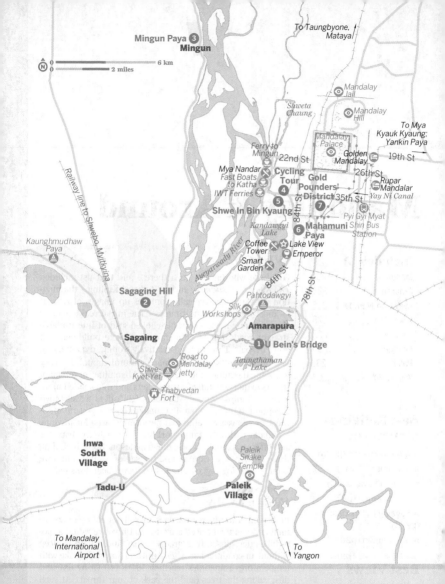

Mandalay & Around Highlights

1 Join the dawn monk parade crossing the world's longest teak bridge, Amarapura's iconic **U Bein's Bridge** (p224)

2 Look over pagodas and the Ayeyarwady River from atop **Sagaing Hill** (p228), an important religious site

3 Climb **Mingun Paya** (p230), a king-sized unfinished stupa reached by a boat ride from Mandalay

4 Escape Mandalay's big-city bustle with our **cycling tour** (p211)

5 Potter around Mandalay's less-known monasteries, including the beautiful teak masterpiece, **Shwe In Bin Kyaung** (p209)

6 Arrive by 4am at **Mahamuni Paya** (p208) as attendants brush the teeth of the country's most famous buddha image

7 Discover the wealth of crafts being made, including edible sheets of gold-leaf, in the **Gold Pounders' District** (p209) around 36th St

Mandalay city streets are laid out on a grid system and numbered from east to west (up to 49th) and north to south (over 50th). A street address that reads 66th (26/27) means the place is located on 66th St between 26th and 27th Sts. Corner addresses are given in the form 26th at 82nd St. Some of the longer east–west streets can also take names once they cross the Shweta Chaung (Shweta Canal) heading west. Hence 19th St becomes Inwa St, 22nd St becomes Pinya St, 26th St becomes Bayintnaung Rd and 35th St becomes Yangyiaung Rd. But even here the numbered address system still works.

The 'downtown' area runs roughly from 21st St to 35th St, between 80th St and 88th St. Across the tracks, 78th St is developing into the main site for big shopping malls; 73rd St is also bustling as it leads down to the university. Major east–west thoroughfares include 26th and 35th Sts plus 19th St east of the moat.

History

According to Burmese myths, Buddha himself visited Mandalay Hill (see p201) and also found time to scuttle up a riverside bluff (p225) in the guise of a chicken. In less legendary epochs, Mandalay didn't actually take shape as a city until 1857. Its brief, if momentous, period as a tailor-made Burmese capital lasted from only 1861 until the British take-over in 1885. However, several other post-Bagan capitals lay very close to today's city (see p224). On several occasions new kings sought to build their legacy by founding a new capital, often transporting building materials with them, meaning little remained at the old site. The longest lasting of these was Inwa, known to Europeans as Ava.

MANDALAY

📞 02 / POP C1,100,000 / ELEV 244FT

The natural focus of the city is an abrupt hill, rising above a vast moated and walled square. It once contained the sprawling royal city but apart from reconstructed Mandalay Palace at the very centre, this is now a sparse, mostly out-of-bounds area of military encampments. Today the city's centre sprawls for miles, the commercial heart lying south and west of the fort. Quieter monastic districts are further west towards the Ayeyarwady River.

◉ Sights

NORTHERN MANDALAY

If you're fed up with visiting pagodas, this area also has a swimming pool (p210), golf course and **zoo** (Map p204; admission K2000; ☺8am-5pm), the latter built in 1989 to cover a site used during the 1988 demonstrations.

Mandalay Hill   LANDMARK
မန္တလေးတောင်

(Map p204; camera/video fee K500/1000) To get a sense of Mandalay's pancake-flat sprawl, climb the 760ft hill that breaks it. The viewpoint is especially popular at sunset when young monks converge on foreigners for language practice.

For many visitors the 45-minute barefoot climb (all on covered stairways) is a major part of the experience, but you'll need at least a minimum level of fitness. The most common starting point is at the south, either between two giant **chinthe** (guardian lion-dog creatures) or by another stairway starting further southeast where the **Bobokyi Nat** (spirit statue) watches over the entrance. The routes converge a little south of a large **standing Buddha**, who points an outstretched arm towards the royal palace. No, he's not playing Lenin, but rather indicating the location of Myanmar's future capital. According to legend, the Buddha, accompanied by his disciple Ananda, really did climb Mandalay Hill and prophesied that, in the 2400th year of his faith, a great city would be founded below the hill. By our calendar that 2400th year was 1857, the year that King Mindon did indeed decree the capital's move from Amarapura to Mandalay.

Further up is the **Myatsawnyinaung Ordination Hall**. It's a large, forgettable concrete affair that most people walk straight through. But if you cross the hall and look out to the northeast, you'll spy the remnants of a three-storey stone **fort**. Back on the main pathway, steep steps lead past a memorial to Britain's Royal Berkshire Regiment who retook that fort from the Japanese in March 1945.

As you near the summit, the plethora of souvenir stands and 'Hello Water' women

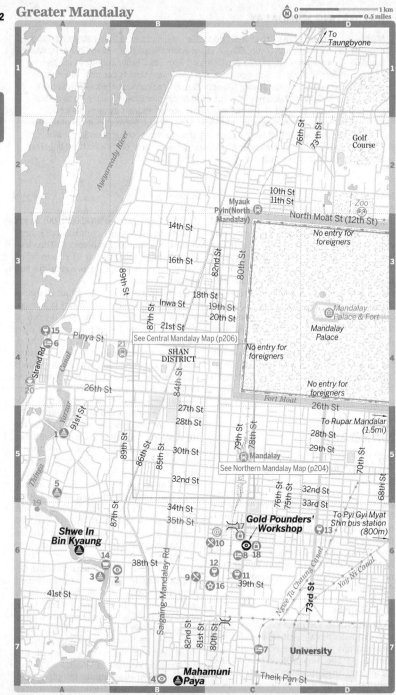

N

0 _____ 1 km
0 _____ 0.5 miles

To Taungbyone

Golf Course

Zoo

Ayeyarwady River

76th St
73th St

10th St
11th St

Myauk Pyin(North Mandalay)

North Moat St (12th St)

14th St

16th St

No entry for foreigners

89th St

82nd St

80th St

18th St
19th St
20th St

Inwa St

87th St

21st St

See Central Mandalay Map (p206)

Mandalay Palace & Fort

Mandalay Palace

15
6

Pinya St

21

Strand Rd

20

Canal

SHAN DISTRICT

84th St

No entry for foreigners

26th St

27th St

28th St

79th St
78th St

No entry for foreigners

Fort Moat

26th St

Yarzar

91st St

1

To Rupar Mandalar (1.5mi)

28th St

29th St

70th St

89th St

86th St

85th St

30th St

32nd St

Mandalay

See Northern Mandalay Map (p204)

76th St
75th St

32nd St

33rd St

68th St

Thinga

5

34th St

35th St

To Pyi Gyi Myat Shin bus station (800m)

13

Gold Pounders' Workshop

@

17

10

8 18

Shwe In Bin Kyaung

14

3

2

87th St

38th St

12

9

16

11

39th St

Saigaing-Mandalay Rd

Ngwe Ta Chaung Canal

73rd St

Yay Ni Canal

41st St

82nd St
81st St
80th St

7

University

4

Mahamuni Paya

Theik Pan St

becomes ever more dense. This means it's all too easy to miss the small penultimate stupa, in front of which a contemporary statue depicts ogress **San Dha Mukhi** offering forth her severed breasts. That's the sort of display that might have alarmed a more squeamish man, but according to legend, her bizarre feat of self-mutilation impressed Buddha so much that he ensured her reincarnation 2400 years later as King Mindon.

If you aren't up to the 45-minute each-way walk, it's possible to take a taxi (blue/normal taxi K8000/10,000) using a long switchback road (allegedly built with forced labour) that brings you within an escalator ride of the summit. Along the same route there are also very occasional shared pickup shuttles charging a hefty K1000 per person. They leave from near the giant chinthe entrance. These shuttles have usually ceased before sunset. Beware that police don't like letting motorbikes up Mandalay Hill. Some motorcycle-taxi drivers even claim to have lost their bikes for giving it a go while a few foreigners have received fines for riding their rental bikes up.

Shwenandaw Kyaung BUDDHIST MONASTERY
ရွှေနန်းတော်ကျောင်း

(Golden Palace Monastery; Map p204; admission $10 combo ticket) Lavished in carved panels this fine teak monastery-temple was originally built as the royal apartment of King Mindon, who died inside it in 1878. Reputedly unable to cope with Mindon's ghost, his successor, King Thibaw, had the building dismantled, carted out of the palace complex and reassembled outside the walls, where it was converted into a monastery (1880). It's a good thing he did, as all the other palace's royal buildings were later lost to WWII bombs.

At one time the building was gilded and decorated with glass mosaics. These have long gone and some exterior panels have weathered badly or been removed or replaced, but those inside are still in excellent condition, particularly the 10 Jataka (past-life stories of the Buddha).

Atumashi Kyaungdawgyi BUDDHIST TEMPLE
အတုမရှိကျောင်း

(Atula; Map p204; admission $10 combo ticket; ⊙9am-5pm) This unusually shaped temple is a series of diminishing stupa-dotted terraces over an arched base decorated with peacock

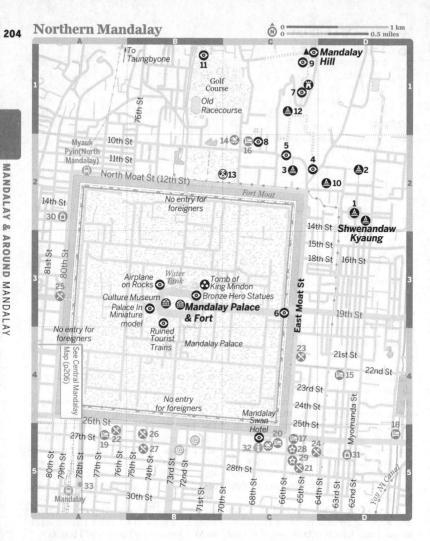

motifs. When built in 1857, it housed a famous Buddha image clothed in royal silk clothing and with a huge diamond set on its forehead. However, the image was stolen following the 1885 British takeover, and the monastery was gutted by fire five years later. What you see today is a 1996 reconstruction.

Kyauktawgyi Paya   BUDDHIST TEMPLE
ကျောက်တော်ကြီးဘုရား
(Map p204; 12th St, 66/68; admission free; ⏰5am-8pm) At the heart of this large 19th-century complex is a 900-tonne Buddha, 26ft tall and dressed in royal attire. Carved from a single

block of marble, it reputedly took 10,000 men 13 days to transport it from a canal to the present site before its dedication in 1865. Outer halls are edged in mirror tiles. Look for the little subshrine room displaying a giant alms bowl and colourful renderings of King Mindon's 1865 visit. Mandalay's biggest festival is held here for seven days in October.

Moat & Fortress Walls   FORTIFICATIONS
(Map p204) Seen from the air, Mandalay seems to have a vast 2.5km square cut out of its middle. In fact, that's the **Mandalay Fort**, ringed by a 230ft-wide **moat** and crenellated

MANDALAY SIGHTS

26ft-high **walls** cut from deep red-brown stone. The walls are punctuated at regular intervals with **gatetowers** topped by pyramids of fancifully carved woodwork. The overall effect isn't quite as impressive as you might anticipate, in part because of the sheer length and regularity of the walls, but the scene creates photogenic reflections in the moat, and in certain long-zoom angles the watchtowers appear to stretch to infinity. Built in 1857, the fort was a walled city within a city where the relative locations of the teak houses represented the residents' status within the social hierarchy. At the centre was the royal palace.

Mandalay Palace　　　　　　　　PALACE
မန္တလေးနန်းတော်

(Map p204; admission $10 combo ticket; ⊘entry 7.30am-4.30pm) Before 1885, the fortress walls enclosed a gigantic royal city. The British ejected the Burmese elite from their teak houses and deported King Thibaw, then demolished part of the original city to create a parade ground and turned the centrepiece palace complex into a governor's residence and club. Much later, during fierce WWII fighting in March 1945, the palace itself caught fire and was destroyed leaving nothing of the original. Today the area within the walls is mostly a vast tree-shaded army camp. However, foreign visitors can visit the central palace, which was completely rebuilt in the late 1990s, reputedly using forced labour. Foreigners may enter the fortress area only through the east gate (by trishaw, taxi, bicycle etc), and due to army sensibilities are allowed only within the oval palace loop plus along the road that leads there directly (even though there's no obvious physical barrier to venturing down some other roads).

The reconstruction is impressive for its scale (over 40 timber buildings) and completeness, but less so for its artistry and the peeling paint on its corrugated metal roofs. Start by getting a general overview by climbing the curious spiral **watchtower**, but

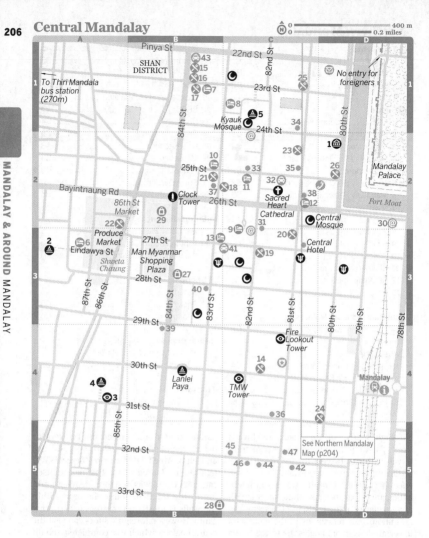

MANDALAY & AROUND MANDALAY

beware of dangerously missing and rotting floorboards.

The **throne room** is the palace's most striking building, a soaring multi-layered pyramid of gilt filigree. Linked behind this is the 'Hall of Victory', then the so-called **Glass Palace** (aka Central Palace), where the kings lived. It was so named not because of any windows, but because King Thibaw slept in a four-poster bed made with glass pillars. This bed still exists, and is today displayed at the **Culture Museum**, the westernmost building within the palace oval, which was once Chief Queen's Audience Hall. The mu-

seum also includes 13 life-sized models of former cabinet members in traditional attire and some great vintage photos: the Burmese envoys to France must have caused a stir in costumes that even Gaultier couldn't have topped.

Many other buildings within the oval are open but empty. Outside the oval (and thus out of bounds), you might spy the **tomb of King Mindon**, ruined narrow-gauge **trains** that once ferried tourists around, sheds containing over 600 stone inscription slabs and a small **airplane** on some rocks in the trees.

CENTRAL MANDALAY

The downtown area is not the city's most beautiful. However, it is easy enough to escape into fascinating tree-shaded back alleys further west (see Cycling Tour, p211). And even amid the smoggy central grid of lacklustre five-storey concrete ordinariness lurk many pagodas, striking churches and notable mosques. The colourful, sculpture-crusted *gopuram* (monumental tower) of **Sri Krishna Temple** might excite you if you've never been to southern India or Singapore.

Eindawya Paya
BUDDHIST TEMPLE

(Map p206; Eindawya St, 88/89; admission free) Built in 1847 by King Pagan Min, Eindawya is ranged around a typical gilded pagoda off a street where shops sell all the gear a monk would need. Little visited, its importance is as the site of one of Myanmar's many cultural battles before independence. In 1919 a group of Europeans had defied the Buddhist ban on shoe-wearing within Eindawya and were forcibly evicted by outraged monks. For their pains, four monks were convicted by a colonial court, and one, U Kettaya, received a life sentence. (So please take your shoes off!)

Setkyathiha Paya
BUDDHIST TEMPLE

(Map p206; 30th St, 85/86) Hidden behind shopfronts for most part, this large elevated pagoda complex includes a 'golden rock' look-alike and a sacred bodhi tree planted by U Nu, Myanmar's first post-independence prime minister. However, it is best known for an impressive 17ft-high seated bronze Buddha, cast in 1823 by King Bagyidaw.

THE $10 COMBO TICKET & HOW TO DODGE IT

Rather than paying individual entry fees, most of Mandalay area's key sites are paid for collectively by buying a $10 combo ticket at any of the sites involved. Looking something like an undernourished credit card, the ticket has a scratch-and-reveal PIN number that is supposedly entered into a computer to be linked with your name and purchase date. According to text on the ticket, it is valid a week from first use, though certain entry booths insist that this is a mistake and claim that it is only really valid for four (even three) days. But as there's no date written on the ticket anyway, and as few of the sites' computers are actually on line, you're unlikely to be challenged.

While the $10 fee isn't unreasonable for the large range of attractions covered, many visitors feel uncomfortable that the fee goes to the government (Archaeology department; see p21). If you go to Mandalay Palace, Atumashi Kyaungdawgyi, Shwenandaw Kyaung or key sites at out-of-town Inwa, you won't have a shot of visiting without paying. But trickery can get you at least a peep into several others while substitution can show you equivalent free gems. Random discoveries and lesser-known sights are often more interesting than the commercialised tourist 'must sees' anyway. Consider the following tactics:

» The south entrance (not west) of Kuthodaw Paya (p210) has ticket checkers, who sit at a table and chat away until they leave work at 5pm. If avoiding them seems too 007 for you, the similarly designed adjoining Sandamuni Paya (p210) is free and features plenty more slab-in-stupa monuments.

» The teak Shwenandaw Kyaung (p203) can be spied with your zoom from outside the unobtrusive fence, but you won't get in without a ticket. South of the centre, however, the equally impressive 'teak monastery' Shwe In Bin (p209) is ticket-free.

» According to attendants on Mandalay Hill, the combo ticket is no longer required there, but should you find otherwise, Yankin Paya (p231), 3 miles east, makes a fine alternative for sunset viewing and sees far fewer foreigners.

Shwekyimyint Paya   BUDDHIST TEMPLE
(Map p206; 24th St, 82/83) Founded in 1167 by Prince Minshinzaw, exiled son of King Alaungsithu, Shwekyimyint considerably predates Mandalay itself. It's famous for an original Buddha image consecrated by the prince and for other images collected by later Myanmar kings that were relocated here after the British occupied Mandalay Palace. However, these images are shown to the public only on important religious occasions. Shwekyimyint is tucked away behind the strikingly modern Kyauk Mosque.

Cultural Museum & Library   MUSEUM
(Map p206; 80th St, 24/25; admission $5; ☉10am-4pm Tue-Sat) This dowdy, poorly lit three-room collection displays archaeological finds, Buddhas and a bullock cart. It's ludicrously over-priced.

GREATER MANDALAY

Mahamuni Paya and the Stone Carvers' Area are conveniently visited as part of a day trip to Amarapura, Inwa or Sagaing. There's a whole series of monasteries in the area west of 85th street, between 35th and 41st Sts. Also very pleasant for random exploration is the area somewhat further north, which is covered in our cycling tour, p211.

TOP CHOICE **Mahamuni Paya**   BUDDHIST TEMPLE
မဟာမုနိဘုရား:
(Map p202) The star attraction of this massive complex is its highly venerated 13ft-high **seated Buddha image**, one of Myanmar's most famous. Many locals believe that it is 2000 years old. Over the centuries so much votary gold leaf has been applied by the (male) faithful that the figure is now entirely covered in a knobbly 6in-thick layer of pure gold. Entirely, that is, apart from his radiantly gleaming face, which is lovingly polished daily at 4am. The statue is a relative newcomer to Mandalay. It was seized from Mrauk U (p287) by the Burmese army of King Bodawpaya, who dragged it back here in 1784. The epic story of this feat is retold in a series of 1950s paintings in a **picture gallery** across the pagoda's inner courtyard to the northeast. Bodawpaya also nabbed a collection of Hindu-Buddhist **Khmer bronze figures**, which were originally pilfered centuries earlier from Angkor Wat, and reached Mrauk U by a series of *other* historical thefts.

Legend claims that many figures were melted down in the 1880s to make cannons for Mandalay's defence against the British. But six rather battered figures remain, enshrined in a drab concrete building on the northwest side of the inner courtyard. The most impressive are two images of the Hindu god Shiva (one painfully emasculated) and another of the multi-headed elephant, Airavata. Locals enthusiastically rub parts of the image, believing that any affliction on the corresponding part of their own body will thus be cured.

Mahamuni Paya is an endlessly popular place of pilgrimage with thousands of faithful arriving daily, including countless family groups bringing their colourfully robed kids for coming-of-age celebrations. The human scene is often more memorable than the mainly recent architecture – the original 1784 temple burnt down a century later. Today the central Buddha sits beneath a soaring multi-tiered golden shrine roof. It is approached through long concrete passageways crammed with stalls selling all manner of religio-tourist trinkets. More interesting sets of Buddha images are sold in the side arcade leading to the (young) **bodhi tree**.

Near the compound's northeast exit are a merrily kitsch **clock tower** and the odd little **Maha Buddhavamsa world Buddhism museum**.

TOP
CHOICE **Shwe In Bin**
Kyaung   BUDDHIST MONASTERY
ရွှေအင်ပင်ကျောင်း
(Map p202; 89th St, 37/38) If you wanted a place for quiet meditation in Mandalay, you couldn't find a better spot than this beautiful teak monastery. Commissioned in 1895 by a pair of wealthy Chinese jade merchants, the central building stands on tree-trunk poles and the interior has a soaring dark majesty. Balustrades and roof cornices are covered

WOMEN & MAHAMUNI

Only men are allowed in to apply gold leaf to Mahamuni's torso. Female devotees kneel close by, but get only a glimpse of the crowned image whether directly or on the surreally static TV monitors. Some ladies believe that desegregation is overdue. One local grandmother told us, 'Lord Buddha never said anything like this, and I'd so much like to put gold leaf on the Buddha image myself!'

in detailed engravings, a few of them mildly humorous. 'Remove your shoes' signs are placed at the compound entrance, but you don't actually have to do so until reaching the approach stairs.

Gold-Pounders' District   WORKSHOPS
Most of the one-inch-square gold-leaf sheets you see worshippers putting onto shining Buddha images are laboriously hammerpounded for hours by hand in one of Mandalay's 70 or so workshops, centred on 36th St between 77th and 79th Sts. Many are in back-alley houses, but there are two souvenir-shop showrooms, King Galon (Map p202; 36th St, 77/78; ◷7am-7pm) and Golden Rose (Map p202; 36th St, 78/79; ◷7am-7pm), where English-speaking staff patiently talk you through the process while muscle-bound gold-beaters hammer out an insistent, thumping rhythm. It's free and fascinating, and there's no sales pressure (though the gold leaf sheets do make popular souvenirs – from K2000 for 10).

Stone Carvers   WORKSHOPS
(Map p202) West of Mahamuni Paya there are a whole series of workshops where you can see slabs of rock being blasted, chipped and polished into Buddhas of all sizes. Souvenir carvings are also made, notably little marble elephants. You can spot several workshops along the Sagaing–Mandalay Rd when driving to Amarapura.

Ma Soe Yein Nu Kyaung   BUDDHIST MONASTERY
(Map p202; 39th St, 87/88) Across the creek from Shwe In Bin, this large monastery isn't architecturally outstanding, but it does have its own 'Big Ben' clock tower and is building a unique multi-storey concrete pavilion. More notably it has long been noted for the politically forthright views of its monks, albeit less so since the 2007 protests, after which many younger monks were encouraged to return to their homes.

Tingaza Kyaung   BUDDHIST MONASTERY
(Map p202; 92nd St, 34/35) Somewhat dilapidated, this appealingly lived-in teak monastery has some carved wooden details. Across the yard, a shaded open-air trio of sinuous Buddha figures have been weathered into almost abstract ghosts.

Jade Market   MARKET
(Map p202; 87th St, 39/40; admission $1; ◷8am-5pm) This heaving grid of cramped walkways is a shoulder-to-shoulder mass of jade traders. It feels rather sketchy, but not all the deals

THE WORLD'S BIGGEST BOOK

Around the gilt-and-gold stupa of mid-19th-century **Kuthodaw Paya** (Maha Lawka Marazein Paya; Map p204; admission $10 combo ticket; ⊙24hr), you'll find 729 text-inscribed marble slabs, each housed in its own small stupa and together presenting the entire 15 books of the Tripitaka. Another 1774 similarly ensconced marble slabs (collected in 1913) ring the nearby **Sandamuni Paya** (admission free; ⊙8.30am-5pm) with Tripitaka commentaries. Collectively these slabs are often cited as the 'World's Biggest Book'. Producing the Kuthodaw set alone required an editorial committee of over 200. When King Mindon convened the 5th Buddhist Synod here he used a team of 2400 monks to read the book in a nonstop relay. It took them nearly six months to finish.

are rip-offs. If you don't know your jade and don't want to pay the $1 entry (not always enforced), it's still interesting to see the cutting and polishing of jade pieces that takes place just outside along the market's eastern flank. Or retreat to the octagonal **Unison Teahouse** (38th at 87th St; snacks K500-1500; ⊙5am-1am) to watch more furtive-looking jade merchants discussing deals over a cuppa.

🏃 Activities

Swimming

The Mandalay City and Mandalay Swan hotels both allow nonguests to use their attractive outdoor pool for $5 per day. Behind the zoo, the outdoor, Olympic-sized **Yatanaban Swimming Pool** (Map p204; admission K2000; ⊙6am-6pm) is OK, but don't use the diving board or you'll pike yourself into a fountain.

At the base of the Shan Hills beyond Yankin, 18-hole **Yedagon Taung** (www.myanmargolf.com/yedagontaung_golf_club.htm) is arguably the most attractive of Mandalay's three golf courses. **Shwe Mann Taung Golf Resort** (Map p204; ☎60570; 9-/18-holes $15/30, gear rental $10) is also lovely and sits handily close to Mandalay Hill. There's a driving range nearby.

🎓 Courses

Dhamma Mandala   MEDITATION CENTRE
(☎39694; www.mandala.dhamma.org; Yaytagun Hill) Spacious centre several miles from

Mandalay offering regular 10-day Vipassana courses (bilingual) on a donation basis. Bookings usually close two weeks ahead. Website gives schedules.

🎉 Festivals & Events

Traditional *pwe* (festivals), big and small, happen all the time – for weddings, birthdays, funerals and holidays, and in side streets and at pagodas. Ask a trishaw driver if they've passed one. Major festivals include the following:

» **Mahamuni Paya pwe** In early February thousands of people from nearby districts make pilgrimages to Mahamuni (see p208).
» **Mingun Nat Festival** Pays homage to the brother and sister of the Teak Tree, who drowned in the river while clinging to a trunk. Fifth to 10th days of the waxing moon of Tabaung (February/March).
» **Sagaing Waso festival & Paleik Festival** The Sagaing Waso festival and then the big Paleik festival take place in the two weeks following the Waso full moon (June–July).
» **Taungbyone Nat Pwe** This massive festival is held in August about 12 miles north of Mandalay. It honours the so-called Muslim Brothers, Byat-wi and Byat-ta, two of the most famous *nat* from the Bagan era. Celebrations culminate on the full moon of Wagaung.
» **Irinaku Festival** (Yadanagu) A week after Taungbyone Nat Pwe worshippers move to just south of Amarapura to honour the brothers' mother Popa Medaw.
» **Thadingyut** Central Mandalay's biggest festival at Kyauktawgyi Paya (p225) lasts seven days in early October.

🛏 Sleeping

Aside from our listings, many more Chinese-type hotels in the blocks south of 27th St offer generally mediocre to poor midrange rooms for $20 to $30. None of the cheapest local guesthouses takes foreigners.

Unless otherwise stated, all room rates include breakfast and a bathroom with hot water. However, in budget places, don't be surprised if your air-con or hot water isn't working. Most midrange hotels have rooms that are every bit as dowdy as budget hotels, but add a lift (handy in the heat given that most hotels are at least five storeys) and perhaps a doorperson or two. In the high-end bracket only a handful of choices are really appealing.

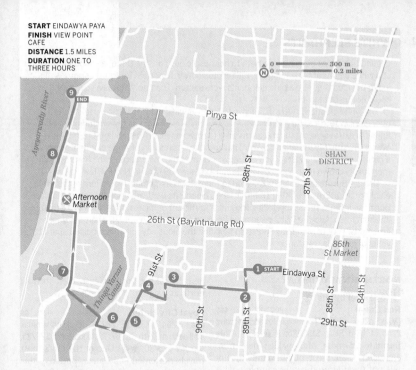

Cycling Tour

West Mandalay

> If central Mandalay's fumes and traffic are getting you down, jump on a bike and pedal out into the web of back lanes to the west. Random encounters are likely to be a highlight, but there's plenty of interest at every turn. This suggestion is just one of many possibilities.

Start at the west exit of **1 Eindawya Paya**, descend shady 89th St one block, then veer right just before a **2 crocodile bridge**. The bridge represents Ngamoe Yeik, the faithful servant of tragic Burmese-chronicle hero Min Nandar, who made his last journey in the friendly crocodile's jaws.

Take the east-west narrow lane between old monastery residences, some wooden, others colonial-style with pillar-mouldings. At the T-junction two blocks later, swing round the south side of **3 Khin Makantaik monastery**, take a left at the T-junction and ride through interesting alleyways where **4 locals turn sugar cane into jaggary** (mornings only).

Turn south on winding 91st St, possibly stopping to nibble a delicious coconut-filled doughnut (K250) at typically unpretentious **5 Aung Pyemoe ('Who Dares Wins') teahouse**. Opposite, a mirror-fronted colonnade leads into **6 Chanthaya Paya**, whose most precious Buddha image supposedly dates back to the reign of Indian emperor Ashoka. The pagoda's main golden stupa is particularly photogenic in afternoon light when seen reflected in the Thinga Yarsar Canal from across a long teak footbridge.

Pass two **7 ceramics shops**, then turn west at 26th St to reach the **8 Ayeyarwady riverside** where it's endlessly fascinating to watch the plethora of cargo boats loading and unloading.

Enjoy the scene more serenely with a beer in hand from **9 View Point cafe**.

WHITE ELEPHANTS

Legend has it that before giving birth to her auspicious son, the Buddha's mother dreamt of a white elephant presenting her with a lotus flower. In certain Buddhist countries this led to the idea that rare albino elephants were sacred. Their holy status also meant they could not be put to work.

The white elephants were expensive to feed yet without any practical use. Western observers in 19th-century southeast Asia saw white elephants as the embodiment of financial extravagance, and the term came to mean as much in standard English. However, in Burma/Myanmar and Siam/Thailand, the possession of white elephants remains a potent symbol of kingship: you can view several of the specimens – which are actually more pinky brown than white – outside Yangon (see p39) and in Nay Pyi Taw (see p140).

Certain Burmese monarchs referred to themselves as 'golden-footed lord of the white elephant'. In 1885 one of King Thibaw's white elephants died, an omen that superstitious Burmese interpreted as foretelling the king's imminent demise at the hands of a British invasion force. And the Brits' insensitive decision to drag the elephant's carcass unceremoniously out of Mandalay Palace so horrified the pious city folk that it helped spark 10 years of guerrilla resistance.

NORTHERN MANDALAY

TOP CHOICE Hotel by the Red Canal

BOUTIQUE HOTEL $$$

(Map p204; ☏61177; www.hotelredcanal.com; 22nd at 63rd St; r $135-186; ✹@🛜✹) This intimate 25-room faux palace has more character than most other Mandalay hotels put together and comes complete with neo-traditional roof gables and a trickling 'stream'. The interior is dotted with Asian knick-knacks, there's a floral welcome and cocktails are free to guests from 6pm to 7pm. It's tucked away on a dusty back road beside a small canal that does indeed turn red in some seasons. Credit cards are accepted with 10% commission, but only on 24 hours' notice.

TOP CHOICE Peacock Lodge

GUESTHOUSE $$

(Map p204; ☏61429, 09 204 2059; www.pyin oolwin.info/peacock.htm; peacocklodge@gmail. com; No 5 60th St, 25/26; s/d $18/24; ✹) One of Myanmar's great homestay-style inns, the Peacock's charming retired hosts treat many guests like part of the family, maybe showing you their fascinating old photos ('granddad' was a British-era mayor of Mandalay). There are four spacious rooms in the main 1960s home overlooking a lotus-filled canal. There's also a bungalow room off the mango-shaded garden, where tables are set for a well-prepared breakfast. In the cool season, three simpler rooms without air-conditioning (single/double $12/14) are available in an attached bamboo house. It's peaceful and comfy without being posh. Great value. Get

here by taking 26th St east, then turning north at a sign to 'Hotel Treasure'.

Royal City Hotel

HOTEL $$

(Map p204; ☏31805, 28299; royalcity@winmax mail.net.mm; 27th St, 76/77; standard s/d $20/25, superior $25/30; ✹@) One of the city's most traveller-oriented midrange options, this tall, narrow 19-room tower has windows all round, simple but effective bathrooms and a lift that works when electricity allows. Superior rooms have bathtubs and stronger, quieter air-conditioning. Breakfast can be taken on a flower-decked outdoor/indoor roof garden, which is one of Mandalay's finest.

Sedona Mandalay

HOTEL $$$

(Map p204; ☏36488; www.sedonahotels.com.sg; 26th at 66th St; superior/deluxe $130/170; ✹✹) The large, open-plan lobby is as alluring as the sprawling outdoor pool behind, but rooms can feel a little ordinary for the price. The big plus in some deluxe rooms is the view staring straight down the eastern moat towards Mandalay Hill. You can pre-book rooms online (sometimes discounted to $70 on www.agoda.com), but in situ credit cards are no longer accepted. The business is a Singaporean joint venture.

Mandalay View Inn

GUESTHOUSE $$

(Map p204; ☏61119; www.mandalayviewinn.com; 66th St, 26/27; r $42-54; ✹) Converted from a two-floor 1960s villa, this 12-room guesthouse feels cosier and more personable than most hotels. Carved wooden panels enliven the decor, but bathrooms are small and dated, there are a few signs of wear, and rooms

105 and 206 are windowless. You can use the small swimming pool at the co-owned Hotel by the Red Canal. Credit cards are accepted by advance agreement (10% commission).

Mandalay Hill Resort Hotel
HOTEL $$$

(Map p204; ☑35688; www.mandalayhillresortho tel.com; 10th St; s/d from $120/144; ❋❉) This Thai-owned resort hotel sits near the base of Mandalay Hill set in a garden twinkling with oriental umbrella-lamps. There's a lovely outdoor pool and the breathtaking spa area feels like an Indiana Jones treasure trove. Overloaded lifts climb from the bejewelled lobby to nine storeys of rooms, which conform to international resort-style specs, but with less flair.

CENTRAL MANDALAY

The nearest thing to a 'backpacker zone' is a three-block area around the Nylon Hotel in Central Mandalay. Don't imagine Khao San Rd. These are ordinary-looking streets where several cheaper hotels happen to be licensed for foreigners. There's no banana-pancake strip, and only a few (mostly unspectacular) restaurants have menus in English. Several hotels here can help you organise transport, and outside you'll often find a motorbike and/or trishaw driver who speaks some English. You might need to book ahead to get the hotel you want, especially in December, January and April.

Mandalay City Hotel
HOTEL $$

(Map p206; ☑61700, 61911; www.mandalaycity hotel.com; 26th St, 82/83; r $52-60; ❋@❉❉) Walking past you'd never guess that this enticing palm-shaded oasis lay just behind all the dreary buildings of 26th St. The airy, cream-tiled lobby is entered across a fish pond, there's an attractive outdoor pool (nonresidents $5) and rooms are neat and professionally maintained. Choose 'garden view' rooms as the alternative rear rooms have frosted-glass windows with no view whatsoever.

Royal Guest House
BACKPACKER GUESTHOUSE $

(Map p206; ☑31400, 65697; 25th St, 82/83; s/d $10/15, with shared bathroom $5/10; ❋) Putting a lot of effort into a little space, the Royal is the Mandalay cheapie that fills first. Gloss paints in multiple pastel colours, little carved panels and a frontage of pot-plants and foliage, all help set the place apart from its lacklustre budget competition, though bed quality is somewhat inconsistent and cheap rooms can be seriously small.

Silver Star Hotel
HOTEL $$

(Map p206; ☑33394, 66786; www.silverstarhotel mandalay.com; 27th at 83rd St; s/d $25/28, cnr room $27/30; ❋@) A vast step up on most of Mandalay's dreary midrange hotels, the Silver Star isn't particularly stylish but it's spotlessly clean with pine furniture and creamy yellow walls. The lift works and the rooms are bright, especially the corner rooms ($2 extra).

ET Hotel
HOTEL $

(Map p206; ☑65006, 66547; tmchomdy@mand alay.net.mm; No 129A 83rd St, 23/24; s/d $14/18, without bathroom $6/12; ❋@) The only thing extraterrestrial in the 27-room ET is the glow of the lone fluorescent bulb against the mint-green walls in clean but dated rooms. However, beds are comfy, showers hot and the unusually helpful staff understand travellers' needs. The air-conditioning might even work once in a while. On the roof are a few cheaper rooms and a couple of deck chairs in which guests can sun themselves.

Nylon Hotel
HOTEL $

(Map p206; ☑33460; 25th at 83rd St; s/d with fan $7/12, with air-con $10/15; ❋@) Mandalay's long-term backpacker standby is a no-nonsense 25-room, five-floor tower (no lift). Decently tiled rooms come with solar-heated showers and are more likely to have windows than rooms at the similarly priced Garden Hotel next door.

Classic Hotel
HOTEL $

(Map p206; ☑32841, 61891; 23rd St, 83/84; s/d $9/15; ❋) Don't be fooled by the name or the modernist facade. Rooms here are simple, mainly windowless boxes with little charm beyond their price and location.

Sabai Phyu Hotel
BACKPACKER HOTEL $

(Map p206; ☑32297, 39997; 81st St, 25/26; s/d $10/13, shared bathroom $6/10; ❋) Friendly service and a rooftop area with a few sunny lounger-chairs make up for seriously lacklustre rooms, which are most acceptable on the 3rd floor. The 1st-floor cheapies are padlocked prison cells, which won't put anyone in a holiday mood.

AD 1 Hotel
BACKPACKER HOTEL $

(Map p206; ☑34505; Eindawya Rd, 87/88; s/d $8/16, with air-con $12/24; ❋) Simple, functional rooms just off vibrant 'onion market street', hidden in the approach lane to Eindawya Pagoda. Beware if asking a taxi to take you here – to local ears 'AD 1' sounds very much like '81' (ie 81st St).

RIVER BEDS

If you want to sleep on a river boat, there are several upmarket choices.

Amara (www.amaragroup.net/de/river/river-de) Two seven-cabin teak boats, traditionally styled but recently built, make three-night cruises to Bagan (Amara I s/d/full-charter €720/980/4480, Amara II €950/1360/6550) and six-night trips between Mandalay and Bhamo (Amara I €1620/2240/11,200, Amara II €2200/2980/14,900).

GMT (☏01 392552; www.myanmartravelagent.com; 1st fl, 343 Bo Aung Kyaw St, Yangon) Tailor-made private live-aboard cruises for couples or small groups in relatively simple converted local boats, with chef and crew. This is great for stopping off at minor riverside villages and for spotting ultra-rare Irrawaddy dolphins on the Bhamo–Mandalay trip ($1600 per person for a five-day trip, minimum two passengers). Not usually available Mandalay–Bagan.

Pandaw (www.pandaw1947.com) A 60-year-old riverboat with teak and ironwood floors refitted into an upmarket 16-berth cruiser.

Road to Mandalay (Map p200; www.orient-express.com/web/rtm/road_to_mandalay.jsp) This 43-berth liner is huge by Ayeyarwady standards and includes an onboard swimming pool and wellness centre. In tourist season it does mostly Bagan–Mandalay, but in midsummer there are Bhamo trips too. Be aware that its start/end point is at Shwegyet (Golden Fowl) jetty near Sagaing Bridge, so visiting Mandalay requires a one-hour drive, and the 'cruise' to Mingun is on a different boat – something you could have easily organised for yourself at a fraction of the cost.

GREATER MANDALAY

TOP CHOICE **Ayarwaddy River View Hotel** HOTEL $$
(Map p202; ☏72373; ayarwaddyriverviewhotel@gmail.com; Strand Rd, 22/23; d $30-42, ste $81; ❀@🛜) Brand new in March 2011, this hotel has 56 tasteful and restrained rooms. They're partly panelled in wood and all are sizeable with good, if fashion-neutral, bathrooms. Price (four categories) depends on size and view. And what a view! Front-facing rooms look across the river towards distant Mingun, rear-upper ones overlook the city, Mandalay Hill and the Shan uplands. Enjoy the lot, 360 degrees, from the rooftop bar.

Rupar Mandalar BOUTIQUE RESORT $$$
(off Map p202; ☏61555; www.ruparmandalarresort.com; No A-15 53rd St at 30th St; d/ste $200/600; ❀@🛜❄) This stunning 16-room complex set in tropical foliage melds timeless neo-traditional features with modern design flair in indulgent teak rooms. Even the gym has teak walls. The suites are wonderful for families, sleeping six in three fully equipped ensuite sub-bedrooms, which share two extensive lounges and a kitchenette. The two swimming pools are inviting, and guests qualify for a free 15-minute Thai massage in the spa. The main downside is the odd location way out on Mandalay's eastern outskirts amid incongruously counterpointed nouveau riche houses, stagnant ponds and light industrial wreckage.

Hotel Mandalay HOTEL $$
(Map p202; ☏71582; 78th St, 37/38; d $35-50, ste $60-120; ❀🛜❄) A seven-storey business-style hotel whose well-tended rooms feature goldfish-bowl wash basins and heart-shaped wall lamps. Perks include indoor swimming pool, gym, buffet breakfast and free in-room wi-fi. Next door is City Mart supermarket, and there's an array of dining possibilities nearby.

Golden Mandalay HOTEL $$
(Map p200; ☏61488, 09 680 6414; http://homepage.mac.com/hr_weber/golden_mandalay/index.html; 19th St at Ye Zarni Rd; s/d $17/23; ❀) This homely cluster of bungalow-style rooms is attractively set amid palms, and there's a small dining terrace that's perched above a canal. Rooms are large, and though carpets are rough, there's plenty of character in the form of bamboo patchwork designs and pictures. Golden Mandalay is easy to miss. It's unsigned just east of Police Station No 1 before 19th St crosses the canal. Book ahead.

Great Wall Hotel HOTEL $$
(Map p202; ☏68460; No 901 78th St, 42/Theik Pan; d $40-50; ❀) A six-floor tower whose fair-value rooms have power showers, partly wood-panelled walls and plastic covers still protecting the upholstery. Mostly aimed at Chinese visitors. The $40 rooms suffer thundering road noise.

✕ Eating & Drinking

Mandalay's dining scene lacks the charm and variety of Yangon's or even Pyin Oo Lwin's, but there are several new semi-stylish cafes and a few faithful old standbys. Surprisingly, few of these are near the main downtown traveller area. There's a sprinkling of decent if tourist-centric options towards the southeast east corner of the palace moat. Things are much livelier south of the centre, notably down 78th St (university district around the Theik Pan St crossing), along 73rd St (31st to 35th St) and spread more thinly beside Kandawgyi Lake.

NORTHERN MANDALAY

TOP CHOICE Too Too Restaurant BURMESE $
(Map p204; No 79 27th St, 74/75; meals from K2500; ☺10am-8.30pm) Too Too's dining area is an uninteresting box room hidden away in a side alley, but many consider it *the* place in Mandalay for home-style local fare. Meals are picked from a buffet-like spread, but the set price covers only one main curry, one side dish, rice and soup. Extras cost K500 to K1000.

Ko's Kitchen THAI $$
(Map p204; ☑31265; 80th at 19th St; soups & dishes K3560-5000, snacks K2500, rice K600; ☺11.30am-2.30pm & 5.30-10pm; ✻🍴) Ko's cooks a wide selection of Thai dishes, including Lao/ north Thai chilli-dips and the usual curries and noodles, plus a particularly tasty crispy catfish salad with mango and cashews (K4000). It's in an art deco building, but the peach-coloured interior is starting to look a little tired, and dirty glass dividers rather defeat the point of a show kitchen.

BBB WESTERN $$
(Map p204; ☑73525; 76th St, 26/27; meals K5500-7250, burgers K2750, beer K1650; ☺9am-10pm; 🍴) Tablecloths, attentive waiters and a pitched wooden ceiling create the feel of an old-world ski-lodge. Food includes many fish and seafood options, which are competent and elegantly presented without being truly gastronomic. Decent Burmese red wine costs K2500 per glass.

Green Elephant BURMESE $$
(Map p206; ☑61237; 27th St 64/65; mains/extras/rice 6000/2400/1200, set menu per person K8000; ☺8.30am-3pm & 5-9.30pm; ✻🍴) Consistently recommended for regional cuisine. A few tables are within a Pyin Oo Lwin-style colonial-era building full of period relics. Others spill out into a bamboo-tufted garden and a bigger pavilion for group dining.

Spice Garden INDIAN $$
(Map p206; ☑61177; Hotel on the Red Canal, 22nd St at 63rd; mains $3-8, beer $4; ☺6am-10.30pm; 🍴) Spread over two storeys this luminously bright, wooden-framed restaurant serves up some of Mandalay's most authentic Indian food, along with set-menu European and Burmese dinners ($10 to $15). Fair value, though the drinks can get pricey. Appealing garden seating also available.

Café City WESTERN $$
(Map p206; ☑61237; East Moat Rd 20/22; meals K5500-6600, burgers K2200, draught beer K1200; ☺9am-10.30pm; 🍴) Neon and old enamel signs add to the feeling of a comfortable, latter-day American diner. Food choice (steaks, pizza, English triangular sandwiches) supports the idea, but there's plenty that's more imaginative including the delicious, very generous coconut basted fish kebabs. Good coffee too (espresso K1000). It's popular with wealthy locals on a casual family outing.

Marie-Min VEGETARIAN $$
(Map p206; off 27th St, 74/75; dishes K1300-2000, rice K300; ☺8.30am-9pm, closed Jun; 🍴) On an upper balcony above an antiques shop on a residential alley, the friendly English-speaking owners have tailored a short menu to their stated principles: 'Be kind to animals by not eating them.' Highlights include all-day breakfasts, guacamole, veg curry, stomach-safe lassis (K1500) and delicious aubergine dip. If you're hungry, you'll probably need to order two dishes.

Peacock Lodge BURMESE $$
(Map p206; ☑61429; see p204; set dinner K8000; ☺by arrangement) Real home-cooked Burmese meals cooked to order are served beneath giant parasols in the guesthouse's lovely peaceful garden. However, you'll need to order a day in advance.

A Little Bit of Mandalay BURMESE, CHINESE $$
(Map p206; ☑61295; 65th St 27/28; mains K4000-5000, rice K1000, set menu per person K9000, beer K3500; ☺11am-2.30pm & 5-9.30pm; 🍴) Wooden bucket-lamps, back-lit parasols and plinking local harp melodies bring atmosphere to this tourist-oriented pavilion restaurant with a bamboo-weave roof. Bringing your own wine incurs a modest K2000 corkage charge.

CENTRAL MANDALAY

V Café/Skybar INTERNATIONAL $$
(Map p206; 25th St at 80th St; mains/burgers K5000/2000, espresso/draught beer/cocktails

DINING DOWNTOWN

In the downtown traveller zone there's a disappointing lack of inspirational dining. The following reviews offer a selection of places to fill the stomach if you lack the transport to head further afield. But don't expect anything special. For something more interesting, get on your bike. And don't forget a head torch for the journey home!

Nay (Map p206; 27th at 82nd St; ⊙5-11.30pm) and Sri Karaweik (Map p206; 23rd at 81st St; ⊙5pm-1am) are roadside tables that appear only in the evenings, but keep serving curry snacks (K250-1000) with fresh chapattis (K150 each) unusually late. Nylon Ice Cream Bar (Map p206; 83rd St, 25/26; ice cream K500-1500, beer K1700; ⊙8am-10pm) is another ultra-simple pavement-table meeting place, but it opens all day and offers shakes, lassis and beer, as well as fully perfumed durian ice cream.

Crusty shop-restaurant Mann (Map p206; 83rd St, 25/26; dishes K1500-2000, rice K300, beer K1600; ⊙10am-10pm) has concrete floors, beer posters and scraggy hunting trophies, and remains an eternally popular meeting place for foreigners, due more to its location than its average Chinese fare.

Bakeries Gold Medal (Map p206; 30th St 81/82) and SB (Map p206; 80th St at 31st St) sell bagged-up super-soft bread and sticky cakes in Japanese style.

Pyi Taw Win (Map p206; 81st St 24/25; BBQ items K200-1800; ⊙8am-10.30pm) is a standard but central beer station for barbecues, cold draught beer (K600) and Premier League football (soccer).

There's a gaggle of Shan restaurants around the 84th/23rd St corner where Karaweik (Map p206) teashop (unsigned in English) whips up Shan noodles (K600) and semi-sweet tandoori-naan bread (K100), which is ideal for tea-dipping. Golden Shan (Map p206; buffet K3000) has an all-you-can-eat buffet, while Lashio Lay (Map p206; per plate K500-900, rice K300) offers a pre-cooked spread.

NVC (Map p206; Nepali Food; 81st St, 26/27; meals K1000-2000; ⊙8am-9pm) serves a daily changing K2000 pure-veg Nepali *thali* (multi-curry meal) in a bare concrete box of a shop. No eggs, no alcohol.

For fresh veg, head to the produce market (Map p206; 86th St, 26/28).

K800/1000/3000; ⊙9am-10.30pm; ❋▥) The most central of Mandalay's new breed of air-conditioned Western cafe-bars, V offers wicker-frame sofa seating and semi-successful attempts at 1970s decor. Food options include pasta, Mexican stir-fry, fish dishes, tempura, burgers and pizza. When open, the rooftop bar has views across the walled fort towards distant Mandalay Hill.

GREATER MANDALAY

Mya Nandar   BURMESE, CHINESE $$
(Map p200; ☎66110; Strand Rd, 26/35; mains K1600-4000; ⊙9am-11pm; ▥) The food can sometimes be a little bland, but the river views from the back-terrace tables are hard to beat. You'll need to book if dining during the free 7.30pm puppet show (in the bigger wedding-style main hall).

View Point   BAR $
(Map p202; Strand Rd; draught beer K600; ⊙9am-11pm) The name doesn't lie. Whether sunset-watching or spying distant Mingun by day, the river views to the west are magnificent,

while to the south there's the endlessly fascinating mayhem of loading and unloading riverboats. From 7pm loud karaoke changes the atmosphere completely. Open air, very limited food.

JJ Café 2   BAR $$
(Map p202; 38th St at 78th St; cocktails/draught beer K2800/1200, meals K3800-5000; ⊙9am-10.30pm; ❋▥) Boldly modern angular planes counterpoint wicker lounge chairs and traditional carved figurines in this stylish Mandalay retreat. The low-lit ground floor has live music from 7pm daily except Saturday. Upstairs is brighter, calmer and better for conversation.

Uncle Chan's   BEER STATION $
(Map p202; 35th St, 72/73; barbecue items K300-1800; draught beer K600; ⊙8am-10pm) A cut above most typical beer-barns and less totally male-dominated, there's a wide range of eating possibilities here, but the prime attractions are the polar-cold brews in super-frosty mugs. Stretching several blocks up 73rd St from here are several equally lively eating and drinking spots.

Sin Chun Yin
BARBECUE $

(Map p202; 36th St, 80/81; barbecue items K300-1600; draught beer K600; ☻9am-10pm) Although it looks like any normal beer station, the stuffed grilled fish is as good as you'll find anywhere – almost boneless and with a great tamarind dipping sauce. If you're looking for a suaver option, try Sylvia Cafe across the road.

Shwe War Thar
THAI, HALAL $$

(Map p202; 82th St 38/39; meals K2500, beer K2500; ☻10am-9pm) Wooden booth seats on the ground floor, a karaoke lounge upstairs and a rooftop 'coffee garden' that's open from 5pm.

Super One
BEER STATION $

(Map p202; 80th St at 38th; draught beer K400; ☻8.30am-9.30pm) This cheap, cheerful and essentially male-only place is handily located for quaffing draft Spirulina beer while waiting for the Moustache Brothers' performance to start. Minimal food.

KANDAWGYI LAKE
Kandawgyi Pat Rd forms a causeway across large Kandawgyi Lake, starting from the Sagaing–Mandalay road around 900yd southwest of Mahamuni Temple. Dotted along it you'll find a restaurant shaped like a royal boat and a scattering of cafes in various price ranges. It all adds up to an alternative nightlife centre, but for visitors it's handiest as a refreshment stop when heading home from Amarapura or Sagaing, especially via the quieter riverside route.

Coffee Tower
CAFE $$

(Map p200; Kandawgyi Pat Rd; mains K2500-4500, juice K700-1200; ☻2pm-2am) An open-air cafe on a stilt pier over the waters, ideal for a good espresso (K700), iced latte (K1500) or fresh strawberry shake (K1000). Simple yet popular and with decent food. Open very late.

Smart Garden
BURMESE $$

(Map p200; Kandawgyi Pat Rd; mains K3000-6000, beer K2000) Attractive thatched pavilions in a lakeside garden, but no English spoken and no draught beer.

Emperor
BEER STATION $

(Map p200; Kandawgyi Pat Rd at 85th St; draught beer K1000) This simple beer station comes to life after dark when the trees are beautifully lit with orange paper lanterns. Snooker tables available; live acoustic music sets from around 7pm.

☆ Entertainment

A-nyeint
A-nyeint is a form of vaudeville folk opera with dance, music, jokes and silly walks.

Moustache Brothers
COMEDY

(Map p202; 39th St, 80/81; donation K8000; ☻8.30pm) Officially banned but presently tolerated, this world-famous *a-nyeint* troupe has suffered a string of prison sentences for their jokes and rants against the Myanmar government. These days the shows include slightly indulgent self-parody, but they remain one of Mandalay's greatest talking points for Western visitors. See boxed text, p218.

Dance, Music & Puppet Shows
Evening shows, professionally performed but aimed squarely at tourist audiences, have helped rekindle interest in Burmese traditional dance and puppetry. The most authentic performances are set to a six-piece 'orchestra' led by a distinctively wailing *hneh* (an oboe-like instrument). The other musicians play gamelan-style gong arrangements and percussion, notably a circle of tuned mini-drums known as a *sai-wai*. As well as those listed below, you can see a selection of performances during dinner shows at several upmarket hotels, and there's a free puppet show at Mya Nandar riverside restaurant.

Mandalay Marionettes
PUPPET SHOW

(Map p204; www.mandalaymarionettes.com; 66th St, 26/27; admission K10,000; ☻8.30pm) On a tiny stage, colourful marionettes expressively recreate tales based on the Buddhist Jataka and Yamazat (Ramayana), with occasional bursts of visual humour. Read the leaflet for an overview of what you're about to see. Occasionally a sub-curtain is lifted so that you can briefly admire the skill of the puppeteers' deft hand movements. The troupe has travelled and performed internationally.

Mintha Theater
DANCE

(Map p204; www.mintheater.com; 27th St, 65/66; admission K8000; ☻8.30pm Jul-Mar) Colourfully costumed dancers give human form to many of the scenes you may have seen depicted by puppets at Mandalay Marionettes. Explanations here are somewhat clearer, but the show lacks the flashes of humour. Seeing both is worthwhile if you can spare a second evening. Some shows include a remarkable (if entirely discordant) display of cane-ball skills as an off-beat extra.

MANDALAY ENTERTAINMENT

MOUSTACHE BROTHERS – FROM SLAPSTICK TO SATIRE

In Myanmar jokes can get you into serious trouble, as the internationally celebrated Moustache Brothers found out the hard way. In 1996 they performed at an Independence Day celebration at Aung San Suu Kyi's Yangon compound, telling politically tinged jokes about Myanmar generals. For two of the three 'brothers' (Par Par Lay and Lu Zaw), the result was arrest and seven years' hard labour. In 1997 several Hollywood comedians (including Rob Reiner and political comedian Bill Maher) wrote to the government in protest. Meanwhile, the third brother, Lu Maw, kept the Mandalay show going with the help of his wife.

After their release in 2002, the reunited Moustache Brothers remained 'blacklisted' from playing at outside events (marriages, funerals, festivals and so on). However, they played a series of gala performances at home attended – inevitably – by government agents with video cameras. The regional commander soon summoned Par Par Lay and told him not to perform at home anymore. When he got home, some Westerners had already gathered for that night's show, and he and his family imaginatively decided to perform without costumes and makeup. Thus the show went on for the tourists (and the 'KGB' people – Lu Maw's nickname for Myanmar's military intelligence). They explained they were merely 'demonstrating' a performance, since they couldn't do a 'real' one without costumes. Somehow, it worked.

'They've ordered us to stop six times', Lu Maw told us. 'It goes in one ear and out the other. That's our job!'

Some costumes have since returned, but the job has become exclusively for foreigners: locals who attended would probably be followed by police, but tourists experience no backlash. Following the September 2007 demonstrations, Par Par Lay suffered another month in jail, but the shows have never stopped: they're still performed in a single room with just a dozen or so plastic chairs a yard away from the performers.

The Show Today

The only English-speaker, Lu Maw, kneels over an antique microphone stand and uses word-boards to help listeners decipher his thick accent. The hour-long show slithers between slapstick, political satire, Myanmar history, traditional dance and how to tie up your *longyi*. Plenty of material also highlights the troupe's notoriety, from Lu Maw's wife as cover star of an ageing Lonely Planet guide to a video clip from the film *About a Boy*, in which Hugh Grant's character mentions Par Par Lay. Par Par Lay promptly appears on stage wearing handcuffs – a cameo role to which the former troupe leader has been relegated by his lack of English. The players are undoubtedly courageous, but not all visitors are bowled over by the show. Some might even agree with Lu Maw's jocular taunt: 'Do show for tourist very easy, just one hour. I rip you off, you are sitting duck'. Some 'jokes' are little more than smirking insults, wife-baiting or frequently repeated colloquialisms. And it all culminates with a shameless T-shirt sales drive. But love it or loathe it, this is a unique experience and a Mandalay classic.

Nightlife

Mandalay has no nightclubs, so if locals suggest 'dancing' they probably mean witnessing a 'model show' – a popular local entertainment where young ladies sing to a karaoke-style recorded backing tape accompanied by the clapping and whooping of waiters who try to get the mood upbeat. Generally there's no cover charge beyond beer and food costs. Examples include Lake View (Map p200) beside Kandawgyi Lake and Yatanaban Restaurant (Map p204; draught beer K800) beside Yatanaban swimming pool, near Mandalay Hill Resort. Both also have karaoke; model shows start around 7.30pm.

Shopping

Big shopping malls are mushrooming up on 78th St near the train station.

Arts & Crafts

Mandalay is a major crafts centre, and probably the best place in the country for traditional puppets and hand-woven embroidered tapestries. Beware: items may be scuffed up or weathered to look much older than they are. Handicraft places will generally have to pay commissions to drivers or guides, so prices may prove better if you visit alone.

Handicraft specialists include Aurora (Map p202; 78th St, 35/36), Garuda (Map p204; 80th St at 15th), Soe Moe (Map p202; 36th St, 77/78) and Sunflower (Map p204; Marie-Min, 27th St, 74/75). There are numerous **silk workshops** and a couple more handicraft emporia along main Sagaing road in Amarapura (p224). **Puppets** are sold at Moustache Brothers and Mandalay Marionettes. Good-value items can be found at the stone carvers' workshops (p209), and there are several interesting shops on 36th St beside the gold-leaf-pounding workshops (p209).

Shwe Pathein
SOUVENIRS
(Map p202; No 141 36th St, 77/78; ☺8am-5pm) Sells Pathein-style parasols (K4000 to K8000) and bark animal portraits (from K4000).

Rocky
SOUVENIRS
(Map p204; Sein Win Myint; 27th St, 62/63; ☺8am-9pm) Various handicrafts including stuffed 'gold-thread' tapestries, plus gems and jade.

Sut Ngai
FABRIC
(Map p206; 33rd St, 82/83) Sells Kachin fabrics and costumes, aimed mainly at Kachins themselves rather than tourists.

Markets
Zeigyo
MARKET
(Map p206; 84th St, 26/28) This downtown market offers wall-to-wall stands selling just about everything Myanmar. The Chinese communist-style architecture dates from the early 1990s after a disastrous 1988 fire destroyed an earlier model. This market should be replaced in a few years by a vast 25-storey tower mall, currently under construction.

Night market
MARKET
(Map p206; 84th St, 26/29) Vendors selling food, music, army hats and clothes imported from China block off the street as dusk approaches – a worthy wander.

ℹ Information
Internet Access
Internet cafes are fairly common along 27th St and are scattered widely around the city centre, but most are appallingly slow.

Acme-Net (Map p206; 26th St, 78/79; per hr K500; ☺9am-9pm) Better connection than most and adept with proxy servers.

Dream Land (Map p204; 27th St, 72/73; per hr K400; ☺9.30am-11pm; ❄) Good connection and AC, free drinking water.

Money
EXCHANGE Most guesthouses will change pristine US$ cash, but for rates approaching Yangon levels, ask at gold shops such as **Shwe Hinn Thar** (26th St 84/85; ☺10am-4pm), beside the clock tower, or travel agencies such as **Seven Diamond Express** (Map p206; ☎22365; 32nd St, 82/83). Marie-Min vegetarian restaurant also offers decent rates.

CREDIT CARDS Nowhere in Mandalay gives cash advances. If you're out of dollars and need a room, the Mandalay View Inn and the Hotel by the Red Canal accept credit cards at 10% commission if you pay one day ahead.

Post
DHL (Hotel Mandalay, 78th St, 37/38; ☺8.30am-5.30pm Mon-Fri, 8.30am-12.30pm Sat) Costs from $80 for the cheapest document-only package to Europe.

Main post office (Map p206; 22nd St, 80/81; ☺10.30am-4pm)

Telephone
Local/national calls cost K100/200 per minute from PCO street stands. Royal Guest House and Royal City Hotel both offer international calls for $2 per minute.

CTT Telephone Office (Map p206; 25th St, 80/81; calls to Europe/Australasia/North America per min $4/4/5; ☺7am-8.30pm) Anonymous-looking room for expensive international calls.

Tourist Information & Travel Agencies
Daw San San Aye (Map p206; ☎31799; Hotel Dynasty, 81st St, 24/25; ☺7.30am-8pm) Very obliging, fair-priced air-ticket sales booth.

Seven Diamond (Map p206; ☎30128, 72828; 82nd St, 26/27; ☺8am-9pm) Helpful agency that can pre-book flights by email request, change money at good rates and organise airport-bound shared taxis. Henry speaks great English.

MTT (Map p204; ☎60356; 68th at 27th St; ☺9am-5pm) The government-run travel company doubles as tourist office selling city maps (K200) as well as transport tickets and permit-needing tours. See p21 for a discussion of the implications of using government-run agencies and services such as MTT and Myanma Airways.

Websites
Lonely Planet (www.lonelyplanet.com/myanmar-burma/mandalay) Head here for planning advice, author recommendations, traveller reviews and insider tips.

ℹ Getting There & Away
Schedules and prices change frequently.

Air

A daunting 28-mile drive south of the centre, Mandalay's huge, gleaming airport is nominally international, thanks to two daily flights to Kunming, China. All other services are domestic.

The government-run **Myanma Airways** (MA; Map p206; ☑36221, 87458; 81st St, 25/26; ☺9am-2pm) has a lacklustre reputation and sells its own tickets directly, generally only possible one day ahead. Use an agency for Air Mandalay (AM), Asian Wings (AW), Bagan Air (BA) or Air Kanbawza (AK) – the latter two airlines owned by Tay Za (p26) and Aung Ko Win (p373) respectively.

Boat

Unless otherwise stated, all boat services listed start from or near Gawein Jetty (Strand Rd at 35th St), the exact point varying somewhat according to river levels.

BAGAN

For a readers' report of a boat ride to Bagan, see p120. There are several options:

GOVERNMENT SLOW BOAT (deck/cabin $12/33) Departs at 5.30am Wednesday and Sunday, taking 13 to 15 hours when water levels are OK. Should you beach on a sandbank (quite possible in February and March) it might take a day longer. Buy tickets one day before sailing at **IWT** (Map p200; ☑36035; 35th St; ☺sales 10am-2pm). See p21.

MALIKHA 2 ($36, nine hours) A private express boat with view deck. It departs 7am on certain days in season. Frequency varies widely from 24 trips a month in January to barely one per week in March. Book ahead through hotels, agents or **Malikha Travels** (☑72279; www.malikha -rivercruise.com; 26th St, 82/83)

SHWEI KENNERY ($33, nine hours) Similar to Malikha 2, but runs to Bagan only a few times per season. See p221.

CRUISE BOATS River lovers can opt for one of several sleep-aboard tours (see boxed text, p214). These tend to be very pricey and are sold as part of a package. Read very carefully what's on offer. Some packages are as long as five days, four nights, but as the journey itself takes only a few hours, such packages may simply be using the boat as a hotel while doing over-priced land-based tours. Is that really what you want?

KATHA & BHAMO

GOVERNMENT FERRY ITW ferries to Bhamo (deck/cabin $9/54, three to five days) depart at 6am on Monday, Thursday and Saturday. Useful stops en route include Kyaukmyaung ($4, 11 to 15 hours) and Katha (deck/cabin $7/42, at least two full days). Carefully read the boxed text on p239 before jumping aboard. Tickets are sold on departure. Double-check schedules with **IWT** (Map p202; ☑36035; 35th St). See also p21.

FAST BOAT Departures are at 5am once every two days to Katha (K45,000, around 14 hours), where you'd have to change boats for Bhamo.

MANDALAY AIR ROUTES

Sample rates with peak-season schedules

DESTINATION	PRICE $	FREQUENCY	AIRLINES
Bhamo	45	Thu, Sun	MA
Heho	42	several daily	AM, AW, BA, AK
Homalin	55	Tue	MA (permits required)
Kalay(myo)	85	Mon, Fri	AW
Kengtung	95	Sat (via Tachilek)	BA
		Tue	MA
Khamti	70	Sun	MA (permits required)
Kunming	281	2 daily	China Eastern
Lashio	70	irregular	AW
Myitkyina	95	Mon, Tue, Thu, Fri, Sun	BA
	70	Mon, Wed, Fri, Sat	MA
Nyaung U (Bagan)	42	daily	AM, AK, BA
Putao	105	Tue, Sun	BA (permits required)
Tachileik	95	daily	BA
	65	Thu, Sat	MA
Yangon	92	several daily	AM, AW, BA

Mandalay has three bus stations:

» **Thiri Mandalar bus station** (Map p202; 89th St, 22/24) Relatively central. Buses for Monywa, Shwebo and Bhamo (though foreigners can't use the latter).

» **Pyi Gyi Myat Shin bus station** (off Map p202; 60th St 35/37) Two miles east of centre. Buses for Hsipaw, Lashio and Mu-se.

» **Main (Kwe Se Kan) bus station** Six miles south of centre, this serves all other major destinations, including Yangon, Bagan, Kalaw and Taunggyi. Allow 45 minutes for the K3000/5000 motorbike/blue-taxi ride to get to the bus station from downtown and plenty more time to find the right bus in the mayhem.

Buying Tickets

Pre-booking long-distance bus tickets is wise. The easiest way to do that is through your hotel, but check how much commission is charged (typically K350 to K1500). Bus companies each have their own city-centre ticket office: booking there saves you going all the way to the bus station twice. If you're trying to save money, this will be the best deal, especially if you use a company that provides a 'ferry' (minibus transfer to the bus station), saving you the taxi/motorbike fare. But double-check ferry conditions – some will leave you far too much (or occasionally too little) connecting time to justify the financial saving. Many such agents are on 32nd St. **Shwe Mann Thu** (Map p206; ☑22365; 32nd St, 82/83) has a particularly wide choice of destinations and has several 'ferries' costing K500 per head (last at 3.30pm).

Buy tickets one day ahead from **Shwe Eyama** (☑09 680 0243; Strand Rd). The booth's sign is in Burmese, but a second sign above it says Panlon Co Ltd in English. Nearby, **MGRG** also advertise a Mandalay–Katha–Bhamo service, but that wasn't operating at the time of research.

SHWEI KENNERY Higher-standard express boat aimed at the tourist market. Enquire for schedules and prices at **Sun Far Travel & Tours** (Map p204; ☑69712; No H, 30th St, 77/78; ☺9am-5pm Mon-Fri, 9am-noon Sat & Sun).

CRUISES Several of the Bagan cruise operators (p214) also do occasional Bhamo–Mandalay trips.

MINGUN

Boats start at 9am from Mayan Chan Jetty. See p231.

PYAY

Government ferries (deck/cabin $10/20; see p21) depart Tuesday and Saturday at 5.30am taking around four days. Bring mat and sleeping gear. Tickets sold on board at departure. Double check schedules with **IWT** (Map p202; ☑36035; 35th St).

Bus & Shared Taxi

Two of Mandalay's three highway bus stations are infuriatingly distant from the city centre. Shared taxis, where available, aren't quite as expensive as they might seem at first glance because most offer door-to-door (or at least centre-to-centre) service, saving expensive taxi rides to/from bus stations at either end of your journey.

BAGAN

Journey time is around eight hours from the main bus station. Choice is limited.

Shwe Mann Thu (Map p206; ☑22365; 32nd St, 82/83) has buses at 8am (K9000) and 4.30pm (K8000), with 'ferries' to the bus station departing their office at 7am and 3pm.

Nyuang U Mann has buses without air-con at 8.30am and 9pm (K8500, eight hours) as a last resort.

HSIPAW, LASHIO & MU-SE

BUS Buses use the **Pyi Gyi Myat Shin bus station** (off Map p202; 60th St 35/37), with central agencies clustered on 83rd St, 22/23, but relatively few companies will accept foreigners on buses bound for Lashio or beyond. Most buses leave between 5.30am and 6.30am, but if you sleep in, there are still two Hsipaw-specific buses departing at 3pm operated by **Ye Shin** and **Duhtawadi** (Map p206; ☑61938; 31st St, 81/82). Duhtawadi ticket holders can get a connecting transfer from the city centre office to the bus station 1½ hours before bus departure time.

SHARED TAXI Duhtawadi also organises shared taxis to Hsipaw (K15,000, five to six hours), departing from their city office most days around 8.30am. If there is no Hsipaw car, take one bound for Lashio, operated by **Shwe Li Oo** (Map p206; ☑33280; 32nd St, 81/80) back/front seat K15,000/17,000 at 6.30am, 8am and 9am and **Shwe Li Shan** (Map p206; 84th St, 22/23) back/front K18,000/21,000 when full.

KALAW & TAUNGGYI (FOR INLE LAKE)

BUS Almost all buses to Taunggyi (K10,000 to K12,000, around 11 hours) run overnight via Kalaw and the Inle Lake junction. Operators include the following:

» **Shwe Taung Yo** (Map p206; ☎09 5311918; 32nd St, 82/83) At 6pm (K12,000 with 4pm transfer).

» **Taung Paw Thar** (Map p206; ☎09 91028717; 32nd St, 81/82) At 6.30pm (K12,000 with 4pm transfer).

» **Shwe Mann Thu** (Map p206; ☎22365; 32nd St, 82/83) At 7.30pm (K10,000, no well-timed transfer).

» **Chandar Aung** (Map p206; 24th St, 81/82) Operates the only day-time bus (no air-conditioning), but currently refuses to carry foreigners.

SHARED TAXI The only public-transport option for foreigners that isn't overnight is a shared taxi from **Aung Yedana** (☎24850; 25th St, 81/82) leaving for Taunggyi (front/back seat K27,000/25,000) around 8am. Price includes pick-up from any central Mandalay hotel. Add K8000 to be dropped off in Nyaungshwe.

KYAUKME

Yedena (Map p206; ☎36196; 81st St, 31/32) Has a 1pm bus to Kyaukme (K4000) from the **Pyi Gyi Myat Shin bus station**.

MONYWA

Hourly buses depart between 7am and 4pm (K1700, 3¼ to four hours) from the relatively central **Thiri Mandalar bus station** (Map p202; 89th St, 21/22), operated by several companies including Mahanwe, AGB and **Yadanabon** (☎61500). In the past some drivers have proved reluctant to allow foreigners on the bus.

PYIN OO LWIN

SHARED TAXI Regular departures (back/front seat K5000/6000, two hours) from the corner of 27th and 83rd Sts (Map p206). Alternatively have your hotel book for you with **Shwe Mann May** (☎38685) or other operators.

PICK-UP TRUCKS Depart when full. They operate (front/back K3000/2000) till mid-afternoon from the corner of 28th and 83rd Sts (Map p206).

SHWEBO

Buses depart roughly hourly (K1700, three to four hours) until mid-afternoon from Thiri Mandalar bus station. Companies include **Aung Nang Man** (☎72193).

TAUNGOO

Shwe Mann Thu departs at 9pm (K9000, eight hours) from the main bus station. No 'ferry'.

YANGON

Countless companies operate air-conditioned buses (K10,400 to K12,000, around 10 hours).

Most run overnight, leaving Mandalay between 5pm and 8.30pm, but there are also daytime buses. Options include the following:

Shwe Mann Thu (Map p206; ☎22365; 32nd St, 82/83) Departures at 6am, 7am, 8am, 9am, 7pm, 8.30pm and 9.30pm.

Shwe Mandalar Express (Map p206; ☎73211; 32nd St, 81/82) Departures at 8am, 5pm, 7pm and 8pm, with bus-station transfer at 3pm.

Mann Shwe Pyi (Map p206; ☎09 6502246; 32nd St, 82/83) Departures at 8.30am, 8pm and 8.30pm, with free bus-station transfer at 5pm. Comfy air-conditioned buses with recliner seats and free drinking water.

Train

The **train station** (Map p206; 30th St, 78/79) is relatively central, saving a long commute to an outlying bus station. Just inside the main ground-floor entrance, an **MTT sub-office** (⊙9.30am-6pm) can sell tickets at 10% commission if the queues upstairs look too daunting.

❶ Getting Around

To/From the Airport

Neither city buses nor pick-up trucks go to the airport. **Seven Diamond Express** (p206; ☎22365; 32nd St, 82/83) charges only K10,000/4000 per car/person in private/shared taxis, but booking a day ahead is advised. Cheaper hotels will order you an airport taxi for K12,000. Taxis on the street might charge more, as they'll find it hard to get a return ride. From the airport, you'll pay K10,000 to town if you use one of the counters on the arrivals floor. Freelance taxis are liable to charge more.

Bicycle

On foot, Mandalay's vast size can rapidly become overwhelming. Buses are confusing and motorcycle/taxi fares can mount up. Renting a bicycle is a good solution for random exploration. You can rent one for around K1500 per day from ET Hotel, a shop opposite the Royal Guest House and from Mr Jerry.

Motorcycle & Taxi

Mr Jerry (Map p206; 83rd St, 25/26; ⊙8am-6.30pm) rents drive-your-own motorcycles at K10,000 per day. Motorcycle taxis are reasonably easy to find near hotels and on downtown street corners. Clunky old Toyota Corolla taxis can be found outside bus stations, but Mandalay's distinctive 'blue taxis' cost about half as much. These are teeny Mazda pick-up trucks with room for four or so in the covered cab. Reckon on around K2000 to the Gawein Jetty from downtown. Charter all day for about K15,000/20,000 in town/to the ancient cities (Amarapura, Inwa and Sagaing). Guesthouses can help you find a reliable taxi or motorcycle driver.

Sample fares (ordinary/upper class/sleeper):

DESTINATION	PRICE ($)	DURATION (HR)	DEPARTURE
Hsipaw	4/7/-	10	4am
Monywa	3/-/-	5¼	6.15am
Myitkyina	10/27/30	22+	noon, 4.15pm
	14/31/36	16-20	4.30am
Naba (for Katha)	6/13/16	11¾	noon, 4.15pm
Nyaung U (Bagan)	4/10/-	8	9pm
Yangon	15/35/40	15¼	9.45pm
	11/30/33	16	5am, 5.30am, 6am

Bus & Pick-Up Trucks

If you're in any kind of hurry, just take a motorbike taxi. But should you have time to spare and aren't too worried about not getting quite where you wanted to go, Mandalay's packedfull, antiquated buses and pick-ups can be a fun experience. Some, though by no means all, display route numbers, but these are only written in local script, the background colour can prove significant and some vehicles don't follow the route their number implies. Ask, ask, ask... A good place to try your luck is a jammed junction just north of the Zeigyo market (Map p206). Useful routes from near here:

» **Route 4** Heads along the north moat, getting close to the base of Mandalay Hill.

» **Route 5** (touts may cry 'Yeyji' or 'Yankin Taung') Along the southern moat, up past Cafe City then east on 19th St.

» **Various** (touts cry 'Payagyi') Heads south to Mahamuni Paya.

» **White 2 on a blue background** (cries of 'Mayanja') Heads west on 26th St to the Mingun ferry, sometimes continuing south to Gawein Jetty.

» **Pick-ups to Amarapura, Sagaing and the main bus station** Leave when very full from along 84th St (Map p206), south of the market.

Trishaw

Traditionally the main form of city transport, trishaws are steadily disappearing from the city centre, and rumour has it that during 2012 they might be phased out altogether. Sample fares:

» City centre to Thiri Mandalar bus station, K500

» City centre to base of Mandalay Hill, K1500.

» All day hire from around K8000.

English-speaking drivers include eloquent **Ko Re** (koore6070@gmail.com for appointments) and **Mr 'Take it Easy'**, who waits outside the Central Hotel (27th St, 80/81).

AROUND MANDALAY

For many visitors, the historic sites around Mandalay trump anything in the city itself. Iconic attractions include U Bein's Bridge in Amarapura, Mingun's gigantic stupa stub, Sagaing's temple-studded hills and horse-cart rides to Inwa's wonderful teak monastery.

To visit Inwa's main sites and Amarapura's Bagaya Kyaung, you'll need to show or buy Mandalay's 'Archaeological Zone' $10 combo ticket (see p208). A separate $3 ticket for Mingun and Sagaing is patchily enforced. No one checks for tickets at the other sites.

Apart from one hotel in Sagaing, there's no foreigner-licensed accommodation near any of the sights around Mandalay. There are eateries in Mingun, in Sagaing and at either end of U Bein's Bridge.

Although there are crushed-full pick-up trucks from Mandalay to Sagaing and Amarapura, they won't get you close to the main sights, and even the most tight-fisted traveller will be well advised to visit by motorcycle (chauffeured or self-drive), taxi or bicycle (if you're not afraid to sweat). River boat is also an option for Mingun, which is rather too far for a bicycle day trip.

A full-day ride by motorcycle/blue taxi (around K12,000/18,000) might include the main highlights of Amarapura and Sagaing, plus waiting time at the ferry dock while

WHICH CAPITAL WHEN

CAPITAL	FROM...	NOTES
Inwa (Ava)	1364	
Taungoo	1555	
Inwa (Ava)	1636	
Shwebo	1752	then called Mokesebo
Sagaing	1760	
Inwa (Ava)	1764	
Amarapura	1783	
Inwa (Ava)	1823	
Amarapura	1841	following the 1838 earthquake
Mandalay	1861-85	the British later banished the royals to India

you explore Inwa by horse-cart. Pay slightly more to be driven around Inwa, to add Paleik or to substitute Mingun for Inwa. Doing the whole lot in one day would be exhausting – and quite impossible if you wanted to do the Mingun boat. Ideally, make two or three more modest day trips.

Amarapura

အမရပူရ
☑ 02 / POP C35,000

Myanmar's penultimate royal capital, Amarapura (pronounced amuRA-puRA) means 'City of Immortality', though its period of prominence lasted less than 70 years (from 1783). Starting in 1857, King Mindon dismantled most of the palace buildings and shipped them 7 miles north to Mandalay, which was to become the new capital according to a Buddhist prophesy. These days Amarapura is essentially a spread-out suburb of Mandalay, but it's leafy and attractively set on a wide, shallow lake, named for an ogre who supposedly came looking for Buddha here. The lake is crossed by an iconic wooden footbridge. Several other scattered attractions can be visited, but they're widely spaced, so a bike or taxi is almost essential.

⊙ Sights

TOP CHOICE **U Bein's Bridge**   WOODEN FOOTBRIDGE
ဦးပိန်တံတား

The world's longest teak footbridge gently curves 1300yd across shallow **Taungthaman Lake**, creating one of Myanmar's most photographed sites. In the dry season it feels surreally high and mostly crosses seasonal vegetable gardens. But at the height of summer the lake rises several feet and laps just below the floor planks. Just a few of the 1060 poles on which it stands have been replaced by concrete supports.

A great time to visit the bridge is just after sunrise when hundreds of villagers and monks commute back and forth across it. The light is often best around an hour before sunset, but by then there will be a large number of tourists and trinket sellers. A popular visiting tactic is to walk across the bridge then return by paddle-boat (K3000) as the sun is setting. However, as boats are usually only available at the bridge's western end (where tour buses arrive), you'll need to make pick-up arrangements before you walk across. Or simply ask your taxi/motorbike driver to drop you at the eastern end. In the dry season a track along the southeast side of the lake is passable by motorbike.

Amarapura

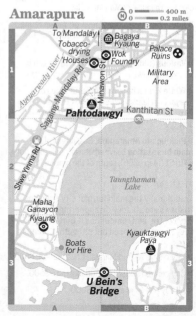

Technically, U Bein's Bridge is part of Mandalay's $10 combo ticket (see p208). In reality nobody checks.

Around the Bridge

Near either end of the bridge there's a selection of viewpoints, plus food stalls where you can buy noodles, tea and roasted crab.

Kyauktawgyi Paya
BUDDHIST TEMPLE
ကျောက်တော်ကြီးဘုရား

Around 200yd beyond the eastern end of side of U Bein's Bridge, this 1847 pagoda, built by Pagan Min, was supposedly modelled on the larger Ananda Pahto at Bagan (p156), but its five-tiered roof makes it look more like a Tibetan/Nepali temple. While the paya doesn't have the perfectly vaulted roofs or the finer decorations of the original, it does have a serene seated Buddha image and some well-preserved frescoes in the four approaches. The southern entry ceiling depicts some bossy, English-looking figures in bamboo hats.

Maha Ganayon Kyaung
BUDDHIST MONASTERY

Just west of the bridge, this sprawling monastery is home to several thousand young monks. Founded around 1914, it's renowned as a centre for monastic study and strict religious discipline, and for most of the day it's a pleasantly meditative place. But at about 11am, busloads of tourists arrive to gawp while the whole monastery sits down to eat, their silence pierced by the endless rattle of camera shutters. Worth avoiding.

Other Sights

Pahtodawgyi
BUDDHIST STUPA
ပုထိုးတော်ကြီး

This vast bell-shaped pagoda was erected by King Bagyidaw in 1820. It's the tallest structure for miles around (185ft), a mesmerising white apparition that seems to float above the water when viewed from across the lake. Climbing half-way to the upper terrace affords great views, showing the plethora of *hti* (stupa pinnacles) glittering through the Amarapura tree-scape. However, women aren't allowed up.

Bagaya Kyaung
BUDDHA MUSEUM
ဘားကရာကျောင်း

(admission $10 combo ticket) This 1996 reconstruction of an early-19th-century monastery has plenty of flying wooden filigree roofwork, which looks exciting from afar. However, on closer inspection the work looks ham-fisted and the collection of 19th-century Buddha images will appeal only to specialists. In the area around here you'll find a **foundry** where giant woks are hammered into shape, there are several distinctive **tobacco drying barns** and, hidden away at the edge of a military encampment, it's possible to glimpse the sorry ruins of some former **palace** buildings.

Ayeyarwady Bridges

Linking Sagaing and Amarapura are two parallel bridges, each with multiple metal-framed spans. The newer three-span, four-lane highway bridge was completed in 2005. The 1934 British-engineered, 16-span **Ava Bridge** carries the railway and a narrower road. In 1942 the British demolished two spans of this bridge to deny passage to the advancing Japanese. It wasn't repaired until 1954.

If you cross the Ava Bridge, you'll probably be charged the Mingun–Sagaing $3 fee. However, if approaching from the eastern side, you can stop before the checkpoint and look down to glimpse **Thabyedan Fort**, one of three chunky if far-from-dramatic forts built as a last ditch defence against the British advance in 1885.

Shwe-kyet-kay
STUPAS, VIEWPOINT
ရွှေကြက်ကျ

(Map p228) One of the best places from which to appreciate Sagaing is from across the river at this little bluff with a cascade of small stupas. It's part of a pair with the bigger Shwe-kyet-yet on a gentle rise across the road. The name, meaning Golden Fowl's Run, relates to a legend that in a previous life the Buddha-to-be had lived here as a golden chicken and had fluttered up the hillock to evade royal trappers. The Buddha-bird's younger brother had chosen the riverside bluff.

Inwa (Ava)
အင်းဝ

For over half of the past 650 years, Burma's royal capital was Inwa (Mandalay $10 combo ticket required). Yet nowadays the site is a remarkably rural backwater of empty fields sparsely dotted with widely spaced ruins, monastic buildings and stupas. It's a world away from the city bustle of Mandalay, and for many, exploring by plodding old horse cart is all part of its charm. At the time of research, the $10 combo ticket

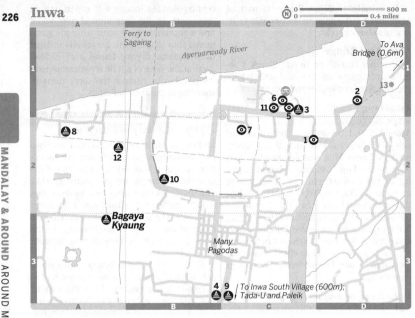

Inwa

⊚ Top Sights

⊚ Sights

ⓘ Transport

was checked only for those entering Bagaya Kyaung and Maha Aungmye Bonzan. However, if you don't have the pass, your cart-driver or motorbike-pilot will expect you to pay up to avoid getting him into possible trouble.

The local **Inwa Nat Pwe** festival culminates on the full moon of Tabaung (February/March).

History

In 1364, Inwa got its first of four turns as Burmese capital when Sagaing, across the river, fell to the Shan. Inwa's kings quickly set about re-establishing Bamar supremacy, which had been in decline since the fall of Bagan. Inwa means 'Mouth of the Lake', but the site has also been known less modestly as 'City of Gems' (Ratnapura in classical Pali, Tadanabon in Burmese). The Europeans knew the city as Ava, and indeed dealt with Burma under the moniker 'Kingdom of Ava' even after the royal court abandoned Inwa for Amarapura (in 1841) and eventually Mandalay.

⊚ Sights

Only three main sites are at all tourist-oriented, though at each of those the drinks vendors and postcard peddlers can be annoyingly insistent.

TOP
CHOICE **Bagaya Kyaung**   WOODEN MONASTERY
ဘားကရာကျောင်း
By far Inwa's most memorable individual attraction is this 1834 teak monastery supported on 267 teak posts, the largest 60ft

high and 9ft in circumference. The prayer hall's soaring interior is cool and dark, feeling genuinely ancient. Its stained timbers are inscribed with repeating peacock and lotus-flower motifs. Despite the constant flow of visitors, this remains a living monastery with globes hung above the little school section to assist in the novices' geography lessons.

There are a few interesting stupas in the fields surrounding the monastery. Some horse-cart drivers will get tetchy if you linger too long, but you could breeze through Bagaya and walk out to the stupas – no postcard vendors out there.

Nanmyin
WATCHTOWER

အင်း:ဝမျှော်စင်

The 90ft 'leaning tower of Inwa' is all that remains of King Bagyidaw's palace complex. The upper portion was shattered by the 1838 earthquake and the rest has taken on a precarious tilt that is noticeable when you're climbing the steps. The tower is neither beautiful nor especially high, but wide views from the top are great for getting your bearings amid the widely scattered sights. As it's not a religious site, you can keep your shoes on.

Maha Aungmye Bonzan
MONASTERY

မဟာအောင်မြေဘုံစံ

Built, unusually, of stucco-covered brick, this 1822 royal monastery temple is a rare survivor from the Ava era. The faded, lumpy structure looks attractive in cleverly taken photographs, but in the harsh midday sun the main attraction is the cool afforded by its ultrathick walls and the bats flitting through its empty undercroft. Sales folk at the entrance can be especially persistent. It is also known as the Ok Kyaung or the Me Nu Ok Kyaung.

Behind, the antique two-storey monks' residence is crumbling, and a footpath leads to river gardens with views across to Sagaing.

Beside the monastery is the more fanciful **Htilaingshin Paya**, an attractive array of stupas, some dating back to the Bagan period and recently part-gilded.

OTHER SIGHTS

Shwedigon Paya & Nogatataphu Paya
GIANT STUPAS

Rising above the palm-speckled horizon, the tips of two enormous stupas are visible for miles around. Golden **Shwedigon** is tucked into the southwest corner of Inwa's moated central 'island' while recently revamped **Nogatataphu** lies around 200m beyond the Bagaya monastery turning. There's a tiny tea-shop at its entrance.

Yedanasini Paya
STUPA RUINS

This small but photogenic ensemble brings together a sitting Buddha and a handful of old brick stupas shaded by a giant flame tree. Horse carts go right past it en route to Bagaya Kyaung.

City Walls
RUINS

Old Inwa was protected by rivers to north and east, canals to south and west and ringed by city walls. Much of the canal and several sections of wall remain, including some chunky rampart sections above the southern canal. By horse-cart tour the only bit you're likely to see is the heavily reconstructed **Gaung Say Daga** (Hair-Washing Gate).

Le-htat-gyi Paya
PAGODA RUIN

Forgotten in fields around 1.3km south of the moat are a series of forgotten, decaying old stupas. Across the road from the large gilt bell-stupa of **Sandamuni Paya** is the four-storey stub of the once huge **Le-htat-gyi Paya**, which has been fissured by earthquakes, but retains a fair amount of stucco detail. If you arrive by road from Tada-U, you'll drive right by, but horse-cart tours won't come anywhere near this far south.

ⓘ Getting There

There are three possible ways to access Inwa.

MAIN RIVER FERRY Unless otherwise stated, any tour or taxi-hire that includes Inwa will assume you want to visit the site by horse-cart. They will therefore drop you at a small jetty about 1km south of Ava Bridge, from which shuttle ferries take just two minutes to get to the other side, where cart drivers await. Ferries depart as soon as there are a few passengers (usually every few minutes). Pedestrians pay K1000 return, motorcyclists K1500. No one-way reductions. Cars can't cross. Double fares apply after 6pm. In the rainy season, ferries start further north near Thabyedan Fort beneath Ava Bridge.

BY ROAD Take the new (dusty, unfinished) airport highway 4.5km south of the Ava Bridge junction. Around 200m beyond a major river bridge, but before Tada U, turn right. Wind through Inwa South Village taking a right at both T-junctions (600m then another 600m). Pass Le-htat-gyi and reach the moat 3.5km after leaving the highway. Loop around the moat clockwise for the easiest access to the main sights.

FERRY FROM SAGAING A little passenger boat crosses from Sagaing, but it operates infrequently and might refuse to take foreigners.

❶ Getting Around

A three-hour horse-cart tour visiting the three main sites costs K5000 for one or two people. For many visitors horse-cart tours are a major part of the Inwa experience, the carriages avoiding noise pollution and creating picturesque scenes themselves along the tree-lined tracks. However, carts are undeniably slow moving and somewhat limiting. Bringing your own bicycle or motorbike from Mandalay can prove an attractive alternative.

Sagaing

စစ်ကိုင်း

☏072 / POP C40,000

As you cross the Ayeyarwady on the busy new bridge, Sagaing's uncountable white-and-gold stupas shimmer alluringly on a series of hillocks that rise behind the almost flat town centre. No individual pagoda stands out as a particular must-see, but taken together the whole scene is enthralling. A highlight is walking the (sometimes steep) tree-hung stairways that lead magically past monasteries and nunneries to viewpoints from which you can survey the river and yet more stupas.

History

Named for the trees hanging over the river, Sagaing became the capital of an independent Shan kingdom around 1315, after the fall

of Bagan had thrown central Myanmar into chaos. Its period of importance was short, for in 1364 the founder's grandson, Thado Minbya, hop-scotched the capital to Inwa. From 1760 Sagaing enjoyed just four more years as capital, but the town's significance from then on became more spiritual than political. Today it is home to some 6000 monks and nuns, and is a place where many Myanmar Buddhists go to meditate when stressed.

◉ Sights

SAGAING HILL

စစ်ကိုင်းတောင်

(admission Sagaing/Mingun $3 ticket)

Stupa-topped hillocks coalesce into Sagaing Hill, a long tree-dappled north–south ridge that starts around 1½ miles north of the market area. If you drive to the top, you

Sagaing

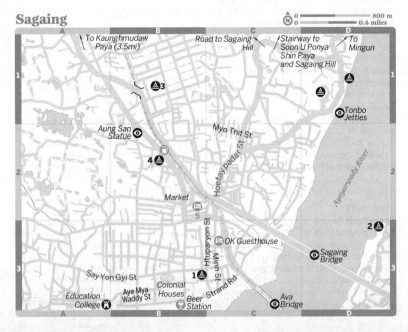

Sagaing

will probably be charged $3 for a Mingun–Sagaing ticket, and on the way back to the market, your taxi driver will probably stop off at one of the **silver shops** where repoussage artisans bang away at various pieces. Alternatively there are several pedestrian access stairways, including one from the Mingun road, where nobody is likely to check tickets.

Soon U Ponya Shin Paya   BUDDHIST TEMPLE
This 'early offering shrine' is the most important of the temples on Sagaing Hill's southern crown and the first you'll come to on climbing the southern stairway. Its central 97ft-high gilded stupa was originally built in 1312. Legends claim that the structure magically appeared overnight, built by the king's faithful minister Ponya in a superhuman flurry of activity inspired by a magical Buddha relic that he'd found in a betel-nut box. The myth fancifully claims that Ponya himself was of supernatural parentage, his father having 'flown' to Sagaing from the Himalayas millennia before, arriving to a curious communion with the Buddha, seven hermits and a flower-bearing orang-utan. Burmese genealogy is never boring.

Notice the bronze rabbit that serves as a collection box in the rather gaudy Buddha hall. And don't miss the views from the balcony area of the small associated snack bar.

Umin Thounzeh   BUDDHIST TERRACE
North of Soon U Ponya Shin, Umin Thounzeh (literally 30 Caves) is one of the more distinctive complexes on the main hilltop, a colourful crescent-shaped colonnade within which there are 45 Buddha images.

Tilawkaguru   CAVE TEMPLE
Accessed from a dead-end road at the southwest base of the hill, this mural-filled cave complex dates originally from 1672. Until recently it was a popular site for visitors and was especially appealing when lit only by candles. However, at the time of research, opening times had become sporadic.

TOWN CENTRE
The market area isn't especially charming, but further south it's pleasant to cycle along Strand Rd with several fine old **colonial-era buildings** lining its north side and views across to Inwa from the Ayeyarwady riverfront. A block inland from here, **Htuparyon Paya** is a gigantic stupa originally built in 1444. It's unusual for having three circular storeys each incorporating arched niches. Across Yonegyi St, a garden of garish statues includes a particularly fearsome red cobra.

North of the market area **Thacheiselik** has a large golden stupa and **Shwezigon** is a huge bell-shaped brick stupa, currently undergoing a massive renovation.

NORTHWEST OF CENTRE
Five miles northwest of central Sagaing, **Kaunghmudaw Paya** is a vast gilded pudding of a stupa rising 150ft high. It was built in 1636 to commemorate Inwa's establishment as the royal capital. According to local tradition, the king agonised interminably over how to shape the stupa. His queen, tired of hubby's indecisiveness, ripped open her blouse and, pointing to her breast, said: 'Make it like this!' Less romantic scholars claim it was actually modelled after the vast Suvarnamali Mahaceti (Ruwanwelisaya) stupa in Anuradhapura, Sri Lanka. Kaunghmudaw is distantly visible from Sagaing Hill and easy to spot as you drive past en route to Monywa.

🛏 Sleeping & Eating
To make a more in-depth exploration of Sagaing's leafy pagoda paths some travellers opt to stay in the town's one foreigner-licensed hotel. However, while central, it's a long walk from the main stupa area and management doesn't rent bicycles or motorbikes, so you'd be wise to bring your own from Mandalay.

Happy Hotel   HOTEL **$$**
(☑21420; standard s/d $15/25, superior $20/30, deluxe $30/40; ❄) On a small town-centre backstreet tucked behind the market. The best deal in this two-part complex are the mid-priced 'superior' rooms with comfy mattresses, fridge and modest bathrooms. Standard rooms are contrastingly old-fashioned with lumpy beds. The sizeable **Chinese restaurant** (veg/non-veg mains K2500/5000) is partly a gift shop, and there's a cheaper Burmese eatery next door.

❶ Getting There & Away
Sagaing is about 12 miles southwest of Mandalay. Authorities may check/sell the Sagaing-Mingun $3 ticket at the old Ava Bridge, but there's no such check if you use the new Sagaing Bridge, used by most Sagaing-Mandalay pick-up trucks.

Mingun

မင်းကွန်း

☑72 / POP C1000

Home to a trio of unique pagodas, Mingun (admission Sagaing/Mingun $3 ticket) is a compact riverside village that makes a popular half-day excursion from Mandalay. The journey is part of the attraction, whether puttering up the wide Ayeyarwady or rollercoastering from Sagaing along a rural lane through timeless hamlets of bamboo-weave homes.

◉ Sights

Mingun Paya   STUPA RUIN
မင်းကွန်းဘုရား

Started in 1790, Mingun Paya (or Pahtodawgyi) would have been the world's biggest stupa had it been finished. In fact, work stopped when King Bodawpaya died in 1819. That left only the bottom third complete. But that is still a huge structure – a roughly 240ft cube on a 460ft lower terrace – which is often described as the world's largest pile of bricks. And for added drama, there are several deeply cut cracks caused by an 1838 earthquake. Across the road, just the haunches remain of two vast brick **chinthe** (half-lion, half-dragon guardian deities) that would have guarded the pagoda.

Mingun

0 ——— 200 m
0 ——— 0.1 miles

Hsinbyume Paya

Ayeyarwady River

Mingun Bell

Buddhist Nursing Home

Mingun Paya

Ticket Booth   Chinthe Ruin

Snack Restaurants   Chinthe Ruin

Settawya Paya   Poing

Pondaw Paya

Climbing to the top of Mingun Paya affords predictably fine views across the river towards hazily distant Mandalay, but despite the structure's dilapidated state, you must go barefoot, which can be very painful on soft Western feet.

To see the giant structure without its foreground of snack shops and ticket booth, walk the path around the back – best in afternoon light.

To see what Mingun Paya would have looked like had it ever been completed, have a quick look at diminutive **Pondaw Paya**, 200yd south at the end of the tourist strip.

Mingun Bell   GIANT BELL
မင်းကွန်းခေါင်းလောင်း

Continuing his biggest-is-best obsession, in 1808 Bodawpaya commissioned a gigantic bronze bell. Weighing 55,555 *viss* (90 tonnes), it's 13ft high and over 16ft across at the lip, making it the world's largest uncracked bell (Moscow has a bigger one but it's split and not hung). Another unusual feature of the Mingun Bell is that you can scramble beneath and stand within while some helpful bystander gives it a good thump.

Across the road, a Buddhist nursing home for family-less elderly folk is always glad of donations.

Hsinbyume Paya   BUDDHIST STUPA
ဆင်ဖြူမယ်ဘုရား

Built in 1816, possibly using materials pilfered from Mingun Paya, this unusual pagoda is supposedly a representation of the Sulamani Paya. That, according to the Buddhist plan of the cosmos, stands atop Mt Meru, the mountain that stands at the centre of the universe. The stupa is surrounded by seven wavy whitewashed terraces representing the seven mountain ranges around Mt Meru. At the top, one Buddha sits directly behind another; the small one behind was beheaded by raiders looking for gold but when it was fixed, locals worried that Buddha's head was tilted too low, so they made another.

Settawya Paya   BUDDHIST SHRINE
စက်တော်ရာဘုရား

Hollow and lacking finesse, this 1811 shrine contains a 'footprint' of the Buddha. How can one be sure it's real? Well, who else had feet a yard long with conch-shell toes and a floral heel? A lovably naive rank of sitting *nat* statues leads down to the riverbank behind.

Mingun is so small that it can feel oppressively touristy, especially if you arrive with the 9am boat and follow the crowd along the main drag, overloaded as it is with drinks sellers and oil-painting vendors. But you can easily bypass most of these by simply walking around the monuments on dusty paths to the west. This route makes particular sense in the afternoon when the sun lights the west-facing side of Mingun Paya. By then tourist numbers will already be greatly diminished following the return of the 1pm boat. But the bricks of Mingun Paya will be scalding hot after soaking up a full day's sun.

In the past the Mingun-Sagaing combo-ticket was sold as you boarded the ferry in Mandalay. However, since the Sagaing-Mingun road has been upgraded, the $3 fee is now half-heartedly collected instead at the east side of Mingun Paya. If you don't want to climb the stupa, you'll probably avoid paying anything.

AROUND MANDALAY PALEIK

✖ Eating

There are half a dozen snack shacks around Mingun Paya entrance, but only Poing, further south, has a river view and draft Spirulina beer (K700).

ⓘ Getting There & Away

BOAT The **Tourist Boat Association** (☏63596) has a daily riverboat service from Mandalay departing at 9am (K5000 return) and taking about one hour from the western end of 26th St in Mandalay (Map p202). These boats return from Mingun at 1pm. If there are less than five passengers or if you want different departure times, you can rent a small/larger boat for K25,000/40,000.

MOTORBIKE Now that the road has been mostly asphalted, it is increasingly popular to ride to Mingun by motorbike (around 25 minutes from Sagaing) as part of an ancient cities loop.

Paleik

ပုလဲ

☏02 / POP C2500

At 11am daily, local families and tourists converge on Paleik's modest temple, the rather kitschy Yadana Labamuni Hsu-taung-pye, to see the bathing and feeding of three giant pythons, which give it the widely used nickname, the Snake Pagoda (Hmwe Paya). The pythons appeared from the nearby forest in 1974 and never left. Predictably much of the statuary now celebrates Buddha getting cosy with snakes.

Arguably more impressive than the python-fest is Paleik's almost entirely overlooked collection of over 300 close-packed stupas in varying states of repair, many from the Konbaung period. They're easy to find. Simply walk five minutes south from the snake temple.

Paleik is about 12 miles south of Mandalay, a mile west of the annoyingly busy Mandalay–Yangon road. If you're heading to Inwa or Sagaing, there's a tree-shaded cross-country lane that links the Yangon road to Ava Bridge, so you don't need to go all the way back to Amarapura.

Yankin Hill

ရန်ကင်းတောင်

Around three miles east of Mandalay, this pagoda-dotted hillside lacks the historical pedigree of other regional attractions but makes a pleasantly simple, untouristy short excursion from Mandalay.

Yankin Paya BUDDHIST TEMPLES

After crossing a long, flat swath of paddy fields, 19th St suddenly swings abruptly right at the foot of Yankin Hill. A covered stairway here takes you steeply up in 10 minutes to a pagoda where feeding a couple of **domesticated stags** supposedly brings you Buddhist merit. Pagoda walkways turn south along the ridge-top, eventually ducking down into a **rocky cleft** where devotees splash water on tacky gold fish statues that lie at the feet of a Buddha image. The main attraction of the hill is the **view**, which takes in a wide sweep of rice fields to the west and the Shan foothills behind.

Mya Kyauk Kyaung BUDDHIST MONASTERY

From the foot of the Yankin Paya access stairway, backtrack 300yd towards Mandalay then turn north and go another 300yd north to find this modern monastery with its dazzlingly distinctive brassy stupa. Mya Kyauk is famed for its subterranean source of moderately alkaline mineral water, found by faith-led digging in 1998. The water supposedly 'promotes IQ and ameliorates diabetes, constipation, gout and morning sickness'. The only way to try it is to first seek an audience with the head monk, Bhaddanta Khaymar Sarya, who may deign to give you a bottle of it. Before opening the bottle, try holding it up to the sunlight and play. If you hit on the right angle, the light projects an image reminiscent of the monastery stupa onto the back of the label. 'Magic', claim the locals. Or at least good bottle design.

❶ Getting There & Away

Some route 5 Mandalay pick-up trucks come out as far as Yankin. By bicycle it's a straightforward if somewhat traffic-blighted ride, almost dead straight along 19th St. By car or motorbike you can drive to the top of the hill by continuing around and winding up from the south and east.

Northern Myanmar

Best Places to Stay

» Dat Taw Gyaik Waterfall Resort, (p256)

» Mr Charles Guest House, (p260)

» Malikha Lodge (p267)

» Basic village homestays around Hsipaw (see p262)

» Friendship Hotel, Bhamo (p243)

Best Places to Eat

» Club Terrace (p254)

» Kiss Me, (p237)

» Woodland (p254)

» Feel (p254)

Why Go?

Fascinating northern Myanmar covers a vast area but for now foreigners without special permits are essentially limited to two main out-and-back routes. One of these climbs rapidly from Mandalay to the British-era summer capital of Pyin Oo Lwin (Maymyo) then continues across the rolling Shan plateau to Lashio. The relatively cool days and crisp cold evenings are refreshing and hikes take visitors into timeless Lisu, Palaung and Shan hill-villages, notably around Hsipaw.

The second main option is taking a multiday ride along the mighty Ayeyarwady (Irrawaddy) River. You'll need to allow a week or so if doing the whole stretch between Myitkyina and Mandalay, but shorter versions are possible starting from Bhamo or Katha, the setting of George Orwell's *Burmese Days*. The main attractions are the people you'll meet and the lazy, mesmerising journey.

Far beyond Myitkyina lie the snow-capped peaks of Myanmar's Himalaya. However, getting anywhere near there means joining expensive pre-organised fly-in/fly-out tours via Putao for which permits take at least two weeks to arrange.

When to Go

November is probably the best time for boat travel on Ayeyarwady, with temperatures comfortable but water levels still high. As the season proceeds and river levels fall, boats take longer and larger ferries may need to stop at night to avoid hidden sandbanks. As in Mandalay, the Ayeyarwady valley might have mildly nippy nights in midwinter but days are warm and it gets progressively hotter into April before the rains start in May or June. The Shan Plateau offers an easy escape to cooler days and nights that can feel positively cold in the middle of winter. In Putao and the far north, rain is least likely in November and December but temperatures can dip almost to freezing. Snow can hinder serious climbing expeditions which are best timed for September or October despite the rain which makes far-north roads almost impassable.

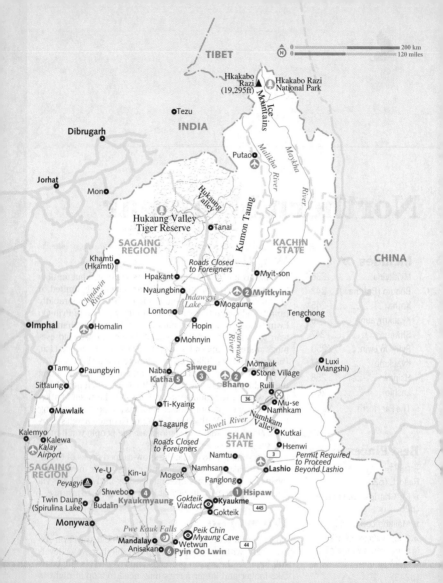

Northern Myanmar Highlights

1 Walk into unspoilt Shan and Palaung villages from lovable **Hsipaw** (p258), a laid-back plateau town with princely connections

2 Spend lazy days drifting down the mighty Ayeyarwady River starting from **Myitkyina** (p236), with its colourful market and dazzling festivals,

or from pretty little **Bhamo** (p242)

3 Be one of just a tiny handful of foreigners who jump ship at **Shwegu** (p244) to discover the town's historic island monastery and forest of mini-pagodas

4 Investigate the ancient pottery traditions of **Kyaukmyaung** (p246)

5 Discover George Orwell connections in sleepy riverside **Katha** (p245)

6 Take the cool upland air at **Pyin Oo Lwin** (p250), the old British summer capital of Myanmar

People

The north is sparsely populated and ethnically complex, with many minority groups dominating a series of pro- and anti-government local administrations and regional armed forces.

Northeast of Mandalay you'll find many Shan people (as in eastern Myanmar; see boxed text, p196) along with the related Wa and the Palaung who see themselves semi-religiously as the guardians of Burmese tea production (see boxed text, p262). Lashio and several other border areas have large Chinese populations who mostly retain their language even after generations of living in Myanmar.

North of Mandalay lies Kachin State where 'minorities' (notably Kachin and Shan) form an overall majority. Shan folk here are divided into five subgroups all prefixed 'Tai-'. Meanwhile, as an ethnic term, Kachin is generally synonymous with speakers of the Jingpaw (Jingpo) language. However, by Myanmar's official definition, it also covers at least five other groups including Rawang and Lisu. The Lisu language is written in a sci-fi capitalised Latin script with many inverted letters and 'vowel-free' words (hello is 'hw hw'). Over the past century, many Kachin and a majority of Lisu have converted to Christianity, their former animist beliefs now largely reduced to colourful folklore as seen in two great festivals at Myitkyina (p236).

In the Himalayan foothills are minuscule populations of various Tibetan tribal peoples including the Taron, Asiatic pygmies who now number barely a dozen and are limited to Naungmun in Myanmar's northernmost tip.

Dangers & Annoyances

Since Burma's independence, the north has witnessed a whole smorgasbord of low-level uprisings and ethnic separatist movements. Tourists won't be allowed near any flash points so for most visitors these are a political curiosity rather than a serious danger, though the closure of whole areas of the region is an obvious annoyance. Many insurgency conflicts that had rumbled on since the early 1960s, were mothballed after a 1994 ceasefire that brought de facto recognition of ethnic administrations over the areas their armies controlled. The KIA (Kachin Independence Army) is still said to control most of Kachin State away from main rivers and rail lines. Shan rebels continue to fight sporadically with the United Wa State Army (UWSA), one of the formations that emerged after the 1989

implosion of the Burmese Communist Party. Quite who's fighting who can change dramatically, as was seen after 2008 when the controversial new constitution demanded an end to private armies. The previously pro-government UWSA and autonomous Kokang (an ethnic Chinese grouping) both baulked at the idea of turning their forces into border guards under Myanmar Army command. The result was a major government army assault on Kokang in 2009.

MYITKYINA & THE UPPER AYEYARWADY

Snaking across Kachin State like a fat yellow python, the mighty Ayeyarwady River provides the main transport route between a series of gently interesting port towns, isolated villages and gold-panning camps. While no individual sight is world beating, the journey itself is a stepping down of gears that many visitors find unforgettable. Unlike boat rides from Mandalay to Bagan, ferries on the upper Ayeyarwady are used almost entirely by locals. Slowly chugging days provide an opportunity to interact with local people in a way that is often impossible on dry land. That's especially true of the bigger, slower (government-run) Inland Water Transport (IWT) ferries. A phrase book and a bottle of Grand Royal can be useful tools to help break the ice.

Note that the Ayeyarwady isn't scenically dramatic in the way of, say, the Nam Ou in neighbouring Laos, but the landscape does reach several modest crescendos as rolling fields and distant sand banks alternate with forest-dappled 'defiles'.

Myitkyina

မြစ်ကြီးနား

♪ 074 / POP C40,000

The capital of Kachin State, Myitkyina lacks much in the way of real sights but it's an engaging multicultural place, home to Kachin, Lisu, Chinese and Burmese. The low-rise architecture is predominantly bland but many mature trees give shade and there's a fair scattering of part-timber houses. Citizens seem unguardedly keen to assist visitors, with local Christians particularly keen to practise their English.

Most visitors jump straight onto an Ayeyarwady River boat out (see boxed text, p239), but the town is also host to two of Myanmar's most colourful 'ethnic' festivals.

NAVIGATING MYITKYINA

The town spreads for miles but the central area is a manageably compact grid. Walking out of the train station, Waing Maw St heads east reaching the river bank in five short blocks. Parallel but four blocks further north is Zei Gyi Rd, the junction marked by one of Myitkyina's two clock towers. Zei Gyi runs east to the market and river, west across the tracks passing very close to the YMCA (follow the tracks north), Hotel United (second block then north), Three Star Hotel (fifth block then north) and plentiful restaurants. Parallel to Ze Gyi four blocks further north, Si Pin Thar Yar St also crosses the railway. The main road then swerves northwest to become Pyi Htaung Su Rd, the road to the airport and Sinbo ferry jetty. But if you instead continue in a northerly sweep on Thakhin Phay Net St, you'll reach the museum and, eventually, Manao Park and Jing Hpaw Thu restaurant.

◎ Sights & Activities

Produce Market   MARKET
(☉5am-5pm) This riverside market specialises in colourful heaps of Chinese fruit and local fresh vegetables. Many of the latter arrive by canoe and are then lugged up the rear stairway on shoulder poles. At dawn this creates an unforgettable scene with more open boats gliding in across shimmering golden water backed by a rising sun.

Directly southwest is the architecturally drab **main market** (☉8.30am-5pm).

Hsu Taung Pye Zedidaw   BUDDHIST TEMPLE
This gilded 'wish-fulfilling' pagoda is the town's most eye-catching religious building, sitting on the banks of the Ayeyarwady River at the north end of Zaw John (Strand) Rd. Opposite its stupa, a 98ft-long **reclining buddha** and nearby standing equivalent (both 'housed') were funded by a Japanese soldier who had served here in WWII. They partly commemorate 3400 of his comrades who died.

Kachin State Cultural Museum   MUSEUM
(Yon Gyi St; admission $2; ☉10am-3.30pm Tue-Sun) Displays Kachin and Shan costumes and the usual assortment of instruments, farming tools and ethnological artefacts.

Aung Ze Yan Aung Paya   PAGODA
Just east of the airport, this pagoda is noteworthy for its arcing ranks of around 1000 little buddhas sitting in the grounds.

☞ Tours

U Myint Oo ('Marcus'; ☎23009, 09 240 1314; khaingkhaingsoesann@gmail.com; A2 Construction Bldg, Yan Aung Mien St) Born in Italy, 'Marcus' speaks excellent English, arranges car rental and leads upper-range private tours, some using a snazzy new 4WD SUV-truck.

Snowland Tours (☎23499; snowland@mpt mail.net.mm; Wai Maw St) Two blocks east of the station, this helpful agency can book flights and arrange customised tours.

Sher Mohammad Khan (☎09 4700 0174) English-speaking driver who can take you around in his 1940s US Jeep, a vehicle that his father originally drove here across the Ledo Rd during WWII.

✸ Festivals & Events

Lisu New Year   CULTURAL
Started in 2011 this big three-day bash unites Lisu folks from all across Kachin

State and Xishuangbanna (China) in a very colourful, if comfortably slow-moving fair. The event is entirely untouristy, unless you count the many costumed Lisu villagers snapping photos of one another – varied regional Lisu costumes being markedly different. Highlights include barefoot climbing of a knife tower and have-a-go stalls to try out your prowess on a traditional crossbow. Held before the February full moon.

Manao Festival   CULTURAL
Originally a way to propitiate the local *nat*, this is now a nationally important gathering of the six Kachin tribes for feasting and costumed dances, performed in Manao park (north of centre) where the large Native American–style totem poles remain in place year round. Accommodation will be stretched at this time. Observers get into the festival mood by drinking copious quantities of rice beer. Held on and around 10 January, Kachin State Day.

🛏 Sleeping

In Myitkyina, nowhere named 'Guesthouse' takes foreigners and the town's two riverside hotels can't be recommended: the Nanthida is run down and slated for conversion into offices while the potentially lovely Sumpra is also in need of some TLC and likely to be rebuilt in 2012 (it's also inconveniently far north of town towards the Ayeyarwady Bridge). Apart from the YMCA and the cheap, but rather sorry, New Light Hotel (singles/doubles $10/15), all other options are variations on the typical Chinese-style hotel.

Hotel United   HOTEL **$$**
(☎22085; 38 Thit Sa St; s/d/f $25/30/40; ❄) Brand new and slightly more refined than most of the Chinese hotels, it's beside the better known Hotel Pantsun, a block west of the YMCA and the railway line. It's close to several eateries yet reasonably quiet.

Xing Xian Hotel   HOTEL **$$**
(☎22281; xingxianhotel@mptmail.net.mm; 127 Shan Su North; standard s/d $20/30, superior s/d $25/35; ❄) Two giant vases and a cabinet of jade trinkets welcome you into this quiet, friendly decade-old hotel that's two blocks south and west from the jetty (or four blocks south from the market). Walls are getting grubby in some of the 30 rooms, but the best 'superior' options (upper-floor corners) are bright and well equipped. Staff here are unusually obliging, informal bicycle rental is

possible (K3000 per day) and the location is central yet quiet, just a block from the river.

YMCA   HOSTEL **$**
(☎23010; mka-ymca@myanmar.com.mm; YMCA St; s/d/ste $12/16/20, s/d with shared bathroom $8/13; ❄@) The 'Y' is an ageing half-timbered place whose main attractions are low prices and the very helpful English-speaking staff who can prove to be a valuable source of information. However, conditions are pretty basic and beneath the starched white sheets, the beds are lumpy. The family suite is no less grungy but it's the size of an apartment, sleeps three and comes with kitchenette.

Two Dragons Hotel   HOTEL **$$**
(☎23490; Zay Gyi St; s $25-35, d $35-45; ❄) While marginally the smartest city centre option, the difference in quality isn't always quite enough to justify the heavy mark-up and some rooms, while well equipped, are inconveniently configured. Central but somewhat noisy.

🍴 Eating

Traditionally Kachin food is noted for using relatively little oil in contrast to Burmese cuisine. Classic dishes include *chekachin* (steamed chicken pasted with spices and wrapped in a banana leaf), *sipa* (mixture of freshly steamed vegetables sprinkled with sesame powder) and *nakoo-che* (hot-sour fish with bamboo shoots). Wash it down with *kaung-ye,* a cloudy semi-sweet pink-brown beer made from sticky rice.

As well as the places reviewed here, there is a wide range of accessible (if fairly standard) eateries along Zaw Gyi St west of the rail tracks.

TOP CHOICE Kiss Me   BURMESE **$**
(Zaw John Rd; snacks K500-1500; ⊙6am-9pm) Popular with Myitkyina's wind-combed fashionable youth, this is at first glance just a simple stilted riverside pavilion with low wooden stalls. Yet quite unexpectedly it turns out some of Myanmar's very best snack-food. The 'banana roll' is as delicate a fritter as you'll find and comes with a wonderful tangy tamarind dipping sauce. And don't miss their fabulous *gyin tok* a divine flavour explosion that is quite possibly the best crunchy ginger salad you'll ever taste.

Jing Hpaw Thu   KACHIN **$$**
(Riverside; dishes K1500-3000; ⊙9am-10pm) Considered the top place for real Kachin food, you'll probably need local help finding (and

NORTHERN MYANMAR MYITKYINA

Which Boat?

IWT FERRIES

These two-/three-storey craft are the cheapest option and the best for interacting with locals but they're slow, unreliable and government-owned.

» **Routes** They run three times a week between Bhamo and Mandalay with stops in Shwegu, Katha, Ti Kyaing, Tagaung and Kyaukmyaung. They do not proceed further north than Bhamo. Timetables are guesswork and ferries can be a day or more late so don't be in a hurry.

» **Tickets** Ticket purchasing procedures vary by port but foreigners always need to pay with pristine US dollar bills, sometimes at the relevant IWT office. Agency bookings aren't possible and there are no seat reservations, indeed no seats whatever, just cold metal decks.

» **Comfort** You'll generally need to sleep aboard at least one night, maybe three nights northbound from Mandalay to Bhamo. A few simple cabins are available ($54, shared toilet) but most folk travel deck class (maximum fare $9) for which you'll need your own mat and bedding.

» **Provisions** Snacks and drinks are sold aboard but they are comparatively pricey. Cheaper provisions are available once or twice a day when the ferry docks at intermediate ports: sales-folk swarming aboard peddling fish on a stick, noodles and curries while other vendors await on the shore.

FAST BOATS

Long covered motor boats carrying between 30 and 80 passengers. Departures are predictable and regular, either daily or at least every second day.

» **Routes** Fast boats make one-day hops on the following sectors, always travelling by day (each sector will be in a different boat): Myitkyina–Sinbo (daily), Sinbo–Bhamo (daily), Bhamo–Shwegu–Katha (daily) and Katha–Mandalay (every second day).

» **Tickets** Usually purchased just before departure, or one day before for Katha–Mandalay.

» **Comfort** The wooden bench seats are small and often partly broken. Sitting on the flat roof can be more comfy if you have sufficient sunscreen but that's not always an option. You'll need to sleep at local hotels and guesthouses, which are very basic in Sinbo and Katha.

» **Provisions** Bring plenty of drinking water. North of Bhamo there may be a lunch stop but this can be cancelled if they are behind schedule and there are no vendors en route, so bring your own snacks. South of Bhamo, villagers aggressively peddle cheap meal-bags during brief intermediate halts.

LOCAL BOATS

Similar to fast boats but making shorter, local journeys and often dangerously overloaded. Foreigners are typically forbidden to use these.

CRUISE BOATS

Several cruise companies offer Ayeyarwady trips, albeit rarely more than a few times per year. On such journeys your interaction with locals will be minimal. See the boxed text on p214 for full details.

Which Direction?

Southbound: The rare handful of travellers who venture this way generally head south. That's a sensible decision as you'll be going with the current and each leg is quicker, though if you're sticking with fast boats, the total number of days you'll need remains the same.

Northbound: Each leg takes more of your day and IWT ferries will take up to two days longer northbound. You will almost certainly not meet any other foreigners on northbound boats.

When to Go?

Boats run all year between Mandalay and Bhamo.

» Journeys are fastest in autumn when water levels are high.

» In the winter tourist season there's rarely a problem finding space aboard. Journey times lengthen as the river levels fall. By February, sandbanks mean that the IWT ferry will have to moor overnight, adding up to a day to southbound journey times.

» April is difficult with boats packed full of local travellers and ferries seriously overloaded.

» Bhamo to Myitkyina can prove difficult due to very low water from May to July.

» In summer, rain and high winds can make the passage very uncomfortable.

Where to Start/Finish?

North of Mandalay there are essentially only four realistic start/finish points for foreigners on the Ayeyarwady adventure:

» **Myitkyina** Has the most reliable (if heavily booked) air connections plus several daily trains from Mandalay. Decent accommodation is available. Myitkyina to Bhamo is the least touristed river section and a forced stay in Sinbo is a great excuse to stay in a tiny roadless local village, if you can cope with the very basic accommodation there.

» **Bhamo** No rail or bus link to Mandalay and the only air connection is an unpredictable twice-weekly Myanma Airways flight (not recommended). However, accommodation is good and you could fly to Myitkyina and connect to Bhamo by road. Bhamo to Katha is the most popular single section of river trip due to the (brief) drama of the second defile. Shwegu, part way, is an off-beat highlight.

» **Katha** Popular for its George Orwell connections but accommodation is basic. Three daily trains connect to Mandalay albeit at antisocial times and from a railhead 18 miles away. River scenery south of Katha is initially lovely but there's no easy jump-off point till Kyaukmyaung.

» **Kyaukmyaung** Jumping off at this very interesting pottery town can make sense if you're heading for Bagan, which you can reach across country via Shwebo, Monywa and Pakokku. Continuing by boat to Mandalay you'll pass Mingun but IWT ferries won't stop there.

How Long Will It Take?

The minimum time from Myitkyina to Mandalay by fast boat would be four days, or five if you arrived in Katha on the wrong day (services not daily). Adding a day in Katha is highly advised anyway, as is one day in Bhamo and one in Shwegu. You could save one day by doing the Myitkyina–Bhamo section by road. If the dates work out (three sailings a week), the IWT ferry makes a more relaxing alternative to the fast boat on the Katha–Mandalay section but takes a day longer southbound, maybe two days longer northbound.

What Will I Need?

» Plenty of time

» A blanket and mat for IWT overnight boats

» A cushion for fast boats

» Several passport and visa photocopies (not essential for the boats themselves but needed for some excursions and time-savers at police checks in places you might stop off at)

How Much Will It Cost?

Factors to consider:

» Budget accommodation for foreigners is limited in Myitkyina and Bhamo.

» Fast-boat tickets are pricier than many travellers anticipate: the Myitkyina to Mandalay fast-boat fares add up to K66,000.

» IWT ferries are cheaper but less frequent.

» Be sure to bring sufficient cash – like anywhere in Myanmar there is no way to get cash transferred and while pristine US dollars can be exchanged in Myitkyina, Bhamo and Katha, rates will be relatively poor.

ordering at) this attractive riverside place, hidden at the end of an improbable suburban alley north of the Manao Park (around 2 miles north of the centre). There's also a more central branch but it's without any of the charm.

River View   CHINESE $

(Riverside; dim sum K500-700; ☺6am-10pm) Forgo your half-hearted hotel breakfast and stroll over to watch the sun rise from this open riverside terrace whose dim sum are the best in town. Numerous alternative snacks are available and there's a karaoke section at night. It's directly south of the main vegetable market.

Win Thu Zar   BEER STATION $

(Zyo Gyi St; draught beer K500; ☺10am-10pm) Facing the main market this attractive beer garden turns out typical barbecue offerings.

Royal Kiss   BAKERY, CAFE $

(Swon Para Bwan St; snacks K500, coffee K600-1000; ☺9am-8pm) This conspicuous bright-orange bakery bakes fluffy pastries and serves fresh fruit juices and real coffee (macchiatos K700). It's near Myanma Airways.

Bamboo Field Restaurant   CHINESE $$

(313 Pyi Htaung Su Rd; dishes K5000-9000, burgers K2000; ☺9am-10pm) On the main airport road, four blocks northwest of the YMCA, the 'attraction' of this overpriced barn-like 'restobar' is the nightly beauty-pageant-cum-karaoke show by local girls (from 6.30pm).

Night Market   STREET FOOD $

(Aung San Rd & Wai Maw St; ☺4.30-9.30pm) Stalls with various typical meals plus some Kachin and Shan specialities.

ⓘ Information

The YMCA sells a K500 map of greater Myitkyina and has a better street map on their wall (albeit mostly in Burmese) that you can photograph.

MCC (Yan Aung Mien St; internet per hr K500) Fast connection, though several other internet places are more central.

ⓘ Getting There & Away

Air

On arrival by air in Myitkyina you'll be half-heartedly quizzed by immigration police in the terminal building. Then you walk out of the airport compound *before* collecting your luggage. Don't panic – bags are delivered to a shed just outside the airport gates.

Air Bagan (AB; ☎20308; Swon Para Bwan St; ☺9am-5pm Mon-Fri, 9am-noon Sat & Sun) Book early.

Myanma Airways (MA; ☎22545; ☺bookings 8am-9.30am one day before flight) Tucked just off Swon Para Bwan St, a half-block south of Air Bagan, 200yd north of Myitkyina's 'second' (one-pole) clock tower. Schedules can be erratic, rather like the maintenance of their government-owned aircraft.

There are flights to Myitkyina from the following destinations:

Mandalay Monday, Tuesday, Thursday, Friday and Sunday ($95, AB); Monday, Wednesday, Friday and Saturday ($60, MA).

Nay Pyi Taw Monday, Wednesday, Friday and Saturday ($95, MA).

Putao Monday ($35, MA), Tuesday and Sunday ($60, AB). With pre-arranged permits/tour only.

Yangon Monday, Tuesday, Thursday, Friday and Sunday ($140, AB); Monday, Wednesday, Friday and Saturday ($125, MA)

TRANSPORT OPTIONS TO MYITKYINA

The following table provides a quick comparison of the various ways of getting to Myitkyina from Mandalay. Ferry options will be faster southbound and in the rainy season (see boxed text, p239 for more details). All boat-ferry options require intermediate stops.

TYPE OF TRAVEL	DURATION	FARE	FREQUENCY
Air	70min	$60-95	nine flights weekly
Bus	not permitted	not permitted	not permitted
Fast boats	4-5 days	K66,000 total	see boxed text p239
Fast boats & bus	2-plus days	K48,000 total	alternate days on one section
Ferry & boats	6-plus days	K30,000 plus $7	three ferries weekly
Ferry & bus	5-plus days	K12,000 plus $7	three ferries weekly
Train	16-40hr	$10-30	three daily

INDAWGYI LAKE

About 110 miles southwest of Myitkyina, placid Indawgyi is the largest natural lake in Myanmar. The lakeshore is ringed by rarely visited Shan villages, and the surrounding Indawgyi Wetland Wildlife Sanctuary provides a habitat for more than 120 species of birds, including shelducks, pintails, kingfishers, herons, egrets and the Myanmar peacock.

The serene Shwe Myitsu Pagoda, on an island off Nam Tay village, seems to float on the surface of the lake. The central, gilded stupa was constructed in 1869 to enshrine Buddha relics transported here from Yangon. Pilgrims visit in droves for the Shwe Myitsu Pwe, held during the week before the full moon of Tabaung (March), at which time the lake waters are low enough for a walk along a seasonal causeway to the pagoda.

During festival time you might be allowed to camp or bed down at Nam Tay monastery. At other times, however, the only licensed guesthouses are 12 miles away in Lonton. Both are pretty basic. Indawa 2 (per person $10) has three rooms with attached bathroom and is owned by a military family. Indawmaha (per person K7000) has eight rooms in a stilt building right at the water's edge but is even more simple. Boat drivers want around K70,000 for day trips around the lake, or K20,000 for a return trip to the pagoda. Land-based tours around the lake shore are much cheaper.

Two of the daily Myitkyina–Mandalay trains stop in **Hopin**, which is roughly halfway between Myitkyina and Katha. From Hopin, overloaded pick-ups leave very occasionally for the excruciatingly uncomfortable 28-mile trip to Lonton (K3000, 3½ hours). The alternative, chartering a 4WD for a three-day, two-night trip from Myitkyina (return or dropping you in Katha), will likely cost several hundred dollars. There's a very rough road that continues all the way to Khamti via the casino-filled jade-mining boom town of **Hpakant** (Pakkan) but foreigners can't go anywhere beyond **Nyaung Bin** without very hard-to-score permits.

NORTHERN MYANMAR AROUND MYITKYINA

Boat

The daily express boat, *TO Sinbo*, departs around 8.30am (local/foreigner K4000/8000, five hours) from Talawgyi pier. That's a 20-minute, K5000 three-wheeler ride from town. In Sinbo you'll usually need to stay the night in the ultra simple guesthouse before continuing next morning to Bhamo. For more information on boat travel, see p239.

Bus

The only bus route open to foreigners is the Myitkyina–Bhamo route (K12,000, six hours) leaving Myitkyina at 7.30am from a dusty bus stand, just north of the centre off Tha Khin Net Phay Rd. Before getting aboard it's essential to prepare five photocopies of the visa and ID pages from your passport to hand out at the various checkpoints en route. Attractive scenery.

Train

There are three daily trains to Mandalay (ordinary/upper/sleeper $10/27/30). Fast train '38 Down' departing 4.30am should arrive in Mandalay at 8.30pm. The slower '56 Down' (departs 9.45am) and 58 Down (departs 1.45pm) stop at Naba (for Katha, ordinary/upper $4/11, 9½ hours) and Hopin (ordinary/upper $2/6, 4½ hours) where you could hop out for a few days to make the very off-beat excursion to Indawgyi Lake (see boxed text). All three trains stop in Shwebo (Mandalay fares apply). Ordinary class is designed for sardine wannabes. Bring a blanket for the cold nights, and motion sickness pills for the incredible bouncing over warped rails.

ℹ Getting Around

Motorised three-wheelers (called thonbeecars: *thoun* means 'three', *bein* means 'wheel') carrying up to four people charge K3000 to/from the airport, K6000 to the boat jetty for Sinbo.

Staff at the Xing Xian Hotel rent two bicycles to guests. The YMCA can show you a nearby stall that rents motorcycles for K10,000 per day.

Around Myitkyina

MYIT-SON & JAW BUM

မြစ်ဆုံ

About 27 miles north of Myitkyina, Myit-Son marks the point where the Mayhka and Malikha Rivers come together to form the Ayeyarwady. It's considered a local 'beauty spot', though 'intriguing' describes the ravaged scene better than 'beautiful'. The confluence point is distantly overlooked by a series of rough snack- and teahouses, a big dumpling-shaped golden pagoda and a traditional Kachin longhouse rebuilt as a 'cultural emblem'. However, more interesting is the nearby purgatory of gold-panning outfits churning up the muddy stream in accompanying **Tang Phray** village using semi-mechanised bamboo-tower conveyor belts. You'll have to hurry to see any of this. A vast dam project will eventually put the whole area under water, pagoda, village and all. The surreally neat **Aung Nge Tang** 'model village', 11km south of Myit-Son, is being built to rehouse the displaced villagers but so far looks far from big enough to help all those affected.

The road north of Myitkyina (bound eventually for Putao) has been newly rebuilt as far as the dam construction site, but the last 11km to Myit-Son are horrendously bumpy. You'll need a photocopy of your passport and visa to hand to a police checkpoint en route. A motorbike/taxi from Myitkyina costs around K15,000/50,000 return (1½ hours each way). For a token extra fee you can detour 1 mile off the main road at Nawng Nang village to comically named **Jaw Bum**. Its name translates as 'praying mountain' but it's really only a fairly modest hill, a sacred site for Kachin and Lisu Baptists. In spite of its religious connections, most visitors here are amorous local couples who climb a repulsively ugly six-storey concrete **viewing tower** to observe and drop litter on a sweep of rural scenery.

Myitkyina to Bhamo

Travelling by boat, the first day is through low lying scenery that is not immediately memorable but has the bonus of a forced stay in appealing Sinbo, a village that's wonderfully unspoilt apart from the piles of riverside rubbish that mar almost every habitable area along the route. The Sinbo to Bhamo section, on smaller (25 plank-seat) longboats, spends most of the route traversing the Ayeyarwady's First Defile where the river cuts through hills shaggy with forest-bamboo mix, the boat stopping at isolated sandbanks to pick up gold-panners, rattan harvesters and cantilever fishermen. In the dry season the access into Bhamo can be complicated by weaving through a maze of very shallow sandbars.

SINBO
POP C1700

Taking the river route between Myitkyina and Bhamo you'll be forced to spend a night in this delightfully car-less riverside village. Though conditions aren't luxurious, the stop is actually a blessing in disguise – for some travellers one of the highlights of the river trip. Founded as a teak station for the Scottish firm Steel Brothers, Sinbo is a neat grid of unpaved streets, the mostly wood and part-timber houses set amid coconut and toddy palms. There are no must-see sights but river views are mesmerising from the muddy lane that climbs between the trio of old stupas and the 1919 British Officers' Bungalow (now fenced and out of bounds for military use) at the south end of town. On arrival from Myitkyina, boats are usually met by **Hla Tun**, the manager of the one ultrasimple **guesthouse** (bed/dinner/breakfast K3000/2000/1500). It has eight hardboard-separated sleeping spaces over a party dining room featuring portraits of Buddha, Jesus and Avril Lavigne. Delicious dinners are cooked by Hla Tun's wife on a simple wood-stove out back.

Bhamo (Banmaw)

ဗန်းမော်
☑074 / POP C25,000

For most travellers, Bhamo ('ba-more'; Banmaw), is just a staging post on the river journey to Myitkyina or Mandalay. However, it's an attractive little town that rewards at least one day's rest-stop. The bustling central **riverfront** (Kannar Rd) features several old stained-teak houses and is overhung with magnificent mature 'rain trees', so named because their lovely pink flowers bloom in the monsoon season. At the southern end of this riverfront are dealerships selling great stacks of clay-pots including simple water carriers from Shwegu and giant glazed amphorae from Kyaukmyaung. Two short blocks east then one north on Lammataw Rd brings you to the main market (Thiri Yadana) from which Sinbyushin St leading west becomes the main road to Myitkyina and China. It quickly passes Post Office St (for Grand Hotel, turn right after one block), the **pre-dawn vegetable market** and Letwet Thondaya Rd (for the Friendship Hotel, turn left after the second block). Around 500m further is the large, photogenic complex of **Theindawgyi Paya** featuring an elongated golden bell-shaped gilded stupa. It's best admired from the southeast across a pond lined with processing concrete monk statues.

About 3 miles north of town, beyond the military enclave, the much more historic **Shwe Kyina Pagoda** has two gold-topped stupas and marks the site of the 5th-century Shan city of **Sampanago** (Bhamo Myo Haung, Old Bhamo). Almost nothing remains of the old city, though locals remember numerous remnant bricks and posts remaining into the 1950s. If you know what you're looking for you can still make out a section of 10ft-high mud rampart where the lane around the monastery cuts through it to the east, but you'll probably need a guide and the site is hardly memorable. Far more impressive is the awesome seasonal **bamboo bridge** (return toll with bicycle K300) that allows you to make your precarious way across the wide Tapin River. A nice cycle ride is to continue over the bridge for half an hour west through timeless **Sinkin village** and on to a brickworks from which a 10-minute stairway climb takes you up **Theinpa Hill** past a meditation hall to a stupa with very attractive **panoramas**.

☞ Tours

Sein Win (🖉in China 0086-692 927 8557) This English-speaking guide (K15,000 per day without transport) is an eccentric septuagenarian. His front room is dominated by the helicopter he designed and built but never flew for want of a sufficiently powerful engine. At least not yet.

🛏 Sleeping

Only two options accept foreigners. Both are central.

TOP CHOICE Friendship Hotel HOTEL $
(🖉50095, in China 0086-692 687 6670; Letwet Thondaya Rd; s/d/tr with shared bathroom $7/14/21, s/d with air-con $20/25; ❋🐾) This large, comfortable Chinese-style hotel is truly excellent value for money with plenty of little extras including in-room coffee, free water fill-ups, satellite TV and a basket of complimentary toiletries. Even the basic rooms are well maintained, better ones have good linens and decent mattresses and all qualify you for the excellent buffet breakfast served in an appealing rooftop cafe. Helpful manager Moe Naing speaks fluent English. There's an internet room but don't count on a connection.

Grand Hotel HOTEL $$
(🖉50317, in China 0086-692 688 1816; Post Office Rd; s/d $15/20; ❋) Grand indeed is its modern lobby and blue-glass facade but the rooms are altogether more down-to-earth, and while reasonably well equipped, they are let down by their musty bathrooms.

✗ Eating

There's a great new place for Burmese curry-spreads (K2000) directly beside Friendship

Hotel (south) while on the short diagonal street cutting behind that hotel (northeast) you'll find a busy cafe, a popular beer-station and barbecue place and a servery for pre-cooked Muslim-Indian curries.

Sein Sein CHINESE $
(Kannar Rd; veg/nonveg dishes K1500/2000, rice K300; 🍴) The old-fashioned dining room, rough round tables and beer-poster decor promises little. However, the reliable Chinese food is widely considered the best in town, there's a menu in English (no prices) and there's Dagon beer on draught (K600). It's near the IWT office, and tantalisingly close to the river but without views.

Arthan TEAHOUSE $
(Kannar Rd; snacks K200; ⊗5.30am-7pm) Just south of the riverbank pot-sellers' stalls, this very basic teahouse is the only one with views of the Ayeyarwady.

ℹ Information

Free town maps are available for guests at the Friendship Hotel. They are extremely useful, if misleadingly out of scale towards the edges.

The prefix 🖉0086-692 denotes 'China numbers', which should be dialled from another China-line phones (0086-692 numbers) to avoid paying international call rates.

ℹ Getting There & Away

Air
Theoretically the clunky government aircraft of **Myanma Airways** (🖉50269; Kantawgyi St) fly to Yangon ($120) via Mandalay ($45) on Thursday and Sunday. Ticket sales are only possible from 8am to 9.30am and 1pm to 4pm, one day before flying. Their office is three blocks east of the market, up Sinbyushin St then half a block south.

Boat
IWT FERRIES Pre-purchase tickets at **IWT** (🖉50117; Strand Rd; ⊗9am-5pm), the wooden mansion with brick-columned overhang that's set back opposite the Sikh Temple, just north of the central riverfront area. Departures (7am on Monday, Wednesday and Friday) are from a jetty 2½ miles south of central Bhamo. Don't forget mats and bedding (see boxed text, p239). Costs and very approximate timings (southbound, dry season):

Shwegu ($2, five hours)
Katha ($4, 10 to 12 hours)
Kyaukmyaung ($9, 22 to 30 hours).
Mandalay (deck/cabin $9/54, 30 to 50 hours)

FAST BOATS In the rainy season most boats are faster and there may be a direct seasonal fast boat to Mandalay departing at dawn.

Katha Services (K15,000, around eight hours) via Shwegu (K7500, 2½ hours) depart 8.30am from the northern end of the central waterfront.

Myitkyina Two-day trip starts with the 9.30am boat to Sinbo (p242, K7000, six hours), departing from the middle of the central waterfront.

Bus & Pick-Up Trucks

Myitkyina Bus leaves at 7am (K12,000, six hours) from Bawdi St, around 400m south of Friendship Hotel. Book one evening ahead (hotels can help) and prepare five photocopies of your visa and passport for checkpoints.

Mandalay via Shwegu No foreigners.

Train

A Katha–Bhamo railway is under construction.

❶ Getting Around

LOCAL TRANSPORT Motorcycle/three-wheeler taxis cost K1000/2000 to the airport, K2000/3000 to the IWT ferry dock.

BICYCLE Rent from **Breeze Coffee & Cold** (Letwet Thondaya Rd; per day K2000; ◷8.30am-7pm), a small shop almost opposite Friendship Hotel.

PICK-UP TRUCKS Intervillage pick-ups (called 'Hilux' after the vehicle brand) are an unusual mongrel where the rear section is a goods carriage with seats fixed high on the roof as though for a safari. Dangerously top-heavy.

Around Bhamo

Popular with Chinese visitors and local weekenders, Stone Village is a picnic spot where a thatched-roof karaoke restaurant overlooks a mountain stream cascading between large boulders. The scene is pretty enough but only really worth the trip if you're desperate for a time-filler. If so, do also take a look at some of the water-powered cottage industries in Kyauk Sahan, the village where Stone Village's half-mile access track branches off the newly cobbled China-bound road, 15 miles east of Bhamo. The China-bound road branches off the Bhamo–Myitkyina road at Momauk where there are teahouses and (just east) some attractive rice-paddy scenes.

Bhamo to Katha

Between Bhamo and Shwegu, the scenery reaches a modest climax in the short Second Defile where the Ayeyarwady passes through a wooded valley with a rocky cliff face at one section (often described misleadingly as a gorge).

SHWEGU

ေရႊဂူ

♩074 / POP 15,000

Every year around a dozen foreign travellers jump ship at historic Shwegu, a long ribbon of township, known for its elegantly unfussy **pottery** and for the fabled Shwe Baw Kyune monastery on mid-river Kyundaw ('Royal') Island. Few locals speak English.

◉ Sights

Shwe Baw Kyune   BUDDHIST MONASTERY

Although at first glance this monastery looks ostensibly 20th-century, historians say it was built in the 13th century while monastic fables suggest that the place was founded some two millennia ago when an Indian prince turned up with seven holy bone fragments of the Buddha. These are now encased within small buddha statuettes that have become lumpily unrecognisable with centuries of added gold leaf and form the monastery's priceless main treasure (dattaw).

However, for non-Buddhists, visiting the monastery is far more interesting for its extraordinary array of over 7000 closely packed stupas, ancient and modern, which fill the eastern end of the island. Some are whitewashed, others gilded and many more are mere piles of antique bricks with just traces of former stucco detail. Most appear to have been suffocated for years by foliage, Angkor Wat style. The bushes were recently cut back to reveal the spectacle, but getting to the outlying stupas is very uncomfortable barefoot given all the stubble and thorns (carry your sandals).

Hidden here and there are dozens of tiny buddha statues and the odd brick-and-stucco lion. The whole scene is made even more photogenic by a series of pyathak (stepped towers) that flank the monastery's central golden tipped stupa. And the island setting, with its tree shaded village of wooden stilt houses, makes for a wonderfully peaceful environment. There's a big local festival here in the week leading up to full moon of Tabaung.

Old Shwegu   NEIGHBOURHOOD

Shwegu town is a narrow riverside strip extending around 3 miles along the Ayeyarwady's rubbish strewn southern bank. Around 400yd west of the central jetty is an area of relatively old town including several wooden houses along the riverfront road. A block inland from there are the hotels on a busy new road but behind there is an area of tree-shaded footpaths and alleys that forms an intriguing pottery district. Here, in household compounds, Shwebo's archetypal *tau ye-u* (drinking water pots) and *subu* (football-sized piggy banks) are formed and fired in kilns of carefully heaped rice-husks.

An Daw Paya
BUDDHIST TEMPLE

This eye-catching ornate pagoda lies in a rural mainland field, directly across the river from Shwe Baw Kyune and around 2 miles east of central Shwegu. Motorcycles charge K1000 to get there but finding one to come back can be tricky.

🛏 Sleeping & Eating

Two guesthouses face each other where Bhamo–Mandalay buses stop. **Mya Myint Mo** (☑52134; per person K4000) is the better deal but given the bureaucratic headache that hosting foreigners causes the owners, you shouldn't expect an over-enthusiastic welcome. Rooms are basic, but survivable, turquoise boxes sharing simple bathroom facilities. It's 10 minutes' walk from the jetty area: walk west, turn left at the roundabout then right and it's 50yd beyond the entrance to Mingala Monastery amid a gaggle of teahouses and snack stalls.

ⓘ Getting There & Away

Fast boats leave for Bhamo (K7500, 2½ hours) around 1.30pm and Katha (K9000, four hours) around 11.30am. Foreigners may not take the other local village-to-village boat services. Curiously, Shwegu agents were prepared to sell us tickets on the normally locals-only Bhamo–Mandalay bus services that arrive southbound around 3pm. However, we have no confirmed reports of any foreigner successfully completing the Shwegu–Mandalay trip by road.

ⓘ Getting Around

From a logging jetty 300yd west of An Daw Paya, an open longboat ferries passengers across to Shwe Baw Kyune (K500/4000 per person/boat, four minutes). A much more convenient option is to charter your own boat directly from Shwegu's central jetty taking around 15 minutes each way. A K10,000 return charter should include several hours' wait while you explore the island.

Katha

ကသာ

☑074 / POP C12,000

Literature lovers and boat bums may enjoy this small but lively Ayeyarwady port town.

It's a forced stop if you're travelling the river in fast-boat hops, a pleasant optional hop-off if you're on the IWT ferry, and there's a rail link to Mandalay if you're fed up with the river altogether. The guesthouses and various boat ticket sales booths are close together along three short central blocks of Strand Rd, the attractive curving riverside road.

⊙ Sights

In 1926 and 1927, Katha was briefly home to British colonial police officer Eric Blair. Better known by his pen name, George Orwell, Blair used the outpost as the setting for his novel *Burmese Days*. Several Orwell-related buildings that featured in the book are still standing but none are marked as such and none are commercialised tourist attractions, so ask politely before trying to barge in. The half-timbered former **British Club**, now used as an association office, is tucked away 100yd behind the 1924 **Tennis Club** on a street appropriately called Klablan (Club St). A block north the 1928 **DC's House** was actually completed just after Orwell's stay but its unmistakable style would fit McGregor and its sorry state of decline is symptomatic. Three families now live within and Daw Wei Wei Dwin sometimes shows visitors into the original (much decayed) hall-drawing room. Two blocks south, Orwell would have lived at the comfy, two storey **police commissioner's house**, which is still used as such (so it's not advisable to knock on the door). Directly northwest, the Orwell-era **St Paul's Anglican Church** collapsed in 2007 and has now been replaced by a new church part-sponsored by troops from the Royal Sussex Regiment in appreciation of the hospitality they received in Katha during Christmas 1944.

There are several attractive temples at the southern end of town near the prison.

🛏 Sleeping & Eating

Only two of Katha's guesthouses accept foreigners. Neither have private bathrooms nor offer breakfast. Both are within 60yd of each other on the riverfront and both are best (albeit noisy) if you can score one of a handful of rooms with river views.

Ayarwady Guest House
GUESTHOUSE $

(☑25140; Strand Rd; per person K5000-7000) The better of the two, the Ayarwady is an old wooden rooming house with half-heartedly whitewashed hardboard room dividers, but the better options have windows and cleaning is relatively thorough. The owners speak a little English.

Annawah Guest House
GUESTHOUSE $

(📞25146; Strand Rd; per person K5000) Annawah is more off-puttingly chaotic than the Ayarwady: its downstairs rooms are dark, upstairs ones include some truly minuscule cupboard-like bed-spaces and the ragged stairway bodes ill. However, a couple of upper, front-facing rooms are OK for a night or two. The pot-bellied owner speaks no English but is a distinctive character and bears a few passing similarities to Orwell's antihero U Po Kyin.

Sein Restaurant
CHINESE $$

(veg/meat/fish dishes K1200/2000/4000; ⊗8am-8pm; 🖼) This older two-room shophouse has a degree of character in its older half and serves consistently good Chinese fare. It's just off the night-market street, three streets inland from the Ayarwady Guest House.

Shwe Sisa
BEER STATION $

(Strand Rd; draught beer K600; ⊗9am-10pm) Brew with a view. Perched over the riverside a block southwest of the guesthouses, Shwe Sisa also barbecues fresh tasty 'Slavia' fish, said to have invaded the Ayeyarwady River having been originally introduced from Yugoslavia.

❶ Getting There & Away

Boat

IWT FERRY

Tickets are only available around an hour before departure, bought from the **IWT office** (📞25057; Strand Rd) opposite the main jetty.

Mandalay Departs around 5pm Monday, Wednesday and Friday (deck/cabin class $7/42). Takes around 40 hours in the dry season (two nights aboard), much less when water is high and the boat can sail by night.

Bhamo Departs Monday, Thursday and Saturday, timings unpredictable ($4).

FAST BOAT

Mandalay Departs every second day at 5am, arrives around 6.30pm (K36,000).

Bhamo Departs daily at 8am (K15,000); arrives in Shwegu at 1.30pm and Bhamo around 4pm.

Train

The nearest train station on the Mandalay–Myitkyina mainline is at Naba, 16 miles west of Katha. There is a daily Katha–Naba connecting train (1¼ hours) leaving Katha at 1pm and Naba at 9am. Local buses (K1000) also connect the two towns timed to meet arriving trains. A chartered Katha–Naba taxi costs around K30,000.

Trains from Naba (according to the station-master in Katha):

Northbound Departures 11.30pm and 3.30am (plus 7.30am local) to Hopin and Myitkyina.

Southbound Departures 6pm and 10.30pm (plus 2.30pm local) to Shwebo and Mandalay.

Katha to Kyaukmyaung

IWT ferries tend to sail the section south of Katha in the dark, but the area has some of the Ayeyarwady's more appealing landscapes with several pagoda-topped hills and thatched villages. The first stop is **Ti Kyaing** (pronounced 't'chine'; Htigyaing,) where a double row of riverfront thatched wooden stilt houses leads north from the jetty, a monastery hill rises directly above and there's a large reclining Buddha on the next hill northeast.

Further south the landscape becomes more monotonous towards **Tagaung**, which gave its name to a whole era of Burmese history, but has not much to show for it.

Kyaukmyaung

📞075 / POP C10,000

ကျောက်မြောင်း

The last major IWT stop before Mandalay is Kyaukmyaung, famous for its distinctive glazed pottery. That is produced in the delightful **Ngwe Nyein** district, a 20-minute stroll south along the Ayeyarwady riverside from central Kyaukmyaung's attractive triple-stupa, **Nondo Zedi**. Traffic en route is mainly a procession of ox carts carrying faggots or rice husks for pot-firing.

Beyond **Letyway Kyaunggyi** monastery you'll see almost every open space filled with large amphorae waiting to be shipped on river barges. Homes, some of them old wooden affairs with distinctive portal-arches, double as storefronts selling vases, jugs and mustard pots (from K200). Although some are vivid green (notably big owl-figure vases) archetypal Kyaukmyaung designs are usually glazed a rich glossy brown that's casually daubed swirls of beige-yellow, the latter apparently taking its colour from old batteries.

The pottery district stretches nearly a mile further south, to and beyond the brutal gash of the new Ayeyarwady bridge site. En route are a few crumbling old stupas while a block or two inland, several 'factories' are housed in bamboo thatched barns. These

IRRAWADDY DOLPHINS

The Irrawaddy dolphin is one of Myanmar's most endangered animals. This small cetacean has a short, rounded snout like a beluga whale and hunts using sonar in the turgid waters of lakes and rivers. In the past, dolphins and humans were able to coexist quite peacefully – there are even reports of dolphins deliberately herding fish into nets – but the use of gill nets and the poisonous run-off from gold mining has driven the dolphin onto the critically endangered list. A 2003 survey estimated a population of just 59 dolphins in the river for which they are named. Yet sightings do still occur and since 2005 a 45-mile stretch of river south of Kyaukmyaung has been designated as a dolphin protection zone.

can shelter as many as 60 potters working at hand-turned or foot-turned wheels. Visitors are generally welcome to nose around and you'll also see kilns, drying yards and piles of rough clay being chopped.

🛏 Sleeping & Eating

Kyaukmyaung has one ultra simple **guest-house** (per person K1500) but it isn't licensed for foreigners so you'll normally be expected to sleep in nearby Shwebo, 18 miles west. However, the plodding local police will usually make exceptions if your river ferry happens to arrive here at an antisocially late hour. The guesthouse, unmarked in English, is down an alley just inland from the main junction (riverside and Shwebo roads). Almost at the ferry jetty, the restaurant marked with a diamond graphic is run by local character Sein Win who speaks some English.

ℹ Getting There & Away

Southbound Katha–Mandalay express boats usually get here midafternoon, arriving at a central jetty three minutes' walk north of Nondo Zedi. IWT river ferries also stop here but timings can be highly erratic. Buses to Mandalay (K2200, four hours) via Shwebo (K500, one hour) depart at 5.45am, 6.45am and 7.45am from the market area, just inland from Nondo Zedi. Other buses and pick-ups to Shwebo leave at least hourly until 3pm.

ရွှေဘို

📞 075 / POP C40,000

Between 1752 and 1755, the leader of little Moksobo village, Aung Zeya, revived Burmese prestige by fighting off both Manipuri and Bago-Mon armies. Rebranding himself King Alaungpaya (or Alaungmintayagyi), his short reign transformed formerly obscure Moksobo into glittering Shwebo ('Golden Leader'), which became, until his death in 1760, the capital of a newly reunified Burma. These days Shwebo makes relatively little of its royal history and few foreign tourists bother making a special excursion to see its recently reconstructed palace. However, if you're jumping off an Ayeyarwady ferry at Kyaukmyaung, Shwebo makes a pleasant enough staging point from which to reach Bagan (via Monywa and Pakokku) without returning to Mandalay. Shwebo is locally famed for snakes and *thanakha* (see boxed text) and some visitors consider it good luck to take home some earth from 'Victory Land', as Shwebo has been known since Alaungpaya's time.

◉ Sights

Shwe Daza Paya   BUDDHIST TEMPLE

As you approach from the south, central Shwebo's skyline is given a very alluring dazzle by a collection of golden pagoda spires. These cluster around the extensive, 500-year-old Shwe Daza Paya and look equally evocative when viewed from the rooftop of the Win Guest House. Closer to, however, the complex feels a little anticlimactic. Across the road, **Chanthaya Paya**

SHWEBO THANAKHA

Wherever you go in Myanmar you'll find hawkers selling *thanakha*, the sandalwood-like logs that are ground to a paste and smeared on the skin as ubiquitous sun-block and moisturiser. However, Shwebo's *thanakha* is considered the country's sweetest smelling, forms the subject of a famous folk song and if you want a gift to delight guesthouse grandmas elsewhere in Myanmar, you won't find better. You'll find it sold on the southern approach cloister to Shwe Daza Paya.

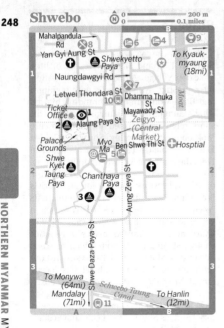

Shwebo

⊚ Sights

1 Palace Museum	A1
2 Schwebon Yadana	A2
3 Shwe Daza Paya	A2

🛏 Sleeping

4 Shwe Phyu Guest House	B1
5 Win Guest House	A2
6 Zinwailar Guesthouse	B1

🍴 Eating

7 Eden Culinary Garden	B1
8 SSD Garden Restaurant	A1

🍷 Drinking

9 Melody Music Garden	B1

ℹ Transport

10 Buses to Kyaukmyaung	A1
11 Main Bus Station	A3

north of town where the moat is crossed by a road causeway near **Maw Daw Myin Tha Paya**, a pagoda built by Alaungpaya and guarded by giant *chinthe*.

🛏 Sleeping

Win Guest House　　　　　　HOTEL **$$**
(☎22049; Aung Zeya St; s/d $20/30, with shared bathroom $10/20) Fresh, clean and unusually airy, the standard rooms are boxy but bright and share communal showers that are spotless and spacious. A handful of top-floor rooms have private bathroom, air-conditioning and satellite TV (but no hot water). Some English is spoken and the staff is reasonably accustomed to dealing with foreigners. The nobby-looking 2007 building is handily close to the market area.

Shwe Phyu Guest House　　　　HOTEL **$**
(☎22264; Yan Gyi Aung St; s/d K12,000/20,000, with shared bathroom K7000/14,000) Better rooms have an en-suite squat, cold shower, cobwebs and geckos. Floors are neatly tiled and the manager speaks English but the road outside is as noisy as the beer station opposite. The similar Zinwailar Guesthouse, nearby, has a couple of rooms with air conditioning.

🍴 Eating & Drinking

Open-air food stands set up shop around the market, especially after dusk. There's a sprinkling of restaurants along Aung Zeya

has an abandoned wooden monastery dormitory that's precariously close to collapse.

Shwebon Yadana　　　　　　　PALACE
(admission incl Hanlin $5; ⊙7.30am-5.30pm) The city's most striking buildings are a pair of towering gold-painted wooden throne rooms, nine-tiers high. These would have been the centrepiece of the King Alaungpaya's 1753 palace complex. However, in the British era, the originals were replaced by a jail. What you see today are recently reconstructed structures. They are undoubtedly photogenic but have no furnishings and if you're not planning on visiting Hanlin (p249), the entry fee seems farcically high – try peeping over the wall from the west to get an idea for free. If you do pay up, the ticket also includes entry to a two-room **museum** displaying assorted archaeological finds, manuscript chests and Alaungpaya's royal palanquin.

Old City Moat　　　　　NEIGHBOURHOOD
In its 18th-century heyday, the palace was at the heart of an enormous walled city. The wall is now almost entirely invisible but some sections of the wide **moat** are well preserved. The road to Kyaukmyaung crosses one section beside **Yan Gyi Aung Park** but more attractive is the area around 2 miles

St, with many beer stations in the northern quarter and along Yan Gyi Aung St.

Eden Culinary Garden
CHINESE $

(Aung Zeya St; veg/meat mains K1500/2500; ⊘7am-9pm; ⊡) The English-language menu is a rarity, typical Chinese fare comes in large portions with soup and small salad, and the Western 'breakfasts' include hamburger. The restaurant's pleasant courtyard twinkles with fairy lights in the foliage though it isn't really quite a garden.

SSD Garden
CHINESE $$

(Shwekyettho Pagoda Rd; mains K2000-4000; ⊘11am-9pm) Peaceful and spacious with similar food to Eden but little English.

Melody Music Garden
BEER STATION $

(Yan Gyi Aung St; draught Tiger K750; ⊘9am-10pm) Ice-cold beer and partially obscured moat views. Bring mosquito repellent.

❶ Information

TSS Internet (Ben Shwe Thi St; per hr K400; ⊘8am-last customer) Connection better at night

❶ Getting There & Away

Bus

MAIN BUS STATION

Mandalay At least hourly until 3.30pm (K1700, three to four hours). Bumpy sections.

Monywa Minibuses plus some buses at least hourly from 5am to 1pm plus 3pm (K1100, 3½ hours). After the potholed first hour the route is smoother and offers a very attractive view of rural life.

MARKET AREA

Kyaukmyaung Departs roughly half-hourly on decent asphalt (K500, one hour).

Train

Mandalay Departs 7.05pm, midnight, 2am and 6.10am (ordinary/1st class $2/4, 3½ to five hours)

Myitkyina Via Naba (for Katha) and Hopin (for Indawgyi Lake). Departs at 3pm, 7.25pm and 10.17pm (cheapest). Fast train (ordinary/upper/sleeper $11/26/29) departs 7am, arrives 8pm; doesn't stop at Naba.

❶ Getting Around

A trishaw or motorbike ride from either station to the centre costs around K1000. Hotel staff can often arrange informal bicycle hire.

HANLIN
POP C4000

ဟန်လင်း

An almost imperceptible rise means that the diffuse, very attractive village of Hanlin (Halingyi, Halin, Halim) sits very slightly above the pan-flat surrounding plains. For centuries this geographical advantage has been deeply significant and the site has been inhabited for millennia. The few foreign visitors who do brave seriously rough roads to get here, come to visit the area's various archaeological diggings. But before leaving Shwebo be sure to visit Shwebon Yadana and warn the archaeological office there that you will be visiting Hanlin. Otherwise, your unannounced arrival is likely to conjure up a band of police, immigration officers and assorted try-to-help guides, scrambling to find someone who can sell you a ticket and verify your identity.

Archaeological Zone
ARCHAEOLOGICAL SITES

(admission $5, free with Shwebon Yadana ticket) Crowning the rise above Hanlin village and surveying the plains for a surprising distance, archaeologists have found large, low sections of brickworks that once formed part of a wall enclosing a complex that was 2 miles wide and 1 mile long, dating back to the Pyu era (4th to 9th centuries AD). In total there are, so far, 32 excavation sites scattered over many miles, many of which have yielded pottery and coins from various epochs. Several excavated grave sites can be visited. To nonspecialists, these tend to look relatively similar (metal-roofed barns covering in-situ skeletons whose depth is a guide to their antiquity), so if you don't want to spend hours seeing everything, consider making a beeline for Site 29 where one can still see the ornaments and weapons with which the bodies were buried.

The excavations are thinly spread over several square miles, so you'll need wheels. To find the way, an archaeology department fixer should accompany you (K1000 extra) but if you can't cope with an all-in-Burmese experience, freelance local guide Toe Myint can speak basic English and may offer to accompany you for around K5000. Key-holders at each sub-site also expect a tip, which is a good way of benefiting the community (your $5 entry fee goes to the government's archaeology department).

Hanlin Village
VILLAGE

Coming all this way without visiting the archaeological sites would seem inexplicable, but Hanlin village is nonetheless a magical place in its own right. Unpaved ox-cart tracks link an incredible plethora of decaying old stupas that create the feeling of an untouched mini-Bagan. This is best appreciated when the scene is viewed from behind Maung San Monastery with its obvious golden *zedi*.

Near the market is a collection of inscribed steles and stone slabs in now-forgotten Pyu script. Within the Nyaung Kobe Monastery (donation expected), a museum room displays various ancient, but unlabelled, archaeological finds. Another minor attraction is the little hot spring area where villagers collect water from circular concrete-sided well-pools and bathe in two bigger basin-pools.

❶ Getting There & Away

Hanlin is about 12 butt-kicking miles southeast of Shwebo. Follow the canal beside the bus station for 6 miles to Bo Tè village, then turn left (across the canal) on the first significant road. This soon degenerates into an outrageously rutted ox-cart track that is very slowly being regraded. Fork left at the only other junction. Coming by car or three-wheeler would be excruciatingly uncomfortable on these tracks. It's marginally less painful by motorcycle: with a driver you'll pay at least K12,000 return from Shwebo.

MANDALAY TO LASHIO

For an easy escape from the heat and smog of Mandalay, do what the colonial Brits always did – nip up to Pyin Oo Lwin. And once you've got going, why not continue further across the cool Shan Plateau to discover some of Southeast Asia's most satisfying short hill-tribe treks from Kyaukme or Hsipaw. But bring a decent fleece: although days are warm, it gets chilly after dark and can be downright cold at 5am when buses depart and markets are at their candlelit best.

Pyin Oo Lwin
ပြင်ဦးလွင်

☎ 085 / POP C70,000 / ELEV 3445FT

Founded by the British in 1896, the town was originally called Maymyo ('May-town'), after Colonel May of the 5th Bengal Infantry and was designed from its inception as a place to escape the Mandalay heat. Following the Indian-raj terminology for such places, it

has ever since been known as a 'hill station', though in fact it's almost entirely flat (just at raised elevation). After the construction of the railway from Mandalay, Maymyo became the summer capital for the British colonial administration, a role it held until the end of British rule in 1948. The name was changed after the British departed but numerous colonial half-timbered buildings remain. So too do the descendents of the Indian and Nepali workers who came here to lay the railway line.

In later decades, Pyin Oo Lwin was famous mostly for its fruit, jams, vegetables and fruit wines. And the huge military academies, built here to train the soldiers of the Tatmadaw (Myanmar Army). However, as Myanmar gets a new breed of nouveau riche, Pin Oo Lwin is once again becoming a popular weekend and hot-season getaway. The town is seeing a burst of investment, roads are getting busier and construction is beginning to fill up the once generous tree-shaded spaces between mansions in the wealthy southern quarter. Come quickly to experience what's left of the old calm.

◎ Sights

Getting around town by horse and cart adds to the nostalgic atmosphere, and by suitably manoeuvring the buggy you can add foreground interest to photos of the various colonial buildings.

Town Centre

Marking the town centre is the Purcell Tower a 1936 clock tower which thinks that it's Big Ben, judging from its quarter-hourly chimes. Around 6am, the pretty Maha Aung Mye Bon Thar Pagoda insists on broadcasting Buddhist lectures through its loudspeakers just in case you weren't already awake. The most important central pagoda is Shwezigone Paya, though it's not worth a special detour.

The red brick, Anglican All Saints' Church (Ziwaka St; ⊙services at 8.30am Sun, 7am Wed) was originally built in 1912 as the regimental church for Maymyo.

GARDENS AREA

TOP CHOICE National Kandawgyi Gardens
PARK
အမျိုးသားကန်တော်ကြီးဥယျာဉ်

(Nandan Rd; adult/child under 12yr/camera $5/2/1; ⊙8am-6pm) Founded in 1915 (though only officially recognised from 1924), this lovingly maintained 435-acre botanical garden features more than 480 species of flowers, shrubs and trees. For casual visitors its most appeal-

Factors to consider:

» If you want to cross the Chinese border, you'll need to get permits and do weeks of planning (see the boxed text, p267)

» Flying to/from Lashio is worth considering as a quick, comfortable way to link Hsipaw with Inle Lake or Yangon.

» The Mandalay–Lashio railway journey is extraordinarily slow and bouncy enough to inspire seasickness. However, it does offers trainspotters the joy of crossing the remarkable Gokteik Viaduct (see boxed text, p256) between Kyaukme and Pyin Oo Lwin.

» Cool, fresh Pyin Oo Lwin is barely two hours' drive from Mandalay.

» Contrary to what most Mandalay guesthouse owners will tell you, there is now an afternoon bus to Hsipaw (leaving Mandalay at 3.30pm).

ing aspect is the way flowers and overhanging branches frame views of Kandawgyi Lake's wooden bridges and small gilded pagoda. Admission costs include use of the swimming pool, visits to the **aviary** (⊘8am-5pm), **orchid garden**, **butterfly museum** (⊘8.30am-5pm) and the bizarre **Nan Myint Tower** (⊘lift operates till 5pm). Looking like a space-rocket designed for a medieval Chinese Emperor, this 12-storey structure offers panoramic views which are better appreciated from the external staircase than through the grease-smeared windows of the observation deck.

Annoyingly you can't use your bicycle to get around the extensive site so bring walking shoes and allow around two hours to do it justice. Using the southern entrance slightly reduces the walking you have to do. By 6pm either gate will likely be locked so watch the time – there are no closure warnings.

The garden's two entrances are both on the eastern side of Kandawgyi Lake, around a mile south of smaller Kandawlay Lake.

National Landmarks Garden MUSEUM
(adult/child $4/2; ⊘8am-6pm) This extensive hilly park is dotted with representations of famous landmarks from around Myanmar, in a selection of different scales. Some are pretty tacky. The entrance is across the main road from National Kandawgyi Gardens, a little to the north of their southern (main) entrance. There is also an **amusement park** (adult/child $4/2; ⊘8am-6pm) around 500 yard further north.

Circular Road NEIGHBOURHOOD
A good sprinkling of Pyin Oo Lwin's trademark colonial era buildings lie dotted amid the southeastern woodland suburbs as you'll see if you cycle Circular or Forest

Roads round to the Candacraig Hotel or the splendid **former Croxton Hotel** (Gandamar Myaing Hotel; Circular Rd). Some look like 1920s British homes, others like Louisiana plantation houses and the biggest have the air of St Trinian's, as with **Number 4 High School** (Circular Rd) and the **Survey Training Centre** (Multi-Office Rd). Up near the Shan Market, a fine half-timbered mansion is now a **Seventh Day Adventist Church** (Cherry St).

Chan Tak CHINESE TEMPLE
(134 Forest Rd) This large, classically styled, if mostly modern, Chinese temple comes complete with ornate stucco dragons, rock gardens, a vegetarian buffet restaurant, landscaped ponds and a seven-layered Chinese-style pagoda.

Candacraig Hotel HISTORIC BUILDING
(Thiri Myaing Hotel; ☑22047; Anawrattha Rd; s/d $42/48) Formerly the British Club, this classic colonial pile comes complete with side turrets and is set in attractively manicured gardens. It makes a popular film set for Burmese movie-makers. However, many locals believe the building to be haunted, and Westerners tend to avoid it due to its government affiliation (see p21), so it is not unusual to find the eight slightly discoloured guest rooms mostly unoccupied. Disappointingly there's no raj-redolent bar.

🏃 Activities

The 18-hole **Pyin Oo Lwin Golf Club** (☑22382; Golf Club Rd; green fee $10, caddy $4, club hire $5, shoe hire $1; ⊘6am-6pm) is one of Myanmar's better golf courses. However, it's government run (see p21) and has a strict dress code with collars, caps and rubber-spiked shoes compulsory.

Pyin Oo Lwin

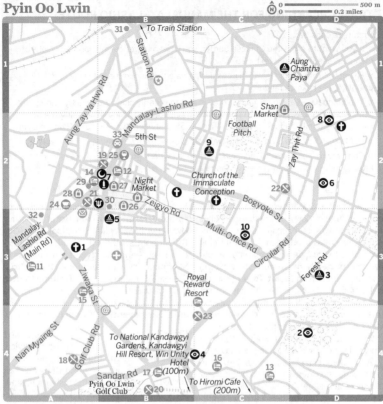

🛏 Sleeping

Many of Pin Oo Lwin's cheaper hotels aren't licensed to accommodate foreigners. Staying in the leafy gardens area south of the centre is a distinctively Pyin Oo Lwin experience; however, before heading out there, consider renting a bicycle. And carry a head-torch – those roads get very dark at night. Staying centrally is less evocative but more convenient for transport, shops and internet cafes.

Unless otherwise stated, breakfast is included in quoted rates.

TOWN CENTRE

Bravo Hotel BOUTIQUE HOTEL **$$**

(📞21223; www.bravo-hotel.com; Mandalay-Lashio Rd; r $25) Earthenware amphorae, ornate teak chests and carved gilded panel-work create the idea of a boutique hotel, a notion maintained (if somewhat diluted) in the comfortable rooms by brick- or bamboo-effect wallpaper. There are a few early

signs of wear but this remains a great value midrange option with breakfast served on the rooftop with its wide city views. Fridge and air-conditioning but no heating. When demand is low, single occupancy costs $15.

Golden Dream Hotel HOTEL **$**

(📞21302; 42/43 Mandalay-Lashio Rd; s/d $6/12, with shared bathroom $5/10) For the price this is about the best you'll find – perfectly survivable and while the colours aren't pretty, the walls are reasonably clean and beds not unbearably saggy. There are even windows in most rooms unlike the gruesomely discoloured, yet similarly priced, Grace 2 Hotel next door.

PALACE HILL

Aureum Governor's House HOTEL **$$$**

(📞21901; www.aureumpalacehotel.com/pyinool win-index.htm; off Mandalay Hwy; bungalows/ste $75/180) Whatever you may think of tycoon Tay Za, there's no doubt that this painstak-

⊙ Sights
1	All Saints' Church	A3
2	Candacraig Hotel	D4
3	Chan Tak	D3
4	Former Croxton Hotel	C4
5	Maha Aung Mye Bon Thar Pagoda	B3
6	Number 4 High School	D2
7	Purcell Tower	B2
8	Seventh Day Adventist Church	D2
9	Shwezigone Paya	C2
10	Survey Training Centre	C3

⊜ Sleeping
11	Aureum Governor's House	A3
12	Bravo Hotel	B2
13	Dahlia Motel	C4
14	Golden Dream Hotel	A2
15	Grace Hotel 1	A3
16	Royal Parkview Hotel	C4
17	Tiger Hotel	B4

⊗ Eating
18	Club Terrace	A4
19	Family Restaurant	B2
20	Feel	B4
21	Golden Triangle Café	A2
22	Sain Mya Ayar	C2
23	Woodland	C4

⊝ Drinking
24	Golden Lion	A2
25	Win Thu Zar	B2

⊜ Shopping
26	Central Market	B2
27	Liqueur Corner	B2
28	Pacific World Curio	A2

ⓘ Transport
29	Bike Shop	A2
30	Gandamar Land Handicrafts	B2
31	Pickup to Mandalay	B1
32	Pick-ups to Mandalay	A3
33	Share-Taxi Stand	B2
	Soe Moe Aung	(see 33)
	Win Yadana	(see 33)

ingly precise recreation of the former British governor's mansion is a considerable achievement. However, only five suites are within the main half-timbered mansion, with the remaining accommodation being in stylish but modern bungalows at the bottom of the extensive grounds (electric buggy links).

GARDENS AREA

Royal Parkview Hotel　　　　　HOTEL **$$**
(☏22641; royalparkview107@gmail.com; 107 Lanthaya St; standard s/d/tr $30/35/50, deluxe s/d $40/45; ❄☎) Still one of Pyin's most characterful mid-range options, there's neither royalty nor park views here, but long ceiling drapes create a fashionable edge to the restaurant and the complex is surrounded by trees and handkerchiefs of meticulously nurtured lawn. Rooms vary considerably in style and standard but all are attractive, most have terrace seating and the best deluxe ones have stone-clad showers, gift-wrapped curtains and miniature private 'gardens'.

Win Unity　　　　　HOTEL **$$**
(☏23079, 8 Nandar Rd; s/d/tr from $40/45/50; ❄@☎) Brand new in 2010, this semi-smart villa-hotel has sparkling clean rooms with matching softwood furniture, air-conditioning in superior rooms (add $5) and bathtubs in deluxe (add $12). It's just north of Kandawgyi Lake but with no views. Around the corner, the upmarket **Pyin Oo Lwin Hotel** (☎) is nearing completion.

Kandawgyi Hill Resort　　　　　HOTEL **$$$**
(☏21839; Nandar Rd; d/tr $65/80) Five of the 15 rooms are within a 1921 British-era house whose lounge is disappointingly plain but whose key asset is a delightful terrace and sitting deck commanding a large sweep of garden leading down to the lakefront road. The rest are well-spaced, well-appointed bungalows with wicker chairs on the terrace. It's one of very few hotels to have heating (important in January) and residents get free entry to the botanical gardens (both are Tay Za owned), saving $10 on a double room.

Grace Hotel 1　　　　　GUESTHOUSE **$**
(☏21230; 114A Nan Myaing Rd; s/d/tr $12/24/36) The major attraction here is the lovely garden with plenty of space to sun yourself, albeit on ageing, uncushioned loungers. The rooms aren't sophisticated but they're large with high ceilings and are good value for single travellers. Bicycles/motorbikes are available for rent for K3000/8000 per day.

TAY ZA IN PYIN OO LWIN

If you're worried about supporting government-affiliated businesses (see p21), you'll be a little stumped in Pyin Oo Lwin, where the town's foremost attraction, the Kandawgyi National Gardens, is now owned by Tay Za's Htoo Group as are most of the best hotels (Governor's House, Kandawgyi Lodge, Candacraig).

Dahlia Motel   GUESTHOUSE $

(☏22255, 105 Eidaw Rd; s/d/tr from $10/15/25, s/d with shared bathroom $5/10) The Dahlia is a friendly if nonaesthetic clump of coloured concrete buildings offering about the cheapest beds you'll find in the leafy 'burbs. Balconies are disappointingly designed to overlook a concrete car-park and some rooms are tatty with mildewed bathrooms, though others are quite acceptable – so look carefully. Water runs hot...eventually.

✗ Eating

The city centre has countless cheap, ordinary restaurant-teahouses and simple cafes, both along the main road and around the Central Market where a night market sees three blocks of Zaigyo St fill with **snack-food stands** (snacks from K200; ☺5.30-9pm). There's also a row of cheap eateries (Melody, Khitsan, Emperor) beside TKY Internet. However, if you can spend a little more money, a handful of stand-out restaurants can make dining in Pyin Oo Lwin a real pleasure.

[TOP CHOICE] **Club Terrace**   SOUTHEAST ASIAN $$

(☏23311; 25 Golf Club Rd; veg/nonveg mains K2500/3500, rice K600; ☺7am-9pm) Pyin Oo Lwin's most romantic restaurant occupies a gorgeous half-timbered colonial bungalow with tables spilling out onto the garden terrace. The food favours scrumptiously authentic Thai flavours but if you're chilli-intolerant there are also some Malaysian options and even fish and chips. Extensive wine selection. Shan noodles breakfasts cost K1200.

Woodland   EUROPEAN, THAI $$

(53 Circular Rd; mains K3000-6000; ☺9am-9.30pm; 🛜) This fashion conscious, if eclectic, design statement includes electric-blue panelling and a glass wall that reveals an aviary. The menu covers mostly European and Thai territory cooked with panache and served with flare. There's also a cocktail bar and free wi-fi.

Feel   EUROPEAN, PAN-ASIAN $$

(☏22083; off Nandar Rd; mains K2500-6000; ☺8.30am-9.30pm) The upmarket yet casual lakeside setting is an obvious attraction. And the vast range of excellent food lives up to the promise with well-honed local, Thai, Chinese and European flavours and occasional forays into sushi and sashimi that get the thumbs up from Japanese diners. Reservations are occasionally advisable for dinner. The comfy waterside cafe-terrace serves real espressos (K1400) and a plethora of cocktails (K2200 to K3600) but can get pretty cold on winter evenings.

Golden Triangle Café   BAKERY, CAFE $

(Mandalay-Lashio Rd; cakes, sandwiches & pizzas K500-2000; ☺7am-10pm) This upbeat Western-flavoured cafe occupies a column-fronted late-colonial building full of ceiling fans and big blackboard menus. It serves a range of coffees (K500 to K1800), juices, cakes, sandwiches, pizzas and burgers.

Family Restaurant   BURMESE, THAI $

(off Mandalay-Lashio Rd; meals K1500-5000; ☺9.30am-9pm) The decor is bland, if bright, and there's no alcohol (food is halal) but the delicious curry spread (K1500 to K2500) comes with complimentary rice, soup, pappadams and a 10-dish smorgasbord of salad vegies, side dishes, chutneys and dips. Pricier Thai and Chinese options are also available.

Sain Mya Ayar   CAFE, CHINESE $

(Zay Thit Rd; snacks/meals K500/2000; ☺6am-9pm) This family cafe fills a new pavilion in the small front yard of a modest half-timbered colonial-era house. Snack on dim sum (K500), delicious strawberry juice (K1000) and assorted cakes (K25 to K200 per piece).

🍸 Drinking

Hiromi Cafe   CAFE

(☏22685; 55D Aing Daw Rd; ☺8.30am-5.30pm) This cute, tiny timber cafe with fireplace and wrought-iron chairs is ideal for a coffee or glass of homemade plum wine while exploring the leafy lanes.

Tiger Hotel   BAR

(Golf Course Rd; beer K700; ☺8am-10pm) Thatched drinking pavilions attractively set between banana trees.

Win Thu Zar BEER STATION
(Mandalay-Lashio Rd; beer K500; ⌚8.30am-9pm) Standard male-dominated beer hall notable purely because it serves tastily smooth Spirulina 'anti-ageing' beer on draught (see boxed text, p134).

Golden Lion CAFE
(Mandalay- Lashio Rd; coffee K200; ⌚8am-4pm) Locally grown coffee is roasted out back and sold by the packet as well as cup-by-cup in this cheap, if dowdy, government shop-cafe (see p21).

Shopping

Central Market MARKET
(Zeigyo Rd; ⌚7am-5pm) Sample Pyin Oo Lwin's famous (if seasonal) strawberries, damsons, plums, passionfruit and other fruit, fresh, dried or as jams and wine.

Liqueur Corner ALCOHOL
(⌚7am-8pm) Booze shop stocking some local fruit wines

Pacific World Curio ANTIQUES, CRAFT
(75 Mandalay-Lashio Rd; ⌚8am-6pm) The best of several curio shops selling local 'antiques' and crafts

Information

Pyin Online (www.pyinoolwin.info)

Skynet (4th St; internet per hr K500; ⌚9am-10pm) Unusually fast internet...sometimes.

TKY Internet (per hr K500; ⌚9am-8pm) Handy for Grace Hotel 1.

Getting There & Away

Air

There's an airport at Anisakan but no commercial flights.

Bus, Pick-Up Trucks & Shared Taxi

Various Yangon-bound air-conditioned buses (K11,500 to K15,000, 13½ to 16 hours) depart between 2pm and 5pm from the farcically inconvenient main bus station **Thiri Mandala** (☎22633), hidden behind the gigantic Pyi Chit Pagoda, 2 miles east of the Shan market (K1500 by motorbike taxi). It's 600yd off the Lashio highway, on a road that branches southeast near the San Pya Restaurant. Beside that is Shi May clothing shop, which doubles as bus stand for the 7am and 4pm minibuses to Hsipaw (K4000). At around 7.30am shared taxis to Hsipaw and Kyaukme (back/front seat K14,000/16,000) also depart from here with pick-up trucks (K5000) starting from across the road (also 7.30am).

For Mandalay pick-ups (front/back K3000/2000 for foreigners, K2000/1500 locals) depart frequently from Thiri Mandala starting at 5am and becoming rarer in the later afternoon. More conveniently central, some pick-ups start from the petrol pump roundabout and a few start near the train station. At least three companies offer shared taxis (back/front K6000/6500). **Win Yadana** (☎22490) and **Soe Moe Aung** (☎21500) cars start across from 4th St. **Lwin Man** (☎21709) starts near the Central Market. Alternatively, pre-arrange a hotel pick-up (K500 extra). They'll generally drop you at any central Mandalay address for no extra cost.

Train

Eastbound Departs at 8.50am for Lashio (ordinary/upper $4/8, 10 hours) via the dramatic Gokteik Viaduct (two hours; see the boxed text, p256), Kyaukme ($2/4, four hours) and Hsipaw ($2/4, six hours).

Westbound If it's on time (rare!) the train to Mandalay ($2/3, 3½ hours) sits in Pyin Oo Lwin station for 1½ hours before finally leaving at 5.40pm.

Getting Around

'WAGONS' Pyin Oo Lwin's signature horse-drawn buggies are colourfully decorated and highly photogenic. Reckon around K1500 for a short trip across town, K12,000 for an all-day tour. Driver **Myou Min Thein** (☎09 204 5461) speaks a little English.

THREE-WHEEL PICK-UPS These congregate outside the market; around K2000 to Kandawgyi Gardens.

MOTORCYCLE TAXIS These are easiest to find beside Bravo Hotel. Also around K2000 to Kandawgyi Gardens. For longer hires, consider engaging English-speaking Bahein at **Gandamar Land Handicrafts** (main market stall AA5/6), who acts as guide and motorcycle driver for much the same price as you'd pay for any motorcycle taxi, eg K6000 including wait for Anisakan Falls.

BICYCLE The unmarked **bike shop** (Mandalay-Lashio Rd; ⌚7am-6pm) beside Grace II hotel rents bicycles (K3000 per day, K4000 for 24 hours).

Around Pyin Oo Lwin

TOWARDS MANDALAY

Anisakan Falls WATERFALL
အနီးစခန်းရေတံခွန်
(admission free) About 1.5 miles north of Anisakan village, the plateau disappears into an impressively deep wooded amphitheatre, its sides ribboned with several waterfalls. The most impressive of these is the gorgeous three-step **Dat Taw Gyaik** whose last stage thunders into a shady splash pool beside a small pagoda on the valley floor.

THE GOKTEIK VIADUCT

A highlight of the long, slow Mandalay–Lashio train ride is the mighty Gokteik Viaduct (ဂုတ်ထိပ်တံတား) about 34 miles northeast of Pyin Oo Lwin. Constructed in 1901 by contractors from the Pennsylvania Steel Company it bridges the Gokteik Gorge, a densely forested ravine that cuts an unexpectedly deep gash through the otherwise mildly rolling landscape. At 318ft high and 2257ft across, it was the second-highest railway bridge in the world when it was constructed, and remains Myanmar's longest. Trains slow to a crawl when crossing the viaduct to avoid putting undue stress on the ageing superstructure, which, despite some 1990s renovation work, still creaks ominously as trains edge their way across.

In either direction, the best views are from north-facing windows, that is the left side if you're heading towards Lashio. It's also visible through the trees for some time as the train winds down from the plateau and there are fine views from parts of Gokteik station (near the viaduct's western end) but beware that the train only stops there very briefly. Theoretically taking photographs of the viaduct is banned for 'security reasons', but in reality nobody seems to care.

To get here from Pyin Oo Lwin take the main Mandalay highway. In Anisakan town take the second asphalted turn right (signposted) and keep right past the first large pagoda. At the end of this road a pair of basic shack-restaurants mark the start of a forest trail along which the falls' base are reached by a 45-minute trek. While the way isn't too difficult to find, employing one of the sales kids as guide (K1000) can prove helpful especially if taking the 'alternative' route back (very steep, almost a climb).

The falls are best photographed in afternoon light from the lower view-terrace of the fabulous (but government affiliated) **Dat Taw Gyaik Waterfalls Resort** (☑50262; cottages $250) on other side of the amphitheatre. Each of its eight luxurious wooden bungalows comes with a stocked drinks cabinet and a large balcony equipped with loungers and a two-person spa tub from which to enjoy partial waterfall views. To find the resort take the easternmost asphalted turn north off the Mandalay–Pyin Oo Lwin highway in Anisakan (signposted for a meditation centre) and turn left immediately after crossing the railway.

CyberCity   NEW TOWN

About 12 miles south of Pyin Oo Lwin at Yatanarpon, CyberCity is part university town, part 21st-century Potëmkin village where most of the numerous high-tech factories are said to be just shells with signboards and oddments of trade waste left conspicuously outside to look genuine. The long term idea is to incubate industries here and attract inward investment once international sanctions fade.

TOWARDS KYAUKME

If you're driving to Kyaukme/Hsipaw, none of the following is more than a 2-mile detour from the main road but visiting by public transport will prove awkward. A round-trip half-day tour by motorcycle-taxi to all of the above from Pyin Oo Lwin should cost around K10,000. Sites are reviewed from west to east.

Aung Htu Kan Tha Paya   BUDDHIST TEMPLE

Although only finished in March 2000, this dazzling pagoda is by far the region's most impressive religious building. It enshrines an enormous 17-ton white-marble buddha statue that fell off a truck bound for China in April 1997. After several attempts to retrieve the buddha failed, it was decided that the statue 'had decided to stay in Myanmar'. Eventually cranes were used to yank him up the hill and a dazzling new golden pagoda was built for him. He is now draped in gilt robes and sits in a temple interior that's an incredible overload of gold. The pagoda is on a hilltop, just south of the Lashio-bound highway, around 15 minutes' drive beyond Pyin Oo Lwin's vast Defense Forces Technological Academy compound. If you reach the toll gates you've gone half a mile too far.

Pwe Kauk Falls   WATERFALL

ပွေးကောက်ရေတံခွန်

(admission K500, camera fee K300) Called Hampshire Falls in British times, Pwe Kauk is a fan of small weirs and splash pools rather than a dramatic waterfall but the forest glade setting is pretty. A series of little wooden bridges, souvenir stands and children's play areas add to the attraction for local families but undermine any sense of natural serenity. It's a two-minute drive down a steep, easily missed lane excursion off the Hsipaw road that starts directly north of Aung Htu Kan Tha Paya.

December Strawberry Farm   REST STOP
This invitingly stylish complex of new thatched pavilions on a rolling roadside lawn 2½ miles beyond Aung Htu Kan Tha Paya offers an easy stop for motorists to get a meal or taste locally produced fruit wines.

Myaing Gyi   VILLAGE
After descending a loop of hairpins, the Hsipaw road reaches pretty Myaing Gyi where a photogenic monastery climbs a wooded hillside. Two minutes' drive beyond the roadside Wetwun Zaigone Monastery is equally photogenic with a fine array of stupas and Balinese-style pagodas behind a gigantic old banyan tree.

Peik Chin Myaung   BUDDHA CAVE COMPLEX
ပိတ်ချင်း‌မြောင်း|‌ကျောက်မဲ
(admission/camera free/K300; ⊙6.30am-4.30pm) Many Buddha caves are little more than rocky niches or overhangs but Peik Chin is much more extensive. It takes around 15 minutes each way to walk to the cave's end (longer when crowded) following an underground stream past a whole series of colourfully painted scenes from Buddhist scriptures interspersed with countless stupas and buddha images. There are a few sections where you'll need to bend over to get beneath dripping rocks but most of the cave is high-ceilinged and adequately lit so you don't need a torch. It can feel sweaty and humid inside. No shorts or footwear permitted.

The access road is around 2½ miles east of Myaing Gyi, just beyond the green sign announcing your arrival in Wetwun town. Turn right through a lion-guarded gateway arch then descend inexorably for another 2 miles to the large parking area thronged with souvenir stalls.

Kyaukme
ကျောက်မဲ
☑082 / POP C85,000 / ELEV APPROX 900M
Pronounced 'chao-may', Kyaukme is a low-rise district centre with a gently attractive central market area bracketed by monastery-topped hills, each only 15 minutes' walk away using steep, covered stairways. The main at-

traction is hiking and motor-biking options into surrounding Shan and Palaung hill villages (see boxed text, p258). Although Kyaukme is rather bigger than Hsipaw, the town is far less accustomed to travellers and there's only one foreigner-licensed guesthouse. Kyaukme means 'black stone', fitting a folkloric belief that its citizens were dishonest traders of precious (or not so precious) gems.

🛏 Sleeping & Eating
A Yone Oo Guest House (☑40183; Shwe Phi Oo Rd; s/d from $15/18, luxury $25/30, with shared bathroom from $4/8) is the only accommodation for foreigners. The cheapest options are basic bed-spaces with hardboard separators – noisy, and the shared squat toilets are across the yard. Pay a few dollars more per person and the beds are better, walls are thicker and the shared bathroom has hot water. The luxury rooms set around the rear courtyard are vastly better appointed and come with fridge, air-conditioning and heater but so too do the slightly larger, decently maintained $18 doubles, arguably the best deal here. Management speaks some English. Evenings, the hotel has a barbecue stall out front. There's a greater dining choice around the cinema, three blocks south.

ⓘ Getting There & Away
Bus
Buses to Hsipaw (7am, noon and 4pm) plus the 7am air-conditioned bus to Lashio start from the southwest corner of the market, two blocks south of the guesthouse.

Four buses to Mandalay all leave around 5.30am from a bus terminal, just across the rail tracks, around 10 minutes further north. Mu-se–Hsipaw–Mandalay buses mostly stay on the AH16, bypassing Kyaukme by over a mile, though some halt at the Mao or Nentang Dan restaurants for lunch (a K1500 motorcycle ride from town).

Taxi & Motorcycle
Oddly, a taxi to Mandalay (typically K60,000) is more expensive from Kyaukme than from Hsipaw and there's no share taxi system. The guesthouse can help you organise motorcycle rentals. Note that the gem-mining town of Mogok is now completely off limits to foreigners – if you travel too far along the road running north from Kyaukme, you will be turned back. The rough Kyaukme to Namhsan road is closed to foreigners northbound.

Train
From the guesthouse the train station is a 10-minute walk west then north.

TREKKING FROM KYAUKME

Typical walking destinations have an unspoilt charm that challenges even those around Hsipaw. But Kyaukme itself is pretty spread out so most treks start with a motorcycle ride to a suitable trailhead. This is typically included in guide-fees, which cost around K25,000 for a couple plus K15,000 per additional walker. For longer motorbike trails you'll need to add K10,000 per day for bike rental plus petrol.

Naing-Naing (☎09 4730 7622; naingninenine@gmail.com), nicknamed '9-9', is Kyaukme's best-known guide. He has a fascinating background and an extensive knowledge of the entire area. The guesthouse has copies of his hand-drawn hiking and biking schematic regional map. **Thura** (☎09 4730 8497; www.thuratrips.tl) has also been recommended.

Eastbound Departs 1.50pm for Hsipaw (ordinary/upper class $2/4, two hours)
Westbound Departs 11.25am for Mandalay ($3/6, 10½ hours) via Gokteik Viaduct (2½ hours) and Pyin Oo Lwin ($3/6, five hours).

Hsipaw
သီပေါ

☎082 / POP C54,000 / ELEV APPROX 700M

The trickle of foreigners who make it to Hsipaw ('see-paw' or 'tee-bor'), mostly arrive for hill-tribe treks that are easy to organise and handily short yet 'unspoilt' in a way you'll rarely find around Kalaw or anywhere in northern Thailand. Hsipaw itself is smaller yet more historic than Lashio or Kyaukme. It has just enough tourist infrastructure to be convenient yet it still feels thoroughly genuine. Though architectural remnants are fairly limited, this was once a Shan royal city. Local historians claim that 19th-century prince Sao So Chae was knighted by Queen Victoria while the last *sawba* (Shan prince), Sao Kya Seng, became the tragic hero of a book by his Austrian wife (see boxed text, p259).

◉ Sights & Activities

The present town centre, Tyaung Myo, only dates back to the early 20th century. The main monasteries, stupas and former palace lie on higher ground around a mile further north in Myauk Myo.

Central Riverfront NEIGHBOURHOOD
Hsipaw's riverside **produce market** (◷4.30am-1pm) is most interesting before dawn when the road outside is jammed with hill-villagers (Shan, Palaung, Lisu) selling their wares: all will have cleared away by 7am. Between here and the large **central market** (◷8am-5pm) are four column-fronted 19th-century **godowns** (warehouses, one now used as a schoolroom) and a **banyan tree** worshipped by locals as a *nat* (spirit) shrine, though reverence doesn't prevent the nearby riverbank being used as a smelly rubbish tip.

Mahamyatmuni Paya BUDDHIST TEMPLE
(Namtu Rd) South of the central area, **Mahamyatmuni Paya** is the biggest and grandest pagoda in the main town. The large brass-faced buddha image here was inspired by the famous Mahamuni buddha (p208) in Mandalay. He's now backed by an acid-trip halo of pulsating coloured lights that would seem better suited to a casino.

Myauk Myo NEIGHBOURHOOD
Towards the northern edge of town, Hsipaw's oldest section today has a village-like atmosphere and two delightful old teak monasteries. The multifaceted wooden **Madahya Monastery** looks particularly impressive when viewed across the palm-shaded pond of the **Bamboo Buddha Monastery** (Maha Nanda Kantha), whose 150-year-old lacquered buddha is made from bamboo strips (now hidden beneath layers of gold). Around and behind lie a few clumps of ancient brick stupas, some being overwhelmed by vegetation in vaguely Angkor Wat style. The nickname for this area, **Little Bagan**, blatantly overplays the size and extent of the sites but the area is undoubtedly charming.

To get here cross the big bridge on Namtu St heading north. Turn first left at the police station, then first right and fork left. Take this lane across the railway track then follow the main track as it wiggles.

To return by an alternative route, take the unpaved track east behind the Bamboo Buddha monastery, rapidly passing **Eissa Paya** (where one stupa has a tree growing out of it). You'll emerge near **Sao Pu Sao Nai**, a colourful shrine dedicated to the guardian *nat* of Hsipaw. Rather than turning left into the shrine, turn right and you'll reach Namtu Rd a little north of the railway.

Several years ago, one of the most interesting Hsipaw experiences used to be a visit to the fading 1924 Shan palace-villa in the company of the charming Mr Donald, nephew of Sao Kya Seng, who had been the area's last *sawbwa* (Shan prince). Sao Kya Seng vanished during the 1962 military takeover, an event powerfully described by his wife, Inge Sargent, in the book *Twilight over Burma: My Life as a Shan Princess*. History in Myanmar has a habit of repeating itself. In 2005 Mr Donald was himself arrested and sentenced to 13 years in prison. The dubious charges were of 'operating as an unlicensed tour guide and defaming the State', but few doubted it was part of a coordinated crackdown on tribal leaders. In 2009 Mr Donald was conditionally released, but with nine years probation. Reportedly the probation conditions specify that if he so much as talks to a foreigner he'll be sent back to jail. So please don't think it a clever wheeze to visit him by climbing over the heavily chained palace gates. If you want to get an idea of the palace's design, a safer alternative is to head to Hsipaw's Don Bosco Catholic Seminary, whose main building was created by the same architect in a similar 1920s suburban-English style.

Sunset Hill
VIEWPOINT

For sweeping views across the river and right over Hsipaw, climb to **Thein Daung Pagoda** also known as Five Buddha Hill or, most popularly, Sunset Hill. It's part of a steep ridge that rises directly behind the Lashio road, around 1½ miles south of Hsipaw. Cross the new river bridge, follow the main road left then take the laterite track that starts with a triple-crowned temple gateway around 300m beyond. There's a small English sign at the gateway. The climb takes around 15 minutes. At the time of research it was possible to loop back to central Hsipaw along a horribly dusty road on the river's east bank, passing an attractive timber monastery building before crossing the river on a pontoon bridge north of the sports field. However, the pontoons are scheduled for removal during 2011 or 2012.

Bawgyo Paya
BUDDHIST TEMPLE

Five miles west of Hsipaw, this pagoda is of great significance to Shan people and gets overloaded with pilgrims who arrive en masse during the annual **Bawgyo Paya Pwe** culminating on the full moon day of Tabaung (February/March).

The pagoda's current incarnation is an eye-catching 1995 structure of stepped gilded polygons, within which the dome supposedly incorporates genuine rubies. The name translates loosely as 'Dad come and get me', and the original pagoda was built centuries earlier by a heartbroken Shan king who had married off his daughter, warrior-princess Saw Mun La, to the Burmese king as part of a Shan-Burma peace deal. The Burmese king adored her but, as the seventh wife in his harem, her presence and growing favour

caused trouble. Jealous concubines set about denouncing her as a spy. The king didn't fall for the lies but realised that he'd better get her out of his court before the other wives murdered her. The plan should have worked, but on the long, arduous route back to her father's court she fell ill. The Shan king was sent for but arrived to find her already dead of a mystery sickness. The point where she died became the site of a pagoda to underline Shan-Burmese friendship.

It's beside the Hsipaw–Kyaukme road: you'll get a brief glimpse from the right-hand windows of any Kyaukme- or Mandalay-bound bus.

🏃 Activities

Hiking

Each of the guesthouses can organise guides (around K10,000 per day) to take you on a range of fascinating treks into the hills above town visiting Shan, Palaung and Lisu villages. Mr Charles Guest House (p260) is especially well organised and most evenings there'll be someone sitting on the front terrace to answer questions about the various options. Generally a next-day departure is possible if you don't want anything too adventurous. Pankam (see boxed text, p262) is a good one-/two-day choice. Trekking without a guide is less satisfying (very few villagers speak English) but it is possible – get someone to write down your destination in local script before departing. Most villages have motorcycle tracks too, so it may be possible to pay a villager to drive you back if you're fed up, though finding a bike isn't always straightforward.

Hsipaw

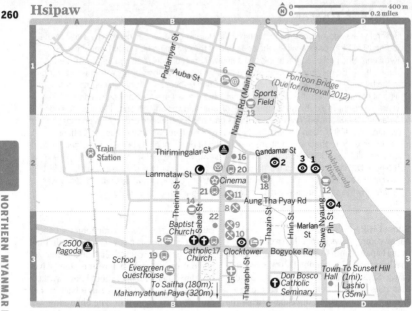

Workshop Visits

If you don't fancy walking so far, there are various workshops and mini factories around town, where you can see locals carrying out cottage industries like weaving, noodle manufacturing, dipping-candle making, cheroot rolling and even popcorn popping. All these are marked on the map in the reception at Mr Charles Guest House. Or find a guide to combine a few workshop visits with, perhaps, a field-stroll to Parpeit village and hot springs.

🛏 Sleeping

TOP CHOICE Mr Charles Guest House HOTEL **$**
(☑80105; 105 Auba St; s/d from K10,000/15,000, with shared bathroom K4500/9000, air-con r from K22,000; ❄) This well-run travellers' magnet covers all bases from simple, hard-bedded backpacker basics to relatively snazzy new-block rooms where every extra Kyat you pay gets something slightly nicer. For air-conditioning and balcony reckon K22,000. Fancy bath fittings and more contemporary decor start at K30,000. Staff can arrange all manner of transport, treks and tours and each building has an enticing communal upstairs balcony where guests swap travel stories late into the evening. Dollars can be changed at

poor rates. Breakfast is included but served in the yard (bring a blanket!)

Golden Doll/Mr Kid GUESTHOUSE **$**
(☑80066; 124 Bogyoke Rd; s/d $6/10, with shared bathroom $5/8) The obliging, if laid-back, family welcome makes this feel like an overgrown homestay. Conditions are basic and there are a handful of coffin-box singles (normally for locals only) but several rooms have been revamped, some with half-timber effects, others with wooden panelling and most with fine new mattresses. However, the shared bathrooms are dimly lit and across the yard.

Nam Khae Mao GUESTHOUSE **$**
(☑80077; nkmao@myanmar.com.mm; 134 Bogyoke Rd; s/d from K11,000/13,000, with shared bathroom K4000/8000) The cheapest bare-box rooms come with bubbling paintwork and shared squat toilets. En suite rooms are more presentable and the best K18,000 rooms have air-conditioning and hot water, though they are accessed off a communal TV room that's often packed full of local guests.

🍴 Eating & Drinking

A selection of dining options is strung out along Namtu Rd. Most are relatively basic having made few attempts to gentrify their old wooden or half-timbered shophouses. Eateries scattered south of the town hall along the road towards the Lashio bridge are even more rickety. Several cafes double as de facto bus stands, such as the Duhtawadi Cafe.

Street vendors outside the cinema sell *moun-ou-khalei* (rice-flour balls) and *kaukpout* ('cow-po') rounds of pounded sticky brown rice that are barbecued then sprinkled with jaggary and sesame.

San SHAN, CHINESE $
(Namtu Rd; meals K1000-2500, barbecue items from K100; ☺8am-9.30pm) It's under-lit and far from stylish but cosier than many alternatives; the barbecue is well stocked, large Dali beers cost only K800 and there's a bilingual picture menu of other options.

Best Place CAFE $
(Aung Tha Paya St; shakes K500-800; ☺7am-10pm) In this archetypal part-timbered teahouse, 'Mr Shake' speaks English while his wife whizzes up scrumptious lassis using grated coconut and Pyin Oo Lwin strawberries (seasonal).

Law Chun ('Mr Food') CHINESE $$
(Mr Food; Namtu Rd; mains K1000-4000; ☺8am-8.45pm) 'Mr Food' stands out very obviously from the pack due to its bright white, if far from atmospheric, interior. The Chinese food is reliable and there's draught Dagon beer on tap.

Valentines ICE-CREAM PARLOUR $
(Sabal St; shakes K500; ☺11am-9pm) Cold drinks, shakes and ice creams in a clean,

modern, if over-cutesy, environment with kiddy-chairs on the pavement and relatively little passing traffic to disturb you.

La Wün Aung CAFE $
(Namtu Rd; mains K800-1500; ☺6am-10pm) One of several low-key teahouse bars that hide the sports field but make amends by screening international football matches. Being handy for Mr Charles Guest House and open relatively late, it gets plenty of traveller business.

Black House Coffee Shop CAFE $
(23 Shwe Nyaung Pin St; coffee from K800, banana cake K500; ☺6am-6pm) The airy, 75-year-old teak shophouse is backed by a wide river-facing yard, a delightful, if relatively unsophisticated, place to linger over a coffee made from Shan beans grown in Taunggyi.

❶ Information

The guesthouses are good sources of reliable advice about things to do and see. A remarkable source of local information and history is Ko Zaw Tun, who is known locally as Mr Book, as he runs a small **book stall** (Namtu Rd; ☺7am-8.15pm) opposite the entrance to the Central Pagoda (which his own family helped to build).

There are several internet cafes but connection breaks down frequently.

❶ Getting There & Away
Bus & Pick-Up Trucks

There's no single bus stand. Instead buses leave from a confusing plethora of shops/cafes notably

Khaing Dhabyay (📞80349; Mandalay Rd), Ye Shin (📞80159; Namtu Rd) and helpful Duhtawa-di Cafe (📞80116; Lanmataw St), which can also organise taxis when cars are available. Apart from services listed here, other through buses between Lashio/Mu-se and Mandalay often stop for lunch or snacks at Ah Kong Kaik ('Myanmar Traditional Food'; cnr Namtu & Bogyoke Rds).

Magwe/Pyay 9am from Khaing Dhabyay (K12,000/16,000).

Mandalay Departs at 5.30am (air-con expresses from Duhtawadi, Yetagon and Ye Shin, K5000, around six hours), 6.30am (slow bus from Duhtawadi), 9am (air-con from Khaing Dhabyay, K5000) continuing to Magwe (K12,000) and Pyay (K16,000).

Kyaukme Departs from Duhtawadi corner (K1000, one hour) at 8am, 9.30am, 11am, noon (air-con ex-Lashio), 3pm, 4.20pm (air-con ex-Lashio). There's also an 8am minibus from Pwai (Namtu Rd).

Yangon A Mangshwe Pyi bus bound for Yangon (K14,500, 15 to 18 hours) calls at the Khaing Dhabyay shop around 1pm.

Shared Taxi

Mandalay (front/back seat K13,000/11,000, whole car K45,000) from the Duhtawadi Cafe around 7am.

Kyaukme Charter only, K25,000.

Lashio Charter only, K40,000.

Train

Hsipaw's tiny train station is across the tracks from the end of Thirimingalar St.

Eastbound Departs 3.15pm for Lashio (lower/upper class $2/4, 4½ hours)

Westbound Departs 9.40am to Mandalay ($4/9) via Kyaukme ($1/2), Naungkhio ($1/2) and Pyin Oo Lwin ($3/6).

ⓘ Getting Around

Trishaws rides start from K500; they wait by the market. Bicycles can be rented from Mr Charles and Nham Khae Mao guesthouses. Saifha (📞80566; Minepon St; ⏰7am-5pm) rents out 125CC motorcycles for between K8000 and K10,000 per day. So do Mr Charles and Nham Khae Mao guesthouses.

Around Hsipaw

NAMHSAN
နမ္မတ္
POP 32,000 / ELEV 5249FT

High in the Shan Hills, Namhsan is a fascinating ridge-top town that looks out over

PANKAM VILLAGE TREK

The sizeable, traditional Palaung ridge-village of Pankam makes a deservedly popular short-trek destination from Hsipaw. While other villages have better views, a key advantage here is that the charming young head man, O Maung, speaks good English and his family readily offers bed-and-dinner to walkers in their archetypal teak home (K6000 per person). Walking up from Hsipaw takes around five hours at a very modest pace, crossing flat fields before climbing through timeless stilt-house hamlets including Na Lowe, Na Muu, Man Piet and Beng Puie. In each Shan settlement en route you'll find a *kin-gyiao*, a wooden phallus placed above a buried urn of vegetable oil to ensure field fertility. Villages are protected from evil spirits by gateways with crossed wooden knife symbols. And, beside the main temple in Pankam, you'll find a classic shrine-box where a nativity-style doll-scene depicts the legendary bestowal of tea seeds upon the Palaung in the 12th century. The Buddha-like figure represents Burma's 'traveller king' Alaungsithu who had come to the Shan mountains in search of rubies, before eventually turning into a powerful *nat* spirit after his murder in 1167! Here, Alaungsithu is seen handing out tea seeds to kneeling Palaung leaders. One such chief, embarrassed by the hole in his black baggy trousers, covered the hole with one hand and so rudely received the gift with the other – politeness required receiving gifts with both hands. This jolly legend gave rise to the Palaung name for tea, Lapet, a contraction of Latopet (one hand). And to this day the Palaung tribe see tea cultivation as a semi-divine raison d'etre – as well as good business.

From Hsipaw there are several ways to visit Pankam: as part of a multiday trek, hiking out and back in two days, or trekking in one day then engaging one of the villagers to run you back on a motorbike (around K3000 to Hsipaw, but K8000 back). With a guide (recommended) you can start by simply crossing the fields northwest of Mr Charles Guest House. Without a guide it's easier to take the road towards Mandalay for 1 mile then branch right beside a lone noodle shack where the main road swerves sharp right at the far edge of Hsipaw. Then keep asking!

a sea of rucked-up mountain ridges and plunging ravines. The surrounding slopes are covered by tea plantations that are the mainstay of Namhsan's economy. Two possible one-day return hikes take you up to superb viewpoints at Taung Yo monastery and atop Loi San ('Ruby Mountain'). The scenic (if rough) journey to reach Namhsan from Hsipaw is an attraction in itself while trekking back again to Hsipaw (two nights and three days) is an ideal way to stay in timeless villages en route. Hsipaw's Mr Charles Guest House can help suggest guides. Namhsan has a very simple guesthouse (per person K3000) and in the past, some locals have offered homestays.

❶ Getting There & Away

Shared jeeps to Namhsan (K6000) run at least five times a week from Kyaukme bus stand picking up passengers in Hsipaw (same price) by pre-arrangement on ☏09 4730 6067. Ask your guesthouse to call for you. From Hsipaw, renting your own jeep will cost around K60,000.

The beautiful but tough motorbike ride takes almost four hours: the route is signed at a roundabout 17 miles towards Namtu from Hsipaw. Maps show a direct Namhsan to Kyaukme secondary road. Part of this road is out of bounds to foreigners and you won't get through the halfway checkpoint if you're heading to Namhsan. However, returning that way you might make it. Ask local advice before trying this.

Lashio

 လားရှိုး
☏082 / POP C130,000 / ELEV 2805FT

Lashio (pronounced '*lar*-show') is a sprawling market town with a significant Chinese population. You're most likely to come here for the airport – the nearest to Hsipaw. Or, if you've managed to organise the necessary permits, to meet your guide for the four-hour drive to the Chinese border at Mu-se (see boxed text, p267). Lashio is a large but unassuming place that straggles up a gently sloping valley ringed by dragon-backed ridges, abrupt hillocks and terraced vegetable plots. Once the seat of an important Shan *sao pha* (sky lord), the town played a pivotal role in the fight against the Japanese in WWII. It was the starting point of the Burma Road, which supplied food and arms to Chiang Kai-Shek's Kuomintang army. Not much evidence of either historical period remains today, and most of the city's old wooden homes were destroyed in

a disastrous 1988 fire. However, a few interesting pagodas survive amongst the lacklustre 20th-century architecture.

⊙ Sights & Activities

Lashio's sights wouldn't warrant a significant detour but there's plenty to investigate should you find yourself here for a day.

Thatana (Sasana) 2500-
Year Paya   BUDDHIST STUPA
Lashio's most evocative sight, this small gilded stupa gleams alluringly among ridge-top trees above the town centre. It was reportedly built by Sao Hon Phan, the last Shan 'sky king'. Mist-layered after dawn, the town looks its best from the stupa's terrace. Walking up here takes around 20 minutes following the second lane that slopes northeast after the Kachin Baptist Church. The fastest way back down is a long steep stairway passing a large, distinctive concrete ball monument called Khabar Aye.

Central Lashio   NEIGHBOURHOOD
A few decrepit old wooden buildings and an eye-catching central mosque aren't quite enough to bring a photogenic quality to predominantly concrete central Lashio. However, the pre-dawn morning market (Bogyoke Rd; ⊙4.30am-7am) is particularly endearing when many vegetable sellers light their wares with flickering candles. Between the large main market and the Nannhaewon Amusement Park, is the eye-catching Mahamyatmuni Paya (La Ma Daw St), an open-sided pavilion enshrining a dazzle-faced seated Buddha along the lines of Mandalay's Mahamuni. If you walk towards the Hsipaw bus stand you'll pass the pretty 1994 Maha Bodayaong temple, whose unrefined seven-storey church-like tower offers decent townscape views – assuming you find a monk who'll let you climb it.

Quan Yin Shang   CHINESE TEMPLE
Part way up the wooded ridge at the southern edge of town, this large temple-nunnery is the principal place of worship for Lashio's large Chinese community. Squint briefly at the main buildings and they appear to be olde-worlde Chinese temples with classic tip-tilted traditional roofs. However, on closer inspection they are somewhat gaudy 20th-century versions while the flanking brick nuns' residences are contrastingly dour. The main prayer hall contains a trio of buddha-like

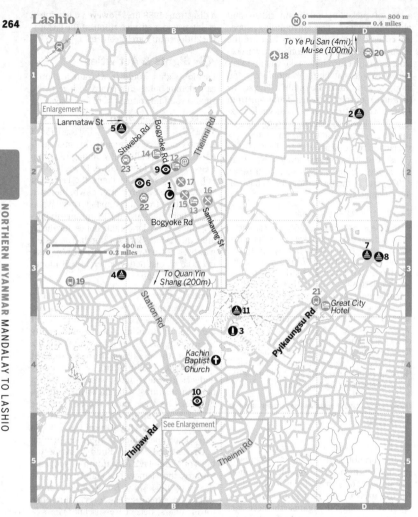

figures held aloft on gilded, disembodied hands. You might find visiting Quan Yin Shang worthwhile to discover the surrounding low-rise back-streets and for glimpses of ridge and karst horizons. From the market area, three-wheel pick-ups charge K3000 return.

Mansu Paya   BUDDHIST MONASTERIES
Beyond the bus station, the main road bends between the two halves of the gold and stucco Mansu Paya, said to be over 250 years old. One side of the monastery is archetypal Shan, the other is Burmese with a notable octagonal stupa. Hidden by school buildings

just off the main road, around a mile further north, is another century-old Shan monastery, Kamenjaung Paya.

Ye Pu San   HOT SPRINGS
ရေပူစမ်း
(local/foreigner K100/$3, parking K500) This popular local bathing place is a pea-green artificial pond ringed by a handful of stalls and crossed by a rickety pair of rough plank bridges. The water is perfectly bathwater-warm and the rural agricultural setting is pleasant enough but it's hard to justify the hefty foreigner entry fee or the K3000 each

Lashio

way pick-up hire to get here (4 miles from town, a mile or so off the Mu-se road).

World Peace Pagoda   BUDDHIST TEMPLE
(Hsipaw Rd) This massive new golden stupa on the far western edge of town is visible for a short time (on the right) from the Hsipaw-bound bus.

🛏 Sleeping

Room rates in Lashio are the same for singles and doubles, and don't include breakfast.

Thi Da Aye   HOTEL $
(✆22165; Thiri Rd; budget/standard/air-con r from $5/15/18, tr from $18; ❄) Standard rooms are clean, if functional, high-ceilinged boxes but for minimal extra cash the newest rooms (small/suite $20/30) are a vast step up in quality with new tiled floors, good bathrooms and very comfy mattresses. The cheapest

basement dives are, in contrast, musty with saggy beds, sorry little squat-toilet cubicles and headless showers.

Royal Ground   HOTEL $
(✆25516; Theinni Rd; r with shower/bath $17/19; ❄) Clean, all-air-con motel-like place with 35 rooms on two floors that extend well back from the busy road. Showers in some are a little rusty and little English is spoken but it's next door to the town's most central internet cafe.

Ya Htaik   HOTEL $
(✆22655; Bogyoke Rd; fan/air-con r $15/18, ste $25; ❄) Fair-sized rooms are perfectly bearable and beds are comfy but the puke green walls are off-putting and several fittings are in need of a little freshening up. Suites are bigger but not better, apart from a balcony in some. The lift shaft still has no lift.

🍴 Eating

There are a selection of food stalls around the junction of Theinni Rd and Bogyoke St, and many many more appear after 5pm as part of the bustling **night market** (⊙5pm-9pm). Shan specialities here include pig-organ hotpots, Shan noodle soup and savoury cakes made from steamed purple sticky rice and sesame seeds.

Sun Moon Café   CHINESE, THAI $
(Bogyoke Rd; meals K1500; ⊙9am-9pm) Above an over-lit bakery, this is about the brightest, cleanest and most Western-friendly eatery in central Lashio albeit without any real hint of style. The picture menu helps you guess what you're ordering.

Royal Restaurant   CHINESE $
(Samkaung St; barbecue items per stick from K100, meals K1000-8000; ⊙11am-10pm) Every bit as grubby and uninviting as most of the downmarket central eateries, but the barbecue food's fine and you can wash it down with draught Myanmar Beer (K650). The all-in-Burmese menu also offers whole fish (K5000), hotpot (K8000) and fried rice (K1000).

ℹ Information

ST Internet (Theinni Rd; per hr K500; ⊙8am-10pm)

ℹ Getting There & Away
Air
Asian Wings operates a new hopper flight on a Yangon–Heho–Mandalay–Lashio–Tachileik

route but as yet this is a public charter with no fixed schedule. Yangon to Lashio costs around $135, Mandalay to Lashio $70. Air Kanbawza has announced plans for Lashio flights in future.

On arrival don't panic if your baggage doesn't appear in the tiny terminal building while you're being quizzed by immigration officers: in fact bags are disconcertingly delivered to a shed outside the airport compound gate.

Bus

Long distance services use the **Main Bus Station** (Pyikaungsu Rd) opposite the Great City Hotel, about 1 mile north of centre. Services include:

Mandalay Air-con buses depart at 8am and 6pm (K5000, eight hours), travelling via Pyin Oo Lwin (six hours) and Kyaukme (three hours)

Mu-se Regular buses (four hours) and a good road but foreigners are never allowed.

Nay Pyi Taw Departs 6am (K9000, 14 hours).

Taunggyi Departs 7am (K15,000, 15 hours). However, most long-distance bus companies are highly reluctant to sell tickets to foreigners, citing the dangers to the driver of your presence (should he crash he faces a serious backlash).

The local bus station, 300m west of Daowadengda Pagoda, is a series of shophouses doubling as bus offices. The first one on the right offers useful services to Hsipaw (K1500, two hours) at 9.30am, 11am, 12.30pm and 2.30pm. Ideally buy tickets a couple of hours ahead.

Taxi

Shared taxis wait in front of the main bus station (mostly before 10am), charging K35,000 per person to Taunggyi, between K13,000 and K15,000 per person to Mandalay (eight hours) depending on the season (assuming four in a car). There's no discount if you get off in between at Hsipaw (two hours), Kyaukme (three hours) or Pyin Oo Lwin (six hours). By arrangement most will pick up at your hotel.

Train

Lashio's miniature train station is 2 miles north of the market, a K1500 pick-up ride. At 5am the one daily train departs to Mandalay (ordinary/upper class $6/12, 16 hours) via Pyin Oo Lwin ($2/4, four hours) and Hsipaw ($4/8, 11 hours). Ticket sales only start at 4.30am the same morning.

ⓘ Getting Around

From the Theinni Rd–Bogyoke St junction, shared three-wheeler pick-up trucks (K300) shuttle down past the bus station and Mansu pagodas, terminating at a major junction ('Lashio Gyi') half a mile east of the airport. Occasional shared rides from there run to the hot springs. Chartered three-wheelers costs around K1500 per hop within town. Taxis from the airport ask a steep K5000.

THE FAR NORTH

Myanmar's far northern range of Himalayan 'Ice Mountains' is one of the world's least-known 'last frontiers'. Hkakabo Razi (19,295ft), the nation's loftiest summit, is over a half a mile higher than Mont Blanc and had never been climbed until 1996. Perhaps that's not surprising given that the trek to reach its base camp took almost a month. The surrounding Hkakabo Razi National Park is considered a treasure trove of biodiversity. Landscapes here are similar to those found in the Indian state of Arunachal Pradesh – steep forests, ridges of peaks bursting through the snowline and deep valleys carved by fast-flowing mountain rivers. Further south is the Hukaung Valley Tiger Reserve (www.panthera.org/programs/tiger/ tigers-forever/Myanmar), which, at 6748 square miles, is larger than all of India's tiger reserves put together.

The far north has sparse populations of Kachin, Rawang, Lisu and even a handful of Taron, the only known pygmy group in Asia. Set well back from the higher peaks, the only settlement of any size is Putao, an oddly diffuse place that has a market but no other real sense of a town centre. This was the site of the isolated British WWII military outpost, Fort Hertz, though there's no fortress to visit.

Today the region still feels (and genuinely is) entirely cut off from the rest of Myanmar. This may change as the airport runway gets extended and new tourism facilities are being developed. But for now, to get even the briefest possible glimpse, you'll have to do an organised 'tour', costing from around $600 per person for the shortest four-day option. That will get you to one or two photogenic suspension footbridges and some unspoilt rural villages, though the latter aren't markedly different from similar settlements elsewhere in rural north Myanmar. Unless you trek for many days further, the Himalayan horizon will remain fairly distant, and might stay hidden altogether by rain clouds. So is it worth the trouble? That really depends on how you value exclusivity. If you're comparing tourist numbers, Putao makes Bhutan look like a veritable Benidorm.

The best time to visit is from October to April, when daytime temperatures are quite pleasant and nights are cold but rarely freezing.

The border crossing between **Mu-se** and **Ruili** (Shweli) in China is nominally open to travellers. However, getting to Mu-se requires a permit that will take at least two weeks to be issued and even then is only available if you book a package including car, driver and guide through Myanmar Travels & Tours (MTT) in Yangon (p69) or Mandalay (p219). This will cost around $200 from Lashio where your guide will collect you at a pre-designated hotel. You'll need to have your Chinese visa already. In reverse you'll need to organise things through a travel agency in Kunming where there's also a **Myanmar consulate** (☏0871-360 3477; www.mcg-kunming.com; Room A504, Long Yuan Hao Zhai, 166 Wei Yuan Jie; ⏰8.30am-noon & 1-2pm Mon-Fri).

Permits are also required for the appallingly rough Mu-se–Namhkam–Bhamo road. MTT Mandalay (p219) can fix things and provide a Lashio–Bhamo vehicle for $350/370/390 (one/two/three passengers) but again you'll need at least two weeks prep time. It might take much longer.

👉 Tours

For foreign visitors the only way to visit is on a pre-arranged tour. Allow ample time for organising practicalities as your agency will need to obtain permits that usually take an absolute minimum of two weeks to issue, often much longer. The cheapest tours usually cost from around $150 per person per day (minimum four days) plus flights to Putao. Tour package fees generally include food, permits and excursions and/or treks.

In the dry season, an appealing part-day activity is a boat trip along sections of the deep green Malikha River alternating between rapids and calm pebble-bottomed shallows and passing beaches, sculpted rocks, unspoilt villages and rainforest jungle-sections. When water levels are higher, white-water rafting is a possibility. This might be combined with an interesting excursion to Machanbaw (40 minutes' drive from Putao). With an attractive setting beside the mirror-calm Malikha River, Machanbaw was the district's former colonial administrative centre and retains a well-spaced scattering of older British-era buildings.

Tours typically include some trekking. Even for just a two-day walk you'll probably get porters, a good cook and accommodation provided en route whether camping or in a very basic village homestay or cabin. Longer treks include a 14-day hike to the peak of 11,926ft **Mt Phon Kan Razi**, for views over the Myanmar Himalaya and the Mishimi Hills of neighbouring Arunachal Pradesh. For an excellent visual impression of the route's attractions and challenges see www.hsdejong.nl/myanmar/putao.

Don't underestimate the rigour of hiking here. Even the shortest loop includes long days of fairly strenuous gradients, a high chance of leeches and you'll need to be prepared for damp, cold weather.

🛏 Sleeping & Eating

In coming years, a major expansion in facilities can be expected if Putao develops as planned into Myanmar's ecotourism gateway. For now, however, unless you're allowed to stay at the basic **'army' guest-house** (www.traveltomyanmar.com/hotel_putao. htm), all tours start and finish with at least one night at either the stunning but secretive and massively expensive Tay Za–owned **Malikha Lodge** (www.malikhalodge.com), around an hour's drive from Putao, or at the more affordable **Putao Trekking House** (www.putaotrekkinghouse.com), a perfectly decent place but with some inconsistencies and indifferent food served in a glaringly lit dining hall. The cabin rooms are designed so that the small verandahs face a central lawn rather than the distant mountain horizon.

ⓘ Getting There & Away

AIR Twice weekly Air Bagan flights to Putao cost around $180 from Yangon, $120 from Mandalay and $60 from Myitkyina but without tour permits you won't be allowed to board the plane. Tours can be organised through Malikha Lodge, **Journeys** (www.journeysmyanmar.com), MTT (p69) and assorted Yangon agencies.

Road transport from Myitkyina would be appallingly rough but isn't permitted anyway for foreigners. Locals claim that there are only around 20 cars in the whole Putao area.

Western Myanmar

Best Places to Stay

» Royal Beach Motel (p272)

» Pleasant View Resort (p272)

» Shwe Thazin Hotel (p277)

» Mrauk U Princess Hotel (p284)

Best Places to Eat

» Pleasant View Islet Restaurant (p273)

» Gisspanadi (p278)

» Mondi stand (p278)

» Moe Cherry (p285)

Why Go?

Travelling in Rakhaing (Arakan) State, bordering Bangladesh and cut off from the rest of Myanmar by a 600-mile long mountain range, almost feels like you're in a different country – which, in fact, it once was. The landscape is tropically lush, proud locals speak the Rakhaing language, the food comes with more chilli, and the mix of cultures reflects the Indian subcontinent.

Few tourists head this way and most who do confine themselves to the relaxing resorts of Ngapali Beach where the pristine sand is lapped by the turquoise waters of the Bay of Bengal. The more adventurous head to the state's scrappy, atmospheric capital Sittwe (Akyab) and the old Rakhaing capital of Mrauk U (Myohaung), an amazing archaeological site, studded with hundreds of temples.

Looming to the north is elusive, underdeveloped Chin State, a richly traditional area where travel requires government permits, although it's easy to get a taste of Chin life at riverine villages accessed on boat trips from Mrauk U.

When to Go

Those wishing to risk the heat or rains outside the high season (November to March) will find that downpours or jellyfish will discourage much fun at Ngapali Beach. Sittwe and Mrauk U receive more rain than most of the country – about 200in per year. Sudden rainstorms during the monsoon season (mid-May to mid-September) are dangerous if travelling by boat to Mrauk U, or between Sittwe and Taunggok. Cyclones and tropical storms tend to occur just before and after the rainy season.

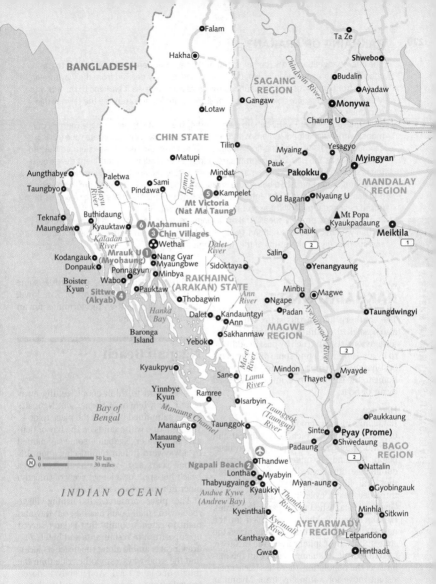

Western Myanmar Highlights

1 Lose yourself amid hundreds of ruined temples and fortifications in timeless **Mrauk U** (p279), former grand capital of Rakhaing

2 Savour the squid and other seafood at beautiful **Ngapali Beach** (p270), Myanmar's top beach destination

3 Boat to **Chin villages** (p286) upriver from Mrauk U, where tattoo-faced women lead you around by the arm

4 Wander about one of Myanmar's most exotic scenes: Sittwe's morning **central market** (p275)

5 Sort out a permit to climb **Mt Victoria** (p287), the country's second-highest peak

6 Hire a jeep in Mrauk U and drive to **Mahamuni Paya** (p287), original home of one of Myanmar's most venerated images of Buddha

RAKHAING OR ARAKAN?

The interchangeable terms Rakhaing and Arakan are frequently used and refer to the people, the state and the local language. Arakan is actually derived from the way foreign visitors from centuries ago pronounced the word Rakhaing. As it harkens to the era when Mrauk U was a regional powerhouse, English-speaking locals often use the term with a particular pride.

Names aside, there's still debate over whether the Rakhaing are actually Bamar (Burmans) with Indian blood, Indians with Bamar characteristics or a separate race (as is claimed locally). Although the first inhabitants of the region were a dark-skinned Negrito tribe known as the Bilu, later migrants from the eastern Indian subcontinent developed the first Hindu-Buddhist kingdoms in Myanmar before the first Christian millennium. These kingdoms flourished before the invasion of the Tibeto-Burmans from the north and east in the 9th and 18th centuries. The current inhabitants of the state may thus be mixed descendants of all three groups: Bilu, Bengali and Bamar.

The Rakhaing proudly speak 'Arakan', a language they claim birthed Bamar (and it's certainly related). But the national government uses Bamar in state communications and supposedly forbids study of the Rakhaing script.

RAKHAING STATE

The southern half of this state, which can also be spelled 'Rakhine', is the only part that foreign tourists can reach by bus, in addition to by air. Here you'll find some of Myanmar's best beaches. The northern part of the state, home to the capital Sittwe, must be accessed by air or boat.

History

Rakhaing's historical roots are linked to those of northern India, which held political and cultural sway over the region for centuries before the land fell under Bagan's (Pagan's) dominance during medieval times. In 1430 the local king Naramithla returned after three decades in exile in the Bengali city of Guar and established a new capital at Mrauk U, from where Rakhaing was ruled for the next 400 years. When the British annexed the state in 1826, the capital was moved to Sittwe.

With ethnic Rakhaing making up the majority of the population, there has been a persistent move for autonomy from Myanmar since Independence. In the 2010 election, the Rakhaing Nationalities Development Party (RNDP) had 35 of its candidates elected across the national and local assemblies, making it one of the most successful of the ethnic parties.

In October 2010 Rakhaing's coast was battered by Cyclone Giri, killing over 150 and leaving another 70,000 people homeless. Unlike when Cyclone Nargis hit in 2008, the government took steps to ensure the safety of those in Giri's path, evacuating some 50,000 people from the port of Kyaukpyu, under development as the terminus for an oil pipeline to China.

Ngapali Beach

ငပလီ

☑43

It feels weird to think about 'getting away from it all' while in Myanmar, but Ngapali's idyllic palm-lined beach is the place to do it. With pristine white sands on the Bay of Bengal's blue water, Ngapali – some say named by a wayward Italian reminiscing about his Napoli years ago – serves as the country's beach hot-spot for a jet-set crew of (mostly) older Europeans and rich locals.

The place preserves its fishing-village roots with small boats heading out day and night to catch a bounty that is later served up superfresh in restaurants and hotels. Ox-drawn carts amble along the beach as locals find the sand-ways a smoother ride than the rough one-lane road. And barely a dozen bungalow-style resorts over 2 miles gives a lot of space on the beach.

Even at the height of the season, Ngapali is a snoozy, early-to-bed place. But this could soon change, as several new big resorts are in the works and Tay Za (see p26) is said to be bankrolling the extension of the airport, to be completed in the next three years, to enable direct flights from Bangkok and Singapore.

Peak season is from November to March. Things get even quieter in rainy season (mid-May to mid-September) when flights dip to twice a week and most hotels either shut up shop or keep open only a handful of rooms.

⊙ Sights & Activities

South of the hotels, and easily reached barefoot by the beach, is the rustic fishing village of Jade Taw, where small fish dry on bamboo mats across the beach. Even further south is the bigger village of Lon Tha and an inlet of the same name, backed by a sweeping curve of mangrove and sand facing south.

On a bayside hill east of Lon Tha is a modest white stupa. It's worth seeing for its glorious panoramic views – and for the adventure to reach it. To get there, turn left at the town junction (near the market). The road runs parallel to the boat-filled bay and quickly degenerates into a path too sandy to ride on; if you're on a bike, leave it with a local. About five minutes or so after passing a small bridge, you reach the hill steps to the stupa.

Four-hour snorkelling trips (per person incl boat, mask & snorkel K15,000), arranged by any hotel or directly with boat owners on the beach, usually depart at 7am or 8am to catch the clearest water. Most trips take in a few spots around (private) 'Pearl Island' off the south end of the beach. The coral's not super, but there are plenty of bright red and blue fish to follow. Some snorkellers bring along fishing rods to drop a line.

You'll need deeper pockets to board the expat-run Barracuda (www.myanmaraquatic tourism.com; half day/day trip $200/400), a cute 32ft-long boat accommodating six, for a big game fishing adventure. It can also be hired for picnic trips to private beaches. Bookings can be made at Lin Thar Oo Lodge.

Upscale hotels offer golfing outings to the nine-hole government-owned Ngapali Golf Course (green fee $10) for about $30.

🛌 Sleeping

If you're on a budget, brace yourself: Ngapali's cheapest bed is $20, with very few rooms at this price. There are good midrange

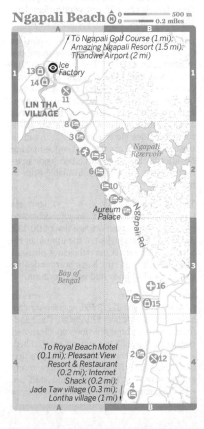

Ngapali Beach

options from $35 up. The 'Top End' here covers rooms for $100 and over.

If there's somewhere you particularly want to stay, plan ahead; during high season (November to March) some hotels can get booked out, sometimes way in advance. A few places hike up their rates over the peak Christmas and New Year period, and also drop them if open during the rainy season. Nearly all hotels include airport transfer and breakfast in their rates. Where there isn't 24 hour electricity we note the times the power kicks in.

TOP CHOICE Pleasant View Resort　RESORT $$$

(☑42511, in Yangon 01-393 086; www.pvrngapali. com; r $100; ✳@) Ngapali's best balance of price and style, the Pleasant View lives up to its name with a brilliant location at the far southern end of the beach, close to the fishing village. The 26 rooms, all sea facing, are simply but chicly decorated with a TV, a minibar and a hot-and-cold shower. The power clicks on from 2pm to 7am and the resort also offers beachside massages for $12.

Royal Beach Motel　HOTEL $$

(☑42411, in Yangon 01-544 484; www.royal beachngapali.com; s/d from $35/40) More cosy and personable than other midrange places, the wooden-floored rooms at this complex have lounge chairs on the deck, and there's a small bell by the door that staff chime when they call. It also has a great restaurant. Unlike most hotels, it's set a bit back from the beach, with a grove of palms providing easy-breezy, day-round shade. Higher-priced rooms face the water.

Sandoway Resort　RESORT $$$

(☑42244, in Yangon 01-294 612; www.sandoway resort.com; deluxe $180, garden-view/sea-view cottages $240/300, villas $300-340; ✳@≋) With palm-shaded walkways leading past well-tended gardens and ponds, this Italian–Myanmar joint venture offers lovely two-storey bungalows with lofty ceilings and appealing craft details. You get no TV, but there's a massive communal screening room for movies, comfortably set out with padded armchairs. There's also a mezzanine library with a couple of free internet terminals above a bar, next to a giant pool. It charges $10 for the transfer from the airport. Rates almost double during 22 December to 15 January and dip slightly in October, April and May.

Amata Resort & Spa　RESORT $$$

(☑42177, in Yangon 01-665 126; www.amataresort. com; r from $120, cabana cottage/sea-view villa $195/315; ✳@≋) Owned by a Yangon sea captain, this swish complex of gorgeous two-storey cabanas and rooms (request rooms 701 and 702 for their brilliant beach views) is Ngapali's most stylish, although it loses points for less than stellar maintenance. Still, it's a very appealing, friendly resort set back from the beach in lush gardens with a handsome Morris 8 and wood-panelled Wolseley outside for show. Ngapali's lone tennis court ($7) is next to the business centre, offering wi-fi access for $15 for the duration of your stay.

Bayview Beach Resort　RESORT $$$

(☑42299, in Yangon 01-504 471; www.bayview -myanmar.com; garden-view/sea-view bungalows $150/160; ✳@≋) This luxurious German–Myanmar joint venture occupies a nice strip of beach, with a rare on-the-beach bar. The 45 swanky bungalows have an inviting, basic layout, and lounge chairs on the private deck. Guests can rent out windsurfers, kayaks and catamarans ($5 to $10 per hour).

Laguna Lodge　HOTEL $$

(☑43122, in Yangon 01-501 123; www.lagunalodge -myanmar.com; r $50-60) For a 'house on the beach' feel, the 12-room Laguna, run by a German chef, goes rustic with dark-wood, open-shuttered windows and huge balconies. Mosquito nets hang over the big beds and a giant circular window in the bathroom provides views through the room to the beach. There are tea- and coffee-making facilities in the rooms and a beachside massage service. Electricity is available 6pm to midnight.

Thande Beach Hotel　HOTEL $$$

(☑42788, Yangon 01-546 225; www.thandebeachho telmyanmar.com; garden-view/sea-view r $110/130; ✳@≋) The least stylish of the upmarket resorts, the Thande is nevertheless a pleasant place to bunk, offering a spa surrounded by gardens and a handy mid-beach location.

Memento Resort　HOTEL $$

(☑42441, in Yangon 01-228 556; ngapalimementore sort@gmail.com; s/d from $20/25; ✳) The handful of rooms without sea views are clean and cheap (for Ngapali), but may offer only a bed, a cold-water shower and a fan. They're fine for a short stay. There's several more comfy and beach-facing rooms too, and staff are eager to please. Power available from 5.30pm to 7am.

Lin Thar Oo Lodge
HOTEL $$

(☎42322, in Yangon 01-503 721; www.lintharoo
-ngapali.com; s/d from $30/35; ❋) Offers 20
mostly sea-facing, simple, cottage-type
rooms, the more expensive have a minibar,
a TV and air con. Three basic rooms ($25)
with a fan and cold-water showers are set
back from the beach in a concrete block.
Electricity is on from 6pm to 6am.

Silver Beach Hotel
HOTEL $$

(☑in Yangon 01-381 898; www.silverbeachhotel
ngapali.com; r/ste $65/100; ❋@) At the beach's
north end, Silver Beach is the cheapest way
to go for 24-hour electricity. The prim, red-
roofed cottages conjure up the look of a
1950s British holiday camp, with dated furnishings and facilities to match.

Amazing Ngapali Resort
RESORT $$$

(☎42011, in Yangon 01-203 500; www.amazing-ho
tel.com; s/d from $120/125; ❋☎❋) Favoured by
tour groups, the spacious and well-equipped
36 double-storey villas at this resort near
the airport all face the beach. You're isolated
here, though, from the more appealing Nga-
pali Beach several miles south.

Under construction at the time of research,
but looking promising, are the luxurious
Tamarind Resort next to the Aureum Palace
and the 28 bungalow Amara Ocean Resort
(www.amaragroup.net; d from $350; ❋@❋❋) run
by a Burmese-Myanmar couple and the only
hotel north of Thandwe Airport.

✖ Eating & Drinking

Cheap, fresh and plentiful, Ngapali's sea-
food (particularly fresh squid dunked in
spiced ginger-and-garlic sauce) ranks eas-
ily among Myanmar's best dining. The long
lights that line the western horizon offshore
at dusk are fishing boats using bulbs to at-
tract squid.

A dozen family-run restaurants of vary-
ing quality cluster outside the gates of ho-
tels. These have practically identical menus
(posted in English) and prices. A dish of
crab, squid or barracuda starts from K2000
or K2500, barbecued tiger prawns are K3500
to K5000, and lobster is K15,000 and up.
Food is more nicely prepared and presented
inside the hotels – but you'll generally pay
more for this.

TOP CHOICE Pleasant View
Islet Restaurant
SEAFOOD, BAMAR $$

(near Pleasant View Resort; dishes K4000-K10,000;
☺lunch & dinner) Set on a rocky islet at the

beach's south end (you may have to wade
through knee-deep surf to get to it), this stylish eatery serves very tasty seafood at a better price than most hotels. It's also perfect
for sunset cocktails and nibbles.

TOP CHOICE Sandoway Resort
Restaurant
ASIAN, EUROPEAN $$$

(Sandoway Resort; dishes $6-48; ☺7am-10pm) An
elegant place to dine by the beach with the
most creative menu among the big resort
restaurants. The Italian co-owners ensure
that the pasta ($10 to $14) is made al dente
and you can also dip into local dishes, such
as *laphet thoke* (tea-leaf salad; $6).

Htay Htay's Kitchen
BAMAR, CHINESE $$

(Ngapali Rd; dishes K1500-K3500; ☺7am-11pm)
At the north end of the beach, this restaurant and gift shop is run by a very friendly
couple. Expect the usual grilled seafood and
curries as well as some more unusual items,
such as various types of tempura and a salad
and drinks made using giant lemons from
Mrauk U as an ingredient.

Brilliance
BAMAR, SEAFOOD $$

(dishes K1500-4000; ☺7am-10pm) This is a sim-
ple place, but it serves fairly brilliant seafood
that's far more reasonably priced than in the
big hotels.

Two Brothers Restaurant
BAMAR, SEAFOOD $$

(Ngapali Rd; dishes R3000-7000; ☺noon-9.30pm)
One of the more reliable operations on the
Ngapali Rd strip, with a touch more class
in its overall presentation. Tables have natty
blue-and-white tablecloths and there's wine
available.

Amata Resort Restaurant
INTERNATIONAL $$$

(Amata Resort; dishes $8-20; ☺7-10am, 11am-2pm
& 6.30-10.30pm) This hotel restaurant over-
looks the pool and beach. It serves pretty
good pizzas ($8 to $10) and a real-deal beef
burger ($8).

Lili's Bar
INTERNATIONAL $$

(Laguna Lodge; meals $4-6; ☺7am-11pm) A cute
spot in the palm-shaded sand with a lazy
dog or two lolling around, fake turtles, generous plates of pasta and $2 *mojitos*.

Catch/Sunset Bar
INTERNATIONAL $$$

(Bayview Beach Resort; dishes $5-24) Bayview's
restaurant is called Catch and is located
away from the beach, but everyone eats
from the Catch's menu by dining at Sunset
Bar, which *is* by the beach. It's good for fil-
lets of barracuda, burgers and pizzas.

If you're planning on connecting to Sittwe from Ngapali Beach by boat, you're most likely going to have to overnight in Taunggok. Only a couple of very basic guesthouses near the bus station take foreigners. Be prepared at the **Royal Guest House** (☏61088; r K6000) for lumpy beds and no hot water.

Shopping

The broad souvenir selection at Htay Htay's (see p273) is worth a browse and you can watch fabric weavers working on looms at the rear.

Ngapali Art Gallery (www.ngapaliartgallery.com; ☯9am-6pm) In Lin Tha Village, just beyond the north end of Ngapali Beach, is the atelier and gallery of San Naing whose mainly abstract canvases are priced from $100 to around $4500.

Gallerie Htein Lin Thar (☯9am-9pm) Next to Ngapali Art Gallery and representing a range of artists selling colourful works. A gift shop and cafe were in the process of being set up when we dropped by.

Wai Bar La (Main Rd, near entrance to Sandoway Resort; ☯8am-8pm) Attractive wood carvings by the son of the craftsman who decorated the Sandoway Resort.

❶ Information

Ngapali Dispensary (☏42233; ☯9am-noon, 1-4pm) is a charity-built clinic across from Sandoway Resort with English-speaking staff.

Upscale hotels allow nonguests to use their **internet** (per 30 minutes/hour $3/6) or there's a small **internet shack** (one hour K3000; ☯9am-9pm) opposite the Pleasant View Resort. Most hotels can place **international calls** ($6 per minute).

❶ Getting There & Away
Air

Thandwe airport is named for the town 4 miles inland, but is closer to Ngapali village. Hotel buses meet planes typically offering free transport to Ngapali Beach.

Both **Air Bagan** (☏42429) and **Air Mandalay** (☏42404) serve Yangon ($78 to $86; daily; 50 mins) and Sittwe ($65 to $71; daily; 40 mins) Air Mandalay offer a daily connection from (but

not to) Heho/Inle Lake ($116; one hour). Connections are less frequent from May through September.

Boat

Catch a bus to Taunggok. Fifty miles or so north of Thandwe, Taunggok is a stopping-off point for travellers between Pyay (Prome) and Thandwe by bus, or for catching the **Malikha Express** (☏60127; $40; nine hours) boat to Sittwe at 7am on Monday, Wednesday and Saturday.

Bus

Aung Thit Sar (☏65363) run daily buses to Yangon via Thandwe and Pyay (K15,500; 17 to 18 hours); you'll pay the same if you only go as far as Pyay (12 hours). Tickets are sold by hotels in Ngapali Beach, and the bus will pick you up from your accommodation. The road – particularly between Taunggok and Pyay – has the reputation of being one of Myanmar's hardest, bounciest, most stomach-churning trips. Bring warm clothes, as the ride over the mountains at night gets cold. For more details see p146.

The other just-as-rough option to Yangon (K15,500; 17 to 18 hours) is via Gwa (supposedly eight hours).

❶ Getting Around

Pick-up trucks run frequently from Thandwe to Ngapali Beach and on to Lon Tha village (K400, one hour). Catch one in either direction on the main road.

Bicycles can be rented from most hotels for K2500 per day; and a few motorbikes are available for K15,000.

Thandwe

သံတွဲ
☏43 / POP C50,000

Located about 4 miles inland to the northeast of Ngapali Beach, Thandwe fills a hilly valley with its low-key streets. It's been a key Rakhaing town for many centuries. When the British stationed a garrison here around the turn of the 20th century, they twisted the name into Sandoway.

There are no licensed places to stay and eating boils down to noodles around the market, or rice-'n'-curry restaurants on side streets a block north and south. While not a major destination, Thandwe makes for a nice visit if you're staying at Ngapali Beach and fancy a change of scene.

Sights

Housed in a former British jail in the centre of town, the **Thandwe market** (◎6am-4pm) is where a handful of daytripping guests from beach resorts go in search of a 'real deal' market. Vendors sell medicinal herbs, clothes, textiles, some souvenirs, hardware and free-market consumer goods. Across the street on the north side is the **Suni Mosque**, Thandwe's largest of five.

Three golden stupas stand on hilltops at four points around Thandwe. None are spectacular in themselves (and all the names rhyme with each other), but each offers excellent viewpoints of the town's tin roofs, peeking out of a sea of palms and hills.

The tallest, **Nandaw Paya**, a mile west of the market, was supposedly erected in AD 761 by King Minbra to enshrine a piece of a rib of the Buddha. The long shrine facing the stupa to the south houses some nice woodcarving reliefs of Buddha's life.

Just east of town, right across a small river about half a mile from the market, the **Sandaw Paya** was supposedly built in AD 784 by Rakhaing King Minyokin to house a Buddha hair, and was rebuilt by the Burmese in 1876.

Across the river (north past the bus station and east on a stone road about 1.3 miles from the market), the **Andaw Paya** is the lowest stupa but has revealing glimpses of the river's fork from the hills east. It claims to house a Buddha molar relic and dates from AD 763.

❶ Getting There & Away

Pick-up trucks from Ngapali run every 30 minutes (K500; one hour). Pick-ups to Taunggok (K2500; four or five hours) run several times daily from a small station a couple of hundred yards north of the bus station (across the river).

Sittwe (Akyab)

စစ်တွေ

♪43 / POP C200,000

Rakhaing's capital Sittwe (pronounced 'Sit-TWAY' by Burmese, 'Sigh-TWAY' by Rakhaing) may look scrappy but it sits in an incredible spot – where the wide, tidal Kaladan River kisses the big fat Bay of Bengal. Most foreign travellers skedaddle to Mrauk U as soon as possible. Those willing to linger here will find a lot to like.

There's good sunset viewing at dusk, plus a fish and fresh produce market that's one of Myanmar's more fascinating. You're also likely to be swarmed by chatty monks at one of the Buddhist museums in town. The mix of locals – Rakhaing, Muslims, Indian Hindus, Burmese – is also more pronounced here than in other major Myanmar cities.

History

Prior to the Burmese invasion of the Mrauk U kingdom in 1784 there was little more than a village here. Fifty years later, Sittwe's economy underwent a boom when British forces took over during the first Anglo–Burmese War. The British moved the state capital here from Mrauk U and named the place Akyab after the local pagoda, Ahkyaib-daw.

Incoming wealth from cargo trade with Calcutta fuelled the construction of some fine colonial mansions, but much of the grace was lost under heavy WWII fighting between the British and Japanese forces.

Today, the town's economy is set to benefit from the construction of a new harbour – a joint venture between Myanmar and India – next to the municipal market and a rail link to Ann-Minbu which will go via Mrauk U.

Sights

Most of Sittwe's action runs along the Main Rd, which parallels the Kaladan River. The airport is about 1.5 miles southwest of the centre; the main boat jetty is about 2 miles north.

Central Market   MARKET
(Strand Rd; ◎6am-6pm) Focussed on the 1956 municipal market building, there's lots going on here from dawn up to noon and beyond – it's well worth popping by before your boat or plane leaves. Head straight past *longyi*, fishing net and vegetable stands to the fish and meat area, where stingrays and gutted eels and drying sharks make quite a scene. In the bay, small boats jostle for space to unload their catch.

A few blocks north is the **Rice Market**, with tiny lanes between the water and Strand Rd filled with simple wood homes, where traders hawk brown and sticky rice – some bound for Bangladesh.

View Point   BEACH
(Strand Rd) The riverside Strand Rd leads about 1 mile south to a smashing location called the **View Point** where you can sip on a beer or fresh coconut as the sun sets over the Bay of Bengal. Just west, in front of a closed naval base, is a broad, grey-brown sand **beach** that has a tricky undertow, where a few swimmers lose their lives each year.

Sittwe (Akyab)

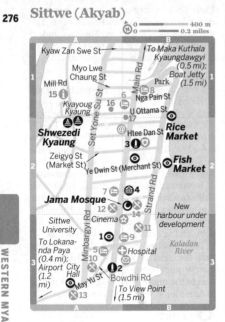

Lokananda Paya BUDDHIST TEMPLE

လောကနန္ဒာဘုရား:

(May Yu St) You can't miss this big golden pagoda between the airport and the centre, endowed by General Than Shwe himself in 1997. Its gilded, cavernous worship hall held aloft by decorated pillars is pretty spectacular. Rakhaing State Day is staged here.

On the west side of the compound is a small ordination hall, which houses the intriguing Sachamuni Image, a bronze buddha, the surface of which is entirely encrusted with mini-buddhas. Apparently the image dates from 24 BC and is said to have been found by Mrauk U fishers in recent years. It was moved from Mrauk U by the government in 1997.

Rakhaing State Cultural Museum MUSEUM

(Main Rd; admission $2; ⏰10am-4pm Tue-Sat) The government-run Rakhaing State Cultural Museum features two floors of Rakhaing cultural goodies that benefit from just enough English subtitles. On the ground floor, diagrams and artefacts detail Rakhaing's origins (around 3000 BC) and four key periods (Dhanyawadi, Vesali, Lemro and Mrauk U), compelete with useful renderings and models.

Upstairs are displays on local customs (such as models showing off some of the 64 traditional Mrauk U royal hairstyles – all of which look pretty similar) as well as drawings illustrating key moves you may need for Rakhaing wrestling.

Jama Mosque MOSQUE

(Main Rd) Next to the museum, this impressive 1859 building could have been ripped out the pages of *Arabian Nights*. Sadly, it appears little used by the town's Muslim community and is haunted by desperate looking beggars. There's a good restaurant in its courtyard.

FREE **Maka Kuthala Kyaungdawgyi** MUSEUM

(Large Monastery of Great Merit; Main Rd; ⏰7am-9pm) Monk U Bhaddanta Wannita spent 49 years collecting old coins and buddha images from monasteries to protect them from thieves. Some of his collection is displayed in his former monastery, which is housed in (of all things) a grand, century-old British colonial mansion about half a mile north of the centre. The dusty, eclectic museum upstairs contains cases of old banknotes, buddhas and votives (candleholders) and coins from the Mrauk U and other ancient periods, plus many bone relics of head monks, kept in small tins. Plenty of friendly English-speaking monks will follow you around. On the ground floor is a bronze statue of U Bhaddanta Wannita.

If you're interested in this kind of thing, there's also the government's **Buddhistic Museum** (Baw Dhi St; admission $5) closer to the airport.

Shwezedi Kyaung   BUDDHIST MONASTERY
ရွှေစေတီကျောင်း
(U Ottama St; admission free; ⊘24hr) Partly housed in a picturesque, ramshackle colonial-era building on a backstreet, this monastery is well worth searching out, particularly during Buddhist festivals. This was the monastery of U Ashin Ottama (1880–1939) a leader of the Burmese independence movement during British colonial rule, who died during imprisonment for his political activities. In September 2007 monks at this monastery followed in his footsteps and took part in the protest marches then happening across the country.

Don't miss the **Fruit Bat Trees** around Sittwe University, where hundreds of fruit bats slumber during the day then head off at dusk – there's a great view of their migration from the roof of the Shwe Thazin Hotel. Nearby, at the foot of Main Rd is **New Clock Tower**, a painted concrete pillar topped with pagoda style hat. The Victorian-era **Old Clock Tower** is a rusting, yet handsome iron affair on Main Rd, just west of the Central Market.

★ Festivals & Events

The **Rakhaing State Day** (a Saturday in mid December) is staged at Lokananda Paya, with traditional wrestling, bamboo pole climbing and tug-of-war – it's well worth delaying a departure to see it. Locals may tell you the real Rakhaing day is December 31, 'when Mrauk U fell – it's more a day to grieve'.

⌂ Sleeping

At the three budget options, all of which could use more love, electricity runs from about 6pm to 11pm. The far more comfy midrange options include round-the-clock generators.

(✆23579; www.shwethazinhotel.com; 250 Main Rd; s/d $30/35; ✳) A bit more polished than Noble, the Shwe Thazin is proud of a 5th-floor restaurant, and (higher up) a lookout deck, good for glimpses of those fruit bats at dusk. Rooms are clean and modern (with mini-balconies), if not overly stylish.

Noble Hotel   HOTEL **$$**
(✆23558; 45 Main Rd; noble@myanmar.com.mm; s/d $25/35; ✳) This modern hotel has small but clean carpeted rooms with a desk, a teapot and a satellite TV with a few movie channels. Nothing fancy, but the best deal for recovering from the boat ride back from Mrauk U. There's no lift, so ask for a room on one of the lower floors – unless you need a workout climbing the stairs.

Mya Guest House   GUESTHOUSE **$$**
(✆22358, 23315; 51/6 Bowdhi Rd; s/d $20/30) A bit off Main Rd, this guesthouse and tea garden is dominated by a century-old, blue-and-red mansion once home to a British lawyer who is said to have put the first Mercedes on Sittwe streets. The main building now houses students, but a new brick building to the side offers simple, spacious, tiled rooms, with fans and private bathrooms (no hot water).

Prince Guest House   GUESTHOUSE **$**
(✆22539, in Yangon 09 503 4780; http://mrauku prince.com/sittweprince.htm; 27 Main Rd; s/d

THE ROHINGYA

One controversial topic of conversation on Sittwe's streets is the state's Rohingya minority. The Myanmar government denies the existence of this group, which consists of anywhere between 750,000 and 1.5 million Muslims (and not to be confused with another local Muslim group, the 'Rahkaing Muslims').

According to Amnesty International and the Arakan Rohingya National Organisation (www.rohingya.org), Rohingya – who speak a Bengali dialect – are routinely subjected to persecution in Myanmar, including arbitrary taxes, forced labour, forced relocation, rape and murder. Within Rakhaing, Rohingya must seek permission just to travel to the next village. For more about this issue, see the Kaladan Press Network (www.kaladanpress.org).

DAY TRIPS FROM SITTWE

Have a day to spare? Consider taking one of the following boat trips, both of which can be arranged by Khine Pyi Soe (p279). The most potentially interesting is to the weaving village **Wabo** (K60,000, plus $20 for an English-speaking guide) a 90-minute boat ride from Sittwe, to see Rakhaing-style *longyi* being made; the Rakhaing are known in Myanmar as skilled weavers who can produce intricate designs in their cloths. The other is to hilly **Baronga Island** (K60,000), across the wide Kaladan River, to see a typical fishing village.

$6/12) English-speaking staff with some handy travellers' advice make up for the rather dingy rooms (small, with a fan and a mosquito net and coil) and shared bathrooms you'll want to wear sandals in. Check a few rooms before choosing – some are better than others. There's also a lone 'family room' with private bath and air-con (running from 7pm to 11pm only) that is $10/$15 per single/double.

New Palace Hotel   HOTEL **$**
(📞21996; 5 Main Rd; s/d from $10/16) Is everything else full? Little is new about the Palace. Rooms are rundown and a bit depressing. Spring a few extra dollars for the brighter rooms on the upper floors.

✕ Eating & Drinking

TOP CHOICE **Gisspanadi**   CHINESE, RAKHAING **$**
(Minbargyi Rd; dishes K2000-4500; ⏰6am-10pm) This friendly, family Chinese-Burmese restaurant – along a strip of eateries, just east of city hall – is a standard spot, busy with local men sitting over tables of fried fish fingers (better than they sound), grilled prawns and Myanmar beer bottles.

Mondi Stand   RAKHAING **$**
(May Yu St; bowl K200; ⏰6am-6pm) *Mondi* is the Rakhaing-style fish noodle soup downed by locals for breakfast. It's similar to *mohinga* but comes with chillies not peanuts, and often eel not fish. Sittwe's best – many claim – is served at the tiny *mondi* stand facing the city hall. If you're feeling frisky ask for the ultra spicy *abu shabu*. Students from the nearby university pour in for lunch.

Mya Teahouse   BAMAR **$**
(51/6 Bowdhi Rd; tea K200; ⏰6am-5pm) Sit on bright-blue plastic chairs under shady trees amid the potted plants and flowers at this delightful teahouse: a perfect place to revive over a cuppa with various sweet and savoury snacks. Good for a breakfast of fried rice or *mohinga*, too.

Utingdameer   INDIAN **$**
(Main Rd; meal K1000; ⏰10am-3pm) At the back of the compound in which the Jama Mosque sits, this family-run canteen dishes up a bargain lunch of several tasty curries and vegetable dishes with rice.

Moe Pearl   TEAHOUSE, BAKERY **$**
(80 Main Rd; cakes K100-200; ⏰6am-7pm) Run for 20 years by the same Chinese family, this smart little bakery and cafe is a good spot to stock up on biscuits, cakes and savouries for journeys, or to rest and enjoy a tea or coffee.

River Valley Seafood Restaurant   CHINESE, RAKHAING **$$**
(5 Main Rd; set meals K300-5000; ⏰7am-10.30pm) Popular with many foreigner visitors, Sittwe's fanciest restaurant offers open-air space and wall murals, including a large blown-up photo of a tattooed-faced Chin woman. The menu lists many seafood options, plus a handful of spicy Rakhaing-style dishes. Some waiters wear bowties.

May Yu   CHINESE, RAKHAING **$$**
(Strand Rd) Seafood spot done up like a Caribbean shack, with a blue-and-green wood house and plank-board deck facing the water.

View Point   RAKHAING **$$**
Simple restaurant on Bay of Bengal, 1.5 miles south of the centre via Strand Rd.

ℹ Information

You are highly likely to encounter a certain local tout (at the time of research going by the name of Mr Learn) when you arrive (and no matter how you arrive, he'll find you). His rates for boat transfers are not above the norm but he will try to secure commissions for arranging whatever you do (such as boats to Mrauk U or hotels in Sittwe). He's harmless, but persistent enough to annoy some travellers. Also see www.lonelyplan et.com/myanmar-burma for further information on travelling in Myanmar.

Outside the generator-run midrange hotels, electricity runs generally from 6pm to 11pm only. In the rainy season, clouds can sometimes cut telephone communication. Sittwe's **hospital**

(☎23511; Main Rd) and **post office** are both near the new clock tower.

Internet Access

KISS (Main Rd; K500 per hr; ⊙noon-9pm) Has webcams and plenty of terminals, though connections can be sloooow.

Travel Agencies

Khine Pyi Soe (☎23159, 09 851 61162; 25 Mill Rd) Housed in the home of a former karate teacher, this unlikely agency can arrange boats to Mrauk U (K130,000 return; the boat waits up to three nights while you explore Mrauk U) and various day trips (p278).

❶ Getting There & Away

Overland routes between Sittwe and Yangon (as well as to Mrauk U) are closed to foreigners. The following information is for the dry season – schedules are different in the wet season and from year to year, so double check everything well in advance.

Air

Sittwe's airport is about 1.5 miles west of the centre. Taxis (K2500 to K3000) and trishaws (K1000) await flights.

In peak season **Air Mandalay** (☎21638; U Ottama St) and **Air Bagan** (☎23113) fly daily to Yangon ($108; one hour 25 mins) and Thandwe ($78; 40 mins).

Flight schedules are erratic. Before leaving Sittwe, you must reconfirm your booking – your hotel should be able to help.

Boat

TO MRAUK U The only way to/from Mrauk U for foreigners is by boat. There are a few options.

You will have offers for a **private boat** (from $120; five to six hours) – a simple tarp-covered boat with flat deck, a few plastic chairs and a very basic toilet – before you can get out of the airport. Generally a boat can fit four to six people, with a driver who will wait with the boat for two or three nights. Ask ahead about the cost if you decide to stay another day in Mrauk U, which often happens. If you arrive in Sittwe in the afternoon, don't expect to be able to leave on such boats until early the next day.

The double-decker **ferry** to Mrauk U ($4, six to seven hours) is run by the government's **Inland Water Transport** (IWT; ☎23382), which has an office 90yd west of the Mrauk U jetty, though there's no need to buy tickets in advance. Ferries depart Sittwe Tuesday and Friday, and return from Mrauk U on Wednesday and Saturday. Deckchairs are available for rent (K500) and there's a stall serving basic food. We're told there's also a similar private ferry service ($10) leaving Sittwe on Monday and returning on Tues-

day. See p22 before deciding to use government-run services.

The fastest boat is the **Shwe Pyi Tan** (☎09-8628145; $15; two hr) that departs Sittwe at 3pm on Monday and Wednesday and Mrauk U at 7am on Tuesday and Thursday.

TO TAUNGGOK **Malikha Express** (☎24248, 24037; Main Rd; ⊙9am-5pm) sells tickets for the 130-person fast boat for Taunggok ($40, nine hours), which departs at 7am on Monday, Thursday and Saturday. The boat stops in the island port town of Kyaukpyu ($20) for 30 or 40 minutes for lunch.

Mrauk U (Myohaung)
မြောက်ဦး

☎043 / POP C50,000

'Little Bagan?' Not by a long shot. Myanmar's second-most-famous archaeological site, Mrauk U (pronounced 'mraw-oo') is a centuries-old city of hundreds of temples around which village life thrives. The temples – previously mistaken for forts due to thick bunker-style walls built against the fierce Rakhaing winds – are smaller and younger than Bagan's. Being here is as much about seeing temples in the gorgeous scenery of rounded hillocks as about mingling with the goatherds and vegetable farmers who live around them (unlike Bagan).

Much of the locals' daily activity seems to be taken up with water trips. Instead of the usual clay pots or rectangular oil cans, Mrauk U residents carry shiny aluminium water pots (imported from Bangladesh) on their hips or heads.

You're likely to have many temples to yourself: in a good year, only about 3500 to 4000 foreign visitors come. The site's remote location, a five to seven hour boat ride up a creek of the Kaladan River, and lack of government promotion, means this is unlikely to change in the short term.

MRAUK U FEES

For foreign visitors to Mrauk U there's an archaeological site 'entry fee' of $5; this is usually collected at the Shittaung Paya or at the boat jetty; on the government ferry you'll be asked to show proof of payment before leaving. But many people arriving and leaving by private boats manage to avoid paying the fee with little consequence. The palace site museum also charges $5 for entry.

For visitors coming on pre-arranged private boats, it's necessary to let the driver know how much time you'll need in Mrauk U (though it can often be changed, with an extra charge). Two full days is the minimum necessary to see the area; add on another for the day trip to the Chin villages (recommended) and another if you plan to explore on your own after you've seen the greatest hits.

History

Mrauk U (meaning, bizarrely, Monkey Egg) was the last great Rakhaing capital for 354 years, from 1430 to 1784, when it was one of the richest cities in Asia. In its heyday, it served as a free port, trading with the Middle East, Asia, Holland, Portugal and Spain. The Portuguese Jesuit priest, A. Farinha, who visited in the 17th century, called it 'a second Venice' while other visitors compared it to London or Amsterdam. Little remains of the European quarter, Daingri Kan (about 3 miles south of Mrauk U's current centre) other than ruins and a Hindu temple.

The Mrauk U dynasty was much feared by the peoples of the Indian subcontinent and central Myanmar. Japanese Christians fleeing persecution in Nagasaki were hired as bodyguards for the king. At Mrauk U's peak, King Minbin (1531–53) created a

naval fleet of some 10,000 war boats that dominated the Bay of Bengal and Gulf of Martaban. Many of Mrauk U's finest temples (Shittaung, Dukkanthein, Laymyetnha and Shwetaung) were built during his reign.

In the late 18th century, the Konbaung dynasty asserted its power over the region and Mrauk U was integrated into the Bamar kingdoms centred on Mandalay.

After the First Anglo–Burmese War of 1824–26, the British Raj annexed Rakhaing and set up its administrative headquarters in Sittwe, thus turning Mrauk U into a political backwater virtually overnight.

A rare incidence of the military bowing to popular opinion occurred here in late 2010 when a few brave locals protested against the planned route of a new railway linking Sittwe with Minbu, construction of which was damaging temples and sites within the archaeological area. The project was halted and the railway's route changed.

⊙ Sights

The original site of Mrauk U is spread over 17.5 sq miles, though the town today and bulk of the temples to visit cover a 2.7-sq-mile area. With a bike, a packed lunch and

Mrauk U (Myohaung)

Top Sights

	Andaw Paya	B1
	Bandoola Kyaung	C3
	Dukkanthein Paya	B1
	Kothaung Paya	D2
	Mahabodhi Shwegu	C1
	Shittaung Paya	B1

Sights

1	Haridaung Paya	B2
2	Laksaykan Gate	C3
3	Laungbanpyauk Paya	B1
4	Laymyetnha Paya	B1
5	Palace Museum	B2
6	Peisi Daung Paya	D2
7	Phraouk Paya	D2
8	Pitaka Taik	B1
9	Ratanabon Paya	C1
10	Ratanamanaung	C2
11	Sakyamanaung Paya	C2
12	Shittaung Pillar	B1
13	Shwetaung Paya	C2

Sleeping

14	Golden Star Guest House	B2
15	Mrauk U Princess Hotel	A3
16	Nawarat Hotel	B2
17	Prince Hotel	D2
18	Royal City Guest House	B3
19	Shwe Thazin Hotel	B2
20	Vesali Resort Hotel	D2
21	Waddy Htut Guest House	B2

Eating

22	For You	B2
23	Hay Mar	B3
24	Moe Cherry	C2

Shopping

25	L'amitie Art Gallery	B1

Information

26	Dr Aye Maung Zan	B3

Transport

27	Bicycle Rental Shop	B3
28	Horse Cart Stand	C2
29	Jeep Stand	B2
30	Jetty	B3

the stamina for exploration, you could take any path for DIY adventures.

NORTH GROUP

For many, this area is the pick of the litter for Mrauk U, with all sites within walking distance. There are a couple of food stalls and a gift shop below Shittaung.

Shittaung Paya BUDDHIST TEMPLE
ရှစ်သောင်းဘုရား

The usual starting point is at Mrauk U's most complex temple, the Shittaung (Sittaung in Burmese); if you've not paid it already, the $5 zone fee is collected here (see boxed text, p279). You'll also be asked for a 'donation' of K3000 to cover the interior illumination of this temple, Andaw Paya and Dukkanthein Paya.

King Minbin, the most powerful of Rakhaing's kings, built Shittaung in 1535. It's a frenzy of stupas of various sizes; some 26 surround a central stupa. Shittaung means 'Shrine of the 80,000 Images', a reference to the number of holy images inside (the actual tally is more like 84,000, though some have since been stolen). Thick walls, with windows and nooks, surround the two-tiered structure.

Outside the temple

Beside the southwest entrance stairway, and inside a locked mint-green building, is the much-studied **Shittaung Pillar**, a 10ft sandstone obelisk brought here from Wethali by King Minbin. Considered the 'oldest history book in Myanmar' (by the Rakhaing at least), three of the obelisk's four sides are inscribed in faded Sanskrit. The east-facing side likely dates from the end of the 5th century. The western face displays a list dating from the 8th century, outlining Rakhaing kings from 638 BC to AD 729 (King Anandacandra).

Lying on its back next to the pillar is a cracked, 12ft-long **sandstone slab** featuring an engraved lotus flower (a Buddhist motif) growing from a wavy line of water and touching an intricately engraved *dhammacakka* (Pali for 'Wheel of the Law').

Along the outer walls, several **reliefs** can be seen engraved (some are hard to reach); a few on the south side are rather pornographic.

Inside the temple

Inside the temple's **prayer hall** you'll see several doors ahead. Two lead to passageways that encircle the main buddha image in the cave hall (which is seen straight ahead).

The far left (southwest) doorway leads to the outer chamber, a 310ft passageway with sandstone slabs cut into six tiers. Over 1000 sculptures show a lot of detail of Rakhaing customs (eg traditionally dressed dancers, boxers and acrobats), beasts of burden, and hundreds of Jataka (scenes from Buddha's past 550 lives). At each corner are bigger figures, including the maker King Minbin and his queens at the southwest corner. The passage opens in the front, where you can step out for views.

Next to the outer chamber entry is a coiling inner chamber leading past scores of buddha images in niches, passing a Buddha footprint where – it's said – Buddha walked during his post-enlightenment. Once you get to the dead end, double back to the hall, and see if you can feel the passageway becoming cooler. Some claim it does, symbolising the 'cooling effect' of Buddhist teachings.

Andaw Paya
BUDDHIST TEMPLE

အံတော်ဘုရား

Immediately northeast of Shittaung stands a smaller, eight-sided monument with a similar linear layout: rectangular prayer hall to the east, multispired sanctuary to the west. Sixteen *zedi* (stupas) are aligned in a square-cornered U-shape around the southern, northern and western platforms. As at Shittaung, small windows admit light and ventilation, but here the fluorescent glare is dimmer. Two concentric passageways are lined with buddha niches; in the centre of the shrine, an eight-sided pillar supports the roof.

The original construction of the shrine is ascribed to King Minhlaraza in 1521. King Minrazagyi then rebuilt Andaw in 1596 to enshrine a piece of the tooth relic supposedly brought from Sri Lanka by King Minbin in the early 16th century.

Dukkanthein Paya
BUDDHIST TEMPLE

ဒုက္ကသိမ်ဘုရား

Across the road to the west of Shittaung, the Dukkanthein (also spelled Htuk Kant Thein) smacks of a bunker (with stupas). Wide stone steps lead up the south and east side of the building considered to be an ordination hall; take the east side steps to reach the entrance. Many consider this to be Mrauk U's most interesting pagoda.

Built by King Minphalaung in 1571, Dukkanthein's interior features spiralling cloisters lined with images of buddhas and common people (such as landlords, governors, officials and their spouses) sporting all of **Mrauk U's 64 traditional hairstyles**. The passageway nearly encircles the centre three times before reaching the sun-drenched buddha image, now lit by Christmas-style lights too.

The poorly restored Laymyetnha Paya, 90yd north, looks a bit like a squashed-up version of the Dukkanthein, but was actually built 140 years earlier.

Mahabodhi Shwegu
BUDDHIST TEMPLE

မဟာဗောဓိရွှေဂူ

This squat hilltop temple, northeast of Ratanabon Paya in a quiet area with fewer villagers (and visitors), is located past two gold hilltop *zedi* and a covered water well. Its narrow passageway leads to a 6ft central buddha and four buddhas in niches. The best are the 280 Jataka scenes, depicting the *tribumi* – Buddhist visions of heaven, earth and hell – including acrobats, worshippers, and animal love scenes (!) engraved onto either side of the arched entry walls also.

Ratanabon Paya
STUPA

ရတနာဘုံဘုရား

This massive stupa (sometimes called Yadanapon), just north of Andaw Paya, is ringed by 24 smaller stupas. It was apparently built by Queen Shin Htway in 1612. During WWII a bomb nailed it, but it had already been picked at by treasure hunters attracted by the name, which means 'accumulation of treasure'. Renovations later repaired the enormous bomb-made crack and reinserted the tall *chattra* (spire).

Laungbanpyauk Paya
BUDDHIST TEMPLE

လောင်ပွန်းပြောက်ဘုရား

Back on the road, and 100yd north, is this octagonal, slightly leaning *zedi* built by King Minkhaungraza in 1525. An unusual feature is its outer wall, adorned with Islamic-inspired glazed tiles in the shape of large flowers.

Pitaka Taik
BUDDHIST LIBRARY

ပိဋကတ်တိုက်

At the end of the road, 180yd north, this compact, highly ornate stone building is one of the seven Mrauk U libraries left out of the original 48. Covered over by a blue-and-maroon shelter, it was built in 1591 by King Minphalaung as a repository for the Tripitaka (Three Baskets; the Buddhist canon), which was received from Sri Lanka in the 1640s. It's wee – only 13ft long and 9ft high.

PAMELA GUTMAN

An Honorary Associate in the Department of Art History at the University of Sydney, and author of *Burma's Lost Kingdoms: Splendours of Arakan*, Pamela Gutman has been travelling to Myanmar since the early 1970s when she began work on her PhD on Rakhaing's ancient art, architecture and inscriptions. The following are her top temple picks in Mrauk U:

» **Shittaung Paya** (p281) Regarded as the repository of Rakhaing national identity.

» **Dukkanthein Paya** (p282) For its mysterious buddha-lined passageways.

» **Andaw Paya** (p282) For its remarkable collection of sculptures.

» **Mahabodhi Shwegu** (p282) An example of the early style of Buddhist sculpture at Mrauk U and for its representation of the Buddhist heaven, earth and hell. If you look carefully you can spot some erotic carvings on the buddha's throne – very naughty for a Buddhist temple!

EAST GROUP

This area stretches a mile or so east of the palace walls.

Kothaung Paya
BUDDHIST TEMPLE

ကိုးသောင်းဘုရား

One of Mrauk U's highlights, this restored temple is a mile or so east of the palace. At 230ft by 250ft, it's Mrauk U's largest temple. Built in 1553 by King Minbin's son, King Mintaikkha, to outdo his pop's Shittaung by 10,000 images ('Kothaung' means 'Shrine of 90,000 Images'), much of it was found in fragments. Legends vary – that lightning or an earthquake in 1776 destroyed it, jewel-seekers overturned walls, or that it was built with inferior stones by a superstitious king bent on beating a six-month timeline.

The outer passageway is lined with thousands of bas reliefs on the walls and buddha images (some headless). Stairways lead up to a top terrace, once dotted with 108 stupas.

Get here either on the winding road to Sakyamanaung (just north of Moe Cherry), veering right at one fork, or from the east–west road from the market, veering left before the bridge.

Sakyamanaung Paya
BUDDHIST TEMPLE

သက္ကမာန်အောင်ဘုရား

Roughly half a mile northeast of the palace walls, and behind Shwegudaung hill, this graceful Mon-influenced *zedi* was erected in 1629 by King Thirithudhammaraza. At this later stage, stupas were built more vertically and ornately than before.

The lower half of the well-preserved 280ft *zedi* features a multitiered octagonal shape as at Laungbanpyauk Paya, but beyond this the bells revert to a layered circular shape mounted by a decorative *hti* (umbrella-like

top). You'll see brightly painted, half-kneeling giants at the west gate.

Looking over Shwegudaung hill (back to the west) **Ratanamanaung** offers fine views. From the path off the road, villagers will probably walk with you towards Ratanamanaung.

Peisi Daung Paya
BUDDHIST TEMPLE

ပိသိတောင်ဘုရား

On a hill immediately south of Kothaung, sits this unrestored four-door pagoda, housing four sandstone buddha images. Push your way past the rubble and cobwebs for the wondrous views from the top. It's up to you whether you believe the locals who claim that it has the honour of keeping testicle relics of the Buddha.

Returning to town you'll pass the **Phraouk Paya**, another hilltop pagoda.

PALACE SITE & AROUND

Just east of the main strip of Mrauk U village, the one-time royal palace of Mrauk U now is mostly crumbling walls (though the outer walls still stand 11.5ft high).

According to the legend, King Minbin's astrologers advised a move here in 1429 after the palace at Launggret had been invaded by 'poisonous snakes and evil birds'. His representatives witnessed some strange things at this spot – an old guy playing a flute pointed to a cat-chasing rat and then a snake-biting frog – apparently suggesting its soil as being worthy of a king. Construction began in 1430 (though some sources say it didn't start until 1553).

Palace Museum
MUSEUM

(admission $5; ⊙9am-4pm Mon-Fri) Just inside the palace's western walls is the Department of Archaeology's museum, which houses

ⓘ BOOKS ABOUT MRAUK U

There are several useful books on Rakhaing history and Mrauk U. Myar Aung's paperback *Famous Monuments of Mrauk-U* (2007; K3500) is sold at a couple of places in Mrauk U, including the Bandoola Monastery and the Waddy Htut Guest House; it has lots of photos but its poorly translated text isn't the easiest to follow. Far better is Pamela Gutman's scholarly *Burma's Lost Kingdom: Splendours of Arakan* (2006), Tun Shwe Khine's artful *A Guide to Mrauk U* (1993) and U Shwe Zan's more detailed *The Golden Mrauk U: An Ancient Capital of Rakhine* (1997), all of which you should search out before heading to Mrauk U.

buddha images, inscribed stone slabs (a 15th-century one features ancient Arabic writing), cannons, Wethali-era coins and a helpful model of the Mrauk U site. Old photos on the walls include a before-restoration shot of Ratanabon's crack. Items are signed in English, although foreign scholars note that the dates on some pieces should be taken with a pinch of salt. If you come on a weekend, ask next door for the key.

Haridaung Paya   BUDDHIST TEMPLE
ဟာရိုတောင်ဘုရား:
Built around 1750, this small white temple with particularly good westward views, is on a hilltop just north of the palace walls. It's a good place to get your bearings or to view sunset.

SOUTH GROUP
South of the palace site and across the river are evocative, easy-to-lose-your-way back lanes through thatched-hut villages and a host of pagodas. About half a mile south, the Laksaykan Gate leads to the eponymous lake, a source of clean water.

Bandoola Kyaung   BUDDHIST MONASTERY
ဗန္ဓုလကျောင်:
Climb the steps to view this rambling hilltop monastery, home to yet another of buddha's many scattered molars, a relic brought here from Sri Lanka in the 16th century. The complex is also known as the Sanda Muni Phara Gri Kyaung, after the Sanda Muni, a buddha statue said to have been cast from

the precious metal leftover from making the Mahamuni buddha (p287).

Legend has it that this 4ft image was encased in cement in the 1850s to protect it from pillaging British troops, and then forgotten about for over a century. In April 1988 one of the glazed eyes dropped out, revealing the metal statue below. It's now housed in a new building to the rear of the main hall packed with more ancient buddha images that the monks will happily explain to you. They will also point out a large copper roof tile (used as a table top), saved from Mrauk U's palace after the Burmese carted the rest off to Mandalay back in the 18th century.

Shwetaung Paya   BUDDHIST TEMPLE
ရွှေတောင်ဘုရား:
Southwest of the palace, the 'Golden Hill Pagoda' is the highest in Mrauk U; you can see it for nearly half the trip from Sittwe. Built by King Minbin in 1553, it's accessed by a few trails largely lost under thick vegetation. This is a good spot from which to view sunrise.

🎊 Festivals & Events
One of the most interesting times to visit Mrauk U is during the huge weeklong paya pwe (pagoda festival) held near Dukkanthein Paya (p282) in mid-May which includes music, dance, traditional wrestling and boat racing.

🛏 Sleeping
Generators keep power going most of the day and night at some guesthouses; otherwise expect power to be on only from 7am to 3pm and 6pm to 11.30pm.

TOP CHOICE Shwe Thazin Hotel   HOTEL $$
(☎24200, ext 50168, 09 850 1844; www.shweth azinhotel.com; Sunshaseik Quarter; r from $50; ❄) This new complex offers the best balance of price, comfort and location. There's a small but welcome amount of artistic design in its chalet-style rooms, all of which are en-suite with a satellite TV and a fridge.

Mrauk U Princess Hotel   RESORT $$$
(☎50232, 09 850 0556; www.mraukooprincessre sort.net; s/d $170/194; ❄@) Mrauk U's most luxurious digs, the Princess offers 21 beautifully decorated wooden villas with fresh flowers adorning the bed, the bathtub and tables. Gardens and ponds (mosquitoes!) surround the villas and the central monastery-like restaurant and spa. Rates include

breakfast and dinner, and it's the town's only hotel with an internet connection.

Vesali Resort Hotel
HOTEL $$

(☏24200, ext 50008, in Yangon 01-526 593; myathiri@mptmail.net.mm; s/d $40/45) Though removed from the bulk of the temples and town, the Vesali's 18 snazzy bungalows offer dark-wood floors, vaulted bamboo ceilings, mosquito nets, private decks and modern bathrooms. Rooms come with battery-powered lamps. There's an inviting restaurant up front along with gardens, and behind is a path up to Shwetaung Paya.

Royal City Guest House
HOTEL $$

(☏24200, ext 50257; www.newpalacehotelsittwe.com/royal-city.htm; Minbar Gyi Rd, r s/d $15/20, bungalow s/d $25/30; ❋) This place is conveniently located on the road between the jetty and the market, but skip the cell-like rooms in the main building in favour of the smart, new brick bungalow-style rooms across the road. The air con comes on only from 6pm to 11pm but it claims to have 24 hour hot water.

Nawarat Hotel
HOTEL $$

(☏24200, ext 50077, in Yangon 01-578 786; s $40-50, d $50-60; ❋) Offering all-night electricity, the Nawarat's 30-room motel-style complex, a short walk from the (out of sight) Shittaung Paya, suffers a bit in atmosphere. The walled-off compound consists of boxy bungalow rooms with air-con, satellite TVs and glow-in-the-dark stars on some ceilings. Identical, cheaper rooms get power 6pm to 6am only.

Golden Star Guest House
GUESTHOUSE $

(☏24200, ext 50175, 09 850 1664; 116 Min Bar Gree Rd; per person $5-15) Across from a small reservoir, is Mrauk U's best cheap deal, with little Rakhaing-style figurines and private cold-water bathrooms in most of the 13 basic rooms. The English-speaking manager is very helpful, sometimes adding a free lunch for long stayers. Two 'traditional house' rooms out the back look out into a palm forest (these are $15).

Prince Hotel
GUESTHOUSE $

(☏24200, ext 50174, in Yangon 09 501 9114; www.mraukuprincehotel.com; r $15 & 25) Half a mile southeast of the market, this leafy complex of nine bungalows sits below a hill in a leafy garden. The rustic bungalows are a bit aged for the price, but the family who run it are extremely hospitable, and the wife is an excellent cook. They can also arrange good trips to the Chin villages.

Waddy Htut Guest House
GUESTHOUSE $

(☏24200, ext 50240; r $5-30) This modern-style two-floor house has an OK mix of options – basic rooms with shared bath ($5), a well-lit 'family room' with sofa, a few beds and a balcony ($30, but negotiable). Rates don't include breakfast but there's a teahouse next door and the market is around the corner.

✖ Eating

There are a few local restaurants facing the market to the west of the Mrauk U market, serving basic Chinese food. The Gamone Phyu restaurant at Mrauk U Princess Hotel and the one at the Vesali Resort Hotel are both very good and open to nonguests.

[TOP CHOICE] Moe Cherry
BAMAR, RAKHAING $

(☏24200, ext 50177; dishes K1000-2000, beer K1500) This friendly, traveller-focused, two-storey restaurant, east of the palace walls, serves a few meals and what's on offer changes nightly. There's a deliciously Rakhaing edge to the chicken curry, prawn and vegie dishes (cauliflower's the best). They're open 'anytime: this is our home' and the restaurant also arranges area tours.

For You
BAMAR, RAKHAING $

(dishes K1000) Two blocks north of the market (via the road from the jetty), this plain, concrete-floor restaurant is based at the ground level of a traditional wood house. It serves good noodles (with an egg on top) and cans of Myanmar beer.

Hay Mar
BAMAR $

(dishes K1000) This simple teahouse beside the main jetty is a good spot to watch the comings and goings on the river while tucking into simple dishes, such as fried rice, chicken and vegetables. The owner, Aung Zan is the local Mr Fix-it – offering boat rides back to Sittwe (from $20 per person) and Chin Village trips (K50,000).

🛍 Shopping

Stalls outside the Shittaung Paya sell some souvenirs. Aung Zan at Hay Mar teahouse can also guide you to a weaver in the village – a short walk or bike ride south of the jetty – who has attractive textile pieces for sale (K2500 to K15,000).

L'amitie Art Gallery ART GALLERY

(paintings $35-100; ⊙7am-7pm) Located in a simple hut opposite the Dukkanthein Paya, L'amitie (French for 'friendship') is hung with attractive canvases in oils and pastels created by the 54-year-old ex civil servant, Shwe Maung Thar and his son, Khine Minn Tun (29).

The paintings are of landscapes and pastoral scenes (that skillfully capture the light and tranquillity of Mrauk U), still-life compositions of vegetables, and portraits. Shwe Maung Thar also painted the ceiling panels in the central hall of Shittaung Paya.

In 2000 Trevor Wilson, Australia's ambassador to Myanmar at the time, met Shwe Maung Thar and was so impressed with his work that he helped arrange gallery shows in Canberra in 2005 and 2007. Shwe Maung Thar's canvases have also been displayed at a gallery in Vienna and a couple of galleries in Yangon.

Whether you buy or not, Shwe Maung Thar is very happy to chat.

❶ Information

In case of an emergency, the hospital at Sittwe is your best bet. For minor bruises and stomach upsets, friendly **Dr Aye Maung Zan** (☑24200, ext 50032; Main Rd), south of the market, speaks English.

Mrauk U's only **internet** connection is at the Mrauk U Princess Hotel ($4 per hour).

The town shares a handful of telephone lines, so most local numbers add on an extension. To make an international call head to stalls around the market offering connections via cell phones.

❶ Getting There & Away

BOAT For information on boat services to Mrauk U, see p279.

The Mrauk U **Jetty** is about half a mile south of the market. If you don't want to get back by government ferry, it's often possible to jump aboard a fellow traveller's boat and share costs for the ride. Negotiating a one-way 'private boat' ride may be possible too ($20).

❶ Getting Around

HORSE CART Rides around the temples costs about K10,000 per day (the stand is just southeast of the palace site).

JEEP Usually fitting four plus a driver, a jeep ride (arranged by your hotel or from the stand on the north side of the palace site) should be K4000 between the jetty and hotels, K18,000 around Mrauk U, or K30,000 to the Lemro River or Mahamuni Paya.

TRISHAW & BICYCLE Rides between the jetty and hotels are K2000. Hotels can get you a bicycle for K2000 or K3000, or you could rent one for K1500 from the **shop** south of the bridge leading to the central market.

Around Mrauk U

The temples are only a part of the area's attractions. Tack on a few extra days here to enjoy a relaxing boat ride down the Lemro River to Chin villages, or to venture out to a couple of archaeological and religious sites north of Mrauk U that are of particular pride for locals.

CHIN VILLAGES

The day trip from Mrauk U to various Chin villages scattered along the nearby Lemro River is recommended. The boat ride is nicer than the one to Mrauk U from Sittwe because of the chance to observe life (up close) on and along the river. You can usually stop off at one of the peanut, chilli or bean farms – located on islands or on the riverside – that you pass on the way. Time your trip for Tuesday or Saturday to attend the busy morning market at the village of Pan Mraun.

These boat trips don't quite reach Chin State, but they do provide an opportunity to meet elderly Chin women who have tattooed faces (p310). This traditional practice ended a couple of generations ago; unlike the sad situation of Padaung women (p192), these chatty, proud, old women are the last of their kind.

You may feel ambivalent about taking photos but the women we met didn't seem to mind posing, having made a conscious decision to use their unique and soon-to-disappear looks as a way of attracting tourists and earning money for the betterment of their impoverished communities. Simple weavings are sold in the villages and without tourist donations (you should plan on donating a few thousand kyat) it's highly unlikely that there would be a school building, let alone salaries for the teachers who work there.

❶ Getting There & Away

BOAT Typical trips, which your guesthouse or hotel can help arrange, begin at 7am or 8am and include a two- to three-hour boat ride each way, and an hour or so at a couple of villages. The charge is $90 and includes jeep transfers to the boat, a simple lunch and an English-speaking guide for a boat accommodating up to four passengers. There's not much in the way of food or drink to buy in the Chin villages so pack any extra snacks and water you'll need.

WETHALI

ဝေသာလီ

Almost 6 miles north of Mrauk U are the remains of the kingdom of Wethali (aka Vesali, or Waithali in local parlance). According to the Rakhaing chronicles, Wethali was founded in AD 327 by King Mahataing Chandra. Archaeologists believe that this kingdom lasted until the 8th century. Little remains of the oval-shaped city (and apparently some buildings were damaged purposely for road-building materials in recent years). The walls of the 1650ft by 990ft central palace site are reasonably well preserved.

The main attraction for visitors en route to Mahamuni Paya is the so-called **Great Image of Hsu Taung Pre** (Pye), home to a 16.5ft Rakhaing-style sitting buddha. It's said to be carved from a single piece of stone and date to AD 327 (but most visitors argue the features look more modern).

Regular transport is rare. It's possible to reach here by bicycle (take the sign that says 'VSL' and 'you are here' east from the main road).

MAHAMUNI PAYA

မဟာမုနိဘုရား:

Some local Rakhaing recount, with fresh, fiery passion, how the Bamar King Bodawpaya sent soldiers to dismantle and remove the Mahamuni buddha in 1784. Originally housed here at the Mahamuni Paya, 25 miles north of Mrauk U and just north of the former ancient capital of Dhanyawady, the image is one of the country's most famous and venerated. Although the buddha now resides in Mandalay (p208), its original site remains a fascinating place to visit.

Some Rakhaing believe the image was cast when Buddha visited the area in 554 BC. Others say King Bodawpaya unknowingly took a counterfeit back to Amarapura (to which it was originally relocated) and the true one rests under the banyan tree at the site's southwest corner. The Rakhaing don't let go easily.

The current Konbaung-style shrine dates from the 19th century, as earlier ones were destroyed by fire. The Mahamuni buddha is gone, but 'Mahamuni's brother' is now one of three fine golden images resting inside. Down the steps, near the south walls of the shrine, is a small **museum** (free) with a couple of dozen relics and engraved stones.

The hilltop golden stupas visible (barely) to the east, are the first indication that you're close to **Salagiri Hill**, the fabled site Buddha

visited in 554 BC. It's as close as you'll get, as the area is closed to foreigners.

The easiest way to get to the site from Mrauk U is by hired jeep (K35,000; three hours one way); you should be able to stop at Wethali along the way.

CHIN STATE

Hilly, sparsely populated and severely lacking infrastructure, much of Chin State (ချင်းပြည်နယ်) is off limits to travellers. The people and culture exhibit a mixture of native, Bengali and Indian influences similar to that found among the Rakhaing, with a much lower Bamar presence; for more on the Chin see p308.

All visits to Chin State require government permission and the presence of a licensed guide – something that will take at least 20 days, and more likely a month, to arrange.

There are a couple of options to mingle with Chin people just outside Chin State that don't require government permits: villages near Mrauk U in Rakhaing State and a flight from Mandalay to Kalaymyo (Kalay), a half Chin town in Sagaing Region just northeast of Chin State.

Mt Victoria (Nat Ma Taung)

ဝိတိုရိယတောင် (နတ်မတောင်)

As long as you're with a licensed guide, one of the few areas of Chin State on the tourist radar is **Mt Victoria** (Nat Ma Taung), roughly 80 miles west of Bagan. The 10,016ft (3,053m) mountain, Myanmar's second highest, stands amid a 279 sq mile national park and is a prime spot for **birdwatching**. It's best visited in November when the rhododendron bushes that cover the slopes are in full bloom.

Several tour agencies have itineraries covering Mt Victoria, including Yangon-based **Bike World Explores Myanmar** (☑09 513 4190; www.bwemtravel.com) offering both trekking and cycling tours to the mountain; and the experienced Yangon-based guide **Mr Saw** (☑09 4929 2258; www.toursmyanmar.com; saww.myanmar@googlemail.com).

Saw charges $550 per person from Nyaung U (Bagan) for a five-day (four-night) trip including car, driver, guide, accommodation (minimum two people per trip).

The loop from Nyaung U starts with a seven-hour ride to Mindat town – across

WESTERN MYANMAR MT VICTORIA (NAT MA TAUNG)

the Ayeyarwady (Irrawaddy) River on rough roads. The next day it's seven more hours to Kampelet at the foot of the mountain, where you trek up to the summit (3 miles one way). It's possible to camp overnight on the mountain and it's an eight-hour ride back to Nyaung U from Kampelet.

Longer itineraries, including visits to the region to take part in the Chin National Day celebrations (usually held around 20 February) and an overland journey from Mrauk U, can be also be arranged.

Kalaymyo (Kalay)

ကလေး

It's remote, and not particularly exciting, but travellers with hopes to mingle with Chin folk can fly to Kalaymyo (often called Kalay) without government permission. The town – 9 miles long, rarely more than two blocks wide and about 62 miles from the Indian border – offers few sights beyond a central market and a pagoda. It's more interesting to see its half Burmese, half Chin population and its slender setting, ringed by far-off, lush mountains.

Foreigners who do make it here are typically Christian missionaries ministering to the Chin (who are 95% Christian and live in the western half of town). The Chin folk sometimes refer to Kalaymyo as 'Zomi'. There's some local debate on who lived here first, Bamar or Chin. No women have tattooed faces here.

Across the street from the airport is **Taung Za Lat Hotel** (☑073-21463; Bogyoke Rd; s/d from $15/20) the lone hotel licensed for foreigners. Be prepared for grubby rooms with balconies, fans, screened windows and squashed 'squitoes left on the walls. More expensive rooms are slightly bigger but not really worth it.

In theory, both Myanma Airways ($105) and Air Bagan ($152) offer at least a couple of flights a week here from Yangon (2 hours), but the schedule depends on demand, so be prepared for last-minute changes and cancellations. The same applies to flights from Mandalay (from $45; one hour).

Understand Myanmar (Burma)

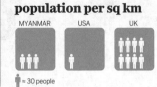

population per sq km

MYANMAR   USA   UK

👤 ≈ 30 people

Myanmar (Burma) Today

Roadmap to Democracy?

In October 2010 Myanmar went to the polls for its first national election in 20 years, part of the generals' plan for a 'discipline flourishing democracy'. Following the victory of the military-backed Union Solidarity & Development Party (USDP), National League for Democracy (NLD) leader Aung San Suu Kyi was released from her latest stint of house arrest – and instantly jumped into the fray, and rounds of interviews with the international media, reminding people of the 2100 other political prisoners still in detention.

To everyone's surprise, a new national flag was unveiled at the end of the year, while in February 2011 a quasi-civilian parliament convened for its initial sessions, replacing the military regime's State Peace and Development Council (SPDC). A new president, former general and old prime minister Thein Sein, was 'chosen' by the elected reps to take over from Senior General Than Shwe, Myanmar's supreme ruler for the past two decades.

When the new parliament was sworn in at the end of March and a new head of the military, Min Aung Hlaing, was announced, a tick appeared against the seventh, and final, step on the junta's 'roadmap to democracy'. In response, neither the US nor the EU fully dropped their sanctions against Myanmar, but both softened their stance – the former appointing Derek Mitchell as a special envoy, the latter easing travel restrictions on key members of the new government.

A 'Deeply Flawed' Election

Has much changed in Myanmar? Over 30 different political parties did manage to jump through a considerable number of hoops to contest the election, including the National Democratic Force (NDF), a breakaway group from the NLD that, unlike its parent party, decided to participate in the poll. However, few were surprised by the results, which saw the

» GDP per capita: $435

» Cost of a mobile phone SIM card: $1000

» Internet users: 0.1% of the population

» Political Prisoners: 1994 (June 2011; source www. aappb.org)

Travel Literature

The Trouser People Journalist Andrew Marshall retraces the steps of Sir George Scott, who traversed unmapped corners of British Burma in the late 1800s. **Golden Earth** Norman Lewis's account of his trip through Burma in the turbulent 1950s.

Finding George Orwell in Burma Sarah Larkin's evocative and perceptive travelogue recounts Orwell's days here as a colonial policeman, as well as the modern-day plight of Myanmar.

Documentaries

Burma VJ About the monks' uprising in 2007. **Burma Soldier** The journey of a Burmese soldier from junta supporter to democracy activist. **This Prison Where I Live** Covers the plight of political prisoner Zargana.

belief systems
(% of population)

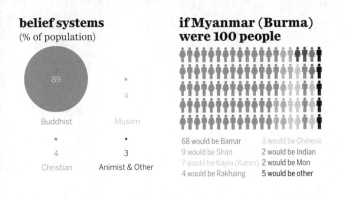

89 Buddhist

4 Muslim

4 Christian

3 Animist & Other

if Myanmar (Burma) were 100 people

68 would be Bamar
9 would be Shan
7 would be Kayin (Karen)
4 would be Rakhaing

3 would be Chinese
2 would be Indian
2 would be Mon
5 would be other

The graphics above are based on data from the CIA World Fact Book, which differs from the data of the Myanmar government; see p316 for more on Myanmar

USDP triumph, amid numerous reports of serious interference with the voting process. The UN called the election 'deeply flawed' and many other respected commentators (among them US President Barack Obama and British Ambassador to Burma, Andrew Heyn) expressed concerns that it was neither free nor fair.

However, most of the new political parties and civil capacity building organisations (civic value educational bodies), such as Myanmar Egress (www.myanmaregress.org) fervently believe that participating in the election was worthwhile – however flawed the result may have been. In their view, a 'political space' had opened up for them for the first time in two decades. These groups are now looking towards the next election, scheduled for 2015, as a chance to expand that space. One hopeful development was the government's initiation of talks with NLD leader Aung San Suu Kyi in August 2011.

A New Government?

Under the 2008 constitution Myanmar is divided into seven regions (where the Bamar are in the majority) and seven states (minority regions, namely Chin, Kachin, Kayah, Kayin, Mon, Rakhaing and Shan States). In addition there are six ethnic enclaves (Danu, Kokang, Naga, Palaung, Pa-O and Wa) with a degree of self-governance.

A quarter of the seats both at the national and state level are reserved for unelected military candidates; this gives the military a casting vote on any constitutional change because these require a parliamentary majority of more than 75%. One outcome of the election is that in four of the seven state legislatures (Chin, Kayin, Rakhaing and Shan) ethnic parties hold over 25% of the seats, theoretically allowing them to call special sessions or initiate impeachment proceedings against local public officials.

Top Downloads

Irrawaddy (www.irrawaddy.org) Focuses on politics and culture.
Mizzima (www.mizzima.com) A nonprofit news service run by Myanmar journalists in exile.
Transnational Institute (www.tinyurl.com/4y2vphq) Politics and social issues.

Top Fiction

Burmese Days George Orwell depicts small-town Burma of the 1920s, damning colonialism along the way.
The Glass Palace Amitav Ghosh's novel is a fictionalised, but accurate, account of Burma's history.

The Piano Tuner Daniel Mason's elegant adventure story is about a London piano tuner who heads off into Burma's jungles in the 1880s to repair a famous instrument.

At the time of writing, much of the daily mechanics of government, including how the national and state legislatures will interact and the role of the military, remained unclear. Seasoned observers, such as Macquarie University academic Sean Turnell, are sceptical of the notion that Than Shwe has relinquished power, believing that behind the scenes he continues to be the government's puppet master.

A Land of Rumours

Myanmar's national parliament is made up of the 440-seat People's Assembly (*Pyithu Hluttaw*) and the 224-seat Upper House (*Amytha Hluttaw*). There are also seven state legislatures.

Whoever is in charge, it's pretty clear they've got quite a job on their hands to revive the country's fortunes. Yangon may have a few flashy shopping malls and wi-fi-enabled cafe-bars where fashionably attired youths sip cappuccinos and jabber into mobile phones, but the vast majority of people in Myanmar remain the poorest in Southeast Asia. According to Sean Turnell from Macquarie University in Sydney, the economy 'is unbalanced, unstable and devoid of the institutions and attributes necessary to achieve transformational growth.' Transparency International (www.transparency.org) places Myanmar behind only Somalia as the most corrupt country in the world, and along many of the country's borders the longest running civil war in modern history continues to spark and flare.

Reporters Without Borders (http://en.rsf.org) nails Myanmar as a 'censor's paradise', but also notes that the local media did a professional and creative job covering the 2010 election and Aung San Suu Kyi's release. Still, most locals glean what they can about the machinations of power in their country from the tried and trusted channels of gossip and rumour. While in Bagan on research in February 2011, we heard it whispered that billionaire Tay Za (see p26) had been involved in a helicopter accident hundreds of miles north in the Himalaya Mountains near Putao. A few days later the rumour was confirmed on the internet. That's how news travels in Myanmar.

Dos & Don'ts

» Do remove shoes on entering a Buddhist site or home. Dress respectfully: no shorts, short skirts or exposed shoulders.

» Don't touch somebody on the head (including a child).

» Don't pose with or sit on buddha images.

» Don't point your feet at anyone or anything – apologise if you accidentally brush someone with your foot.

» Don't speak politics with locals unless they raise the subject first.

» Do ask before your photograph anyone.

Greetings

» Greet someone by saying *mingala-ba*, meaning 'auspiciousness be upon you'.

» Use a person's full name – locals don't have surnames

» Shake hands or pass money with your right hand, with left hand 'holding up' your right arm.

History

The roots of Myanmar's present complex, tragic situation can be traced back through its convoluted history. Spanning several millennia, Myanmar's history involves a bewildering cast of people and competing kingdoms.

Long before the British took control of Burma in three waves in the 19th century, the area was ruled over by several major ethnic groups, with the Bamar only coming into prominence in the 11th century. Britain managed the mountainous border regions separately from the fertile plains and delta of central and lower Burma, building on a cultural rift between the lowland Bamar and highland ethnic groups that lingers today. Civil war erupted between minority groups after independence in 1948, and in pockets of the country the unrest continues today.

General Ne Win wrested control from the elected government in 1962 and began the world's longest-running military dictatorship, pursuing xenophobic policies – such as nationalising most of the country's industries and business, severely curtailing international trade, only allowing 24-hour visas for tourists (later extended to a week) and controlling all books and magazines allowed into the country – that isolated Burma from the rest of the world. State socialism ruined the economy, necessitating several major currency devaluations, the last of which sparked mass, peaceful street protests in 1988.

The prodemocracy marches saw Aung San Suu Kyi emerge as the leader of the National League for Democracy (NLD). The military used violence to stop the marches, then, to everyone's surprise, called a national election. It thought it couldn't lose. But at the 1990 election the NLD won 82% of the assembly seats. The military simply refused to transfer power and threw many elected politicians into jail.

In the years since, Myanmar's trade with its neighbours (particularly Thailand and China) and its membership of Asean, have enabled the government to withstand increased international scorn and Western sanctions. The military's aggressive reaction to the 2007 protests (the

Outrage: Burma's Struggle for Democracy by Bertl Lintner is one of several works by the long-time Bangkok-based foreign correspondent and Burma expert, exploring the machinations of Myanmar's military government.

failed 'Saffron Revolution') and its inaction following Cyclone Nargis in 2008, the worst natural disaster ever to befall the nation, have caused it to become even more despised and feared.

Elections for a civilian government in 2010 and the release of Aung San Suu Kyi from house arrest have provided a glimmer of hope for some. But for others it's just business as usual in Myanmar, with the military as much in control as it has been for the past half century.

Pre-Colonial Burma

The Earliest Inhabitants

Archaeologists believe humans have lived in the region as far back as 75,000 BC. The limestone Padah-Lin Caves in western Shan State contain paintings that could be 13,000 years old, and there's evidence that local farmers had domesticated chickens and made bronze by 1500 BC. At least 2500 years ago, the area was a key land link between traders from India and the Middle East and China. Ancient Greeks knew of the country too.

In 2003 the BBC reported the finding of a 45-million-year-old fossil (possibly the anklebone of a large ape-like animal) in central Myanmar that might just prove the area to be the birthplace of *all* humans. The implication of this research, written up in an academic paper by paleontologist Laurent Marivaux of the University of Montpellier II, is that our primate ancestors may have had Asian rather than African origins. Not surprisingly, the military government was happy to embrace this interpretation.

The First Burmese Empire

Bagan was nearly 200 years old when its 'golden period' kicked off – signalled by an energetic, can-do King Anawrahta taking the throne in 1044. His conquest of the Mon kingdom and the adoption of Buddhism inspired a creative energy in Bagan. It quickly became a city of glorious temples and the capital of the First Burmese Empire. For more on the history of Bagan, see p150.

Anawrahta's successors (Kyanzittha, Alaungsithu and Htilominlo) lacked his vision, and the kingdom's power slowly declined. In 1273 King Narathihapate made the diplomatic mistake of offending the growing power of Kublai Khan by executing his envoys. When the Mongols invaded in 1287, Narathihapate fled south to Pyay (Prome) where he committed suicide.

In the ensuing chaos, Shan tribes (closely related to the Siamese) from the hills to the east grabbed a piece of the low country, while the Mon in the south broke free of Bamar control and re-established their own kingdom.

KING

Remembered as *Tayokpyay Min*, or 'the King who Ran Away from the Chinese', Narathihapate was also known for his gluttonous appetite, demanding 300 varieties of dishes at his banquets.

AD 754	849	1044	1057
Nanzhao soldiers from Yunnan, China, conquer the hill tribes in the upper reaches of the Ayeyarwady River and challenge the Pyu who ruled from the city of Sri Ksetra.	Bagan is founded on the site of a once-thriving Pyu city; its first name may have been Pyugan, something recorded 200 years later by the Annamese of present-day Vietnam.	Anawrahta slays his brother, takes the throne in Bagan and starts organising his kingdom to kick off the 'golden period' of the First Burmese Empire.	Having subdued the Shan Hills, Anawrahta's armies sack the ancient Mon city of Thaton and bring back 30,000 people to Bagan, including the Mon king, Manuha.

The Second Burmese Empire

It would be another 200 years before the Bamar were able to regroup to found their second empire. During this time a settlement of Bamar refugees in central Taungoo survived between Mon to the south and the Shan to the north and east, by playing the larger forces off against each other.

In the 16th century, a series of Taungoo kings extended their power north, nearly to the Shan's capital at Inwa, then south, taking the Mon kingdom and shifting their own capital to Bago. In 1550 Bayinnaung came to the throne, reunified all of Burma and defeated the neighbouring Siamese so convincingly that it was many years before the long-running friction between the two nations resurfaced.

Following Bayinnaung's death in 1581 the Bamar's power again declined. The capital was shifted north to Inwa in 1636. Its isolation from the sea – effectively cutting off communication around the kingdom – ultimately contributed to Myanmar's defeat by the British.

Thant Myint-U's *River of Lost Footsteps* is a must-read historical review that recounts kings' blunders and successes, while adding occasional family anecdotes of Burma's early days of independence.

HISTORY PRE-COLONIAL BURMA

The Third Burmese Empire

With all the subtlety of a kick to the groin, King Alaungpaya launched the third and final Burmese dynasty by contesting the Mon when the latter

ORIGINAL KINGDOMS

Four major precolonial ethnic groups peppered Burma's flatlands with their kingdoms for centuries, while smaller ethnic groups lived – mostly untouched – in the remote hills beyond. The early histories that are attached to these groups are a mix of fact and legend: see p157 for an archaeologist's perspective.

Pyu Arriving from the Tibeto-Burman plateau and/or from India around the 1st century BC, the Pyu established the first major kingdom of sorts, with city-states in central Myanmar including Beikthano, Hanlin and Sri Ksetra (Thayekhittaya). In the 10th century, Yunnanese invaders from China enslaved or scared off most Pyu.

Rakhaing Also known as Arakanese, these people claim their kingdom was well under way by the 6th century BC. Certainly it was in full force by the 15th century, when their Buddhist kingdom was based in Mrauk U and their navy controlled much of the Bay of Bengal.

Bamar Also known as Burmans, these people arrived from somewhere in the eastern Himalaya in the 8th or 9th century, supplanting the vanquished Pyu and establishing the cultural heartland of Myanmar as it's still known. Centuries of conflict with the Mon erupted after their arrival. Although the Bamar came out on top, the result was really a merger of the two cultures.

Mon This race, who may have originated from eastern India or mainland Southeast Asia, settled fertile lowlands on the Ayeyarwady (Irrawaddy) River delta across Thailand to Cambodia. They developed the area as Suvannabhumi (Golden Land), with their Burmese kingdom centred around present-day Thaton coming into existence around the 9th century.

1084	1273	1290s	1315
Kyanzittha continues the reforms started by his father Anawrahta, including developing the Burmese written language; he's succeeded in 1113 by his grandson, Alaungsithu who rules until 1167.	In a curious gesture of diplomacy against far-superior forces to the north, the Burmese in Bagan slay Tartar ambassadors, prompting a peeved Kublai Khan to invade 14 years later.	Marco Polo becomes possibly the first Westerner to travel in central Burma (then known to foreigners as Mien), and publishes an account of his travels in 1298.	After the collapse of Bagan, Sagaing becomes the capital of a Shan kingdom. The capital moves to Inwa in 1364 and stays there intermittently until 1841.

took over Inwa in 1752. Some say Alaungpaya's sense of invincibility deluded the Burmese into thinking they could resist the British later on.

After Alaungpaya's short and bloody reign, his son Hsinbyushin charged into Thailand and levelled Ayuthaya, forcing the Siamese to relocate their capital to what would eventually become Bangkok. Hsinbyushin's successor, Bodawpaya (another son of Alaungpaya), looked for glory too, and brought the Rakhaing under Burmese control. This eventually led to tension with the British (who had economic interests in Rakhaing territory) that the dynasty would not outlive.

Colonial Burma
Wars with the British

With eyes on fresh markets and supply sources in Southeast Asia, Britain wrested all of Burma in three decisive swipes. In the First, Second and Third Anglo–Burmese Wars they picked up Tanintharyi (Tenasserim) and Rakhaing in 1824, Yangon and southern Burma in 1853, and Mandalay and northern Burma in 1885.

The first war started when Burmese troops, ordered by King Bagyidaw, crossed into British-controlled Assam (in India) from Rakhaing to pursue refugees. General Maha Bandula managed some minor victories using guerrilla tactics, but eventually was killed by cannon fire in 1824. Burmese troops then surrendered. The Treaty of Yandabo, helped by the translator of missionary Adoniram Judson (whose name is still on many Baptist churches in Myanmar), gave Rakhaing and Tenasserim to the British.

Published in 1925, GE Harvey's *History of Burma* gives a chronological rundown of Myanmar's kingdoms from the Pyu era until 1824, faithfully recounting many fanciful legends along the way.

THREE KINGS

Lording it over a military parade ground in Myanmar's capital of Nay Pyi Taw are giant statues of the three kings considered the most important in Burmese history:

» **Anawrahta** (1014–77) The creator of the First Burmese Empire ascended the throne in Bagan in 1044. He unified the Ayeyarwady Valley and held sway over the Shan hills and Rakhaing at the same time as introducing key religious and social reforms that form the basis of modern Burmese culture.

» **Bayinnaung** (1516–81) Aided by Portuguese mercenaries, this king of Taungoo is famed for unifying Burma for its 'second empire' and conquering Ayuthaya, the capital of Siam (Thailand), in 1569. Since 1996, his likeness has ominously looked over Thailand from near the border at Tachileik.

» **Alaungpaya** (1714–60) With no royal roots, this hometown hero of Mokesebo (Shwebo) founded the Konbaung dynasty and created the second largest empire in Burmese history. His reign lasted only eight years, ending when he died – some say from poisoning – on retreat from Siam, after being turned back by rains.

BERNARD NAPTHINE/LONELY PLANET IMAGES ©

» Buddha statues, Mrauk U

1433

Rakhaing's ruler, Naramithla establishes a new capital at Mrauk U, which, over the course of the next few centuries, grows into a grand city of temples and international commerce.

1472

The great Mon King Dhammazedi takes the throne, unifies the Mon, moves the capital from Inwa to Bago (Pegu), and sets up diplomatic contact with Europe.

1527

The Shan, who had exercised increasing control over the area following the fall of Bagan, defeats the kingdom at Inwa and rules Upper Burma for 28 years.

Two Burmese kings later, Bagan Min started his reign in the same manner that many did: with mass executions to rid the capital of his potential rivals. An 1852 incident involving the possible kidnapping of two British sea captains (some argue it never happened) gave the British a welcome excuse for igniting another conflict, and an opportunity for more land. The British quickly seized all of southern Burma, including Yangon and Pathein (Bassein). They then marched north to Pyay (Prome), facing little opposition.

The Final Two Kings

The unpopular Bagan Min was ousted in favour of the more capable and revered Mindon Min, who moved the capital to Mandalay. Palace intrigues, including the murder of Mindon's powerful half-brother by Mindon's own sons, stayed the king's hand in naming his successor. When Mindon suddenly died following an attack of dysentery in 1878, the new (rather reluctant) king, Thibaw Min, was propelled to power by his ruthless wife and scheming mother-in-law. The following massive 'massacre of kinsmen' (79 of Thibaw Min's rivals) made many British papers. Alas, previous kings hadn't had to face the consequences of world media attention, and this act did little to generate public backlash in the UK against Britain's final, decisive war against the Burmese.

In 1885 it took Britain just two weeks to conquer Upper Burma, exile Thibaw and his court to India and establish control over all the country. The conflict is sometimes called 'the war over wood', as Britain's victory allowed it to secure rights to Burma's plentiful teak forests. Direct colonial rule was implemented only where the Bamar were the majority (ie in the central plains). The hill states of the Chin, Kachin, Shan, Kayin and Kayah were allowed to remain largely autonomous – a decision that would have ramifications in the run up to independence in 1948 and beyond.

The Impact of British Rule

Burma was henceforth administered as part of 'British India'. A flood of Indian immigrants were allowed into the country, where they acted like second colonisers: building businesses and taking rare, low-level government jobs from the hostile indigenous population. In 1927 the majority of Yangon's population was Indian. Chinese immigration was also encouraged, further subjugating and marginalising the Burmese people.

Cheap British imports poured in, fuelled by rice profits. Many key cities and towns were renamed by the British with Yangon becoming Rangoon, Pyay became Prome and Bagan was renamed Pagan.

Much of Burma was considered a hardship posting by British colonial officials, who found the locals difficult to govern. On the other hand, many of the British officials were incompetent and insensitive, and refused to

One of the biggest meteor showers in modern history filled Burma's sky in 1885. Locals saw it as an omen of the end of their kingdom.

Despite a British-held ban against visiting Buddhist sites (because of the tradition of visitors being asked to remove their shoes), aviator Amelia Earhart visited them anyway (and took off her shoes).

1540	1551	1599	1760
Lower Burma is reunified after Tabinshwehti, the ambitious and young king of Taungoo, defeats the Mon kingdom at Bago – helped by Burmans fleeing the Shan in Inwa.	Bayinnaung becomes king and, having conquered the Shan in 1557, reunifies all of Myanmar as the Second Burmese Empire; his forces take the Siam capital of Ayuthaya in 1569.	Following his defeat of Bago, the King of Rakhaing grants the Portuguese mercenary Filipe de Brito e Nicote governorship of the port of Syriam (Thanlyin), which he controls until 1613.	Burmese King Alaungpaya, having conquered Inwa, Pyay (Prome), Dagon (which he renames 'Yangon') and Tenasserim (Tanintharyi), fails to take Ayuthaya in Siam and dies during the retreat.

REVOLUTIONARY MONKS

In 1919, at Mandalay's Eindawya Paya, monks evicted Europeans who refused to take off their shoes. The British, sensing that this 'Shoe Question' was the start of a nationalist movement, sentenced the monk leader, U Kettaya, to life imprisonment. This would not be the last involvement of the *sangha* (Buddhist brotherhood) in politics.

U Ottama, a monk who had studied in India and returned to Burma in 1921, promoted religious liberation as a way to bring the independence movement to the attention of the average local Buddhist. After numerous arrests, U Ottama died in prison in 1939. Another monk, U Wizaya, died in prison in 1929 after a 163-day hunger strike, which began as a protest against a rule that forbade imprisoned monks from wearing robes.

In the footsteps of these martyrs to the nationalist cause strode the brave monks who, risking arrest and worse, marched the streets in 2007. Monks currently account for 256 of Burma's 1994 political prisoners and include the 31-year-old U Gambira, one of the organisers of the 2007 protests, who is serving a sentence of 68 years.

honour local customs such as removing shoes to enter temples, and thus causing grave offence to the majority Buddhist population. Inflamed by opposition to colonial rule, unemployment and the undercutting of the traditional educational role of Buddhist monasteries, the country had the highest crime rate in the British Empire. And apart from constructing railroads and schools, the British built prisons, including the infamous Insein prison, the Empire's largest (and still in use by the current government).

The Burman (1882) and Burma: A Handbook of Practical Information (1906) by colonial adventurer Sir J George Scott remain today in print and still provide an insight into the nation's culture.

Rise of Nationalism

Burmese nationalism burgeoned in the early days of the 20th century, often led by Buddhist monks. University students in Yangon went on strike on National Day in 1920, protesting elitist entrance requirements at British-built universities. The students referred to each other as *thakin* (master), as they claimed to be the rightful masters of Burma. One *thakin* – a young man called Aung San – was expelled from university in 1936 for refusing to reveal the author of a politically charged article.

Growing demands for self-government and opposition to colonial rule eventually forced the British to make a number of concessions. In 1937, Burma was separated administratively from India and a new legislative council including elected Burmese ministers was formed. However, the country continued to be torn by a stuggle between opposing political parties and sporadic outbursts of anti-Indian and anti-Chinese violence.

1784	1813	1826	1852
Alaungpaya's son, Bodawpaya defeats Rakhaing, hauling off the revered Mahamuni Buddha image (supposedly cast during Buddha's legendary visit to the area in 554 BC) to Inwa.	Adoniram Judson, a Baptist missionary from Massachusetts, arrives to convert souls and translate the Bible; thanks to his influence, Myanmar has the third-largest number of Baptists worldwide.	The Treaty of Yandabo concludes the First Anglo-Burmese War that had begun two years previously; the British annex Rakhaing and Tanintharyi (Tenasserim) and demand an indemnity of £1 million.	Britain uses several minor offences to kick-start the Second Anglo-Burmese War for control of Lower Burma; Mindon Min overthrows his half brother and sues for peace.

Aung San & WWII

More famous in the West as Aung San Suu Kyi's father, Bogyoke (General) Aung San is revered as a national hero by most Myanmar people and his likeness is seen throughout the country. Aung San Suu Kyi, who was only two when he died, called him 'a simple man with a simple aim: to fight for independence'.

Aung San was an active student at Rangoon University; he edited the newspaper and led the All Burma Students' Union. At 26 years old, he and the group called the 'Thirty Comrades' looked abroad for support for their independence movement. Although initially planning to seek an alliance with China, they ended up negotiating with Japan and receiving military training there. The 'Thirty Comrades' became the first troops of the Burmese National Army (BNA) and returned to Burma with the invading Japanese troops in 1941.

By mid-1942 the Japanese had driven retreating British–Indian forces, along with the Chinese Kuomintang (KMT), out of most of Burma. But the conduct of the Japanese troops was starting to alienate the Burmese. Aung San complained at Japan's 15th Army headquarters in Maymyo (now Pyin Oo Lwin): 'I went to Japan to save my people who were struggling like bullocks under the British. But now we are treated like dogs.'

Aung San and the BNA switched allegiance to the Allied side in March 1945. Their assistance, along with brave behind-enemy-lines operations by the 'Chindits', an Allied Special Force, helped the British prevail over the Japanese in Burma two months later. Aung San and his colleagues now had a their chance to dictate post-war terms for their country.

Post-Colonial Burma
Towards Independence

In January 1947, Aung San visited London as the colony's deputy chairperson of the Governor's Executive Council. Meeting with the British Prime Minister Clement Attlee, a pact was agreed, under which Burma would gain self-rule within a year.

A month later, Aung San met with Shan, Chin and Kachin leaders in Panglong, in Shan State. They signed the famous Panglong Agreement in February 1947, guaranteeing ethnic minorities the freedom to choose their political destiny if dissatisfied with the situation after 10 years. The agreement also broadly covered absent representatives of the Kayin, Kayah, Mon and Rakhaing.

In the elections for the assembly, Aung San's Anti-Fascist People's Freedom League (AFPFL) won an overwhelming 172 seats out of 225. The Burmese Communist Party took seven, while the Bamar opposition,

---

WWII Sites in Myanmar

» Start of Burma Rd, Lashio, Northern Myanmar

» Taukkyan War Cemetery, North of Yangon

» Thanbyuzayat War Cemetry, Mon State

» Meiktila, Central Myanmar

HISTORY POST-COLONIAL BURMA

Armed Forces Day (27 March) commemorates the Burmese soldiers' resistance against the Japanese army in WWII.

1857

Mindon Min moves Upper Burma's capital from Inwa to a newly built city at the foot of Mandalay Hill, thus fulfilling a purported 2400 year-old prophecy by Buddha.

1862

Bahadur Shah Zafar, the last emperor of India, is exiled with his family to Yangon, which the British call Rangoon. He dies in 1858, and is buried in secrecy.

» Kuthodaw Paya (p210); built by Mindon Min in 1857

MIXED FEELINGS ABOUT THE TATMADAW

'Born of the people and one with the people': that's how former Senior General Than Shwe describes Myanmar's army, the Tatmadaw. Other commentators, including the academic and former diplomat Andrew Selth, author of *Burma's Armed Forces: Power Without Glory*, call it a 'state within a state'.

From a small and disunited force at the time of independence, the army has grown to nearly half a million soldiers. It takes care of its troops and their dependants by providing subsidised housing and access to special schools and hospitals. The military also owns two giant corporations – the Union of Myanmar Economic Holdings (UMEH) and Myanmar Economic Corporation (MEC) – whose dealings extend into nearly every corner of the economy.

Small wonder that for many families, having a son (it's rarely a daughter, although there are some roles for women in the army) who is a solider results in much appreciation for the financial security it brings. Many other people in Myanmar live in fear of the army, but there are others who continue to respect the institution for the role it originally played in securing independence for the nation.

Summing up such divided feelings is none other than Aung San Suu Kyi who, in an interview for the *Financial Times* said, 'I was brought up to be fond of the military, to believe that everybody in military uniform was, in some way or other, my father's son. This is not something that you can just get rid of. It stays with you.'

led by U Saw, took three. (U Saw was Burma's prime minister between 1939 and 1942, and was exiled to Uganda for the rest of WWII for secretly communicating with the Japanese following a failed attempt to gain British agreement to Burmese home rule.) The remaining 69 seats were split between ethnic minorities, including four seats for the Anglo-Burman community.

On 19 July 1947, the 32-year-old Aung San and six aides were gunned down in a plot ascribed to U Saw. Some speculate that the military was involved, due to Aung San's plans to demilitarise the government. Apparently U Saw thought he'd walk into the prime minister's role with Aung San gone; instead he took the noose, when the British had him hanged for the murders in 1948.

As many as 250,000 people of Indian and Chinese descent left Burma in the 1960s. Anti-Chinese riots in Yangon in 1967 also resulted in hundreds of Chinese deaths.

U Nu & Early Woes

While Myanmar mourned the death of a hero, Prime Minister Attlee and Aung San's protégé, U Nu, signed an agreement for the transfer of power in October 1947. On 4 January 1948, at an auspicious middle-of-the-night hour, Burma became independent and left the British Commonwealth.

1866	1885	1886	1920
Mindon's sons conspire against the heir apparent – beheading him in the palace – prompting Mindon to pick Thibaw, who showed no interest in the throne, as his successor.	The Third Anglo–Burmese War results in the end of the Burmese monarchy, as Britain conquers Mandalay, sending Thibaw and his family into exile in India.	Burma becomes an administrative province of British-ruled India, with its capital at Rangoon; it takes several years for the British to successfully suppress local resistance.	Students across Burma strike in protest against the new University Act, seen as helping to perpetuate colonial rule; the strike is celebrated today by National Day.

Almost immediately, the new government led by U Nu had to contend with the complete disintegration of the country, involving rebels, communists, gangs and (US-supported) anticommunist Chinese KMT forces.

The hill-tribe people, who had supported the British and fought against the Japanese throughout the war, were distrustful of the Bamar majority and took up armed opposition. The communists withdrew from the government and attacked it. Muslims from the Rakhaing area also opposed the new government. The Mon, long thought to be totally integrated with the Burmese, revolted. Assorted factions, private armies, WWII resistance groups and plain mutineers further confused the picture.

In early 1949 almost the entire country was in the hands of a number of rebel groups, and there was even fighting in Yangon's suburbs. At one stage the government was on the point of surrendering to the communist forces, but gradually fought back. Through 1950 and 1951 it regained control of much of the country.

With the collapse of Chiang Kai-Shek's KMT forces to those of Mao Zedong, the tattered remnants of the KMT withdrew into northern Burma and mounted raids from there into Yunnan, China. But being no match for the Chinese communists, the KMT decided to carve their own little fiefdom out of Burmese territory.

The First Military Government

By the mid-1950s, the government had strengthened its hold on the country, but the economy slipped from bad to worse. A number of grandiose development projects succeeded only in making foreign 'advisers' rather wealthy. In 1953 Myanmar bravely announced that aid or assistance from the USA was no longer welcome, as long as US-supplied Chinese KMT forces were at large within the country.

U Nu managed to remain in power until 1958, when he voluntarily handed the reins over to a caretaker military government under General Ne Win. Considering the pride most of the country had in the Burmese army, which had helped bring independence, this was seen as a welcome change.

Freed from the 'democratic' responsibilities inherent in a civilian government, Ne Win was able to make some excellent progress during the 15 months his military government operated. A degree of law and order was restored, rebel activity was reduced and Yangon was given a massive and much-needed cleanup. According to Thant Myint-U, Ne Win's first period of government was 'the most effective and efficient in modern Burmese history'.

The Burmese Road to Socialism

Sadly, the same would not be true for the general's second, much more extended, stint at Burma's helm. As promised, the military allowed free

HISTORY POST-COLONIAL BURMA

Following Ne Win's military coup in 1962, the country started closing off the outside world, limiting foreigners' visits to just 24-hour visas, later extended to a week.

U Nu, Burma's first prime minister, was also a devout Buddhist who banned the slaughter of cows after winning the 1960 election. His autobiography *Saturday's Son* was published in 1975.

elections to held in December 1960 and the charismatic U Nu regained power with a much-improved majority, partly through a policy of making Buddhism the state religion. This, and politically destabilising moves by various ethnic minorities to leave the Union of Burma, led Ne Win to order an army coup and abolish the parliament in March 1962.

U Nu, along with his main ministers, was thrown into prison, where he remained until he was forced into exile in 1966. Meanwhile, Ne Win established a 17-member Revolutionary Council and announced that the country would 'march towards socialism in our own Burmese way', confiscating most private property and handing it over to military-run state corporations.

Nationalisation resulted in everyday commodities becoming available only on the black market, and vast numbers of people being thrown out of work. Ne Win also banned international aid organisations, foreign language publications and local, privately owned newspapers and political parties. The net result was that by 1967, a country that had been the largest exporter of rice in the world prior to WWII, was now unable to feed itself.

Riots & Street Protests

Opposition to Ne Win's government eventually bubbled over into a strike by oil workers and others in May 1974 and, later that same year, riots over what was seen as the inappropriate burial of former UN secretary-general, U Thant in Yangon. Responding with gunfire and arrests, the government regained control and doggedly continued to run the country – further impoverishing the people with successive demonetisations.

In late 1981 Ne Win retired as president of the republic, retaining his position as chair of the Burmese Socialist Programme Party (BSPP), the country's only legal political party under the 1974 constitution. But his successor, San Yu, and the government remained very much under the influence of Ne Win's political will.

Even though the Burmese standard of living was on a continual downward spiral, it wouldn't be until 1988 that the people again took to the streets en masse, insisting that Ne Win had to go. Even the surprise retirement by Ne Win as BSPP chairperson in July 1988, and his advocating of a multiparty political process, was insufficient to halt the agitation of the people. Public protests reached a climax on the auspicious date of 8 August 1988 (8-8-88), after which the government steadily moved to crush all opposition, killing an estimated 3000 and imprisoning more. Tens of thousands, mainly students, fled the country.

Slorc Holds an Election

In September 1988, a military coup (widely thought to have had the blessing of Ne Win) saw the formation of the State Law & Order Restoration

SAO HEARN HKAM

Patricia Elliott's *The White Umbrella* (www.whiteumbrella.com) is the fascinating true story of Shan royal Sao Hearn Hkam, wife of Burma's president and founder of the Shan State Army.

1947	**1948**	**1958**
Having gained independence from Britain and rallied ethnic groups to a 10-year deal where they could secede from Burma by 1958, Aung San and six colleagues are assassinated by rivals.	On 4 January the country gains independence as the Union of Burma with U Nu as the prime minister; immediately it is destabilised by various ethnic and political conflicts.	A split in the AFPFL causes parliamentary chaos; U Nu barely survives a no-confidence vote and invites General Ne Win to form a 'caretaker government' which lasts until 1960.

FRANK CARTER/LONELY PLANET IMAGES ©

» *Independence Monument*

Council (Slorc). Slorc's leader, General Saw Maung, commander in chief of the military, promised to hold a multiparty election within three months.

Although 235 parties contested the election (which was delayed until May 1990), the clear front runner from the start was the National League for Democracy (NLD). The NLD was led by several former generals, along with Aung San Suu Kyi (daughter of hero, Aung San), who had made such a public impression at rallies during the 1988 protests. For more about Aung San Suu Kyi's role in the democracy movement, see p352.

In the run up to the election, Slorc tried to appease the masses with construction programmes, adding a coat of paint to many buildings in Yangon and abandoning socialism in favour of a capitalist economy. In 1989, it changed the name of the country to Myanmar, then placed Aung San Suu Kyi under house arrest and detained many other prodemocracy leaders.

Convinced it had effectively dealt with the opposition, the government went ahead with the country's first election in 30 years. The voter turnout – 72.59% – was the highest in Myanmar's history. The result was a resounding victory for the NLD, which took 392 of the 485 contested seats (or about 60% of the vote), with the military-backed National Unity Party gaining just 10 seats with just over 25% of the vote.

The 1988 demonstrations were sparked by a students' fight at the Rangoon Institute of Technology (that's right, RIOT) that ended with police intervening and some students being killed.

Post-1990 Myanmar
NLD Under Attack

Slorc barred the elected members of parliament from assuming power, decreeing that a state-approved constitution had to be passed by national referendum first. In October 1990 the military raided NLD offices and arrested key leaders. A handful of elected members managed to escape the country – and set up the National Coalition Government of the Union of Burma (www.ncgub.net) with Sein Win, nephew of Aung San, as its leader.

Some commentators wondered if the election was a ruse to get members of the opposition out in the open, where they could be more easily crushed. Either way, in 1995 Slorc deemed it safe enough to release Aung San Suu Kyi; at the same time many other high-level dissidents, including the NLD's Tin U and Kyi Maung, were also released from prison.

For several months Aung San Suu Kyi was allowed to address crowds of supporters from her residence. In May and September 1996, a congress of NLD members was held in a bold political gambit to show that the party was still an active force. The military junta responded by detaining hundreds who attended the congress; the street leading to Suu Kyi's residence was also blockaded, prohibiting her from making speeches at her residence.

In 1998 Suu Kyi attempted to leave Yangon to meet with supporters, but was blocked by the military and forcibly returned to the city. A second attempt to drive to Mandalay in September 2000 again saw the Lady (as

1962	1964	1978	1988
Following the coup by Ne Win, a peaceful student protest at Rangoon University is suppressed by the military, with over 100 students killed and the Student Union building dynamited.	All opposition political parties are banned, commerce and industry are nationalised and Ne Win begins the process of isolating Myanmar from the rest of the world.	General San Yu succeeds New Win as Burma's president but Ne Win remains the ultimate ruler, even after his resignation from the Burmese Socialist Programme Party in 1988.	Civilian unrest grows as living standards continue to fall. On 8 August, huge nonviolent marches end with the military killing over 3000 protestors; the military promise to hold democratic elections.

she is affectionately known) detained at a military roadblock. After spending six days in her car by the roadside, Suu Kyi was once again placed under house arrest. Save for barely a year between 6 May 2002 and 30 May 2003, she would spend the next decade shut away from the public.

Than Shwe Takes Over

In the 1990s, after years of isolation from the rest of the world, the junta actively tried to launch Myanmar as a tourist destination. But there was a disappointing turnout for the official 'Visit Myanmar Year 1996' (partly due to the tourism boycott launched by the NLD and others). Increased sanctions from the West led the government to seek other sources of income: namely from trade with China, India and Thailand.

Khin Nyunt, head of military intelligence and a protégé of Ne Win (who died, disgraced and living in obscurity, in 2002), became Prime Minister in 2003. Khin Nyunt took the lead on the junta's seven-step 'roadmap towards discipline-flourishing democracy'. But in 2004 hardliner Senior General Than Shwe ousted Khin Nyunt and many of his fellow intelligence officers; at a secret trial Khin Nyunt was sentenced to 44 years in jail and is believed to currently be under house arrest.

Than Shwe: Unmasking Burma's Tyrant by Benedict Rogers is an unauthorised biography of the secretive senior general who, many believe, still calls the shots in Myanmar.

Than Shwe initially promised to continue the transition to democracy, but instead his activity showed a focus on negotiating multimillion-dollar trade deals with China, India and Thailand, and importing weapons and military know-how from Russia and North Korea.

In 2005, an entirely new capital city was created in the arid fields near Pyinmana, a move widely viewed as enormously expensive and wasteful, including by China, a nation otherwise disinclined to comment on the activities of its neighbour and trade partner. The junta named the city-in-the-making Nay Pyi Taw (Royal Capital), leaving little doubt that Than Shwe's strategies and inspirations were aligned less with the modern world than with Burmese kings of centuries past.

The 'Saffron Revolution'

In mid-2007, natural gas prices rose by 500% (and petrol by 200%), leading to price hikes for everything from local bus tickets to rice. In late August a group of '1988 generation' protestors were arrested for staging a march against the inflation. On 5 September, when monks denounced the price hikes in a demonstration in Pakokku, the protests escalated. The military responded with gunfire and allegedly beat one monk to death.

In response, the All Burma Monks Alliance (ABMA) was formed, denouncing the ruling government as an 'evil military dictatorship' and refusing to give alms to military officials (a practice called *pattam mikkujana kamma*). By 17 September daily marches began, swelling in numbers across major cities including Yangon, Mandalay, Meiktila and Sittwe.

1990	1995	1997	2000
In May the National League for Democracy (NLD), led by Aung San Suu Kyi, conclusively wins the first nationwide election in three decades, but the military refuses to relinquish power.	Aung San Suu Kyi released from house arrest. The government uses forced labour to ready some sites for 'Visit Myanmar Year'; NLD and other activist groups launch a tourism boycott.	US and Canada impose investment ban on Myanmar. State Law & Order Restoration Council (Slorc) changes name to the State Peace & Development Council. Myanmar joins Asean.	The EU intensifies its economic sanctions against Myanmar, citing continued human rights abuses in the country. Aung San Suu Kyi again under house arrest until May 2002.

As David Steinberg points out in *Burma/Myanmar: What Everyone Needs to Know,* the Saffron Revolution was neither saffron nor a revolution. Burmese monks wear maroon (not saffron) coloured robes for a start. The revolutionary part of the events of 2007 was that, for the first time, they were broadcast via smuggled out videos on satellite TV or the internet. 'For the first time in Burmese history, violent suppression by the state was not simply a matter of rumour but was palpably visible', writes Steinberg. For a nail-biting account of how such incendiary video evidence was captured, watch the Oscar-nominated documentary *Burma VJ* (www.burmavjmovie.com).

Unexpectedly, monk-led crowds were allowed to pray with Aung San Suu Kyi from outside her house gates on 22 September. Two days later, anything from 50,000 to 150,000 protestors marched through the streets of Yangon in what would become known as the 'Saffron Revolution'. All the while the government watched, photographing participants.

On 26 September the army began shooting protestors and imposed a curfew. A monk was beaten to death, monasteries were raided and 100 monks were arrested. The following day, a soldier was caught on video fatally shooting Japanese photographer, Kenji Nagai at the southwest corner of Sule Paya Rd and Anawrahta Rd in central Yangon (Nagai may have been mistaken for a local, as he was wearing a *longyi*). Two days later, with around 3000 people arrested and 31 people dead, the protests were quashed, and an unsettled quiet hung over Myanmar's cities.

Legend has it that Buddha gave eight of his hairs to a couple of visiting Burmese merchants 3000 years ago. They are enshrined in Yangon's Shwedagon Paya.

Cyclone Nargis

In the aftermath of the 2007 demonstrations, Than Shwe made promises to fend off outside criticism. First, he finalised the long-delayed new constitution, which had been under discussion since 1993 and which included a provision that the generals would not be legally held to account for crimes against the population committed during their governing period. Second, he announced a national referendum for it on 10 May 2008. But on 2 May a natural disaster took hold, as Cyclone Nargis – the second-deadliest cyclone in recorded history – tore across an unaware Ayeyarwady Delta.

Cyclone Nargis' 121mph winds, and the tidal surge that followed, swept away bamboo-hut villages, leaving over two million survivors without shelter, food or drinking water. Damages were estimated at $2.4 billion. Yangon avoided the worst, but the winds (at 80mph) still overturned power lines and trees, leaving the city without power for two weeks.

The government was widely condemned for its tepid response to the disaster. Outside aid groups were held up by a lack of visas and the

BUDDHA

2002	2003	2004	2006
In March, Ne Win's son-in-law and three grandsons are arrested for plotting to overthrow the junta; Ne Win is placed under house arrest and dies 5 December, aged 91.	Aung San Suu Kyi and NLD members are attacked by pro-government mobs in northern Myanmar; up to 100 are killed. 'The Lady' is again placed under house arrest.	Having brokered a ceasefire agreement with Karen insurgents, Prime Minister Khin Nyunt, the moderate voice in the military who outlined a seven-point 'roadmap' for democracy, is arrested.	General Than Shwe and the government move the capital from Yangon to Nay Pyi Taw, a new city in central Myanmar.

NUCLEAR AMBITIONS?

In June 2011, the US Navy turned back a North Korean vessel presumed to be carrying military cargo bound for Myanmar. According to a report in the *Christian Science Monitor*, experts had linked the vessel to previous shipments to Myanmar, with whom North Korea is suspected of cooperating in a program for enriching uranium for nuclear warheads.

According to Aung Lynn Htut, a former senior intelligence officer in Myanmar's Ministry of Defence and a defector to the US in 2005, the country had secretly re-engaged with North Korea as far back as 1992 to gain missile and nuclear-weapon technology. These allegations appeared to be backed up by US diplomatic cables, leaked by Wikileaks in 2010, detailing the presence of North Korean technicians in Myanmar, helping the regime to build some kind of missile facility.

The cables don't confirm conclusively what Myanmar and North Korea are up to, but as the BBC reported 'they do provide a fascinating insight into the jigsaw of information on which Western intelligence is based'.

Myanmar military's refusal to allow foreign planes to deliver aid. Locals stepped into the breach, heroically organising their own relief teams. In the meantime, the government kept the referendum more or less on schedule, outraging many locals and outside observers.

Several months afterward, a group organised by Asean and the UN to analyse the disaster documented 84,537 deaths and 53,836 missing people – 138,373 in all, 61% of whom were female. Other estimates are even higher, suggesting 300,000 were lost. Children, unable to withstand the inflow of water, were most vulnerable to drowning.

A New Constitution

Even before the cyclone, activist groups and NLD members had urged the public to vote 'no' at the referendum to change the constitution. They feared that it would enshrine the power of the generals. Others worried that not voting would only deepen the military hold on the government and leave no wiggle room for other political parties to contribute.

Voting took place in two rounds during May 2008, while a reported 2.5 million people still required food, shelter and medical assistance. The military announced that 98.12% of those eligible had voted and that 92.48% had approved the new constitution – even though very few would have even seen the document in advance of the referendum.

With Than Shwe's 'roadmap towards discipline-flourishing democracy' in place, and yet another reason found to keep his nemesis, Aung San Suu Kyi, under house arrest (beyond her scheduled release in 2009), Myanmar's first general election in 20 years went ahead in November 2010.

Everything is Broken by Emma Larkin is an eye-opening account of the regime's response to the worst natural disaster to befall Myanmar in modern history.

NARGIS

2007	2008	2010	2011
Following fuel price hikes, monk-led protests hit Myanmar's streets; after 50,000 march in Yangon in September the government brutally cracks down on this 'Saffron Revolution', killing at least 31.	Cyclone Nargis tears across the delta, killing an estimated 138,000 and leaving many more without homes. Two days later (sticking to schedule), a referendum on constitutional reform takes place.	NLD boycott October elections but many other parties decide to take part; few are surprised when the military-backed USDP wins. Aung San Suu Kyi released in November.	Myanmar achieves seventh and final step on 'roadmap to democracy' when former general Thein Sein is sworn into office as President, heading up a quasi-civilian government.

People of Myanmar (Burma)

Ethnically speaking, multicultural Myanmar is more salad bowl than melting pot. The government recognises 135 distinct ethnic groups that make up eight official 'major national ethnic races': Bamar, Shan, Mon, Kayin (Karen), Kayah, Chin, Kachin and Rakhaing. The DPS tourist maps of the country depict cute cartoon characters of each of these races dressed in their traditional attire, and the incredible thing is that as you travel through Myanmar, you're quite likely to see people wearing similar, if not identical, attire.

Variations in dress are just a hint of the differences between Myanmar's diverse ethnic populations. This chapter provides background on the major ethnic groups that visitors are most likely to encounter or read about.

The 1983 census records 69% of the population as Bamar, 8.5% Shan, 6.2% Kayin, 4.5% Rakhaing, 2.4% Mon, 2.2% Chin, 1.4% Kachin, 1% Wa and 0.4% Kayah.

Main Ethnic Groups

Historically, Myanmar's diverse ethnic make-up has been delineated by its topography. The broad central plain, with the Ayeyarwady (Irrawaddy) River and Myanmar's most fertile soil, has been populated by

MYANMAR'S CYCLE OF LIFE

In *From the Land of Green Ghosts: A Burmese Odyssey*, Pascal Khoo Thwe writes that, growing up in the Shan hills, traditional family life meant that the 'earth is round at school and flat at home', meaning some aspects of modern life are left, along with your shoes, outside the door.

Families in Myanmar tend to be large, and the birth of a child is a big occasion. While boys are coddled more, girls are equally welcomed, as they're expected to look after parents later in life. You might find three or four generations of one family living in a two- or three-room house. Some thatched huts in the countryside have generators, powering electric bulbs and pumping life into the TV a couple of hours a night; many don't. Running water outside the cities and bigger towns is rare.

About three-quarters of the population farm, so much of local life revolves around villages and the countryside. Here, national politics or dreams of wealth can pale in comparison to the season, the crop or the level of the river (used for bathing, washing and drinking water). Everywhere, people are known for helping each other when in need, and call each other 'brother' and 'sister' affectionately.

In *Finding George Orwell in Burma*, Emma Larkin recounts how a Mandalay cemetery worker saved dirt from a moved gravesite so that just in case the family ever returned they could have 'some soil from around the grave'. Death, of course, is a big deal, though mourned for less time than in much of the West. To miss a funeral is an unimaginable faux pas. If a heated argument goes too far, the ultimate capper is to yell: 'Oh yeah? Don't come to my funeral when I die!'

whichever group was strongest – usually the Bamar (Burmese) in the past few hundred years. Most ethnic groups continue to live in some sort of troubled isolation in the mountains lining much of Myanmar's international borders, notably the Shan, Kayah and Kayin in the east; the Kachin to the north; and the Chin and Rakhaing to the west.

As in many other ethnically (and religiously) diverse countries, feelings of pride and prejudice cause friction between Myanmar's ethnic groups. Ask a Bamar (or a Shan or a Kayin) their opinion about their countryfolk of different ethnic or religious backgrounds and you'll get an idea of what kinds of challenges governments in Myanmar down the ages have faced in their efforts to keep the peace and preserve the borders.

Khin Myo Chit's English-language *Colourful Myanmar* highlights many customs and traditions of Myanmar life and is available in many Yangon bookshops.

Bamar

'The one single factor which has had the most influence on Burmese culture and civilisation is Theravada Buddhism.'
Aung San Suu Kyi, Freedom from Fear

Also known as Burman or Burmese, the Bamar make up the majority (69% according to 1983 census data) of the population. Thought to have originally migrated from the Himalaya, the Bamar ruled much of what is now Myanmar from Bagan (Pagan) by the 11th century. When the British conquered Myanmar in the 19th century, it was the Bamar who had to relinquish the most. Many ancient court customs and arts were lost when the Bamar monarchy was abolished.

Despite an enduring attachment to older animist beliefs in *nat* (spirits) the Bamar, from trishaw drivers to senior generals, are devout Buddhists. Monks are highly respected and the media reports daily on the merit-making of top officials at the country's principal Buddhist places of worship – continuing a tradition of patronage started by Burmese monarchs.

Coming of age (*shinbyu*) is a major event in Bamar/Buddhist culture with parades around villages and towns for boys about to enter monasteries as novice monks, and both girls and boys having their ears pierced. For more on Buddhist traditions see p338.

The military and current government stopped short of making Buddhism the state religion (as Prime Minister U Nu did in 1960). However, nation-building efforts have included establishing the Bamar language (Burmese) as the language of instruction in schools throughout Myanmar, so most non-Bamar speak Burmese as a second language.

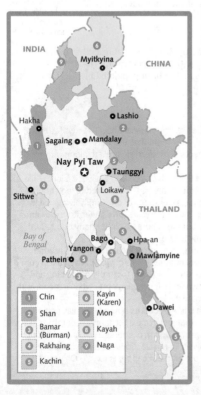

Chin

The Chin inhabit the mountainous region (mostly corresponding with Chin State) that borders India and Bangladesh to the west. Chin State is restricted to travellers, but can be visited with government permission.

Of Tibeto-Burman ancestry, the Chin people call themselves Zo-mi or Lai-mi (both terms mean 'mountain people'), and share a culture, food and language with the

Zo of the adjacent state of Mizoram in India. Outsiders name the different subgroups around the state according to the district in which they live, for instance Tidam Chin, Falam Chin and Haka Chin.

In the past, the Chin, as with most highland dwellers, led labour-intensive lives, and their relatively simple traditional dress reflected this. Men wore loincloths in the warmer months and draped blankets over themselves when the weather turned cool. The women wore poncho-like garments woven with intricate geometric patterns. These garments and Chin blankets are highly sought after by textile collectors today.

Traditionally the Chin practise *swidden* (slash-and-burn) agriculture. They are also skilled hunters, and animal sacrifice plays a role in important animistic ceremonies: the state has the largest proportion of animists of any state in Myanmar. Even so, some 80% to 90% of Chin are believed to be Christian, mainly following the efforts of American missionaries during the British colonial period. However, with the present-day activities of government-sponsored Buddhist missions in the region, the traditional Zo or Chin groups are fading fast. Many Chin have also fled west to Bangladesh and India.

The Chin National Front (www.chinland.org) would like to create a sovereign 'Chinland' out of parts of Myanmar, India and Bangladesh.

Kachin

Like the Chin, the Kachin are part of the Tibeto-Burman racial group. Based mainly in Kachin State, they are divided into six ethnic sub-groups (Jingpaw, Lawngwaw, Lashi, Zaiwa, Rawang, Lisu) among which the Jingpaw are the most numerous. Also traditionally animist, the Kachin were heavily targeted by Christian missionaries during colonial times (about 36% of the population are Christian, mostly Baptist and Catholic).

As much of Kachin State lies above the tropic of Cancer, the climate is more extreme – stifling hot in the summer months and downright cold in the winter – and the Kachin seem to have abandoned their traditional dress for Western clothes that can be easily changed to suit the seasons.

For more about the Kachin see the websites of the Kachin National Organisation (www.kachinland.org) and the Kachin Post (www.kachinpost.com).

UNHAPPILY TOGETHER

During colonial rule the British managed to keep animosity between ethnic groups under control by utilising the carrot of semi-autonomy or the stick of arrest and imprisonment. Over a century later, little has changed.

Insurgencies between the Tatmadaw (Myanmar Army) and minority ethnic groups that smouldered for five decades after independence have been largely quelled. Groups that signed ceasefire agreements with the government (the Kachin, Kayah etc) have been granted limited economic autonomy. In advance of the 2010 election five ethnic ceasefire groups had agreed to integrate their troops into a Border Guard Force under Tatmadaw control; eight had refused.

Those who continue to fight (including some Shan and the Kayin) are dealt with severely. The government has long operated its 'four cuts' system of denying insurgents food, financing, recruiting and intelligence. This scorched-earth policy has, according to the UK Burma Campaign, resulted in the displacement of up to half a million people with as many as 300,000 fleeing across borders into refugee camps mainly in Thailand, India and Bangladesh. In 2003, the US State Department investigated and found credible reports of systematic military rapes of Shan and other ethnic groups.

Some observers of politics in Myanmar predict that, given a choice, many of Myanmar's ethnic groups would opt for independence and break away from Bamar-controlled Myanmar. As Thant Myint-U writes in *The River of Lost Footsteps*, 'the prospects for peace are remote, the possibilities of renewed violence perhaps greater.'

Against this background it is significant that following her release in 2010, Aung San Suu Kyi expressed her desire for a second Panglong Conference: it was at the first Panglong Conference in 1947 that her father forged the fragile agreement between Myanmar's ethnic groups that lead to Burma's independence.

THE WOMEN WITH TATTOOED FACES

The most extraordinary (but no longer practised) Chin fashion was the custom of tattooing women's faces. Chin facial tattoos vary according to tribe, but often cover the whole face – starting at just above the bridge of the nose and radiating out in a pattern of dark lines that resemble a spider's web. Even the eyelids were tattooed. A painful process, the tattooing was traditionally done to girls once they reached puberty.

Legend has it that this practice was initiated to keep young Chin maidens from being coveted by Rakhaing princes whose kingdom bordered the southern Chin Hills. But it's just as likely that the tattoos were seen as a mark of beauty and womanhood. One proud old Chin woman we met told us that she was just seven when she started pestering her parents to have her own facial inking.

Efforts by Christian missionaries and a government ban on facial tattoos in the 1960s has resulted in the practice dying out. But in some Chin villages (particularly in the more traditional southern areas) live a handful of tattooed grannies; see p286 for details on how to visit these places.

About the only vestige of Kachin dress that foreign visitors are likely to encounter are men's *longyi* (sarong-style lower garment) of indigo, green and deep-purple plaid. During festive occasions, Kachin women sport finely woven wool skirts decorated with zigzag or diamond patterns, and dark blouses festooned with hammered silver medallions and tassels.

Following independence from Britain, Kachin relations with the Burmese-run government were increasingly precarious. After the military coup in 1962, the Kachin Independence Army (KIA) was formed under the Kachin Independence Organisation (KIO). These two organisations effectively ran the state on an economy based on smuggling and narcotics until a ceasefire agreement was struck in 1994.

Since the 2010 election when some pro-KIO politicians were barred from standing, the situation has again turned volatile. In July 2011 fighting with the Tatmadaw broke out in the state again, forcing, according to human rights groups, some 10,000 people to flee.

Author Alan Rabinowitz shows much of the local life in the Kachin hills in his fascinating *Life in the Valley of Death*.

Kayah

Also known as the Karenni or Red Karen, the Kayah are settled in the mountainous isolation of Kayah State – an area closed to travellers.

As with many of Myanmar's ethnic groups that traditionally practised animism, the Kayah were targeted for conversion to Christianity by Baptist and Catholic missionaries during the colonial period. The name 'Red Karen' refers to the favoured colour of the Kayah traditional dress and the fact that their apparel resembles that of some Kayin (Karen) tribes – a resemblance that caused the Kayah to be classified by colonisers and missionaries as 'Karen'.

Today the Kayah make up a very small percentage of the population of Myanmar – perhaps less than 1% – and the vast majority lead agrarian lives. A significant number of Kayah also live in Thailand's Mae Hong Son Province.

Little Daughter: A Memoir of Survival in Burma and the West is the autobiography of Zoya Phan (written with Damien Lewis), a Kayin woman who is the international coordinator of the UK Burma Campaign and who spent many years as a child living in refugee camps.

Kayin (Karen)

No one knows for sure how many Kayin (also known as Karen) there are in Myanmar. This ethnic group numbers anything between four and seven million and is linguistically very diverse, with a dozen related but not mutually intelligible dialects. Originally animists, it's now reckoned that the majority are Buddhists, with around 20% Christian and a small percentage Muslim.

The typical dress of both the Kayin men and women is a *longyi* with horizontal stripes (a pattern that is reserved exclusively for women in other ethnic groups). A subgroup of the Kayin live on both sides of the Thai-Myanmar border; it's here that you'll likely encounter the Padaung tribe, a sub-group of the Kayin, whose women are best known for the brass neck rings they wear. See p192 for more about Padaung women.

The only major ethnic group to never sign peace agreements with the Myanmar military, the Kayin are an independent-minded people; the Karen National Union (KNU) is the best known of the insurgency groups. However, the sheer diversity of the many Kayin subgroups has made it impossible for them to achieve any real cohesion. Buddhist Kayin often side with the Buddhist Bamar against their Christian Kayin kin; also in the 2010 election a variety of ethnic parties managed to secure 43.5% of the state legislature.

Visit Karenni Homeland (www.karennihomeland.com) to find out more about the people living in one of the poorest and least accessible parts of Myanmar.

A 2011 report by the Netherlands based Transnational Institute (www.tni.org/briefing/burmas-longest-war-anatomy-karen-conflict) on Myanmar's longest running insurgency concludes that the KNU 'is facing serious political and military challenges. It has lost control of most of its once extensive "liberated zones" and has lost touch with most non-Christian Karen communities. Already greatly weakened militarily, the KNU could be ejected from its last strongholds, should the Burma Army launch another major offensive.'

Presently the only place in Kayin State that travellers can visit is the regional capital Hpa-an.

Mon

The Mon (also called the Tailing by Western historians) were one of the earliest inhabitants of Myanmar and their rule stretched into what is now Thailand. As happened with the Cham in Vietnam and the Phuan in Laos, the Mon were gradually conquered by neighbouring kingdoms and their influence was waned until they were practically unknown outside present-day Myanmar.

The Independent Mon News Agency (http://monnews.org) covers Mon and Burmese affairs.

As in Thailand, which also has a Mon minority, the Mon have almost completely assimilated with the Bamar and in most ways seem indistinguishable from them. In the precolonial era, Mon Buddhist sites

THE WA

The remote northeastern hills of Shan State – the homeland of the Wa – are off limits to tourists. During British colonial times, these tribal people – living in fortified villages, speaking dozens of dialects and having a reputation for being permanently unwashed and frequently inebriated – were hated and feared. A status they have yet to throw off.

The British distinguished two mains groups of Wa according to how receptive they were to the coloniser's attempts to control them. The 'Wild Wa' were headhunters, and decorated their villages with the severed heads of vanquished enemies to appease the spirits that guarded their opium fields. (Apparently they only stopped the practice in the 1970s!)

The so-called 'Tame Wa' allowed the colonisers to pass through their territory unimpeded, yet the area inhabited by the Wa – east of the upper Thanlwin (Salween) River in northern Shan State – was never completely pacified by the British.

For decades the 30,000-strong United Wa State Army (UWSA) has controlled this borderland area, gathering power and money through the production of opium and methamphetamine; the US labelled the UWSA a narcotics trafficking organisation in 2003. Nevertheless, the UWSA struck a ceasefire deal with the military regime in 1989 and the territory under their control looks set to be designated a special autonomous region for the Wa under Myanmar's new constitution.

including Yangon's Shwedagon Paya were appropriated by the Bamar (though the Golden Rock is still in Mon State), and Mon tastes in art and architecture were borrowed as well.

Today the Mon only make up just over 2% of the population of Myanmar, but Mon art and culture have influenced that of the Bamar quite thoroughly, as a trip to the Mon Cultural Museum in Mawlamyine will attest.

Rakhaing

Rakhaing Cultural Relics

» Temple ruins, Mrauk U

» Mahamuni Buddha image, Mandalay

» Rakhaing State Culture Museum, Sittwe

The Rakhaing (also spelled Rakhine and formerly called Arakanese) are principally adherents of Buddhism; in fact, they claim to be among the first followers of Buddha in Southeast Asia. Their last ancient capital was centred at Mrauk U in Rakhaing State, which borders Bangladesh.

The Rakhaing language is akin to Bamar but, due to their geographical location, they have also absorbed a fair amount of culture from the Indian subcontinent. In the eyes of most Bamar, the Rakhaing are a Creole race – a mixture of Bamar and Indian – a perception that Rakhaing strongly resent. It is true though that the local culture exhibits a strongly Indian flavour particularly when it comes to food and music. The Rakhaing are skilled weavers and are known in Myanmar for their eye-catching and intricately patterned *longyi*.

Rakhaing State also has a minority population of Muslim Rakhaing, as well as the Rohingya (see p277), another Muslim people not recognised as citizens of Myanmar by the government.

Shan

To find out more about the Shan and issues in Shan State read the Shan Herald Agency for News (www.shanland. org).

The biggest ethnic group in Myanmar after the Bamar, the Shan, most of whom are Buddhists, call themselves Tai ('Shan' is actually a Bamar word derived from the word 'Siam'). This name is significant, as the Shan are related ethnically, culturally and linguistically to Tai peoples in neighbouring Thailand, Laos and China's Yunnan Province. In fact, if you've spent some time in northern Thailand or Laos and learned some of the respective languages, you'll find you can have a basic conversation with the Shan.

Traditionally, the Shan wore baggy trousers and floppy, wide-brimmed sun hats, and the men were known for their faith in talismanic tattoos. Nowadays Shan town-dwellers commonly dress in the Bamar *longyi*, except on festival occasions, when they proudly sport their ethnic costumes.

In former times the Shan were ruled by local lords or chieftains called *sao pha* (sky lords), a word that was corrupted by the Bamar to *sawbwa*. Many Shan groups have fought the Bamar for control of Myanmar, and

THE MOKEN

Also known as sea gypsies, or Salon in Burmese, the Moken live a nomadic life drifting on the ocean winds around the Myeik Archipelago, Tanintharyi (Tenasserim) Division. Numbering around 2000 to 3000 individuals, scientists believe they have been floating around these islands since at least 2000 BC.

Totally at home on the water, Moken families spend almost all their time on wooden boats, called *kabang*. As the boys come of age they build their own boats, and as the girls come of age and marry, they move away from their parents' boat.

Breathing through air hoses held above the water surface, the Moken dive to depths of up to 200ft in search of shellfish. For all their skill, this can be a lethal activity with divers dying in accidents each year, mainly from the bends caused by rising too quickly to the surface.

Like almost every ethnic minority in Myanmar, the Moken have suffered greatly under military rule; reports from the late 1990s talk of how almost all Moken were subjected to forced relocations to onshore sites. For more information see www.projectmaje.org/gypsies.htm.

The Naga are mainly settled in a mountainous region of eastern India known as Naga-land, but significant numbers live in the western Sagaing Region between the Indian border and the Chindwin River.

When the British arrived in the mid-19th century, the Naga were a fragmented but fearsome collection of tribes. Headhunting was a tradition among them and for many decades they resisted British rule, though a lack of cooperation between the tribes hindered their efforts to remain independent. After nearly 17,000 Naga fought in WWI in Europe, a feeling of unity grew, which led to an organised Naga independence movement.

The Naga sport one of the world's most exotic traditional costumes. Naga men at festival time wear striking ceremonial headdresses made of feathers, tufts of hair and cowry shells, and carry wickedly sharp spears.

The only way to visit the Naga in Myanmar is on a government-organised trip during the Naga new year in January. It's easier, and more rewarding, to visit on the Indian side of the border, where the majority of Naga live.

a few groups continue a guerrilla-style conflict in the mountains near Thailand.

Other Peoples

Apart from the Wa (see p311), Myanmar's constitution has set aside 'self-administered zones' for the Naga, Danu, Pa-O, Palaung and Kokang.

Figures from the 1983 census also show there were 233,470 Chinese, 428,428 Indians, 567,985 Bangladeshis and 42,140 Pakistanis living in Myanmar. This data is sure to be grossly inaccurate today, especially with regard to the Chinese. In recent years there's been a massive influx of Chinese people into northern Burma, evident in Mandalay and certainly in border towns such as Mong La, where the yuan is the local currency.

In Andrew Marshall's *The Trouser People* the intrepid author goes in search of the Wa's creation myth lake of Nawng Hkeo.

Women in Myanmar

In *Letters From Burma*, Aung San Suu Kyi writes that a baby girl is as equally celebrated as a baby boy, as they're believed to be 'more dutiful and loving than sons'. Girls are educated alongside boys and, by university age, women outnumber men in university and college enrolment. Most white-collar professions grant women six weeks paid maternity leave before birth and one or two months afterwards.

Myanmar women enjoy equal legal rights to those of men, can own property, do not traditionally change any portion of their names upon marriage and, in the event of divorce, are legally entitled to half of all property accumulated during the marriage. Inheritance rights are also equally shared.

Rights on paper, however, don't always translate into reality. In the current parliament only 20 out of 659 members are women, and it's rare that you'll find women in other positions of power in Myanmar including, crucially, in the military. As the author Nu Nu Yi said in an interview with *The Irrawaddy* on the occasion of International Women's Day in 2011, men in Myanmar 'don't want to give important decision-making positions to women.'

When it comes to religion, women certainly take a back seat. Many people in Myanmar – women as well as men – believe the birth of a girl indicates less religious merit than the birth of a boy, and that only males can attain *nibbana* (for a woman to do so, she first has to come back as a man!) A few Buddhist shrines, including Mandalay's Mahamuni Paya, have small areas around the main holy image that are off limits to women.

White Lotus Press (www.whitelotuspress.com) publishes books in English on the various people of Myanmar.

Just as boys between the ages of five and 20 usually undergo a pre-puberty initiation as temporary novice monks, girls around the same age participate in an initiatory ear-piercing ceremony (often called 'ear-boring' in Burmese English). Some also become temporary nuns at this age, but nuns are not as venerated in Myanmar as monks.

Saw Myat Yin, the insightful author of *Culture Shock! Burma*, express-es a viewpoint common among Myanmar women, who see their role as equal but 'supportive and complementary...rather than in competition', and that 'if they accept a role a step behind their menfolk, they do so freely and willingly.'

Politics, Economics & Sanctions

Regardless of the many questions raised about the fairness of the process, the 2010 elections have changed the political landscape in Myanmar. After decades of military dictatorship, there's now a quasi-civilian government and many new political parties, the most significant of which represent ethnic minorities. Declared illegal by the ruling powers, the National League for Democracy (NLD) continues to function, in the eyes of both locals and the international community, as the main opposition force and champion of democracy. It's hard to know whether the elections are a token attempt by the government to appease critics or a substantive step along the path to an open and democratic society.

The political situation post-election is certainly more complex, and the country's economy is yet another can of worms. Having first disastrously dabbled in socialist economics – and very nearly lost control of the country in 1988 because of it – the military was saved at the eleventh hour by trade deals for raw materials cut with neighbouring countries. Enormous revenue has been gained from the export of natural gas, and government figures now posit double-digit economic growth for Myanmar, which doesn't exactly tally with the country's status as one of the poorest in the world.

In the meantime, the debate and policy differences continue in the outside world over economic sanctions: their efficacy in persuading the government to become more democratic and stop violating human rights, and whether they generally help or harm ordinary people in Myanmar.

Politics
The Government/Military

Over the last 50 years, Myanmar's rulers (aka the military) have adopted a variety of guises. They started out as the Burma Socialist Programme Party (BSPP) in 1962, which morphed into the State Law and Order Restoration Council (Slorc) in 1988, which was then renamed the State Peace and Development Council (SPDC) in 1997. In the run up to the 2010 election many in the upper echelons of the military resigned their posts to become candidates for the military-backed Union Solidarity and Development Party (USDP), which, to nobody's surprise, was the victor at the polls.

The names and some faces may have changed, but few people inside or outside Myanmar believe that the military have relinquished control. The Burma Campaign UK points out that 'More than 80% of MPs come

David Steinberg's *Burma/Myanmar: What Everyone Needs to Know* sheds light on many aspects of the country's complex situation via a series of concise and understandable Q&As on history and culture.

Guy Delisle's *Burma Chronicles* is a graphic account of the year that the Canadian cartoonist spent in Myanmar with his wife, an administrator for Medecins Sans Frontières (MSF). It's both amusing and horrifying, covering topics ranging from electricity outages to the heroin shooting galleries in Chinese-owned jade-mine towns.

THE FICTION OF MYANMAR STATISTICS

'Facts are negotiated more than they are observed in Myanmar', writes David Steinberg in *Burma/Myanmar: What Everyone Needs to Know*. 'Statistics are often imprecise or manipulated, caused by internal political considerations or insufficient data, and biased externally by a lack of access to materials.' Under such circumstances, economic policy becomes pretty much guesswork.

Even a basic figure such as Myanmar's population is elusive. The Chinese news agency Xinhua quotes the government's 2009 official figure of 59.12 million, while the Asian Development Bank has it at 58.84 million and the CIA World Factbook at 54 million.

Sean Turnell, an expert on Myanmar's economy at Sydney's Macquarie University, isn't surprised by this 10% spread. 'The last full census was back in 1913', he says, pointing out that all subsequent attempts at a head count, including the oft-quoted census of 1983, have been compromised by lack of data from parts of the country experiencing rebellions and unrest.

Where we give population figures in this guide, they should only be taken as estimates that try to gauge the relative size of different towns and cities. Statistics provided by the Myanmar government should be regarded at best as an indicator and at worst as pure fiction.

Ethnic Politics in Burma: The Time for Solutions, a report by the Transnational Institute (http://tinyurl.com/3o4pcqs) makes for sobering reading on a land in political transition and ethnic crisis.

from the military or pro-military parties. In the new and all-powerful National Defence and Security Council, only one of its eleven members is genuinely civilian, and that member comes from the pro-military Union Solidarity and Development Party.' A post-election report from the International Crisis Group (www.tinyurl.com/6e4omqk) is more cautiously hopeful, noting that while 'changes are unlikely to translate into dramatic reforms in the short term…they provide a new governance context, improving the prospects for incremental reform.'

Many people continue to speculate about the role of Than Shwe, who retired as the head of the military in March 2011. It's commonly thought he continues to pull strings from behind the scenes in much the same way that Ne Win once did. Than Shwe, however, will be well aware of Ne Win's fate: the one-time strongman of Myanmar died in 2002, unceremoniously buried, with some of his family jailed for their alleged roles in planning a coup a few months earlier. The constitution contains provisions to stop attempts to prosecute Than Shwe and other top military brass for crimes committed under their watch – but the rule of law has counted for little in Myanmar over the last half century.

National League for Democracy

Founded on 27 September 1988, the National League for Democracy (NLD; www.nldburma.org) is the best known of Myanmar's pro-democracy organisations, thanks to its iconic leader Aung San Suu Kyi. It won the 1990 election in a landslide victory that the ruling junta ignored; many of its members were subsequently thrown into prison; others went into self-imposed exile (see p303).

Bribery is part of *all* business in Myanmar. The owners of one private guesthouse owner told us they have to bribe their tax official. 'We pay the tax man 25% of the taxes we would have paid. He's a very rich man.'

Unhappy with the revised constitution pushed through by the government in 2008, the NLD called for a boycott of the October 2010 elections, in turn causing the military junta to declare the party illegal. This decision caused a division within the NLD that resulted in senior members of the organisation, Dr Than Nyein and Khin Maung Swe, leaving to form the National Democratic Force (NDF), a party that did contest the 2010 poll.

Since the election the NDF has split into two factions, with some elected MPs committed to staying in the new party and others stating that at any upcoming election they would rejoin the NLD.

Other Political Parties & Opposition Groups

The NDF ended up with 16 elected members taking seats in the national and state legislatures, compared to 883 seats for the military-backed USDP. Among the 16 ethnic parties who also won seats were the Shan Nationalities Democratic Party (SNDP; 57 seats), Rakhaing Nationalities Development Party (RNDP; 35 seats), All Mon Region Democracy Party (AMRDP; 16 seats), Chin Progress Party (CPP; 12 seats) and the Pao National Party (CPP; 10 seats). There are also parties representing the Kayan, Kayin, Taaung (Palaung) and Wa.

In addition to the parties listed above, there are a further 18 ethnic parties who either didn't win seats or chose not to contest the election, *plus* about 20 other unregistered opposition groups, some of whom – such as the Kachin Independence Army – are fighting the government. All of this shows how complicated the ethnic political struggle in Myanmar has become. Tackling this situation to achieve national reconciliation (see p309) is considered by many, including Aung San Suu Kyi, one of the most pressing political problems that Myanmar faces, since it's a pre-requisite for improving the everyday lives of the country's citizens.

A ray of hope is that representatives of many of the ethnic parties have welcomed the chance – the first they've had in over 20 years – to participate in national and local government. In the ethnic states some of the ethnic parties captured significant percentages of the vote (p291).

Political Prisoners & Human Rights

Aung San Suu Kyi may have been released in November 2010, but as she and many others keep pointing out, over 2000 other political prisoners remain under detention in Myanmar. According to the Assistance Association for Political Prisoners (www.aappb.org), which keeps a running tally of the detainees, the 'arbitrary arrest and detention of political activists and ordinary people for their perceived opposition to the regime continues unabated'. Human Rights Watch (www.hrw.org) has documented how these prisoners are routinely mistreated, tortured and 'deprived of health resources, food and contact [with family and friends]'.

Bad as this is, it pales in comparison with the litany of human-rights abuses that are taking place in the government's war with various armed ethnic groups in the border regions. In the Shan State, according to the UK Burma Campaign and others, there is 'widespread use of rape as a weapon of war against ethnic minorities, the forced displacement of over

Nowhere to Be Home, edited by Maggie Lemere and Zoë West, presents 22 oral histories of Myanmar citizens gathered from those living in the country and those in exile. The stories are often heartbreaking, and the book includes very useful appendices on current affairs, history and politics.

ACTIVIST WEBSITES

Many groups have websites that outline Myanmar's prodemocracy movement and provide details about ongoing human-rights abuses.

Amnesty International (www.amnesty.org) Provides regular updates on the status of 1994 political prisoners being held behind bars.

Burma Campaign UK (www.burmacampaign.org.uk) One of the more outspoken campaign groups, which is in favour of targeted sanctions.

Burma Global Action Network (BGAN; www.burma-network.com) In the wake of the 2007 monk-led anti-government protests, BGAN was founded through the creation of the Facebook group 'Support the Monks' Protest in Burma'.

Burma Voices (www.burmavoices.com) A database of stories and photos of people who have first-hand knowledge of the situation in Myanmar.

Free Burma Coalition (www.freeburmacoalition.org) Run by Myanmar-exile figure Zarni. Includes links to Myanmar-related news.

Network Myanmar (www.networkmyanmar.org) Committed to people-to-people contact and dialogue on issues surrounding Myanmar.

one million refugees and internally displaced people, tens of thousands of child soldiers, and the abundant use of forced labour'. In March 2010, the UN special rapporteur on Myanmar, Tomás Ojea Quintana, recommended that the UN consider establishing a Commission of Inquiry into war crimes and crimes against humanity in the country.

Economics

You needn't spend much time in Myanmar to realise how profoundly dysfunctional its economy is. The country is rich in natural resources – including gas, oil, teak, and precious metals and gems – yet its people are among the poorest in Asia, most struggling to get by on an income of less than $2 a day. Ask about the price of one of the clapped-out secondhand cars on the roads, or about the cost of real estate in Yangon, and you'll be shocked by the sky-high figures, a reflection of ongoing inflation, which has seldom been under 25% per annum over the last decade.

The *Economist* reported that K1.8 trillion, 23.7% of Myanmar's 2011's budget, is earmarked for military spending, compared to 4.3% for education and 1.3% for healthcare. When it comes to financing such expenditure, Sean Turnell, of Burma Economic Watch, notes that the government's favourite method has been to print money. Hence the inflation rates and the lack of faith in the local currency that has created a black market for US dollars.

Deeper mining of Myanmar's *Alice in Wonderland* economics reveals that thanks to its emergence as a major regional exporter of natural gas, the country has been running substantial trade surpluses since 2004; its foreign-exchange reserves at 2010 were estimated to reach over $6 billion. As Myanmar specialist David Steinberg notes, the country's economic crisis is 'not with funding but with knowledge of economic affairs, priorities and distribution of the state's considerable present and future resources'.

Trading Partners

Shunned by the West, Myanmar has wasted no time cutting trade deals with its immediate neighbours, several of whom are themselves not shining paragons of democracy. Despite Western sanctions against timber and jade, these materials are reportedly exported to China, Thailand and Singapore, then used to make furniture and jewellery for export.

The flow of foreign investment isn't likely to slow soon. India is spending about $100 million developing a port in Sittwe to access more fuel reserves in the Bay of Bengal, supposedly worth up to $4 billion a year. The Shwe gas reserves off the coast are projected to earn up to $24 billion over the next 20 years. Thailand is spending $10 billion to develop a new seaport in Dawei and transport connections to it, while China will pay most of the costs of a massive highway from Kunming in China to a new seaport at Kyaukpyu, giving western China increased access to international trade routes.

On occasion Asean (Association of Southeast Asian Nations) officials have frowned over Myanmar's behaviour – even expressing 'revulsion' over the violent response to the September 2007 protests – but this has seldom been followed with action. One-time adviser to George W Bush on Asia, Michael J Green likened Myanmar to a 'crazy drunk' on a block of Asean homes: it would take their unified confrontation to get the bottle away. At the time of research, Asean was considering whether to allow Myanmar to take on Asean's chairmanship in 2014; the country skipped its turn in the lead role in 2006 because of international pressure over its poor human-rights record.

Tourism's Economic Impact

While the government once hoped tourism would provide a steady source of hard currency, it's become clear as time has passed that the

Where China Meets India – Burma and the New Crossroads of Asia is Thant Myint-U's new book, scheduled for publication in late 2011; it's about the historic and current connections between the three countries.

Fiery Dragons: Banks, Money lenders and Microfinance in Burma by Sean Turnell explains how Myanmar went from one of the richest countries in Southeast Asia to one of its poorest within the space of a century.

government doesn't depend on it. As Ma Thanegi, a former aide to Aung San Suu Kyi, puts it, 'tourism is peanuts for the generals', particularly when contrasted with the billions being earned for exports of gas, teak and – surprisingly – beans and pulses (estimated by Sean Turnell to account for $920.4 million in exports in 2009–10).

In neighbouring Thailand around 6% of GDP, or about $14 billion annually, comes from tourism. Myanmar earns, at most, 0.7% of its GDP through tourism (calculated using CIA statistics and proboycott activists' estimates of the government receiving $100 million per year).

While fellow Asean countries see many more tourists, visitor arrivals in Myanmar have been on the rise following the lows experienced after the protests in September 2007 and Cyclone Nargis in May 2008. In 2010 close to 300,000 tourists passed through Yangon International Airport, an increase of nearly 30% on 2009. According to the Bangkok-based Pacific-Asia Travel Association (www.pata.org), Asians make up about two-thirds of the arrivals, Europeans 22% and Americans 8%.

One the main deterrents to the growth of this sector of Myanmar's economy was the tourism boycott, launched during Visit Myanmar year in 1996; the NLD called off that boycott in 2010, but still urge visitors to avoid joining package groups and cruises when visiting the country.

The Sanctions Debate

Since 1988, economic sanctions, implemented mainly from the US, EU, Canada and Australia, have been deployed against individuals and industries in an attempt to force political and social change in Myanmar. Loopholes allowed some companies – such as UK's Premier Oil, France's Total and USA's Unocal – to continue to help develop offshore gas fields. Stronger international sanctions were implemented in 1997 by the US, when it banned new investment by American companies in Myanmar. Strident lobbying and threats of consumer boycotts forced some major companies (including PepsiCo, Heineken, Carlsberg and Levi Strauss) either to pull out or decide against investing in the country.

Around 70% of Myanmar's population lives in rural areas and relies on farming for its livelihood. A third of the population lives below the poverty line.

The Stone of Heaven by British journalists Adrian Levy and Cathy Scott Clark is an investigation into jade, both its history as a precious stone and the current horrifying circumstances surrounding its mining in Myanmar.

THE GEM BUSINESS

Myanmar generates considerable income from the mining of precious stones – including rubies, jade and sapphire – and metals such as gold and silver. There is controversy surrounding this mining, with reports of forced labour and dangerous working practices.

Mining areas are not open to foreigners, including Mogok (Sagaing Region), Pyinlon (Shan State), Maingshu (Shan State), Myaduang (Kayah State) and parts of Kachin State. Following the September 2007 protests, the EU added sanctions specifically against the purchase of gems and precious stones, which is supposed to be a government monopoly.

The finer imperial jade or pigeon-blood rubies can only be purchased at exclusive dealer sessions during the government-sponsored Myanmar Gems, Jade & Pearl Emporium, held three or four times a year in Nay Pyi Taw; the 13-day Emporium in November 2010, netted sellers $1.4 billion.

Still, many visitors manage to buy stones from unlicensed dealers, who far outnumber those who are licensed. The government turns a blind eye to most domestic trade; Mandalay's jade market (p209) is an example.

There are many tales of visitors buying cheap gems and selling them for huge profits in the West. Beware of scams: we've heard of a foreigner spending $2000 on worthless stones hawked as jade in Mandalay.

If any stones are found when your baggage is checked on departure, they may be confiscated unless you can present a receipt showing they were purchased from a government-licensed dealer.

In November 1999, the UN International Labour Organization took the unprecedented step of recommending sanctions against Myanmar, because of its use of civilians for forced labour and treacherous tasks of porterage for the military (including serving as 'human landmine detectors').

TESTING TIMES FOR THE MEDIA

Media censorship in Myanmar has been routine since the military takeover in 1962, giving locals years of practice of using gossip, short-wave radios, satellite-TV dishes and computers to find out what their government doesn't want them to know. Local journalists have also become braver at pressing the envelope of what is permitted. In early 2011 the government signalled that censorship would be eased, with coverage of issues, including health, technology and entertainment, no longer requiring pre-publication approval by the Press Scrutiny and Registration Division (PSRD).

The following is an overview of Myanmar's main media outlets:

Print

To get a sense of what passes for news, thumb through the English version of the *New Light of Myanmar,* which features generals' visits to plants and monasteries on the front page and little else of interest inside. The English-language weekly *The Myanmar Times* is a bit bolder, but just as friendly to the government; its former editor and co-owner, Australian Ross Dunkley was found guilty of assault and immigration offences in June 2011, a verdict he is set to appeal.

Neither of these papers is the only source of printed news for locals, who have access to over 150 privately owned newspapers and magazines. Many news magazines are weeklies because the current bureaucracy involved in submitting all articles to the PSRD makes daily publication practically impossible.

Editors have not been averse to publishing stories they know will have consequences. Reporters Without Borders noted that following Aung San Suu Kyi's release at least 10 publications were suspended for periods of one to three weeks for according, in the words of the government censor, 'too much importance' to the story. There's concern that the proposed shift to a more informal Chinese-style of censorship might cause editors to become more cautious about publishing such news at all, as they will become personally responsible for the articles.

TV & Radio

There are three free-to-air TV channels (MRTV, Myawady TV and MRTV-3), but many locals prefer to get their news from overseas radio broadcasts by the BBC's World Service, VOA (Voice of America) and RFA (Radio Free Asia; www.rfa.org) or from satellite-TV channels such as BBC World, CNN and Democratic Voice of Burma (DVB; www.dvb.no), whose brave video journalists (VJs) risk imprisonment to film events in Myanmar and smuggle them out of the country. It's believed that there are over 10 million daily viewers of DVB in Myanmar (we saw the channel screened in the lobby of one hotel on our research trip) and the work of DVB's VJs is covered in the Oscar-nominated documentary *Burma VJ.*

Internet

In 2009 the Committee to Protect Journalists (www.cpj.org) ranked Myanmar as the worst country in the world in which to be a blogger, citing, among others, the case of Maung Thura, who is serving a 59-year prison term for circulating video footage after Cyclone Nargis in 2008. Internet cafes face strict operating rules, and many sites, including that of Lonely Planet, are blocked; see p363 for details on how people get around this.

Despite the dangers, the internet is an increasingly popular and important means of news and communication in Myanmar. One of the most fascinating events we attended during our research in the country was Barcamp Yangon (www.barcampyangon.org), a user-generated conference on all things related to IT and the internet. Over two days, some 4700 people of all ages attended the event, during which topics such as blogging, computer coding and security were openly discussed.

What to call the Republic of the Union of Myanmar (to use its official name as of 2011) has been a political flashpoint since 1989. That was the year in which the military junta decided to consign Burma, the name commonly used since the mid-19th century, to the rubbish bin, along with a slew of other British colonial-era place names, such as Rangoon, Pagan, Bassein and Arakan.

The UN recognises Myanmar as the nation's official name; Myanmar is more inclusive than Burma, given that its population isn't by any means 100% Burman. However, nearly all opposition groups (including the NLD), many ethnic groups and several key nations including the US continue to refer to the country as Burma. As Aung San Suu Kyi told us (see p354), 'I prefer Burma because the name was changed without any reference to the will of the people.'

In this book, the default name for the country is Myanmar, with Burma used for periods before 1989 and where it's the name of an organisation, ie Burma Campaign UK. 'Burmese' refers to the Bamar people (not to all the country's population, which we term 'the people of Myanmar'), the food and the language.

All member nations were advised to review their links with Myanmar and ensure they did not support forced labour there.

In 2001 Japan controversially defied the embargo on nonhumanitarian aid to Myanmar. As an incentive for the regime to press ahead with reconciliation talks with Aung San Suu Kyi, Japan offered $28 million in technical assistance to repair the Baluchaung hydroelectric power plant in Kayah State.

Following Aung San Suu Kyi's third arrest in 2003, the US imposed full economic sanctions, which resulted in foreign banks in Myanmar packing up and leaving. (The wording of the EU's sanctions, however, allowed France's Total gas company to continue operating there.) Critics of the use of sanctions argue that these measures hurt the local workforce. After the strengthening of the US sanctions, many Myanmar garment factories, virtually all of which are privately owned, closed down, reportedly leading to the loss of up to 60,000 jobs.

The controversy surrounding sanctions boils down to how effective they have been in forcing the pace of change. Thant Myint-U argues that a 'policy of isolating one of the most isolated countries in the world – where the military regime isolated itself for the better part of 30 years, and which indeed has grown up and evolved well in isolation – is both counterproductive and dangerous'.

'The regime is the biggest sanction by far', says Sean Turnell, explaining why the international community shies away from doing business with Myanmar. The absence of the rule of law, rampant corruption, and what Turnell terms 'wilfully inept economic management' are sufficient on their own to discourage business and investment, without the imposition sanctions, which have become largely symbolic.

This is clearly not a view shared by the government, who lay the blame for their citizens' economic hardships at the foot of the sanction-imposing countries. Many opposition political parties in the country would like to see sanctions go too. However, the NLD has refused to drop its call for continued economic sanctions until the new government has demonstrated progress and change toward meaningful democracy and human rights.

The tourism boycott worked, at least judging by its original goal: Myanmar received fewer than 200,000 visitors during its Visit Myanmar Year (1996), well below the government's initial target of 500,000.

In its Press Freedom Index for 2010, Reporters Without Borders (http://en.rsf.org) tagged Myanmar one of the world's most repressive countries towards journalists.

Environment & Wildlife

A bit bigger than France and slightly smaller than Texas, Myanmar covers 261,228 sq miles. It borders (clockwise from the west) Bangladesh, India, Tibet, China, Laos and Thailand, with 1199 miles of coastline facing the Bay of Bengal and the Andaman Sea. Within the country's borders is extraordinary diversity, a slice of almost every habitat but desert. From frozen alpine country to steamy jungles, blushing coral reefs to open grasslands, you name it, Myanmar's got it. Scientists continue to discover new species here, but at the same time, the country's lack of environmental standards is killing off many others.

One end of the 1860-mile-long Himalaya mountain chain, formed when the Indian and Eurasian tectonic plates collided 140 million years ago, extends to Myanmar's Kachin State.

Geography

Myanmar's south is similar to Malaysia and its north to northern India or China. The centre is an overlap of the two, producing 'zones' whose uniqueness is manifest in the scenery and creatures that hop around in it.

The area southwest of Yangon is a vast delta region notable for its production of rice. Paddy fields are also an ever-present feature of Myanmar's central broad, flat heartland, known as the 'dry zone' for its lack of rain. This area is surrounded by protective mountain and hill ranges. Most notable are the rugged Kachin Hills, which serve as the first steps into the Himalaya to the north; Hkakabo Razi, on the Tibetan border, which at 19,295ft is Southeast Asia's highest mountain; and Mt Victoria (Nat Ma Taung), west of Bagan in Chin State, which rises to 10,016ft.

Three major rivers – fed by monsoon downpours and melted Himalayan snows from Nepal and India – cut north to south through the country. The 1240-mile-long Ayeyarwady (Irrawaddy) River, one of Asia's most navigable big rivers, feeds much of the country's rice fields. It connects lower Myanmar (based around Yangon) with upper Myanmar (around Mandalay). North of Mandalay, the Chindwin River connects the hills to the north, while the Thanlwin (Salween) River leads from China to the Gulf of Mottama, through Myanmar's east. Also, the Mekong River passes by on the short border with Laos.

According to the Asean Centre for Biodiversity (www.asean biodiversity.org), Myanmar is home to 300 species of mammal, 400 species of reptile and around 1000 bird species.

Flora & Fauna

Myanmar, which sits on a transition zone between the plants and creatures of the Indian subcontinent, Southeast Asia and the Himalayan highlands, is a biodiversity hotspot. However, the troubled politics of the country over the last century have made it difficult for researchers to gain an accurate picture of the current state of the country's wildlife.

Animals

When Marco Polo wrote about Myanmar in the 13th century, he described 'vast jungles teeming with elephants, unicorns and other wild beasts'. Though Myanmar's natural biodiversity has no doubt altered considerably since that time, it's difficult to say by just how much.

The most comprehensive wildlife survey available was undertaken by the Bombay Natural History Society (www.bnhs.org) between 1912 and 1921 and published as the *Mammal Survey of India, Burma and Ceylon*. In Myanmar *The Wild Animals of Burma*, published in 1967, is the most 'recent' work available and even this volume simply contains extracts from various surveys carried out by the British between 1912 and 1941, with a few observations dating to 1961. The US-based Wildlife Conservation Society (www.wcs.org) has engaged in a number of localised surveys, primarily in the far north, over the past few years, but currently nobody is attempting a full nationwide stocktake of plants and animals.

As with Myanmar's flora, the variation in Myanmar's wildlife is closely associated with the country's geographic and climatic differences. Hence the indigenous fauna of the country's northern half is mostly of Indo-Chinese origin, while that of the south is generally Sundaic (ie typical of Malaysia, Sumatra, Borneo and Java). In the Himalayan region north of the Tropic of Cancer (just north of Lashio), the fauna is similar to that found in northeastern India. In the area extending from around Myitkyina in the north to the Bago Mountains in the central region, there is overlap between geographical and vegetative zones – which means that much of Myanmar is a potential habitat for plants and animals from all three zones.

Distinctive mammals found in dwindling numbers within the more heavily forested areas of Myanmar include leopards, fishing cats, civets, Indian mongooses, crab-eating mongooses, Himalayan bears, Asiatic black bears, Malayan sun bears, gaur (Indian bison), banteng (wild cattle), serow (an Asiatic mountain goat), wild boars, sambar, barking deer, mouse deer, tapirs, pangolin, gibbons and macaques. Sea mammals include dolphins and dugongs.

Reptiles and amphibians include 27 turtle species (of which seven are found exclusively in Myanmar), along with numerous snake varieties, of which an astounding 52 are venomous, including the common

See www.national geographic.com/ adventure (search for 'Rabinowitz') for an in-depth interview with Alan Rabinowitz, the man who has done more for conservation in Myanmar than anyone else.

ENVIRONMENT & WILDLIFE FLORA & FAUNA

MYANMAR'S ECO TREASURE CHEST

Myanmar has long intrigued scientists who believe that many critically endangered species, or even species that are new to science, might be living in closed-off parts of the country. As remote parts of the country have opened up, the scientists' hopes have been proven correct.

In 2010, the BBC reported the discovery of a new species of primate, since dubbed the Burmese snub-nosed monkey. It's estimated there's a population of between 260 and 330 of these monkeys living by the Mekong and Thanlwin rivers in Kachin State.

In 2009, a team of World Conservation Society scientists discovered five Arakan forest turtles amid thick stands of bamboo in a sanctuary set up originally to protect elephants. Previously this critically endangered species, less than a foot long and with a light brown shell, had only been seen in museum specimens and a handful of captive examples.

The Kitti's hog-nosed bat, also known as the bumblebee bat, is another rare species discovered in Myanmar in 2001. At a length of 1.25in to 1.5in and weighing in at just 0.07oz, the world's smallest bat, as well as potentially the world's smallest mammal (it vies with the Etruscan pygmy shrew for this honour), was previously thought to live only in a tiny part of western Thailand.

The stunningly bright Gurney's pitta is a small bird that underwent a dramatic decline during the 20th century, until only a single population in Thailand was known. However, it was also discovered in Myanmar in 2003, giving hope that it may also be able to survive.

In 1999, another previously unknown species, the 25lb, 20in-tall 'leaf deer', or 'leaf muntjac' was confirmed in northern Myanmar. The tiny animal is so called because it can be wrapped up in a large leaf.

SAVING THE BIG CATS

A rare example of wildlife conservation has been Myanmar's establishment of the Hukaung Valley Tiger Reserve, which was doubled in size in 2010 to 8452 sq miles. Conservationists estimate that as few as 50 tigers survive in the area that could in theory support several hundreds more.

Instrumental in helping establish the reserve was Dr Alan Rabinowitz, president and CEO of the US-based NGO **Panthera** (www.panthera.org) and a former executive director at the Wildlife Conservation Society (WCS). In a 2008 interview in the *Myanmar Times*, Rabinowitz applauded the government for creating the park and helping to make eco-tourism to the area a viable alternative to killing tigers for illegal trade. 'If tourists come and spend money to see wildlife, then the local people start feeling that wildlife is more valuable alive than dead', he said.

Even though local hunters get a fraction of the $100,000 or so that can be made when a tiger is butchered into separate parts, the amounts are large enough for villagers to build a house or make other major changes to their lives.

Another step forward has been a preliminary agreement with the ethnic minority Wa people who control the border areas of northeast Myanmar to stamp out the sale of tiger and other big-cat parts in markets in border towns such as Mong La and Tachileik. A 2010 report prepared by the wildlife-trade monitoring group **Traffic** (www.traffic.org) showed that such items as tiger and leopard skin, bones, paws, penises and teeth were commonly available and consumed mainly by Chinese traders. Tiger bone wine is apparently a popular drink with those out for sex in these 'wild east' border towns.

Panthera is also spearheading the Tiger Corridor Initiative, a cross-border, 4660-mile-long 'genetic corridor' for tigers stretching from Bhutan to Malaysia, with a large part of the corridor passing through Myanmar. The idea has been presented to the UN and endorsed by the King of Bhutan.

---

cobra, king cobra (hamadryad), banded krait, Malayan pit viper, green viper and Russell's viper. This makes Myanmar home to more venomous snakes than any other country in the world.

Myanmar is rich in birdlife, with an estimated 687 resident and migrating species. Coastal and inland waterways of the delta and southern peninsula are especially important habitats for Southeast Asian waterfowl.

An excellent resource on feathered friends in Myanmar is provided by www.birdlife indochina.org.

Endangered Species

Of some 8233 known breeding species (of which 7000 are plants) in Myanmar, 132 of these (animals, birds and plants) are endangered, including the flying squirrel, tiger and three-striped box turtle.

There are believed to be anything from 4000 to 10,000 Asiatic elephants living in the wild throughout Myanmar. Their numbers are steadily dropping, primarily due to logging, which leads to habitat destruction. Ironically, domesticated or captive elephants are widely used by the logging industry to knock down the forests on which their wild cousins depend. However, the creature's usefulness could be its very saviour: Myanmar has the largest population of domesticated elephants (around 4000) in the world.

To find out more about the plight of elephants in Myanmar, see the report compiled in 2006 for Eleaid (www.eleaid. com).

Both the one-horned (Javan) rhinoceros and the Asiatic two-horned (Sumatran) rhinoceros are believed to survive in very small numbers near the Thai border in Kayin State. The rare red panda (or cat bear) was last sighted in northern Myanmar in the early 1960s but is thought to still live in Kachin State forests above 6500ft.

Deforestation poses the greatest threat to wildlife, but even in areas where habitat loss isn't a problem, hunting threatens to wipe out the rarer animal species. Wildlife laws are seldom enforced and poaching remains a huge problem in Myanmar.

Plants

As in the rest of tropical Asia, most indigenous vegetation in Myanmar is associated with two basic types of tropical forest: monsoon forest (with a distinctive dry season of three months or more) and rainforest (where rain falls more than nine months per year). It's said there are over 1000 plant species endemic to the country.

Monsoon forests are marked by deciduous tree varieties, which shed their leaves during the dry season. Rainforests, by contrast, are typically evergreen. The area stretching from Yangon to Myitkyina contains mainly monsoon forests, while peninsular Myanmar to the south of Mawlamyine is predominantly a rainforest zone. There is much overlapping of the two – some forest zones support a mix of monsoon forest and rainforest vegetation.

In the mountainous Himalayan region, Myanmar's flora is characterised by subtropical broadleaf evergreen forest up to 6500ft; temperate semi-deciduous broadleaf rainforest from 6500ft to 9800ft; and, above this, evergreen coniferous, subalpine snow forest and alpine scrub.

Along the Rakhaing and Tanintharyi (Tenasserim) coasts, tidal forests occur in river estuaries, lagoons, tidal creeks and along low islands. Such woodlands are characterised by mangroves and other coastal trees that grow in mud and are resistant to seawater. Beach and dune forests, which grow along these same coasts above the high-tide line, consist of palms, hibiscus, casuarinas and other tree varieties that can withstand high winds and occasional storm-sent waves.

The country's most famous flora includes an incredible array of fruit trees, over 25,000 flowering species, a variety of tropical hardwoods, and bamboo. Cane and rattan are also plentiful.

Myanmar holds 75% of the world's reserves of *Tectona grandis,* better known as teak (*kyun* in Burmese). This dense, long-wearing, highly prized hardwood remains one of Myanmar's most important exports, despite sanctions being placed on its import to the US and the European Union.

Alan Rabinowitz's *Beyond the Last Village: A Journey of Discovery in Asia's Forbidden Wilderness* (2001) details the author's attempts to set up wildlife reserves in Myanmar's northern areas.

TOP PARKS & RESERVES

PARK	SIZE (SQ MILES)	FEATURES	BEST TIME TO VISIT	PERMIT NEEDED?
Hkakabo Razi National Park (p266)	1472	highest mountain in Myanmar; forests; rare species such as takin, musk and black barking deer, and blue sheep	Oct-Apr	yes
Indawgyi Wetland Wildlife Sanctuary (p241)	299	Southeast Asia's largest lake, 120 species of birds	Jan-Apr	no
Inle Wetland Bird Sanctuary (p186)	642	floating agriculture, birdlife, otters, turtles	Year-round	no
Moeyungyi Wetlands (p85)	40	125 species of birds	Nov-Apr	no
Mt Victoria (Nat Ma Taung) National Park (p287)	279	second-highest mountain in Myanmar, rare birds and orchids	Nov-Mar	yes
Popa Mountain Park (p127)	50	extinct volcano, unique dry-zone ecosystem, monkeys	Nov-Mar	no

COOKING UP AN ECO SOLUTION

Dawn over a Myanmar village: the mist you see is not the evaporation of dew, but the smoke from firewood- and charcoal-fuelled cooking stoves. According to Win Myo Thu, founder of the Myanmar NGO **Ecodev** (www.ecodev-mm.com), 90 per cent of Myanmar's population relies on firewood for cooking and each household consumes some three tons of wood a year – all of which is putting pressure on Myanmar's forests, particularly in the dry zone.

To tackle the problem, the A1 stove, an energy efficient cooking stove developed by Myanmar's Forest Research Institute (FRI) has been distributed in the dry zone by Ecodev. The stoves cost around $2 each and cut a household's consumption of firewood by one ton a year. With over 300,000 now in use, and 5000 a month being sold, a market has been established for this simple energy-saving device.

National Parks

By an optimistic account, about 7% of Myanmar's land area is made up of national parks and national forests, wildlife sanctuaries and parks, and other protected areas. However, such protection on paper is rarely translated into reality without the backing of adequate funds and effective policing.

A 2009 report by environmental watchdog Global Witness found a dramatic decrease in the illegal timber trade between Myanmar and China, but notes smuggling still continues.

Apart from the parks and reserves covered in the table below and reviewed in full elsewhere in this guide, you may also want to enquire with specialised travel agents about visits to the 103-sq-mile Chattin Wildlife Sanctuary and the 620-sq-mile Alaungdaw Kathapa National Park, both in Sagaing Region northeast of Mandalay, and both partly created to protect the endangered thamin, a species of Eld's Deer.

Environmental Issues

Myanmar has little in the way of an official environmental movement. However, recycling and making use of every little thing is part of most people's daily life, disposability only being a luxury of the rich.

Essentially no environmental legislation was passed from the time of independence in 1948 until after 1988. Since then, government dictums, such as recent efforts to 'green the dry zone' and protect wildlife, have been more words than action. 'They may have laws on the books but they mean extremely little', says Sean Turnell, an expert on Myanmar's economy at Sydney's Macquarie University.

Deforestation

Myanmar supposedly contains more standing forest, with fewer inhabitants, than any other country in Indochina. That said, it's also disappearing faster than almost anywhere else in Asia, and Myanmar's forests remain the most unprotected in the region.

In 2009 the Korea International Cooperation Agency (KOICA) launched a three-year programme worth $1.5 million for a reforestation project in Myanmar's dry zone.

Much of Myanmar's forest has fallen to the axe – for fuel and for timber exports (both legal and illegal) or due to clearing for farming. One of the most troubled areas is the so-called 'dry zone', made up of heavily populated Mandalay, lower Sagaing and Magwe divisions. Little of the original vegetation remains in this pocket (which is about 10% of Myanmar's land, but home to one-third of the population), due to growth in the area's population and deforestation.

The problem isn't new. Much of Britain's 19th-century industrialisation, as well as the train tracks made here in Myanmar, were built from Burmese timber. Following the 1988 putting down of the prodemocracy protests, the government relaxed timber and fishing laws for short-term gain, ultimately causing more long-term problems.

Air & Water Pollution

You don't need to be a scientific expert to sniff the air pollution in Yangon and Mandalay. According to a spokesperson for Ecodev (www.ecodev-mm.com), a local NGO, studies by the National Commission for Environmental Affairs pegged air quality in these cities at below World Health Organisation standards.

Uncontrolled gold and other mining means that the release of pollutants into rivers and the sea is steadily increasing. The most noticeable aspect of pollution to travellers will be the piles of non-biodegradable waste, such as plastic bags, dumped at the edge of towns and villages and seen fluttering across the fields. Bans on the production and sale of polythene bags and cord exist in both Yangon and Mandalay but they are not strictly enforced.

Dams & Pipelines

In the last decade the authorities have embarked on a series of hydroelectric dam projects along the country's major rivers, creating a crescendo of economic, social and environmental problems. Trumping the fuss made over the ongoing construction of the Tamanthi Dam on the Chindwin River, which has so far forced the relocation of many tribal Kuki villages and threatens the habitat of rare wildlife species, is the Myitsone Dam, the biggest of seven large dams currently planned on the Mali, the N'Mai and the Ayeyarwady rivers.

The government has said it wants to make hydropower its sole source of electricity by 2030 but critics believe the majority of the power generated will be exported to neighbouring countries.

There's also concern among environmentalists about the development of oil and gas fields off Myanmar's coast and the impact this is having on fragile eco-systems as pipelines are built across the country to send the fossil fuels to Thailand and China.

Find out about Myanmar's rivers and the environmental problems they face at Burma Rivers Network www.burmarivers network.org, an umbrella gro.

Earthrights International (www.earthrights.org) documents human rights and environmental abuses in Myanmar, focusing in particular on the controversial Yadana gas pipeline.

ENVIRONMENT & WILDLIFE ENVIRONMENTAL ISSUES

Eating in Myanmar (Burma)

Burmese food suffers from a bad rap – a rather unjustified bad rap in our opinion. While Burmese food can be somewhat oily, and lacks the diversity of cuisine in neighbouring Thailand, with a bit of advice and background knowledge we're confident you'll return from Myanmar having savoured some truly tasty and memorable meals.

A Burmese Meal

T'ămìn (rice), also written as *htamin*, is the core of any Burmese meal. Rice is served with a variety of dishes that characterise Burmese cuisine, a unique blend of Burmese, Mon, Indian and Chinese influences. These dishes use a variety of local, largely plant- and seafood-based ingredients, and as with other Southeast Asian cuisines, an effort is made to balance the four primary flavours: sour, salty, spicy and bitter.

Although these foundations are relatively simple, one of the pleasures of eating an authentic Burmese meal is the sheer variety of dishes at a single setting, something that rivals even Thai food. Upon arriving at any *Myanma saa thauk sain* (Burmese restaurant), and having chosen a curry (see box, p329), fried dish or salad, a succession of side dishes will follow. One of these side dishes is invariably soup, either an Indian-influenced *peh-hìn-ye* (lentil soup, or dhal), studded with chunks of vegetables, or a tart leaf-based *hìn-jo* (sour soup). A tray of fresh and par-boiled vegetables and herbs is another common side dish; they're eaten with various dips, ranging from *ngăpí ye* (a watery, fishy dip) to *balachaung* (a dry, pungent combination of chillies, garlic and dried shrimp fried in oil). Additional vegetable-based side dishes, unlimited green tea and a dessert of pickled tea leaves and chunks of jaggery (palm sugar) are also usually included.

Good Yangon restaurants at which to experience this type of Burmese dining include Aung Thukha (p60), Feel Myanmar Food (p58) and Danuphyu Daw Saw Yee Myanma Restaurant (p58).

> Food is so enjoyed in Myanmar that standard greetings to friends and foreigners include *sar pyi bi lar?* (have you eaten your lunch yet?) and *bar hin ne sar le?* (what curry did you have for lunch?).

Burmese Specialities

One of the culinary highlights of Burmese food is undoubtedly *ăthouq* – light, tart and spicy salads made with raw vegetables or fruit tossed with lime juice, onions, peanuts, roasted chickpea powder and chillies. Among the most exquisite are *maji-yweq thouq*, made with tender young tamarind leaves, and *shauq-thi dhouq*, made with a type of indigenous lemon. Shwe Mei Tha Su (p59) in Yangon does an excellent take on the latter. In fact, the Burmese will make just about anything into a salad, as *t'ămìn dhouq*, a savoury salad made with rice, and *nangyi dhouq*, a salad made with thick rice noodles, prove.

A popular finish to Burmese meals and possibly the most infamous Burmese dish of all is *leq-p'eq* (often spelled *laphet*), fermented green tea leaves mixed with a combination of sesame seeds, fried peas, dried shrimp, fried garlic, peanuts and other crunchy ingredients. The slimy-looking mass of leaves puts some foreigners off, but it's actually quite tasty once you get beyond the dish's exotic appearance. A more user-friendly version of the dish is *leq-p'eq thouq,* where the fermented tea and nuts are combined in the form of a salad with slices of tomato and cabbage and a squeeze of lime. The dish is a popular snack in Myanmar, and the caffeine boost supplied by the tea leaves makes the dish a favourite of students who need to stay up late studying.

Noodle dishes are prized by the Burmese and are most often eaten for breakfast or as light meals between the main meals of the day. The general word for noodles is *hkuauq-swèh.* The most popular noodle and unofficial national dish is *moún-hìn-gà* (often spelled *mohinga*), thin rice noodles served in a thick fish and shallot broth and topped with crispy deep-fried vegies or lentils. *Mohinga* is available just about everywhere, but our favourite bowl is at Myaung Mya Daw Cho (p61) in Yangon. *Moún-di* (also known as *mondhi*) are spaghetti-like noodles served with chunks of chicken or fish. Another popular noodle dish, especially at festivals, is *oùn-nó hkauq-swèh,* Chinese-style rice noodles with pieces of chicken in a broth made with coconut milk.

Most, if not all, of these noodle dishes can be sampled at the Yangon teahouses Lucky Seven (p63) and Thone Pan Hla (p63).

Regional & Ethnic Variations

Local cuisine can be broadly broken down into dishes found in 'lower Myanmar' (roughly Yangon and the delta), with more fish pastes and sour foods; and 'upper Myanmar' (centred at Mandalay), with more sesame, nuts and beans used in dishes.

In Mandalay and around Inle Lake, it is also fairly easy to find Shan cuisine, which is somewhat similar to northern Thai cuisine. Popular dishes are *k'auq sen* (Shan-style rice noodles with curry) and various fish and meat salads. Large *maung jeut* (rice crackers) are common throughout Shan State.

One of the seminal works on Myanmar cuisine is *Cook and Entertain the Burmese Way,* by Mi Mi Khaing, available in Yangon bookshops.

OIL SPILL

Burmese food has a reputation for being oily. We won't deny this, but in its defence will posit that much of this is the fault of the curries.

The centrepiece of any Burmese meal, *hi'n* (Burmese-style curries) are generally cooked until the oil separates from all other ingredients and rises to the top. The Burmese term for this cooking method is *s'i pyan,* 'oil returns', and the process ensures that the rather harsh curry paste ingredients – typically turmeric, tomatoes, ginger, garlic, onions and shrimp paste – have properly amalgamated and have become milder. Some restaurants also add extra oil to maintain the correct top layer, as the fat also preserves the underlying food from contamination by insects and airborne bacteria while the curries sit in open, unheated pots for hours at a time.

The good news is that all this oil isn't necessarily meant to be eaten, and it's usually easy enough to work around it. Those who've been burned by the spiciness of Thai food will be pleased to learn that Burmese curries are the mildest in Asia – in fact, most cooks don't use chillies in their recipes. It's also worth mentioning that the most common curry proteins you'll encounter are fish, chicken, prawns or mutton. Relatively little beef or pork is eaten by people in Myanmar – beef because it's considered offensive to most Hindus and Burmese Buddhists, and pork because the *nat* (spirits) disapprove.

Most importantly, it's crucial to keep in mind that a curry only constitutes a single element of a Burmese meal. The side dishes, which include various soups, salads, dips and fresh herbs, often have little or no oil.

An Introduction to Myanmar Cuisine (2004) by Ma Thanegi is an excellent source of Myanmar recipes, both sweet and savoury.

Shàn k'auq-swèh (Shan-style noodle soup), thin rice noodles in a light broth with chunks of chilli-marinated chicken or pork, is a favourite all over Myanmar, but is most common in Mandalay and Shan State. A variation popular in Mandalay, called *myi shay,* is made with rice noodles and is often served with pork. Another Shan dish worth seeking out is *ngà t'ămìn jìn,* 'kneaded fish rice', a turmeric-tinged rice dish. Both of these dishes and more are available at Yangon Shan restaurants 999 Shan Noodle Shop (p58) and Inlay Amathaya (p62).

Mon cuisine, most readily available in towns stretching from Bago to Mawlamyine, is very similar to Burmese food, with a greater emphasis on curry selections. While a Burmese restaurant might offer a choice of four or five curries, a Mon restaurant will have as many as a dozen, all

A TASTE OF HOME: TIN CHO CHAW

It was my husband's first trip to Myanmar, and I was eager to show Chris my country of birth and the much-loved food of my childhood. One dish I particularly wanted to share was *let thoke*, which can be translated as 'hand-mixed'. It can roughly be described as a salad because all the ingredients are tossed in a dressing, but unlike salads in the West, it is hearty and substantial.

So when my cousin asked what we wanted to eat, naturally, I suggested *let thoke*. I have made *let thoke* for my husband many times at home, but this was the first time he had the chance to taste *let thoke sone. Sone* means an assortment or variety, and is a dish you assemble yourself, with all the ingredients laid out on the table. As the name suggests, it is mixed and eaten with your hands.

We arrived at my cousin's house early to help with the preparations, but all the ingredients were already sliced, chopped and cooked. Concerned that my husband would be uncomfortable sitting on the floor, my cousin started to move a large table toward the kitchen, but we assured her we were used to sitting on the floor. We washed our hands and sat down on a bamboo mat. Chris gave me a look that asked, Are we eating on our own again? I reminded him that as guests, we ate first and my cousin's family would eat afterwards, so we must leave enough. Eating while our hosts watched was an unnerving experience for Chris. He felt he was being rude eating first, but I explained that, as good hosts, this was their way.

My cousins kept saying 'Please eat, don't be polite', so I started and took a small amount of each ingredient: rice mixed with chilli oil, flat rice noodles, vermicelli, egg noodles, mung-bean noodles mixed with turmeric oil, boiled sliced potatoes, Shan tofu, deep-fried tofu, fried garlic and fried onions. These I mixed with a small handful of thinly sliced white cabbage and chopped coriander. The cabbage gave the dish a crunchy texture while the coriander added freshness to an otherwise carbohydrate-heavy meal.

Next came the seasonings: a teaspoon of pounded dried shrimp and a spoonful of roasted chickpea powder. The powder helps emulsify the dressing, which is comprised of oil infused with fried onion, tamarind liquid, a squeeze of lemon juice and a generous dash of fish sauce. Finally I cautiously added some crushed roasted chillies, and to the amusement of my cousin, Chris heaped a generous amount on his plate.

Once all the ingredients were assembled, I used the fingertips of my right hand to mix and toss, mashing the potatoes, making sure all the ingredients were combined. A quick taste and I added a little more lemon before being satisfied. Chris spent the next five minutes adding small amounts of fish sauce, lemon and tamarind. He felt it did not taste the same as mine and I told him that's the fun of making *let thoke*: each person adjusts the flavours according to his or her own personal taste.

Of all our food experiences in Myanmar, *let thoke* was the most memorable. For Chris, *let thoke* summed up the flavours of Burmese food: a balance of salty, sour and spicy. For me, the taste evoked memories of the food I ate while growing up in Yangon. It also reminded me that food always tastes better when mixed with your hands.

Tin Cho Chaw is the author of hsa*ba, a Burmese cookbook and website (www.hsaba.com)

» A fork is held in the left hand and used as a probe to push food onto the spoon; you eat from the spoon.

» Locals tend to focus on the flavours, not table talk, during meals.

» If you're asked to join someone at a restaurant, they will expect to pay for the meal. Expect to do likewise if you invite a local out for a meal.

lined up in curry pots to be examined. Mon curries are also more likely to contain chillies than those of other cuisines.

Rakhaing (Arakan) food most resembles dishes found in Bangladesh and India's Bengal state, featuring lots of bean and pulse dishes, very spicy curries and flatbreads. Minn Lane Rakhaing Monte & Fresh Seafood (p60) in Yangon is a good place to sample Rakhaing-influenced seafood and noodles.

In towns large and small throughout Myanmar you'll find plenty of Chinese restaurants, many of which do a distinctly Burmese (eg oily) take on Chinese standards. Despite being the most ubiquitous type of dining in Myanmar (upcountry this is often the only kind of restaurant you'll find), it's probably the least interesting.

Indian restaurants are also common, although much more so in Yangon than elsewhere. Most are run by Muslim Indians, a few by Hindus. Excellent chicken *dan-bauq* (biryani), as well as all-you-can-eat vegetarian *thali* served on a banana leaf, is easy to find in the capital. The Myanmar people call Indian restaurants that serve all-you-can-eat *thali* 'Chitty' or 'Chetty' restaurants.

Pregnant women, stay away from bananas! According to local beliefs, your baby will be born overweight if you indulge while pregnant.

Sweets

The typical Burmese dessert is often little more than a pinch of pickled tea leaves or a lump of palm sugar (jaggery). You can visit places making jaggery and toddy (see p333) on the road between Bagan and Mt Popa (see p128). Bagan is also famous for its tamarind flakes, delicious candies made from the dried pulp of the sweet-sour fruit and wrapped in twists of white paper; they're made in Chauk, an hour's drive south of Bagan on the way to Salay.

More substantial sweet dishes, generally referred to as *moún* (sometimes written *moun* or *mont*), are regarded as snacks, and are often taken with equally sweet tea in the morning or afternoon.

Prime ingredients for Burmese sweets include grated coconut, coconut milk, rice flour (from white rice or sticky rice), cooked sticky rice, tapioca and various fruits. Some Burmese sweets have been influenced by Indian cooking and include more exotic ingredients such as semolina and poppy seeds. In general, Burmese sweets are slightly less syrupy sweet than those of neighbouring Thailand, and often take a somewhat familiar form, such as *bein moun* and *moun pyit thalet,* Burmese-style pancakes served sweet or savoury.

A good place to sample Burmese sweets in Yangon is from the street-side vendors (see p61) who set up every afternoon in front of the FMI Centre.

Drinks
Nonalcoholic Drinks

Black tea, brewed in the Indian style with lots of milk and sugar, is ubiquitous and cheap, costing K250 per cup at the time of research. See below for more about the very Burmese institution of teahouses. If this is not to your liking, ask for Chinese tea, which is weak and comes without milk.

Many restaurants will provide as much weak Chinese tea as you can handle – for free if you order some food. It's a good, safe thirst-quencher, and some people prefer it to regular Burmese tea.

Soft drinks cost more, but are reasonable by Asian standards. Since the privatisation of industry there has been a boom in new made-in-Myanmar soft-drink brands, including Fantasy, Lemon Sparkling, Max, Star, Fruito and Crusher. They taste pretty much the same as their Western counterparts.

Real coffee is limited to a handful of modern Western-style cafés in Yangon and other large cities. As a result, coffee drinkers will find themselves growing disturbingly attached to the 'three-in-one' packets of instant coffee (the 'three' being coffee, milk and sugar), which you can have in teahouses for about K250.

> The website hsa*ba (www.hsaba.com), written by cookbook author Tin Cho Chaw, a contributor to this chapter, includes a blog that regularly features Burmese recipes.

Alcoholic Drinks

In the past the people of Myanmar were not big drinkers. This was due to a lack of disposable income, but also to the consumption of alcohol being looked down upon by the many Burmese Buddhists who interpret the fifth lay precept against intoxication very strictly. However, with the advent of 'beer stations' – places that serve cheap draught beer – the number of urban locals who can afford a few glasses of beer after work is on the rise.

Beer

Apart from international brands such as Tiger, ABC Stout, Singha, San Miguel and other beers brewed in Thailand and Singapore (typically costing K1700 for a 375mL can or bottle), there are a couple of Myanmar brews. These include long-established, joint-venture Myanmar Beer, which is slightly lighter in flavour and alcohol than other Southeast Asian beers (to the palate of at least a couple of researchers). A more watery beer is Mandalay Beer. If you order it, some waiting staff may double-check to see if you meant 'Myanmar' beer. Founded in 1886, Mandalay Brewery, in Yangon, also produces the New Mandalay Export label, which is the best-tasting local beer. Some fine, newer brands brewed in Myanmar include Dagon and Skol.

> Fountain of youth in a bottle! Spirulina Beer, made from lake algae near Monywa, is revered for its 'anti-ageing' qualities (less so for the slightly sweet aftertaste).

Among the locals, Myanmar draught is the favourite; a glass of it will set you back only K500 or so.

Liquors & Wines

Very popular in Shan State is an orange brandy called *shwe leinmaw*. Much of it is distilled in the mountains between Kalaw and Taunggyi. It's a pleasant-tasting liqueur and packs quite a punch. Near Taunggyi, there's a couple of vineyards making wine (p191) and in Pyin Oo Lwin there are several sweet strawberry-based wines.

There are also stronger liquors, including *ayeq hpyu* (white liquor), which varies in strength from brandylike to almost pure ethyl; and *taw ayeq* (jungle liquor), a cruder form of *ayeq hpyu*. Mandalay is well known for its rums, and there is also, of course, the fermented palm juice known as toddy.

DRINKING WATER

Drink water in Myanmar only when you know it has been purified – which in most restaurants it should be. You should be suspicious of ice, although we've had lots of ice drinks in Myanmar without suffering any ill effects. Many brands of drinking water are sold in bottles and are quite safe, but check the seal on the bottle first. A 1L bottle, usually kept cool by ice or refrigerator, costs about K300 or K400 at most hotels.

Throughout central Myanmar and the delta, *t'àn ye* (or *htan ye; palm juice*) or toddy is the farmer's choice of alcoholic beverage. *T'àn ye* is tapped from the top of a toddy palm, the same tree – and the same sap – that produces jaggery (palm sugar). The juice is sweet and nonalcoholic in the morning, but by midafternoon it ferments naturally into a weak, beerlike strength. By the next day it will have turned. The milky, viscous liquid has a nutty aroma and a slightly sour flavour that fades quickly.

Villages in some areas have their own thatched-roof toddy bars, where the locals meet and drink pots of fermented toddy. The toddy is sold in the same roughly engraved terracotta pots the juice is collected in, and drunk from coconut half-shells set on small bamboo pedestals. Some toddy bars also sell *t'àn-ayeq* (toddy liquor, also called jaggery liquor), a much stronger, distilled form of toddy sap.

Where To Eat & Drink

Myanmar has three dining/drinking scenarios: what's in Yangon (including many expat-oriented, high-end choices); what's in other oft-visited places, including Mandalay, Bagan, Inle Lake and Ngapali Beach (many traveller-oriented menus, with Thai and pizza); and everywhere else.

Food can be quite cheap (from K1200 or K2000 for a full stomach) if you stick to roadside restaurants with their curry-filled pots or pick-and-point rice dishes. It's worth mentioning that these restaurants, though cheap, don't always meet international hygiene standards. That said, you're usually looking at K3000 to K5000 for a meal. In many mid-sized towns, there are basic stands and maybe a Chinese restaurant or two – and that's it.

Listings in this book are divided into three price brackets: **budget ($)**, meal less than $3 (about K2550); **midrange ($$)**, $3 to $15 (about K2550 to K12,750); and **top end ($$$)**, more than $15 (about K12,750).

Quick Eats

The bulk of Myanmar eateries are basic, with concrete floors, a wide-open front for ventilation and often a menu in English. Burmese eateries are busiest (and many say freshest) at lunch. No menus are necessary at most; just go to the line of curries and point to what you want. A meal comes with a tableful of condiments, all of which are automatically refilled once you finish them. An all-you-can-eat meal can start at as little as K1500.

Another abundant option is the (usually) hole-in-the-wall Indian (often Muslim) curry shop, which sometimes serves vegie dishes only and no beer.

Like most Southeast Asians, the people of Myanmar are great grab-and-go snackers. Stands at night markets, selling a host of sweets and barbecued meals and noodles, get going around 5pm to 8pm or later. Generally you can get some fried noodles, a few pieces of pork, or sticky rice wrapped in banana leaf for a few hundred kyat.

Myanmar's fruit offerings vary by region and season. Don't miss Pyin Oo Lwin's strawberries and Bago's pineapples. Mango is best from March to July; jackfruit from June to October.

Restaurants

Most restaurants keep long hours daily, usually from 7am to 9pm or until the last diner wants to stumble out, their belly full of curry or beer.

Chinese restaurants are found in most towns and most have similar sprawling menus, with as many as 50 rice or noodle and chicken, pork, lamb, fish, beef or vegetable dishes, usually without prices indicated. Vegie dishes start at around K800 or K1000; meat dishes about K1200 or K1500.

More upmarket restaurants – some serving a mix of Asian foods, others specialising in one food type, such as pizza or Thai – can be found in Bagan, Mandalay, Inle Lake and especially Yangon. Also, most top-end hotels offer plusher eating places, sometimes set around the pool. Such comfort is rarer to come by off the beaten track.

Drinking Venues

You'll be hard-pressed to find anything resembling the Western concept of a bar or pub. Most drinking is done at dark shophouse restaurants or open-air barbecue restaurants, sometimes cutely called 'beer stations' in Burmese English. Opening hours are therefore the same as for restaurants. All but Muslim Indian restaurants keep cold bottles of Tiger and Myanmar Beer handy (charging from K1700 in basic restaurants and up to K3000 or so in swankier ones). It's perfectly fine to linger for hours and down a few beers.

Men and women don't often intermingle at restaurants, so in many places you may see red-faced men lingering over a slowly massing number of empty bottles, with full ones always kept nearby by waiting staff.

Teahouses

Teahouses are an important social institution in Myanmar, a key meeting place for family, business associates or conspirators speaking of potentially freer times. Locals like to sit and chat while sipping tea – sometimes for hours. They're also a great place for breakfast (see p334), as many also serve noodles, fried snacks or pastries. 'Morning teahouses' typically open from 6am to 4pm, while evening ones open from 4pm or 5pm and stay open till 11pm or later.

Servers in teahouses around Myanmar are 'tea boys', poor kids from the countryside who bring snacks and drinks to tables. They work daily in exchange for room, board and several dollars a month. One told us: 'Some day I hope to be a tea maker or a teahouse manager.'

Vegetarians & Vegans

Vegetarians will be able to find fare at most restaurants in Myanmar. Many Burmese Buddhists abstain from eating the flesh of any four-legged animal and, during the Buddhist rain retreat around the Waso full moon, may take up a 'fire-free' diet that includes only uncooked vegetables and fruit. Even meaty barbecues have a few skewered vegetables that can be grilled up. The easiest way to convey your needs is saying 'I can't eat meat' (ǎthà mǎsà-nain-bù). Some Indian or Nepali restaurants are vegan.

Throughout the regional chapters, we highlight some particularly good vegetarian options or restaurants.

Habits & Customs

At home, most families take their meals sitting on reed mats around a low, round table about 1ft in height. In restaurants, chairs and tables are

---

BREAKFAST OF CHAMPIONS

Virtually every hotel fee in Myanmar includes some sort of breakfast, but the offerings are usually very basic and/or barely palatable attempts at Western food such as toast and a fried egg. With this in mind, it's worth exchanging the comfort of the hotel bubble for breakfast at a Myanmar-style teahouse. These places are not only cheap and delicious, but also an authentic slice of Myanmar daily life.

Teahouses are the best place to dig into the world of Burmese noodle dishes. *Mohinga* is usually available as a matter of course, but other more obscure noodle dishes offered at teahouses include *oùn-nó hkauq-swèh* (a wheat noodle dish with a coconut-milk broth), *myi shay* (a Shan-influenced noodle soup with pickled tofu and pork) and *nangyi dhouq* (a salad of wide rice noodles). Burmese-style teahouses that serve these dishes are also likely to serve fried rice and *t'ǎmìn dhouq* (rice salad), also great for breakfast.

Indian/Muslim-owned teahouses often specialise in deep-fried dishes such as the ubiquitous samosas and *poori* (deep-fried bread served with a light potato curry), as well as oil-free breads such as dosai (southern Indian-style crepes) and *nanbya* (nan bread), the latter often served with a delicious pigeon pea-based dip. And Chinese-style teahouses often feature lots of baked sweets as well as meaty steamed buns and yum cha-like nibbles.

See p63 for our shortlist of Yangon teahouses.

more common. The entire meal is served at once, rather than in courses. In basic Burmese restaurants, each individual diner in a group typically orders a small plate of curry for himself or herself, while side dishes are shared among the whole party. This contrasts with China and Thailand, for example, where every dish is usually shared.

Traditionally, Burmese food is eaten with the fingers, much like in India, usually with the right hand (but using the left doesn't seem to be taboo as it is in India). Nowadays, it's also common for urban Myanmar people to eat with a *k'ăyìn* (or *hkayin*; fork) and *zùn* (tablespoon). These are always available at Burmese restaurants and are almost always given to foreign diners.

If you eat at a private home, it's not unusual for the hostess and children to not join you at the table.

Eat Your Words

For some general Burmese phrases and pronunciation guidelines, see the Language chapter.

Food Glossary
Typical Burmese Dishes

ămèh·hnaq	အမဲနှပ်	beef in gravy
ceq·thà·ăc'o·jeq	ကြက်သားအချိုချက်	sweet chicken
ceq·thà·gin	ကြက်သားကင်	grilled chicken (satay)
ceq·thà·jaw jeq	ကြက်သားကြော်ချက်	fried chicken
hìn	ဟင်း	curry
ămèh·dhà·hìn	အမဲသား·ဟင်း	beef curry
ceq·thà·hìn	ကြက်သားဟင်း	chicken curry
ăthì·ăyweq·hìn/ *thì·zoun·hìn·jo*	အသီးအရွက်ဟင်း၊ သီးစုံဟင်းချို	vegetable curry
hìn·jo	ဟင်းချို	soup (clear or mild)
s'an·hlaw·hìn·jo	ဆန်လှော်ဟင်းချို	sizzling rice soup
s'éh·hnămyò·hìn·jo	ဆယ်နှစ်မျိုးဟင်းချို	'12-taste' soup
móun·di	မုန့်တီ	*mount-ti* (Mandalay noodles and chicken/fish)
móun·hìn·gà	မုန့်ဟင်းခါး	*mohinga* (noodles and chicken/fish)
móun·s'i·jaw	မုန့်ဆီကြော်	sweet fried-rice pancakes
móun·zàn	မုန့်ဆန်း	sticky rice cake with jaggery (palm sugar)
myì shay	မြီးရှည်	Shan-style noodle soup
ngà·dhouq	ငါးသုပ်	fish salad
ngà·baùn·(douq)	ငါးပေါင်း(ထုပ်)	steamed fish (in banana leaves)
t'ămìn	ထမင်း	rice
kauq·hnyìn·baùn	ကောက်ညှင်းပေါင်း	steamed sticky rice
oùn·t'ămìn	အုန်းထမင်း	coconut rice
t'ămìn·gyaw	ထမင်းကြော်	fried rice
t'ădhi·móun	ထန်းသီးမုန့်	toddy-palm sugar cake
weq·thăni	ဝက်သနီ	red pork

Meat & Seafood

ămèh·dhà	အမဲသား	beef
ceq·thà	ကြက်သား	chicken

Until 2008's Cyclone Nargis devastated much of the rice crop in the Delta region, Myanmar was the world's sixth largest producer of rice.

For short videos on various Burmese food-related topics, from cooking Burmese dishes to eating in Myanmar, search for 'meemalee's kitchen' on YouTube.

k'ăyú	ခရု	shellfish
ngà	ငါး	fish
ngăk'u	ငါးခူ	catfish
ngăshín	ငါးရှဉ့်	eel
ngăthălauq·paùn	ငါးသေလောက်ပေါင်း	carp
pin·leh·za/ye·thaq·tăwa	ပင်လယ်စာ၊ ရေသတ္တဝါ	seafood
pyi·ji·ngà	ပြည်ကြီးငါး	squid
weq·thà	ဝက်သား	pork

Vegetables

bù·dhì	ဘူးသီး	zucchini/gourd
ceq·thun·ni	ကြက်သွန်နီ	onion
gaw·bi·douq	ဂေါ်ဖီထုပ်	cabbage
hìn·dhì·hìn·yweq	ဟင်းသီးဟင်းရွက်	vegetables
hmo	မှို	mushrooms
hngăpyàw·bù	ငှက်ပျောဖူး	banana flower
kălăbèh	ကုလားပဲ	chick peas
k'ăyàn·dhì	ခရမ်းသီး	eggplant/aubergine
k'ăyàn·jin·dhì	ခရမ်းချဉ်သီး	tomato
moun·la·ú·wa	မုန်လာဥဝါ	carrot
pàn·gaw·p'i	ပန်းဂေါ်ဖီ	cauliflower
p'ăyoun·dhì	ဖရုံသီး	pumpkin
pèh·dhì	ပဲသီး	beans
pyaùn·bù	ပြောင်းဖူး	corn (cob)

Fruit

àw·za·thì	ဩဇာသီး	custard apple ('influence fruit')
ceq·mauq·thì	ကြက်မောက်သီး	rambutan ('cocksomb fruit')
cwèh·gàw·dhì	ကျွဲကောသီး	pomelo
dù·yìn·dhì	ဒူးရင်းသီး	durian
lain·c'ì·dhì	လိုင်ချီးသီး	lychee
lein·maw·dhì	လိမ္မော်သီး	orange
meq·màn·dhì	မက်မန်းသီး	plum (damson)
măjì·dhì	မန်ကျည်းသီး	tamarind
nănaq·thì	နာနတ်သီး	pineapple
ngăpyàw·dhì	ငှက်ပျောသီး	banana
oùn·dhì	အုန်းသီး	coconut
pàn·dhì	ပန်းသီး	apple ('flower fruit')
shauq·thì	ရှောက်သီး	lemon
t'àw·baq·thì	ထောပတ်သီး	avocado ('butter fruit')
than·băya·dhì	သံပရာသီး	lime
thiq·thì/ăthì	သစ်သီး၊ အသီး	fruit
thăyeq·dhì	သရက်သီး	mango
thìn·bàw·dhì	သင်္ဘောသီး	papaya ('boat-shaped fruit')

Spices & Condiments

ceq·thun·byu	ကြက်သွန်ဖြူ	garlic
gyìn	ဂျင်း	ginger
hnàn	နှမ်း	sesame

Rudyard Kipling famously referred to *ngapi*, the Burmese fermented fish condiment, as 'fish pickled when it ought to have been buried long ago'.

Cooking Myanmar Food (www.cookmyanmarfood.wordpress.com) features a growing list of Myanmar food recipes, including recipes for most of the more famous Burmese dishes.

hnìn·ye	နှင်းရည်	rose syrup
kǎlà·t'àw·baq	ကုလားးထောပတ်	ghee
kùn·ya	ကွမ်းယာ	betel quid
meiq·thǎlin	မိတ်သလင်	galangal (white gingerlike root)
mye·bèh·(jaw)	မြေပဲ(ကြော်)	peanuts (fried)
nan·nan·bin	နံနံပင်	coriander
ngan·pya·ye	ငံပြာရည်	fish sauce
ngǎyouq·thì	ငရုတ်သီး	chilli
ngǎyouq·ye	ငရုတ်ရည်	chilli sauce
oùn·nó	အုန်းနို့	coconut cream
p'a·la·zé	ဖါလာစေ့	cardamom
paun·móun	ပေါင်မုန့်	bread
pèh·ngan·pya·ye	ပဲငံပြာရည်	soy sauce
t'àw·baq	ထောပတ်	butter
tha·gu	သာကူ	sago/tapioca
t'oùn	ထုံး	lime (for betel)
s'à	ဆား	salt
s'ǎnwìn	ဆနွင်း	turmeric
sha·lǎka·ye	ရှာလကာရည်	vinegar
thǎjà	သကြား	sugar
to·hù/to·p'ù	တိုဟူး	တိုဖူး	tofu (beancurd)

Cold Drinks

ǎyeq	အရက်	alcohol
bi·ya/tǎbǎlìn	ဘီယာ	တစ်ပုလင်း	beer
can·ye	ကြံရည်	sugarcane juice
lein·maw·ye	လိမ္မော်ရည်	orange juice
nwà·nó	နွားနို့	milk
oùn·ye	အုန်းရည်	coconut juice
p'yaw·ye/ǎ·è	ဖျော်ရည်	အအေး	soft drink
s'o·da	ဆိုဒါ	soda water
t'àn·ye	ထန်းရည်	toddy
than·bǎya·ye	သံပုရာရည်	lime juice
ye-	ရေ	water
ye·thán	ရေသန့်	bottled water ('clean water')
ye·è	ရေအေး	cold water
ye·jeq·è	ရေကျက်အေး	boiled cold water
ye·nwè	ရေနွေး	hot water

Hot Drinks

kaw·fi	ကော်ဖီ	coffee
dhǎjà·néh	သကြားနဲ့	with sugar
nó·s'i·néh	နို့ဆီနဲ့	with condensed milk
nwà·nó·néh	နွားနို့နဲ့	with milk
lǎp'eq·ye·jàn/	လက်ဖက်ရည်ကြမ်း		green tea (plain)
ye·nwè·jàn	ရေနွေးကြမ်း	
leq·p'eq·ye	လက်ဖက်ရည်	tea (Indian)

If you're having issues with onion breath in Myanmar, it's because the Burmese allegedly consume the most onions per capita of any country in the world.

Although Myanmar is a food surplus producer, the World Food Programme estimates that as much as 17% of the population are undernourished.

Religion & Belief

Faith and superstition go hand in hand in Myanmar. About 89% of the people of Myanmar are Buddhist, but many also pay heed to ancient animist beliefs in natural spirits or *nats*. Locals are proud of their beliefs and keen to discuss them. Knowing something about Buddhism in particular will help you better understand life in the country.

Freedom of religion is guaranteed under the country's constitution. However Buddhism is given special status. Myanmar's ethnic patchwork of people also embraces a variety of other faiths, among which Islam and Christianity are the most popular.

When Myanmar locals go on holiday its often in the form of a pilgrimage. Ma Thanegi describes one such trip in *The Native Tourist: In Search of Turtle Eggs*.

Buddhism

The Mon were the first people in Myanmar to practise Theravada (meaning Doctrine of the Elders) Buddhism, the oldest and most conservative form of the religion. King Asoka, the great Indian emperor, is known to have sent missions here (known then as the 'Golden Land') during the 3rd century BC. A second wave is thought to have arrived via Sinhalese missionaries between the 6th and 10th centuries.

By the 9th century the Pyu of northern Myanmar were combining Theravada with elements of Mahayana (Great Vehicle) and Tantric Buddhism brought from their homelands in the Tibetan Plateau. During the early Bagan era (11th century), Bamar king Anawrahta decided that the Buddhism practised in his realm should be 'purified' from all non-Theravada elements. It never completely shed Tantric, Hindu and animist elements, but remains predominately Theravada.

All religious groups are barred from engaging in political activities and accepting funds from foreign sources.

RELIGIOUS CONFLICTS

Friction between religious groups in Myanmar is not uncommon. In February 2001, riots between Buddhists and Muslims broke out in Sittwe, followed a few months later by ones in Taungoo that, according to Human Rights Watch, resulted in nine Muslim deaths including three children, the destruction of 60 homes and looting of Muslim-owned shops.

As David Steinberg notes in *Burma/Myanmar: What Everyone Needs to Know*, these riots are 'usually based on some perceived insult by a Muslim to Buddhism or to a Burmese woman'. There is also the ongoing problem of the government's non-recognition of the Muslim Rohingya minority, which is very controversial among most locals in Rakhaing State (see p277).

Relations between each of the religions hasn't been helped by the fact that within government Buddhists tend to attain higher rank more easily than non-Buddhists. There has also been a programme of building pagodas in border regions including the Christian area of Kachin State bordering China and the Muslim areas of Rakhaing State bordering Bangladesh.

For information on violations to religious freedom in Myanmar, read the 2006 US State Department report at www.state.gov/g/drl/rls/irf/2006/71335.htm.

At temples and shrines, look out for the following hand signs of buddha images, each has a different meaning:

» **Abhaya** Both hands have palms out, symbolising protection from fear.

» **Bhumispara** The right hand touches the ground, symbolising when Buddha sat beneath a banyan tree until he gained enlightenment.

» **Dana** One or both hands with palms up, symbolising the offering of *dhamma* (Buddhist teachings) to the world.

» **Dhyana** Both hands rest palm-up on the buddha's lap, signifying meditation.

» **Vitarka or Dhammachakka** Thumb and forefinger of one hand forms a circle with other fingers (somewhat like an 'OK' gesture), symbolising the first public discourse on Buddhist doctrine.

RELIGION & BELIEF

Theravada vs Mahayana

Theravada Buddhism (also followed in Cambodia, Laos, Sri Lanka and Thailand) differs from Hinduism, Judaism, Islam and Christianity in that it is not centred around a god or gods, but rather a psycho-philosophical system. Today it covers a wide range of interpretations of the basic beliefs, which all start from the enlightenment of Siddhartha Gautama, a prince-turned-ascetic and referred to as the Buddha, in northern India around 2500 years ago.

In the Theravada school, it's believed that the individual strives to achieve *nibbana* (nirvana), rather than waiting for all humankind being ready for salvation as in the Mahayana (Large Vehicle) school. The Mahayana school does not reject the other school, but claims it has extended it. The Theravadins see Mahayana as a misinterpretation of the Buddha's original teachings. Of the two, the Theravada is more austere and ascetic and, some might say, harder to practise.

During the U Nu period, Buddhism functioned as a state religion, as embodied in such catchphrases as 'the Socialist Way to Nibbana'.

Buddhist Tenets

Buddha taught that the world is primarily characterised by *dukkha* (suffering), *anicca* (impermanence) and *anatta* (insubstantiality), and that even our happiest moments in life are only temporary, empty and unsatisfactory.

The ultrapragmatic Buddhist perception of cause and effect – *kamma* in Pali, *karma* in Sanskrit, *kan* in Burmese – holds that birth inevitably leads to sickness, old age and death, hence every life is insecure and subject to *dukkha*. Through rebirth, the cycle of *thanthaya* (*samsara* in Pali) repeats itself endlessly as long as ignorance and craving remain.

Only by reaching a state of complete wisdom and nondesire can one attain true happiness. To achieve wisdom and eliminate craving, one must turn inward and master one's own mind through meditation, most commonly known in Myanmar as *bhavana* or *kammahtan*.

The monkhood, numbering around 400,000 and collectively known as the *Sangha*, is seen as the nation's only real civil institution.

Devout Buddhists in Myanmar adhere to five lay precepts, or moral rules (*thila* in Burmese, *sila* in Pali), which require abstinence from killing, stealing, unchastity (usually interpreted among laypeople as adultery), lying and intoxicating substances.

In spite of Buddhism's profound truths, the most common Myanmar approach is to try for a better future life by feeding monks, donating to temples and performing regular worship at the local paya (Buddhist monument) – these activities are commonly known as 'merit making'. For the average person everything revolves around the merit (*kutho*, from the Pali *kusala*, meaning 'wholesome'), one is able to accumulate through such deeds.

Monks & Nuns

Every Buddhist Myanmar male is expected to take up temporary monastic residence twice in his life: once as a *samanera* (novice monk) between the ages of 10 and 20, and again as a *hpongyi* (fully ordained monk) sometime after the age of 20. Almost all men or boys aged under 20 'take robe and bowl' in the *shinpyu* (novitiation ceremony).

All things possessed by a monk must be offered by the lay community. Upon ordination a new monk is typically offered a set of three robes (lower, inner and outer). Other possessions a monk is permitted include a razor, a cup, a filter (for keeping insects out of drinking water), an umbrella and an alms bowl.

> Bright red robes are usually reserved for novices under 15, darker colours for older, fully ordained monks.

In Myanmar, women who live the monastic life as *dasasila* ('10-precept' nuns) are often called *thilashin* (possessor of morality) in Burmese. Myanmar nuns shave their heads, wear pink robes and take vows in an ordination procedure similar to monks. Generally, nunhood isn't considered as 'prestigious' as monkhood, as nuns generally don't perform ceremonies on behalf of laypeople, and keep only 10 precepts – the same number observed by male novices.

In mornings, you'll see rows of monks and sometimes nuns carrying bowls to get offerings of rice and food. It's not begging. It's a way of letting locals have the chance of doing the deed of *dhana,* thus acquiring merit.

Temples & Monasteries

> For more on Buddhism, check www.dharmanet.org or www.accesstoinsight.org.

Paya (pa-*yah*), the most common Myanmar equivalent to the often misleading English term 'pagoda', literally means 'holy one' and can refer to people, deities and places associated with religion. Often it's a generic term covering a stupa, temple or shrine.

There are basically two kinds of paya: the solid, bell-shaped *zedi* and the hollow square or rectangular *pahto*. A *zedi* or stupa is usually thought to contain 'relics' – either objects taken from the Buddha himself (pieces of bone, teeth or hair) or certain holy materials.

The term *pahto* is sometimes translated as temple, though shrine would perhaps be more accurate as priests or monks are not necessarily in attendance. Mon-style *pahto*, with small windows and ground-level passageways, are also known as a *gu* or *ku* (from the Pali-Sanskrit *guha,* meaning 'cave').

Both *zedi* and *pahto* are often associated with *kyaung* (Buddhist monasteries), also called *kyaungtaik* and *hpongyi-kyaung*. The most important structure on the monastery grounds is the *thein* (a consecrated hall where monastic ordinations are held). An open-sided resthouse or *zayat* may be available for gatherings of laypeople during festivals or pilgrimages.

FOUR NOBLE TRUTHS & THE EIGHTFOLD PATH

The Buddha taught four noble truths:
1 Life is *dukkha* (suffering)
2 *Dukkha* comes from *tanha* (selfish desire).
3 When one forsakes selfish desire, suffering will be extinguished.
4 The 'eightfold path' is the way to eliminate selfish desire.

The eightfold path consists of:
1 Right thought
2 Right understanding
3 Right speech
4 Right action
5 Right livelihood
6 Right exertion
7 Right attentiveness
8 Right concentration

Nat Worship

One of the most fascinating things about Myanmar is the ongoing worship of the *nat* (spirit being). Though some Buddhist leaders downgrade the *nat,* the *nat* are very much alive in the lives of the people of Myanmar.

History

Worship of *nats* predates Buddhism in Myanmar. *Nats* have long believed to hold dominion over a place (natural or human-made), person or field of experience.

Separate, larger shrines were built for a higher class of *nat,* descended from actual historic personages (including previous Thai and Bamar kings) who had died violent, unjust deaths. These suprahuman *nat,* when correctly propitiated, could aid worshippers in accomplishing important tasks, vanquishing enemies and so on.

Early in the 11th century in Bagan, King Anawrahta stopped animal sacrifices (part of *nat* worship at Mt Popa) and destroyed *nat* temples. Realising he may lose the case for making Theravada Buddhism the national faith, Anawrahta wisely conceded the *nat's* coexistence with Buddha.

There were 36 recognised *nat* at the time (in fact, there are many more). Anawrahta sagely added a 37th, Thagyamin, a Hindu deity based on Indra, whom he crowned 'king of the *nat*'. Since, in traditional Buddhist mythology, Indra paid homage to Buddha, this insertion effectively made all *nat* subordinate to Buddhism. Anawrahta's scheme worked, and today the commonly believed cosmology places Buddha's teachings at the top.

Worship & Beliefs

In many homes you may see the most popular *nat* in the form of an unhusked coconut dressed in a red *gaung baung* (turban), which represents the dual-*nat* Eindwin-Min Mahagiri (Lord of the Great Mountain Who Is in the House). Another widespread form of *nat* worship is exhibited through the red-and-white cloths tied to a rear-view mirror or hood ornament; these colours are the traditional *nat* colours of protection.

Some of the more animistic guardian *nat* remain outside home and paya. A tree-spirit shrine, for example, may be erected beneath a particularly venerated old tree, thought to wield power over the immediate vicinity. These are especially common beneath larger banyan trees *(Ficus religiosa),* as this tree is revered as a symbol of Buddha's enlightenment.

A village may well have a *nat* shrine in a wooded corner for the propitiation of the village guardian spirit. Such tree and village shrines are simple, dollhouse-like structures of wood or bamboo; their proper placement is divined by a local *saya* (teacher or shaman), trained in spirit lore. Such knowledge of the complex *nat* world is fading fast among the younger generations.

Spirit possession – whether psychologically induced or metaphysical – is a phenomenon that is real in the eyes of locals. The main fear is not simply that spirits will wreak havoc on your daily affairs, but rather that one may enter your mind and body and force you to perform unconscionable acts in public.

Nat Festivals

On certain occasions the *nat* cult goes beyond simple propitiation of the spirits (via offerings) and steps into the realm of spirit invocation. Most commonly, this is accomplished through *nat pwe* (spirit festivals), special musical performances designed to attract *nat* to the performance venue.

RELIGION & BELIEF

Many Buddhist temples in Myanmar have their own *nat-sin* (spirit house) attached to the main pagoda.

The written Burmese word *nat* is likely derived from the Pali-Sanskrit *natha,* meaning lord or guardian.

To lure a *nat* to the *pwe* takes the work of a spirit medium, or *nat-gadaw* (*nat* wife), who is either a woman or, more commonly, a male transvestite who sings and dances to invite specific *nat* to possess them. The *nat* also like loud and colourful music, so musicians at a *nat pwe* bang away at full volume on their gongs, drums and xylophones, producing what sounds like some ancient form of rock and roll.

Every *nat pwe* is accompanied by a risk that the invited spirit may choose to enter, not the body of the *nat-gadaw,* but one of the spectators. One of the most commonly summoned spirits at *nat pwe* is Ko Gyi Kyaw (Big Brother Kyaw), a drunkard *nat* who responds to offerings of liquor imbibed by the *nat-gadaw.* When he enters someone's body, he's given to lascivious dancing, so a chance possession by Ko Gyi Kyaw is especially embarrassing.

Once possessed by a *nat,* the only way one can be sure the spirit won't return again and again is to employ the services of an older Buddhist monk skilled at exorcism – a process that can take days, if not weeks. Without undergoing such a procedure, anyone who has been spirit possessed may carry the *nat* stigma for the rest of their lives. Girls who have been so entered are considered unmarriageable unless satisfactorily exorcised.

> Those with a general fear of *nat* will avoid eating pork, which is thought to be offensive to the spirit world.

Islam

Although official statistics say that 4% of Myanmar's population follow Islam, according to a 2006 US government report on religious freedom in Myanmar, local Muslim leaders believe the more accurate figure is approximately 20%. Either way, Muslims have been part of Myanmar's religious fabric from at least the 9th century, and possibly as far back as the 6th century in Rakhaing State.

Waves of Indian immigration under British colonial rule boosted the local Muslim population. This was slashed during WWII when many Indians fled the country, and again from the start of military rule in 1962 when ethnic Indians were expelled from the army and marginalised in society.

THE POWER OF SUPERSTITION

Men wearing *longyi* are commonplace in Myanmar. But when Than Shwe and other senior military figures showed up at a nationally televised ceremony in February 2011 wearing decorative *acheik,* the female version of the sarong-like garment, eyebrows were raised. A fashion faux pas? Not according to one Yangon-based astrologer quoted in *Time* who claimed the generals were indulging in *yadaya*: magic. The rumours go that by wearing the women's *acheik,* the generals were hoping either to fulfil a prophesy that a woman would one day rule Myanmar, or cancel out Suu Kyi's feminine power.

Superstitions run deep in Myanmar. Many people consult astrologers to find mates and plan events. According to Benedict Rogers, author of a biography of Than Shwe, the retired senior general has seven personal astrologers at his call, several of whom are tasked with focussing their darker arts on his chief nemesis, Aung San Suu Kyi.

On a less dramatic level, Myanmar astrology, based on the Indian system of naming the zodiacal planets for Hindu deities, continues to be an important factor in deciding proper dates for weddings, funerals, ordinations and other events. Burma became independent at 4.20am on 4 January 1948, per U Nu's counsel with an astrologer.

Numerology plays a similar role with both eight and nine being auspicious numbers. The Burmese word *ko* (nine) also means 'to seek protection from the gods'. General Ne Win was fascinated with numerology, especially that relating to the cabalistic ritual Paya-kozu (Nine Gods). In 1987 he introduced 45-kyat and 90-kyat notes, because their digits' sum equalled nine.

Occurring at the height of the dry and hot season, around the middle of April, the three-day Thingyan (Water Festival) starts the Myanmar New Year. As in Thailand's Songkran, the event is celebrated in a most raucous manner – by throwing buckets of cold water at anyone who dares to venture into the streets. Foreigners are not exempt!

On a spiritual level, Myanmar people believe that during this three-day period the king of the *nat* (spirit beings), Thagyamin, visits the human world to tally his annual record of the good deeds and misdeeds humans have performed. Villagers place flowers and sacred leaves in front of their homes to welcome the *nat*. Thagyamin's departure on the morning of the third day marks the beginning of the new year, when properly brought-up young people wash the hair of their elder kin, buddha images are ceremonially washed, and *hpongyi* (monks) are offered particularly appetising alms food.

Although the true meaning of the festival is still kept alive by ceremonies such as these, nowadays it's mainly a festival of fun. In cities, temporary stages called *pandal* (from the Tamil *pendel*) are erected along main thoroughfares, with water barrels ready to douse all passersby; for more on the Thingyan see p11.

RELIGION & BELIEF

Christianity

The CIA World Fact Book says 4% of Myanmar's population are Christians. Anglican, Baptist and Catholic missionaries have been active in Myanmar for over 150 years. Going even further back there were communities of Christians among the Japanese who fled to Arakan (Rakhaing State) in the 16th century and the Portuguese Catholics (and later Dutch and French mercenaries and prisoners of war) who arrived in the early 17th century.

Ethnic groups that traditionally practised animism have proved more receptive to conversion to Christianity, especially the Kayin, Kachin and Chin.

Other Religions

Among the other religions encountered in Myanmar are Hinduism, practiced among locals of Indian descent, the various traditional religions of Chinese immigrants down the ages, and animism among the small tribal groups of the highlands.

The Jewish community in pre-WWII Rangoon numbered around 2500 and the city once had a Jewish mayor (as did Pathein). Burma was also the first Asian country to recognise Israel in 1949. However the military coup and its aftermath encouraged most to leave, and today Yangon has only about 25 Jews. Even so the city's 19th-century Moseah Yeshua Synagogue (p42) is beautifully maintained.

Officially Myanmar is 1% animist, 1.5% Hindu, 4% Christian and 4% Muslim; others believe that non-Buddhists may account for 30% of the population.

Arts & Architecture

For centuries the arts in Burma were sponsored by the royal courts, mainly through the construction of major religious buildings that required the skills of architects, sculptors, painters and a variety of craftspeople. Such patronage was cut short during British colonial rule and has never been a priority since independence.

However, there are plenty of examples of traditional art to be viewed in Myanmar, mainly in the temples that are an ever-present feature of town and countryside. The locals are just as likely as any other people to take time out to enjoy themselves at a puppet show, watch traditional dances at festivals or catch up on the latest episode of their favourite Korean soap opera on TV.

Architecture

It is in architecture that one sees the strongest evidence of Myanmar artistic skill and accomplishment. Myanmar is a country of *zedi*, often called 'pagodas' in English. Wherever you are – boating down the river, driving through the hills, even flying above the plains – there always seems to be a hilltop *zedi* in view. Bagan is the most dramatic result of this fervour for religious monuments – an enthusiasm that continues today, as the mass rebuilding of temples at the site attests.

Traditionally, only *zedi, gu* and *pahto* (see p340) have been made of permanent materials. Until quite recently all secular buildings – and most monasteries – were constructed of wood, so there are few old ones left to be seen. Even the great royal palaces, such as the last one at Mandalay, were made of wood. No original ones remain and the reconstructions are often far from faithful reproductions.

Zedi Styles

Early *zedi* were usually hemispherical (the Kaunghmudaw at Sagaing near Mandalay) or bulbous (the Bupaya in Bagan). The so-called Mon-style *pahto* is a large cube with small windows and ground-level passageways; this type is also known as a *gu* or *ku* (from the Pali-Sanskrit *guha*, meaning 'cave'). The more modern style is much more graceful – a curvaceous lower bell merging into a soaring spire, such as the Shwedagon Paya in Yangon or the Uppatasanti Paya in Nay Pyi Taw.

The overall Bamar concept is similar to that of the Mayan and Aztec pyramids of Mesoamerica: worshippers climb a symbolic mountain lined with religious reliefs and frescoes.

Style is not always a good indicator of the original age of a *zedi,* as Myanmar is earthquake-prone and many (including the Shwedagon) have been rebuilt again and again. In places such as Bagan and Inthein, near Inle Lake, ruined temples have been rebuilt from the base up with little

Best Buddhist Buildings

» Shwedagon Paya, Yangon

» Ananda Pahto, Bagan

» Shwenandaw Kyaung, Mandalay

» Shwesandaw Paya, Pyay

» Shittaung Paya, Mrauk U

if no respect for the what the original would have looked like. In Bagan, for example, all *zedi* would have been traditionally covered with white or painted stucco, not left as the bare brick structures they are today.

Other Buildings

Although so little remains of the old wooden architectural skills, there are still many excellent wooden buildings to be seen. The people of Myanmar continue to use teak with great skill, and a fine country home can be a very pleasing structure indeed.

While many buildings erected during the British colonial period have been demolished or are facing the wrecking ball, those that survive are often well worth seeking out. They range from the rustic wood-and-plaster Tudor villas of Pyin Oo Lwin to the thick-walled, brick-and-plaster, colonnaded mansions and shop houses of Yangon, Mawlamyine and Myeik.

An interesting example of a fusion of Myanmar and European styles is the City Hall building in Yangon. Until recently scant attention was paid to preserving colonial architecture – for political as well as economic reasons. In March 2011, *The Irrawaddy* reported that five major colonial-era buildings in Yangon (the former Prime Minister's Office, and the former Ministries of Energy; Hotels and Tourism; Immigration and Population; and Commerce) would be preserved in an effort to attract more tourists.

One Yangon colonial-era building that has already been nicely spruced up through private donations and overseas grants is the Moseah Yeshua Synagogue.

Amazing Wood Structures

» Shwenandaw Kyaung, Mandalay
» U Bein's Bridge, Amarapura
» Bagaya Kyaung, Inwa
» Youqson Kyaung, Salay
» Pakhanngeh Kyaung, Pakokku

Sculpture & Painting

Early Myanmar art was always a part of the religious architecture – paints were for the walls of temples, sculpture to be placed inside them. Many pieces, formerly in paya or *kyaung,* have been sold or stolen and, unfortunately, you'll easily find more Myanmar religious sculpture for sale or on display overseas than in Myanmar.

In the aftermath of the 1988 demonstrations, the government forbade 'selfish' or 'mad art' that didn't have clear pro-government themes. One artist, Sitt Nyein Aye, spent two months in custody for sketching the ruins of the former student union, which Ne Win had blown up in 1962.

Most contemporary Myanmar artists now play safe with predictable tourist-oriented works. The government's posters – anti-AIDS, antidrugs, pro-traffic safety, or just pro-government! – are occasionally interesting pieces of propaganda artwork, but you shouldn't expect any of the Socialist Realist élan of the former Soviet Union, Vietnam or North Korea.

Old Myanmar Paintings in the Collection of U Win is one of the illustrated publications of the Thavibu Gallery (www.thavibu. com) specialising in Burmese art.

Traditional Crafts

Apart from the following, other Myanmar crafts you may come across are paper parasols, silver and metalware, and wood carvings. For tips on shopping for traditional crafts, see p27.

Kammawa & Parabaik

Kammawa (from the Pali *kammavacha*) are narrow, rectangular slats painted with extracts from the Pali Vinaya (the Pitaka) concerned with monastic discipline; specifically, extracts to do with clerical affairs. The core of a *kammawa* page may be a thin slat of wood, lacquered cloth, thatched cane or thin brass, which is then layered with red, black and gold lacquer to form the script and decorations.

The *parabaik* (Buddhist palm-leaf manuscript) is a similarly horizontal 'book', this time folded accordion-style, like a road map. The pages are made of heavy paper covered with black ink on which the letters are engraved.

The bronze Mahamuni Buddha, in Mandalay's Mahamuni Paya, may date back to the 1st century AD and is Myanmar's most famous Buddhist sculpture.

ARTS & ARCHITECTURE

Lacquerware

The earliest lacquerware found in Myanmar can be dated to the 11th century and sported a very Chinese style. The techniques used today are known as *yun,* the old Bamar word for the people of Chiang Mai, from where the techniques were imported in the 16th century (along with some captured artisans) by King Bayinnaung. An older style of applying gold or silver to a black background dates back to, perhaps, the Pyay era (5th to 9th centuries) and is kept alive by artisans in Kyaukka, near Monywa.

Many lacquerware shops include workshops, where you can see the long-winded process involved in making the bowls, trays and other objects. The craftsperson first weaves a frame (the best-quality wares have a bamboo frame tied together with horse or donkey hairs; lesser pieces are made wholly from bamboo). The lacquer is then coated over the framework and allowed to dry. After several days it is sanded down with ash from rice husks and another coating of lacquer is applied. A high-quality item may have seven to 15 layers altogether.

The lacquerware is engraved and painted, then polished to remove the paint from everywhere except from within the engravings. Multicoloured lacquerware is produced by repeated engraving, painting and polishing. From start to finish it can take up to five or six months to produce a high-quality piece of lacquerware, which may have as many as five colours. A top-quality bowl can have its rim squeezed together until the sides meet without suffering any damage or permanent distortion.

Lacquerware centres

» Kyaukka, near Monywa

» Myinkaba, Bagan

» New Bagan (Bagan Myothit), Bagan

Burmese Crafts: Past and Present by Sylvia Fraser-Lu details the foundations of Myanmar's artistic traditions and catalogues the major crafts from metalwork to umbrella making.

Tapestries & Textiles

Tapestries *(kalaga)* consist of pieces of coloured cloth of various sizes heavily embroidered with silver- or gold-coloured thread, metal sequins and glass beads, and feature mythological Myanmar figures in padded relief. The greatest variety is found in Mandalay, where most tapestries are produced.

Good-quality *kalaga* are tightly woven and don't skimp on sequins, which may be sewn in overlapping lines, rather than spaced side by side, as a sign of embroidery skill. The metals used should shine, even in older pieces; tarnishing means lower-quality materials.

AUNG SOE MIN, YANGON GALLERY OWNER

Is art in Myanmar different from elsewhere? Myanmar artists are still influenced by traditional art. A main part of Burmese art is surrealistic ideas that have existed since a long time ago. And because of the colours in Burma, the art has bright colours. Burmese art has a lot of potential because we've been closed for a long time.

How would you describe the art scene in Yangon? There's no national art museum in Burma yet. But you can see works by famous artists such as U B Nyan and U Ngwe Gaing at the National Museum. There are also private galleries, such as Baikthano Gallery.

Can artists survive only doing art, or do they have to take other jobs as well? Most artists can survive on their paintings, but many also do illustration and design for books, magazines and advertisements. Artists in other cities can depend on tourists to buy art, but here we have to depend on locals.

Are Myanmar artists exposed to much international art? Until 1962, artists in Myanmar were in touch with the outside. But now we've been closed for a long time. But since about 2003 we can see anything on the internet.

Does art ever get political in Myanmar? Yes, a lot. People everywhere are always trying to express themselves and they don't care about the risk.

Myanmar is a poor country; people have to worry about food, health, etc. When you consider this, is art really important? Every human likes some sort of art. Even very poor people buy paintings from the street or frame ads or calendars at home.

Tribal textiles and weavings produced by the Chin, Naga, Kachin and Kayin can also be very beautiful, especially antique pieces. Among traditional hand-woven silk *longyis, laun-taya acheik,* woven on hundred spools, are the most prized.

Dance & Theatre

Myanmar's truly indigenous dance forms are those that pay homage to the *nat* (spirit being). Most classical dance styles, meanwhile, arrived from Thailand. Today the dances most obviously taken from Thailand are known as *yodaya zat* (Ayuthaya theatre), as taught to the people of Myanmar by Thai theatrical artists taken captive in the 18th century.

The most Myanmar of dances feature solo performances by female dancers who wear strikingly colourful dresses with long white trains, which they kick into the air with their heels – quite a feat, given the restrictive length of the train.

An all-night *zat pwe* involves a re-creation of an ancient legend or Buddhist Jataka (life story of the Buddha), while the *yamazat* pick a tale from the Indian epic Ramayana. In Mandalay, *yamazat* performers even have their own shrine.

Myanmar classical dancing emphasises pose rather than movement and solo rather than ensemble performances. In contrast the less common, but livelier, *yein pwe* features singing and dancing performed by a chorus or ensemble.

Most popular of all is the *a-nyeint pwe,* a traditional *pwe* somewhat akin to early American vaudeville, the most famous exponents of which are Mandalay's Moustache Brothers.

Classical dance-drama is performed nightly at Mandalay's Mintha Theater and occasionally at the National Theatre in Yangon.

Marionette Theatre

Youq-the pwe (Myanmar marionette theatre) presents colourful puppets up to 3.5ft high in a spectacle that many aesthetes consider the most expressive of all the Myanmar arts. Developed during the Konbaung period, it was so influential that it became the forerunner to *zat pwe* as later performed by actors rather than marionettes. As with dance-drama, the genre's 'golden age' began with the Mandalay kingdoms of the late 18th century and ran through to the advent of cinema in the 1930s.

The people of Myanmar have great respect for an expert puppeteer. Some marionettes may be manipulated by a dozen or more strings. The marionette master's standard repertoire requires a troupe of 28 puppets including Thagyamin (king of the gods); a Myanmar king, queen, prince and princess; a regent; two court pages; an old man and an old woman; a villain; a hermit; four ministers; two clowns; one good and one evil *nat;* a Brahmin astrologer; two ogres; a *zawgyi* (alchemist); a horse; a monkey; a *makara* (mythical sea serpent); and an elephant.

It's rare to see marionette theatre outside tourist venues in Yangon, Mandalay or Bagan.

The Illusion of Life: Burmese Marionettes by Ma Thanegi gives readers a glimpse of the 'wit, spirit and style' of this traditional Burmese performance art.

Music

Much of classical Myanmar music, played loud the way the *nat* like it, features strongly in any *pwe*. Its repetitive, even harsh, harmonies can be hard on Western ears at first; Myanmar scales are not 'tempered', as Western scales have been since Bach. Traditional Myanmar music is primarily two dimensional, in the sense that rhythm and melody provide much of the musical structure, while repetition is a key element. Subtle shifts in rhythm and tonality provide the modulation usually supplied by the harmonic dimension in Western music.

Classical Music

Classical music traditions were largely borrowed from Siam musicians in the late 1800s, who borrowed the traditions from Cambodian conquests centuries earlier. Myanmar classical music, as played today, was codified by Po Sein, a colonial-era musician, composer and drummer who also designed the *hsaing waing* (the circle of tuned drums, also known as *paq waing*) and formalised classical dancing styles. Such music is meant to be played as an accompaniment to classical dance-dramas that enact scenes from the Jataka or from the Ramayana.

Musical instruments are predominantly percussive, but even the *hsaing waing* may carry the melody. These drums are tuned by placing a wad of *paq-sa* (drum food) – made from a kneaded paste of rice and wood ash – onto the centre of the drum head, then adding or subtracting a pinch at a time till the desired drum tone is attained.

In addition to the *hsaing waing*, the traditional *hsaing* (Myanmar ensemble) of seven to 10 musicians will usually play: the *kye waing* (a circle of tuned brass gongs); the *saung gauq* (a boat-shaped harp with 13 strings); the *pattala* (a sort of xylophone); the *hneh* (an oboe-type instrument related to the Indian *shanai*); the *pa-lwe* (a bamboo flute); the *mi-gyaung* (crocodile lute); the *paq-ma* (a bass drum); and the *yagwin* (small cymbals) and *wa leq-hkouq* (bamboo clappers), which are purely rhythmic and are often played by Myanmar vocalists.

> Myanmar dance scholars have catalogued around 2000 dance movements, including 13 head movements, 28 eye movements, eight body postures and 10 walking movements.

Folk

Older than Myanmar classical music is an enchanting vocal folk-music tradition still heard in rural areas where locals may sing without instrumental accompaniment while working. Such folk songs set the work cadence and provide a distraction from the physical strain and monotony of pounding rice, clearing fields, weaving and so on. This type of music is most readily heard in the Ayeyarwady Delta between Twante and Pathein.

Rock & Rap

Western pop music's influence first came in the 1970s, when singers such as Min Min Latt and Takatho Tun Naung sang shocking things such as Beatles cover versions or 'Tie a Yellow Ribbon Round the Old Oak Tree'. This led to long-haired, distorted-guitar rock bands such as Empire and Iron Cross (aka IC) in the 1980s. Two decades later, no-one's bigger than Iron Cross – try to see them live (you're sure to see them on videotape at teashops or on all-night buses). Another big band is Lazy Club who played concerts in the US in 2009.

> The beautifully painted little parasols you see around Myanmar are often made in Pathein – in fact they're known as *Pathein hti* (Pathein umbrellas).

Bands such as these (all of whom usually sing in Burmese, even if they have English names) have a stable of several singers who split stage time with the same backing band. Iron Cross, for example, features one of Myanmar's 'wilder' singers, Lay Phyu, but it can also tone it down as a

---

TRADITIONAL BURMESE MUSIC CDS

These music CDs can generally be found outside Myanmar:

» **Mahagitá** *Harp & Vocal Music from Burma* (2003; Smithsonian Folkways)

» **Music of Nat Pwe: Folk & Pop Music of Myanmar** (2007; Sublime Frequencies)

» **Pat Waing** *The Magic Drum Circle of Burma* (1998; Shanachie)

» **U Ko Ko** *Performs on the Burmese Piano* (1995; Ummus)

» **Various artists** *Burma: Traditional Music* (2009; Air Mail Music)

» **White Elephants & Golden Ducks** *Enchanting Musical Treasures from Burma* (1997; Shanachie)

It's not just journalists who can fall foul of government censors in Myanmar. Writers of fiction, movie makers, performing and visual artists and singers all have to watch out, too. Back in 1988, popular singer Mun Awng, originally from Kachin, was forced into exile after participating in anti-government demonstrations. His *Battle for Peace* album was recorded in Thailand in the 1990s and he contributed to *For the Lady*, a 2004 benefit CD in support of Aung San Suu Kyi that also includes tracks by U2 and the Indigo Girls.

Rap band 9mm was briefly detained in 2004 for performing political songs written by an anonymous prodemocracy group of exiled and local rappers called **Myanmar Future Generations** (MFG; www.mmfg.netfirms.com/index2.html).

Sometimes the Big Brother tactics of the censors verge on the ridiculous. In 1998 blues singer Nyi Pu had to rename his debut *Everything's Going to Be Good* to *Everything's Good;* a few years later, Iron Cross' Myo Gyi changed his *Very Wild Wind* album to a tamer *Breeze*. And when censors wouldn't go for a literal translation of Eminem's lyric ('shake that ass') in Sai Sai's cover version in 2007, Sai Sai sang 'shake that water pot' *(o lay, hloke pa ohn!).*

backing band for the poppier stuff of other singers. One local aficionado explains: 'There's no competition between a band's many singers. They help each other. Our rock singers don't throw TVs out the windows. On stage they jump around and all, but offstage they're very good-natured.'

Female singers like Sone Thin Par and actor Htu Aeindra Bo (www. htunaeindrabo.com) win fans for their melodies – and looks – but the most interesting is rapper Phyu Phyu Kyaw Thein, a sort of 'Sporty Spice', who has fronted both Iron Cross *and* Lazy Club. Other rappers include Min Min Latt's son, Anega, now busting beats with other big-name rappers Barbu, Myo Kyawt Myaung and heart-throb Sai Sai. Songs often deal with gossip, or troubles between parents and kids. Thar Soe is a popular hip-hop singer whose 2007 hit 'I Like Drums' merged *nat* music with trance.

Yangon is the best place to catch a show; look out for advertisements in local publications and on billboards and leaflets.

Literature

Religious texts inscribed onto Myanmar's famous *kammawa* (lacquered scriptures) and *parabaik* (folding manuscripts) were the first pieces of literature as such, and began appearing in the 12th century. Until the 1800s, the only other works of 'literature' available were royal genealogies, classical poetry and law texts. A Burmese version of the Indian epic *Ramayana* was first written in 1775 by poet U Aung Pyo.

The first Myanmar novel *Maung Yin Maung Ma Me Ma,* an adaptation of *The Count of Monte Cristo* by James Hla Kyaw, was published in 1904. Eric Blair (aka George Orwell) worked in Myanmar from 1922 to 1927 as a policeman, an experience that informed his novel *Burmese Days,* first published in 1934. Sharply critical of colonial life in the country, it is one of the few English-language books still widely available in Myanmar (unlike Orwell's *1984* and *Animal Farm,* political works that are not to the generals' tastes).

More recently, Myanmar-born Nu Nu Yi Inwa, one of the country's leading writers with at least 15 novels and over 100 short stories to her name, made the shortlist for the 2007 Man Asian Literary Prize with *Smile As They Bow*. The story, set at the Taungbyon Festival held near Mandalay, follows an elder gay transvestite medium who fears losing his much younger partner to a woman in the heat of the week-long festivities.

For other novels in English set in Myanmar see p290.

The U2 song *Walk On* from the 2001 album *All That You Can't Leave Behind* is about and dedicated to Aung San Suu Kyi.

Cinema

Myanmar has had a modest film industry since the early 20th century and it continues today producing low-budget, uncontroversial action pics, romances and comedies that are a staple of cinemas, village video-screening halls and DVD sellers across the country. There's even an annual Academy Awards ceremony that is one of the country's biggest social events.

You'll need to look to film-makers outside Myanmar for movies and documentaries that tackle some of the country's more controversial topics. Among recent documentaries available on video or doing the festival rounds are Nic Dunlop's *Burma Soldier* (www.breakthrufilms.org/burma -soldier/), the moving story of a military recruit, who loses two limbs to land mines and switches sides to become a democracy activist; Rex Bloomstein's *This Prison Where I Live* (http://thisprisonwhereilive.co.

MYANMAR'S SPORTING LIFE

Martial arts are perhaps the longest-running sports that the people of Myanmar have patronised: the oldest written references to kickboxing in the country are found in the chronicles of warfare between Burma and Thailand during the 15th and 16th centuries. The British introduced football (soccer) in the 19th century and it remains Myanmar's most popular spectator sport.

Football

The 11-team **Myanmar National League** (http://myanmarnationalleague.com) was launched in 2009. A US embassy cable released by WikiLeaks revealed that Senior General Than Shwe had thought it would be politically more popular to instruct crony businesses to create this league rather than spend US$1 billion on buying Manchester United, as his grandson had advised. Local TV broadcasts European games and tea-shops are invariably packed when a big match is screened.

Martial Arts

Myanma let-hwei (Myanmar kickboxing) is very similar in style to *muay thai* (Thai kick-boxing), although not nearly as well developed as a national sport.

The most common and traditional kickboxing venues are temporary rings set up in a dirt circle (usually at *paya pwe* rather than sports arenas). All fighters are bare-fisted. All surfaces of the body are considered fair targets and any part of the body except the head may be used to strike an opponent. Common blows include high kicks to the neck, elbow thrusts to the face and head, knee hooks to the ribs and low crescent kicks to the calf. Punching is considered the weakest of all blows and kicking merely a way to soften up one's opponent; knee and elbow strikes are decisive in most matches.

Before the match begins, each boxer performs a dancelike ritual in the ring to pay homage to Buddha and to Khun Cho and Khun Tha, the *nat* whose domain includes Myanmar kickboxing. The winner repeats the ritual at the end of the match.

Chinlon

Often called 'cane ball' in Burmese English, *chinlon* are games in which a woven rattan ball about 5in in diameter is kicked around. It also refers to the ball itself. Informally, any number of players can form a circle and keep the *chinlon* airborne by kicking it soccer-style from player to player; a lack of scoring makes it a favourite pastime with locals of all ages.

In formal play six players stand in a circle of 22ft circumference. Each player must keep the ball aloft using a succession of 30 techniques and six surfaces on the foot and leg, allotting five minutes for each part. Each successful kick scores a point, while points are subtracted for using the wrong body part or dropping the ball.

A popular variation – and the one used in intramural or international competitions – is played with a volleyball net, using all the same rules as in volleyball except that only the feet and head are permitted to touch the ball.

uk), which includes interviews conducted with the Burmese comic Zargana in 2007 before he was sentenced to 35 years in jail for his political activities; and the Oscar-nominated *Burma VJ*.

Filmed in the summer of 2009, *Altered Focus: Burma* (www.hotknees. com/media/Altered_Focus.php) is a 19-minute documentary following three young British film-makers and skateboarders as they share their love of skateboarding with local enthusiasts in Yangon and volunteer to teach English at a school in Mandalay. There is politics here but it's great to see something about people in Myanmar having some fun, as well as to discover Yangon's skate park just opposite the national football stadium.

John Boorman's *Beyond Rangoon*, a political tract/action flick set during the 1988 uprisings, had Georgetown, Penang, do a credible turn as the nation's then-turbulent capital. It starred several Myanmar actors, including Aung Ko, who plays an elderly guide to Patricia Arquette's American tourist galvanised into political activist. Another Myanmar actor, Win Min Than, was cast opposite Gregory Peck in 1954's *The Purple Plain*, the most credible of several WWII dramas set in Myanmar.

Fighting more recent wars is Sylvester Stallone who returned to one of his most famous roles in *Rambo* (2008). This time Vietnam Vet John Rambo takes on the Tatmadaw, a whole platoon of which he mows down at the movie's climax with a jeep-mounted machine gun!

It's a cert that no such dramatics will be part of Luc Bresson's *The Lady*, in production during the research period of this book. The documentary *Lady of No Fear*, directed by Anne Gyrithe Bonne, also focuses on Aung San Suu Kyi. For more about both productions, see p352.

Myanmar's lack of copyright laws means those same DVD sellers will happily offer you the latest Hollywood or overseas product; during our 2011 visit all the Oscar nominees and more were available.

The inaugural Burmese Arts Festival (http://burmeseartsfestival.com), held in London in 2010, featured many contemporary artists, including the Burmese Theatre Workshop and former political prison Htein Lin.

ARTS & ARCHITECTURE

Aung San Suu Kyi

Since her release from house arrest in November 2010, Aung San Suu Kyi has been busy. She has been on the cover of *Time* and been profiled in countless other publications; met with ambassadors and addressed global movers and shakers at Davos (www.tinyurl.com/5wfxzbn); and even guest-directed the 2011 Brighton Arts Festival (www.brightonfestival.org) in the UK. The Lady – as she is known as in Myanmar and by her millions of supporters around the world – appears as poised, eloquent and media-savvy as any politician in the digital age.

The daughter of a national hero, Aung San (see p299), the 66-year-old Nobel Peace Prize winner has spent 15 out of the 21 years since 1989 shut away from the public as a prisoner of conscience. At the time of research, while at liberty in Yangon, she is highly unlikely to leave the country, since the current regime would certainly not allow her to return.

Before circumstances thrust her onto the global stage in 1988, Suu Kyi was primarily a wife, mother and academic. In 1990 the National League for Democracy (NLD), the party that she continues to lead, won the general election by a landslide, yet was denied power by a military junta that before, and ever since, has sought to demonise, imprison and sideline Suu Kyi. She is easily the most famous Burmese person alive and has been compared to Nelson Mandela and Mahatma Gandhi for her

According to local custom, Aung San Suu Kyi's name, like that of all Burmese, should be spelled out in full. It's also commonly preceded by the honorific title Daw. Through this chapter we follow the international convention of shortening her name to Suu Kyi.

AUNG SAN SUU KYI: BOOKS, MOVIES & THE INTERNET

There are many sources of information on Aung San Suu Kyi. On the internet there are the Daw Aung San Suu Kyi Pages (www.dassk.org) and the site of the NLD (www.nldburma.org).

Suu Kyi's interviews in 1995 and 1996 with journalist and former Buddhist monk Alan Clements, described in *The Voice of Hope* (1997), often intermingle politics and Buddhism; it's available as an audio book from www.useyourliberty.org.

Freedom from Fear (1991) is a collection of Suu Kyi's writings and those of supporters on topics ranging from her father to the Nobel Prize acceptance speech delivered by her son Alexander. *Letters from Burma* (1997) features a year's worth of weekly essays Suu Kyi wrote on Burmese culture, politics and incidents from her daily life for the Japanese newspaper *Mainichi Shimbun*.

The best biography of several is Justin Wintle's *The Perfect Hostage* (2007), an impressively researched account of her life and times, and of modern Burmese history, which paints a very believable, likeable 'warts and all' portrait of Suu Kyi.

On the cinematic front, Luc Bresson's *The Lady* is a bio-pic released in 2011 based on Suu Kyi's life between 1988 and 1999 when her husband Michael Aris died; it stars Malaysian actress Michelle Yeo as Suu Kyi.

Covering similar ground, but in documentary format, is *Lady of No Fear*, directed by Anne Gyrithe Bonne, which was finished before Suu Kyi's release in 2010 and includes interviews with close friends and colleagues about the famously private woman.

patient, nonviolent activism. She embodies what the people of Myanmar call *awza* – charisma and powerful moral authority.

Family & Influences

Aung San Suu Kyi was born just two years before the assassination in July 1947 of her father, Aung San, leader of the Burma Independence Army and the key architect of the country's independence. Aung San had met Suu Kyi's mother, Ma Khin Kyi, a nurse, while recuperating from malaria in Rangoon General Hospital in 1942.

Her father's premature death was not the only family tragedy: in 1953 Suu Kyi's elder brother Lin drowned accidentally at the age of eight (there was also an elder sister Chit, but she had died when only a few days old in 1946, a year before Suu Kyi's birth). Later, Suu Kyi would become estranged from her eldest brother Aung San Oo, an engineer who emigrated to the US; in 2001 he unsuccessfully tried to sue her for a share of their mother's home – 54 University Ave, Yangon, where Suu Kyi has spent the many years of her house arrest.

Her parents' political activism and example of public service had an enormous influence on Suu Kyi. 'When I honour my father, I honour all those who stand for the political integrity of Burma', she writes in the dedication to her book *Freedom from Fear*. In the essay *My Father*, she says he was 'a man who put the interests of the country before his own needs' – something Suu Kyi has also done.

Suu Kyi's mother was also a prominent public figure in newly independent Burma, heading up social planning and policy bodies, and briefly acting as an MP, before being appointed the country's ambassador to India in 1960. Suu Kyi finished her schooling in New Dehli, then moved to the UK in 1964 to study at Oxford University. It was in London at the home of Lord Gore Booth, a former ambassador to Burma, and his wife that Suu Kyi met history student Michael Aris.

Beautiful Love Story

Luc Bresson, director of the biopic *The Lady,* calls Suu Kyi and Aris's courtship and marriage 'probably the most beautiful love story I've heard since Romeo and Juliet.' When Aris went to Bhutan in the late '60s to work as a tutor to the royal family and continue his research, Suu Kyi was in New York, working at the UN; they corresponded by post. After their marriage on 1 January 1972 in London, Suu Kyi joined him Bhutan. Five years later they were back in Oxford, Aris teaching at the university, Suu Kyi a mother to two boys – Alexander and Kim.

From that period, her friend Anna Pasternak Slater remembers, in the essay she contributes to *Freedom from Fear,* the future leader of Burma's democracy movement as a thrifty housewife, 'laboriously pedalling back from town, laden down with sagging plastic bags and panniers heavy with cheap fruit and vegetables' or 'running up elegant cut-price clothes' on her sewing

19 June 1945
A baby girl is born in Yangon and named after her father (Aung San), paternal grandmother (Suu) and mother (Khin Kyi); the name means 'a bright collection of strange victories'.

1960
Daw Khin Kyi is appointed Burma's ambassador to India. Suu Kyi accompanies her mother to New Delhi, where she continues her schooling.

1964
Moves to the UK to study at Oxford University. Meets future husband, Tibetan scholar Michael Aris, at London home of her 'British parents' Lord Gore Booth and his wife.

1967
Graduates with a third-class degree in politics, philosophy and economics. Daw Khin Kyi retires to Yangon.

1969–71
Moves to New York for postgraduate studies, but ends up working for the UN alongside family friend and 'emergency aunt' Ma Than E and Secretary-General U Thant.

1972
Marries Aris and joins him in Bhutan, where he is tutoring the royal family. Suu works as research officer in Bhutan's Royal Ministry of Foreign Affairs.

1973–77
The couple return to the UK for the birth of their first son, Alexander. They take up residence in Oxford, where their second son, Kim, is born in 1977.

machine. Historian and author Thant Myint-U also recalls dropping by the Aris' home in 1984: 'Michael sat contentedly and quietly smoking his pipe, their kids playing in the room nearby' while Suu Kyi gave him 'polite and somewhat schoolmarmish' advice on his educational options. 'In later years', he writes, 'I felt I had a sense of the happy life both she and Michael had given up.'

Pasternak Slater, like many others since, recognised Suu Kyi's 'courage, determination and abiding moral strength', qualities that were already in evidence in some of the 187 letters Suu Kyi wrote to Aris in the eight months before their marriage. In one she asks '...that should my people need me, you would help me do my duty by them.' That moment came in March 1988. Suu Kyi's mother had suffered a stroke.

Return to Burma

Suu Kyi immediately packed her bags to return to Yangon (Rangoon), and Aris had 'a premonition that our lives would change would for ever'.

Meanwhile there was growing turmoil in Burma as students and others took to the streets calling for a change of government. Back in Yangon, where injured protestors were brought to the same hospital her mother was in, it was something Suu Kyi could not ignore, especially when political activists flocked to her mother's home on Inya Lake to seek her support.

IN HER OWN WORDS

On 28 December 2010, Austin Bush, co-author of this guide, interviewed Aung San Suu Kyi by phone.

We've decided to use both names for our book, but which do you prefer, Myanmar or Burma? I prefer Burma because the name was changed without any reference to the will of the people.

You were previously opposed to foreign tourists visiting Myanmar, but appear to have softened this stance over the last few years. How do you feel now about foreign tourists visiting Myanmar? I think the NLD came to this decision about six or seven months ago. We are not in favour of group tourists, but don't mind if individuals come to Burma. Foreign tourists could benefit Burma if they go about it in the right way, by using facilities that help ordinary people and avoiding facilities that have close links to the government.

Can foreign tourists do anything to benefit the move towards democracy in Myanmar? If they would like to meet people working for democracy, then it might help.

Why are there so many areas restricted to tourists in Myanmar? Do you think this will change in the near future? I'm not quite sure. Along the border areas, it's because hostilities might break out again. It might have something to do with the fact that there aren't enough facilities for tourists in remote areas.

To many visitors, Yangon can appear as if it's caught in a time warp. In your experience as someone who grew up there, how has the city changed over the years? I haven't noticed any great changes since I've been under house arrest. The changes I've noticed are that there are many people using handphones, which I hadn't seen seven years ago. But the streets and buildings appear the same.

The museum dedicated to your father, located in his former home, appears to be closed. Do you know why? I don't think they want to encourage people to go there. They don't want to remind people too much of my father. Officially they haven't allowed portraits of my father to be hung in government offices over the last decade, probably because of the association with me and also because of how my father regarded the role of the army.

What's your favourite part of the city? It's been a long time since I've been able to explore Yangon. Shwedagon is very important, and the Sule Pagoda, but I spend much of my time at the NLD office.

It was at this point, as the street demonstrations continued to mount, that Suu Kyi decided to join the movement for democracy. Her speech at Shwedagon Paya on 26 August 1988, with her husband and sons by her side, electrified the estimated crowd of half a million, and sent ripples of excitement and hope throughout the country. Elegantly attired, the trademark flowers in her hair, the 43-year-old Suu Kyi brought a hitherto-unseen sophistication to Myanmar politics as she launched what she called 'the second struggle for national independence'.

The brutal reaction of the military brought the protests to an end a month later.

Braving the Generals

Suu Kyi, however, was just getting started, and in September 1988 she joined several former generals and senior army officers (including Tin Oo, army chief of staff in the 1970s, who had been jailed for his role in an abortive coup in 1975) to form the NLD. As the party's general secretary, she travelled around the country attending rallies.

Her assistant at the time, Win Htein, a former army captain, recalls how she had 'a real ability to connect to the people', while a diplomat quoted in the *New York Times* said her very name was 'magic' among the public. In April 1989, while campaigning in the town of Danubyu, she came up against soldiers who threatened to shoot her and her supporters; with great courage she continued to move forward and calmly asked that they be allowed to pass. Only at the last minute did a senior officer step in and order the men to lower their guns (it's a scene reimagined in the movie *Beyond Rangoon*).

In July 1989 Aung San Suu Kyi, who by now had become the NLD's primary spokesperson, was placed under house arrest for publicly expressing doubt about the junta's intentions of handing over power to a civilian government, and for her plans to lead a march in Yangon to celebrate Martyr's Day. Her status as Aung San's daughter saved her from the fate of many other NLD members, who were imprisoned in the country's notorious jails.

With her husband and sons by her side, Suu Kyi went on a hunger strike for 12 days to gain an assurance that her jailed supporters would not be tortured. None of this stopped the NLD from decisively winning the general election of May 1990.

A Prisoner of Conscience

Aris left Yangon with their sons on 2 September 1989. Suu Kyi would see either Alexander or Kim for over two and a half years. Her husband was allowed to spend one more fortnight with her over Christmas in 1989, a time he described as 'among the happiest memories of our many years of marriage'.

At any moment during her years of arrest, Suu Kyi knew that the authorities would let her walk free to board a flight to return to her family in the UK. But once she left Burma she knew she would never be allowed to return, and she would not accept permanent exile. It was a sacrifice in which her family supported

1985–87
At Kyoto University, Suu Kyi researches her father's time in Japan; she also registers at London's School of Oriental and African Studies for a doctorate in Burmese literature.

1988
Returns to Yangon in March to care for her mother, who has suffered a stroke; in September becomes secretary-general of National League for Democracy (NLD).

1989
At her mother's funeral in January she swears to serve the people of Burma until her death. Stands for election in February; placed under house arrest in July.

1991
Wins Nobel Peace Prize; sons accept it on her behalf. Pledges she will use $1.3 million prize money to establish health and education trust for Burmese people.

1995
Released from house arrest, resumes campaigning for the NLD, but her movements are restricted. At year's end she sees Aris for what will be the final time.

1996
In November her motorcade is attacked in Yangon, the windows of the car she is travelling in is smashed by a mob; despite presence of security forces no one is arrested.

1999
Suffering terminal prostate cancer, Aris is refused entry to Burma and dies in the UK. After his funeral, sons Kim and Alexander are allowed to visit their mother briefly.

THE SWIMMER

For an example of how a visitor's actions, well-meaning or otherwise, can affect a local in Myanmar, you need look no further than John Yettaw's unauthorised meeting with Aung San Suu Kyi. On 3 May 2009, the 53-year-old Vietnam vet, retired bus driver and Mormon strapped on homemade flippers and paddled his way across Inya Lake to the democracy leader's home; he had attempted a meeting the year before, but had been blocked that time by her two housekeepers. This time, however, Suu Kyi took pity on the exhausted American and allowed him to stay, even though she knew such a visit violated the terms of her house arrest.

Speaking to a reporter for the *New Yorker* in 2010, she said 'I felt I could not hand over anybody to be arrested by the authorities when so many of our people had been arrested and not been given a fair hearing.' When he left two days later, Yettaw was fished out the lake by government agents. Following a trial, he was sentenced to seven years in prison, only to be released a few days later to return to the US. Aung San Suu Kyi and her two housekeepers, meanwhile, were sentenced to three years of hard labour, commuted to 18 months of house arrest – sufficient to keep the NLD leader out of the way during the 2010 elections.

her, acting as her proxies to accept from the European Parliament in January 1991 the Sakharov Prize for freedom of thought, and the Nobel Peace Prize in October of the same year.

As the international honours stacked up (the Simón Bolivar Prize from Unesco in June 1992; the Jawaharlal Nehru Award for International Understanding in May 1995), Suu Kyi maintained her strength and spirits by meditating, reading (in *Letters from Burma* she writes how she loves nothing more than relaxing over a detective story), exercising, practicing piano, and listening to news on the radio. From May 1992 until January 1995 she was also permitted regular visits from her husband and sons.

Five Years of Freedom

Much to the joy of her supporters at home and abroad, as well as her family, the government released Suu Kyi from house arrest in July 1995. She was allowed to travel outside Yangon with permission, which was rarely granted. During her subsequent five years of freedom, she would test the authorities several times with varying degrees of success.

The last time she would see her husband was in January 1996. A year later he was diagnosed with prostate cancer, which would prove to be terminal. Despite appeals from the likes of Pope John Paul II and UN Secretary General Kofi Anan, the generals refused to allow Aris a visa to visit his wife, saying that Suu Kyi was free to leave the country to tend to him. Aris died in an Oxford hospital on 27 March 1999, his 53rd birthday; over the telephone he had insisted Suu Kyi remain in Burma where many political prisoners and their families also relied on her support.

The following decade was marked by more extended periods of house arrest punctuated by shorter spells of freedom. A couple of intercessions by UN special envoys resulted in talks with military leaders and the release of hundreds of political prisoners, but no real progress on the political front – nor release for the woman who had become the world's most famous prisoner of conscience.

Run-Up to Elections & Release

On 22 September 2007, at the height of the failed 'Saffron Revolution' (p304), the barricades briefly came down along University Ave, allowing the protestors to pass Aung San Suu Kyi's house. In a powerful scene, later recounted by eyewitnesses and captured on mobile-phone footage, the jailed NLD leader was briefly glimpsed at the gate of her compound, tears in her eyes, silently accepting the blessing of the monks.

A couple of meetings with a UN envoy, Ibrahim Gambari, and members of the military later that year failed to result in Suu Kyi's release. Her house arrest was extended a year in 2008 and then by a further 18 months in August 2009 following her encounter with John Yettaw (see box, p356).

With the 2010 election in the bag, the regime finally saw fit to release her, announcing in the *New Light of Myanmar* that she had been pardoned for 'good conduct'. Suu Kyi mocks the government's English language mouthpiece as the 'The New Blight of Myanmar', so it's a fair assumption she didn't take too seriously the same paper's insistence, a few months later, that she and her supporters would come to a 'tragic end' for their continued calls for sanctions and a 'second Panglong Conference' to discuss ethnic issues.

An Unpredictable Future

Emerging from house arrest in November 2010, Suu Kyi addressed a jubilant crowd. 'I'm going to work for national reconciliation. That is a very important thing', she said, adding, 'There is nobody I cannot talk to. I am prepared to talk with anyone. I have no personal grudge toward anybody.'

Initially, Suu Kyi's offer fell on deaf ears. However, in August 2011, the regime began to take a more conciliatory approach. At the time of writing there have been two rounds of talks between Suu Kyi and a government minister in which both sides agreed 'to cooperate on national stability and development'. Also, for the first time since 2003, the NLD leader has been allowed to travel out of Yangon on political business. On a trip to Bago, thousands of well-wishers lined the streets, and in the nearby town of Tha Nat Pin, where she opened a library, Suu Kyi told the assembled crowd 'We can develop this country only when we all work together.'

'It's still not very clear still what her role is going to be', says Thant Myint-U, commenting on the much more complex nature of Myanmar politics today versus the united opposition that existed back in the 1990s. Aung Zaw, editor of the *Irrawaddy*, sums up the situation when he says that Suu Kyi 'steps into the fray at a time when the NLD requires fresh ideas and strong leadership'. Conscious of this, Suu Kyi has repeatedly reached out to, and mentioned the work of, younger NLD and democracy supporters in the many interviews and speeches she has given since her release.

How long will Aung San Suu Kyi remain at large? Nobody knows, least of all Suu Kyi herself. 'I want to do as much as I can while I'm free', she said in a January 2011 interview with *Time*. Over two decades since she mounted that podium at Shwedagon Paya, and despite everything she has undergone since, the Lady's determination to fight for democracy and freedom for the people of Myanmar appears undiminished.

AUNG SAN SUU KYI

2000
Begins second period of house arrest in September; a month later starts secret talks with the junta, facilitated by UN special envoy Rizali Ismail.

2002
Released in May; returns to campaigning around Yangon and in late June makes a triumphant visit to Mandalay, her first trip to Myanmar's second-largest city since 1989.

2003
In May, while touring northern Myanmar, Suu Kyi and 250 NLD members are attacked by a pro-junta mob; at least 70 people are killed. Another period of house arrest follows.

2007
In September she makes a fleeting appearance, greeting protesting monks at her gate. In October a meeting with UN envoy Ibrahim Gambari is followed by talks with NLD and regime reps.

2008
Suu Kyi's detention is extended for another year in May despite this contravening Myanmar's law requiring a person to be put on trial or released within a five-year period.

2010
Released on 13 November, six days after the general election; 10 days later, is reunited with son Kim, who brings her a puppy as a present.

2011
Suu Kyi gives the prestigious Reith Lectures on BBC Radio (www.bbc.co.uk/programmes/b0126d29) and journeys to Bagan with her son Kim, her first time out of Yangon in eight years.

Survival Guide

Directory A–Z

Accommodation

Myanmar has hundreds of privately run hotels and guesthouses licensed to accept foreigners. To get the licence they supposedly must keep at least five rooms and reach a certain standard. In fact many are simple family-run guesthouses or mini-hotels, sometimes with just a mosquito net, a fan that turns off at midnight (when the generator does) and a cold shower down the hall.

In key destinations (eg Yangon, Bagan, Inle Lake, Mandalay, Ngapali Beach), you'll find high-end affairs with bungalow-style rooms, swimming pools, tennis courts and fancy restaurants. In between (but closer to budget in quality) are modern, hit-or-miss Chinese-style hotels that follow familiar templates: tiled rooms with air-con, a refrigerator and a private bathroom with hot water.

Nearly all accommodation choices include breakfast in their rates. Staff at most can also change money, arrange laundry service (starting at K1000 per load at budget guesthouses), rent bikes, arrange taxis, sell transport tickets and find you local English-speaking guides.

At night, all hotels and other accommodation options must fill in police forms on behalf of all guests, which include the details of your passport and visa. Hotels will not have to keep your passport.

Prices

Hotels and guesthouses quote prices in US dollars. Typically you can pay in kyat too, but at an unfavourable exchange rate, so it's worth keeping dollars ready for accommodation expenses. Prices quoted at budget and midrange hotels include all taxes; top-end hotel prices often don't include up to 20% in taxes and service charges. A handful of top-end hotels in Myanmar accept credit cards. There are lower rates or it's possible to bargain a little at most hotels during the low season (March to October).

Listings in this book are ordered by author preference and divided into three groups with regard to price:

» **Budget ($)** Doubles under $20 (under about K17,000)

» **Midrange ($$)** Doubles $20 to $60 (about K17,000 to K51,000)

» **Top End ($$$)** Doubles over $60 (over about K51,000).

Business Hours

Government offices, including post offices and telephone centres, are open Monday to Friday 9.30am to 4.30pm. Shops open Monday to Saturday from 9.30am to 6pm or later (sometimes only half-day Saturday). Restaurants open 8am to 9pm, while internet cafes open noon to 10pm. In this book we spell out opening hours where they differ from those above.

Children

Travelling with children in Myanmar can be very rewarding as long as you come well prepared with the right attitude, the physical requirements and the usual parental patience. Lonely Planet's *Travel with Children* contains useful advice on how to cope with kids on the road. Special attention is paid to travel in developing countries.

People in Myanmar love children and in many instances will shower attention on your offspring, who will find ready playmates among their

---

BOOK YOUR STAY ONLINE

For more accommodation reviews by Lonely Planet authors, check out hotels.lonelyplanet.com/Myanmar. You'll find independent reviews, as well as recommendations on the best places to stay. Best of all, you can book online.

PRACTICALITIES

» Connect (when it's working) to the electricity supply (230V, 50Hz AC). Many hotels have generators (some run at night only). Local power sources in many towns are scheduled for night hours only.

» Read the English-language newspaper *Myanmar Times,* which offers some useful travel and entertainment information, and the government mouthpiece *New Light of Myanmar.*

» Bring a short wave radio and listen, like many locals, to BBC and VOA broadcasts.

» Watch satellite TV rather than the state controlled broadcast channels – you'll often find CNN, BBC World and other news and entertainment channels at hotels.

» Petrol is sold by the gallon; distances are in miles, not kilometres; 1 Burmese *viss* or 100 *tical* = 3.5lb; 1 *gaig* = 36in.

local counterparts. It may, however, be confusing for some children seeing young locals working at restaurants and teahouses.

Practicalities

» Due to Myanmar's overall low level of public sanitation, parents ought to lay down a few ground rules with regard to maintaining their children's health – such as regular hand-washing – to head off potential medical problems.

» Children should especially be warned not to play with animals they encounter, as a precaution against rabies.

» Nappies (diapers) are hard to come by outside Yangon, and it's wise to bring all the nappies or formula you'll need for the trip from home.

» Most high-end hotels and restaurants will have highchairs available.

» When travelling with children, it may be more comfortable getting about by private car (p378).

Sights & Activities

» Kids often get a thrill from little things such as rides on trishaws and in horse carts. Inle Lake boasts trips in dugout canoes, and the ancient

cities outside Mandalay also offer fun, brief boat trips.

» Big Buddhist sights and ancient ruins can make for good learning experiences, including Yangon's Shwedagon Paya, the reclining buddhas in Bago, or the 10-storey buddha in Pyay. You can climb into the back of the lacquered buddha image at Nan Paya in Salay.

» Some kids might dig ruins of old palace walls and moats, which you can see at places like Bagan and Mrauk U.

» Indulge in some face painting by trying on *thanakha* (yellow sandalwood-like paste), which is sold and applied from sidewalk stands around the country.

» There are zoos in Yangon, Nay Pyi Taw and Mandalay as well as excellent birdwatching at the Moeyungyi Wetlands near Bago.

» Traditional puppet shows are performed in Yangon, Bagan and Mandalay as well as other places.

» The beaches at Ngapali, Chaung Tha and Ngwe Saung are all sure to be winners with kids wanting to splash in the sea and play on the sand.

» Myanmar's festivals, such as Thingyan in mid-April with its throwing of water, and Taunggyi's fire-balloon festival in October or November, can be a lot of fun.

» Consider asking about a local orphanage – there are many – so your children can play with kids their own age. The local kids would love it.

Climate

Mandalay

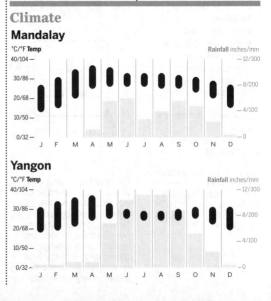

Yangon

Customs Regulations

For the vast majority of visitors, clearing customs is a breeze, but it's important to be aware of the restrictions. Any foreign currency in excess of $2000 is supposed to be declared upon entry. Besides personal effects, visitors are permitted to bring duty free:

» 400 cigarettes
» 100 cigars
» 250g of tobacco
» 0.5L of perfume.

It's not a problem to bring a camera, video camera, laptop or mobile phone. You cannot bring in antiques, pornographic materials or narcotic drugs (obviously).

Export Restrictions

The following items cannot legally be taken out of the country:

» prehistoric implements and artefacts
» fossils
» old coins
» bronze or brass weights (including opium weights)
» bronze or clay pipes
» *kammawa* or *parabaik*
» inscribed stones
» inscribed gold or silver
» historical documents
» religious images
» sculptures or carvings in bronze, stone, stucco or wood
» frescoes (even fragments)
» pottery
» national regalia and paraphernalia.

Technically you have to show approval from various government agencies to bring out books, videos or DVDs, though this is very unlikely to be enforced.

Electricity

230V/50Hz

230V/50Hz

Power outages occur everywhere, Yangon and Mandalay included. Many smaller towns have short scheduled periods for electricity, usually a few hours in the afternoon and evening (power always seems to be available if Myanmar TV is airing a premiership soccer game!). Many hotels and shops run generators 24 hours, others keep them on only a few hours (eg 6pm to midnight, and a few hours in the morning)

Embassies & Consulates

The generals moved the capital from Yangon to Nay Pyi Taw in 2005, but foreign embassies and consulates stayed behind in Yangon. Check the government's **Ministry of Foreign Affairs** (www.mofa.gov.mm) for more information.

Australia (☑01-251 810, 01-251 809; fax 01-246 159; 88 Strand Rd)

Bangladesh (☑01-515 275; 11B Than Lwin Rd, Kamayut)

Cambodia (☑01-549 609; 25 New University Ave Rd, B3/4B)

Canada Affairs handled by Australian embassy or Canadian embassy in Bangkok (☑+66 (0)2 636 0540)

China (☑01-221 281; 1 Pyidaungsu Yeiktha Rd, Dagon)

France (☑01-212 178; fax 01-212 527; 102 Pyidaungsu Yeiktha Rd, Dagon)

Germany (☑01-548 951; fax 01-548 899; 9 Bogyoke Aung San Museum Rd)

India (☑01-243 972, 01-391 219; 545-547 Merchant St)

Indonesia (☑01-254 465, 01-254 469; 100 Pyidaungsu Yeiktha Rd)

Israel (☑01-515 155; fax 01-515 116; 15 Kabaung Rd, Hlaing Township)

Italy (☑01-527 100; 3 Inya Myaing Rd)

Japan (☑01-549 644; 100 Nat Mauk Rd)

Korea (☑01-510 205; 97 University Ave Rd, Bahan)

Laos (☑01-222 482; A1 Diplomatic Quarters, Taw Win St)

Malaysia (☑01-220 249; 82 Pyidaungsu Yeiktha Rd)

Nepal (☑01-545 880; fax 01-549 803; 16 Nat Mauk Rd)

Netherlands Affairs handled by German embassy or Neth-

erlands embassy in Bangkok
(☎+66 (0)2 309 5200)
New Zealand Affairs handled by UK embassy
Pakistan (☎01-222 881; 4A Pyay Rd)
Philippines (☎01-558 149; 50 Sayasan St)
Singapore (☎01-559 001; 238 Dhama Zedi Rd)
Sri Lanka (☎01-222 812; 34 Taw Win St)
Thailand (☎01-226 721; 94 Pyay Rd, Dagon)
UK (☎01-256 438, 01-370 863; fax 01-380 322; 80 Strand Rd)
USA (☎01-536 509, 01-535 756; fax 01-650 306; 110 University Ave, Kamayut)
Vietnam (☎01-511 305; 72 Than Lwin Rd, Bahan)

Gay & Lesbian Travellers

Homosexuality has an ambiguous legal status in Myanmar. Under a section of the Penal Code of 1882–88, 'carnal intercourse against nature' is punishable with imprisonment of up to 10 years. While this law is rarely enforced, it renders gays and lesbians vulnerable to police harassment. This said, a local woman walking with a foreign man will raise more eyebrows than two same-sex travellers sharing a room.

Gay and transgendered people in Myanmar are rarely 'out', except for 'third sex' spirit mediums who channel the energies of *nat* spirits (see p341). As elsewhere, it can be seen as a bit of a cultural taboo, though most of Myanmar's ethnic groups are known to be tolerant of homosexuality, both male and female. Some Buddhists, however, believe that those who committed sexual misconducts (such as adultery) in a previous life become gay or lesbian in this one. Muslim and Christian Myanmar communities may object to homosexuality but, as they form relatively

small minorities, they rarely foist their perspectives on people of other faiths. Public displays of affection, whether heterosexual or homosexual, are frowned upon.

Check **Utopia-Asia** (www.utopia-asia.com) for some Yangon scene reports; it also publishes a gay guide to Southeast Asia, including Myanmar.

A few foreign travel agencies specialise in 'gay tours' – meaning a standard tour on which gay or lesbian travellers can feel comfortable they'll check into gay-friendly hotels. (Many of the guides are openly gay, too.) Agencies with trips to Myanmar include **Purple Dragon** (www.purpledrag.com) and **Mandalay Travel** (www.mandalaytravel.com).

Insurance

A travel-insurance policy is a very wise idea, though not all companies cover travel to Myanmar. There is a wide variety of policies and your travel agent will have recommendations.

Worldwide travel insurance is available at www.lonelyplanet.com/travel_services. You can buy, extend and claim online anytime – even if you're already on the road.

Internet Access

Getting online in Myanmar is possible, especially in the big cities – look for reviews with either an @ or a 🛜 icon for places with internet-ready computers or wi-fi access respectively. During research for this guide, we even found internet access in relatively remote locations such as Mrauk U.

However, with tightly squeezed bandwidth, blocked sites and power outages it can often be a frustrating and ultimately fruitless exercise to send and receive emails or check

various sites. Also, in March 2011, Skype and other VoIP (Voice over Internet Protocol) calls were banned by the authorities at internet cafes.

Ingenious locals have come up with ways around government censorship of sites: typing https://before a site URL can sometimes give you access. However, proceed cautiously as internet shop owners can get into big trouble if they're found to be allowing access to prohibited sites.

There's no censorship (so far) of Facebook or gmail, so set up one of these accounts if you want to stay in contact with the outside world while travelling in the country.

Legal Matters

You have absolutely no legal recourse in case of arrest or detainment by the authorities, regardless of the charge. Foreign visitors engaging in political activism risk deportation or imprisonment. If you are arrested, you would most likely be permitted to contact your consular agent in Myanmar for possible assistance.

If you purchase gems or jewellery from persons or shops that are not licensed by the government, you run the risk of having them confiscated if customs officials find them in your baggage when you're exiting the country.

Journalists often claim a different profession in order to get a visa, and they risk deportation if authorities suspect that they're researching a political exposé while in the country.

Forming public assemblies is illegal. Drug trafficking crimes are punishable by death.

Many foreigners (like Jonathan Rambo in a certain eponymous film) foolishly enter Myanmar illegally from northern Thailand, but not all succeed in avoiding arrest.

Maps

The best available is the 1:2,000,000 Periplus Editions *Myanmar Travel Map,* a folded map with plans for Mandalay, Yangon and the Bagan area, or the ITMB 1:1,350,000 *Myanmar (Burma).* Another choice is the 1:1,500,000 Nelles *Myanmar,* a folded map on coated stock. Good places to buy maps online include International Travel Maps and Books (www.itmb. com) and East View Map Link (www.maplink.com).

Myanmar-based Design Printing Services (DPS; www.dpsmap.com) prints useful tourist maps of Myanmar, Yangon, Mandalay and Bagan; get a free one online. Sometimes these maps are sold locally for about K1000 or given away by tour agencies.

In Yangon you can pick up the full-colour, folded *Tourist Map of Myanmar,* published on coated stock by DPS, from many hotels and bookshops. Sometimes you can grab one free at the Yangon Airport arrival hall.

The Myanmar government's Survey Department publishes a very good 1:2,000,000 paper sheet map of the country, simply entitled *Myanmar.* It's big and the uncoated paper decays rapidly. You can find it on Bogyoke Aung San Rd in Yangon, just east of the market.

Money

See p12 for details on costs in Myanmar and p23 for tips on spreading your budget through the private sector rather than giving it to the government.

ATMs, Credit Cards & Travellers Cheques

None of Myanmar's few ATMs accept overseas cards. Credit cards and travellers cheques are also useless in Myanmar, a situation that is

KYAT & DOLLARS

Prices in this book alternate between kyat (K) and US dollars ($), depending on the currency in which prices are quoted. Be careful to keep some US dollars with you in case you're turned back by a strict museum cashier who will not take kyat. For more information, see p364.

unlikely to change in the near future.

However, a couple of high-end hotels in Yangon and Mandalay do accept credit cards, and sometimes give cash back – albeit with a hefty surcharge.

Banks

There was a mass emigration of foreign banks from Myanmar following the 2003 sanctions by the EU and USA. The few national banks that remain are of little use to travellers, as official exchange rates massively overvalue the kyat.

Currency

Myanmar's national currency, the kyat (pronounced 'chat') is divided into the following banknotes: K1, K5, K10, K20, K50, K100, K200, K500, K1000 and K5000; you'll rarely come across the smaller denominations and if you do they're often in tatters.

The US dollar acts as an alternative currency with most guesthouses and hotels quoting prices and accepting payment in the greenback. If you choose to pay in kyat, it will be at a disadvantageous rate (perhaps a difference of K50 or K100 to the dollar). Some hotels, shops and government ferry clerks give change in kyat or with torn

US bills that you can't use elsewhere in Myanmar.

Government-run services (such as archaeological sites, museums and ferries) and flights are paid for in US dollars or FEC notes (see p365).

Items such as meals, bus tickets, trishaw or taxi rides, bottles of water or beer and market items are usually quoted in kyat.

Moneychangers

Avoid the official exchange counters, which undercut black-market rates substantially (K7 per dollar, rather than K850).

You will be asked to 'change money' many times on your trip. Technically, the only reasonable way to buy kyat is through the 'black market' – meaning from shops, hotels, travel agents, restaurants or less reliable guys on the street. You can change US dollars or euros in Yangon, but generally only US dollars elsewhere.

The $100 bill gets a better exchange rate than a $50 or $20, and so on. And supposedly the exchange rate is marginally better early in the week (Monday or Tuesday).

It's safest to change money in hotels or shops, rather than on the street. The moneychangers standing around just east of the Mahabandoola Garden in Yangon have a reputation for short-changing new arrivals.

Never hand over your money until you've received the kyat and counted them. Honest moneychangers will expect you to do this. Considering that K5000 is the highest denomination (roughly $5.90), you'll get a lot of notes. Moneychangers give ready-made, rubber-banded stacks of a hundred K1000 bills. It's a good idea to check each note individually. Often you'll find one or two (or more) with a cut corner or taped tears, neither of which anyone will accept. We heard from some travellers that Yangon moneychangers have asked for a 'commission'.

Many travellers do the bulk of their exchanging in Yangon, where you can get about K100 more per dollar than elsewhere, then carry the stacks of kyat around the country. Considering the relative safety from theft, it's not a bad idea, but you *can* exchange money elsewhere.

Also, when paying for rooms and services in US dollars, check your change carefully. Locals like to unload slightly torn bills that work fine in New York, but will be worthless for the rest of your trip in Myanmar.

FECs

Some government businesses, such as Myanma Airways and museums, may still quote prices in Foreign Exchange Certificates (FECs). Since one FEC is equal to $1 there is absolutely no value in you acquiring them.

Tipping, Donations & Bribes

Tipping is not customary in Myanmar, though little extra 'presents' are sometimes expected (even if they're not asked for) in exchange for a service (such as unlocking a locked temple at Bagan, helping move a bag at the airport or showing you around the sights of a village).

It's a good idea to have some small notes (K50, K100, K200) when visiting a religious temple or monas-

tery, as donations may be requested and you may wish to leave one even if it's not.

In the past, many travellers have offered a little 'tea money' to officials in order to help expedite bureaucratic services such as visa extensions or getting a seat on a 'sold out' flight. You shouldn't have to do this. If you overstay your visa, you'll often pay a $3 'fee' for the paperwork, in addition to the $3 per day penalty. See p370 for more details.

See also p366 for details on the 'commissions' paid to guides and drivers.

Photography

There should be no problem bringing a camera or video camera into Myanmar, although a huge contraption that looks like a portable movie set *will* attract attention. Photo-processing shops and internet cafes can burn digital photos onto a CD, but you should have your own adapter. Colour film – Fuji and Kodak – is widely available.

Avoid taking photographs of military facilities, uniformed individuals, road blocks, bridges and opposition political offices, including those of the NLD and Aung Sang Suu Kyi's home in Yangon.

Most locals are very happy to be photographed, but always ask first. If you have a digital camera with a display

screen, some locals (kids, monks, anyone) will be overjoyed to see their image. It's also very easy and cheap to get digital photos turned into prints that can then be given to people as presents.

Some sights, including some paya and other religious sites, charge a camera fee of K100 or so. Usually a video camera fee is a little more.

For tips on how to shoot photos, pick up Lonely Planet's *Travel Photography*.

Post

Most mail out of Myanmar gets to its destination quite efficiently. International-postage rates are a bargain: a postcard is K30.

Officially, post offices across Myanmar are supposed to be open from 9.30am to 4.30pm Monday to Friday.

DHL Worldwide Express (☎01-664 423; www.fastforward.dhl.com; 7A Kaba Aye Pagoda Rd, Yangon; ☺8am-6pm Mon-Sat) is a more reliable way of sending out bigger packages (though you can send only documents to the USA because of sanctions). Packages begin at $80 (1.1lb/0.5kg); documents at $72.

Marine Transport Service (☎01-256 628; mts@yangon.net.mm; MGW Centre, 170/176 Bo Aungkyaw Rd) can ship freight boxes if you end up going nuts on puppets.

Public Holidays

Major public holidays:

Independence Day (January 4)

Union Day (February 12)

Peasants' Day (March 2)

Armed Forces Day (March 27)

Workers' Day (May 1)

National Day (October or November)

Christmas (December 25)

BRING NEW BILLS!

We cannot stress enough the need to bring pristine 'new' US dollar bills to Myanmar – that means 2006 or later bills that have colour and are in absolutely perfect condition: no folds, stamps, stains, writing marks or tears. Anything else may be rejected by moneychangers, hotels, restaurants, shops and museums.

While $100 bills get the best exchange rates, it's also a good idea to bring lots of small dollar bills – ones, fives and 10s – and to use them to pay for your hotel and other charges directly.

YANGON PICK-UP

Shipping goods abroad from Myanmar is very expensive (and impossible if you live in the US, due to sanctions). If you want a few puppets, but are worried about breaking them along the way, many shops around the country will package your gifts and arrange to deliver them to a Yangon hotel by bus for a minimal fee.

Safe Travel

Considering all the bad news that trickles out of Myanmar, it may sound like a rather unsafe country to visit. For the vast majority of visitors, the reality is quite the opposite.

Bugs, Snakes, Rats & Monkeys

Mosquitoes, if allowed, can have a field day with you. Bring repellent from home, as the good stuff (other than mosquito coils) is hard to come by. Some guesthouses and hotels don't provide mosquito nets. See also entries on malaria (p384) and dengue fever (p384).

Myanmar has one of the highest incidences of death from snakebite in the world. Watch your step in brush, forest and grasses. See p386 for information on what to do if you're bitten.

Rats aren't all that rampant. Family-run guesthouses, like regular homes, might have a rodent or two. Wash your hands before sleeping and try to keep food out of your room. If you trek in Shan State and stay in local accommodation, you may hear little footsteps at night.

In a few sites, such as Hpo Win Daung Caves, near Monywa or Mt Popa near Bagan,

you'll have monkeys begging for snacks. Take care as bites are possible. See p384 for precautions against rabies.

Crime

All over Myanmar, police stations have English signs up that ask: 'May I help you?' It's easy to smirk at, but supposedly some of the restrictions to travel around Myanmar are based on the government's desire to keep foreigners out of harm's way.

Locals know that the penalties for stealing, particularly from foreigners, can be severe. Most travellers' memories of locals grabbing their money are of someone chasing them down to return a K500 note they dropped. If someone grabs your bag at a bus station, it's almost certainly just a trishaw driver hoping for a fare.

Insurgents & Bombs

In recent years, including in 2011, there have been a handful of bombings, usually linked with insurgent groups, in Yangon and elsewhere. None have targeted foreigners.

Despite treaties between the government and most insurgent groups, signed in the late 1990s, violent incidents on the Myanmar-Thai border could erupt at any time, particularly in and around Tachileik. Land mines on the Myanmar side of the border are another threat. Most travel advisories warn against travel to this area, most of which is restricted for foreigners.

In Kayin State, splintered Kayin groups live in a potential battleground between the Karen National Liberation Army and government troops. The section of the Myanmar border in a restricted area of Kayin between Um Phang and Mae Sariang occasionally receives shelling from Myanmar troops in pursuit of Kayin (also known as Karen) or Mon rebels.

The presence of Shan and Wa armies along the Thai-Myanmar border in northern

Mae Hong Son makes this area dangerous. The Wa have reportedly sworn off drug production, but there's still plenty of amphetamines and opium crossing some border areas.

In the past there have been reports of bandits holding up vehicles at night, most commonly in the Tanintharyi (Tenasserim) division in southeastern Myanmar, but also near Taungoo. We've not heard of foreigners being targeted.

Politics

The message is clear: allow locals to introduce the subject of politics and proceed to talk with discretion if they do.

Since Aung San Suu Kyi's release in 2010, driving by her house in Yangon has become much easier, but you should think twice about stopping to take photos there and especially at any NLD office. You are not only risking trouble (possible deportation), but implicating your taxi driver too.

Guides, trishaw drivers, vendors and hotel staff are often able to talk at length with foreigners without suspicion. Some can be surprisingly frank in their views. Teahouses carry the reputation as being open-discussion forums for some locals – but not all. Again, let the locals lead the conversation in that direction.

Restricted Roads

Many overland roads are closed to foreigners. However, in places you can enter there are surprising levels of freedom to stop and look around where you want. The map on p380 shows the main routes that are openly accessible, though this can change.

Scams & Hassle

Myanmar touts are pretty minor league in comparison with others in the region. Most hassle is due to commissions. These small behind-the-scenes payments are made, like it or not, for a taxi, trishaw driver or guide who takes you to a hotel, to buy a puppet or even to eat some rice.

When arriving at a bus station, you're likely to be quickly surrounded by touts, some of whom will try to steer you to a particular hotel that offers them a commission. Be wary of claims that your chosen place is 'no good', though in some cases we found that trishaw drivers who had warned us that 'foreigners can't stay there' ended up being correct. If you know where you want to go, persist and they'll take you.

Be wary of fanciful offers of jade or other gems as some are filled with worthless rock or concrete mixture.

Many people may approach to say 'hello' on the street. In some cases, they're just curious or want to practise some English. In other cases the conversation switches from 'what country you from?' to 'where you need to go?' It's all pretty harmless.

You'll be asked to change money frequently. See p364 for tips on doing so with caution.

Spies

At some point on your trip (and you'll probably never know when), the authorities will be watching you. This is even more likely to happen when you go to more off-the-beaten-track places, where authorities are less used to seeing foreigners.

Transport & Road Hazards

The poor state of road and rail infrastructure plus lax safety standards and procedures for flights and boats means that travelling can sometimes be dangerous. Government-operated Myanma Airways (MA) has a sketchy safety record, and there are reports that some MA aircraft have been used by Air Bagan. The rickety state of Myanmar's railway also doesn't inspire much confidence. It's not much better on the roads where safety often seems to be the last consideration of both drivers and pedestrians.

Proceed with caution when crossing any road, particularly in cities where drivers are unlikely to stop if they are involved in an accident with a pedestrian. Traffic drives on the right in Myanmar, but the majority of cars are right-hand-drive imports, which add to the chance of accidents occurring. Factor in the poor state of roads and the even poorer state of

GOVERNMENT TRAVEL ADVICE

The following government websites offer travel advisories and information on current hot spots:

» **Australia** (www.smarttraveller.gov.au)

» **Canada** (www.voyage.gc.ca)

» **New Zealand** (www.safetravel.govt.nz)

» **UK** (www.fco.gov.uk/travel)

» **USA** (travel.state.gov/travel)

many clapped-out vehicles and you have a recipe for potential disaster.

Telephone

Local Calls

Most business cards in Myanmar list a couple of phone numbers, as lines frequently go dead and calls just don't go through.

Local call stands – as part of a shop, or sometimes just a table with a phone or two on a sidewalk – are marked by a drawing of a phone and can be found all over Myanmar. A local call should be K100 per minute.

To dial long distance within Myanmar, dial the area code (including the '0') and the number.

A useful resource is the **Myanmar Yellow Pages** (www.myanmaryellowpages.biz).

International Calls

Official telephone (call) centres are sometimes the only way to call overseas, though sometimes this can be done on the street through vendors offering use of their mobile phones.

Generally, it costs about $5 per minute to call Australia or Europe and $6 per

SAFETY GUIDELINES FOR HIKING

We've heard about some travellers finding new paths and staying in the hills for a week or more. Most, however, stick with day trips. Here are a few points to consider before lacing up the boots:

» Hike with at least one companion; in most cases it's best to hire a guide.

» Do not venture by foot into areas restricted to foreigners; ask around before taking off.

» Camping in the hills is not technically legal, as foreigners must be registered nightly with local authorities by owners of 'licensed accommodation'.

» Trail conditions can get slippery and dangerous, especially in the rainy season.

» Walk only in regions within your capabilities – you're not going to find a trishaw out there to bring you back.

minute to phone North America. You'll usually be asked to pay in US dollars. In March 2011, the authorities banned Skype and other internet-based call services at internet cafes, as the lower rates charged for such calls was impacting the revenue made at government call centres.

To call Myanmar from abroad, dial your country's international access code, then ☑95 (Myanmar's country code), the area code (minus the '0'), and the five- or six-digit number. Area codes are listed below town headings throughout the book.

Mobile Phones

Mobile phone numbers begin with ☑09. There's no international roaming in Myanmar, so in most cases your mobile (cell) phone will be useless here. You'll see a lot of them in use, though. This is a serious status symbol, considering the SIM card alone officially costs K1.5 million (around $1685) and much more on the black market.

For a short period in 2010 it was possible to buy a prepaid SIM card for a GSM phone with $20 of credit (expiring in a month); they were provided by a Tay Za company. During our research in 2011 these were not available, although $50 cards (with credit expiring in three months) were widely on sale for use in CDMA phones. You can find a CDMA 450 phone for as little as $50 in Yangon.

Time

The local Myanmar Standard Time (MST) is 6½ hours ahead of Greenwich Mean Time (GMT/UTC). When coming in from Thailand, turn your watch back half an hour; coming from India, put your watch forward an hour. The 24-hour clock is often used for train times.

Toilets

Toilets, when you need them most (at bus stops or off the highway), are often at their worst. Apart from most guesthouses, hotels and upscale restaurants, squat toilets are the norm. Most of these are located down a dirt path behind a house. Usually next to the toilet is a cement reservoir filled with water, and a plastic bowl lying nearby. This has two functions: as a flush and for people to clean their nether regions while still squatting over the toilet. Toilet paper is available at shops all over the country, but not often at toilets. Some places charge a nominal fee to use the toilet.

Note that, other than at top-end hotels, the plumbing in flush, sit-down toilets is not equipped to flush paper. Usually there's a small waste basket nearby to deposit used toilet paper.

It's perfectly acceptable for men (less so for women) to go behind a tree or bush (or at the roadside) when nature calls.

Note that buses and smaller boats usually don't have toilets.

Tourist Information

Government-operated **Myanmar Travels & Tours** (MTT; http://myanmartravelsandtours. com) is part of the Ministry

---

LIVING ON MYANMAR TIME

Chances are that your bus or train will roll in late, but much of Myanmar actually does work on a different time system. Buddhists use an eight-day week in which Thursday to Tuesday conform to the Western calendar but Wednesday is divided into two 12-hour days. Midnight to noon is 'Bohdahu' (the day Buddha was born), while noon to midnight is 'Yahu' (Rahu, a Hindu god/planet). However, it's rare that the week's unique structure causes any communication problems.

The traditional Myanmar calendar features 12 28-day lunar months that run out of sync with the months of the solar Gregorian calendar. To stay in sync with the solar year, Myanmar inserts a second Waso lunar month every few years – somewhat like the leap-year day added to the Gregorian February. The lunar months of Myanmar are Tagu, March/April; Kason, April/May; Nayon, May/June; Waso, June/July; Wagaung, July/August; Tawthalin, August/September; Thadingyut, September/October; Tazaungmon, October/November; Nadaw, November/December; Pyatho, December/January; Tabodwe, January/February; Tabaung, February/March.

Traditionally, Burmese kings subscribed to various year counts. The main one in current use, the *thekkayit,* begins in April and is 638 years behind the Christian year count. Therefore, the Christian year of 2011 is equivalent to the *thekkayit* of 1373. If an ancient temple you see sounds way too old, it may be because locals are using the *thekkayit.*

Another calendar in use follows the Buddhist era (BE), as used in Thailand, which counts from 543 BC, the date that Buddha achieved *nibbana.* Hence AD 2011 is 2554 BE.

of Hotels & Tourism and the main 'tourist information' service in the country. Those who want to avoid using government services should avoid the tours and services offered here, including train or plane ticket sales. MTT offices are located in Yangon, Mandalay, New Bagan and Inle Lake. Other than at Yangon, these offices are pretty quiet, and often the staff have sketchy knowledge on restricted areas. There are no MTT offices abroad.

Much of the tourist industry in Myanmar is now privatised. Travellers who want to arrange a driver, or have hotel reservations awaiting them, would do well to arrange a trip with the help of private travel agents in Yangon. Many Myanmar 'travel agents' outside Yangon only sell air tickets.

Travellers with Disabilities

With its lack of paved roads or footpaths (even when present the latter are often uneven), Myanmar presents many physical obstacles for the mobility-impaired. Rarely do public buildings (or transport) feature ramps or other access points for wheelchairs, and hotels make inconsistent efforts to provide access for the disabled (exceptions include the Strand Hotel and the Traders Hotel in Yangon, which both have some ramping).

For wheelchair travellers, any trip to Myanmar will require a good deal of planning. Before setting off, get in touch with your national support organisation (preferably with the travel officer, if there is one). Also try the following:

Accessible Journeys (☏800-846 4537; www.disabilitytravel.com) In the US.

Mobility International USA (☏541-343 1284; www.miusa.org) In the US.

Nican (☏02-6241 1220; www.nican.com.au) In Australia.

VISA FEES

The vast majority of visitors should apply for a tourist visa. Former Myanmar citizens and their blood relatives are eligible for 'Social' visas, which can be extended at the Immigration Department in Yangon for $36 for up to six months. The following table lists fees, which are converted into local currency depending on which embassy you apply at.

VISA TYPE	FEE	VALIDITY OF VISA
tourist (single entry)	$20	28 days
social (single entry)	$30	28 days
social (multiple entry)	$150	6 months
work (single entry)	$30	10 weeks
work (multiple entry)	$150	10 weeks
meditation (single entry)	$30	3 months

Tourism for All (☏0845 124 9971; www.tourismforall.org.uk) In the UK.

Visas

All nationalities require a visa to visit Myanmar, and to get one your passport must be valid for six months beyond the date of your arrival.

See p375 for more information on entering Myanmar overland from Thailand or China, including details of short-term visas (with very limited access to Myanmar) available at the borders. Special permission is required to leave the country overland from Tachileik to Thailand.

Note that Myanmar doesn't recognise dual nationalities.

Applications

Don't apply too early, as all visas are valid for up to three months from the date of issue. However, don't leave it till the last minute either, as most embassies and consulates need at least two weeks to process an application. Starting the process a month in advance is the safe bet.

There are slight differences between the application procedures at Myanmar embassies in different countries. Some require two forms to be filled out – the general application and a work history form – others just the general application. Some require two passport photos, others only one. Postal applications are usually OK, but it's best to check first with your nearest embassy about its specific application rules.

It's best to proceed on the assumption that embassies will scrupulously check the background of anyone applying for a tourist visa. It's unwise to list your occupation as any of the following: journalist, photographer, editor, publisher, motion-picture director or producer, cameraperson, videographer or writer. Of course, plenty of media professionals (even high-profile ones) do get into the country – usually by declaring a different profession on the visa application; we've found 'consultant' works.

Myanmar foreign missions may also be suspicious of anyone whose passport shows two or more previous visits to Myanmar in a five-year period. Obviously the government can't believe anyone would want to visit Myanmar more than once

VISA ON ARRIVAL?

In 2010, Myanmar test-ran a tourist-visa-on-arrival system for flights into Yangon, but at the time of our research in early 2011, it didn't appear to be operating, despite many websites making it seem as if it still did.

We have since heard that visas on arrival are once again available at Yangon Airport, but only in very specific circumstances. To get one, you need to enter Myanmar on the scheduled Myanmar Airways International flights from either Guangzhou or Siem Reap.

or twice! In cases such as these you'll need more of a reason than simply 'tourism' for receiving another visa. Be creative.

Extensions & Overstaying Your Visa

Tourist visas cannot be extended and you can run into problems if you choose to stay longer than the allotted 28 days. Hotels are obliged to report travellers whose visas have expired to the authorities and, if found to have not done so, will be in trouble themselves.

Also, you may have difficulties with airport immigration if you're planning domestic flights, particularly in far-flung airports (like Sittwe or Myitkyina). If you do overstay, it's wise to stick with land routes and places within easy access of Yangon, as we've heard stories of such tourists being instructed to leave the country immediately when discovered by the authorities.

All this said, overstaying your visa a few days – even a week or so – is possible. At research time, Yangon Airport's immigration charged $3 per day, plus a $3 'registration fee' for visitors who go over the allotted 28 days. Have exact change ready (they're not likely to change your $100 bill and they won't take kyat) and arrive early enough to fill out the necessary forms.

Volunteering

Official opportunities to volunteer are greatly limited. A list of NGOs that may have volunteering opportunities can be found on www.ngoinmyanmar.org, although mostly their postings are for specific experienced workers (often in medicine). Don't let this sway you. Everyone in Myanmar wants to learn English, and few can afford to. Ask in towns or villages to sit in at an English class.

One or two smaller operations have fought their way through government- and sanction- inspired red tape and set up low-key projects to improve lives. The following are able to accept both skilled and unskilled volunteers, but give them as much advance notice as possible.

Growing Together School (gt.camp@gmail.com) Swiss-run project with two schools based in and around Yangon. It generally requires volunteer trained and untrained teachers and builders and handypeople for at least six weeks.

Eden Centre for Disabled Children (☑640 399; www.edencentre.org) Myanmar-run NGO working to better the lives of disabled children in the city.

Myanmar Charity Group (www.myanmarcharitygroup.org) Provides assistance for the education and general welfare of disabled and orphaned children.

Unicef (www.unicef.org/myanmar/index.html) Runs various programs to protect children and improve public health.

Women Travellers

As in most Buddhist countries, foreign women travelling in Myanmar are rarely hassled on the road as they might be in India, Malaysia or Indonesia. However, we have heard a few reports of sexual harassment. Dressing modestly should help reduce this risk: wear a local *longyi* instead of a skirt above the knee, and any old T-shirt instead of a spaghetti-strap singlet.

Few Myanmar women would consider travelling without at least one female companion, so women travelling alone are regarded as slightly peculiar by the locals. Lone women being seen off on boats and trains by local friends may find the latter trying to find a suitably responsible older woman to keep them company on the trip.

If you didn't bring tampons, one good place to find them is Yangon's City Mart Supermarket.

'Ladies' (per the posted signs in certain areas) cannot go up to some altars or onto decks around stupas, including the one affording a close-up look at the famous Golden Rock at Kyaiktiyo, or apply gold leaf on the Buddha image at Mandalay's Mahamuni Paya. Also, women should never touch a monk; if you're handing something to a monk, place the object within reach of him, not directly into his hands.

Most locals tend to visit teahouses, restaurants or shops with members of the same sex. Asian women, even from other countries, travelling with a Western man may encounter rude comments.

Transport

GETTING THERE & AWAY

Entering the Country

If you're arriving by air, and have your visa ready (see p369) and a valid passport with at least six months of validity from the time of entry in hand, you should have no trouble entering Myanmar.

Arriving and departing by land from China and Thailand is possible, but not very practical. Regular tourists are not allowed to enter Myanmar by land or sea from Bangladesh, India or Laos. For more on border crossings see boxed text, p375.

There is no requirement for you to show an onward ticket out of the country in order to enter Myanmar.

Air

Airports & Airlines

Practically all international flights arrive at Yangon (Rangoon) airport (RGN); there's also a connection to Kunming in China from Mandalay airport (MDL). The most common route to Yangon is via Bangkok, though there are direct flights with several other regional cities such as Singapore and Kuala Lumpur.

The following airlines have regular international links. See p373 for a list of domestic carriers.

Air Asia (airline code FD; ☑01-251 885; www.airasia. com; Park Royal Hotel, 33 Ah Lan Paya Pagoda Rd, Dagon) Twice daily to/from Bangkok and Kuala Lumpur.

Air China (airline code CA; ☑01-505 024; www.airchina. com; B13/23 Shwe Kanayei Housing, Narnattaw Rd) Five times weekly to/from Beijing and Kunming.

Air India (airline code AI; ☑01-253 601; http://home. airindia.in; 127 Sule Paya Rd) Kolkata (Calcutta) on Monday and Friday.

Bangkok Airways (airline code PG; ☑01-255 122; www. bangkokair.com; Sakura Tower, 339 Bogyoke Aung San Rd) Four times weekly to/from Bangkok.

China Airlines (airline code CI; www.china-airlines.com) Three times weekly to/from Taipei.

Malaysia Airlines (airline code MH; ☑01-2410 0720; www.malaysiaairlines.com; Central Hotel, 335/337 Bogyoke Aung San Rd) Daily to/from Kuala Lumpur.

Myanmar Airways International (airline code 8M; ☑01-255 260; www.maiair. com; Sakura Tower, 339 Bogyoke Aung San Rd) Unaffiliated with the government's Myanma Airways. Flies to/from Bangkok, Gaya, Guangzhou, Kuala Lumpur, Siem Reap, Singapore. There are plans to add Delhi, Hong Kong, Kunming, Seoul and Tokyo flights to its schedule.

Silk Air (airline code MI; ☑01-255 287; www.silkair.com; Sakura Tower, 339 Bogyoke

---

CLIMATE CHANGE & TRAVEL

Every form of transport that relies on carbon-based fuel generates CO_2, the main cause of human-induced climate change. Modern travel is dependent on aeroplanes, which might use less fuel per kilometre per person than most cars but travel much greater distances. The altitude at which aircraft emit gases (including CO_2) and particles also contributes to their climate change impact. Many websites offer 'carbon calculators' that allow people to estimate the carbon emissions generated by their journey and, for those who wish to do so, to offset the impact of the greenhouse gases emitted with contributions to portfolios of climate-friendly initiatives throughout the world. Lonely Planet offsets the carbon footprint of all staff and author travel.

DEPARTURE TAX

Myanmar locals pay K500, but foreigners pay $10 departure tax, which is not included with your air ticket. Have the US dollars in hand when leaving the country. You pay at the window in the entrance hall, before you check in. Kyat are not accepted. There is no departure tax for domestic flights.

Aung San Rd) Daily to/from Singapore.

Thai Airways (airline code TG; ☎01-255 499; www.thaiair. com; Sakura Tower, 339 Bogyoke Aung San Rd) Daily to/from Bangkok.

Vietnam Airlines (airline code TG; ☎01-255 066; www. vietnamairlines.com; Sakura Tower, 339 Bogyoke Aung San Rd) Five times weekly to/from Hanoi and twice weekly to/from Ho Chi Minh.

Tickets

Airlines offer discounted tickets via the internet depending on how far in advance you book. Good deals are often available from Bangkok, Kuala Lumpur and Singapore on budget airlines such as Air Asia and Silk Air. If you're flying around the region, look into Bangkok Airways Discovery Airpass.

Once in Myanmar you can only buy international tickets from travel agents or airline offices in Yangon.

Reconfirming Tickets

It's important to reconfirm your outgoing tickets from Myanmar a few days in advance for all airlines other than Thai Airways and Silk Air. If you've forgotten what time your flight is, the inside back page of the *Myanmar Times* lists the week's international flight schedule.

GETTING AROUND

Much of the mountainous areas of Myanmar near the borders is closed, due to conflicts with minority groups or sometimes due to dodgy infrastructure. We have highlighted these places in the destination chapters but situations could change, with routes opening (or closing).

In unrestricted areas, travel methods are remarkably open to visitors. No set itineraries are required and you can pick and choose how you go as you go – taking a bus, plane or train, or crammed pick-up, or hopping onto a giant ferry that drifts at ox-like speed.

Speaking of which, local transport also comes pedpowered, often with trishaws greeting you for rides around town and rental bikes awaiting you at nearly all accommodation. There are horse carts too.

It's worth trying to go by land in Myanmar. Airlines have higher fares – thus more tax money that reaches the government (see p21) – than a bus, not to mention higher carbon emissions.

Many places that are restricted actually *can* be visited with permits provided by the government's Myanmar Travels & Tours (MTT) and a guide. Sometimes this takes several months of advance planning. So don't expect to cross Chin State's rough highways by showing up and asking.

The bulk of this book, of course, focuses on places you can go on your own without any pre-planning. See the map on p380 for transport routes that were open at research time. Reaching some isolated towns such as Kengtung or Sittwe requires jumps by air or boat.

Air

Myanmar's domestic air service features a handful of overworked planes that have busy days, sometimes landing at an airport, leaving the engine on, unloading and loading, and taking off in 20 minutes! This doesn't yield a spot-free safety record (see p367).

Between the main destinations of Yangon, Mandalay, Heho (for Inle Lake), Nyaung U (for Bagan) and Thandwe (for Ngapali Beach), you'll find daily connections. In many other places, there are spotless, largely unused airports serving, well, no flights other than visiting dignitaries on occasion.

As with international flights, domestic flights involve immigration and customs checks.

Airport Codes

Many posted flight schedules around the country only use domestic airport codes, shown in the following table.

AIRPORT	CODE
Bhamo	BMO
Dawei (Tavoy)	TVY
Heho (Inle Lake)	HEH
Homalin	HOX
Kalaymyo	KMV
Kawthoung	KAW
Kengtung	KET
Lashio	LSH
Mandalay	MDL
Mawlamyine	MNU
Myeik	MGZ
Myitkyina	MYT
Nay Pyi Taw	NPT
Nyaung U (Bagan)	NYU
Pathein	BSX
Putao	PBU
Sittwe	AKY
Tachileik	THL
Thandwe (Ngapali Beach)	SNW
Yangon	RGN

Domestic Airlines

Although only one of the domestic airlines is owned outright by the government (Myanma Airways), the other four have known or suspected links. At the very least, all pay hefty government licence and administration fees.

Tay Za (see boxed text, p26) owns Air Bagan; his companies have been targeted directly by outside sanctions. Aung Ko Win, owner of Air Kanbawza, is believed to be a close business associate of Vice-Senior General Maung Aye.

We advise avoiding Myanma Airways – its Fokkers are antiques with the worst reputation for upkeep.

Following is the contact information for airline offices in Yangon; the regional offices are listed in the respective destination chapters.

Air Bagan (airline code W9; ☎01-513 322/422; www.airbagan.com; airline code AB; 56 Shwe Taung Gyar St) Has the largest fleet with six planes.

Air Kanbawza (airline code KZ; ☎01-255 260; Sakura Tower, 339 Bogyoke Aung San Rd) Owned by the same Kanbawza Bank tycoon who owns Myanmar Airways International, this two-plane operation started up in April 2011.

Air Mandalay (airline code 6T; ☎01-525 488; www.airmandalay.com; 146 Dhammazedi Rd) A Singapore-Malaysia joint venture with three planes.

Asian Wings (airline code AW; ☎01-516 654; www.asianwingsairways.com; 34 Shwe Taung Gyar St) Rumoured to be a subsidiary of Air Bagan, this two-plane operation started in January 2011.

Myanma Airways (MA; airline code UB; ☎01-374 874, 01-373 828; www.mot.gov.mm/ma; 104 Strand Rd) Government airline.

Schedules

One Yangon agent told us 'in Myanmar, air routes change in the air'. They're not joking. It's particularly true of MA flights, where dates and departure times are often not written on your ticket, so the airline doesn't have to honour the dates and times for which reservations were originally made. (In some cases, if officials are flying somewhere seats may suddenly open to the public.) Schedules are more reliable on the other airlines, and between main destinations such as Yangon, Mandalay, Nyaung U and Heho, during the high season – but it's essential to always double-check departure times before leaving for the airport.

Tickets

Travel agents sell flight tickets at a slightly discounted rate, so it usually makes little sense to buy directly from the airlines. An exception to this is if you choose to use Air Mandalay. In 2011 the company began its Discover Myanmar Pass covering the four flights on the routing Yangon–Mandalay–Nyaung U–Heho–

Yangon. At $215 plus $28 in taxes it's a slight saving over what you are likely to pay for similar tickets from an agent. There are plans to add Thandwe (for Ngapali Beach) to the pass. Reservation can be made online via the Air Mandalay website with the pass being paid for and picked up from the company's office in Yangon.

One-way fares are half a return fare, and can usually be bought a day in advance. To buy a ticket, you'll need to pay with US dollars or Foreign Exchange Certificates (FECs; see p365), and bring your passport to the travel agent or airline office. It's sometimes difficult to buy a ticket that departs from a town other than the one you are in.

There is no domestic departure tax.

SAMPLE AIRFARES

The following table shows some one-way airfare quotes during peak season for key routes in Myanmar – you may find them for a few dollars cheaper. Fares during the off season (roughly March through October) are about $4 or $5 cheaper.

ROUTE	FARE ($)
Mandalay-Heho (Inle Lake)	43
Mandalay-Nyaung U (Bagan)	43
Nyaung U (Bagan)-Heho (Inle Lake)	62
Thandwe-Sittwe	71
Yangon-Heho (Inle Lake)	91
Yangon-Mandalay	97
Yangon-Nyaung U (Bagan)	91
Yangon-Sittwe	107
Yangon-Thandwe (Ngapali)	78

TOURS

Many foreign-run companies book package tours to Myanmar. In most instances, more money will reach the local people if you travel on your own or arrange a driver and guide from a locally based agent. See p30 for tips on arranging your own tour with agencies in Myanmar.

Travel agents along Bangkok's Khao San Rd offer a host of short-term package trips to Myanmar, some of which are geared more to midrange, locally run hotels than top-end, joint-venture hotels.

Bicycle

You'll sure see a lot of these: bicycles are clearly the number-one means for locals to get around and can easily be hired around the country by visitors.

Around Town

At popular tourist spots in Mandalay, Bagan and Inle Lake you'll see 'bike rental' signs; rates start at K1000 per day; top-end hotels and occasionally more far-flung places charge up to K4000. Most guesthouses in such places keep a few bikes on hand; if not, staff can track one down. Note the condition of the bike before hiring; check the brakes and pedals in particular. Many rental bikes have baskets or bells, but don't expect a crash helmet!

Sturdier Indian, Chinese or Thai imports are around (from $100) if you'd rather buy one. Some tours provide bikes, so you may be able to rent better quality ones from agents (eg Exotissimo in New Bagan).

Apart from in Yangon and Mandalay, vehicular traffic is quite light.

Long Distance

A few visitors bring their own touring bikes into Myanmar. There doesn't seem to be any problem with customs as long as you make the proper declarations upon entering the country.

Gradients are moderate in most parts of Myanmar that are open to tourism. Frontier regions, on the other hand, tend to be mountainous, particularly Shan, Kayin, Kayah and Chin States. You'll find plenty of opportunity everywhere for dirt-road and off-road pedalling. A sturdy mountain bike would make a good alternative to a touring rig, especially in the north, where main roads can resemble secondary roads elsewhere.

WARNING – THINGS CHANGE

The information in this chapter is particularly vulnerable to change, and this is especially so in Myanmar.

In terms of international travel, prices are volatile, routes are introduced and cancelled, schedules change, special deals come and go, and rules and visa requirements are amended. Always check directly with the airline or a travel agent to make sure you understand how a fare (and ticket you may buy) works. In addition, the travel industry is highly competitive, and there are many perks.

The upshot of this is that you should get opinions, quotes and advice from as many airlines and travel agents as possible before you part with your hard-earned cash. The details given in this chapter should be regarded as pointers and are not a substitute for your own careful, up-to-date research.

Some of the key routes around Myanmar:

» Thazi to Inle Lake via Kalaw
» Pyin Oo Lwin (Maymyo) to Lashio via Hsipaw
» Mandalay to Bagan via Myingyan
» Mandalay to either Monywa, Pyin Oo Lwin, Sagaing, Inwa (Ava) or Amarapura

November to February is the best time to cycle in terms of the weather.

If you're bringing your bike, bring the spare parts you need. There are (at least) basic bicycle shops in most towns, but they usually have only locally or Chinese-made parts to equip single-speed bikes. You can also buy lower-quality motorcycle helmets here; many are disturbingly adorned with swastikas – a fad, not a political alliance. Bring reflective clothing and plenty of insurance. Don't ride at night.

Travellers on a bike may end up needing to sleep in towns few travellers make it to, and a lack of licensed accommodation may be an issue. Technically, you will need permission from local immigration to stay at such places. Be patient. Most cyclists get permission from local authorities to stay one night, but the paperwork (coming with some frowns) may take an hour or so to arrange.

It's possible to store your bicycle in the undercarriage storage on buses, though you may have to pay a little extra. On smaller buses it's possible you'll be asked to buy a 'seat' for your bike.

Some bike tours connect the dots of Myanmar's greatest hits – going, for example, up the Pyay highway to Bagan then Mandalay, and back to Yangon via Meiktila and Taungoo. It's more rough going, but nicer riding, to reach some mountainous areas, like Inle Lake. Recommended tours companies:

Bike World Explores Myanmar (☏09 513 4190; www.bwemtravel.com) Yangon-based company that also sells and rents bikes and can offer touring advice. It has eight itineraries from easy day trips around Yangon (from $140) to 10-day adventures in Chin State (from $1128).

Exotissimo (☏01-255 266; www.exotissimo.com) Bangkok-based firm that has offices in Myanmar, and runs high-end cycle tours covering Mandalay to Bagan, the Shan Hills and sights in Mon State.

Spice Roads (☎0066 2 712 5305; www.spiceroads.com) Bangkok-based operation, offering two 14-day itineraries (including eight days of riding) from $2150 per person. One follows part of the old Burma Road from Pyin Oo Lwin to Mandalay.

Boat

A huge fleet of riverboats, remnants of the old 1920s-era Irrawaddy Flotilla Company (IFC), still ply Myanmar's major rivers, where the bulk of traveller-oriented boat travel gets done. Some boats are ramshackle (but certainly lively) government ferries. Others date all the way back to the British era and others still are old-style IFC liners converted for luxury cruises. The main drawback of this mode of travel is speed – or lack thereof. Boat trips for many routes are loosely scheduled in terms of days, not hours.

There are 5000 miles of navigable river in Myanmar, with the most important river being the Ayeyarwady (Irrawaddy). Even in the dry season, boats can travel from the delta region (dodging exposed sandbars) all the way north to Bhamo, and in the wet they can reach Myitkyina.

Other important rivers include the Twante Chaung (Twante Chanel), which links the Ayeyarwady to Yangon, and the Chindwin River, which joins the Ayeyarwady a little above Bagan. The Thanlwin River in the east is only navigable for about 125 miles from its mouth at Mawlamyine, though the five-hour trip to Hpa-an is one of the country's most scenic waterway journeys.

It takes great expertise to navigate Myanmar's waterways. Rapidly changing sandbanks and shallow water during the dry season mean the captains and pilots have to keep in constant touch with the changing pattern of the river flows.

In addition to the rivers, it's possible to travel along the Bay of Bengal between Sittwe and Taunggok (north of Ngapali Beach).

BORDER CROSSINGS

Myanmar's land borders are closed to foreign tourists, except for three specific cases detailed here, each of which is subject to special conditions. No bus or train service connects Myanmar with another country, nor can you travel by car or motorcycle across the border – you must walk across. Have your visa ready before you get to the border (see p369).

Overland links could change at some point in the future. Most of Myanmar's neighbours actively covet Myanmar ports and are planning on investing for infrastructure projects to eventually criss-cross Myanmar by road. This may mean connections from Danang, Vietnam (through Laos and Thailand) to Mawlamyine, and up through central Myanmar, across the Indian border at Morei to New Delhi.

To/From Mae Sai, Thailand
North of Chiang Rai it's possible to cross to Tachileik (p197). Travellers are issued a 14-day entry permit, not a visa, at the border for B500. You can travel to Kengtung, but cannot continue anywhere else (even if you have a regular tourist visa).

Travellers wanting to exit Myanmar here can do so with the 14-day permit, or if they have a permit from Myanmar Travels & Tours (MTT) in Yangon.

To/From Ranong, Thailand
This exit is generally closed for outgoing tourists, though it's possible to cross into Myanmar from Thailand on a 'visa run'. See p105 for more.

To/From Ruili, China
You can only enter or leave Myanmar from this border with China on a package in both directions. Coming from Kunming you should book a multiday 'visa-and-package trip' – you can't go on your own – to cross the border at Mu-se and on to Lashio. It's about Y1400 ($200). Ruili is about 20 hours from Kunming by road, and Lashio is a five-hour trip from the border, but you can stay in Mu-se if necessary.

Heading in the other direction, MTT in Yangon and Mandalay quoted us deals from Lashio to the border, including a permit, guide, car and driver for one/two/three passengers, for $170/220/255. Once across the border, onward connections to Kunming and Dali are straightforward. For more details see the boxed text, p267.

Cargo Ships

Myanma Five Star Line (www.mfsl-shipping.com), the government-owned ocean transport enterprise, is only cargo now, but you can try to see about jumping on a boat to Thandwe, Taunggok or Sittwe, or south to Dawei, Myeik or Kawthoung, at some point in the future.

Ferries & Private Boats

The government-run **Inland Water Transport** (IWT; www.iwt.gov.mm) has 476 boats shifting some 25 million passengers annually. The boats tend to be rather run-down and ramshackle, but provide remarkable glimpses into local river life. Many of the passengers on the long-distance ferries are traders who make stops along the way to pick up or deliver goods.

Along the heavily travelled 262-mile-long Yangon–Pyay–Mandalay route, there are 28 ferry landings, where merchants can ply their trade. IWT offices are usually near the jetty. They can offer information, schedules and fare details, and usually tickets. IWT offices, officially, accept US dollars and FECs only.

Some short trips – for example, between Bagan and Pakokku – are handled with small covered wooden ferries that fit about 25 people. Often there are smaller, private boats you can negotiate to use with the driver. We include private boat services whenever possible. However, because of their size it's not always as safe riding with private boats compared with bigger government ferries. In 2004, a small private boat between Sittwe and Mrauk U capsized during a storm and several Italian tourists were killed.

Only a few riverboat routes are regularly used by visitors. Key routes:

» Mandalay to Bagan (see p120) On the IWT or private boats such as the Malikha

» Mandalay to Myitkyina via Bhamo and Katha (see p241) A few private fast-boat services, but mostly done on the IWT.

» Mawlamyine to Hpa-an (see p101) Daily government ferries.

» Sittwe to Mrauk U (see p279) Small private boats or government ferry.

There is no direct service between Yangon and Mandalay; you have to change boats in Pyay – and the IWT offices seemed to frown on taking passengers on this route. If you make it, take a book or two: it's about two days by boat between Mandalay and Bagan, three more to Pyay, and two more to Yangon. A more feasible long journey, and a more attractive one, is south from Myitkyina.

Luxury Boats

Several luxury ferries travel the upper and lower reaches of the Ayeyarwady River. You can book services with travel agents in Yangon, but keep in mind that many trips are booked out by tour groups and some will be joint-venture operations. For more about these cruises see boxed text, p214.

Amara Cruise (www.myanmar-discovery.de, www.amaragroup.net) Owned by a German and his Burmese wife this company runs cruises from Mandalay to both Bagan (four day, three nights single/double from €720/490) and Bhamo (seven day, six nights single/double from €1620/1120); it also runs a local charity the **Amara Foundation** (www.amara-foundation.com)

Ayravata Cruises (www.ayravatacruises.com) Beautifully restored river steamers are used for this company's trips, which range from one or two days between Manda-

---

SURVIVING LONG-DISTANCE BUS TRIPS

Heed the following points and your long-distance bus trip will, possibly, be more comfortable:

» Bring snacks and drinks by all means but don't worry too much about this. A bottle of water is often handed out on better-quality buses. There are usually no bathrooms on the bus, but frequent toilet-and-refreshment stops (where everyone must get off the bus to prevent anything being stolen) perforate the night – frustrating if you've *just* got to sleep and the bus stops at 3am for 'breakfast'.

» Often the TV blares for much of the trip – usually sticking with Myanmar-made concerts or movies detailing things such as, oh, protagonists dying bloody deaths in car crashes, but the occasional *Raiders of the Lost Ark* slips in.

» Take a jacket or blanket (preferably both) as temperatures can drop substantially at night. And consider earplugs and an eye-mask as well if you plan to grab a little shut-eye between toilet stops.

» Myanmar superstition says that when you're on a journey you shouldn't ask anyone 'How much longer?', or 'Brother, when will we arrive?', as this is only tempting fate.

» Try not to become alarmed when you see how some local passengers hold their breath whenever a bus approaches a particularly dodgy looking bridge.

lay and Bagan (from $280) to 10-day itineraries including sights along the Chindwin River (from $3150).

Journeys Myanmar (www.journeysmyanmar.com) Yangon-based tour agent that can arrange river trips on a wide range of luxury craft, including those listed here, and other options.

Pandaw Cruises (www.pandaw.com) Offers various high-end cruises aboard a replica of the teak-and-brass IFC fleet, such as a 14-night trip between Pyay and Mandalay (from $3683 per cabin, all inclusive) and a 20-day itinerary that charts the Chindwin and upper reaches of the Ayeyarwady ($5828).

Road to Mandalay (www.orient-express.com) Part of the Orient Express group, this joint-venture operation offers cruises from three (from $2290) to 11 days (from $3330), which centre on Bagan and Mandalay.

Bus

Almost always faster and cheaper than trains, Myanmar buses range from luxury air-con express buses, less luxurious but nice buses (without air-con), local buses, and mini 32-seaters. Most are operated by private companies.

Also see p381 for information on pick-up trucks, and the boxed text, p123, for more about the luxury Elephant Coaches that can be hired for transport around the country.

Classes & Conditions

Many long-haul trips, such as those from Yangon to Mandalay, allow the greatest comfort, with new(-ish) air-conditioned express buses – some of which are quite nice. A lot of bus activity happens at night, with buses leaving between 4pm and 10pm or later, and arriving at the final destination in the wee hours (often 5am or 6am). There are a couple of reasons for this: local people can't afford

ROUTE	FARE (K)	DURATION (HR)
Bagan-Taunggyi	10,500	10
Mandalay-Bagan	6500	8
Mandalay-Hsipaw	5000	6
Mandalay-Taunggyi	6000	12
Pyay-Taunggok	10,000	11
Yangon-Bagan	15,000	15
Yangon-Bago (Pegu)	6000	2
Yangon-Chaung Tha Beach	8000	6-7
Yangon-Kyaiktiyo	7000	4½
Yangon-Mandalay	11,000	12-15
Yangon-Pyay	4000	7
Yangon-Taunggyi	11,000	17
Yangon-Thandwe	12,000	17-18

BUS ROUTES

to waste a working day on a bus so prefer to travel overnight; and the buses don't overheat as much by avoiding the punishing midday sun.

If you want extra air-con comfort but don't want to go the whole way on one of these routes, you usually have to pay the full fare (eg going from Mandalay to Taungoo you pay the full fare to Yangon) and will have to deal with the middle-of-the-night arrival time. Similarly, by paying the full fare for the route, you can jump on a bus at a stop along the way, for example catch the Mandalay-to-Yangon bus at Meiktila. Staff at your guesthouse or hotel should be able to help with this.

Similar sized but older buses, with no air-conditioning, make shorter-haul trips, such as direct links from Yangon to Pyay or Taungoo to Yangon.

Local 32-seat minibuses bounce along the highways too. These tend to use the aisles, if not for blokes, for bags of rice, vegies or (worst) dried fish. Sometimes the floor in front of you is filled too, so you'll find your knees to your chin for some bouncy hours. Getting up to stretch your legs while moving just

isn't an option. (Try to sit in the front couple of rows, which sometimes have fewer bags stored, and better visibility.)

Trip durations for all forms of public road transportation are very elastic and buses of all types do break down sometimes. Older buses often stop to hose down a hot engine. Some roads – one-lane, mangled deals (read: *very* rough) – don't help matters, and tyre punctures occur too.

Costs

You can pay kyat for all bus fares. Note, foreigners will pay more than locals – and on occasion the price is 'set' on the spot. Generally minibuses, local 32-seaters, express buses with no air-con, and air-con luxury jobbies charge roughly the same on overlapping routes. The table above shows sample foreigner fares and trip times.

Reservations

From November to February, it's wise to pre-book buses a couple of days in advance for key routes, such as Bagan–Inle Lake. Seat reservations are made for all buses. Ask to see the bus ahead of time to choose the seat you'd like.

Restricted Roads

Foreigners are permitted to buy bus tickets of any class, using kyat, to any destination within or near the main Yangon–Bagan–Mandalay–Taunggyi quadrangle. We also found that buses were easily boarded in most other places in the country, except for a couple of tricky areas, like travel towards the Thai border.

Car & Motorcycle

Visitors not wanting to take planes, or endure overnight-bus bumps, frequently hire a car and driver for the bulk or entirety of a trip. It's a good way to go, though not always cheap. To drive one yourself, permission must be arranged via the government-run MTT and Road Transport Administration Department (RTAD; 01-36113), and you must be accompanied by a local at all times. (Some expats bypass this with registration from the RTAD.)

Driving conditions can be poor but are often better than on many roads in Vietnam, Cambodia and Laos – and traffic is comparatively light compared to

Thai or Vietnamese roads. Of the 15,000 miles of roads in Myanmar, about half are paved; the remainder are graded gravel, unimproved dirt or simple vehicle tracks.

Hiring a Car & Driver

The best place to arrange a driver, perhaps for a full trip, is in Yangon, but it's possible to track down a 'taxi' or 'private car' from most travel agencies and guesthouses around the country, particularly in popular destinations like Bagan, Mandalay and Inle Lake.

When trying to find a car with driver, consider there are three unofficial types of cars:

» **Tourist cars** – these are reasonably new, air-conditioned cars run by a company that provides back-up or repairs in the event they break down. These are the most comfortable – and that air-con is handy when it's dusty and hot out – but the most expensive, running to about $80 to $100 a day, depending on the length of the trip. This price includes petrol for up to 12 hours' driving per day and all of the driver's expenses.

» **Airport taxis** – a midrange option are the so-called 'airport taxis' – often yellow taxis that will be offering

you their service for your trip before you leave Yangon airport. These are older, may or may not have working aircon, and run to about $50 to $60 per day.

» **Private cars** – the cheapest option are 'private cars', run by entrepreneur drivers. These go with windows down (ie no air-conditioning), vary in condition and price dramatically, and there's less chance that you'll have any sort of replacement if the engine goes out midway between Bago and Taungoo. They can be found for as little as $40 or $50 per day. Some travellers tell us of great experiences with this option, others have problems.

There are no car-rental agencies per se, but most travel agencies in Yangon, Mandalay and Bagan – as well as guesthouses and hotels elsewhere – can arrange cars and drivers.

Among the most popular and reliable rental cars in the country are secondhand, reconditioned Toyota Corona hatchbacks imported from Japan from 1988. Such a car can cost a staggering $40,000. A slightly better quality car is the Toyota Chaser (from 1990 to 1992). Myanmar also assembles its own Mazda 'jeeps' (MJs) using 85% local parts. Though mostly a government monopoly, these jeeps make decent off-road vehicles. The old US-made, WWII-era Willys Jeeps that once characterised outback Myanmar travel are becoming few and far between.

Petrol & Tolls

Fuel stations were privatised in 2010, but the government continued to subsidise petrol at K2500 per gallon. Many of the private filling stations are owned by domestic conglomerates such as Htoo Trading and Max Myanmar (see p26), but since they are forced to sell at the artificially capped rate, there has been no incentive for them to ex-

ROAD DISTANCES (miles)

	Yangon	Mawlamyine	Nay Pyi Taw	Nyaungshwe	Mandalay	Myitkyina	Sittwe	Ngapali Beach	Hpa-an	Pyay	Pathein	Nyaung U
Mawlamyine	185											
Nay Pyi Taw	265	335										
Nyaungshwe	420	430	200									
Mandalay	420	500	185	175								
Myitkyina	795	900	515	465	350							
Sittwe	430	590	620	610	605	915						
Ngapali Beach	200	380	460	465	450	760	205					
Hpa-an	155	70	310	480	470	785	565	355				
Pyay	170	355	365	350	335	655	255	120	330			
Pathein	140	315	390	565	615	925	380	165	295	280		
Nyaung U	390	505	195	175	170	495	485	330	470	215	490	
Taunggyi	415	485	200	15	175	495	605	450	445	340	545	175

Approximate distances only

pand their pump networks to meet demand.

The situation has sustained the black market for people to resell petrol they don't need – hence the long lines at the filling stations. By March 2011, the price in central Myanmar at unofficial roadside stalls was around K4800 a gallon, while in Myitkyina (where there are only two filling stations) it had hit a high of K5500. That month the government stepped in to limit sales of the subsidised fuel to 4 gallons per vehicle per day and started issuing ration books.

Another cost to consider when travelling by car is the customary K50 or K100 'toll' collected upon entering many towns and villages throughout Myanmar. Many drivers are adept at handing these to the toll collectors while barely slowing down. The toll for private cars using the new expressway from Yangon to Mandalay is K4500, while to Nay Pyi Taw it's K2500.

Motorcycle

It's occasionally possible to rent a motorbike, though few locals advertise this – and the authorities frown on it since they don't want to deal with the complications of visitors involved in accidents. In Mandalay and Myitkyina, for example, it's K10,000 per day to rent a motorbike. Unlike cyclists, you're required to wear a helmet in most towns.

Hitching

Hitching is never entirely safe in any country in the world, and we don't recommend it. Travellers who decide to hitch should understand that they are taking a small but potentially serious risk. People who do choose to hitch will be safer if they travel in pairs and let someone know where they are planning to go.

One extra reason to avoid hitching in Myanmar is that local drivers may not know which areas are off limits to foreigners and may unwittingly transport them into such areas. In such cases the driver will probably be punished.

Local Transport

Larger towns in Myanmar offer a variety of city buses (ka), bicycle rickshaws or trishaws (saiq-ka, for sidecar), horse carts (myint hlei), ox carts, vintage taxis (taxi), more modern little three-wheelers somewhat akin to Thai tuk-tuks (thoun bein, meaning 'three wheels'), tiny four-wheeled 'blue taxi' Mazdas (lei bein, meaning 'four wheels') and modern Japanese pick-up trucks (lain ka, meaning 'line car'; see p381).

Small towns rely heavily on horse carts and trishaws as the main mode of local transport. However, in big cities (Yangon, Mandalay, Pathein, Mawlamyine and Taunggyi) public buses take regular routes along the main avenues for a fixed per-person rate, usually K25 to K100.

Standard rates for taxis, trishaws and horse carts are sometimes 'boosted' for foreigners. A little bargaining may be in order. Generally a ride from the bus station to a central hotel – often a distance of 1.25 miles or more – is between K1000 and K1500. Rides around the centre can be arranged for between K500 and K800. You may need to bargain a bit. Sometimes first time offers are several times higher than the going rate.

Pick-up Trucks

Japanese-made pick-up trucks feature three rows of bench seats in the covered back. Most pick-ups connect short-distance destinations, making many stops along the way to pick up people or cargo. They are often packed (yet somehow never 'full' according to the driver). Pick-ups trace some useful or necessary routes, such as from Mandalay to Amarapura, from Myingyan to Meiktila, from Bagan to Mt Popa, and up to the Golden Rock at Kyaiktiyo. Unlike buses, they go regularly during the day.

Fares are not necessarily cheaper than those charged for local bus trips of the same length, and prices often go up more after dark. You can, however, pay 25% to 50% extra for a seat up the front. It's often worth the extra expense, if you don't want to do scrunch duty. Sometimes you may share your spot with a monk riding for free; usually you get exactly what you pay for ('the whole front'), unlike in some other parts of Southeast Asia.

Pick-ups often start from the bus station (in some towns they linger under a big banyan tree in the centre) and then, unlike many buses, make rounds through the central streets to snare more passengers.

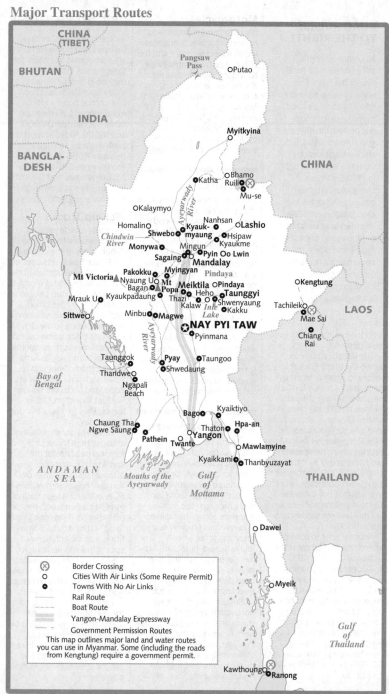

Border Crossing

○ Cities With Air Links (Some Require Permit)

◉ Towns With No Air Links

Rail Route

Boat Route

Yangon-Mandalay Expressway

Government Permission Routes

This map outlines major land and water routes you can use in Myanmar. Some (including the roads from Kengtung) require a government permit.

Tours

Many high-end hotels offer expensive day tours. We list sources for less expensive, private guides throughout this book. Also see p30 for tips on organising a 'DIY package trip'.

Train

There are as many opinions of Myanmar's oft-maligned train service as there are people riding it. For some a train ride on narrow-gauge tracks is like going by horse, with the old carriages rocking back and forth and bouncing everyone lucky enough to have a seat on the hard chairs – sleep is practically impossible; others dig it, as some routes get to areas not reached by road and the services provide a chance to interact with locals. 'It's not as bad as some people say, not as good as you hope,' one wise local told us.

What's certain is that compared to bus trips on the same routes, taking the train means extra travel time, on top of which likely delays (over 12 hours is not unheard of) have to be factored in. It also means extra expense. A 1st-class seat between Yangon and Mandalay is $35; a bus ticket on an air-conditioned bus is about $10. If you're concerned about avoiding government-owned businesses (see p21), then taking the train will also not be on your to-do list.

The Network

First introduced by the British in 1877 with the opening of the 163-mile line between Yangon and Pyay, Myanmar's rail network continues to expand. According to government mouthpiece *New Light of Myanmar,* in 2010 there were 3357 miles of 3.3ft-gauge track and 858 train stations. Extensions to the network, adding another 2264 miles of track, are currently under con-struction from Sittwe in the west to Myeik in the south.

The 386-mile trip from Yangon to Mandalay, via Bago, Nay Pyi Taw and Thazi, is the most popular train ride visitors take – though there are plenty more routes for the adventurous. Others worth considering are Bagan to Yangon, Mandalay (or Pyin Oo Lwin) train to Lashio (or Hsipaw), which takes in hilly terrain the roads miss (Paul Theroux managed to do this back when foreigners weren't supposed to, as described in his book *The Great Railway Bazaar*), and the Yangon-to-Mawlamyine route.

You can also take the poke-along the line from Pyinmana to Kyaukpadaung (31 miles south of Bagan) or the Thazi-to-Shwenyaung branch (7 miles north of Inle Lake). From Yangon lines also run northwest to Pyay, with a branch to Pathein; from Bago there's a branch southeast to Kyaiktiyo (the jumping-off point for the Golden Rock) and on to Mottawa, a short ferry ride from Mawlamyine.

An express line connects Bagan or Nyaung U with Mandalay from where there are three other branch lines: one running slightly northwest across the Ava Bridge and up to Ye-U, one directly north to Myitkyina in Kachin State and one northeast through Pyin Oo Lwin to Lashio in the northern part of Shan State.

Note also that Myanmar trains are classified by a number and the suffix 'Up' for northbound trains or 'Down' for southbound trains. Train numbers are not always used when purchasing tickets.

Classes & Facilities

Express trains offer two classes of passage, upper class and ordinary class, while many trains also offer sleepers. The main difference between ordinary and upper is that the seats recline and can be reserved in the latter, while ordinary class features hard upright seats that can't be reserved. Some trains also offer another class of service called 1st class, which is a step down from upper in comfort.

Sleeper carriages accom-modate four passengers, have air-conditioning that may or may not work, linens and blankets and their own toilet. We had one to our-selves from Bagan to Yangon but it was also sealed off with no through corridor to the rest of the train. If you'd pre-fer to move around the train and meet fellow passengers, an upper class seat will be better.

Long-distance trains have dining cars accessible to passengers in 1st, upper and sleeper class. The food isn't bad – fried rice and noodles. Attendants can also take your order and bring food to your seat or pass it through the window.

Trains stop pretty often too, with vendors on plat-forms offering all sorts of snacks. Bathrooms are basic; there are also sinks to wash hands and brush teeth. At-tendants sometimes hire out bamboo mats to spread on the floor in aisles or under seats if you can't sleep up-right. It can get cold at night, so bring a jacket and/or a blanket.

The express trains are far superior to the general run of Myanmar trains. Other trains are late, almost by rule – tak-ing one 12-hour trip that ends up running as much as 15 hours late is enough for most travellers. The Mandalay to Myitkyina route, though scheduled to take around 24 hours, can take up to 40 hours. Even on the far-more-travelled Yangon–Mandalay route, delays are common particularly in the rainy season when the tracks are prone to flooding.

Reservations

For most major routes you should be able to buy tickets directly at the train sta-tions, using the same ticket windows as the locals. Payment is usually required in US dollars or FECs. Smaller stations sometimes require some perseverance to get a ticket, as agents aren't used to foreigners climbing on.

MTT is supposed to set aside seats for foreigners, which can mean they will have seats when the booking office or station window says that the train is full. A day or two's notice is usually enough to book a seat.

If you want to try your luck at getting a coveted sleeper, you'll need at least a couple of days' notice – longer during the high season (November to March), when berths are sometimes booked weeks in advance. If you hold a seat on a train pulling a sleeper car, you can try to upgrade to a berth after you board by paying the additional fare directly to the conductor.

If you're having trouble buying a ticket or making yourself understood at a train station, try seeking out the stationmaster (*yonepain* in Burmese) – the person at the station who is most likely to speak English and most inclined to help you get a seat.

Health

The following advice is a general guide only and does not replace the advice of a doctor trained in travel medicine.

BEFORE YOU GO

» Pack medications in their original, clearly labelled containers.

» Carry a signed and dated letter from your physician describing your medical conditions and medications, including their generic names.

» If you have a heart condition bring a copy of your ECG taken just prior to travelling.

» Bring a double supply of any regular medication in case of loss or theft.

» Take out health insurance.

Vaccinations

Proof of yellow fever vaccination will be required if you have visited a country in the yellow-fever zone (ie Africa or South America) within the six days prior to entering Myanmar. Otherwise the World Health Organization (WHO) recommends the following

vaccinations for travellers to Myanmar:

Adult diphtheria and tetanus Single booster recommended if none in the previous 10 years.

Hepatitis A Provides almost 100% protection for up to a year. A booster after 12 months provides at least another 20 years' protection.

Hepatitis B Now considered routine for most travellers. Given as three shots over six months. A rapid schedule is also available, as is a combined vaccination with hepatitis A.

Measles, mumps and rubella (MMR) Two doses of MMR are required unless you have had the diseases. Many young adults require a booster.

Polio There have been no reported cases of polio in Myanmar in recent years. Adults require only one booster for lifetime protection.

Typhoid Recommended unless your trip is less than a week and only to developed cities. The vaccine offers around 70% protection, lasts for two to three years and comes as a single shot. Tablets are also available but

the injection is usually recommended as it has fewer side effects.

Varicella (chickenpox) If you haven't had chickenpox, discuss this vaccination with your doctor.

Websites & Further Reading

Lonely Planet's *Healthy Travel – Asia & India* is packed with useful information. Other recommended references include *Travellers' Health* by Dr Richard Dawood and *Travelling Well* by Dr Deborah Mills. Online resources include:

Centres for Disease Control and Prevention (CDC; www.cdc.gov)

MD Travel Health (www.mdtravelhealth.com)

Travelling Well (www.travellingwell.com.au)

World Health Organization (www.who.int/ith/)

IN MYANMAR

Availability of Health Care

Myanmar medical care is dismal, and local hospitals should be used only out of desperation. Contact your embassy for advice, as staff will usually direct you to the best options. Be aware that getting Western-style health care may not come cheap.

If you think you may have a serious disease, especially malaria, do not waste time – travel to the nearest quality facility to receive attention. It is always better to be assessed by a doctor than to rely on self-treatment.

Buying medication over the counter is not recommended in Myanmar, as fake medications and poorly stored or out-of-date drugs are common.

Infectious Diseases

The following are the most common for travellers:

Dengue Fever Increasingly problematic throughout Myanmar. The mosquito that carries dengue bites day and night, so use insect avoidance measures at all times. Symptoms can include high fever, severe headache, body ache, a rash and diarrhoea. There is no specific treatment, just rest and paracetamol – do not take aspirin as it increases the likelihood of haemorrhaging.

Hepatitis A This food- and water-borne virus infects the liver, causing jaundice (yellow skin and eyes), nausea and lethargy. All travellers to Myanmar should be vaccinated against it.

Hepatitis B The only sexually transmitted disease (STD) that can be prevented by vaccination, hepatitis B is spread by body fluids, including sexual contact.

Hepatitis E Transmitted through contaminated food and water and has similar symptoms to hepatitis A, but is far less common. It is a severe problem in pregnant women and can result in the death of both mother and baby. There is currently no vaccine, and prevention is by following safe eating and drinking guidelines.

HIV Unprotected heterosexual sex is the main method of transmission.

Influenza Can be very severe in people over the age of 65 or in those with underlying medical conditions such as heart disease or diabetes; vaccination is recommended for these individuals. There is no specific treatment, just rest and paracetamol.

Malaria While not noted in Yangon or Mandalay, malaria (which can be fatal if untreated) is very much present throughout the rest of rural Myanmar in altitudes below 1000m. Before you travel, seek medical advice on the right medication and dosage for you; note that some areas of the country have strains of the disease resistant to Mefloquine-based drugs. Wherever you are, wear long pants and sleeves and spray insect repellent to prevent bites. Also sleep in air-con or screened rooms with bednets.

Rabies A potential risk, and invariably fatal if untreated, rabies is spread by the bite or lick of an infected animal (most commonly a dog or monkey). Pretravel vaccination means the postbite treatment is greatly simplified. If an animal bites you, gently wash the wound with soap and water, and apply iodine-based antiseptic. If you are not prevaccinated you will need to receive rabies immunoglobulin as soon as possible.

Typhoid This serious bacterial infection is spread via food and water. Symptoms include high and slowly progressive fever, headache, a dry cough and stomach pain. Vaccination, recommended for all travellers spending more than a week in Myanmar and other parts of Southeast Asia, is not 100% effective so you must still be careful with what you eat and drink.

Traveller's Diarrhoea

By far the most common problem affecting travellers is usually caused by a bacteria. Treatment consists of staying well hydrated; use a solution such as Gastrolyte. Antibiotics such as Norfloxacin, Ciprofloxacin or Azithromycin will kill the bacteria quickly.

Loperamide is just a 'stopper', but it can be helpful in certain situtations, eg if you have to go on a long bus ride. Seek medical attention quickly if you do not respond to an appropriate antibiotic.

Amoebic dysentery is very rare in travellers; one sign is if you have blood in your diarrhoea. Treatment involves two drugs: Tinidazole or Metronidazole to kill the parasite in your gut, and then a second drug to kill the cysts.

Giardiasis is relatively common. Symptoms include nausea, bloating, excess gas, fatigue and intermittent diarrhoea. The treatment of choice is Tinidazole, with Metronidazole being a second option.

Environmental Hazards

Air Pollution

Air pollution, particularly vehicle pollution, is an increasing problem, particularly in Yangon. If you have severe respiratory problems speak with your doctor before travelling to any heavily polluted urban centres. This pollution also causes minor respiratory

---

HEALTH ADVISORIES

Consult your government's website on health and travel before departure:

» **Australia** www.smartraveller.gov.au

» **Canada** www.phac-aspc.gc.ca/tmp-pmv/index-eng.php

» **New Zealand** www.safetravel.govt.nz

» **UK** www.dh.gov.uk

» **USA** wwwnc.cdc.gov/travel/

DRINKING WATER

» Never drink tap water.

» Check bottled water seals are intact at purchase.

» Avoid ice.

» Avoid fresh juices – they may have been watered down.

» Boiling water is the most efficient method of purifying it.

» Iodine, the best chemical purifier, should not be used by pregnant women or those who suffer with thyroid problems.

» Ensure your water filter has a chemical barrier, such as iodine, and a pore size of less than four microns.

problems, such as sinusitis, dry throat and irritated eyes. If troubled by the pollution, leave the city for a few days and get some fresh air.

Diving

Divers and surfers should seek specialised advice before they travel to ensure their medical kit contains treatment for coral cuts and tropical ear infections, as well as the standard problems. Divers should ensure their insurance covers them for decompression illness – get specialised dive insurance through an organisation such as **Divers Alert Network** (DAN; www.danseap.org). Have a dive medical examination before you leave your home country – there are certain medical conditions that are incompatible with diving, and economic considerations may override health considerations for some dive operators that operate in Myanmar.

Food

Rather than being overly concerned at street stalls, where food is freshly cooked to order, note that eating in restaurants is the biggest risk factor for contracting traveller's diarrhoea. Avoid shellfish, and food that has been sitting around in buffets. Peel all fruit, cook vegetables and soak salads in iodine water for at least 20 minutes. Eat in busy restaurants with a high turnover of customers.

Heat

Many parts of Myanmar are hot and humid throughout the year. It can take up to two weeks to adapt to the hot climate. Swelling of the feet and ankles is common, as are muscle cramps caused by excessive sweating. Prevent these by avoiding dehydration and excessive activity in the heat.

Dehydration is the main contributor to heat exhaustion. Symptoms include feeling weak; headache; irritability; nausea or vomiting; sweaty skin; a fast, weak pulse; and a normal or slightly elevated body temperature. Treat by getting out of the heat, applying cool wet cloths to the skin, lying flat with legs raised and rehydrating with water containing a quarter of a teaspoon of salt per litre.

Heatstroke is a serious medical emergency. Symptoms come on suddenly and include weakness, nausea, a hot dry body with a body temperature of over 41°C, dizziness, confusion, loss of coordination, fits and eventual collapse and loss of consciousness. Seek medical help and commence cooling by getting the person out of the heat, removing their clothes, and applying cool wet cloths or ice to their body, especially to the groin and armpits.

Prickly heat –an itchy rash of tiny lumps –is caused by sweat being trapped under the skin. Treat by moving out of the heat and into an air-conditioned area for a few hours and by having cool showers. Creams and ointments clog the skin so they should be avoided.

Insect Bites & Stings

Bedbugs Don't carry disease but their bites are very itchy. They live in the cracks of furniture and walls and then migrate to the bed at night to feed on you. You can treat the itch with an antihistamine.

Bees or wasps If allergic to their stings, carry an injection of adrenaline (eg an EpiPen®) for emergency treatment.

Jellyfish In Myanmar waters most are not dangerous. If stung, pour vinegar onto the affected area to neutralise the poison. Take painkillers and seek medical advice if your condition worsens.

Leeches Found in humid rainforest areas. Don't transmit any disease but their bites can be itchy for weeks afterwards and can easily become infected. Apply an iodine-based antiseptic to any leech bite to help prevent infection.

Lice Most commonly inhabit your head and pubic area. Transmission is via close contact with an infected person. Treat with numerous applications of an antilice shampoo, such as Permethrin.

Ticks Contracted after walking in rural areas. If you are bitten and experience symptoms such as a rash at the site of the bite or elsewhere, fever, or muscle aches, see a doctor. Doxycycline prevents tick-borne diseases.

Skin Problems

Fungal rashes are common in humid climates. There are two common fungal rashes that affect travellers. The first occurs in moist areas that receive less air, such as the groin, the armpits and between the toes. It starts as a red patch that slowly spreads and is usually itchy. Treatment involves keeping the skin dry, avoiding chafing and using an antifungal cream such as Clotrimazole or Lamisil. *Tinea versicolor* is also common – this fungus causes small, light-coloured patches, most commonly on the back, chest and shoulders. Consult a doctor.

Cuts and scratches easily become infected in humid climates. Take meticulous care of any cuts and scratches to prevent complications, such as abscesses. Immediately wash all wounds in clean water and apply antiseptic. If you develop signs of infection (increasing pain and redness) see a doctor. Divers and surfers should be particularly careful with coral cuts as they easily become infected.

Snakes

Myanmar is home to many species of both poisonous and harmless snakes. Assume all snakes are poisonous and never try to catch one. Always wear boots and long pants if walking in an area that may have snakes. First aid in the event of a snakebite involves pressure immobilisation with an elastic bandage firmly wrapped around the affected limb, starting at the bite site and working up towards the chest. The bandage should not be so tight that the circulation is cut off, and the fingers or toes should be kept free so the circulation can be checked. Immobilise the limb with a splint and carry the victim to medical attention. Do not use tourniquets or try to suck the venom out. Antivenom is available for most species.

Women's Health

Pregnant women should receive specialised advice before travelling. The ideal time to travel is between 16 and 28 weeks, when the risk of pregnancy-related problems is at its lowest and pregnant women generally feel their best. During the first trimester there is a risk of miscarriage and in the third trimester complications – such as premature labour and high blood pressure – are possible. It's wise to travel with a companion. Always carry a list of quality medical facilities available at your destination and ensure that you continue your standard antenatal care at these facilities. Avoid rural travel in areas with poor transportation and medical facilities. Most of all, ensure that your travel insurance covers all pregnancy-related possibilities, including premature labour.

Malaria is a high-risk disease in pregnancy. WHO recommends that pregnant women do *not* travel to areas with Chloroquine-resistant malaria. None of the more effective antimalarial drugs are completely safe in pregnancy.

Traveller's diarrhoea can quickly lead to dehydration and result in inadequate blood flow to the placenta. Many of the drugs used to treat various diarrhoea bugs are not recommended in pregnancy. Azithromycin is considered safe.

In Yangon and Mandalay, supplies of sanitary products are readily available. Birth-control options may be limited, so bring adequate supplies of your own form of contraception. Heat, humidity and antibiotics can all contribute to thrush. Treatment is with antifungal creams and pessaries such as Clotrimazole. A practical alternative is a single tablet of Fluconazole (Diflucan). Urinary tract infections can be precipitated by dehydration or long bus journeys without toilet stops; bring suitable antibiotics.

Traditional Medicine

Throughout Myanmar traditional medical systems are widely practised. There is a big difference between these traditional healing systems and 'folk' medicine. Folk remedies should be avoided, as they often involve rather dubious procedures with potential complications. In comparison, traditional healing systems such as Chinese medicine are well respected, and aspects of them are being increasingly used by Western medical practitioners.

All traditional Asian medical systems identify a vital life force, and see blockage or imbalance as causing disease. Techniques such as herbal medicines, massage and acupuncture are used to bring this vital force back into balance or to maintain balance. These therapies are best used for treating chronic disease such as chronic fatigue, arthritis, irritable bowel syndrome and some chronic skin conditions. Traditional medicines should be avoided for treating serious acute infections, such as malaria.

Be aware that 'natural' doesn't always mean 'safe', and there can be drug interactions between herbal medicines and Western medicines. If you are using both systems ensure that you inform both practitioners what the other has prescribed.

Language

WANT MORE?

For in-depth language information and handy phrases, check out Lonely Planet's *Burmese Phrasebook*. You'll find it at **shop.lonelyplanet.com**, or you can buy Lonely Planet's iPhone phrasebooks at the Apple App Store.

Burmese is part of the Tibeto-Burman language family. As the national language of Myanmar (Burma), it has over 40 million speakers, of whom more than 30 million use it as their first language. The variety of Burmese of Mandalay and Yangon, spoken throughout the central area of Myanmar, is considered the standard language. Many other languages are spoken in Myanmar, but with Burmese you'll be understood in the whole country.

There are two varieties of Burmese – one used in writing and formal situations, the other in speaking and informal context. The main differences are in vocabulary, especially the most common words (eg 'this' is di in spoken Burmese, but i in the written language). The phrases in this chapter are in the informal spoken variety, which is appropriate for all situations you're likely to encounter. Note that many Burmese nouns are borrowed from English, though the meaning and sound may be somewhat different.

In Burmese, there's a difference between aspirated consonants (pronounced with a puff of air after the sound) and unaspirated ones – you'll get the idea if you hold your hand in front of your mouth to feel your breath, and say 'pit' (where the 'p' is aspirated) and 'spit' (where it's unaspirated). These aspirated consonants in our pronunciation guides are said with a puff of air after the sound: ch (as in 'church'), k (as in 'kite'), ş (as in 'sick'), t (as in 'talk'); the following ones are pronounced with a puff of air before the sound: hl (as in 'life'), hm (as in 'me'), hn (as in 'not'), hng (as in 'sing'), hny (as in 'canyon'). Note also that the apostrophe (') represents the sound heard between 'uh-oh', th is pronounced as in 'thin' and ţh as in 'their'.

There are three distinct tones in Burmese (the raising and lowering of pitch on certain syllables). They are indicated in our pronunciation guides by the accent mark above the vowel: high creaky tone, as in 'heart' (á), plain high tone, as in 'car' (à), and the low tone (a – no accent). Note also that ai is pronounced as in 'aisle', aw as in 'law', and au as in 'brown'.

BASICS

Burmese equivalents of the personal pronouns 'I' and 'you' have masculine and feminine forms, depending on the gender of the person indicated by the pronoun. These forms are marked as 'm/f' in phrases throughout this chapter. Depending on the pronoun (ie 'I' or 'you'), these abbreviations refer to the speaker or the person addressed.

Hello.	မင်္ဂလာပါ။	ming·guh·la·ba
Goodbye.	သွားမယ်နော်။	thwà·me·naw
Yes.	ဟုတ်ကဲ့။	hoh'·gé
No.	ဟင့်အင်း။	híng·ìn
Excuse me.	ဆောရီးနော်။	sàw·rì·naw
Sorry.	ဆောရီးနော်။	sàw·rì·naw
Please.	တဆိတ်လောက်။	duh·şay'·lau'
Thank you.	ကျေးဇူး တင်ပါတယ်။	jày·zù ding·ba·de
You're welcome.	ရပါတယ်။	yá·ba·de
How are you?	နေကောင်းလား။	nay·gàung·là
Fine. And you?	ကောင်းပါတယ်။ ခင်ဗျား/ရှင်ရော။	gàung·ba·de king·myà/ shing·yàw (m/f)

What's your name?
နာမည် ဘယ်လို ခေါ်သလဲ။ — nang·me be·loh kaw·ţhuh·lè

My name is ...
ကျနော့်/ကျမ နာမည်က - - - ပါ။ — juh·náw/juh·má nang·me·gá ... ba (m/f)

Do you speak English?
အင်္ဂလိပ်လို ပြောတတ်သလား။ — ìng·guh·lay'·loh byàw·da'·thuh·là

I don't understand.
နားမလည်ဘူး။ — nà·muh·le·bòo

ACCOMMODATION

Where's a ...?	- - - ဘယ်မှာလဲ။	... be·hma·lè
bungalow	ဘန်ဂလို	buhng·guh·loh
guesthouse	တည်းခိုခန်း	dè·koh·gàn
hotel	ဟိုတယ်	hoh·te

Do you have a ... room?	- - - ရှိသလား။	... shí·ţhuh·là
single	တစ်ယောက်ခန်း	duh·yau'·kàng
double	နှစ်ယောက်ခန်း	hnuh·yau'·kàng
twin	ခုတင်နှစ်လုံး ပါတဲ့အခန်း	guh·ding· hnuh·lòhng· ba·dé·uh·kàng

How much is it per night/person?
တစ်ည/တစ်ယောက် ဘယ်လောက်လဲ။ — duh·nyá/duh·yau' be·lau'·lè

Is there a campsite nearby?
ဒီနားမှာ စခန်းချစရာနေရာ ရှိသလား။ — di·nà·hma suh·kàng·chá·zuh·ya·nay·ya shí·ţhuh·là

DIRECTIONS

Where is ...?
- - - ဘယ်မှာလဲ။ — ... be·hma·lè

What's the address?
လိပ်စာက ဘာလဲ။ — lay'·sa·gá ba·lè

Could you please write it down?
ရေးမှတ်ထားပါ။ — yày·hmuh'·tà ba

Can you show me (on the map)?
(မြေပုံပေါ်မှာ) ညွှန်ပြပေးပါ။ — (myay·bohng·baw·hma) hnyoong·byá·bày·ba

Turn ...	- - - ကွေ့ပါ။	... gwáy·ba
at the corner	လမ်းထောင့်မှာ	làng·dáung·hma
at the traffic lights	မီးပွိုင့်မှာ	mì·pwáing·hma

It's ...		
behind ...	- - - အနောက်မှာ။	... uh·nau'·hma
far away	အရမ်းဝေးတယ်။	uh·yàng wày·de
in front of ...	- - - ရှေ့မှာ။	... sháy·hma
left	ဘယ်ဘက်မှာ။	be·be'·hma
near ...	- - - နားမှာ။	... nà·hma
next to ...	- - - ဘေးမှာ။	... bày·hma
right	ညာဘက်မှာ။	nya·be'·hma
straight ahead	ရှေ့တည့်တည့်မှာ။	sháy·dé·dé·hma

EATING & DRINKING

Can you recommend a ...?	- - - တစ်ခု အကြံပေးနိုင်မလား။	... duh·kú uh·jang·bày· naing·muh·là
bar	အရက်ဆိုင်	uh·ye'·şaing
cafe	ကော်ဖီဆိုင်	gaw·pi·şaing
restaurant	စားသောက်ဆိုင်	sà·thau'·şaing

I'd like a/the ..., please.	- - - လိုချင်ပါတယ်။	... loh·jing·ba·de
table for (four)	(၄)ယောက်စာ စားပွဲ	(lày)·yau'·sa zuh·bwè
nonsmoking section	ဆေးလိပ် မသောက်ရတဲ့နေရာ	şày·lay' muh·thau'·yá· dé·nay·ya

I'd like (the) ..., please.	- - - ပေးပါ။	... bày·ba
bill	ဘောက်ချာ	bau'·cha
menu	မီးနူး	mì·nù
that dish	အဲဒီဟင်းခွက်	è·di hìng·gwe'
wine list	ဝိုင်စာရင်း	waing·suh·yìng

Could you prepare a meal without ...?	- - - မပါဘဲ ပြင်ပေးနိုင်မလား။	... muh·ba·bè bying·bày· naing·muh·là
butter	ထောပတ်	tàw·ba'
eggs	ကြက်ဥ	je'·ú
fish sauce	ငံပြာရည်	ngang·bya·yay
meat	အသား	uh·thà
meat stock	အသားပြုတ်ရည်	uh·thà· byoh'·yay

Do you have vegetarian food?
သက်သတ်လွတ် စားစရာ ရှိသလား။ — the'·tha'·lu' sà·zuh·ya shí·ţhuh·là

What would you recommend?
ဘာအကြံပေးမလဲ။ — ba uh·jang·pày·muh·lè

What's the local speciality?
ဒီမြို့ကစပယ်ရှယ် အစားအစာက ဘာလဲ။ — di·myóh·gá suh·be·she uh·sà·uh·sa·gá ba·lè

Cheers!
ချီးယား။ — chì·yà

Key Words

breakfast	မနက်စာ	muh·ne'·sa
lunch	နေ့လည်စာ	náy·le·za
dinner	ညစာ	nyá·za
snack	အဆာပြေ စားစရာ	uh·şa·byay sà·zuh·ya
fruit	အသီးအနှံ	uh·thì·uh·hnang
meat	အသား	uh·thà
vegetable	ဟင်းသီးဟင်းရွက်	hìng·ţhì·hìng·ywe'
bottle	တစ်ပုလင်း	duh·buh·lìng
bowl	ပန်းကန်လုံး	buh·gang·lòhng
chopsticks	တူ	doo
cup	ခွက်	kwe'
fork	ခက်ရင်း	kuh·yìng
glass	ဖန်ခွက်	pang·gwe'
knife	ဓား	dà
napkin	လက်သုတ်ပုဝါ	le'·thoh'·buh·wa
plate	ပန်းကန်	buh·gang
spoon	ဇွန်း	zòong
teaspoon	လက်ဖက်ရည်ဇွန်း	luh·pe'·yay·zòong

Drinks

(cup of) coffee ...	ကော်ဖီ (၁)ခွက် - - -	gaw·pi (duh·)kwe' ...
(cup of) tea ...	လက်ဖက်ရည် (၁)ခွက် - - -	luh·pe'·yay (duh·)kwe' ...
with milk	နို့နဲ့	nóh·né
without sugar	သကြား မပါဘဲ	ţhuh·jà muh·ba·bè
wine	ဝိုင်	waing
red	အနီ	uh·ni
white	အဖြူ	uh·pyu
beer	ဘီယာ	bi·ya
drinking water	သောက်ရေ	thau'·yay
hot water	ရေနွေး	yay·nwày

Signs

အဝင်	Entrance
အထွက်	Exit
ဖွင့်	Open
ပိတ်ထားသည်	Closed
အခန်းအားရှိသည်	Vacancies
အခန်းအားမရှိပါ	No Vacancies
စုံစမ်းရန်	Information
ရဲစခန်း	Police Station
တားမြစ်နယ်မြေ	Prohibited
အိမ်သာ	Toilets
ကျား	Men
မ	Women
ပူ	Hot
အေး	Cold

milk	နို့	nóh
mineral water	ရေသန့်ဗူး	yay·ţháng·bòo
orange juice	လိမ်မော်ရည်	layng·maw·yay
soft drink	ဖျော်ရည်	pyaw·yay
sugarcane juice	ကြံရည်	jang·yay

EMERGENCIES

Help!	ကယ်ပါ။	ge·ba
Go away!	သွား။	thwà
Call ...	- - - ခေါ်ပေးပါ။	... kaw·bày·ba
a doctor	ဆရာဝန်	şuh·ya·wung
the police	ရဲ	yèh

I'm lost.
လမ်းပျောက်နေတယ်။ — làng·byau'·nay·de

Where are the toilets?
အိမ်သာ ဘယ်မှာလဲ။ — ayng·ţha be·hma·lè

I'm sick.
နေမကောင်းဘူး။ — nay·muh·gàung·bòo

It hurts here.
ဒီမှာနာတယ်။ — di·hma na·de

I'm allergic to (antibiotics).
⟨အင်တီဘားရောတစ်⟩ နဲ့မတဲ့ဘူး။ — (ing·di·bà·yàw·di') né muh·dé·bòo

SHOPPING & SERVICES

Where can I buy (a padlock)?
⟨သော့ခလောက်⟩ ဘယ်မှာ ဝယ်လို့ရမလဲ။ — (tháw·guh·lau') be·hma we·lóh·yá·muh·lè

Numbers

1	တစ်	di'
2	နှစ်	hni'
3	သုံး	thòhng
4	လေး	lày
5	ငါး	ngà
6	ခြောက်	chau'
7	ခုနစ်	kung·ni'
8	ရှစ်	shi'
9	ကိုး	gòh
10	တစ်ဆယ်	duh·şe
20	နှစ်ဆယ်	hnuh·şe
30	သုံးဆယ်	thòhng·ze
40	လေးဆယ်	làe·ze
50	ငါးဆယ်	ngà·ze
60	ခြောက်ဆယ်	chau'·şe
70	ခုနစ်ဆယ်	kung·nuh·şe
80	ရှစ်ဆယ်	shi'·şe
90	ကိုးဆယ်	gòh·ze
100	တစ်ရာ	duh·ya
1000	တစ်ထောင်	duh·towng

Can I look at it?
ကြည့်လို့ရမလား။   jí·lóh yá·muh·là

Do you have any other?
တခြားရှိသေးလား။   duh·chà shí·ţhày·là

How much is it?
ဒါဘယ်လောက်လဲ။   da be·lau'·lè

Can you write down the price?
ဈေးရေးပေးပါ။   zày yày·bày·ba

That's too expensive.
ဈေးကြီးလွန်းတယ်။   zày·ji·lùng·de

What's your lowest price?
အနည်းဆုံးဈေးက   uh·nè·zòhng·zày·gá
ဘယ်လောက်လဲ။   be·lau'·lè

There's a mistake in the bill.
ဒီပြေစာမှာ အမှား   di·byay·za·hma uh·hmà
ပါနေတယ်။   ba·nay·de

Where's a ...?	--- ဘယ်မှာလဲ။	... be·hma·lè
bank	ဘဏ်တိုက်	bang·dai'
internet cafe	အင်တာနက် ကဖေး	ing·ta·ne' gá·pày
market	ဈေး	zày
post office	စာတိုက်	sa·dai'
tourist office	တိုးရစ်ရုံး	dòh·yi'·yòhng

TIME & DATES

What time is it?
အခု ဘယ်အချိန်လဲ။   uh·gòo be·uh·chayng·lè

It's (one) o'clock.
တစ်နာရီ ⟨ရှိပြီ⟩။   (duh·na·yi) shí·bi

It's (two) o'clock.
နှစ်နာရီ ⟨ရှိပြီ⟩။   (hnuh·na·yi) shí·bi

Half past (one).
⟨တစ်နာရီ⟩ ခွဲ။   (duh·na·yi) gwè

morning	မနက် --- နာရီ	muh·ne' ... na·yi
afternoon	နေ့လည် --- နာရီ	náy·le ... na·yi
evening	ညနေ --- နာရီ	nyá·nay ...na·yi
yesterday	မနေ့က	muh·náy·gá
tomorrow	မနက်ဖန်	muh·ne'·puhng

Monday	တနင်္လာနေ့	duh·nìng·la·náy
Tuesday	အင်္ဂါနေ့	ing·ga·náy
Wednesday	ဗုဒ္ဓဟူးနေ့	boh'·duh·hòo·náy
Thursday	ကြာသပတေးနေ့	jà·thuh·buh·dày·náy
Friday	သောကြာနေ့	thau'·ja·náy
Saturday	စနေနေ့	suh·nay·náy
Sunday	တနင်္ဂနွေနေ့	duh·nìng·guh·nway·náy

January	ဇန်နဝါရီလ	zuhn·nuh·wa·yi·lá
February	ဖေဖော်ဝါရီလ	pay·paw·wa·yi·lá
March	မတ်လ	ma'·lá
April	ဧပြီလ	ay·byi·lá
May	မေလ	may·lá
June	ဂျွန်လ	joong·lá
July	ဂျူလိုင်လ	joo·laing·lá
August	သြဂုတ်လ	àw·goh'·lá
September	စက်တင်ဘာလ	se'·ding·ba·lá
October	အောက်တိုဘာလ	ow'·toh·ba·lá
November	နိုဝင်ဘာလ	noh·wing·ba·lá
December	ဒီဇင်ဘာလ	di·zing·ba·lá

TRANSPORT

Public Transport

Is this the ... to (Moulmein)?	ဒါ ⟨မော်လမြိုင်⟩ သွားတဲ့ --- လား။	da (maw·luh·myaing) thwà·dé ... là
boat	သင်္ဘော	thìng·bàw
bus	ဘတ်စ်ကား	ba'·suh·gà
plane	လေယာဉ်	lay·ying
train	ရထား	yuh·tà

At what time's the ... bus?	--- ဘတ်စကား ဘယ်အချိန် ထွက်မလဲ။	... ba'·suh·gà be·uh·chayng twe'·muh·lè
first	ပထမ	buh·tuh·má
last	နောက်ဆုံး	nau'·sòhng
next	နောက်	nau'

One ... ticket to (Taunggyi), please.	(တောင်ကြီး) ---လက်မှတ် တစ်စောင် ပေးပါ။	(daung·ji) ... le'·hma' duh·zaung bày·ba
one-way	အသွား	uh·thwà
return	အသွား အပြန်	uh·thwà uh·byang

At what time does it leave?
ဘယ်အချိန် ထွက်သလဲ။   be·uh·chayng twe'·thuh·lè

How long does the trip take?
ဒီခရီးက ဘယ်လောက် ကြာမလဲ။   di·kuh·yì·gá be·lau' ja·muh·lè

Does it stop at (Bago)?
(ပဲခူး)မှာ ရပ်သလား။   (buh·gòh)·hma ya'·thuh·là

What's the next station?
နောက်ဘူတာက ဘာဘူတာလဲ။   nau'·boo·da·gá ba·boo·da·lè

Please tell me when we get to (Myitkyina).
(မြစ်ကြီးနား) ရောက်ရင် ပြောပါ။   (myi'·ji·nà) yau'·ying byàw·ba

Is this ... available?	ဒီ --- အားသလား။	di ... à·thuh·là
motorcycle-taxi	အငှား မော်တော်ဆိုင်ကယ်	uh·hngà maw·daw·şaing·ke
rickshaw	ဆိုက်ကား	şai'·kà
taxi	တက္ကစီ	de'·guh·si

monument	အထိမ်းအမှတ် ကျောက်တိုင်	uh·tàyng·uh·hma' jau'·taing
museum	ပြတိုက်	pyá·dai'
old city	မြို့ဟောင်း	myóh·hàung
palace	နန်းတော်	nàng·daw
ruins	အပျက်အစီး	uh·pye'·uh·sì
statues	ရုပ်ထု	yoh'·tú
temple	စေတီ	zay·di

Please take me to (this address).
(ဒီလိပ်စာ)ကို ပို့ပေးပါ။   (di·lay'·sa)·goh bóh·bày·ba

Please stop here.
ဒီမှာရပ်ပါ။   di·hma ya' ba

Driving & Cycling

I'd like to hire a ...	--- ငှားချင်ပါတယ်။	... hngà·jing· ba·de
bicycle	စက်ဘီး	se'·bàyng
car	ကား	gà
motorbike	မော်တော်ဆိုင်ကယ်	maw·taw·şaing·ge

Is this the road to (Moulmein)?
ဒါ (မော်လမြိုင်) သွားတဲ့လမ်းလား။   da (maw·luh·myaing) thwà·dé·làng·là

I need a mechanic.
မက္ကင်းနစ်လိုချင်ပါတယ်။   muh·gìng·ni' loh·jing·ba·de

I've run out of petrol.
ဓါတ်ဆီကုန်သွားပြီ။   da·şi gohng·thwà·bi

I have a flat tyre.
ဘီးပေါက်နေတယ်။   bàyng·pau'·nay·de

GLOSSARY

See p335 for some useful words and phrases dealing with food and dining.

Abbreviations

AM – Air Mandalay

DIY – do it yourself

FEC – Foreign Exchange Certificate

IWT – Inland Water Transport

KIA – Kachin Independence Army

KNLA – Karen National Liberation Army

KNU – Karen National Union

MA – Myanma Airways

MTT – Myanmar Travels & Tours

NDF – National Democratic Force

NLD – National League for Democracy

NMSP – New Mon State Party

Slorc – State Law & Order Restoration Council

SPDC – State Peace & Development Council

SSA – Shan State Army

USDP – Union Solidarity & Development Party

UWSA – United Wa State Army

YA – Yangon Airways

acheiq longyi – *longyi* woven with intricate patterns and worn on ceremonial occasions

a-le – opium weights

a-nyeint pwe – traditional variety of *pwe*

Bamar – Burman ethnic group

betel – the nut of the areca palm, which is chewed as a mild intoxicant throughout Asia

Bodhi tree – the sacred banyan tree under which the Buddha gained enlightenment; also 'bo tree'

Brahman – pertaining to Brahma or to early Hindu religion (not to be confused with 'brahmin', a Hindu caste)

chaung – *(gyaung)* stream or canal; often only seasonal

cheroots – Myanmar cigars; ranging from slim to massive, but very mild, as they contain only a small amount of tobacco mixed with other leaves, roots and herbs

chinlon – extremely popular Myanmar sport in which a circle of up to six players attempts to keep a rattan ball in the air with any part of the body except the arms and hands

chinthe – half-lion, half-dragon guardian deity

deva – Pali-Sanskrit word for celestial beings

dhamma – Pali word for the Buddhist teachings; called *dharma* in Sanskrit

eingyi – traditional long-sleeved shirt worn by Myanmar men

flat – covered pontoon used to carry cargo on a river; often up to 98ft long

furlong – obsolete British unit of distance still used in Myanmar; one-eighth of a mile

gaung baung – formal, turbanlike hat for men; made of silk over a wicker framework

gu – cave temple

haw – Shan word for 'palace', a reference to the large mansions used by the hereditary Shan *sao pha*

hgnet – swallow-tailed boat

hintha – mythical, swanlike bird; *hamsa* in Pali-Sanskrit

hneh – a wind instrument like an oboe; part of the Myanmar orchestra

hpongyi – Buddhist monk

hpongyi-kyaung – monastery; see also *kyaung*

hsaing – traditional musical ensemble

hsaing waing – circle of drums used in a Myanmar orchestra

htan – *(tan)* sugar palm

hti – umbrella-like decorated pinnacle of a stupa

htwa – half a *taung*

in – lake; eg Inle means little lake

Jataka – stories of the Buddha's past lives; a common theme for temple paintings and reliefs

kalaga – embroidered tapestries

kamma – Pali word for the law of cause and effect; called *karma* in Sanskrit

kammahtan – meditation; a *kammahtan kyaung* is a meditation monastery

kammawa – lacquered scriptures

kan – *(gan)* beach; can also mean a tank or reservoir

karaweik – a mythical bird with a beautiful song; also the royal barge on Inle Lake; *karavika* in Pali

kutho – merit, what you acquire through doing good; from the Pali *kusala*

kyaik – Mon word for paya

kyauk – rock

kyaung – *(gyaung)* Myanmar Buddhist monastery; pronounced 'chown'

kye waing – circle of gongs used in a Myanmar orchestra

kyi – *(gyi)* big; eg Taunggyi means big mountain

kyun – *(gyun)* island

làn – road or street

lei-myet-hna – four-sided buddha sculpture

Lokanat – Avalokitesvara, a Mahayana Bodhisattva (buddha-to-be) and guardian spirit of the world

longyi – the Myanmar unisex sarong-style lower garment; sensible wear in a tropical climate; unlike men in most other Southeast Asian countries, few Myanmar men have taken to Western trousers

Mahayana – literally 'Great Vehicle'; the school of Buddhism that thrived in north Asian countries like Japan and China, and also enjoyed popularity for a time in ancient Southeast Asian countries; also called the Northern School of Buddhism

makara – mythical sea serpent

mi-gyaung – crocodile lute

mudra – hand position; used to describe the various hand positions used by buddha images, eg *abhaya mudra* (the gesture of fearlessness)

Myanma let-hwei – Myanmar kickboxing

myit – river

myo – town; hence Maymyo (after Colonel May), Allanmyo (Major Allan) or even Bernardmyo

myothit – 'new town', usually a planned new suburb built since the 1960s

naga – multiheaded dragon-serpent from mythology, often seen sheltering or protecting the Buddha; also the name of a collection of tribes in northwest Myanmar

nat – spirit being with the power to either protect or harm humans

nat-gadaw – spirit medium (literally 'spirit bride'); embraces a wide variety of *nat*

nat pwe – dance performance designed to entice a *nat* to possess a *nat-gadaw*

ngwe – silver

nibbana – nirvana or enlightenment, the cessation of suffering, the end of rebirth; the ultimate goal of Buddhist practice

oozie – elephant handler or *mahout*

pagoda – generic English term for *zedi* or stupa as well as temple; see also *paya*

pahto – Burmese word for temple, shrine or other religious structure with a hollow interior

Pali – language in which original Buddhist texts were recorded; the 'Latin' of Theravada Buddhism

pa-lwe – bamboo flute

paq-ma – Myanmar bass drum

parabaik – folding Buddhist palm-leaf manuscripts

parinibbana – literally, final *nibbana;* the Buddha's passing away

pattala – bamboo xylophone used in the Myanmar orchestra

paya – a generic Burmese term meaning holy one; applied to buddha figures, *zedi* and other religious monuments

pe-sa – palm-leaf manuscripts

pin – *(bin)* banyan tree

pi ze – traditional tattooing, believed to make the wearer invulnerable to sword or gun

pwe – generic Burmese word for festival, feast, celebration or ceremony; also refers to public performances of song and dance in Myanmar, often all-night (and all-day) affairs

pyatthat – wooden, multiroofed pavilion, usually turretlike on palace walls, as at Mandalay Palace

Sanskrit – ancient Indian language and source of many words in the Burmese vocabulary, particularly those having to do with religion, art and government

sao pha – 'sky lord', the hereditary chieftains of the Shan people

saung gauq – 13-stringed harp

sawbwa – Burmese corruption of the Shan word *sao pha*

saya – a teacher or shaman

sayadaw – 'master teacher', usually the chief abbot of a Buddhist monastery

shinpyu – ceremonies conducted when young boys from seven to 20 years old enter a monastery for a short period of time, required of every young Buddhist male; girls have their ears pierced in a similar ceremony

shwe – golden

sikhara – Indian-style, corncob-like temple finial, found on many temples in the Bagan area

sima – see *thein*

soon – alms food offered to monks

stupa – see *zedi*

t'ămìn zain – *(htamin zain)* rice shop

Tatmadaw – Myanmar's armed forces

taung – *(daung)* mountain, eg Taunggyi means 'big mountain'; it can also mean a half-yard (measurement)

taw – *(daw)* a common suffix, meaning sacred, holy or royal; it can also mean forest or plantation

tazaung – shrine building, usually found around *zedi*

thanakha – yellow sandalwood-like paste, worn by many Myanmar women on their faces as a combination of skin conditioner, sunblock and make-up

thein – ordination hall; called *sima* in Pali

Theravada – literally 'Word of the Elders' that has thrived in Sri Lanka and Southeast Asian countries such as Myanmar and Thailand; also called Southern Buddhism and Hinayana

thilashin – nun

Thirty, the – the '30 comrades' of Bogyoke Aung San who joined the Japanese during WWII and eventually led Burma (Myanmar) to independence

thoun bein – motorised three-wheeled passenger vehicles

Tripitaka – the 'three baskets'; the classic Buddhist scriptures consisting of the Vinaya (monastic discipline), the Sutta (discourses of the Buddha) and Abhidhamma (Buddhist philosophy)

twin – *(dwin)* well, hole or mine

vihara – Pali-Sanskrit word for sanctuary or chapel for buddha images

viss – Myanmar unit of weight, equal to 3.5lb

votive tablet – inscribed offering tablet, usually with buddha images

wa – mouth or river or lake; Inwa means 'mouth of the lake'

wa leq-hkouq – bamboo clapper, part of the Myanmar orchestra

yagwin – small cymbals

Yama pwe – Myanmar classical dancing based on Indian epic the Ramayana

ye – water, liquid

yodaya zat – Ayuthaya theatre, the style of theatre brought into Myanmar with Thai captives after the fall of Ayuthaya in 1767

yoma – mountain range

youq-the pwe – Myanmar marionette theatre

ywa – village; a common suffix in place names such as Monywa

zat pwe – Myanmar classical dance-drama based on Jataka stories

zawgyi – an alchemist who has successfully achieved immortality through the ingestion of special compounds made from base metals

zayat – an open-sided shelter or resthouse associated with a *zedi*

zedi – stupa, a traditional Buddhist religious monument consisting of a solid hemispherical or gently tapering cylindrical cone and topped with a variety of metal and jewel finials; *zedi* are often said to contain Buddha relics

zei – *(zay* or *zè)* market

zeigyo – central market

behind the scenes

SEND US YOUR FEEDBACK

We love to hear from travellers – your comments keep us on our toes and help make our books better. Our well-travelled team reads every word on what you loved or loathed about this book. Although we cannot reply individually to postal submissions, we always guarantee that your feedback goes straight to the appropriate authors, in time for the next edition. Each person who sends us information is thanked in the next edition – and the most useful submissions are rewarded with a free book.

Visit **lonelyplanet.com/contact** to submit your updates and suggestions or to ask for help. Our award-winning website also features inspirational travel stories, news and discussions.

Note: We may edit, reproduce and incorporate your comments in Lonely Planet products such as guidebooks, websites and digital products, so let us know if you don't want your comments reproduced or your name acknowledged. For a copy of our privacy policy visit lonelyplanet.com/privacy.

OUR READERS

Many thanks to the travellers who used the last edition and wrote to us with helpful hints, useful advice and interesting anecdotes:

Chris, Diana, Hanna, Herbie47, Stefano & Antonio, Lael Ambrose, Yorick Amerlynck, Chris Bain, Jarda Balatka, Michel Baron, Eugene Barsky, Malcolm Battle, Natalie Bell, Patrick Benusiglio, Otto Bertram, Ivan Boekelheide, Edith Bronder, Michael J Bullough, Teri Campbell, Javier Castro Guinea, Marie Catignani, Emma Cave, Anthony Chapin, Marc Cornelissen, Jillian Cowan, Lucilo Crespo, Justin Dabner, Alexandra De Groote, Jonas De Jong, Jasper De Wilde, Kris Demey, Adam Dickson, Joseph Distler, Georgi Djartov, Joe Dochtermann, Diego Domínguez, Anthony D'souza, Natalie Dubach, Melanie Edwards, Daniel Ehrlich, Alex Esch, Denis Favre, Ruth Abraham Fisher, George Fogh, Josh Foreman, Toby & Inbal Frankenstein, Philomene Franssen, Pe Frei, Daniel Gerster, Jeremy Goh, Dan Green, William Green, Natasha Griffiths, Elodie Grossenbacher, Vladimir Gudilin, Guo-hua, Erik Haan, Nathalie Hagestein, Susan Harrold, Ahmar Hashmi, David J Hogarth, Maria Holm, Juanda Ismail, Joerg Jannsen, Els Jodts, Guido Jung, Anna Kaschitza, David Kerkhoff, Daniel Kester, Bill King, Garrett Kostin, Doris Krummenacher, S L, Janelle Langlais, Sabine Langrehr, Tim Laslavic, Julie Lawson, Jessica Lees, Marketa Lepikova, Caroline Liem, Peter Long, Annie Loth, Yokekuen Low, Dudley Mcfadden, Matthew Melia, Nadine Mercan, Andrew Moncrieff, Michael aka Montyman Montague, Martin Morland, Claas Morlang, Susan Mulholland, D Myelnikov, Edith Niedermayr, Pentti Niemi, Stephen Nolan, Robin Nordman, René Olde Olthof, Petra O'Neill, Wiktor Ostasz, Alan Pailing, Lynn Palfrey, Simone Panato, Larisa Pelle, Dieter Petermichl, Alban Plence, Robert Pollai, Marc Postma, Christopher Psomadellis, Harriette Purchas, Denis Riley, Jan Rutten, Ryno Sauerman, Flurina Schaub, Alain Scheuren, Ina-Kristin Schlude, Verena Schuler, Siegfried Schwab, Bill Shaw, Arne Sjunnesson, Lee Smedmor, Frank Smeltink, Leah Stuckings, Charles W Sullivan, Jamie Summers, Bruce Taub, Graham Taylor, Buckley Terpenning, Bill & Coralea Towler, Gerben Van Der Waals, Patricia Van Duijghuijzen, Alex Van Gelder, Mieke Van Hattum, Jan Willem Van Hofwegen, Arie Van Oosterwijk, Ginger Voss, Adrienne Waunch, Erich Weiss, Emelie Wiklund, Kathleen Williams, Htay Win, Jeffrey Witte, Annie Wormald.

AUTHOR THANKS

John Allen

I was very fortunate on this project to work with a brilliant team of authors and have encouraging support from Ilaria, David, Bruce, Simon and the editorial crew at Lonely Planet HQ. A huge thanks to Scotty and Michelle for their hospitality, super agent William, Richard and my driver, Chan. I very much appreciate the time granted and expertise shared by many Burma experts, including Thant Myint-U, Sean Turnell, Bob Hudson, Pamela Gutman, Emma Larkin, Andrew Marshall, Andrew Burke, Lee Hooper, Brett and Kinomar Melzer, Saw Myint Naing, Moses Samuels, Dr Chan Aye, U Zaw Min, Win Myo Thu, Nay Win Maung, Khin Maung Yin, U Thein Lwin, Edwin Briels. Fellow travellers I'd like to thank include Rachel O'Brien, Joan Halifax, Yannick Millet, Dee MacPherson, Bonnie McMillan, Victoria Tofiq, John Greenhalgh, Kornelia Dietrich and Tonny.

Allen John Smith

Thanks to Ilaria Walker, Jon Allen, Jamie Smith, David Connolly, Bruce Evans and Natchaphat Itthi-chaiwarakom, not to mention people on the ground in Myanmar, including Antony, Han and Khaing, Phoekhwarr, the folks at the May Shan Hotel, William Myatwunna, U Myint Thaung, Pyone Cho, Sai Leng and Zayar, as well as those I never had the chance to meet in person, including Daw Aung San Suu Kyi, Kit Young, Tin Cho Chaw and Ma Thanegi.

Jamie Smith

Thanks to Joe Fisher, Saw Tha Hla, Scotty Lazar, Josceline Dimbleby, Johnny Culme-Seymour, Naing-Naing, O Maung, Dani Systermans, Ronald in Pyin Oo Lwin, Sherry Pong, Ehrhart Peter, Meeya, Saskia, San, Stephen, William, Olivia Cullis, Kirsten Jung, Edwin Briels, Brett Melzer, Mr Book, Richard Mayhew and especially Donna Mepham for sharing a tearful shoulder. Eternal thanks and limitless love to my unbeatable family.

ACKNOWLEDGMENTS

Climate map data adapted from Peel MC, Finlayson BL & McMahon TA (2007) 'Updated World Map of the Köppen-Geiger Climate Classification', *Hydrology and Earth System Sciences*, 11, 163344.

Cover photograph: Fisherman on Inle Lake, Nicholas Reuss/Lonely Planet Images. Many of the images in this guide are available for licensing from Lonely Planet Images: www.lonelyplanetimages.com.

This Book

This 11th edition of Lonely Planet's *Myanmar (Burma)* guidebook was researched and written by John Allen, Allen John Smith and Jamie Smith. The previous edition was written by Robert Reid (Bagan & Central Myanmar, Mandalay, Around Mandalay and Western Myanmar); Joe Bindloss (Eastern Myanmar & Northern Myanmar); and Stuart Butler (Yangon, Around Yangon, Southeastern Myanmar and Environment).

Commissioning Editor Ilaria Walker

Coordinating Editor Simon Williamson

Coordinating Cartographer Marc Milinkovic

Coordinating Layout Designer Jacqui Saunders

Managing Editor Bruce Evans

Senior Editors Anna Metcalfe, Susan Paterson, Angela Tinson

Managing Cartographers Shahara Ahmed, David Connolly

Managing Layout Designer Jane Hart

Assisting Editors Carly Hall, Victoria Harrison, Karyn Noble, Saralinda Turner

Cover Research Naomi Parker

Internal Image Research Sabrina Dalbesio

Language Content Laura Crawford, Stephen Nolan, Branislava Vladisavljevic

Thanks to Anita Banh, Ryan Evans, Chris Girdler, Chris Lee Ack, Chris Love, Wayne Murphy, Trent Paton, Averil Robertson, Gerard Walker

index

how to use this book

These symbols will help you find the listings you want:

⊙ Sights	☞ Tours	🍷 Drinking
🏊 Beaches	🎉 Festivals & Events	☆ Entertainment
🏃 Activities	🛏 Sleeping	🛍 Shopping
🤿 Courses	✕ Eating	ℹ Information/Transport

These symbols give you the vital information for each listing:

☏ Telephone Numbers	🛜 Wi-Fi Access	🚌 Bus
⊙ Opening Hours	🏊 Swimming Pool	⛴ Ferry
P Parking	🥗 Vegetarian Selection	Ⓜ Metro
⊖ Nonsmoking	🍴 English-Language Menu	Ⓢ Subway
✳ Air-Conditioning	👪 Family-Friendly	⊖ London Tube
@ Internet Access	🐾 Pet-Friendly	🚊 Tram
		🚆 Train

Reviews are organised by author preference.

Look out for these icons:

TOP CHOICE Our author's recommendation

FREE No payment required

🌿 A green or sustainable option

Our authors have nominated these places as demonstrating a strong commitment to sustainability – for example by supporting local communities and producers, operating in an environmentally friendly way, or supporting conservation projects.

Map Legend

Sights
- 🏖 Beach
- 🛕 Buddhist
- 🏰 Castle
- ✝ Christian
- 🕉 Hindu
- ☪ Islamic
- ✡ Jewish
- ❶ Monument
- 🏛 Museum/Gallery
- 🏚 Ruin
- 🍷 Winery/Vineyard
- 🦁 Zoo
- ● Other Sight

Activities, Courses & Tours
- 🤿 Diving/Snorkelling
- 🛶 Canoeing/Kayaking
- ⛷ Skiing
- 🏄 Surfing
- 🏊 Swimming/Pool
- 🚶 Walking
- 🏄 Windsurfing
- ➕ Other Activity/Course/Tour

Sleeping
- 🛏 Sleeping
- ⛺ Camping

Eating
- 🍴 Eating

Drinking
- ☕ Drinking
- ☕ Cafe

Entertainment
- 🎭 Entertainment

Shopping
- 🛍 Shopping

Information
- 💲 Bank
- 🏛 Embassy/Consulate
- ➕ Hospital/Medical
- @ Internet
- 👮 Police
- ✉ Post Office
- ☎ Telephone
- 🚻 Toilet
- ℹ Tourist Information
- ● Other Information

Transport
- ✈ Airport
- ⊗ Border Crossing
- 🚌 Bus
- 🚠 Cable Car/Funicular
- 🚲 Cycling
- ⛴ Ferry
- Ⓜ Metro
- 🚝 Monorail
- P Parking
- ⛽ Petrol Station
- 🚕 Taxi
- 🚉 Train/Railway
- 🚊 Tram
- ● Other Transport

Routes
- Tollway
- Freeway
- Primary
- Secondary
- Tertiary
- Lane
- Unsealed Road
- Plaza/Mall
- Steps
-)≡(Tunnel
- Pedestrian Overpass
- Walking Tour
- Walking Tour Detour
- Path

Geographic
- 🛖 Hut/Shelter
- 🚨 Lighthouse
- 👁 Lookout
- ▲ Mountain/Volcano
- 🌴 Oasis
- 🌳 Park
-)(Pass
- 🌳 Picnic Area
- 💧 Waterfall

Population
- ◉ Capital (National)
- ◉ Capital (State/Province)
- ● City/Large Town
- ○ Town/Village

Boundaries
- International
- State/Province
- Disputed
- Regional/Suburb
- Marine Park
- Cliff
- Wall

Hydrography
- River, Creek
- Intermittent River
- Swamp/Mangrove
- Reef
- Canal
- Water
- Dry/Salt/Intermittent Lake
- Glacier

Areas
- Beach/Desert
- +++ Cemetery (Christian)
- ××× Cemetery (Other)
- Park/Forest
- Sportsground
- Sight (Building)
- Top Sight (Building)

OUR STORY

A beat-up old car, a few dollars in the pocket and a sense of adventure. In 1972 that's all Tony and Maureen Wheeler needed for the trip of a lifetime – across Europe and Asia overland to Australia. It took several months, and at the end – broke but inspired – they sat at their kitchen table writing and stapling together their first travel guide, *Across Asia on the Cheap*. Within a week they'd sold 1500 copies. Lonely Planet was born.

Today, Lonely Planet has offices in Melbourne, London and Oakland, with more than 600 staff and writers. We share Tony's belief that 'a great guidebook should do three things: inform, educate and amuse'.

OUR WRITERS

John Allen

Coordinating Author; Bagan & Central Myanmar, Temples of Bagan, Western Myanmar Before his first visit to Myanmar in 2001, 'John' took advice from experts and fellow travellers on whether he should go to what he knew was a brutal military dictatorship. He found a country brimming with beautiful sights and gentle people who were delighted to have the chance to interact with those from beyond their borders. A freelance author and photographer who has produced many guides for Lonely Planet since 1999, including several in Southeast Asia, John was delighted to return to the country a decade later as the coordinating author of this guidebook.

Allen John Smith

Around Yangon, Eastern Myanmar, Southeastern Myanmar, Yangon 'Allen' first visited Myanmar in the late '90s while working as an English teacher in Bangkok. Despite several subsequent visits, never did he suspect that later he'd be authoring the very book that first guided him there. A native of Oregon transplanted to Southeast Asia, Smith is a freelance writer and photographer who likes writing about and taking photos of food most of all, because it's delicious.

Jamie Smith

Mandalay & Around, Northern Myanmar 'Jamie' is the author of several travel guidebooks covering Southeast Asia. And like many frequent visitors to the region, it's Myanmar that has long been his favourite destination thanks in great part to the stoic humanity and spontaneous delight of its long-suffering people. When not researching travel publications, Jamie is most likely to be found in suburban Belgium, coastal England or in Azerbaijani jazz clubs playing the same old blues riffs he learnt 20 years ago in Japan.

Published by Lonely Planet Publications Pty Ltd
ABN 36 005 607 983
11th edition – Dec 2011
ISBN 978 1 74179 469 4
© Lonely Planet 2011   Photographs © as indicated 2011
10 9 8 7 6 5 4 3 2
Printed in China